A GRAMMAR OF SAMARITAN HEBREW

A GRAMMAR OF SAMARITAN HEBREW

Based on the Recitation of the Law in Comparison with the Tiberian and Other Jewish Traditions

A REVISED EDITION IN ENGLISH

BY

ZE'EV BEN-ḤAYYIM

WITH ASSISTANCE FROM

ABRAHAM TAL

THE HEBREW UNIVERSITY MAGNES PRESS, JERUSALEM
EISENBRAUNS, WINONA LAKE, INDIANA

© All rights reserved by The Hebrew University Magnes Press
Jerusalem 2000

Library of Congress Cataloging-in-Publication Data

Ben-Hayyim, Zeev, 1907–
   ['Ivrit va-Aramit nusaḥ Shomron, Kerekh 5. English]
   A grammar of Samaritan Hebrew : based on the recitation of the law in comparison with the Tiberian and other Jewish traditions / by Ze'ev Ben-Hayyim with assistance from Abraham Tal.
       p. cm.
   Includes bibliographical references and index.
   ISBN 1-57506-047-7 (cloth : alk. paper)
   1. Bible. O.T. Pentateuch. Hebrew—Versions—Samaritan.   2. Hebrew language—Grammar.   3. Samaritans—Languages.   I. Tal, Abraham.
II. Title.
BM927.B46 2000
492.4'5—de21
                                                                  00-026491
                                                                       CIP

Printed in Israel

Typesetting and Layout: Daatz, Jerusalem

CONTENTS

Preface to the English Edition   xiii
English Preface to the Original Hebrew Edition   xvii

0   INTRODUCTION   1
0.4   The Samaritan Pentateuch and Its Linguistic Character   3
0.5   Can a Hebrew Grammar be Compiled Solely on the Basis of an Unvocalized Text?   4
0.6   Samaritan Pointing System   5
0.10   Recording a Spoken Language for Grammatical Investigation   10
0.13   Material for the Grammar   13
0.15   Classification of Linguistic Phenomena in Tiberian and Samaritan Hebrew   17
0.18   Arrangement of the Book   21
0.20   Samaritan Script   23
    0.20.3   Alphabet Table   25

PHONOLOGY   29

1.0   Preliminaries   29
1.1   Consonants   30
    1.1.2   Table of Consonants   31
    1.1.4   בפדו"ת   32
       1.1.4.1   Three Points of Articulation of *Waw*   33
    1.1.5   גכ"ך   34
    1.1.6   ש   35
    1.1.7   טצ"ך   37
    1.1.8   אהח"ע   38
1.2   Vowels   43
    1.2.0   Vowel System   43
    1.2.1   Vowel Quantity   44
    1.2.4   Vowel Quality   48
    1.2.6   *a, å*   49
    1.2.7   Samaritan Tradition as Compared with that of the Jews   50

- 1.3 *Šəwa* and Auxiliary Vowels   53
  - 1.3.0 Parallels to the *Šəwa* in Samaritan Hebrew   53
  - 1.3.2 Previous Stages of the *Šəwa*   55
  - 1.3.3 *Šəwa* > Vowel of Any Quality   56
  - 1.3.4 Auxiliary Vowels   57
  - 1.3.6 *Pataḥ Furtivum*   60
- 1.4 Syllabic Structure and Stress   60
  - 1.4.1 Syllabic Rules   61
  - 1.4.2 Diphthongs and Syllable Splitting   62
  - 1.4.3 Ascending Diphthong   63
  - 1.4.4 Descending Diphthong   63
  - 1.4.5 Syllabic Splitting   67
  - 1.4.6 Stress   68
  - 1.4.8 Development of Stress in Tiberian Hebrew   71
  - 1.4.10 Auxiliary Stress   74
- 1.5 Sound Changes   74
  - 1.5.1 Interchanges in the Vowel System   75
    - 1.5.1.1 *i/ə/e*   76
    - 1.5.1.2 *i/a(å)*   76
    - 1.5.1.3 *a/å*   77
  - 1.5.2 Diachronic Study   78
    - 1.5.2.1 *i*   78
    - 1.5.2.2 *a*   80
    - 1.5.2.3 *u*   81
    - 1.5.2.4 *ī, ū*   83
    - 1.5.2.5 *ā > ō*   83
  - 1.5.3 Changes Due to Proximity   86
    - 1.5.3.1 Assimilation   87
    - 1.5.3.2 Dissimilation   90
    - 1.5.3.3 Gemination   90
    - 1.5.3.4 Syncope   92
    - 1.5.3.5 Metathesis   94
    - 1.5.3.6 Neutralization   94

MORPHOLOGY   96

- 2 Verb   96
- 2.0 Preliminaries   96
  - 2.0.1 Root   96
  - 2.0.2 Base   97
  - 2.0.3 Formative   98

2.0.4   Inflection and Derivation   98
2.0.7   Grammatical Classification in Tiberian Hebrew   100
2.0.8   Stem   101
2.0.9   Class   101
2.0.10 Tense in Samaritan Hebrew   102
2.0.13 Table of Perfect Afformatives   103
2.0.14 Table of Imperfect Preformatives   104
2.1 Strong Verb   105
  2.1.1 *Qal*   105
    2.1.1.7   *Qal* B Imperfect   109
  2.1.2 *Hifʿil*   110
  2.1.3 *Piʿel*   112
    2.1.3.1   With Geminated Second Radical   112
    2.1.3.5   With Simple Second Radical (*Piʿel* B)   113
  2.1.4 *Nifʿal*
    2.1.4.1   With Simple Second Radical   115
    2.1.4.6   With Geminated Second Radical (*Nifʿal* B)   117
  2.1.5 *Hitpaʿel*   119
    2.1.5.1   With Geminated Second Radical   119
    2.1.5.3   With Simple Second Radical (*Hitpaʿel* B)   119
2.2 Verbs with אהח"ע Radical   120
  2.2.1 I-Guttural (הח"ע)   120
    2.2.1.1   *Qal*   120
    2.2.1.2   *Hifʿil*   123
    2.2.1.3   *Piʿel*   124
      2.2.1.3.1 With Geminated Second Radical   124
      2.2.1.3.3 With Simple Second Radical (*Piʿel* B)   125
    2.2.1.4   *Nifʿal*   125
    2.2.1.5   *Hitpaʿel*   125
      2.2.1.5.2 With Geminated Second Radical   126
      2.2.1.5.3 With Simple Second Radical (*Hitpaʿel* B)   126
  2.2.2 II-Guttural   127
    2.2.2.1   *Qal*   127
    2.2.2.2   *Hifʿil*   128
    2.2.2.3   *Piʿel*   130
    2.2.2.4   *Nifʿal*   130
    2.2.2.5   *Hitpaʿel*   131
  2.2.3 III-Guttural   131
    2.2.3.1   *Qal*   132
    2.2.3.2   *Hifʿil*   133
    2.2.3.3   *Piʿel*   134

	2.2.3.3.1 With Geminated Second Radical 134

- 2.2.3.3.1 With Geminated Second Radical 134
- 2.2.3.3.4 With Simple Second Radical (*Pi'el* B) 134
- 2.2.3.4 *Nif'al* 135
- 2.2.3.5 *Hitpa'el* 136

2.3 Verbs I-*Aleph* (פ"א) 136
2.4 Verbs I-*Yod* (פ"י) 138
2.5 Verbs I-*Nun* (פ"נ) 144
    2.5.2 Suppletion of the *Qal* and *Nif'al* Stems 144
    2.5.5 Change of *Nif'al* of ע"י and פ"ו to פ"נ 145
    2.5.11 נתן 146
    2.5.12–14 נדד, נטה, נקם, נטר 146
2.6 Verbs II-*Waw/Yod* (ע"ו, ע"י) 147
    2.6.13 Gemination of First Radical in Imperfect 152
    2.6.15 Converted Imperfect 152
2.7 Geminate Verbs (ע"ע) 153
    2.7.2 Five Types in Tiberian Hebrew 154
    2.7.3 Types in Samaritan Hebrew 155
    2.7.7 Vocalization of Preformatives 157
2.8 Verbs III-*Heh* (ל"ה) 158
    2.8.18 חיה, היה 166
    2.8.21 עשה 168
2.9 Tenses and Moods 169
    2.9.1 Tiberian Hebrew 169
    2.9.3 Samaritan Hebrew 170
    2.9.6 Converted Imperfect 171
    2.9.9 Shortened Imperfect (Jussive) 173
    2.9.10 Lengthened Imperfect (Cohortative) 174
2.10 Passive Voice 176
    2.10.2 Disappearance of Internal Passive and Its Substitutes 177
    2.10.5 Remains of Internal Passive 179
    2.10.6 *Qal* Perfect 179
    2.10.7 *Qal* and *Hif'il* Imperfect 180
    2.10.8 *Hif'il* Perfect 181
    2.10.9 *Pi'el* 182
2.11 Imperative 183
    2.11.3 Vocalization of Second Radical 184
    2.11.6 Special Features of Different Verb Classes 185
2.12 Active Participle 187
    2.12.4 Participles of *Qal* 189
    2.12.8 Participle of *Pi'el* and *Hitpa'el* 192
    2.12.9 Participle of *Pi'el* without *Mem* 192

       2.12.10 Participles of *Nif'al*   193
       2.12.11 Special Features of Different Verb Classes   194
2.13   Passive Participle   198
       2.13.2   Three Forms of *Qal* Participle   199
       2.13.6   Special Features of Different Verb Classes   201
2.14   Infinitive   202
       2.14.2   Absolute and Construct Infinitives in Tiberian Hebrew   203
       2.14.4   Infinitive in Samaritan Hebrew   205
       2.14.6   Forms of the *Qal* Infinitive   207
       2.14.11 Infinitive Forms of Other Stems   211
       2.14.13 Special Features of Different Verb Classes   213
2.15   Mixture of Classes and Alternation of Stems   218
       2.15.2   Motivations for the Alternation   219
       2.15.5   *Qal* > *Pi'el*   222
       2.15.6   *Nif'al* with Simple Second Radical > *Nif'al* with Geminated Second Radical   223
       2.15.7   Qal Intransitive > *Nif'al*   223

3   PRONOUN   225

3.1   Personal Pronouns   225
3.2   Pronominal Suffixes   227
       3.2.7   Reconstructed Forms in Stage of Hebrew Common to Samaritan and Tiberian Hebrew   234
       3.2.8   Table of Possessive Suffixes   234
       3.2.9   Table of Object Suffixes   236
3.3   Other Pronouns   236
       3.3.1   Demonstratives   236
       3.3.2   Definite Article ‑ה   238
       3.3.3   Interrogative, Indefinite, and Relative Pronouns   238

4   NOUN   240

4.0   Preliminaries
       4.0.2   Difference Between Pattern and Appearance   240
       4.0.4   Method Applied to Samaritan Hebrew   242
4.1   Simple Noun Patterns   245
       4.1.1   Forms with One Consonant   245
       4.1.2   Forms with Two Consonants   245
       4.1.3   Forms with Three Consonants   250
       4.1.4   Forms with Four or More Consonants   260

  4.1.4.0 Forms with Geminated Second Radical and Similar Forms 260
  4.1.4.11 Quadriradicals 265
  4.1.4.12 Quinqueradicals 265
  4.1.4.13 Compounds 266
 4.1.5 Feminine Patterns 266
4.2 Prefixed Patterns 273
 4.2.1 With -א 273
 4.2.2 With -י 275
 4.2.3 With -מ 276
 4.2.4 With -ת 279
4.3 Suffixed Patterns and Nouns with Suffixes 280
 4.3.2 *i* 281
 4.3.3 *e* 282
 4.3.4 *a/å* 282
 4.3.5 *u* 283
 4.3.6 *im/əm, ən* 283
 4.3.7 *īt/ət* 283
 4.3.8 *āy, åy / ā'i, å'i* 284
 4.3.9 *ām/'ām ('ām), om* 285
 4.3.10 *ån/'ān, on/'ūn* 285
 4.3.12 Suffixes with Geminated *Nun* 287
 4.3.13 Suffix ן- not Preceded by Vowel 288
 4.3.14 *åt – ot* 288
4.4 Ultimately-Stressed Nominal Forms 290
4.5 Gender and Number 294
 4.5.1 Masculine and Feminine Gender 294
 4.5.5 Singular, Dual, and Plural Number 295
4.6 Construct State and Pronominal State 298
 4.6.2.1 Four Types of Declension 300

5 NUMERALS 305

5.0 Cardinal Numbers 305
5.1 From 1 to 10 305
5.2 From 11 to 20 308
5.3 Remaining Cardinal Numbers 308
5.4 Ordinal Numbers 309
5.5 Fractions 310
5.6 Multiplicatives 312

6 PARTICLES   313

6.0   Classification of Particles   313
6.3   Particles with Special Characteristics in Samaritan Hebrew   316

7 SOME POINTS OF SYNTAX   323

7.0   General Remarks   323
7.1   Determination   324
7.2   *He Locale*   326
7.3   את   327
7.4   In the Realm of Sentence Structure   328
7.5   Sentence Types (Verbal/Nominal)   330

8 EPILOGUE   333

8.2   Samaritan Hebrew and Theories of the Samaritan Grammarians   333
8.4   Samaritan Hebrew and Mishnaic Hebrew   335
8.8   Samaritan Hebrew and Aramaic   340

User's Guide to the Inventory of Forms   345

Inventory of Forms   353

Addenda and Corrigenda   465

Abbreviations and Bibliographical References   467

Index of Passages   474

PREFACE

The Hebrew version of this book, *LOT V* (*The Literary and Oral Traditions of the Samaritans V* [Jerusalem, 1977]) enjoyed a favorable reception in biblical and linguistic journals. Its reviews suggested, however, that if its author was interested in the broad dissemination of the work among scholars of Biblical Hebrew and Semiticists, it should have appeared in a "European language" since only a limited number of scholars outside the borders of Israel have a level of competence in modern Hebrew that enables them to utilize fully this book for research or teaching purposes. At the time I was not receptive to this argument, being intensely involved in the investigation of grammatical and lexical aspects of Samaritan Aramaic preparatory to the publication of my edition of תיבת מרקה [*Tībåt Mårqe*] (Jerusalem, 1988). Moreover, I was convinced that a straightforward translation, without the emendations and changes necessary to adapt this work for the foreign language reader, would be inadequate; this task, however, was one that necessitated my active participation.

Now, twenty-two years after the original publication of the Hebrew edition, I am able to place this volume before the English speaking public. The credit for this accomplishment must go to two of my colleagues, Professor Moshe Bar-Asher of the Hebrew University and Professor Abraham Tal of Tel-Aviv University, who approached me in 1990 with the suggestion that *LOT V* be translated into English under my direction and adapted as I saw fit for the non-Hebrew speaking audience. Indeed, there is presently more interest in the Samaritan legacy of Hebrew and Aramaic than when the original was being written. Moreover, the importance of the Samaritan pronunciation of Hebrew has gained wide acceptance as essential for reaching a correct understanding of the processes that affected the development of the Hebrew language in the late Second Temple period. This is the outgrow of the intensified study of the Dead Sea Scrolls on the one hand, and the heightened understanding of Mishnaic Hebrew as it emerges from various manuscripts on the other. I not only expressed this opinion when the Scrolls were first discovered, but I have also tried to bring out this viewpoint in my publications. Upon hearing that I hesitated to undertake such a project at my age, my friends encouraged me both in words and in deeds. Professor Bar-Asher found initial funding for the translation and a publisher for the book upon its completion. Professor Tal, a close colleague in the field of Samaritan studies, volunteered to assist me. Indeed, for me, the idea of disseminating the importance of the Samaritan link and its vital place in the history of the Hebrew language held and still holds seductive power.

From the start I was convinced that the English version did not have to be a word-for-word translation of the Hebrew. Indeed, as it was intended for an audience that was not raised on Hebrew, I found it necessary to introduce various changes, including the vocalization of the Hebrew words used as examples; the addition of translations of Hebrew quotations from post-biblical literature; the expansion or contraction of quotations of this type or others for the readers' benefit as I understood it; the provision of the necessary clarifications or rationales for the topics under discussion. None of these changes, nor the additional structural changes in Chapter Six, make the English edition essentially different either in content or conclusions from the Hebrew original; it simply presents them in English garb. Indeed, the original order of the chapters and subchapters has been retained.

Naturally, the initial step in this project was to arrive at a faithful translation of the Hebrew version, which would then serve as the basis for the requisite changes. The chapters on phonology and verb classes up to ע״ו verbs were translated by Mr. Joel Lerner (from June 1991 to March 1994, with interruptions); the remainder of the book was translated by Mr. Peretz Rodman, who also edited the already translated parts in order to arrive at a consistent style (insofar as possible). At that juncture, my role was primarily to assure the accuracy of the English translation. I did, however, check and recheck many linguistic witnesses, reevaluating their presentation in the grammatical rules, a process instigated by the fact of translation itself, since it is a commonplace that every translation contains an element of interpretation. When dealing with two structurally and semantically distinct languages as Hebrew and English, lack of conformity between the translation and the source has its dangers, for it can detract from the precise formulation of the grammatical rules. I have attempted to prevent this to the extent that my knowledge of both languages allows.

Mr. Rodman must be highly commended not only for his most able translation, but also for his patience with the frequency with which I raised questions in the course of our meetings as to whether a particular English phrase had connotations that made it unsuitable for the chosen context. Mr. Rodman was always able to reach eminently satisfactory solutions.

The manuscript then passed into the hands of Dr. Steven Fassberg from the Department of Hebrew Language at the Hebrew University of Jerusalem. Dr. Fassberg compared the translation with the Hebrew original, paying particularly careful attention to consistency in terminology and bibliographical references. He also prepared the manuscript for publication. I sincerely thank him for his help.

Preface

Since the original publication of *LOT V*, and during the time this volume was in preparation, I had occasion to engage friends and colleagues in conversations on linguistic and textual matters related to the book.

Among them I gratefully acknowledge Moshe Bar-Asher, Joshua Blau, Gideon Goldenberg, and Simon Hopkins of the Hebrew University, and Mordechay Mishor of the Academy of the Hebrew Language.

Last but not least, I offer my profound thanks to Abraham Tal for his invaluable assistance from this project's inception to its completion. I often consulted with him on various matters and showed him the changes I introduced in this edition. He was also kind enough to proofread the entire manuscript prior to its being turned over to the press. The very fact that such an outstanding scholar of Samaritan stood by my side was of immense help, above and beyond the call of collegial friendship. I can do not less than thank him for his help by placing his name, with his permission, on the title page.

I wish to express my thanks to the Federman Foundation (Faculty of Humanities, Institute for Jewish Studies, the Hebrew University of Jerusalem) for its aid at the initial stage in preparing the English translation for this book.

It is also my pleasant duty to thank Professor Sara Japhet, the former head of the Academic Committee of The Hebrew University Magnes Press for agreeing to publish this volume and to the director, Mr. Dan Benovici, for his efforts to make this typographically complex book reader-friendly.

Finally, I feel obliged to express my deepest appreciation and gratitude to Zippora, my lifelong companion, and our children for their patience, encouragement, and support, which enabled me to work on this book.

I wish to conclude my studies on the Samaritan linguistic tradition of Hebrew and Aramaic begun in 1935 with the words of the prophet Isaiah: נֹתֵן לַיָּעֵף כֹּחַ וּלְאֵין אוֹנִים עָצְמָה יַרְבֶּה (Isaiah 40:29).

Z.B.H.

Jerusalem, October 1999 (*Tammuz 5759*)

ENGLISH PREFACE TO THE ORIGINAL HEBREW EDITION

This volume completes the set, "The Literary and Oral Tradition of Hebrew and Aramaic amongst the Samaritans," which I initiated in 1935 in order in order to present the Samaritan tradition of Hebrew and Aramaic in its historical development, according to its ancient literary sources and their present pronunciation, and to offer this to research scholars of the Hebrew language.

My original intention was to devote also a volume to a grammatical description of Samaritan Aramaic, my especial interest in these days, but I came to the realization, while working on the project, that it was not yet feasible to draw up a comprehensive description of this Aramaic, since we lack to this day (a) an edition of the Samaritan Targum drawn up with an eye to the linguistic strata of this Targum; (b) a critical edition of "Tebat Marqah" distinguishing between its later sections, not written in Aramaic at all or only in faulty Aramaic, and its early parts written in living Samaritan Aramaic. I have discussed these two points elsewhere, and thus shall not go into further detail here.

The preparation of a new edition of the Samaritan Targum, undertaken by Dr. A. Tal of Tel-Aviv University, is happily progressing, and my present hope is that, having completed this series, I shall now be able to complete my work on "Tebat Marqah", many years now postponed. These two sources, especially if accompanied by extensive word lists, together with the Aramaic material of "Hammeliṣ" (LOT Vol. II) and of the liturgical poetry (LOT Vol. III part II) as pronounced at present, will provide the solid basis for a Samaritan Aramaic grammar.

I have accordingly refrained from providing a systematic description of the Aramaic, on the basis of the material I have amassed to date, in this set. However, it must be stated that the phonology presented in this volume applies both in general and in detail to Samaritan Aramaic, and this is also true concerning many points of morphological import, *i.e.*, the points found in the material published in Volume III part II.

Thus, instead of a volume of Aramaic grammar, Volume IV is offered, for the reason explained in the introduction to that volume.

Concerning the description of Samaritan Hebrew given in this volume, it should be stated that this description is based on the language-type reflected in their Torah reading, which I heard and learned from priests and other experts of various ages. This reading links up with one of the final stages of Hebrew speech development prior to its cessation in ancient times (v, chapter 8). However, as the Pentateuch is read, so are all Hebrew secular and holy writings read. Thus is this grammatical description aimed at the general structure of Hebrew according to the Samaritan tradition. This applies of course both to phonology and to morphology. On the other hand, the syntax of Samaritan Hebrew and also its vocabulary, ever since the language was subjected to the influences of Arabic, the long-time vernacular of the Samaritans, are a different matter entirely, and research into these two fields has not yet really been undertaken.

This book has been compiled which an eye to the Hebrew language scholar and also to the educated lay student, to whom standard Hebrew grammar is known, and who is interested in acquiring a knowledge of Hebrew grammatical phenomena in a tradition so different as that of the Samaritans.

The Hebrew University *Z. Ben-Ḥayyim*
Jerusalem, October 1976

INTRODUCTION

0.1 The Hebrew language comes down to us in several versions, each ethnic community having its own unique tradition of pronunciation. Even though these traditions are subject to the influence of various vernaculars and sometimes differ markedly from each other, their common basis is evident for all to perceive. All, that is, but the pronunciation of the Samaritans, whose tradition stands apart from the others, unique and surprising. One who hears the Samaritan recitation of the Torah or any of their Hebrew prayers would think he is listening to a distant, foreign tongue. Only here and there would his ear discern a Hebrew word. The Samaritan community's distinctness in matters of belief and law, its devotion to its ancestral ways, and its continual preservation of its ancient ritual practices are so well known as to require no proof. Anyone who has had contact with the Samaritans, and particularly with their priests, know how correct were the Sages when they said, "Every commandment which *Kutim* [Samaritans] have held onto, they practice with much greater scrupulousness than the Jews" (*b. Ḥullin* 4a). A Samaritan scholar has said that, according to their belief, the precise recitation of the Torah in accordance with the rules of grammar, as Moses spoke it aloud from God's own mouth, is a basic commandment (see *LOT* I, 383). This raises the following question: does the Samaritans' tendency to adhere closely to their religious heritage apply also to their unique linguistic tradition? In other words, did the Samaritans carefully maintain their linguistic heritage, as they did their observance of tradition, preserving it from the time when they spoke Hebrew?

A search for the answer to this question in the literature of Hebrew linguistics would be in vain. There are a few scholars who have placed a high value on the Samaritans' linguistic tradition and their pronunciation of Hebrew at the present time, while others, and these are the majority, deny that this tradition has any reliability or value whatsoever and pay no attention to it in weighing issues related to the Hebrew language. Neither camp can fall back on reasoned argument; both rely on surface impressions alone. This is because the nature of the Samaritan linguistic tradition and the measure of its reliability and originality are questions that are almost entirely unexplored, and the relations between that tradition and the Hebrew linguistic traditions of other communities remain completely unexamined.

When in 1935 I found myself unable to find ready answers to these questions, I began to explore the Samaritan tradition and to seek answers to these questions in that tradition itself. I took it upon myself to uncover the Samaritan traditions of Hebrew and Aramaic (Aramaic being the constant companion of Hebrew in matters both secular and sacred among the Samaritans, as it is among the Jews) in their historical development, based on their ancient literary sources and their contemporary pronunciation, placing these in the framework of Hebrew linguistic research.

0.2 The question of the origins of the Samaritans and their relation to the Israelite community are irrelevant to the concerns of this book, except that we may learn from the sources that, even according to the Jewish tradition, the Samaritans of the late 8th century and the 7th century BCE believed in the Mosaic Torah and studied it under the direction of an Israelite priest exiled from Samaria. In other words, the traditions of Pentateuchal study and interpretation in the Samaritan community go back, by all accounts, at least that far, to a period in which Hebrew was a thoroughly vital language, the vernacular of the masses in both Judah and Israel. Just what form the language took then is something of which we have only very limited knowledge, based in part on inscriptions carved in stone and written on ostraca (which are preserved as they were at that time), but mainly on the basis of the Hebrew Bible. The books of the Bible preserved the language only to the extent that the (mainly consonantal) alphabet enabled them to do so, and while the particular spelling is not always contemporary with the books themselves, it does not stray far and does not distort the picture of the language, something that cannot be said of the various systems of pointing. Pointing does, in fact, diverge from the form of the language as spoken by various speakers of Hebrew during First Temple times, particularly inasmuch as it casts a variety of types of speech into a single, uniform mold. As a result, while we may succeed in distinguishing within the biblical books aspects of language particular to First Temple and Second Temple Hebrew respectively in the areas of usage and vocabulary, we are presented with an indivisible portrait of the language that eliminates such distinctions in the areas of phonology and morphology.[1]

0.3 Whether the Samaritans were originally Hebrew speakers or whether they entered the Hebrew speech community only in the eighth century BCE, they took part in all the developments that the language underwent in other Israelite communities: Hebrew as it was in First Temple times, Hebrew as it was in

---

[1] On the historical stratification of Biblical Hebrew, see A. Hurvitz, *The Transition Period in Biblical Hebrew: A Study in Post-Exilic Hebrew and its Implications for the Dating of Psalms* (Jerusalem, 1972 [Hebrew]).

Second Temple times, its further development into what we know as Mishnaic Hebrew, Hebrew as a literary language alongside Aramaic as the spoken vernacular, and later as a literary language alongside Arabic as the spoken vernacular. The Samaritans have never made use of Hebrew alongside a non-Semitic vernacular.

From the Hebrew of the First Temple period, only one literary source has been preserved among the Samaritans: the Torah as preserved in Samaritan Torah scrolls. From the long use of Hebrew as a literary language, the Samaritans have preserved prose prayers and liturgical poems, written at different times and in different styles, some written purely in Hebrew, both words and grammar, and some written in a blend of Hebrew and Aramaic which we may call "Late Samaritan Hebrew" [LSH].[2] Has anything survived of Samaritan Hebrew as it was during the Second Temple period?

0.4 The Samaritan Pentateuch and its Linguistic Character

It is well known that there are thousands of differences between the Jewish and Samaritan Pentateuchs. Scholars have counted more than 6000 variants, tallied according to various systems.[3] For our purposes, we may make do with two categories: (a) intentional variants, whether motivated by considerations of belief and law or literary-editorial considerations (i.e., designed to produce a "smoother" text or one in harmony with a Pentateuchal parallel), and (b) unintentional variants, whether such variants as defective/full spelling and guttural letter substitutions or variants in morphology, both sorts of unintentional variants reflecting a linguistic tradition different in pronunciation, word formation, and sometimes even syntax from that represented by the Jewish Pentateuch (and the Masoretic Bible as a whole). Given that the spiritual center of the Samaritans was throughout the generations in the hill country of Ephraim, in Nablus, and around Mt. Gerizim, we are tempted to attribute the particular features of the language of SP to differences of **dialect** between the Hebrew in use in Ephraim and that current in Judah in general and the Jerusalem area in particular. However, sustained and careful attention to the differences in orthography and word formation reveals that many of the features of SH are the same as those evident in non-Biblical Hebrew literature among the Jews, such as rabbinic literature. Furthermore, now that we have access to a number of

---

[2] I used this term in "Samaritan Poems," 333ff. For a description, see Florentin, *Shomronit*.
[3] Gesenius's categorization of these variants (*De Pentateuchi samaritanae origine*, 26ff.) divides them into eight categories; R. Kirchheim, *Karme Šomron* (Frankfurt, 1851), 32ff. [Hebrew], sets up thirteen categories; Kohn, *Pentateucho Samaritano*, 19ff. listed only three; see also Waltke, *Prolegomena*, 271ff.

biblical works, whole or fragmentary, preserved among the Dead Sea Scrolls, and find there linguistic features similar to SH, it is entirely certain that we cannot ascribe the differences between the Biblical Hebrew of the Jewish Pentateuch and those of SP to differences of **place** alone, but rather to differences of **time**. SP in its written form displays some features of the language as we know it from Second Temple times — more specifically, from the end of that period. As a result of these discoveries, things that were considered generations ago to be peculiar to the Samaritan Pentateuchal tradition turn out to be not so.

In summary, then, SP, the sole literary source extant among the Samaritans that dates from the First Temple period, is presented to us in a linguistic redaction that reveals, to the extent possible, features particular to the Hebrew of the Second Temple period (see especially the chapters on tenses and aspects [2.9] and the passive [2.10]), even though its external appearance, the formation of the letters and the division of words by means of a dot, antedates that of the Jewish Pentateuch.

0.5 Can a Hebrew Grammar be Compiled Solely on the Basis of an Unvocalized Text?

One who wishes to be "free of the bonds of Masorah" and to build a complete grammatical description of Biblical Hebrew on the basis of the text as given in the consonants alone (without the pointing) in the books of the Hebrew Bible, assuming that in this way he will be able to describe the language in its "original" form, meaning its form "before the Masorah" — such a person is indulging in fantasy.[4] After all, there are insufficient data in the unpointed text of the Pentateuch, even in the Samaritan version, which uses *matres lectionis* more

---

[4] Bergsträsser, *Grammatik*, II, p. IV, was indeed of the opinion that the application of a "strict philological criterion" would require that the grammatical description of the Hebrew Bible be based on the consonants of the text alone, but he sensed that such a project was outside the realm of the possible. C. Brockelmann, in his *Stand und Aufgaben der Semitistik (Beiträge zur Arabistik, Semitistik und Islamwissenschaft*, ed. R. Hartmann) (Scheel, 1944), 27, casts doubt on whether a grammar so constructed could achieve worthwhile results. Nonetheless, Klaus Beyer (see the introduction to his *Althebräische Grammatik* [Göttingen, 1969]) undertook the impossible task of "liberating Hebrew from the bonds of Masorah and reconstructing its original pre-exilic form." In fact, this is a grammar of hypothetical Hebrew forms constructed according to the rules and formulas that comparative Semitic grammar established by inference from the various historical Semitic languages — among them the Masoretic form of Hebrew! On what basis, for example, could one learn to distinguish the pattern *qōl* from the pattern *qull* in Hebrew (Beyer, 47ff.) if not from the data provided by the Masoretic distinctions in the declensions of nouns?

There is something amusing and even attractive about the attempts to reconstruct Hebrew undertaken by some scholars, but anyone who wants to know Hebrew from its historical sources should keep his distance from them, or at least would be wise to exercise caution in approaching

frequently than does the Masoretic version, to enable us to recognize the vowel system and other phonological phenomena, not to mention that it provides us little insight into word formation since each *mater lectionis* can be realized by more than one vowel. Contemporary transcriptions into other alphabets, which could provide information about vowels, is available only in miniscule amounts and is limited almost entirely to personal names. The grammarian is, thus, left with only a set of "rules" of the sort generated by comparative linguistics, such as $\bar{o} < \bar{a}$, $e < i$, and short vowels in open syllables at the ends of words are deleted. Such rules enable us to reconstruct that the precursor to שומר is *$\check{s}\bar{a}miru$, or to assume that at some time (what time?) during the First Temple period the form ויאכל looked something like: *$way(y)\bar{o}kil$. All the "rules" of Hebrew generated through comparative linguistics, though, were obtained on the basis of Hebrew as reflected in the Masoretic version, with pointing, so that anyone attempting to reconstruct the form of Hebrew "before the Masorah" on the basis of such "rules" is, willingly or not, bound to use the Masoretic data. Without the traditions of pronouncing the text preserved over the generations among the Jews and the Samaritans, no grammar of Hebrew may be constructed. This is evident from an examination of Hebrew's closest cognate languages, Phoenician and Ugaritic. These are available to us only in written documents with no tradition of pronunciation, at most providing us with sparse hints of pronunication in the spelling and in a few transcriptions of words into other tongues. In every description of the grammar of these languages, then, the unknown is greater than the known in almost each and every category. In fact, without our knowledge of Hebrew as preserved by tradition, it would be impossible for us to undertake any reconstruction of the pronunciation of Phoenician or Ugaritic. Moreover, even in such Hebrew sources as Ben-Sira or the Manual of Discipline of the Dead Sea sect, for which we have no tradition of pronunciation, the categorization of a given noun with a given pattern or of a given verb with a given stem can only be a matter of conjecture.[5]

0.6 Samaritan Pointing System

Among the Jews, the oral tradition of reading the Hebrew Bible aloud, passed down from generation to generation, came to be recorded in the various systems of pointing in the 7th and 8th centuries CE. Even though a gap of centu-

---

them, since there are "rules" of language, the logic of which would make it necessary that certain forms exist when in fact they do not exist and no proof can be established that they ever occurred in the past.

[5] See, for example, on אבה in Ben-Sira, Z. Ben-Ḥayyim, "From the Ben-Sira Entries," *Lĕšonénu* 37 (1973), 216 [Hebrew].

ries divides the graphic recording of the oral tradition from the composition of the last of the biblical books, the pointing generally preserves the living language with remarkable fidelity, at least as it was spoken in the last generations of the use of a Hebrew vernacular. This has been proved by comparative linguistic research and verified by considerable external evidence, such as the transcriptions in the second column of Origen's Hexapla and, later, Jerome's transcriptions — evidence that dates from the last generations of spoken Hebrew and those immediately thereafter.[6] In contrast, no such written form of the Samaritan oral tradition has ever been recorded until our own time. To this day, I know of no manuscript of SP produced by Samaritans for their own use which contains a sytematic, thorough indication of the vowel sounds.[7] While it is true that as far back as the Middle Ages, the Samaritans invented vowel signs, their use, however, never departed from the limited scope of teaching children or preventing errors in pronouncing words in which the spelling allows for more than one pronunciation.[8] Even in this very limited realm, no symbol maintains a uniform shape, and there is no one clear method of indicating the vowels. Let us examine the Samaritan pointing and what can be learned from it about the Samaritan pronunciation of the Torah.

0.7 The usual pointing signs found in Samaritan manuscripts are: 1) ˈ, 2) ¯, 3) ˇ, 4) ˆ, 5) ˂, 6) ˃ (on their order in accordance with the Samaritan tradition see *LOT* II, 309, 323); 7) , 8) ˈ, 9) ˥, 10) ˥, ˥. Signs 1–7 are placed above the letters, 9 and 10 before the letter at its upper part. For example: שְׁמִירִים, אֹדֹּבְרה, אַ֑חַת / אָ֑חַת, (לְפָנֶיךָ) לְפָנֶיךָ, הוּא֫, לָכֶם.[9]

From the Samaritan grammatical works, the oldest of which is certainly

---

[6] For the Hexapla material, see G. Mercati, *Psalterii hexapli reliquiae* (Rome, 1958). This has been researched by several scholars. The most comprehensive treatment is Brønno, *Studien*. On Jerome's transcriptions, see C. Siegfried, "Die Aussprache des Hebräischen bei Hieronymus," *ZAW* 4 (1884), 34–83. The material is also collected in A. Sperber, "Hebrew Based upon Greek and Latin Transliterations," *HUCA* 12–13 (1937/38), 103ff. On the problem of the pronunciation of gutturals in Jerome's transcriptions, see E. Brønno, *Die Aussprache der hebräischen Laryngale nach Zeugnissen des Hieronymus* (Göttingen, 1970).

[7] This statement obviously excludes such manuscripts as that prepared especially for M. Gaster in 1912, MS 35 (2060) of the John Rylands Library in Manchester, pointed by Abiša ben Finās. In the British Museum manuscript of ST, Or 10251, which was also written especially for M. Gaster, the first page is pointed, presumably at Gaster's request.

[8] More symbols were created for teaching purposes, symbols which I have never seen in manuscripts; see *LOT* II, 317. They were never incorporated into the pointing system. The same is true for the later use of a circle over a letter (see *LOT* I, צֹב), which appears in British Museum MS Or 10251, apparently to indicate that the letter is not pronounced (like the Syriac מבטלנא); see Z. Ben-Hayyim, review of E. Robertson, *Catalogue of the Samaritan Manuscripts in the John Rylands Library, Manchester, Vol. II: The Gaster Manuscripts*, *JSS* 14 (1969), 145, n. 1.

[9] Many examples of pointed forms can be found in the *apparatus criticus* to composition III in *LOT* I, 173ff.

Introduction

not earlier than the tenth century, we learn that Symbols 1–6 are a complete set and undoubtedly the original system.¹⁰ Symbols 1–5 represent vowels, while Symbol 6 denotes gemination of consonants. The description of the symbols is given in Arabic terminology in those sources, with illustrative examples drawn from the Pentateuch. From those Arabic terms, the value of Symbol 5, as called in Arabic كسر (i.e., *i*), is entirely clear. Nearly as clear is the value of Symbol 4, known as ضم, which in fact may represent an *u* or an *o* vowel. Symbols 1–3 are collectively labeled فتح (TH פתח), each with its own modifier: ايا ("indication"), اخا ("brotherhood"), and ندا ("exclamation"), which are unknown outside of the aforementioned Samaritan sources, and the phonetic value of each symbol is evident from its name. The examples of specific words provide no assistance, of course, without the ability to establish the type of vowel from the tradition of pronouncing those words. In the later literature, we occasionally find the modifiers "large" (فتحة كبرى), "small" (فتحة صغرى), and "intermediate" (فتحة متوسطة).¹¹ These terms, too, fail to provide us with a clear indication of the value of each vowel, since we cannot determine from the term itself whether it refers to a difference of quantity or a difference of quality, like that indicated by the terms פתח גדול (the normal *pataḥ*) and פתח קטן (usually *seghol*) in the Jewish tradition.

> Note: On the value of Symbol 8, see also Luis F. Girón-Blanc, "Un Signo Controvertido en la Vocalizacion del Pentateucho Hebreo-Samaritano" in J.-P. Rothschild and G. D. Sixdenier, eds., *Études samaritaines: Pentateuque et Targum, exégèse et philologie, chroniques* (Louvain and Paris, 1988), 95–106, and my "Observations" in the same volume, 107–108.

0.8 Symbol 7 is readily recognizable as the Arabic ضم itself, and it, therefore, may substitute for Symbol 4. This symbol achieved more extensive use in later generations. Symbols 9 and 10 appear only with letters for guttural consonants, and in fact they are composed of the Arabic ʿayin with the addition of Symbol 2 or with the addition of the Arabic letter ʾalīf (ا).¹² On this basis alone, even without a knowledge of its pronunciation in SH, we could surmise with reasonable assurance that this symbol indicates the presence of an ʿayin at the place indicated by the symbol, since the guttural consonants were eliminated, according to a variety of literary evidence (see 1.1.8).

---

¹⁰ The Samaritan grammatical texts have been published in *LOT* II, 305ff. The rules have been attributed to אבן דרתה, who lived during the 10th century (*LOT* I, טff., and *LOT* III/2, 20).

¹¹ See *LOT* I, 235, s.v. אדני; ibid., 233, s.v. אבני.

¹² The symbol ʿ is rare and is presumably the original form. In British Museum MS Or 6461, written in 1339/40, I saw at Nu 18:2 אֲחִיךָ (today pronounced *ā'ak*), but in later and recent manuscripts I have seen only the symbol ʿ.

Symbols 7–10, then, are borrowed from the Arabic language, and are, therefore, obviously not part of the original stratum of Samaritan pointing as taught by the various grammatical works mentioned above, which even derive their shapes from the use of the Samaritan "vowel letters" אחהיו״ע.[13]

It is apparent that Symbol 8 (based on the Arabic فتحة?) is a substitute for Symbol 1 or Symbol 2 (based on the Arabic فتحة?), and appearing usually just before the letter, it acquired the specialized use, especially in the later manuscripts, of indicating a vowel unrepresented by a letter in the unpointed text. That vowel is one derived from a *šəwa*, as in לפניך (pronounced *alfânək* in contemporary SH), which, if it were written with an initial א (cf. אזרוע/זרוע!), would be vocalized something like this: אלפניך or אלפניך.

Symbol 2 may also appear above the letter ו to mark it as having consonantal value, as in עשו (today *īšåb*), and above the letter פ to mark its pronunciation as *b*, as in יפל (today *yibbål*). The factor common to both of these uses is the plosive pronunciation of [b] as against [f] and as against [w] or [u/o]. It seems that from the perspective of its **origin**, the horizontal line above the letters ו and פ is not identical to Symbol 3, but seems to be a simplified form of the Arabic شدة.

We may conclude, then, that when the Samaritan pointing was created, it was intended to indicate five vowels and gemination of consonants. Since it did not achieve the status of a recognized, obligatory system among the Samaritans as did the Tiberian pointing among the Jews, the system was not preserved intact in texts of the Pentateuch, and one finds that scribes applied the points received from earlier Samaritan tradition in whatever manner they wished and according to whatever level of knowledge they possessed of that inherited system, and indeed there were scribes who borrowed symbols from Arabic pointing for particular purposes, mixing them with the symbols in the received Samaritan tradition.

0.9 One who pays close attention to the pointing of various words in two important manuscripts of SP, British Museum manuscript Or 6461 from 1339/40, henceforth referred to as א, and MS R 16/41 of Trinity College, Cambridge, from 1482 (?), henceforth referred to as ב, will be surprised by the lack of consistency in marking the vowels. The following are selected vocalized words juxtaposed with their contemporary pronunciation.

א: המאור (Gn 1:16) *ammâ'or*, תוצא (Gn 1:24) *tūṣi*, הרמש (Gn 1:30) *arrēməš*, האבדה (Ex 22:8) *â'ēbiddå*, יאמר (Ex 22:8) *iyyâmər*, גנב (Ex 22:11) *gânəb*, גנב (Ex 22:11) *yiggânəb*, וגר (Ex 22:20) *wger*, תלוה (Ex 22:24) *talwi*, מאתם (Ex 25:3)

---

[13] *LOT* II, 309, 323.

miyyētimma, הׄוֹאל בׄאׇר (Dt 1:5) *uwwål bayyår*, כִיתנוֹת עוׄר (Gn 3:21) *kittånot ūr*, הׄחטאים (Nu 17:3) *'åttå'əm*.

בּמקוּם׃בּ (Lv 6:18) *bammåqom*, בּעמיתו (Lv 5:21) *bammītu*, וּבעׁר (Lv 6:5) *wbār*, ישׁבּע (Lv 5:24) *yiššāba*, וּשׁלם (Lv 5:24) *wšalləm*, יחׁטא (Lv 5:23) *yēṭṭi*, דּבׁר (Lv 5:224) *dēbår*, נעׁשׁה במׁרׁחשת (Lv 7:9) *niyyåši bamrā'ešåt*, צׁוי (Lv 6:2) *ṣåbi*, זאׁת (Lv 6:2) *zē'ot*, אׁתו (Lv 5:24) *ūtu*, אׁחת (Lv 5:26) *'åt*, הׁעשוק (SP Lv 5:23) *å'åšoq*.

Each and every one of the manuscripts is marked by inconsistencies in the use of pointing marks, this being especially noticeable when a particular symbol can be used to refer to different vowels in words very close together in the same passage, and even in the very same word, as in MS ב at Lv 5:23: יחׁטא. While it is true that this inconsistency is defined as measured against Samaritan pronunciation in modern times, everything we know about Hebrew and everything we learn from linguistic research still does not help us to assume that the author of MS א, for example, pronounced יׁגנׁב (Ex 22:11) *yaggånəb* just because the symbol ׁ appearing in the word בׁאׇר (Dt 1:5) and other words indicates an "a" vowel. A careful reading of the list of pointing variants in von Gall, *Pentateuch* and the pointed words cited by Diening will further establish the claim that there is much confusion and disorder in Samaritan pointing.[14] Its history and the patterns of its use in various manuscripts from various times are at present engulfed in too deep a fog to provide the basis for a grammar of Hebrew according to the Samaritan tradition. We are still in need of a sorting of all the pointed words in Samaritan literature, Pentateuchal and extra-Pentateuchal, and a cataloguing of those words by morphological patterns and by the date of the pointing. This would be a worthy goal in and of itself, attainable in our time, now that many collections of Samaritan manuscripts are available in microfilm at the Institute for Hebrew Manuscripts at the Jewish National and University Library in Jerusalem. It should be obvious that such an undertaking was beyond the scope of what could be accomplished in the preparation of the present work. Moreover, the examples cited above suffice to demonstrate that without a detailed and precise knowledge of Samaritan pronunciation of the Pentateuch as chanted in Samaritan worship, there is no chance of deciphering the pronunciation values of the pointing symbols in various words in the various manuscripts. We must of necessity conclude that an awareness of Samaritan pronunciation of the Pentateuch and an awareness of the grammar of SH are a necessary, prior condition for understanding the nature of Samaritan pointing.[15]

---

[14] Examples from Diening: p. 20 בׁאה / באה at Ex 3:9; p. 21 וקראת / וקראׁת at Gn 16:11; p. 29 שׁכן / שׁכן at Gn 26:2, and others. E.g, von Gall at Gn 21:18: ידׁך / יד"ך / ידׁך.

[15] Furthermore, a knowledge of Samaritan pronunciation is necessary even for a proper evaluation of the unpointed text, of the *matres lectionis*, in SH. I have previously commented on this in "*Ha'azinu*," with additional evidence in "Some Problems," 254. We may note here, for example,

0.10 Recording a Spoken Language for Grammatical Investigation

A linguist who sets out to describe a language without a tradition of writing, such as one finds among vernaculars in the Semitic languages as well as others, must first give that language written form. For this purpose it is accepted practice to employ the Latin alphabet with the addition of various diacritical marks to represent phonemes and allophones for which the Latin alphabet alone provides inadequate representation. The form of the technical symbol is of no significance in and of itself, and of the multitude of sets of such symbols available, the linguist will choose the one which is most appropriate to the task at hand or which is accepted among linguists in the same field. The **method** of graphic representation and its limits, however, are an issue the linguist must address.

There are basically two approaches: (a) the researcher makes a written record of whatever he hears — each phoneme, each varied allophone of a phoneme, in an attempt to provide a full, "objective" reflection of the speech process. This approach was taken for decades in describing dialects, in Semitics and elsewhere. However, there are limits to the ability of even the most experienced phoneticist — one who is able to discern many shades of difference between varied realizations of phonemes — to perceive the speech process and report it accurately and precisely. In more than one instance, differences can be found in the recording of phonemes between two phoneticists using the same system of graphic presentation. It has even become clear that "narrow" phonetic rendering sometimes distorts the grammatical description of the language, since it ascribes equal importance to every sound uttered, so that even if a given word is one entity in the perception of the speaker, it may turn out to be recorded in several different forms.[16] (b) The alternative approach is to record speech sounds according to the overall value of each phoneme and to denote it with one constant symbol, even when the recorder perceives varying shades of that sound in different phonetic contexts, as long as this way of representing the phoneme does not distort unique phonological and morphological features dependent upon this phoneme. For example, one may sometimes discern two *l* sounds, one "clear," i.e., alveolo-dental [l], and one "dark," i. e., velar [ɫ] (recorded as ḷ). If no particular aspect of the language is dependent upon this distinction, as is the case with modern Hebrew or with English, then for the linguist who adopts this second approach to transcription, one

---

that in Gn 6:7 we find the variant spellings עשיתים/עשיתם, and in Gn 37:17 שמעתים/שמעתם, because of the identical pronunciations of the two forms in each instance: *'aššītimma, šāmāttimma*. Abū Saʿīd, the grammarian, insisted in his first rule (*LOT* I, 135ff.) that the distincitions be retained in spelling, apparently without effect.

[16] This is exemplified in *LOT* III/1, 10.

symbol suffices for both variants. The same is true for marking the distinction between front *a* and back *å* or between front *i* and central *ï*, in a language where these differences do not mark any perceived linguistic distinction, even though they may be obvious to the listener and can be recorded with precision.

0.11 A decision to adopt the second approach must be based on a painstaking phonological analysis of all the sounds of the language being recorded, in all their real contexts, so that it is possible to recognize the crucial element, the phoneme, and all the realizations of which that phoneme is composed and to give them a consistent, unified graphic expression. That demand for total consistency is very difficult for the grammarian to meet even when trying to present in writing a closed morphological unit, and all the more so when the language under study is not the grammarian's own. His only guide is this: as complete a knowledge as possible of the language being recorded provides the best assurance of fidelity in the written presentation of a spoken language for the grammarian's purposes.[17]

The preceding considerations with regard to methods of transcription were developed in the context of research into living dialects and spoken vernaculars that lack a writing system shaped by their own speakers, which could have been helpful in assessing the native speakers' sense of the sound of the language. There is no essential difference, though, between that and a **pronunciation tradition** of a dead, ancient language which became a sacred language. In shaping the written form of a sacred language, the first approach described above would certainly be ineffective. In fact, it might distort the presentation of the language it intends to describe, because the phonological system of the sacred language is subject to influence and even pressure from that of the vernacular languages of those who employ that "sacred tongue." The phonological system of the sacred language would normally be able to withstand that pressure only enough to preserve the general value of its sounds, not their various shades. From SH the following example may be mentioned: ר is phonemic in SH as it is in Jewish Hebrew. Among the Arabic-speaking Samaritans and among the older Samaritans living among the Hebrew-speaking population of Israel, ר is realized as an alveolo-dental *r*, whereas among some of the

---

[17] In 1904, O. Jesperson wrote (*Phonetische Grundfragen* [Leipzig]): "Erst wenn man eine Sprache so beherrscht, dass man das in Ernst und Scherz Gesprochene versteht und sich selbst in Ernst und Scherz auszudrücken vermag, erst dann kann man recht eigentlich alle ihre lautlichen Verhältnisse beurteilen." This is absolutely true, but unfortunately such knowledge of the values of phonemes in ancient and dead languages cannot be obtained.

Similarly, T. Nöldeke wrote ("Texte," 205), in reference to his *Grammatik der Neusyrischen Sprache* (Leipzig, 1868): "Einen Dialekt von dem ich keine Silbe gehört habe systematisch darzustellen das habe ich in jüngeren Jahren einmal gewagt... so etwas täte ich aber nie wieder."

On the formulation of the written text of SH, from which all the data in the present work are taken, see *LOT* III/1, 11–13.

Hebrew-speaking Samaritans, it is uvular R; which is common among contemporary Hebrew speakers. But even those who pronounce this phoneme as uvular produce an alveolo-dental preceding an "a" vowel, i.e., before a vowel absent from the phonetic system of their spoken language. A linguist who imputes significance to the variant realizations of ר would, it may be assumed, accurately record the different sounds (which are easily discernable), but the differences are based not in SH itself but in the interrelations between their vernacular and SH.[18] This is especially true in regard to vowels. A sacred language, after all, has an exalted status, and SH was a written language from antiquity, with those who employ it in worship (in the recitation of the Pentateuch and in prayer) keen to maintain all its written features in full detail. However, the distinguishing characteristic of SH (and of SA) is the absence of a fully formed and stable system of pointing. Pronunciation has been preserved as an oral tradition passed on from generation to generation. Thus, those aspects of the language not recorded in writing, i.e., primarily, the vowels, are more exposed to the influence of the vernacular.

0.12 Given that my entire goal in describing SH, the Samaritans' sacred language, is to research and bring to light whatever SH has preserved of Hebrew from that distant time when it was a spoken language, before it became frozen in place as a sacred language alone, I have chosen to abandon the approach of "total copying" of what is heard, which I had adopted at first, and I have taken up the second approach, which seems more appropriate for the task at hand. I have been consistent, then, in rendering ק as q even when the written letter was pronounced by a particular informant as a glottal stop (א), and the same for s and t when the emphatic $ṣ$ and $ṭ$ respectively were pronounced, as mentioned in 1.1.7. I have, however, abandoned the distinction between [l] and [ḷ], which is observed in *LOT* III/1, not only because it is phonologically insignificant, but because it has no significance for the history of Hebrew as a living language, just as the distinction between [r] and [R] provides no important data with regard to antiquity, as mentioned above. A particular problem, and a difficult and complex one at that, is presented by systematic distinction between long vowels (such as $ī$, $ē$, and $ā$) and extra-long vowels (such as as $ī:$, $ē:$, and $ā:$). In normal reading and certainly in slow-paced reading, the distinction is entirely obvious, but in a somewhat faster and musical rendition, the distinctions of vowel quantity become quite blurred, and one's ear, more precisely, my own ear, does not discern them. Grammatical analysis demonstrates that whenever two syllables contract into one due to the loss of a guttural consonant (1.2.1d), one can assume that an extra-long vowel will occur. Nev-

---

[18] The same is true of the pronunciation of ק as a glottal stop (1.1.5) and of ט and צ as equivalent to ת and ס respectively (1.1.7).

ertheless, I have felt it best not to follow the path of schematization, which would mean marking extra-long vowels according to the grammatical analysis even contravening my direct impression. Rather, in such circumstances, I have settled for marking normal length alone. This concession can have no influence on grammatical considerations, but it should not be overlooked that the same word might be written sometimes with a long vowel and at other times with an extra-long vowel, e.g., למעלה might sometimes be written *almāla* and sometimes *almā:la*, בחרו sometimes *bā:ru*, sometimes *bāru*, all according to what I heard, or thought I heard, from a particular informant during a particular reading.

In giving written form to the Samaritan recitation of the Torah, I tried to put myself in the position of one who uses that language, and I asked myself: what would that reader preserve in writing and what would he not preserve? The pointing of SP texts by Samaritans at my request, using agreed-upon symbols, as well as other material written by Samaritans, assisted me in determining what is considered of primary importance and what is not (and, therefore, may be ignored in writing).[19] Significantly after I adopted this approach, I found that with regard to the vowels, my choices agreed with what was intended by the pointing system as reflected in MS א of the grammar book written by El'azar ben Pinḥas during the 14th century.[20]

0.13 Material for the Grammar

The sections of Pentateuch and liturgy recorded from oral recitations and published in *LOT* III presumably should be sufficient to form the basis for understanding the structure of SH and of SA in the realm of phonology and morphology. For someone interested in general linguistic aspects of these matters, such as evaluating the status of Samaritan tradition vis-à-vis Jewish traditions or evaluating the Samaritan dialect of Aramaic vis-à-vis the other Palestinian dialects, those texts should suffice, along with occasional additional data. However, for someone who wants to describe thoroughly the language of the Pentateuch as pronounced by the Samaritans, it is necessary to know the Samaritan pronunciation of the entire Pentateuch, from the first verse in Genesis to the last verse in Deuteronomy. For one finds several words written exactly alike in the Pentateuch, which appear to be the very same words, and are indeed so in TH, but which a thoroughgoing knowledge of the Samaritan tra-

---

[19] See *LOT* III/1, 12.
[20] This manuscript is described in *LOT* I, דפff. All the vocalized words in the manuscript are cited with their pointing in the critical apparatus to text III, 175ff.

dition reveals to be different words, whether or not they bear meanings different from one another.²¹ The following are just a few examples:

a. The noun פללים is pronounced in SH *fallāləm* at Dt 32:31 and is taken to mean "see," while at Ex 21:22 it is pronounced *fēlāləm* and understood by the Samaritans as referring to prayers and supplication;

b. The noun מדה (TH מִדָּה) is pronounced *måddå* at Ex 26:2, but at Lv 19:35 *måda*, with the only difference between them in derivation, not in semantics: the first is from an ע"ע root, the second from an ע"י root (and related to the Jewish Hebrew word מָדוֹן; see 4.1.2.8 note 3);

c. The participle of hollow roots in the *Qal* stem is normally constructed in the *fåq* pattern, with the feminine singular and the plural constructed on that basis with the appropriate affixes. Indeed, from the root גו"ר we find *går* (Dt 18:6), *aggår* (Lv 17:13), and other forms, but we also find *gīrəm* (Lv 25:6 and elsewhere)(cf. TH לָנִים alongside לָן). The form *šēkən* = TH שָׁכֵן with the addition of the 3rd masc. sing. pronominal suffix is pronounced *šēkīnu* (שכנו Dt 1:7); with the fem. suffix it would be **šēkīna*, and, thus, **šēkinta* would be the expected parallel to TH שְׁכֶנְתָּה. But the words משכנתה ומגרת ביתה in Ex 3:22 are not pronounced as one would expect on the basis of one's grammatical knowledge alone, **miššēkinta wmiggålīråt bīta*, but instead *maškinta wamgīråt bīta*. Perhaps it is possible with some effort to construct a plausible explanation for the lack of gemination in the ש and the ג in those words, along the lines of *milmēta* מלמטה and *milfånək* מלפניך (see 1.5.3.3e) or *amkinnårət* (TH מִכְּנֶרֶת) (*LOT* III/1, 174), and this may even be likened to the word מְנָיִן (= מִנַּיִן!) in manuscripts and some oral traditions of MH. Two points, however, should not be overlooked: (1) ST and SAV do not reflect the preposition "from" (מן) before the nouns in question, seeing them instead as synonyms in apposition to רעותה (SP: ושאל איש מאת רעהו ואשה מאת רעותה משכנתה ומגרת ביתה); (2) There is in SA a masc. noun מגיר, meaning "neighbor" (e.g., ST to Ex 12:4), and מגירה is the feminine form. The term מגירתה/מגירה occurs in Aramaic only in Palestine, and the root גו"ר meaning "dwell temporarily" as in Hebrew is generally unattested in Aramaic, making it nearly certain that מגירתא/מגירא is a Hebrew loanword in Palestinian Aramaic.²² It seems, then, that the Samaritan reading of מגרת (and the variant מגירת) as a

---

²¹ One aspect of semantic differentiation is whether a particular personal name, originally a single term in form, is pronounced differently when referring to different individuals. For example, עוץ in Gn 10:23 is pronounced *ūṣ*, in accordance with the rule in 4.1.2.13, but in Gn 22:21 *oṣ*, at variance with the rule. The same is true of שכם, pronounced *aškəm* in verses such as Gn 34:24, but in Nu 26:31 *šēkåm*, an instance in which a distinction is drawn in the Tiberian tradition as well (שְׁכֶם in Genesis, שֶׁכֶם in Numbers). On the use of variant pronunciations for the purpose of making distinctions, see also 2.2.1.1.5.

²² Similar phenomena are described in Ben-Ḥayyim, "Contribution," 164. Only a few examples are cited there, and there is still a significant amount of material in SA to be revealed and its relation to Hebrew explored.

substantive preserves the Hebrew word as it was, in the form of a *Hifʿil* participle. It is thus easy to see that just as *wamgīrat* is a participle, so *maškinta* is also a *Hifʿil* participle, which is in accordance with grammatical norms. The fact that a *Hifʿil* verb may bear the same meaning as the *Qal* verb of the same root is not surprising. This has been noted particularly with regard to verbs that express remaining at a certain place, such as Aramaic אבית alongside בָּת in the sense of "stay [someplace] overnight,"[23] Arabic اقــــام in the sense of "remained [someplace]," and Hebrew יאמין (Job 39:24), תרגיע (Dt 28:65), and הרגיעה (Isa 34:14);

d. The usual and expected pronunciation of בנה ("her son") is *bēna*, but in Ex 4:25 it is *binna*. It might seem at first that this is just a variant form like that found in the noun זקן *zāqannu* as against *zāqānimma* (see 4.6.3) [or *šimma* שמא ("the name") as against *ešma* in the modern Aramaic vernacular]. In fact, though, from the Samaritan translations and exegesis we learn that the understanding of the word in question does not derive from the noun בן but from the root בנ"ן. SAV ad loc. translates the word as تبـنـــت, and in ST there are manuscripts that read בנה (not ברה!) or בנואה. The root בנ"ן is what is intended by the Samaritan pronunciation of ויבננהו (SP Dt 32:10) as *wyēbannēʾu*, and the word is understood to refer to adoption of someone as a son (see 2.7.10, n.15). Here in Ex 4:25, the sense of בני"ן is different. In reading *binna*, the Samaritan tradition attempts to extricate itself from a difficulty of interpretation: Zippora, Moses' wife, circumcises her son, even though women are disqualified from performing circumcision since only the circumcised may circumcise. From the words of Munajja b. Ṣadaqa Abū l-Faraj (12th century), we learn that he was aware of a "light" reading of the noun (with simple second radical) and of a "heavy" one (with geminated second radical). He rejected the former because

---

The root גו"ר is homonymous. It denotes (a) neighborhood, and (b) conflict, violence. In Hebrew and Arabic and some other Semitic languages, it occurs in both senses. In Aramaic it generally denotes only adultery. Indeed, it is used constantly to translate the Hebrew root נאף. According to F. Schwally, *Idioticon des chrislich-palästinischen Aramäisch* (Giessen, 1893), 17, this specific use developed from sense (a) i.e., to have sexual relations with a [female] neighbor. Brockelmann (*LS*, 110) accepted this strange etymology, though Aramaic does not express neighborhood by גור, but instead by דור. It must not be forgotten that, differently from fornication (זנא/זנה), adultery means "usurpation of a husband's 'property,'" namely his exclusive sexual rights, thus the Aramaic use of גור is far more probably connected with sense (b). Already Schwally (ibid.) explained גור in Aramaic as a loanword from Hebrew. It is worth mentioning that Hebrew נאף has undergone the same semantic process, if my assumption that נאף is etymologically connected with Arabic VN is correct. The dictionaries of Biblical Hebrew do not present a cognate to נאף, although it is found in the Aramaic inscription of ברדכב of יאדי, as shown in "Sfire," 250. (Cf. also S. A. Kaufman, *The Akkadian Influences on Aramaic* [Chicago and London 1973], 153 n. 64.) The kinship of נאב: נאף: נהב is twofold: phonetic and semantic.

[23] The verb אבית (*Afʿel*) in the sense of בת (*Qal*) is clearly attested in SA (ST Gn 2:23,25 לאבתו/ לאבהתה) and CPA (Schulthess, *Lexicon*, 23). It should be mentioned that parallel to the participle forms מגירתה and משכנתה, one finds in SA משרי לגבון (*LOT* III/2, 286, l. 30) = "dwells among them."

in his opinion the intent of the verse is to tell us that Zippora "cut off the (metaphorical) foreskin of her understanding" [קטעת קלפה תבננהא]."[24] This interpretation derives בנה from the root בנ"ן, which is cognate with the root בו"ן. In any case, it is not at all easy to include the form *binna* in the declension of בן ("son").

It would be easy to compile a long list of words and linguistic forms like the previous example, from which one might learn that for a full understanding of the language of the Pentateuch in the Samaritan tradition and a description of its grammar, i.e., for the purpose of classifying forms within the language, it is necessary to know the pronunciation of the word in question everywhere it appears in the Pentateuch and to know the relationship between pronunciation and interpretation, at least where the pronunciation varies from the norm. In other words, it is an absolute necessity to do the the work of establishing a text with full vocalization before the work of the grammarian, since the Samaritan tradition does not provide us with ready-made materials, as does the Masoretic tradition among the Jews.

0.14 Because of the aforementioned considerations, I was not content to rely on those Pentateuchal and liturgical texts published in *LOT* III/1, but instead I gathered additional oral data from Samaritans about the pronunciation of words throughout the Pentateuch, checking each and every detail several times, particularly at any point where the pronunciation seemed to me in conflict with what my conclusions about the grammar would have led me to expect. After the entire Pentateuch was recorded according to the method described above, it was entered into a computer data base. The difference between the text prepared for the purpose of the present volume and that published in *LOT* III/1 is not only that I have decided to forgo marking the allophone [!], as mentioned previously, but I have also refrained from presenting the flow of recitation, e.g., words blended together due to the sentence stress, vowels lengthened, and certain additions made in the chanted reading at the end of each section (*qiṣṣa*) (see *LOT* III/1, 27). The purpose of the text prepared for the grammatical description required that the words be seen in their standard usage and required disregarding certain phenomena caused by the musical rendition in a liturgical setting. With the aid of the computer, each word in the prepared text was subjected to a thorough grammatical analysis, and lists of words were prepared, classified according to the criteria needed for the gram-

---

[24] The text of the passage dealing with this in MS Sassoon 718 is published (and translated into Hebrew) in *LOT* V, 12ff., with the kind permission of Mr. S. D. Sassoon and with the use of a microfilm from the Institute for Hebrew Manuscripts at the Jewish National and University Library.

Introduction   17

matical description. Thus, along the way to preparing that description, all the material was prepared for a concordance of Biblical Hebrew according to the Samaritan pronunciation. Since a knowledge of how each and every word in SP is pronounced is of interest not only to the linguist, but to the Bible commentator and the scholar of Samaritan religion and law as well, I thought it appropriate to arrange the concordance as a separate book (*LOT* IV) and make it available to interested scholars. However, the nouns and the verbs, more precisely, those words that seemed to me to be in those respective categories, were separated into two sections according to **grammatical** criteria and presented as an addendum to the present study, to supplement the grammatical analysis. After all, the nature of a descriptive grammar is that it deals in general rules and problems, and the examples cited therein are chosen to provide not exhaustive documentation but selective representation. The publication of *LOT* IV eliminates the need to provide references for every example cited, leaving me free to provide such references only for unusual forms, which are usually related to a particular passage, or for instances in which the form illuminates some difference between the Samaritan and Jewish traditions.

0.15 Classification of Linguistic Phenomena in TH and SH

One who approaches the task of composing a grammar of Hebrew finds that, when it comes to dividing the material into section, chapters, and even headings and subheadings, the path ahead has been smoothly paved and well marked for generations. Different grammars of Hebrew are distinguishable not on the basis of major divergences but rather in differences of detail, such as the order in which different parts of speech are treated. The reason for this is that every linguistic phenomenon in the Hebrew Bible has been subjected to comprehensive investigation over the years, to the point where its place in the grammar and lexicon of the Bible are well established. Nevertheless, here and there one may find that the classification of various words or forms is not entirely determined by the established rules underlying the descriptive grammar. Several examples follow:

   a. The form נָזֹרוּ in Isa 1:4 and Ezek 14:5 is usually classified today as a *Nifʻal* from the root זו״ר. The semantics of נז״ר, though, make it possible to interpret נָזֹרוּ as reflecting that root in the *Qal* stem. Indeed, Ibn Janāḥ (*Kitāb al-Mustalḥiq*, 77) considered both possibilities, but arranged it (*Kitāb al-ʼUṣūl*, 422) s.v. נזר using the very same criteria used by those who classify that form as *Nifʻal*. The fact that the root נז״ר in such cognate languages as Arabic and Aramaic has an *a* as the vowel of the second radical provides neither support nor refutation, of course, for any classification of נָזֹרוּ in Hebrew, as we learn from the treatment of יכ״ל in those languages: יְכִל in Aramaic, وَكِلَ in Arabic. One who classifies נָזֹרוּ as does Ibn Janāḥ cannot support the claim of Ben Yehuda (*Thesaurus*, VIII, 3594) s.v. נזר, that "the *Qal* stem is not found in early sources."

b. The forms וְהִצִּיל and וְהִמְלִיט in Isa 31:5 would be defined by today's grammarians as converted perfect 3rd pers. masc. sing. verbs in the *Hifʿil* stem, continuing the infinitive absolutes גָּנֹן and פָּסֹחַ, just as וּבָאתֶם in Jer 7:10 continues the string of infinitives רָצֹחַ הֲגָנֹב, etc., in the preceding verse. Ibn Janāḥ (*Kitāb al-Lūmaʿ*, 336), however, interprets them as infinitives, similar to הֶחֱזִיקִי in Jer 31:31 and הִשְׁמִדָם in Jos 11:14. There is no doubt that TH has a *Hifʿil* infinitive with *ḥireq* as the vowel of the preformative ה (BL, 333i), and such forms are not to be taken as corruptions or errors (*pace* Bergsträsser, *Grammatik*, section on *Hifʿil*, §19, note to paragraph *l*). Which classification is preferable cannot be determined.

c. The form מָאֵן in Ex 7:27 is understood by the common grammars of Biblical Hebrew as a *Piʿel* participle with the preformative מ deleted.[25] In traditional school grammars, however, it is taken to be an adjective and not a verb, and so it is by Ben Yehuda (*Thesaurus*, VI, 2763) as well. When Ibn Janāḥ (*Kitāb al-'Uṣūl*, s.v. מאן) compares that form to וּמַהֵר in Zeph 1:14 and David Qimḥi adds וְשַׁבֵּחַ in Eccl 4:2, they surely classify מָאֵן, too, as a *Piʿel*. (The term صفة, Hebrew תאר, includes what we classify as a participle.) A careful look at all the forms of this verb in the Bible taking into account only the unpointed text, though, shows that the *Piʿel* classification emerges from the Masoretic pointing alone. Had the Masoretic tradition opted to vocalize those verbs in the *Qal* stem, as the unpointed text of Ex 7:27 hints — then the form מָאֵן would occasion no surprise but instead be understand as a *Qal* participle. In this verb as with others, the Masoretes vocalize according to the practice in the later strata of the language, where (in this instance) the *Piʿel* not the *Qal*, was in common use, as the forms ממאנת, ממאנים, and מיאון in the Mishna attest.[26] The Samaritan tradition's treatment of verbs II-guttural (see 2.2.2.0), in fact, provides no reason to assume that מאן here is in the *Piʿel* stem. Quite surprising is that recent scholars have overlooked the presence of a *Qal* form of מאן in Syriac and have adopted farfetched explanations.[27]

In either case, one may conclude that even within the realm of Hebrew in the Tiberian tradition, the classification of a particular form may engender

---

[25] So GKC §52s; BL, 217.

[26] See Ben-Ḥayyim, *Tradition*, 115.

[27] This is especially surprising in regard to Brockelmann, author of *LS*, who suggested (*GvG* I, 264) the clever explanation that אם מאן reflects a haplology and also emended to הַמֵּאֲנִים in Jer 13:10 accordingly. His explanation was adopted by BL, 217, and JM, 154, even though the unpointed verbs in their various forms in the Hebrew Bible and in Syriac make this view unnecessary.

Introduction

controversy. All the more prone to doubt and disagreement are the corresponding issues in Samaritan Hebrew. In what way this is so is the topic of the following section.

0.16 A number of phonological processes in SH, such as the loss of the original short *u* vowel (1.5.2.3), the fusion of guttural phonemes (1.1.8ff.), the interrelations between *e/ə/i* (1.5.1.1), and others, brought about a situation in which certain forms that are distinct in TH are identical in SH. In some instances this identity is maintained throughout a declension or conjugation, in which case classification does not engender particular difficulties. More difficult are those instances in which the absolute forms are identical, while the declined forms reveal the original distinction, but where the absolute forms are unattested in the Masoretic Pentateuch. The resulting difficulties of classification may be illuminated through a few examples:

a. Both the imperative שמח (TH שְׂמַח) in Dt 33:18 and the perfect שמח (TH שָׂמֵחַ; SH reads as *Qal*) in Dt 24:5 are pronounced *šåmå* in SH, following phonological rules. Only context teaches us that we have here two forms that are to be classified differently. Context, however, is insufficient as a guide to the classification of *šāma* שמע in Dt 33:7 as imperative and not perfect, and, in fact, we can infer from its translation in SAV that it was taken to be perfect in this verse (see 7.4.5).

b. The TH forms רֹחַב and רָחָב are both pronounced *råb* in SH, and TH רֹב and רַב are both pronounced *råb*. The same rule would lead us to expect TH עַל to be pronounced **al* (or **'ål*), since the vowel was originally short, as is indicated both by TH and by etymological connections; and with the prepositional -בְּ, the expected pronunciation is *bal* or (especially with the inclusion of the definite article) *bāl*. The phrase אשר לא משכה בעל (Dt 21:3) is pronounced in SH *ēšår lā måšåka bāl*, a pronunciation that would enable us to classify בעל here as we do its TH conterpart בְּעַל — if the pronunciation in other verses were not *ūl* = TH עַל, *olkimma* = TH עֲלֵכֶם. It might appear that we must posit two morphological variants *ūl/al*, but both Samaritan translations render בעל in the phrase in question by independent substantives: ST מסחן = "owner"; SAV فحل ("the male of the cattle"). Note also that ST reads משכה as 3rd fem. sing. perfect (TH *מָשְׁכָה), while SAV reads it as 3rd masc. sing. with a 3rd fem. sing. pronominal suffix (TH *מְשָׁכָהּ). Can a classification of these two words, both the noun and the verb, in the Samaritan oral tradition be made with any certainty?

c. The phrase בנים לא האמן בם (SP Dt 32:20, TH בָּנִים לֹא־אֵמֻן בָּם) is pronounced *bānəm lā å:mən bimma*. Could האמן be a noun אֵמֻן preceded by the definite article, or perhaps a *Hifʿil* infinitive? Here, the Samaritan translations provide no assistance with classification. Both ignore the letter ה and do not employ the definite article in the translation, leaving open the question of whether we are to understand this word as TH אָמֵן (the noun) or הָאֵמֻן (the *Hif'il* infinitive).

d. The word חטאתי in Gn 20:9 is pronounced *ēṭåtti*, not *'åṭīti* as in every other instance in the Pentateuch and as is to be expected of the verb חטא which in most forms behaves like a ל"ה (= ל"י) verb; cf. the vocalizations חֹטֶא (Eccl 8:12) and חֹטְאִים (1 Sa 14:33). One is, thus, likely to classify חטאתי in Gn 20:9 as derived from the noun form חטאה, which also fits well with the aforementioned pronunciation and the syntax of the verse, and in fact that would be a good classification. It must be pointed out, however, that the possibility of classifying that form as a verb cannot be ruled out, since such a verb form is not impossible, even in the verb חטא, even if it is unlikely. It appears that ST translates the form in question by a verb אתח(ע/)יבת; in SAV the manuscripts differ from each other (خطيتي, خطيئتي). Translating חטאתי here as a noun provides evidence for the antiquity of the contemporary pronunciation of the word there, which is at variance with other verses, but no certain grammatical classification can be made.

Similar to this is the pronunciation of נדרה as *nēdårå* at Nu 30:11, as against the anticipated form *nådårå*.

e. Imperfect verbs I-guttural cannot be classifed with certainty as *Pi'el* or *Hif'il* (see 2.2.1.2.2/3). Infinitive construct forms with the prefixes -בַּ, -כַּ, or -לַ, such as *bållot* and *bållūti*, are the same whether they are the equivalent of TH לַעֲלוֹת, בַּעֲלוֹת, and בַּעֲלוֹתִי or of בְּהַעֲלוֹת, לְהַעֲלוֹת, and בְּהַעֲלוֹתִי, and even though in some verses context may help with classification (not necessarily on the basis of the spelling in the Pentateuch), we must keep in mind the possibility that the division of usage between *Qal* and *Hif'il* as we find it in TH may not be the same as in SH for every verb. Thus, in such forms as *yåbbəd* יאבד, neither the spelling nor the meaning in context are useful in classifying the verb as *Pi'el* or *Hif'il*.

0.17 The list of forms of questionable classification is long. It might appear that one would be aided in that task, at least with regard to type (e) in the preceding section, by the spelling of the word in the Pentateuch, but it has long been clear, it seems to me, that the Samaritan oral tradition of the Pentateuch is autonomous, independent of the spelling. On the contrary, sometimes pronunciation is the basis for a given spelling in the Pentateuch.[28] Thus, spelling

---

[28] I have had occasion to comment on this, as against the commonly accepted view, in *Lěšonénu* 15 (1946/7), 76, and *LOT* III/1, 28. A clear demonstration of this is the pronunciation *wyåládti* in Gn 16:11, even though the common spelling is וילדת and not וילדתי; or, alternatively, the spellings ישעל and ישאל alongside ישל (Dt 28:40), which stem from the oral tradition of *yēšā'əl* (see *LOT* III/1, 148). Nonetheless, this was not noticed by Brønno, who took his mistaken assumption so far as to use the spelling to explain the absence of an original *u* or *o* as the vowel of a second radical in the imperfect (and in other forms) and their replacement by *a* (see 1.5.2.3, 1.5.2.7) — SH having no ו in that position in the forms in question ("Samaritan Hebrew and Origen's Secunda," *JSS* 13 (1968), 192–202. See also my article "Some Problems," 254–5 and A. Murtonen, "On the Inter-

alone is insufficient to enable us to make a determination about the grammatical value of a form in SH as pronounced, which is the subject of the grammatical analysis presented in this book. From this we may infer as well that the usual approach to the classification of forms in SH according to accepted criteria for TH is inadequate.[29]

Because my goal is, first and foremost, to provide a **synchronic** description of SH, and only on that basis to take up diachronic issues, especially in relation to TH, I felt obliged to attempt to organize the material presented by the Samaritan tradition using internal criteria. I consulted the Samaritan grammarians here and there, of course (see, e.g., 2.0.8, 2.2.2.0), but did not follow them on every point. In light of this situation in the Samaritan tradition, I felt it appropriate, when necessary, to set out the philological analysis of the data before taking up their grammatical classification, even more than I would otherwise think appropriate in a grammar.

0.18 Arrangement of the Book

A few words should be said here about the arrangement of this book. It is constructed in two parts. The first presents the grammatical description. The second presents the inventory of all noun and verb forms set out according to grammatical considerations, thereby complementing the description. On the assumption that the grammatical description will be employed by readers already familiar with the grammar of Biblical Hebrew in the Tiberian tradition, I have kept the description short where the two traditions are identical or similar, expanding the description where the traditions differ to the extent necessary to explain those differences. This guideline has led to some lack of uniformity in the section on verbs. In the strong verb and the strong verb with guttural radicals, the forms are arranged according to stem (*Qal*, *Piʻel*, etc.), and within each stem the perfect precedes the imperfect. In the weak verbs, this principle has not been followed. Instead, phenomena that display phonological similarities are taken up together in order to minimize repetition. Thus, to choose but one example, in y"y verbs I have not hesitated to mix *Qal*

---

pretation of the *Matres Lectionis* in the Biblical Hebrew," *AbrN* 14 (1973–1974), 71, whose view is in accord with mine.

[29] Macuch went to great lengths in subordinating the classification of data arising from the Samaritan tradition to data arising from the Tiberian tradition when he arranged the noun patterns according to the system used by Bauer and Leander "because the formation of nouns in SH is generally congruent with that of TH" (BL, 376). However, if the difference between the traditions is evident in the verb, it is only more so in the formation of the noun.

imperfects with *Hifʻil* perfects (see 2.7.6). Following the same rule, the imperative, the infinitive, and the participle have been extracted from the framework of stems, with a section devoted to each in turn and the stems subsumed under those categories. The same approach has been taken with the passive and with tenses and moods. This concession to uniformity of presentation, will, I hope, be more than balanced by the gain of giving prominence to the unique features of SH and the problems it presents for Hebrew grammar, which are the primary interest of those who deal with Hebrew linguistics.

0.19 Each word cited as evidence is presented in two forms: its pronunciation, rendered in phonetic script, and its written form, presented here in the "square" ("Assyrian") script. With regard to full spelling versus defective spelling, the form presented here does not necessarily correspond to that found in the Masoretic text unless a reference to a specific verse is given alongside the form. It is well known that there are differences of full/defective spelling in different places in the Hebrew Bible, and the number of differences between SP and the Masoretic Pentateuch is very large. Even within SP, manuscripts display differences on this point in many places. In general, I have chosen the spelling to which the spoken form best conforms. Thus, a word such as אחותי is written with a ו, even though the Jewish version is consistently without the ו in the Pentateuch and in SP it is frequently absent, because the pronunciation ʻa'ūti has been taken into consideration, while a word such as עלת (TH עֹלָת) is written without a ו even though it has a ו in the Masoretic version of Nu 28:24, due to the pronunciation ʻâlåt, which is better represented by the defective spelling.

The pronunciations cited herein are taken from the modern reading of the Pentateuch by the Samaritans. While it is true that the pronunciation of each word in each verse is almost always the same and the differences between trained readers is limited to unimportant details on the fine points of pronunciation and not word formation itself, there are variants in the Samaritan manuscripts that hint, only quite rarely, that in the past there was a reading different from that known today, which reflected a difference in word formation. E.g., ועשירת (Nu 28:5) is usually pronounced *wēšīråt*, but the spellings ועשרית and وعشيريث (*LOT* II, 427) hint at a pronunciation something like *wēšīrət*. The spelling העשוה (or העשואה) in Nu 28:6 accords well with the pronunciation ʻa:šuwʻwā, but the spellings העשויה and its Arabic transliteration معشويه (*LOT* II, 427) do not necessarily do so. At Lv 15:3 SP reads רר בשרו את זובו או חתום בשרו מזובו טמא הוא כל ימי זב בשרו or ...החתים בשרו מזובו טמאתו היא..... The manuscripts differ over החתים/חתום. According to contemporary readers, the primary reading is ʻātom and the secondary one ʻā:təm. Both may be passive participles (2.13.3/4), as ST thinks, but ʻā:təm is also open to a different interpretation. In place of the Masoretic text עלות (Gn 33:13), SP reads אעלת or עלאת, and هلعت (*LOT* II, 410), but the pronunciation is *uwwållåt*, which should be written עולת (see 2.13.6b). It may be conjectured that the spelling variants represent a pronunciation closer to TH than to the modern pronunciation of SH.

This book is concerned with the language as it is reflected in the recitation of the Pentateuch, so that the form pronounced today is always the basis of discussion, and we have not dealt with the question of how the contemporary pronunciation relates to textual variants and what those variants might mean for pronunciation.

Furthermore, it should be noted that the words cited as examples appear without the prefixes -בּ, -כּ, -ל, and -מ, the definite article, and the conjunctive ו- wherever eliminating these prefixes would not harm the word being presented. E.g, עֶשֶׂר is unattested in the Pentateuch; there is only העשר, but the ʿ in the pronunciation *ʿaššər* is appropriate to the form without the definite article as well, which is not the case with a form such as *warfəl* וערפל. Were the latter not found in a liturgical poem without the conjunctive -ו, where it is pronounced *ʿarfəl*, it would be inappropriate to present the word without the prefix due to uncertainty over whether the word begins with ʿ. The words as they appear in the recitation of the Pentateuch are set out in the accompanying inventory of forms.

While writing this book, I kept in mind both the scholar of linguistics and the intelligent layman schooled in Hebrew grammar, who may be interested in knowing about some aspects of Hebrew grammar in a tradition as different as that of the Samaritans. Since the latter reader may be unfamiliar with technical linguistic terms, I have attempted to employ traditional, common grammatical terms, departing from this practice only where absolutely necessary for precision of expression.

0.20 Samaritan Script

0.20.1. The Phoenician alphabet in the 11th and 10th centuries BCE served as the medium for writing both Canaanite (including Hebrew) and Aramaic. Shortly thereafter, the alphabet developed into two different traditions. First to arise was the ancient Hebrew script, with the Aramaic script coming into being about a century later. Each of the two maintained certain inherited traits, but each developed its own unique characteristics as well. The ancient Hebrew script was the sole medium for writing Hebrew during the First Temple period, and only during Second Temple times, according to the traditions of the Jews and the Samaritans, was it supplanted by a type of script that was a descendant of the Aramaic branch. It was from that Aramaic script that the Jewish script known in Jewish sources as "Assyrian" script developed. The adoption of an Aramaic script did not entirely displace the use of the ancient Hebrew script among the Jews. Instead, it reduced the range of uses of that ancient script to a limited list of circumstances (e.g., coins, the writing of the Tetragrammaton, etc.), in which it continued to be in use until the middle of the second century CE.

The ancient Hebrew script, to which a high level of sanctity was ascribed by those who continued to employ it for writing the Tetragrammaton, underwent a diminution of its sanctity among the Jews in later generations, as is evident from *m. Yadayim* 4:5.

Not so among the Samaritans. They continued to employ the ancient Hebrew script for all purposes, sacred and profane, when writing Hebrew, Aramaic, and in later generations even Arabic. The script in use among the Samaritans, then, developed directly from the ancient Hebrew script and is closer to the Hebrew script in use during the Second Temple period, known as Paleo-Hebrew. To put it more precisely, the early form of the Samaritan script is not essentially different from the Hebrew script used by the Hasmoneans.

0.20.2. The Samaritan script has been in use for many generations in two forms, each of which displays a range of variations as is shown in the table below. These forms are known among the Samaritans by Arabic terms not used for the Arabic script.

a. The form known as حرف كامل ("whole letter") or مجلس (*mujallas* "well set") appears in the table below in Columns II–VI. Only this form has been systematically researched so far, especially in its lapidary form, i.e., as it appears in inscriptions carved into stone. It remains in use even now in Torah scrolls and other sacred books, in official documents such as wedding contracts, and in anything that requires visual emphasis, such as the titles of books and of chapters (while the body of the text is written in the cursive script).

b. The form known as نصف الحرف ("half letter") or طرش (*ṭariš* "rapid," "cursive") appears in the table below in Columns VII–X, and is used for quotidian purposes. The Samaritan prayerbook, too, took shape in this cursive script. Its history has not been given proper attention by scholars, one result of which is that it cannot serve as a reliable indicator for the dating of texts written in it. As long as the study of the Firkovich Collection in the National Library of Russia at St. Petersburg has not been completed, it appears that the earliest evidence of this script is from 1513, when the late portion of the Samaritan manuscript of Joshua was written, now located in the University Library of Leiden. The earlier portion, written in the "whole letter" script, dates from 1362/3.

Note: 1. In Jewish sources written in Arabic, the term مجلس is used to refer to the "Assyrian" script. The earliest evidence for this is Maimonides' responsum from the year 1191 (R. Moses b. Maimon, *Responsa*, II, ed. J. Blau [Jerusalem, 1960], 513 [Hebrew]). Traditional Jewish scribes in Morocco have, for generations, used the term تقعيد (derived from a root synonymous with جلس) to signify writing with the "Assyrian" script, while employing the term تعليق ("suspension") for writing in what is known as "Rashi" script. On مجلس and the etymology of this term, see *LOT* V, 262.

2. M. Gaster and Y. Ben-Zvi believed that they had discovered the earliest traces of the Hebrew cursive in a Geniza manuscript from the 11th century. That this view was incorrect is demonstrated in *LOT* V, 263ff. On the other hand, Mr. Binyamim Ṣadaqa informed me in a letter dated 30.4.97 that he has seen in the Firkovich Collection a manuscript written in the cursive script and dated 1202/3.

0.20.3 Alphabet Table
a. The Samaritan letters are presented in the alphabet table in comparison to the Jewish script (the "Assyrian" script) and the ancient Hebrew script from the beginning of the 6th century BCE (Column I).

b. The Samaritan letters appear in the table as they are written by manuscript copyists in certain words. Each letter has been separated from the rest of the word in which it appears and placed in the appropriate space in the table. Their sources are as follows.

> Column II: The handwriting of אבי ברכהתה (אבו אל ברכאת) בר אב זהותה בר אב נפושה צרפתאה [צרפתאה = of Ṣarafand] בר אברהם צרפתאה in 1215/6 CE, in a Torah scroll owned by the Jewish National and University Library in Jerusalem [JNUL], MS Sam 2°6.
> Column III: The handwriting of מרחיב (מפרג) בן יעקב (second half of the 17th century), as it appears at the end of the Bodelian Library's MS Hunt 24 (including Munajja b. Ṣadaqa's المسايل الخلاف).
> Column IV: The handwriting of רצון בן בנימים צדקה of Holon, Israel (see *LOT* III/1, 30), from a list held by the JNUL.
> Column V: The letters of a typewriter owned by ישראל בן גמלאל (גבריאל) צדקה of Holon. Prayerbooks and other works were typed on this typewriter and circulated both within and outside the Samaritan community.
> Column VI: The handwriting of עבד אלעיני דמבני עבדה, the scribe who copied the later portion of MS Leiden Or 249 containing the Arabic Book of Joshua. That portion was written in cursive script in 1513.
> Column VII: like column III.

Column VIII: like column IV.
Column IX: like column V.

c. The names of the letters and their pronunciation are according to contemporary usage, as reflected in the lexicon *Hammeliṣ* (*LOT* II, 440ff.) — that is, no later than the 11th century CE. The names preserved there are: דלאת, גמאל, תאף, שאן, ריש, קוף, צדי, פי, עין, סנכאת, נון, מים, לואת, כאף, יות, טית, חית, זין, וא, היא/הי. The Hebrew spellings of these names reveal something of their pronunciation today.

With regard to the letters and their pronunciation, a few observations should be made:

1. The length of the vowel in closed syllables (reflected nicely by the spelling of the *mater lectionis* א in *Hammeliṣ*) violates the rule generally in force with regard to vowel length in the Samaritan pronunication (see 1.2.1). It is not impossible that in the pronunciation of the names of the letters an earlier stratum of Samaritan syllable structure is preserved. This should not occasion any surprise, for we have found that in proper nouns, and among them the names of letters, often do not change in accordance with rules established later. (Cf. the names of the vowels in Jewish Hebrew, for example.) Their ultimate stress, too, may either be original, predating the shift to penultimate stress (see 1.4.8), or it is designed to maintain a long vowel in a closed syllable. It may even be that the pronunciation of the names of the letters is somewhat artificial, related to the manner in which the alphabet is recited aloud in teaching young children: with strong articulation and striking length. It is difficult to determine whether learning by memorization preserved the traditions of unusual vowel length and stress, or whether it is instead the progenitor of those traditions.

2. The origin of the variants גמאל (in *Hammeliṣ*) / *ga'mān* may be in pronunciation changes alone, but if we note the letter name שאן in comparison with σαν (another name for σίγμα) in Dorian Greek, we may posit that the name *gā'mān* is derived from the same form as the Greek γάμμα. The final *n* is to be understood, then, like the final ן- in such MH words as למען, למטן, and להלן, or the Palestinian Aramaic כדון < כדו (כדהו).

3. The form *lā'bāt* לואת (לבד) is congruent with the Greek name λάβδα, which is earlier than the form λάμβδα.[30]

By citing the similarities to Greek letter names, I do not intend to imply that the Samaritans borrowed their letter names from the Greek, but rather that they reveal a common tradition. This is quite clear, given that the Samaritan

---

[30] E. Schwyzer, *Griechische Grammatik* I (München, 1959), 140, n. 2.

Introduction

ALPHABET

	Ṭariš				Mujallas				
	IX	VIII	VII	VI	V	IV	III	II	I
āˈlāf									
bīt									
gāˈmān									
dāˈlāt									
īy									
bā́									
zēn									
īt									
ṭīt									
yūt									
kā́f									
lāˈbāt									
mīm									
nūn									
sinˈgā́t, sinˈkā́t									
īn									
fī									
ṣā́ˈdīy									
qūf									
rīš									
šān									
tā́f									

names do not end with an "a" sound as do the Greek names. The appearance of that vowel there is a characteristic original to Greek and appears only in Greek.[31]

4. It should be noted that the Samaritan name for the letter ס, *sin'gât* or *sin'kåt*, has a Syriac parallel — *semkat*, which Nöldeke noted as being unattested outside of Syriac.[32] Here is another very interesting detail showing the close relationship between Syriac and SA, which we have noted on earlier occasions (see *LOT* III/2, 161, l. 31).

---

[31] Ibid., 141.
[32] Nöldeke, *Beiträge*, 130.

PHONOLOGY

1.0 Preliminaries

1.0.1 The description of the sound system of SH is based on the pronunciation as performed in contemporary reading from the Pentateuch, but it should be noted that in the area of pronunciation there is no difference between the language of the Pentateuch and the Hebrew language outside it, nor is there any difference between them and the Aramaic one hears in the Samaritan's prayers. Though some written sources indicate that a number of changes in pronunciation have taken place since Aramaic ceased being spoken by the Samaritans — at about the end of the tenth century and the onset of the eleventh[1] (changes which will be discussed systematically, e.g., 1.1.3 or 1.4.7), there is no reason to doubt the assumption that the Hebrew pronunciation heard today on the whole corresponds to what was customary when Aramaic was spoken.[2] Moreover, much of this pronunciation may be ascribed to the period of Samaritan Hebrew speech, towards the end of the Second Temple period and for a few generations after, for certain features have already been hinted at in the Samaritan version of the Pentateuch, and the antiquity of those features in SP has been supported in modern days by biblical and other fragments of the Dead Sea Scrolls. Thus, in phonology, too, there exists in the Samaritan tradition a continuity stretching back to a Hebrew dialect whose chronology and geography are not defineable in precise terms, at least not according to the present state of research.

1.0.2 In the sound system of languages a distinction has been made, for several decades now, between the smallest unit detectable by the ear, or even more so by an instrument of measurement, and the smallest unit in the language able to distinguish between meanings of words and forms. The former is termed a 'phone' (from the Greek φωνή meaning "sound," "speech"), and the latter, a 'phoneme' (from the Greek φώνημα "sound," "speech"). The difference between the two units may be illustrated in Hebrew thus: (a) the relationship

---

[1] See Z. Ben-Ḥayyim, "A Samaritan Inscription of the XIth Cent.," *BJPES* 12 (1946), 81 [Hebrew].
[2] Cf. my article "Samaritan Hebrew," 123. The statement on the *'ayin* there is incorrect. See below 1.1.8.2.

between words such as פנים/בנים indicate that ב and פ are separate phonemes because a differentiation of meaning depends on the difference between them; similarly, גַּנִּים/גַּלִּים shows that ל and נ are separate phonemes; (a) the relationship between forms such as בָּנָה (Gn 5:4) / בָנִים (Gn 3:16) demonstrates that while hard and soft ב are indeed separate phones, they cannot distinguish between meanings. Since the two phones belong to a single unit called a **phoneme** they are customarily termed **allophones** of the phoneme /b/.

The Hebrew term הגה "sound," adopted for grammatical use prior to the acceptance of the distinction between "phone" and "phoneme," is generally used in a broader sense than the precise definition of "phone," though attempts have been made to limit it to the meaning of "phone." In this book the term "sound" will serve in the broader sense equivalent to הגה, and only when the need arises will the more precise terminology be adopted. Similarly, we shall not make use of the symbols differentiating "phone" from "phoneme," e.g., [!] and /l/, to distinguish them from the letter l, unless such distinctions become vital — for words adduced in Latin letters do not refer to their graphic representation (since this is in the Hebrew alphabet!); our discussion deals generally with phonemes.

In *LOT* III/1, 9–12, the elements of the graphic representation of SH (and SA) were described. After the evaluation of the phonetic characteristics of the sounds, their phonematic system was deduced. In this book no use will be made of the symbol [!] for it is clearly an allophone of /l/ (see especially 1.1.7). It must not be forgotten that we are describing the tradition of a sacred tongue, a language of ritual, whereas the Samaritan vernacular is Arabic or (contemporary) Hebrew. Only the phonemic value of sounds are likely to be preserved in a linguistic tradition like that under consideration in this book, whereas the presenting of the precise phonetic values of these sounds is rather a matter of the Samaritan communities vernacular, e.g., the pronunciation of יסכם *yaskəm*/ *yasgəm* (*LOT* III/2, 83, l. 6).

1.1 Consonants

1.1.1 The total number of consonants and semi-consonants in Hebrew as presented by the Tiberian and Babylonian traditions is twenty-nine, and if we compare them to the total number of assumed consonants in Proto-Semitic,[3] we find the number unchanged, for other consonants have developed in this

---

[3] Regarding the nature of the consonants expressed in Arabic by ظ, ض — whether in Proto-Semitic they are $ḍ$ or $ḏ̣$, $ṭ$ or $ṯ̣$ — there are differences of opinion, and this table is not intended to resolve them.

1.0 Preliminaries

type of Hebrew, corresponding in number to those which have vanished. This comparison is, however, inaccurate, for the consonants assumed to have existed in Proto-Semitic are all phonemes, whereas of the consonants occurring in TH and in BH only 23 are phonemes, to which six allophones have been added (in the *b g d k p t* group). In SH there are only twenty phonemes, of which only one — ל /l/ — appears in two allophones, the "soft" [l] and the "hard" [!] (for the symbols, see 0.1.2). Thus, the main difference between SH and TH/BH is the lack of three phonemes: /h/, /ḥ/ and /ś/, and of six allophones: soft *b̲, g̲, d̲, k̲,* and *t̲* and hard *p*.

Note: In the following comparative table the consonants of TH are given in Hebrew letters flanked on the right by SH consonants and on the left by those of Proto-Semitic of which TH and SH are offspring. In Hebrew grammar books, the consonant group ʾ, h, ḥ, ʿ are usually referred to by means of a single term, *gutturals*. We, too, shall do so wherever there is no need for a precise description of their place of articulation, as in the morphology.

1.1.2 Table of Consonants

Place of articulation	Plosive voiced	Plosive unvoiced	Nasal	Lateral	Trill	Fricative voiced	Fricative unvoiced	Semi-consonant
Labial	b ב b	p פ -	m מ m					w ו w
Labiodental						- ב̲ -	- פ̲ f	
Interdental						d̲ ד -	t̲ ת -	
Dental	d ד d	t ת t	n נ n	l ל l	r ר r	z ז z	s ס s	
Alveolar							š ש š	
Palato-alveolar							ś ש -	
Alveolo-velar	ḍ - -	ṭ ט ṭ		- - (!)		ẓ - -	ṣ צ ṣ	
Palatal								y י y
Velar	g ג g	k כ k				ḡ ג -	ḫ כ -	
Uvular	q ק q							
Laryngeal						ʿ ע ʿ	ḥ ח -	
Glottal	ʾ א ʾ						h ה -	

1.1.3 The table reflects the usual pronunciation of SH consonants today. Nevertheless, on occasion, under undefined conditions, entirely by chance and from different readers, variations of the sounds described can be heard, such as an unvoiced ב (b, closely resembling p)⁴ or a bilabial ב (β),⁵ a kind of fricative⁶ ד (ḏ), and, from speakers of Hebrew, even a uvular ר. From written sources — the writings of the grammarians and the transcriptions of Hebrew words in Arabic script — it is clear that the entire consonantal inventory in use today is reduced from the inventory, at least until the fifteenth century,⁷ which was similar to the consonantal inventory of TH and BH with regard to the existence of plosive and fricative b, p, d and t. In addition, we learn that the complete merger of ʾ, h, ḥ, ʿ into a single consonant, an ʾ aleph, which it would seem necessary to assume in light of the interchanges taking place amongst the Samaritans even in SP, not to mention their Aramaic literature, is actually far from complete. The ʿayin is very often pronounced according to fixed rules, as is shown below in paragraph 1.1.8.2. Nevertheless, the consonantal inventory of SH is smaller than that of TH, the main point being that sounds present in TH are lacking in SH, with no compensating additions of any kind.⁸

1.1.4 בפדו״ת. This mnemonic note in Samaritan grammar (*LOT* I, 213) collects a group of consonants, not distinguished by any common *maḫraj* (i.e., place of articulation), but rather by a characteristic of theirs in the past, the twofold pronunciation of each consonant. From a description of their pronunciation in comparison with Arabic and using terms coined by the Jewish medieval grammarians (*LOT* I, 123, 213), it is evident that the plosive/fricative relationship characteristic of TH and BH used to exist in SH as well. From the following examples: בבאם (now pronounced *bābā'imma*), דד (now *dod*), לתת (now *altət*), יעפף (now *yāffəf*),⁹ we can also learn that the conditions regulating their plosive or fricative nature resemble those of TH, the first consonant in these examples having been plosive and the second fricative. From such Arabic transcriptions

---

⁴ Examples are to be found in *LOT* III/2, 30, 224, 253, 278, 279, etc.
⁵ Examples are to be found in *LOT* III/1, 14, 38 l. 13, 59 l. 30; *LOT* III/2, 52, 78, 121, etc.
⁶ See *LOT* III/1, 16.
⁷ The examples adduced below in 1.1.4 are taken from "A Compilation of Variant Readings in SP" (*LOT* II, 408ff.), composed probably in the thirteenth century. A later Leiden manuscript (marked ב in *LOT* I, פו) proposes the fricative ث, ذ in Arabic words, wrongly positioned. Perhaps one is to see it as the end of the distinction in Hebrew and Aramaic as well. Unless the writer considered them equivalent, he would not misuse ث for ث, or ذ for ذ. A fragment of the *Defter* written in the 13/14 century (A. E. Cowley, *The Samaritan Liturgy*, II [Oxford 1909], XIII,) reflects this situation. I owe the following examples to Prof. A. Tal: רתותך (presently *rātūtåk*), בראשית (presently *barāšat*), מדינתה (presently *amdīntå*). Note that a transcription of Samaritan ח, ע ה, into the corresponding Arabic letters like יהוה يـهـوه does not prove their pronunciation (cf. my paper "On the Pronunciation of the Tetragrammaton by the Samaritans," *EI* 3 [1954], 147ff. [Hebrew]). However, the distinction between ث and ث, ذ and ذ in a Hebrew word transcribed in Arabic, as shown above, is not possible unless it has some basis in the Samaritan pronunciation.
⁸ Except, perhaps, for the pronounced version *l* (see 1.1.7). The innovation in articulating *waw* does not add a consonant to the inventory.
⁹ See *Tībåt Mårqe*, 102 (f. 54b, n. 2).

1.1 Consonants 33

as وتردیه (*LOT* II, 409), وتقوا (*LOT* II, 412), وتشته (*LOT* II, 426), we learn that the plosive consonant was retained after *waw conjunctive* (= *consecutive*, see 2.0.1.0). This does not contradict the conditions mentioned above, for there is no vowel intervening between the *waw* and the word proper. In Al'aya's description of the pronunciation of the letters (mid-18th century; *LOT* II, 331ff.), no mention is made of any twofold pronounciation of בפדו״ת. Had that entire description not been aimed at the pronunciation of Arabic consonants (he describes [h] and [ḥ], which had not been pronounced for over a thousand years) but rather at that of SH or SA, it might have been possible to determine with certainty the date before which the twofold pronunciation ceased to apply. The present remains of the early conditions are the shift of fricative ב to fricative פ in the preposition ב: **av* > *af* and, on occasion, elsewhere as well, e.g., *afqåråt* (Lv 19:20), *afšīlå* (Nu 6:19. Cf. also 1.5.3.6), and the shift of the doubled, plosive פ to a plosive ב: יפל = **yippal* > *yibbål*; הפר = **appår* > *abbår*. The fact that *ff* appears in place of *bb* under similar phonetic conditions, such as מפי = *miffi*, מפני = *miffåni*, suffices to show that *bb* has been a substitute for *pp* ever since the ability to pronounce plosive פ was lost in an Arabic-speaking environment. The substitution was felt to be inadequate, and so fricative פ was sporadically maintained outside its original phonetic conditions, and it, too, was a substitute. Today the *ff/bb* relationship is lexicalized.[10]

1.1.4.1 ו is reported to have had a threefold *maḫraj*: two like those of ב in Hebrew and one as it is pronounced in Arabic, (i.e., *w*). In the word וביהם (*LOT* I, 153 MS ה), at present pronounced *wbåbīyyimma*, the three consonants are represented. According to the rule above, it must be assumed that ו was also pronounced *v* (fricative ב).

This sound did not appear, however, in cases of *waw conjunctive* or in the cases adduced below. Today, at any rate, there is no way of defining with precision the conditions under which it occurred. The situation today makes it possible to conclude that at an early stage *w* came to be pronounced *v*, possibly while the Samaritans still spoke Hebrew, and since it coalesced with fricative ב it was included in the process of fricative/plosive interchange, together with בפדו״ת. When it became no longer possible to pronounce fricative ב, the sound vanished in original ו as well and became a plosive ב whether single, as in *īšåb* (עשו), or geminated, as in **tištaḥvi* > **tištåvvi* > *tištåbbi* (תשתחוה).[11] It is

---

[10] We find the same situation in the reading of later prayers and poetry. See Florentin, *Shomronit* 71. It is to be hoped that this study will soon be published and made available for general use.

[11] I first discussed this matter at the First World Congress of Jewish Studies in 1947: "The Samaritan Tradition and its Use in the Study of Hebrew and Aramaic," *Lĕšonénu* 17 (1951–52), 136 [Hebrew].

certain that the *waw conjunctive* was not included in the *w* > *v* process, just as it is clear that *w* in the diphthong *uw* was preserved whenever it was geminated, e.g., *ṣawwåru > ṣuwwåru* (צוארו), **yiwwåləd > yuwwåləd* (יולד),[12] *tuwwēbåt* (תועבת), (*תְּאָוֹות <) *tē'uwwåt? > tēwwåt*. Yet, there are also cases where *w* was preserved despite its occurrence in a different phonetic environment, such as *ammakwå* (המכוה), *walmaqwå* (ולמקוה), *yilwåk* (ילוך), and also *tillawwi* (תלוה). It is possible that *w*, when not in the *uww*- sequence, must be viewed as a substitute for the *v* which vanished over the generations, just as *b* is a substitute for *w* (cf. the discussion of ב vs. פ in 1.1.4).

The Samaritan tradition in SH and SA concerning the articulation of ו is clear evidence of a *w* > *v* process in Palestine, at least during the period of Aramaic speech.[13]

1.1.5 גכ״ך. It should especially be noted that neither in the writings of the grammarians nor in the transliterations into Arabic is there any sign of a twofold pronunciation of כ, ג. The process of spirantization did not affect these two consonants. Furthermore, the fact that when the Samaritans write Arabic in their Samaritan script they do not denote خ and غ by כ, ג respectively with the addition of some diacritical mark, but rather by ה, ע (see *LOT* II, 437), just as it has become the custom to do in Modern Hebrew when transcribing from Arabic, indicates that their one pronunciation, i.e., the plosive one, is not the result of a late process of simplification like that of בפד״ת, but rather an ancient feature. כ, ג probably were never spirantized at all. Cf. Eastern Syriac where the פ has no fricative realization. The series בגדכפ״ת is, thus, not automatically to be dealt with as a single phenomenon. It would appear that the difference in resonance between voiced ג and unvoiced כ was not distinct in the ancient period, a fact reflected in the readings ולנגדי (Gn 21:23); הדוגיפת (Lv 11:19); שרוג (Gn 14:23) for ולנכדי, הדוכיפת, שרוך respectively (see also Ben-Ḥayyim "Tradition," 92, n. 2); the difference between voiced and unvoiced ב and פ vanished entirely; only in the case of ד and ת was the voiced/unvoiced distinction maintained.

There is a common tendency to substitute א for ק as the Samaritans do in speaking Arabic. Such an א does not behave like the original א or like the other guttural sounds which have become א (see 1.1.8). A difference in behavior between א arising from ק and original א is familiar from Arabic dialects as well,[14] a fact which suffices to show that this process of substitution among the

---

[12] For the assimilation of the vowel to *waw*, cf. *kuwwāna* in the Arabic dialect spoken by the Jews of Bagdad (H. Blanc, *Communal Dialects in Baghdad*, [Cambridge, Mass., 1964], 144).

[13] See Ben-Ḥayyim, *Studies*, 105. Pronouncing the *waw* as *v* is undoubtedly the reason for the ב/ה interchange in manuscripts of Rabbinic literature. See Epstein, *Introduction*, 1223–1225. See also Ben-David, "Unusual Vocalization," 254ff.

[14] One finds a true parallel in the Egyptian dialect. See T. F. Mitchell, *Colloquial Arabic: The Living Language of Egypt* (London, 1962), 32. A similar phenomenon is the survival of the *aleph*

Samaritans originates under the influence of their Arabic speech. This, too, took place at a late stage, for today it is not considered acceptable when reading from the Pentateuch,[15] unlike the *f* for *p* substitution which seems to have occurred many generations ago. One may occasionally discern a fricative ק (χ), but the phenomenon is rare and only appears in fluent reading.[16]

1.1.6 The distinction between שׁ and שׂ in TH or between שׁ and שׂ in BH originates in the use of the letter שׁ for two sounds in ancient Hebrew or at least in the type of Hebrew represented by the traditions mentioned above. It must be assumed[17] that the two שׁ sounds were independent consonants *(š, ś)*, i.e., each was a separate phoneme, judging by both comparative grammar and Hebrew phonological considerations. Comparative grammar indicates that there exists a regular interchange between roots containing a שׁ in Hebrew and roots in Arabic (and in some other Semitic languages) displaying an *s*, between roots in Hebrew showing שׂ and Arabic roots with *š*, such as חמשׁ/*ḫms*, עשׂר/*'śr*. Slight deviations from this rule, such as קמשׂ (alongside קמושׁ) and *qumāš*, originating in the transmission of the Bible, do not upset the regularity of these interchanges. The interchanges can be understood properly only as stemming from a heritage common to both (and other Semitic) languages, which evolved in different ways in each of them. Phonological considerations strengthen this assumption as well, for the number of roots and words in which only the distinction between שׁ and שׂ prevents them from becoming homonyms is quite considerable, such as נשׂר/נשׁר, שׂבע/שׁבע, שׂכל/שׁכל, שׂכר/שׁכר. Denying the original distinction between שׁ and שׂ in Hebrew entails assuming homonymity to such an extent that any normal language would be unable to cope with it, especially when no *graphic* distinction makes it any easier. (The distinction made is one of a diacritical point only.)

1.1.6.1 In later times, which cannot be precisely determined, שׂ came to be pronounced like ס in some Hebrew dialects. Signs of this can be discerned in the spelling of certain words in the Bible, such as כעס as against כעשׂ, סטים as against שׂטים, סתיו as against שׂתו in Old Aramaic and شتا in Arabic, which postulate the existence of an older שׂתו; this, too, is the rule in MH. One does, indeed, encounter in MH words and roots with the letter שׂ which are often spelled

---

which developed from an *'ayin* or a fricative *gimel* in the eastern dialects of Neo-Aramaic, even under phonetic circumstances in which original *aleph* disappears (See D. Cohen, "Neo-Aramaic," *EJ* 12, 949).

[15] *LOT* III/1, 16.
[16] *LOT* III/2, 77, l. 28: *wmissaχ* ומסך; 292, l. 61: *yiχfāli* יקפלי.
[17] Unlike the opinion of N. H. Tur-Sinai, *Halašon ve-Hasefer*, I (Jerusalem, 1948), 36, n. 2 [Hebrew]; ibid., 470. See also Ben Yehuda, *Thesaurus*, XIV, s.v. שׂ.

with שׂ in the Bible as well, like עָשָׂה, עָשֹׂר, etc., but reality is reflected in the words whose spelling has changed in contrast to the Bible, like סטה, פסיון (from Biblical פָּשָׂה). It should be remembered that in old manuscripts of Tannaitic sources ס is often found in place of שׂ even in roots appearing frequently in the Bible, such as עסה, עסר, etc.

The שׂ > ס shift in Aramaic led some scholars to consider Aramaic as the source of the development in Hebrew.[18] Others even say that the very graphic distinction between שׁ and שׂ (= ס) was established by the Masoretes according to Aramaic pronunciation.[19] The interchange between *ś* and *s* (including the grapheme שׂ in TH) can be found in the pronunciation of Hebrew by various Jewish communities;[20] in SH however there is only a single sound *š* corresponding to the letter שׂ. The question which automatically arises is whether SH reflects an original living phenomenon in spoken Hebrew, or whether the ancient difference in pronunciation of שׂ became obscure when SH ceased to be a living, spoken Hebrew dialect. The supporters of the second possibility[21] have at their disposal a simple, ready answer, but one which seems to be mistaken. The following facts should be considered: [1] the *ś* > *s* shift took place in SA, just as it did in Jewish Aramaic, but, unlike the Jews, the Samaritans carefully distinguish between *ś* > *š* in SH and *ś* > *s* in SA as is evident in roots common to the two languages, like: עשׂר *âšår* : עסר *âsår*, שׂבע *šāba* (Dt 31:20): דסבע *adsāba* (*LOT* III/2, 215, l. 6), שׂלוי *šalwi* (Nu 11:31): סלוי *sålbi* (*LOT* III/2, 135), שׂער *šār* (Gn 25:25) : סער, תשׂטה *tišṭi* (Nu 5:12): תסטי; [2] it is completely unreasonable to assume that the Samaritans were afraid to deviate from the pronunciation *š* because of spelling, whereas they were not at all afraid of pronouncing ו as a ב, as in their teaching that letters had more than a single place of articulation (see 1.1.4), or of pronouncing as אהח"ע a ו or a י under certain circumstances (see 1.1.8); [3] their adherence to the tradition with regard to this sound in Hebrew, in contrast to their Aramaic vernacular, was so strict that no שׂ/ס interchange is to be found in SP, unlike the situation with the letters אהח"ע or ב/ו. The significance of this is that with regard to this sound SH differed from the language found in Tannaitic literature while both were still spoken languages. The story of the refugees from Ephraim who suffered the death penalty because they were unable to differentiate between שׁבלת and סבלת

---

[18] BL, 114; Ben Yehuda, *Thesaurus*, XIV, 6777.

[19] If the assumption is made that this took place in the roots common to Hebrew and Aramaic (Ben Yehuda, *Thesaurus*, XIV, 6777), this conclusion is obligatory. On the two aspects of שׂ/שׁ in Hebrew, see also the comprehensive study of J. Blau, "'Weak' Phonetic Change and Hebrew *śīn*," *HAR* 1 (1977), 87ff.

[20] This becomes clear according to the comparative table in "Hebrew Grammar," cols. 85–86.

[21] E.g., E. Y. Kutscher, review of *LOT* III/2, *Tarbiẓ* 37 (1968), 411 [Hebrew] and Macuch, *Grammatik*, 128.

(Jud 12:6) is not relevant here, since the question is the שׁ/שׂ relationship and not that of שׂ and ס.²² At any rate, our "sons of Ephraim" (the Samaritans) do not substitute שׂ for ס anywhere. This indicates that the finding of only a single sound in SH marked by a שׂ is neither the fruit of forgetfulness nor that of spoken Aramaic influence upon it, but rather the consequence of a ś > š shift. It must, thus, be concluded that this shift had already existed in SH *before* it came under Aramaic influence, for had ś survived until SA speech became the rule, the fate of ś in SH would most probably have resembled its fate in SA and in MH and thereafter in all Jewish oral traditions, i.e., to coalesce with ס. The frontal allophone of /š/ heard occasionally from readers, like Polish ś (mentioned in *LOT* III/1, 16), is not connected in any way with historical שׂ.

1.1.7 טצ״ק. The common aspect of the place of articulation of טצ״ק is not defined and clear, but rather broad and indefinite, involving the back of the oral cavity. These consonants are usually termed "emphatics." Their common phonological aspect is a feature which determines their contrast with the consonants תס״כ. The contrast is clear, and all etymological attempts overlooking it have been found to be valueless.²³ This is true of literary Hebrew and Aramaic; when pronounced under certain conditions the non-emphatic consonants may sound like their emphatic counterparts, at least as far as *s, t* are concerned (and not *k*). The main condition is the appearance of *s, t* immediately prior to *å, â*, each under its own conditions. Here are a number of examples in Arabic transcription (as devised by the priest אב חסדה בן יעקב [Abū l-Ḥasan], see *LOT* III/1, 122 and *LOT* I, קה), but in place of vowel-pointing (unique in this manuscript) a transcription in Latin letters is provided:²⁴ اياطا *ayyåṭå* היתה (Gn 1:2), اطَّانينِم *attånīnəm* התנינים (Gn 1:21), طاتِّ *tåttiyya* תחתיה (SP Gn 2:21), اطَّ *åttå(h)* אתה (Gn 3:11), وطَاْ ُوكل *wtå'ūkəl* ותאכל (Gn 3:6), اِمِّطافيكت *ammēṭåfēkət* המתהפכת (Gn 3:24), اطمامانُو *iṭmåmånu* התממהנו (Gn 43:10), امطاطِيكما *amṭåṭīkimma* אמתחתיכם (Gn 43:12), وبيطك *wbīṭåk* וביתך (Gn 45:11), كتَّانت *kittånət* כתנת (Gn 37:3) [but: كتَّانوت *kittånot* (Gn 3:21)!], طولدت *tūldåt* תולדת (SP Gn 37:2), نوطر *nūṭår* נוטר (Ex 10:15) [but: اوتر *ūtər* הותיר (Ex 10:15)!], اصُّوباب *aṣṣūbåb* הסובב (Gn 2:11), اياصر *iyyåṣår* יאסר (Gn 42:19), تصرُّو *tiṣṣåru* תסחרו (Gn 42:24), ويَاصب *wyåṣåb* ויסב (Gn 42:24), اياصارو *iyyåṣåru* האסרו (Gn 42:16).

---

²² Regarding the שבלת/סבלת question one should consider the article by E. A. Speiser, "The Shibboleth Incident (Judges 12:6)," *BASOR* 85 (1947), 10–13. Whether Speiser is correct in saying that the affair indicates the survival of Proto-Semitic *ṯ* in a certain Hebrew area, i.e., that in that area the *ṯ* had not yet merged with *š*, or not — this is not relevant to the question of the lack of שׂ in SH.

²³ See Ben-Ḥayyim, "Palestinian Aramaic and Samaritan Poetry," 47.

²⁴ Note that the vowel quantity here is always clear, for it is expressed by Arabic *matres lectionis* with the addition of marks taken from the Samaritan pointing system. However, the Arabic *fatḥa* is used inconsistently, as shown by the comparison of the transcribed word with its actual pronunciation. Between *a* and *å*, I decided in favor of the pronunciation custom.

תסבנה (SP Gn 37:7), *tiṣṣâbinna* تصّابنَ (Gn 44:23), תוסיפון *tūṣīfon* توصيفن (Gn 42:34). I have never encountered the opposite process, i. e., *s*, *t* replacing *ṣ*, *ṭ*.

Similar to this is the "emphatic" (i.e., "dark", like the English *all* or the Arabic *allāh*) ל *l* in SH and SA; the conditions under which it appears, however, are clearly defined: it always appears before *å*, *â* (in certain words I have heard it before ד, ג, ב, קצ"ט and expecially ת, and I have noted this in *LOT* III/1, 13). Combinations such as [lå, lå] cannot exist, nor can [la, lā, li, lī, lū, lo]. But we have encountered صو, طو, طي above. Since, in literary Hebrew and Aramaic, there are no ת/ט, ס/צ interchanges whatsoever, the phenomenon must simply be considered a version of a pronunciation involving the Arabic vernacular. Therefore, in all the words adduced as examples in this book they have been completely ignored, including[25] *l*, though it was listed regularly in *LOT* III/1.

1.1.8 אהח"ע. Fluctuations of אהח"ע in SP provide clear evidence that no later than the end of the Second Temple period the guttural consonants began to weaken, until they apparently merged in a single consonant no later than the fourth century, at a time when the Samaritans spoke Aramaic. For in SA poetry, arranged acrostically, we perceive that a word beginning with אהח"ע can appear instead of any other אהח"ע letter in the alphabet: ע or ח or ה before ב, א or ח or ע after ד, etc.[26] Modern Samaritan pronunciation of SH or SA reveals, however, a more complex picture. In fact, only ה and ח have disappeared, but not א nor ע. The ה may be sounded as part of the production of a final vowel, with no connection whatsoever with the historical ה. The following are examples of this phenomenon, according to Schaade's transcription: *wegdîlah* ואגדילה (SP Gn 12:2),[27] *wyaṣmîh* ויצמיח (SP Gn 2:9),[28] *nibnih* נבנה (Gn 11:4),[29] *fâruh* פרעה (Gn 45:21).[30] I myself managed to hear it on occasion. The use of the ע is extremely limited, as described below in Rule 4. It appears that ה has merged with א under all conditions, and ח with ע, the historical ע/ח behaving like א in most phonetic settings with the exceptions stated in Rule 4. The following are the detailed rules:

1. אל"ף (אהח"ע>), except for the stipulations of Rule 4, appears at the beginning of a syllable: *'illa* אלה, *'inna* הנה, *'ikma* חכמה, *'irbəm* ערבים, *'åraṣ* ארץ, *'åšən*

---

[25] In addition to von Gall's edition of SP, I had before me the papers of my former students, R. Mirkin and H. Shiron, who compared a number of pages of ancient SP manuscripts with regard to interchange of the "guttural" letters, as well as the seminar paper prepared by the late R. Weiss, who contrasted the poetical sections of the Masoretic text with their SP counterparts.

[26] See *LOT* III/2, 90 where אהיה stands at the beginning of the verse reserved for ה, אלית at ח; 94: עבודה at א, עבדתנון at ה, עבדתנה at ח, האן at ע. This is very frequent.

[27] See Diening, *Hebräische*, 40; Kahle, *Geniza*, 325.

[28] See Diening, *Hebräische*, 45; Kahle, *Geniza*, 320.

[29] Kahle, *Geniza*, 324.

[30] Kahle, *Geniza*, 330.

1.1 Consonants

חשן, *'am* עם, *'oṣ* עוץ, *'or* אור, *'ūr* אור (only here in these examples has the אל״ף been marked also at the beginning of a word); *yišrā'əl* ישראל, *kā'ən* כהן, *yišmā'u* ישמעו, *yērē'i* יראה.

2. In medial position between *i, u* and another vowel the א (< אהח״ע) is replaced by a geminated glide: *y* after *i, w* after *u* — such as *miyyādåm* מאדם, *niyyâfåk* נהפך, *miyyēləb* מחלב, *miyyūlåm* מעולם, *ēluwwəm* (< *ēlū'im*) אלהים, *ruwwi* רוחי, *yēšuw'wā* (<*yēšū'a*) ישועה.

3. Between two identical vowels the א (< אהח״ע) disappears, and the vowels merge into a single vowel, such as *nār* (< *nā'ar*) נער, *lēm* לחם, *al'mān* למען, *maśfūt* (< *maśfū'ot*) משפחות [but א which has resulted from dissimilation may remain; see also 1.5.3.2].

4. At the beginning of a word (!) with a historical ח or ע, an *y* may be pronounced only before one of the vowels *a, ā, å, â*, as, for example, *'az* עז, *'am* עם, *'amməš* חמש, *'akom* חכום, *'ābəd* עבד, *'âzâbu* עזבו. There are, however, roots and words beginning with historical ח or ע where no *y* is pronounced, such as *åšən* חשן, *ådəš* חדש, *ārəb* חרב, *az* עז, *at* עת.[31]

5. א (< אהח״ע) and ע (< ח״ע) disappear after the prepositions ב and ל and after *waw copulative*; yet the ע survives after the definite article ה and in *Hif'il* verbs, such as *baš* באש, *waf* ואף, *wad* ועד, (but *'ad* עד), etc., *'ām* העם, (*'am* עם), *'ā:bəd* העבד.

6. In word final position the א (< אהח״ע) disappears: *bārā* ברא, *rēṣa* רצה, *zâru* (also *zârū*) זרוע. (However, as to SA see 1.2.0 note).

7. In syllable final, word medial position, the א (< אהח״ע) generally assimilates to the following consonant, such as *qārāttā* קראת, *yārâttimma* יראתם, *šāmåttā* שמחת, *šāmānnu* שמענו, *zērākkimma* זרעכם, *nēmma* נעמה (Gn 49:15), *bīmma* בהמה. The lack of assimilation in such cases as *mā:ni* מחנה, *nā:ra* נערה, *bī:måtåk* בהמתך does not violate this rule; they may be properly interpreted in accordance with the process described in connection with auxiliary vowels, 1.3.5.

> Note: There are only occasional exceptions to the rules above, such as ע in a word beginning with an א (followed by ח): *'ā* אח, *'ād* אחד, *'āt* אחת, *'ā'əz* אחז (Ex 15:14) and the place name *'åtåd* האטד (Gn 50:10) written also as החטד; or ע in the middle of a word: *â''ād* האחד, *â''āni* העינה (Gn 35:3). These are pseudo-exceptions; see 1.4.5 note. Exceptions which cannot be explained away by means of some other process are the personal name *'izzån* עזן, *mī'âfår* מעפר (Nu 19:17), and the place name *'år''år* ערער, except that the latter might be considered made up of two words. Moreover, in words beginning with an articulated ע, the ע is still pronounced, even after the ה of *Hif'il* and after the definite article ה, see 2.2.1.2.1; 3.3.4.

---

[31] See below 1.1.8.3.

1.1.8.1 The description above raises a question: does it reflect an ancient and reliable linguistic heritage regarding Hebrew and Aramaic in light of the occasional weakening of אהח"ע in SP and of the findings in Aramaic poetry, which render א and ע equivalent? Were the viability of this phenomenon to be denied with regard to the period of Aramaic speech, it would be necessary to attribute it to Arabic influence, but this is extremely problematic: (a) though it is possible that אהח"ע were restored in pronunciation the way they are pronounced in Arabic (and in Samaritan Arabic as well!), i.e., by substitution, just as it is possible that the pronunciation of פ:p ceased as a result of Arabic influence (see 1.1.4), why then was only ע restored, but not ה or ח? Furthermore, how could this restored ע have undergone the permanent change as described above in Rule 2, unlike Arabic custom? (b) How is it possible for ע to be pronounced only under the conditions described in Rule 4, this being applicable to words beginning with ח, too, with clear parallels in ח in Arabic, such as *'ăkǎmu* חכמו, حكم, or to words with *ġ* in Arabic, such as *'ānu* (Nu 21:17), the root of which in Arabic is غنى (sing)? In cases like this, how is Arabic influence possible? The response must be that the pronunciation tradition of אהח"ע as it is today precedes the adoption of Arabic by the Samaritan community, and it is maintained carefully in contrast to the spoken language of the community in this respect just as in others.[32]

The weakening of the gutturals is known to have taken place throughout the Aramaic-speaking world, in both the East and the West, with consequences which differ from one dialect to another. In Mandaic ע coalesced with א while ח merged with ה[33] and this inclination can be detected as a tendency in the Aramaic of the Babylonian Talmud as well;[34] in the living eastern dialects: Ṭūrōyo maintains the gutturals, but the articulation of ע "very closely resembles that of א";[35] in Zacho and Urmi ע is the equivalent of א, whereas ח is pronounced like a fricative כ,[36] the aspect common to them and to Mandaic,

---

[32] In my article "Samaritan Vowel System," 526, I claimed that the present-day Samaritan *'ayin* is part of their Aramaic — rather than their Arabic — linguistic heritage. I, however, no longer hold several of the assumptions I made in that article, *inter alia*, that the *'ayin* is secondary, having first become an *aleph*.

[33] Nöldeke, *Grammatik*, 57.

[34] Epstein, *Grammar*, 18; C. Levias, *A Grammar of Babylonian Aramaic* (New York, 1930), 46–47 [Hebrew].

[35] Thus, according to A. Siegel, *Laut- und Formenlehre des neuaramäischen Dialekts des Ṭûr 'Abdîn* (Hannover, 1923), 62. However, H. Ritter, *Ṭūrōyo: Die Volkssprache der syrischen Christen des Ṭûr 'Abdîn* (Beirut, 1969), does not mention this, but does mention (I, 31) that ' becomes *ḥ* before a non-vocal consonant "according to the rule," such as *bi'to>biḥto* (ביצה). O. Jastrow, *Laut- und Formenlehre des neuaramäischen Dialekts von Midin Im Ṭūr 'Abdîn* (Wiesbaden, 1985), does not mention any changes in *'ayin* at all.

[36] But in words borrowed from Hebrew, *'ayin* and *ḥet* generally survive in the Aramaic of Zacho Jewry. See Y. Sabar, "The Hebrew Elements in the Neo-Aramaic Dialect of the Jews of Zacho in Kurdistan," *Lěšonénu* 38 (1974), 210 [Hebrew].

thus, being the shift of ע towards א and a separate shift of ה/ח. A convergence of ע and א on the one hand, and of ה and ח on the other, is discernible in Hebrew texts with Babylonian vocalization signs, too, in features differentiating between ע/א and ח/ה,[37] probably as a result of their connection with Babylonian Aramaic. In contrast to this, in the western dialects the shift of ח > ע can be recognized in literary texts,[38] while in Kutscher's opinion[39] this took place in the Galilee at the end of the second century (R. Ḥiyya), at the very latest. Now, since many ע < א and ה < ח interchanges can be discerned in several manuscripts of rabbinic (Hebrew) literature, Kutscher concluded that from the sixth century on the pronunciation of ע weakened, too, thus completing the weakening of the gutturals. To complete the picture, in the western Aramaic living dialect of Maʿlūla, the gutturals survive, especially ח and ע; "only א and ה tend to disappear with considerable frequency."[40]

1.1.8.2 The Samaritan tradition in Hebrew and in Aramaic teaches clearly that until the end of the spoken Aramaic period in Palestine the gutturals אהח"ע had not merged into a single sound everywhere and under all circumstances. Just as the Samaritan tradition bears faithful witness to the ח > ע shift by virtue of their special behavior, contrasting with א and ה, so it testifies to the gradual character of the אהח"ע merger into a single consonant. At the stage when the Samaritan tradition underwent that shift in its pronunciation of Hebrew and Aramaic, the shift of ע (including ע < ח) to א with the ע preceding *a, å* in initial position, irrespective of vowel quantity, did not occur. The role played by the vowels *a, å* in maintaining "guttural" pronunciation is well known from the phenomenon known as *pataḥ furtivum,* which does not appear before א (which became silent in word final position!). Since the ע (< ע, ח) is preserved in only a narrow section of its original functions, and a root or a word with initial ע maintains it only under the circumstances mentioned above, whereas under other conditions the ע is replaced by א, e.g., ʿarəm ערים, contrasting with īr עיר contrasting with *lam* לעם, ʿåmåd עמד contrasting with *yåmmåd* יעמד — the ע was apparently seen as an "accompanying sound" to the vowels *a, å,* rather than an independent "consonant" to be pronounced, and so in a poetic acrostic no more attention was paid to the ע than to the א. This concept of an "accompanying sound" has, of course, no bearing on our statement that the ע had phonematic significance. Our statement is based on completely different con-

---

[37] Yeivin, *Babylonian Vocalization,* 290ff.
[38] E. Y. Kutscher collected them in his *Studies in Galilean Aramaic,* trans. M. Sokoloff (Ramat-Gan, 1976), 67ff.
[39] Ibid.
[40] Spitaler, *Grammatik,* 24–25.

siderations: the ע generates distinctions between pairs of words otherwise homophonous, such as *am* = עַם/ *'am* = עָם, *al* = אֶל/ *'al* = עַל, etc.

This situation is reflected nicely in the Samaritan linguistic tradition. On the one hand, this tradition indicates that ח and ע are *matres lectionis* like א and ה and serve as a basis for the development of vowel signs (*LOT* II, 309, 311), while, on the other hand, ח and ע are called "sound guttural consonants," unlike א and ה, "weak guttural consonants" (*LOT* I, 55, ll.16–17).[41]

Even if it has been demonstrated that the Samaritan tradition of the pronunciation of אהח"ע in Hebrew and in Aramaic preceded the Arabic linguistic domination, no limitation has been fixed for the dating of this tradition within the long period of Samaritan Aramaic speech, to say nothing of the Hebrew speech. Yet note: a study of the אהח"ע interchanges in ST manuscripts has not revealed any interchanges of ח with either א or ה, nor has it found any interchanges of ח with either of those two under the conditions in which ע is pronounced today, i.e., in word initial position, before *a, å*.[42] This fact is in need of a reexamination; it requires an explanation.

1.1.8.3 A sound shift anchored in a living language can be expected to be regular; therefore, words beginning with historical ח or ע followed by *a, å*, but in which the modern pronunciation ע is not articulated, need to be explained. This concerns such words as *åzi* חזה, *åzəq* חזק, *ådəš* חדש, *ålåq* חלק, *åmå* חמה, *åqqå* חקה, *åri* חרי, *årəb* חרב, *årəm* חרם, *åšək* חשך, *åšən* חשן, *åməs* חמס, *åməṣ* חמץ, *åṣər* חצר, *az* עז, *am* עם, and also a number of verbs (see 2.2.1.0). The fact that the phenomenon is more common with nouns than with verbs is not the product of chance. It should be recalled that most of the verbal formations are made by means of prefixes, such as the marking of the persons of the imperfect (אית"ן), the מ of the participial forms, the ל of the infinitives and *waw conjunctive* (= *consecutive*), and so ע will not appear in them initially. Thus, the phenomenon is limited to perfect, and to some extent imperative, forms of *Qal, Pi'el* and *Hif'il*, of course, when they appear without a *waw*. The absence of the ע in the cases adduced above should probably be explained in various ways. With regard to nouns it is reasonable to assume that at least some of them did not

---

[41] The description of א, ה, ח, ע by Al-'Ayya (*LOT* II, 331, 333) does not correspond at all to the Samaritan pronunciation; rather, he hands down what he learned from the Arabic grammar books, for ה and ח were certainly no longer pronounced in his days (the eighteenth century!).

[42] The investigations conducted by Mirkin and Shiron (see n. 25 above) were carried out many years ago as part of a study of this question. What is needed is an examination of all the existing spelling differences in the old, important manuscripts in the light of the present day pronunciation, a project which is now possible as a result of the concordance of the Pentateuch according to the Samaritan pronunciation found in *LOT*, IV. It is worth noting that SP at Gen 26:29 reads עתה אתה: *'atta åttå* and no alternate reading is known. To such an extent does the pronunciation preserve the written version.

always have an *a* or *å* vowel where there is one today, i.e., they did not fit the pattern defined by having *a* or *å* follow the initial radical; the modern vowels are derived from *u* (see 1.5.2.3) or result from the development of a *šəwa* into a full *a*, *å* vowel (1.3.3). In some cases, the TH tradition bears witness, e.g., *åšak* חֹשֶׁךְ, *ådəš* חֹדֶשׁ (contrasting with *'ådåš* חָדָשׁ), *åri* חֲרִי. This is the case with *å:līma* (Gn 24:43 הָעַלְמָה), as the Arabic and Aramaic cognates with *u* after the first radical indicate. In other cases, the SH form of the noun is the construct (or suffixed) form of the noun at an earlier stage, i.e., it begins with a *šəwa*, e.g., *åmå* חֵמָה derives from something like TH חֲמַת. This latter phenomenon seems not to have affected verbs, or at least was not decisive with them, for the verbal form with initial *šəwa* in the early stage, i.e., in *Qal* and with pronominal suffixes, is too rare to have attracted unsuffixed forms or forms like *Pi'el* or *Hif'il*. On the other hand, with verbs there is vast opportunity for another type of analogy: the absence of *'ayin* in a form like *åfåṣti* הפצתי (Dt 25:8) is a result of its regular absence in a form like *yå:fåṣ* יחפץ (Dt 25:7). Either way, the fact is that, without any such intention, there developed a distinction between verbs and nouns derived from roots which have ח/ע as their first radical, such as *'ånu* ענו (Nu 21:17) / *ånu* חנו (Nu 2:34), *'årəb* ערב (Ex 8:17)/ *årəb* חרב Gn 31:26).

1.2 Vowels

1.2.0 Medieval Samaritan grammarians taught that "in the Hebrew language according to the Samaritan reading" there are five vowels,[43] and this is indeed the number of vowel phonemes in SH today as well. It is possible to distinguish seven vowels, each of which adopts various shades in accordance with certain adjoining consonants; however, since the adoption of these shades is not of grammatical significance, we do not carefully mark them in writing down words as pronounced by the Samaritans. The following are the seven vowels: *i, ə, e, a, å, o, u* — none of which, except for *ə*, are restricted to a single vowel quantity.

i — if not short, then it is a high-front vowel; if it is short, it is situated lower and tends towards the center.

ə — falls between *i* and *e*, and tends towards the center. It is short and appears only in a closed post-tonic syllable.[44]

e — is a medium-front vowel, semi-open, though sometimes, especially when long, it is a little more closed.

---

[43] *LOT* II, 309 (and similarly 329), where six are discussed, but the *dageš* is included in that number.

[44] There are a few cases where I believe I heard this vowel pronounced by a certain reader in a closed stressed syllable, like *məm* מים (*LOT* III/1, 113), *bər* באר (ibid., 79), *ət* את (ibid., 78).

a — is a low-front vowel: this quality is precise, whenever the vowel is not short. When it is short and appears in an unstressed syllable, it is on occasion higher and sounds somewhat like *æ* (in the IPA notation: ɛ). It is sometimes difficult to distinguish between *a* and the vowel marked *å*, especially in a stressed syllable or when the vowel is in an open post-tonic syllable.

å — is a low vowel, ranging from the center to the back when it is short. When it is long it is clearly a back vowel, and even tends to be rounded. When read slowly and musically, it is rounded by everyone.

o, u — are back vowels. The *u* vowel is somewhat lowered, and on occasion might be heard as *o*, though an ear trained to hear Samaritan does not confuse them.[45] In the use of these two vowels there exists a special relationship: *o* appears almost always in a closed syllable, and is thus **short**, whereas *u* appears in open syllables and is **long**. In this way *o* and *u* are mutually complementary, and this is reflected in the writings of the Samaritan grammarians who speak of a single *ḍamma*. For example: *dor* דור, *dūrot* דורות, *dūrūtīkimma* דורותיכם. However, in an open post-tonic syllable *o* can appear, too. In fact, we are referring to *o* which is a result of a contracted diphthong, such as in the 3rd masc. sing. pronominal suffix, e.g., *yēdo* ידיו, *'ālo* עליו, or in the passive participle *Qal* of the ל"י class, e.g., *galo* and other similar forms. Since the second component of a falling diphthong functions, at least phonemically, as a consonant, the appearance of *o* in this position in the previous stage did not contradict the rule. Rarely is the vowel *u* heard in a closed syllable, such as *mukkå* מכה, (Dt 25:3), *dukka* דכה, (Dt 23:2), *wtuqqå* ותקה, (Gn 12:15). In SP MSS one also finds ויגד (today: *wyiggād*) pointed with the mark of the *ḍamma* in Gn 38:24; Ex 14:5.

> Note: In SA (!) there are remnants of the previous stage, when *o* occurred in final syllables closed with a presently unpronounced guttural, e.g., *fāto* פתחיו (*LOT* III/2, 93) < **fātoḥ* (in Tiberian vocalization פָּתוֹחַ), *šāmo* שמעיו (ibid. 104), *zizzo* זעיו (ibid. 195) < זעוע. However, the expected, regular, development is also attested in *maṣbu* מצבוע (ibid. 260) "(purifying) immersion," *mēlu* מלו (ibid. 152) "fullness." It is worthwhile noting the contrast between the aforementioned SA *fāto*, *mēlu* and SH *fātu* (Nu 19:15), *mē'lū* (Ex 9:8).

1.2.1 There are four degrees of vowel length in SH. Even an untrained ear can easily distinguish three of these, whereas one (the second degree) can be dis-

---

[45] Indeed, Schaade and Ritter (Kahle, 318ff.) registered *ō* instead of *ū* in particular as a long vowel, i.e., generally in an open syllable: *wyā'ômer* ויאמר (ibid., 319), *wyā'ômaer* (320), *tôldat* תולדת (321), *wyā'omer* (320) [but p. 321: *wyā'ûmaer* — Gn 3:13], *tā'ôkel* תאכל (321), *ōtímma* אותם (320), *āšômer* השומר (320 — Gn 4:9). I considered this phenomenon an error in hearing ("Samaritan Hebrew," 120). Indeed, all these forms exhibit *ū* according to the rule cited above.

1.2 Vowels

cerned in a precise, unhurried reading; in a slow reading it tends to be heard as long, and in a hurried reading, as short. In a musically intoned reading vowel length will fluctuate, especially in distinguishing between the third and fourth degrees. Brevity is unmarked whereas length is indicated by a macron. Extra length is marked by adding a colon after the long vowel only where, according to the rules given below, it is not possible to distinguish between this degree and normal vowel length. The following are the degrees of vowel length relevant in SH and SA:

a. **a short vowel** occurs in a closed syllable, whether stressed or unstressed (ə, as noted above [1.2], does not occur in a stressed syllable), e.g., *it* את, *yiqra* יקרא, *wyiššåb* וישב, *deš* דיש, *ser* סיר, *dabbər* דבר, *dabbertimma* דברתם, *am* עם, *'am* עַם, *'ammǝm* עמים, *båd* בד, *dåm* דם, *tåfkimma* טפכם, *yåmmǝm* ימים, *mot* מות, *qol* קול, *rē'oškimma* ראשכם, *miyyoṣ* מחוץ, *aṣṣibbor* הצפור. With regard to short *u*, see the previous paragraph. Ultrashort *u* serves in *waw conjunctive* in a phrase such as *"'ū* but is generally marked *u''ū*, there being no fear of error for it is a rule that no short vowel ever occurs in an open syllable (see 1.2.3).

b. **a somewhat long vowel** occurs in a word final open syllable following the stressed syllable, such as *ammiṣri·* המצרי, *immi·* עמי, *måṣli·* מצליח, *fåru·* פרעה. Only here, in the adduced examples, is the slight lengthening demarked by the dot; elsewhere it is not indicated, both because in fluent reading one does not notice it and also because where it is felt, since the vowel appears in an open syllable, it exists under circumstances in which no originally short vowel could survive, and so is unique and need not be singled out.

c. **a long vowel** occurs in open, stressed or unstressed syllables, except for posttonic syllables. For example: *ī* היא, *īno* אינו, *īnīkimma* עיניכם; *rē'oš* ראש, *rē'ūšu* ראשו, *yērē'i* יראה, *bā* בה, *wtåmmā'u* וטמאו, *šāmā'u* שמעו, *yåmǝm* ימים, *niffādåtå* נפדתה, *ū* הוא, *nūšånåt* נושנת, *å'ūri* אֲחוֹרֵי.

d. **an extra-long vowel**, i.e., a longer than usual vowel, occurs in both open and closed syllables, whether stressed or unstressed, such as: (1) *ī:r* עיר, *bī:mma* בהמה, *wē:nna* והנה, *'å:m* העם, *wē:tnå:ltimma* והתנחלתם, *afqārā:ttu* בקרחתו, *ammå:tti* המחתא (Lv 6:19), *rå:m* = TH רְאֵם, *ū:f* עוף, *lā:ššotkimma* לעשותכם, *wetå:nnåna* ואתחננה; (2) *zē'rī:k* זרעך, *mā'rī:* מראה, *tū'lā:t* תולעת, *šånā:* שנאה, *šå'må:* שמחה, *yå'bū:* יבוא, *mā'nū:* מנוח; (3) *bī:måtåk* בהמתך, *nā:ra* נערה, *rā:* רעה, *må:ni* מחנה, *rå:* ראה, *å:bånəm* האבנים, *å:dåmå* האדמה.

In all the examples above the vowel quantity is denoted by a colon. However, since in words such as those listed in (1) the regular vowel length (3rd level) never occurs, and in words of ultimate stress similar to those listed in (2) the vowel length under consideration always bears the stress, we can give up the colon in favor of simplicity of presentation. And so in the previously cited words written *īr, bīmma, wēnna, zē'rīk, yâ'bū*, etc., the rule mentioned determines which of the vowels is extra-long. In words such as those listed in (3) the colon is vital to distinguish between a long vowel and an extra-long one, for in open syllables preceding the stress or even stressed syllables themselves the regular long vowel may also appear.

In fluent reading it is sometimes difficult to decide in words similar to those listed in (3) whether their vowel is extra-long or of regular length. In such cases we have omitted the colon, for the morphological analysis of the word easily indicates which vowel, phonologically speaking, is involved. The examples above demonstrate clearly that the extra-long vowel is almost always connected with the disappearance of an אהח"ע consonant and the coalescence of two syllables into one, such as: **tūlā'at > tū'lā:t* תולעת, **mâ'âni > mâ:ni* מחנה, **rā'a > rā:* רעה, (contrasting with *rā* רע).⁴⁶ Also involving a syllable reduction are **tūlᵉdāt > (tū:ldåt=) tūldåt* תולדת, **qārᵉbəm > (qā:rbəm=) qārbəm* קרבים (in Dt 20:3), and in SA **kârᵉzən > (kâ:rzən=) kârzən* כארזין (*LOT* III/2, 356, l. 70, alongside *wåmårəm* ואמרים!). But such a feature unrelated to אהח"ע is exceptional.

> Note: According to the system of denotation mentioned above one can mark a second degree vowel appearing in an open post-tonic syllable with the macron, e.g., *fårū* פרעה, without ever confusing it with a fourth degree vowel, which in such a position is always stressed: *mâ'nū* מנוח. For the sake of simplicity, however, I followed the vast majority of such words, which tends to shorten the final vowel in an open post-tonic syllable, and as a result I have not marked the second degree at all.

1.2.2 The Jewish traditions do not behave according to the above description. These traditions, as they are reflected in the Tiberian, the Babylonian and the so-called Palestinian⁴⁷ vocalization systems, do not distinguish between vowel quantities, but rather between vowel qualities. The vowel quantity may be surmised and interpreted on the basis of comparative grammatical considera-

---

⁴⁶ All the rules of vowel quantity also apply to SA, examples being easily found on every page of *LOT* III/2. It is perhaps worth noting that the stressed gentilic suffix in such words as *wråt'tâ* ורתאה (*LOT* III/2, 88, l. 91) originates in the contraction process (see 1.4.6.1), having become obscured in various places. Cf. ibid., 14, 61 (l. 26), 159 (l. 82).

⁴⁷ The Babylonian system is described in detail in Yeivin, *Babylonian Vocalization*, 364ff. The Palestinian system is discussed in Dietrich, *Bibelfragmente*, 111–121; E. J. Revell, *Hebrew Texts with Palestinian Vocalization* (Toronto, 1970) and in the article by Revell, "Studies in the Palestinian Vocalization," *Essays on the Ancient Semitic World*, Toronto, 1971), 51–100.

1.2 Vowels

tions. The Samaritan vocalization system does not distinguish between vowel quantities either, and so the grammarians do not discuss them, but what their vocalization system is undoubtedly aimed at expressing is their reading tradition, and this is absolutely uniform and stable in the performance of every modern Samaritan. We may, according to our experience in other fields of their tradition as well, assume the existence of such a situation at the time their vocalization system was crystalized, too, i.e., at the time they spoke Aramaic.[48] In order to appreciate the relationship between SH and the Hebrew of the Jews insofar as vowels are concerned, we must first study the SH vowel system as described by the grammarians, with regard to vowel quality and vowel quantity.

When the grammarians ascribed five symbols to the vowels, they unquestionably included *u* and *o* as a single entity. These two vowels did not require separate symbols, because they were mutually exclusive.[49] It is the quantitative difference between *u/o* which shows that vowel quantity was not marked in any way. Therefore, it may be claimed that they were familiar with six vowels. With regard to the symbol *ə* which we have used both in SH and SA, there has been no intention, as already noted,[50] to use it to denote an independent vocalic phoneme; we have merely used it to mark what is sometimes heard as *i* and on other occasions as *e* in a closed post-tonic syllable, in the very same word. This part of the /e/ phoneme is assuredly what was intended by Schaade in his inconsistent *e* transcription.[51] It is clear that the Samaritans found no need to invent a special sign for such a sound; thus, one finds in MS א (*LOT* I, 188, 189, l. 7) that this sound is on occasion expressed by *i*, as in בשרך = *bāšārək* (with the addition of a 2nd fem. sing. poss. suffix), on p. 15, while on other occasions, by *e*, as in אתך = *ūtək*, on p. 14 (the vocalization indicates the form with the 2nd fem. sing. suffix אתיך as written next to this word). Thus, we may assume that the vowel system we hear today is expressed in the vowel signs, both qualitatively and quantitatively (see further 2.12.3, n. 120).

1.2.3 Since the syllabic structure of SH (and of SA) is as follows: short vowel (1st degree) occurring only in a closed syllable and a long vowel (3rd degree) only in a non-post-tonic open syllable (in a post-tonic syllable one finds the

---

[48] I have already expressed this opinion in "Samaritan Vowel System," 530.

[49] This feature, or a similar one, is reflected in a number of manuscripts vocalized in the Palestinian system, as I have already noted: Ben-Ḥayyim, *Tradition*, 91, n. 3. Dietrich, *Bibelfragmente*, 116, and Revell, "Studies," 62, overlooked my opinion that the possibility of using a single sign for both *u* and *o* depends on there having been a regular interchange between them.

[50] For the first time in *LOT* III/1, 12. Cf. Ben-Ḥayyim, "Some Problems," 245-246.

[51] E.g., *ǣllûwwèm* אלהים (Kahle, *Geniza*, 320 — Gn 2:18), *errûmeš* הרומש (ibid., 319 — Gn 1:26), *wyǣbǣrrèk* ויברך (ibid., 320 — Gn 2:3), as well as many other forms, corresponding to which the transcription shows *e* in this position. In our system the words are to be written thus: *ēluwwəm, arrūməš, wyēbarrək*.

2nd degree) — there is no possible contrast between vowels of the aforesaid quantitative degrees; vowel quantity is automatically arranged. The short vowel in a closed syllable is replaced by a long one when the syllable is opened (historically speaking, the process is often the opposite!), e.g., *zit* זית: *zītåk* זיתך; *'ad* עד: *'ādi* עדי; *båb* וו: *båbīyyimma* וויהם; *dor* דור: *dūrot* דורות; *qåm* קם: *qåmu* קמו. This is not the case with regard to the relationship of the fourth degree to the above two: this relationship determines meaning, e.g., *il* אֶל: *īl* אַיִל; *'am* עַם: *'ām* הָעָם; *råb* רב: *råb* (=*rå:b*) רחב; *ådåmå* אדמה: *å:dåmå* האדמה; *šåtu* שתו (Ex 33:4); *šå:tu* שחתו (SP Dt 32:5).

It is clearly noticeable that the fourth degree involves the special status of the guttural consonants in SH and SA. The syllables with the extra-long vowels result from the reduction of two syllables into a single one (see 1.1.8c), and it is very doubtful if, at the time the vocalization was determined and certainly for generations thereafter, the two syllables had already become one. On the contrary, it may almost certainly be assumed that the long vowel was not then in existence (see 1.4.7). Either way, when clarifying the status of SH as opposed to Jewish traditions with regard to vowel quantity, the fourth degree is not comparable to any corresponding entity. We may deduce from this that the Samaritan heritage presents us with something which contrasts with the Jewish heritage. In other words: the distinction between a short vowel (in SH the first degree) and a long one (in SH the third degree), even if it had been realized and wherever it was realized, would have had no phonological value at all. The extra length appearing in words without guttural consonants, such as *tūldåt* תולדת, *qārbəm* קרבים (in Dt 20:3) (see 1.2.1) is to be interpreted on the basis of the automatic interchange of a short vowel in a closed syllable with a long vowel in an open syllable, for even had it been deemed necessary to realize a long vowel in a closed syllable — after the syllable became closed as the result of the omission of a vowel — it would have been impossible to do so except by means of an extra-long vowel (cf. the attempt to realize a diphthong, 1.4.2). Morpho-phonematic considerations lead to the assumption that a syllable with an extra-long vowel is to be viewed as if it were still two syllables.

1.2.4 With regard to vowel quality five vowel phonemes, are, thus, to be distinguished in SH (as in SA): *i, e, a, å, u/o*, except that the last of these is problematic. The automatic interchange of *u/o* mentioned in 1.2 does not take place in a post-tonic open syllable, the phonetic distinction even determines meaning, such as *yēdu* = TH יָדוֹ / *yēdo* = TH יָדָיו; *bēnu* = TH בְּנוֹ / *båno* = TH בָּנָיו. It should be noted that occasions on which two words are identical except for *u/o* are extremely rare: in general, singular and plural forms differ from one another not only in *u/o* but also in the overall structure of the noun, e.g., *bēnu* בנו / *båno* בניו. At any rate, one should note that no Samaritan ever reads **dammo*

דמיו but rather *dammu* דמו, a rule applicable to *'*ammo* עמו (with prepositions, e.g., in Lv 21:1; Ex 30:38) replaced by '*ammu* עמו[52] though there do exist SP manuscripts which read עמיו. Perhaps the maintaining of *o* instead of *u* in an unnatural phonetic environment is necessary for the independent existence of the 3rd masc. sing. pronominal morpheme for plural nouns, and wherever it is not needed it is replaced. We may view the two vowels *o*, *u* as conditioned allophones of a single phoneme under the above mentioned restriction.

1.2.5 With regard to the vowels *i* and *e*, the distinction between them is not maintained in closed post-tonic syllables, where they both appear as the vowel *ə*; the rule is that a noun or a verb containing an *i* or an *e* vowel in any other circumstances show a shift of that vowel to *ə* in a closed post-tonic syllable, e.g., *bit* בית: *abbət* הבית; *ger* גר: *aggər* הגר. In addition, words containing the vowel *i* in stressed syllables show a shift of that vowel to *e* when the relevant syllable is no longer stressed, e.g., קציר: *qâṣər, qâṣīråk, qâṣerkimma*; דבר: *dabbər, dabbirti, dabbirtā*, etc., but *dabbertimma*; מהר: *mâ'ertimma, mâ'irtən*. The phonematic opposition between *i* and *e* when they are realized as long vowels (e.g., *īši* = TH אִישִׁי / *ēši* = TH אִשָּׁה) helps to identify the verbal stem of verbs with an initial guttural: *Piʿel* such as *tâbbēdon* תאבדון, or *Hifʿil* like *tabbīdu*, though it is difficult to locate word pairs in the Pentateuch differing only in their *e*/*i* vocalic opposition. One example of such a pair, *ī*/*ē*, is *rīm* = TH רֵחַיִם / *rēm* = TH רֵחֶם.

Examples of vowel-oppositions between *e*, *i* and other vowels:

i: *a*/*å* — *bin* (TH בֵּין) : *ban* (TH בֶּן); *zir* (TH זֵר) : *zår* (TH זָר);
e: *a*/*å* — *ser* (TH סִיר) : *sar* (TH סָר); *den* (TH דִּין) : *dan* (TH דָּן);
e:*o* — *qer* (TH קִיר) : *qor* (TH קוֹר);
ī: *ā*/*å* — *šīr* (TH שָׂעִיר) : *šār* (TH שֵׂעָר); *šīr* (TH שָׂעִיר) : *šår* (TH שָׂעֹר, שְׂעוֹר);
ī:*ū* — *īr* (TH עִיר) : *ūr* (TH עוּר);
ē: *ā*(*å*) — *nēl* (TH נַחַל) : *nāl* (TH נַעַל); *rēm* (TH רֶחֶם) : *råm* (TH רְאֵם); *tēt*, "beneath" (TH תַּחַת) : *tåt*, "in place of" (TH תַּחַת);
ē/*ū* — *bēd* (TH בְּעַד) : *būd* (TH בְּעוֹד).

1.2.6 *a*, *å*. The systematic distinction between the front and the back vowels of all quantities was first made in *LOT* III/2, 61. Since the short vowel *a* tends towards æ (IPA: ɛ), we find it expressed by *e*, and when it is long it is expressed the same way as the back vowel, however, the Samaritan grammarians clearly noted the distinction while teaching the existence of three kinds of *fatḥ* (*LOT* II, 309; "Samaritan Vowel System," 521). The "vocative *fatḥ*" is undoubtedly *ē*, while the other two kinds of *fatḥ* turn out to be the vowels under considera-

---

[52] But in Lv 21:14 the reading is *miyyimu*, i.e., מֵעַמּוֹ. See *LOT* III/1, 68 for my comments.

tion here. The most instructive example, taken from Dt 4:11 for all three *faṯḥ*, is *war bār bēš* = ובהר בער באש (*LOT* III/2, 183, l. 22). From it we learn of an ancient traditional distinction, though it must be admitted that this distinction is especially clear with the long and the extra-long vowels, rather than with the short vowels. On occasion the Samaritans differ with regard to the nature of the *a* or *å* vowel in a closed or an open post-tonic syllable. Most reading variants involve this vowel, as may clearly be seen in SA (*LOT* III/2 critical apparatus, *passim*). For SA the word קללה may serve as an example. In Gn 27:12 it is pronounced *qålålå*, while in other verses *qålåla* (See *LOT* V, 280, corrigendum to p. 203). The sensitivity to the *a/å* distinction can be felt in word pairs differing in meaning, such as *an* = הֶן / *ån* = חֵן, *arba* = ארבע / *arbå* = הרבה, *šaš* = שֵׁשׁ / *šåš* = שָׁשׁ, *šam* = שֵׁם / *šåm* = שָׁם. The reason why the distinction between short *a* and *å* is sometimes obscured is twofold: (1) short *a* tends toward the center of the oral cavity, and as a result there is no clear difference in the place of articulation in various words, especially in the case of certain consonantal proximity;[53] (2) there exists an interchange of *a* in closed syllables /*å* in open syllables (see 1.5.1.3a) in word declensions, which has historical antecedents (1.5.2.2); analogy may be the explanation for *å* appearing where *a* is expected.

In contrast, there is a completely clear distinction between *ā* and *å̄*, *ā:* and *å̄:*, as in *šāma* = שמע / *šåma* = שמח; *'āla* = עולה / *'ålā* = עלה; *rāb* (= *rā:b*) = רעב / *råb* (= *rå:b*) = רחב; *šār* (= *šā:r*) = שֵׁעָר / *šår* (= *šå:r*) = שְׁאוֹר, שָׁעֵר.

Note: For examples of the opposition *ā* : *å̄* to the rest of the vowels, see 1.2.5.

1.2.7 Evaluating the Samaritan tradition from the aspect of its vowels as against the Jewish tradition is extremely problematic. This is because the Jewish vowel heritage is very complex. On the face of it, the three known vocalization systems — the Tiberian, the Babylonian and the Palestinian — which differ from one another both in the forms of the signs adopted to signify vowels and in a number of marking techniques, represent three Hebrew dialects[54] (at least with regard to the vowels). But this is not so. Each of the three vocalization systems is used in writing biblical and other manuscripts which reveal the existence of major and minor variants in denoting the vowels, a situation which necessarily leads to the conclusion that each of those systems was used by Jews who had varying pronunciation traditions.[55] A question thus arises concerning the unit

---

[53] E.g., when there is a *m* nearby, like *måmlål/mamlål* ממלל (*LOT* III/2, 58); *alman/almån* למן (ibid., 76); *mattånåtå/måttånåtå* מתנתה (ibid., 156); otherwise: *wamfaššår/wamfåššår* ומפשר (ibid., 136) and perhaps also *kallå/kållå* כלה (ibid., 156).

[54] It is upon this assumption that Revell's discussion in his article mentioned above (see n. 47) is based.

[55] This is evident with regard to the Tiberian vocalization of Mishna manuscripts, and is very

of Jewish tradition to be used in measuring that of the Samaritans. Without entering into the complexities of each system and comparing SH with them, a general examination will suffice:[56] the number of vowel qualities reflected in all the marking systems is seven, at the most, and five, at the least. Seven qualities are characteristic of the accepted Tiberian system, six reflect the simple Babylonian vocalization, while five are to be found in the works of the Spanish gramarians,[57] which are apparently reflected in the fact that various manuscripts, especially those vocalized in the Palestinian and Tiberian systems, reveal an inconsistent use of the signs for *pataḥ* and *qameṣ* on the one hand, and of the signs for *ṣere* and *seghol*, on the other.[58] The six quality system (the "simple" Babylonian vocalization), if compared with that of the seven, is found to have a single sign parallel to *seghol* and *pataḥ*. If we do not ignore our discussion of the denoting of *o, ū* by a single sign and of the special sign for *ə* (see 1.2.2), we can state that there is no difference at all between the Samaritan tradition and the **six** quality system. A phonematic analysis of the seven quality system (the Tiberian system) reveals, too, that the *seghol* is not an independent phoneme, but rather an allophone of *pataḥ*,[59] the common Samaritan and Jewish heritage thus being based on six vowels. It is, however, an entirely different matter as to whether the Samaritan vowels mark those of the Jews. The truth of the matter is that the problem is limited to one of the Tiberian *seghol* and *pataḥ* as against a single sign in the Babylonian tradition, on the one hand, and the *pataḥ* and *qameṣ* in both traditions as against the Samaritan tradition on the other.

1.2.7.1 The fact that in the ("simple") Babylonian vocalization system the symbol ֶ corresponds to *seghol* and *pataḥ*, as in בַּ֫יִת/בִּ֫ית, בְּרַכְאֵל/בַּ֫רְכָאֵל / מֶ֫לֶךְ/מַ֫לְךְ

---

likely with regard to the fragments vocalized according to the Palestinian tradition, but even the more uniform Babylonian system does not reflect only a single pronunciation.

[56] For details see my "Reflections," and "More About the Seghol."

[57] Finally crystallized in Yosef Qimḥi's system of five "large" and "small" vowels. See my "Rules of Šəwa," 135, n. 2.

[58] Cf., for example, the vocalization of the liturgical poems of הדותה. See J. Yahalom "The Palestinian Vocalization in Hedwata's Qəduštot, and the Language Tradition it Reflects," *Lěšonénu* 34 (1970), 34, 39 [Hebrew].

[59] I have noted this in brief in "Hebrew Grammar," *EJ* 8 col. 93, note. This applies to such forms as וַיָּ֫קֶם as against יָקֵם, just as it does to תְּשׂוּמַת as against תְּשׂוּמָת (the latter without a shift of stress to the penult). From a *phonemic* point of view, the *seghol* in וַיָּ֫קֶם is no different from the parallel vowel in וַיֶּ֫סַר or וַיָּ֫נַח. In both types we find the substitution: *e* (*ṣere*) in a stressed syllable / *a* in an unstressed syllable. The substitution *ṣere* / ֶ is quite common in Babylonian vocalization, but the conditions for that substitution have not been clarified. Examples include: חֶשְׂכָּם (Ex 8:16) / תִקְשֹׁב (Job 33:31), תֶּשְׁחַת (Ps 75:1) / תֵּשַׁחַת (Dt 9:26), הִ֫בֶּן (1Sam 3:8) / אֵ֫סֹר (2 Sam 12:20), and many others (cited by Yeivin, *Babylonian Vocalization*, 567, 653). In Babylonian vocalization, ֶ is certainly not an allophone of *ṣere*. One should not confuse the historical development of a vowel with its phonological status in a synchronic system.

שָׂדֶה / שׂוֹדֶה, בְּרָכְיָה / בֹּרְכֹיָה has been interpreted as meaning that in the Babylonian tradition there was only a single vowel corresponding to the two Tiberian ones, and that this vowel was either (1) a *pataḥ* or a *seghol;* or (2) a vowel midway between the two.⁶⁰ Our opinion is that this is no different from what we said concerning the vowel *a* in SH and SA, and according to the description above in 1.2, it is a phoneme, realized as a low or lowered-middle vowel. The Tiberian tradition did not settle for a generalized marking, but preferred to assign a unique symbol for each shade of this vowel. This assumption is supported by the Yemenite pronunciation.⁶¹ In short, the deliberation as to whether one of the two Tiberian vowels, i.e., the *seghol,* was lost to the Babylonian tradition or never developed at all is a mistaken deliberation, for the Babylonian denotes *pataḥ* and *seghol* together according to the circumstances, just as from the examples of the Samaritan "brotherhood *fatḥ*" (*LOT* II, 309–311) there is clearly but a single vowel; without recourse to the testimony of the Samaritan grammarian we are representing it with the letter *a*, though others have used æ⁶² for the same purpose.

1.2.7.2 It is still commonly assumed that there is a difference between the Babylonian ֿ and the Tiberian *qameṣ* in vowel representation: the Babylonian sign denotes⁶³ *a* (usually *ā*), whereas the Tiberian *qameṣ* denotes a vowel between *a* and *o*, generally represented by the symbol *å*. This assumption is based on a faulty premise: since in the simple Babylonian tradition ֿ serves only where Tiberian *qameṣ* is pronounced *ā* in the accepted ("Sephardic") pronunciation, whereas whenever the *qameṣ* represents *o* the Babylonian tradition uses only *šureq* (or *ḥolem*), the Babylonian ֿ must be *ā*!⁶⁴ This reasoning confuses the question of the pronunciation of ֿ with that of its historical development. Furthermore, the reasoning is based also on the mistaken assumption that the (Sephardic!) distinction between *qameṣ* "gadol" (or "raḥav"), which represents *a*, and *qameṣ* "qaṭan," which is *o*, was customary with the Tiberian vocalizers. There is no trace of such a situation in any writings by the Tiberian Masoretes. The quality of the Tiberian *qameṣ* comes through clearly

---

⁶⁰ See BL, 100, 167, and A. Dotan, "Masorah," *EJ* 16, col. 1443.

⁶¹ Morag, *Yemenite*, 121.

⁶² The symbol *e̩* is also used; see the transcription of Ritter and Schaade (Kahle, *Geniza*, 318ff.) The symbol æ has been employed by Murtonen, *Vocabulary*, and by Macuch, *Grammatik*, but they failed to notice what is unique about this vowel and, thus, used the same symbol for sounds other than the vowel described here.

⁶³ The opinion that the Babylonian *qameṣ* was pronounced *ā* was expressed by S. D. Luzzatto in his work *Philoxenus* (Cracow, 1830²), 98 [Hebrew], and by P. Kahle, *Masoreten des Ostens* (Leipzig, 1913), 159. BL and Bergsträsser, *Grammatik*, accept that view, and it appears that this is also the opinion of Yalon, *Studies*, 1971, 275ff.

⁶⁴ This was first taken into consideration, I believe, by Kahle (see previous note).

from the Masoretic grammatical literature, which links it explicitly with the *pataḥ* (and *seghol*), rather than with the *ḥolem* (or the *šureq*).⁶⁵

As for the pronunciation of the Babylonian ﹷ, there exists the written testimony of Qirqisani of Babylon (10th century) that there is no difference whatever between the pronunciation of the *qameṣ* in the Babylonian tradition and that in the Tiberian tradition.⁶⁶ All data, thus, indicate that the Masoretes, both of Palestine and of Babylonia, intended by their signs a kind of *a*-vowel. The various developments in TH and BH concerning the *qameṣ* will be discussed below in 1.5.2.3.

In using the symbol *å* in SH and SA, the intention was merely to distinguish between this non-front vowel, which is often pronounced in the back of the oral cavity and frequently rounded, and a forward *a*, since there was no more appropriate and available sign, and no thought was given to any links this vowel might have with the *qameṣ* in Jewish traditions⁶⁷ — an *a posteriori* phonological analysis leads to the conclusion that the vowel denoted by *å* in SH and SA is a continuation of the *qameṣ*. It is, thus, a heritage common to TH, BH and SH. Of course, in the passage of time, the conditions governing the use of this vowel in SH changed, as will be shown below in 1.5.1, 1.5.2.2.

1.3 Šəwa and the Auxiliary Vowels

1.3.0 The term *šəwa* refers to an ultrashort vowel, while the absence of a vowel will be termed *šəwa quiescens*.

A comparison of SH with TH and BH reveals an unexpected yet decisive difference between them: the absence of a *šəwa* in SH (and in SA as well). Corresponding to the TH *šəwa* one finds a vowel in SH, as a rule a long vowel in an open syllable and a short one in a closed syllable; furthermore, SH sometimes possesses a vowel corresponding to the *šəwa quiescens*. Since in TH the *šəwa* is a secondary vowel, deriving from a full vowel — usually from an originally short vowel — in accordance with rules of syllabic stress, the absence of

---

⁶⁵ Cf. Baer–Strack, *Dikduke Ha-Teamim* , 34: והשלוש להציב עשויות אֶה אָה אִי — i/e/ "and the triad *qameṣ pataḥ seghol* expresses the vowel נצב. להציב alludes to the term نَصْب for the vowel *a* in Arabic grammar. This was already noticed by D. Yellin, *History of the Hebrew Grammar* (Jerusalem, 1947), 17 [Hebrew]: "the *qameṣ* conjoins with the *pataḥ* and not with the *ḥolem*, thus tending toward Sephardic pronunciation." In the manuscript another order of the vowels can be found; however, the order given above is necessitated by the theory of the medieval grammarians, as I stated in "The Vowels According to R. Sa'adya Ga'on," *Lěšonénu* 18 (1953), 91ff. [Hebrew].

⁶⁶ On the evidence of Qirqisani, see B. Klar, *Studies in Language, Poetry, and Literature* (Jerusalem, 1954), 327, n. 37 [Hebrew]. While this is indirect evidence in that it does not describe the pronunciation of *qameṣ* itself, it is clear evidence, and Yalon's argument against Klar's conclusion (n. 63 above) is unconvincing.

⁶⁷ See my "Some Problems," 247.

the *šəwa* in SH gives it, at first glance, an extremely ancient look. The Hebrew reflected in SH would apparently be of a stage prior to that revealed in TH (and in BH for that matter). Yet, a second look shows that the first impression is erroneous, since it is possible to demonstrate that SH had a *šəwa* at a stage earlier than that before us today — a fact which in no way detracts from the assumption that the stage reflected in SH before us is itself indeed ancient. The existence of *šəwa* in SH was demonstrated years ago.[68] Nevertheless, some scholars hold with Petermann, that the absence of *šəwa* in SH is original.[69] A discussion of the problem of the *šəwa* in SH is necessary in a descriptive grammar, for without an understanding of this question it will be difficult to comprehend processes in SH today. It will be even more difficult to evaluate SH in the light of the Jewish heritage.

1.3.1 The first step is to match SH forms with TH forms with *šəwa* according to its place in the word and according to the SH vowels:

a. **word initial**: *kīli* = כְּלִי, כֶּלִי, *fīri* = פְּרִי, *zīb* (< *zi'ib*) = זאב, *līki* = לכי (SP Gn 19:32 as against TH לכה), *qittårət* = קְטֹרֶת, *lillamməd* = לְלַמֵּד, and similarly *iḥrəf* (< *iḥrəf* <*חֲרֹף*) = חֹרֶף, *irrēš* (< *iḥrəš* <*חֲרֵשׁ*) = חֶרֶשׁ, *mēnūra* = מנורה, *sēgūla* = סגולה and סגלה (SP Ex 19:5, TH סְגֻלָּה), *tēnūfa* = תנופה, *tēbūna* = תבונה, *ye'ūda* = יהודה, *tēdabbər* = תדבר, *abråb* = בְּרֹב, *abyom* = ביום, *afgådlåk* = בגדלך, *al'mān* = למען, *alfåno* = לפניו, *aftuwwəl* = בְּתוֹאֵל, *amdabbər* = מדבר, *aškåbtu* = שכבתו (SP Lv 20:15), and similarly *ašfa* (<*שְׂפָה*) = שָׂפָה, *ašfåm* = שְׂפָם; *båfi* = בפי, *båbåtnək* = בבתנך, *båmūši* = במשה, *kåbåšəm* = כבשים, *kåkål* = ככל, *kånigdu* = כנגדו, *kåniddåtå* = TH כְּנִדָּתָהּ, *båråkå* = ברכה, *ya'ūdət* = יהודית, *kūrā'əm* = כָּרְעֵים and כורעים (e.g., SP Lv 11:21 = TH כרעים); *yūmåt* = TH יְמוֹת (see *LOT* III/2, 270, l. 7; 150) and especially the vowel *u* in SA. For example: *šūmayyå* שומיה=(=שְׁמַיָּא); *bū'rå'y* בוראי (<*בְּרָאִי*) "creature"; *lūkon* לוכן=(< לכן); *yūmåm* יומם, i.e., from יְמָם (see in *LOT* III/2, 137, l. 50 also *īmåm* אימם!),[70] and many other words in SA have ו as against *šəwa* in the Jewish Aramaic grammatical tradition.

[68] See my article, "Penultimate Stress," 153–156.

[69] Petermann, *Versuch*, 10: "Übrigens halten die Samaritaner gleich den Arabern die Vocale in der Flexion fest und lassen sie nicht in Schwa übergehen." But Petermann's opinion does not emerge clearly, since on p. 9 he explained the first vowel in such words as גבול and ברית (that is, *gəbol* and *bərət*): "um ein Wort nicht mit einem vocallosen [!] Consonanten zu beginnen." Nöldeke ("Aussprache," 492) hypothesized that the absence of *šəwa* in SH is a late phenomenon, and even attributed it, mistakenly, to the influence of Arabic (a position I regrettably neglected to consider when preparing the article cited in the preceding note). I have attempted to demonstrate that the phenomenon considerably antedates the period of Arabic speech among the Samaritans by showing that it has a parallel in the language of the Dead Sea Scrolls; see Ben-Ḥayyim, *Tradition*, 94. Macuch (*Grammatik*, 210) offers the opinion that *šəwa* was created in TH under the influence of Aramaic, while the absence of *šəwa* even in SA reflects the influence of Hebrew upon Aramaic. The present discussion makes no attempt to respond to the proofs brought in the article cited in the previous note.

[70] See *LOT* III/2, 150. The index there, 384, s.v. שוא, cites examples of the conversion of *šəwa*

1.3 Šǝwa and the Auxiliary Vowels

b. **word-medial**: In order to limit the details, this section shall include what is known in Hebrew grammar as the *šǝwa medium*, which in the Jewish tradition is *quiescens*[71] but generally corresponds to a vowel in SH. For example: *yūšēbi* = יושבי, *âbērot* = חֲבֵרוֹת, *tåbbē'ūtīyyimma* = טבעותיהם, *âdēni* = אדני, *mâlēki* = מלכי, *âmēri* = אמרי, in SA *amraggēle* (<*מרגלה) (*LOT* III/2, 88, l. 29), *fârâši* = פרשי; *måttânūtīkimma* = מתנותיכם, *bēgâdi* = בגדי, *kâbârâkåt* = כברכת, *sīlâ'ot* = צְלָעוֹת, *båfåtǝl* = בפתיל, and in SA *amraggâlǝn* = מרגלין (*LOT* III/2, 89, l. 8), *miyyūdâni* = מֵעֲדָנִי (*LOT* III/1, 35), *tirruw'wā* (<*tiruwwa'a) = תְּרוּעָה, and in SA, such as *yifrâqinnūkon* = יפרקונכון (*LOT* III/2, 362, l. 17), מתונין (*LOT* II, 511 l. 284) = *måttūnǝn* < מַתְּנִין.

1.3.2 These examples indicate the existence of *šǝwa* in a previous stage of SH insofar as: (a) the vowel of the prepositions ב and ל as well as that of the מ of the participle, varies; it appears before the consonant in such forms as *abyom* ביום and *amdabbǝr* מדבר, or after the consonant in forms such as *båmūši* במשה, *ammâdabbǝr* המדבר, according to the structure of the word. With a ב occurring before ב, מ, or פ, the vowel will always follow the consonant. This is true, too, of the ל appearing before ל as in *lillammǝd* ללמד, *lallēkǝt* ללכת (the consonantal gemination is a separate matter), contrasting with *altǝt* לתת. Preceding a word which formerly had an initial guttural consonant the ב and ל have no vowel at all (see 1.3.3): *bişba* באצבע; *bisdåk* בחסדך; *lūlåm* לעולם (this applies to *waw conjunctive* as well: *wišron* ועשרון etc.; (b) in such forms as *âdēni* אדני, *mâlēki* מלכי, the vowel *e* is not the original vowel of the plural noun according to comparative grammar, just as the *a* of *fârâši* פרשי is not the original vowel of the participle (cf. *yūšēbi* יושבי). In this respect, even where the SH vowel may correspond to the assumed original vowel, one may deduce that the SH vowel in the forms under consideration originates only in *šǝwa*. For example, in verb conjugation: *fåqådå, fåqådu, fa(å)qqēdu, yēfa(å)qqēdu*, and so on. One may say that SH preserves the pausal form, thus maintaining the original vowel before its reduction to *šǝwa*, but it is impossible to make such an assumption with such forms as *tēšallā'u* תשלחו because of the *ā* vowel after the ל, or *yifqådu* etc.,

---

to various vowels in SA. As for the form *yūmåm*, it would seem to be a Hebrew word, יומם, in an Aramaic source, but it is difficult to assume that in the phrase ויומם וליליה (e.g., in the liturgical poem cited in *LOT* III/2, 150, l.39), the first word is Hebrew and the second Aramaic. The assumption that *šǝwa* can become *ū* after *yod* as well is supported by the construct state noun *yūmat* יומת (SP Dt 32:6; TH יְמוֹת) and from the infinitive absolute *yūkål*, constructed in accordance with the פָּעֵל pattern (see 2.4.9, n. 59), as well as from the spellings ירושלם and ירושלים in CPA (Schulthess, *Lexicon*, 87; I am grateful to Prof. M. Bar-Asher for this reference). It must be said, however, that even in CPA, which often converts a *šǝwa* to a *u* vowel, the phenomenon is unusual with י.

[71] Cf. my "Medial *Šǝwa*," 83ff. In Ben-Ḥayyim, *Tradition*, 95, I pointed out that in addition to the Samaritan tradition, we sometimes find a vowel in place of a *šǝwa medium* in the Septuagint, Hexapla, and the Dead Sea Scrolls.

because of the originally long ō, ū vowels (in pause!) which survive in SH; therefore, a form such as *yifqūdu is expected. No trace of such a form exists, of course, in SH.⁷² Just as the vowel ā in the Qal impf. originates in šəwa, so too, probably is the origin of the corresponding vowel in the perfect. And as it is in Qal, so it is, probably, in Pi'el. (c) Exceptional forms which are, nevertheless, well attested in transmission can only be interpreted on the basis of the assumption that their original šəwa was absorbed in them, such as tūldåt תולדת, qārbəm קרבים (Dt 20:3), qānyån קנין (LOT III/2, 152 l. 72) "our possessor," and perhaps yildåtå ילדתה "the mothers" (LOT III/2, 143 l. 103) as well, though in such a form the vowel å̂ is to be expected rather than i; (d) Since the entire process under consideration took place in SA as well — it suffices to mention the vacillation in the development of the vowel aftiyya < פְּתִיחָה (participle) as opposed to fâti פתיח (LOT III/2, 283, ll. 9–10) — and in dialects related to SA, the existence and antiquity of the šəwa never in doubt, why rule it out of SH in its early stages?

The fundamental recognition that the origin of various vowels in Hebrew and Aramaic words according to the Samaritan pronunciation traditions is the šəwa does not mean that in every case it is possible to prove or even to assume a basic form equivalent to that of the Jewish tradition. Without this recognition, however, no basis exists for the comparison of the Samaritan and Jewish heritages, especially with regard to nominal forms, nor is there any way to understand the development of the Samaritan forms from their origins in Proto-Semitic; for once the šəwa became a full vowel, the quality of the latter superseded the original vowel quality inherited from Proto-Semitic because of its high frequency of appearance in the declension of the word. Thus, only by assuming a šəwa can one interpret the formation of šūfåṭ (as against *šāfiṭ > שופט), via šūfåṭəm שופטים, nēbi = נביא, nēzər = נזיר, and many others.

1.3.3 It has been shown above that the šəwa may become a full vowel of any quality, just as the Tiberian Masoretes taught that the šəwa "may serve all of them in reading."⁷³ It is not possible to write out rules for the transformation of the šəwa into any particular vowel in SH. It was originally an ultrashort neutral vowel which adopted different shades of sound under different phonetic conditions. A similar picture⁷⁴ is revealed in the transliteration of Origen's Hexapla, e.g., σεμω שמו (Ps 29:2), τεσσορηνι תצרני (Ps 32:7), βανη בני (Ps 18:46),

---

⁷² This is my response to the argument put forth by my friend Prof. J. Blau, "Marginalia Semitica I," IOS 1(1979), 21, n. 21, asking why I consider forms such as fâqådu in SH to be derived from *faq'dū, and is not derived directly from the stage previous to existence of šəwa.

⁷³ Baer–Strack, Dikduke Ha-Teamim, §34. See also my article "Rules of Šəwa," 135.

⁷⁴ The word "similar" is not intended to give the impression that the vowel is of the same quantity as that of SH. On the pronunciation of šəwa in the Hexapla, see Brønno, Studien, 314ff.

1.3 Šəwa and the Auxiliary Vowels

νακαμωτ נקמות (Ps 18:48), χισους כסוס (Ps 32:9), ιεφφολου יפלו (Ps 18:39), μοσαυε משוה (Ps 18:34). This is so with the transliteration of the Hebrew names in the Septuagint as well, with differences in various manuscripts.[75] Nevertheless, clear rules controlling the vowel quality of the *šəwa* were handed down by the Tiberian Masoretes.[76] These are preserved for the most part to the present day by Yemenite Jews[77] and are also reflected, in the main, in SH word formation, i.e., a fixed custom developed in a certain type of Hebrew in Palestine. The rule of the Tiberian Masoretes was as follows: the *šəwa* is generally pronounced with a *pataḥ* quality; before אהח״ע it assimilates to the vowels following those consonants; before *yod* it assimilates to the *yod*. For example: לְעִיר = לָעִיר, כְּמוֹ = כָּמוֹ, בְּיוֹם = בִּיוֹם, לְעוֹלָם = לְעוֹלָם, etc. (the vocalization professes to indicate vowel quality only). Thus, according to this custom of pronouncing *šəwa* before guttural consonants, SH forms are easily explained, such as *bisba* (באצבע) < *bi'isba*, *bisdåk* (בחסדך) < *bi'isdåk*, *būf* (בעוף) < *bᵘ'ūf*, *lūf* (לחוף) < *lᵘ'ūf*, *yid'dūn* (ידעון) < *yiddᵘūn*, *måš'fūt* (משפחות) < *masfᵘ'ot*, and in SA *yā'dīn* (ידעין) < *yad'īn*. From forms such as *måšfā'ot* משפחות (in the construct form as well, Gn 12:3), *yiddā'u* ידעו (unless we assume this was originally a pausal form), *yišmā'u* (ישמעו), alongside *yišᵉmūn*, we learn that this was not the only way. Similarly, from the rule above we may easily interpret *šiyyåd* (= שִׁיָּד) = *šīd*,[78] *illiyon* (=עליון) < *illiyon*, *kalliyon* (כליון) < *kallⁱyon* (see 4.3.11c), and in SA *bâliyyūtån* (< *bāl'yūtån*) בליותן "our decay"; see *LOT* III/2, 121, l. 70.

> Note 1: The difference in vowel quantity between such forms as *bisba* באצבע and *būf* בעוף depends upon the quantity of the vowel in the word without the preposition; I am aware of the disagreement as to whether to read (in Ex 5:7) *lam* or *lām* לעם, the significance of the disagreement being whether the word is determined (*'ām*) or not (*'am*). See also 2.1.2.6.
> Note 2: The form *bāliti* בליתי (SP Gn 18:12), translated in ST as בליותי, has been categorized in *LOT* IV, 52 as infinitive with regard to TH בְּלֹתִי. Perhaps it would be more appropriate to define it as a substantive like *šēbetkimma* שביתכם (SP Nu 31:19).

1.3.4 Auxiliary Vowels.
All existing Hebrew traditions exhibit a tendency to resolve a consonant cluster (other than a geminated consonant), even if the

---

[75] E.g, Σολωμων/Σαλωμων. See also the sources cited by C. Könnecke, *Die Behandlung der hebr. Namen in der Septuaginta* (Stargard, 1855), 25, and G. Lisowsky, *Transkription der hebräischen Eigennamen des Pentateuchs in der Septuaginta* (Basel, 1949), 126.

[76] For a discussion of the pronunciation of *šəwa* by the Tiberian Masoretes, see Dotan, *Diqduqe Haṭṭě'amim*, passim (see index, s.v. שווא), and on this particular point, see p. 35. See also my article "Medial Šəwa," 135.

[77] See Morag, *Yemenite*, especially the summary on p. 171.

[78] See below n. 89.

cluster splits up into two syllables, a process known in the Hebrew grammatical tradition as "making the the *šəwa quiescens* "*mobile*," i.e., "vocalizing" the consonant.[79] In this way a new vowel springs up where there was no vowel at all. This vowel is customarily called an "auxiliary vowel" because it developed, as it were, in order to facilitate the articulation of the word. The process starts with the evolution of a *šəwa*, and if the *šəwa* develops before a consonant vocalized with a *šəwa* (rather than with a full vowel), Hebrew, which cannot accept two consecutive syllables with *šəwa*, as a rule requires the first *šəwa* to be transformed into a full vowel. This even leads to the quiescence of the (second) *šəwa*, which historically is the reflex of a vowel. This phenomenon is regular in TH when the first consonant of the cluster is a guttural sound, as in יַעֲבֹר : יַעַבְרוּ. Sporadically, the phenomenon also appears when the second consonant of the cluster is of a guttural nature, as in יִצְחָק (Gn 21:6), תִּשְׂחָק (Job 39:18), or even in the absence of any guttural consonant, as in הֲתִמְלֹךְ (Jer 22:15), הַקְּרֵבִין (Ez 40:43), רְצָפַת (Est 1:6). Of this nature is the gemination of a consonant like מִקְדָּשׁ (Ex 15:17), עֲקֻבּוֹת (Ps 89:52) — in the Hexapla εκβωτ, הִרְדִּיפָהוּ (Jud 20:43) מַמְּרוֹרִים (Job 9:18), lest a short vowel be left in an open syllable. The appearance of auxiliary vowels is common in TH, especially in the biblical language, and a phenomenon such as יַעַבְרוּ is to be found other than in clusters containing guttural consonants, such as מִשְׂרְפוֹת, יִדְדֹּם, יִרְמְיָהוּ et al.[80] Its influence is distinctly felt in such Hexapla transliterations as εμαραθ אמרת (Ps 18:31), λεββαβεχεμ לבבכם (Ps 31:25)[81] as well as in the Dead Sea Scrolls, in such forms as יְסוֹמְכוּ, יְשׁוֹפְטֵנִי, יְדוֹרְשֵׁהוּ, and many others.[82] For our purposes it is not important if the ו denotes an ultra-short vowel, as in אֲצָרֶנָּה (Isa 27:3), a short vowel, or a long vowel. The important thing is that it corresponds historically to a zero vowel but undoubtedly denotes some real vowel.

1.3.5 This phenomenon applies to SH as well. Furthermore, it would be im-

---

[79] The phrase used in the responsum of Menaḥem ibn Saruq's pupils (S. B. Robles, *Těšubot de los discipulos de Měnaḥem contra Dunaš ben Labraṭ* (Granada, 1986), 3*, is להניע את החונה, "to mobilize the *šəwa quiescens*." I find it difficult to understand what fault Menaḥem's students found with the vocalization of the *šəwa quiescens* for purposes of poetic meter, since this phenomenon is quite common in the Masoretic pronunciation of the Bible in words with a *ga'ya*, such as הִשְׁחִיתוּ, הִתְעָבוּ (Ps 14:1). On the vocalization of an originally *šəwa quiescens* with a *ga'ya*, see Dotan, *Diqduqe Haṭṭě'amim*, 28ff.

[80] See Yeivin, *Babylonian Vocalization*, 451ff. In TH the phenomenon is extraordinary, such as כְּקָרְבְכֶם (Dt 20:2).

[81] The gemination of the first ב, whether faithfully preserving an ancient form or the result of an error of transmission (see Brønno, *Studien*, 161), is outside our purview here.

[82] This is the dealt with by Yeivin, "The Verbal Forms יִקְטְלֵנוּ, יִקְטוֹלֵנוּ in DSS in Comparison to the Babylonian Vocalization," *Bible and Jewish History*, ed. B. Uffenheimer (Tel-Aviv, 1971), 256ff. [Hebrew], who cites all the relevant material. The opinion that antepenultimate stress existed in the Hebrew of the Dead Sea Scrolls is mistakenly attributed to me there.

1.3 Šəwa and the Auxiliary Vowels

possible to comprehend the development of many word forms without it. Of course, it must be recalled that at the stage under consideration SH had no *šəwa*, but rather a long vowel in an open syllable, which became short when the syllable closed. There is no way to determine the phonetic conditions under which it applied, i.e., the consonants near which it occurred, yet it should be noted that it is to be found in the vicinity of guttural consonants, and is not necessarily realized in the same way as in TH. The following are examples of (a) segholate nouns in TH (in many cases, the second radical is not vocalized in SH either, e.g., *nafšåk* נפשך): *qådēšåk* קָדְשְׁךָ, *kåbåša* כְּבְשָׂה, *åmēnimma* אָמְנָם (see 4.1.3.14), *nåfeškimma* נפשכם; (b) nouns of מ-patterns, such as *måqåša* (< *maqᵃša*) מִקְשָׁה, *måšåge* משגה, *mēṣåba* (< *mᵉsāwā* < *maṣᵃwā*) מצוה, *amšåbbēṣot* (< *mašᵃbēṣot*) = מִשְׁבְּצוֹת (Ex 28:11), *amgåbållot* (< *magᵃballot*) = מִגְבָּלוֹת (Ex 28:14), *amsab'bēt* (< *masᵃpaḥt*) = מספחת (Lv 13:6). Thus, nouns such as משבצות, מספחת, מגבלות, merged with *Pi'el* participial forms, a short vowel followed by a geminated consonant replacing a long vowel in an open syllable. In contrast, such a noun as *tēšåbbəṣ* = תַּשְׁבֵּץ, which cannot be interpreted as a participle and which arose as *tašᵃbeṣ* > *tᵉšabbeṣ* > *tēšabbəṣ*, makes the assumption more feasible that the rest of these nouns were formed in the same way; (c) the special type in verb conjugation — the second imperfect in *Qal* — such as *yēzåkår* (< *yizakar*) יוכר, *wyåfånu* (< *wyifᵃnu*) ויפנו, *tēfēši* (< *tifeši*) תִּפְשָׂה. This entire type is rooted in this process, which became routine, while similar forms in TH, such as יִצְחַק, remained isolated rarities; (d) nouns and verbs with a guttural consonant: *nēgā'u* גִּגְעוּ, *zērā'u* זַרְעוּ, (these may indeed be explained on the basis of their simple forms: *nēga*, *zēra*, but their base is likely to have been *nᵢga'u*, *zᵢra'u*), *målā'imtu* מלחמתו < *malaḥimto* (cf. 4.2.3.9). As usual in TH, verbs I-guttural in the imperfect follow the pattern of *tå:dal* תחדל (< *tahᵃdal*). It is, noteworthy however, that, unlike TH, auxiliary vowels were frequently avoided with gutturals, for forms like *yåmmåd* יעמד, *tēssåm* תחסם (see 2.2.1.1.4a,b) can be accounted for only by means of the contact between the guttural consonant and the one following it, with no interference from forms such as יַעֲמֹד* etc. (see 1.3.5.1a); (e) as in TH and BH — יְדֻרְכוּ, יַעַבְרוּ — the *šəwa* derived from a vowel may vanish even in SH, e.g., *nåfeškimma* < *nafᵉšᵉkimma* = נפשכם, *tåråkkimma* < *tārᵃʰkimma* = טרחכם, and even a full vowel following an auxiliary vowel that had become a full vowel, such as *målåmma* מלחמה from *malaḥma* < *malᵃhama*, and in reverse order *måṣåttånu* מצאתנו < *maṣa'atᵃnū* (see 2.2.3.1.5).

The frequent development of an auxiliary vowel and its influence on the word's vowel pattern led, to a considerable degree, to the shift of nouns from one pattern to another, to such an extent that it is difficult to decide in each case which historical form is realized in a given noun, a situation which prevails in the shift from one verb stem to another, especially in SA, from *Qal* to

60   Phonology

Afʿel, as, e.g., in the verb *artət* רתת (< ארתת) (*LOT* III/2, 86 "to tremble").⁸³

1.3.6 Amongst auxiliary vowels a special case is that of the *pataḥ furtivum*, which appears in TH before אהח״ע after any of the vowels *ḥireq, ṣere, šureq* (including *qibbuṣ*) and *ḥolem*, but not after *qameṣ*. In BH, however, this *pataḥ* appears after ע, and it may appear after *qameṣ* as well, e.g., אֶשְׁמֹעַ, לְמִפְגָּעַ.⁸⁴ In Biblical Aramaic, the vocalization rules of which are generally equivalent to those of Biblical Hebrew, this *pataḥ* does not appear after a *ṣere* before a ה: לֵהּ rather than לֵהַּ! It is clear that this vowel is merely a glide accompanying guttural consonants, part, as it were, of producing the guttural sound, which is on occasion expressed in the vocalization and at other times is not. SH may be able to contribute to a clarification of the question of whether the lack of a sign for this vowel is the equivalent of its not being uttered, i.e., the vowel was sometimes produced and at other times not. There would seem to have been a similar phenomenon in SH, the subject of Abū Saʿīd's eighth rule (*LOT* I, 155). His exposition is indeed fragmentary and not sufficiently clear, but his example *madʾdū* = מדוע would seem to reflect *madʾdū* < **maddūʾu* < **maddūʾuʿ*. It may, thus, be concluded that in SH the phenomenon affected an א at the end of the word, and for that reason the vowel was not specifically an *a*, but rather assimilated to the vowel before the guttural consonant (see further below 1.4.6.1).

1.4 Syllabic Structure and Stress

1.4.0 A comparison of the syllable structure of SH with that of TH leads first to a consideration of vowel quantity in TH. The vocalization itself merely differentiates between vowel qualities, and there is no way of deciding from written texts whether the Masoretes distinguished between the two vowel quantities in their pronunciation. At any rate, it is clear that vowel quantity had no phonemic significance, for, according to TH, it is impossible to find any word pair in which the words differ only in vowel quantity, not in vowel quality. It was the Sephardic grammarians⁸⁵ who passed down a quantitative distinction

---

[83] It is particularly interesting to note the form *aftatta* פתתת (*LOT* III/2, 158, l. 65), which may be understood as *Qal*, as the spelling seems to indicate, or as *Afʿel*, along the lines of *mafta* מפתח (ibid., 71, l. 18). The spelling פתתת alone is insufficient to determine the stem, in view of the fact that there exists not only דזמנת *dazmintå* (ibid., 229, l. 10) but also זמנת *azmintå* (ibid., 325, l. 25) without א, both unquestionably *Afʿel* forms. The development of *šəwa* in this direction explains the fluctuation in the orthography, and even more so the shift from *Qal* to *Afʿel*. On the use of both *Qal* and *Afʿel* stems with the verb פתח in SA, see the index to *LOT* III/2.

[84] Yeivin, *Babylonian Vocalization*, 326ff.

[85] We are taught by the standard grammars of Biblical Hebrew (e.g., JM, 37ff.) that the 12th-

— "large" and "small" vowels — but their pronunciation differed from that of the Masoretes, and not only in vowel quantity. The quantitative differentiation maintained in the grammars of Biblical Hebrew is entirely hypothetical, based on theoretical considerations. However, the evolution of the vowels of TH from Proto-Semitic undoubtedly teaches that at some stage prior to TH a quantitative distinction was actually made. This is sufficiently evident from the fact that originally long vowels normally survive wherever they may appear in the word, whereas originally short vowels become *šəwa* under certain conditions or alter their quality — from *ḥireq* to *ṣere*, from *pataḥ* to *qameṣ* — under certain circumstances. The consequence in TH is that the original quantitative difference is expressed as a qualitative one, such as שָׁמַר, שָׁמֵעַ, in pause שָׁמֹר, שָׁמֵעַ. SH is known to make quantitative vowel distinctions in actual fact, and in certain circumstances quantitative differences have phonematic importance (see 1.2.3). Since, in syllable structure, vowel quantity, rather than quality, is decisive, SH is not to be compared with TH, but rather with a stage preceding TH.

1.4.1 This is the rule in SH: (a) each syllable opens with a consonant (initial glottal stop has not been graphically represented here); (b) if the syllable does not end in a consonant (it is "open") and does not occur after the stress, its vowel is either long or extra-long, e.g., *wīnəf* והניף, *ēzən* אזן, *wlēqa* ולקח, *šāma* שמע, *låšåm* לאשם, *tēnūfa* תנופה, *wrå:* וראה, *å:šåm* האשם (for the quantity of the post-tonic vowel, see 1.2.1b); (c) if the syllable ends in a consonant (it is "closed"), its vowel is either short or extra-long, such as *dammǝm* = דמים, *kâbåš* = כבש, *dūrūtīkimma* = דורותיכם (as against *dor* = דור), *wēnna* = והנה, *fāmmǝm* = פעמים; (d) no syllable opens with a consonant cluster (there is no *šəwa* in SH!) except for the beginning of a word with *waw conjunctive*, e.g., *wlēqa* ולקח, *wṭåbål* וטבל, (see 6.3.4); similarly, no syllable ever closes with a consonant cluster. Such syllables as יָלַדְתְּ, וַיֵּבְךְּ, וַיִּשְׁקְ, cannot occur in SH; instead, we have *wyašqi, wyēbēki, yålådti*.

---

century Jewish grammarian Yosef Qimḥi introduced the division of the vowels (תנועות) and their respective vowel points into "large" (גדולות) and "small" (קטנות) (*Sefer Zikkaron*, 17). These standard treatments overlook the fact that according to this theory, vowel quantity as represented by the vowel points has no absolute value but is instead connected to the situation of the vowel in relation to the stress. A clearer definition of this phenomenon is provided in his son David Qimḥi's book *Mikhlol* (ed. Rittenberg, f. 137): פעמים תאריך ותרחיב קריאת הפתח גם בלא אות גרונית בהיותה המלה מלעיל אבל השוא שבצדו יהי' נח גם כן כמו זָכַרְתִּי, שָׁמַרְתִּי, זָכַרְנוּ... ("Sometimes the pronunciation of the *pataḥ* is lengthened even without a guttural letter when the word bears penultimate stress, but the *šəwa* is quiescent, as in שָׁמַרְתִּי, זָכַרְתִּי, זָכַרְנוּ, etc."). This is not an innovation on the part of Qimḥi other than in terminology; the phenomenon had in fact already been described by the Spanish grammarian Yehuda Ḥayyūj in his *Kitāb Al-Tanqīṭ* (ed. John. W. Nutt, *Two Treatises on Verbs Containing Feeble and Double Letters... and the Treatise on Punctuation...*[London, 1870], III). Cf. my article "Medial *Šəwa*," 135.

Ignoring the extra-long vowel peculiar to SH, it may be said that SH and TH in their early stage are similar in that an open syllable must take a long vowel and a closed syllable, a short vowel, while they differ in that SH does not accept consonant clusters either at the beginning or at the end of a word. The same feature comes to light in the closing of an open syllable according to the rule, if for some reason no long vowel was required in it, yet this feature does not necessarily appear in the same words in both traditions. For example, in TH one encounters גְּמַלִּים but in SH *gāmâləm*; in TH שְׁלָמִים — in SH *šēlamməm*; in TH זְקֵנוּ — in SH *zâqannu* (yet זְקֵנָם = *zâqânimma*!); in TH סְגֻלָּה — in SH *sēgūla*; in TH מְקֻשָּׁה — in SH *māqâša*, etc. A comparison of SH and TH in this respect shows that interchanges of open syllables with those closed by means of a geminated consonant were common in Hebrew structure far more than could be assumed on the basis of TH alone. Furthermore, the comparative situation indicates that such interchanges may have been facultative.

Even without ignoring the existence of a vowel not strictly long in an open post-tonic syllable, the stress in SH can be said to have had no effect at all upon syllable structure, unlike TH, for in this syllable the vowel is not a short one (see 1.2.1).

1.4.2. Diphthongs and Syllable Splitting. In Hebrew grammar the occurrence of a semi-consonant, *waw* and *yod*, and a vowel is termed a diphthong. If the consonant appears first (an ascending diphthong), the syllable does not generally[86] differ from other simple syllables, whereas if it appears second (a descending diphthong), the combination may contract into a simple vowel. Alone among Canaanite dialects, Hebrew according to the Jewish tradition, especially TH, still maintains diphthongs under limited conditions.[87] They may be summarized as follows:

a. If one of the elements of the combination is especially strong, the diphthong does not contract. This strength may express itself [1] in a doubling of the consonant (a heterosyllabic diphthong), as in וַיֹּאמֶר, אַיָּה, חַיָּה, צִוָּה, צַוָּאר; [2] in the length of the vowel (i) whether original vowel length, as in אָבִיו, סְמַכְתִּיו, בָּנוּי, גּוּי; (ii) or long because of tone, as in צָו, קָו, עָנָו, בָּנָיו, מָוְתָה.[88]

---

[86] The exception to this is the *waw consecutive* that has become וּ before a bilabial consonant or a consonant preceding *šəwa* in TH, by a process of *wa>wu* as well as the verb יְהוּא (Eccl 11:3) which developed from *יְהוּו and is developed further in MH יְהֵא, תְּהֵא by analogy to forms with original *wū*.

[87] For details of these rules, consult the standard grammars. The formulation given here does not appear in the grammars of which I am aware. The diphthong rules stated here relate to the relationship of alternation between the diphthong and vowel that developed from it; they do not provide an answer to the question of why TH has, e.g., מִקְנֶה < *maqnay* but also such forms as מָתַי and אֲדֵי. In SH both types display a contraction to a single vowel: *maqni, mēti*.

[88] In fact, the form בָּנָיו is not derived in the same way as עָנָו etc., since the origin of the diph-

1.4 Syllabic Structure and Stress

b. When the syllable permitting the existence of the diphthong is closed with a consonant (above and beyond the consonantal element of the diphthong itself), the diphthong, according to the accepted pronunciation, breaks down into two syllables, as in מָ֫וֶת, בַּ֫יִת, עָלַ֫יִךְ. It seems that originally some sort of diphthong expansion took place here, something similar to *maw^et (< *maw^ut). This process parallels that by which the "segholate" forms evolved.

c. Under all other conditions the diphthong contracts to a vowel, yet there are exceptions to these rules, such as עוֹלָה, הַיְצָא (in opposition to a[2]), שׁוֹר < šawr (in opposition to b), עֲבָרִים < עִבְרִיִּים as opposed to a[1]). From such fluctuations such as לָחוֹת /(MH) לְחַיִן, דּוּדִים/דּוֹדִים, אוֹן/אָוֶן, צִים/צִיִּים, גִּיא/גַּיְא, שָׂדֶה/שְׂדֵי, we learn that in Biblical Hebrew there was a strong tendency towards contraction according to TH as well. SH contracts historical diphthongs to a greater degree, but, on the other hand, new diphthongs evolved there. The valid rule in SH is that the diphthong persists when the consonant is geminated and contracts when such is not the case. If it was felt necessary to maintain it, the diphthong split into two syllables. The diphthongs in SH behave as follows:

1.4.3. Ascending Diphthong (a) tends to be maintained in any position of the word, but (b) is likely to contract if its consonantal element is preceded and followed by identical vowels, e.g., wišron וְעִשְׂרוֹן in TH וְעֶשְׂרוֹן (see 1.3.3), wâ'əb והב in TH וְהָב, wafsi ופסי in TH וְפִסִי, šalwi (SP Nu 11:31 שלוי), yifqåd יפקד, yēšši יעשה, yåmmåd יעמד, yūmåm יומם. (b) *ūn = עון, which probably developed from < *ᵃ'won (ᵃ'won = TH עָוֺן), in declension (see 1.3.3) 'an'nā = ענהה (SP Dt 22:29, TH עֲנָהּ) from *'annayā as עשאה / עשיה in MH. Similarly, the SA gentilic suffix 'å or 'ā, as in qåm'mâ קמאה (< קמיה), råt'tâ רתאה "the merciful" and see 1.5.3.2. No contraction is, of course, possible after ו has become b (< v); the diphthong itself ceases to exist in such cases: mēsåba < *mᵉsåwa < מִצְוָה, mēsåbot מצוות (see 1.3.5b), וויהם båbīyyimma, in SA sålbi סלוי (SH שלוי), etc.

A comparison of the forms â'īti (< *âyīti) הייתי, â'ītå היית with ayya היה raises the possibility that the gemination has evolved in order to prevent diphthong contraction and distortion of the form into â:. (cf. râ: ראה). In this case there was no morphological element to geminate, but rather a mere phonetic one. The same is true for the word יי (1.4.4.1).

1.4.4. Descending Diphthong (a) persists only when the consonantal component is geminated; SH is noteworthy for the developments of diphthongs where there were previously none and where they do not appear in TH.

---

thong in forms such as בָּנָיו is from a triphthong ayw < ay(h)ū (*banayhū), even though in TH the endings of the surface forms בָּנָיו and עֲנָו are the same. This is not true in the stage just preceding TH: a form such as *binahū developed into בְּנוֹ by reduction — ahū > aw — and contraction of that diphthong to ō.

1. Historical diphthongs, such as *ṣuwwâru* TH צֻוָּארוֹ, *yuwwâləd* TH יִוָּלֵד, *'ayyəm* TH חַיִּים, *'ayyå* TH חַיָּה, *âyyå* TH הָאַיָּה; in SA: *qayyâmayyå* קעימיה (*LOT* III/2, 78, l. 17).

2. New diphthongs, such as *sinnuwwârəm* TH סַנְוֵרִים, *tirruw'wā* TH תְּרוּעָה, *ēluwwəm* אלוהים, *kuwwi* כחי, *šiyyåd* TH שֵׁיד,[89] *šiyyol* TH שְׁאוֹל, *miyyimmu* TH מֵעִמּוֹ, *'ālīyyimma* TH עֲלֵיהֶם, *yayyən* TH יַיִן.

With regard to the diphthong containing *w*, it should be noted that the combination *uww* prevents the original *w* from shifting to *b* (< *v*); it also preserves an original short *u*; furthermore, other short vowels, *a* (צואר), *i* (יולד), shift to *u* as they assimilate to the consonantal component of the diphthong.

Regarding the sequences *iyyi*, *īyyi*, the original *iyyi* (in the plural form of the gentilic suffix) contracts: *iyīm* > *īm*, in SH > *əm*, e.g. *ibrəm* — עברים, *fålištəm* — פלשתים. Similarly the sequence formed as a result of the elimination of a guttural, as **miy'yīr* > *mīr* — מעיר, **miy'yīš* > *mīš* — מאיש, **miyyīdåt* > *mīdåt* — מעדת. In both of these types, the sequence ends in an extra-long *ī*. Nevertheless, the new sequences with a short vowel, formed as a result of the elimination of guttural consonants, persist. The sequence with a long vowel *īyyi* only appears with the suffixes -יהן, -יהם and the difference between it and the sequence *iyyi* is clearly audible. Wherever I have written down *īyyi*, the *yod* is not marked in the Arabic transcription[90] with a *šadda* (gemination mark); similarly, my informant refrained from marking it with a *dageš* when he was asked to vocalize a word, unlike the sequence *iyyi*. However, the unusual length of the *i* vowel in such forms as *'ālīyyimma* is accompanied by the addition of a *yod* which is what I wrote down in my records.[91]

(b) The diphthong contracts (if it does not split into two syllables, see below) under all other conditions:

Historical *aw* becomes *o* in closed syllables and in the 3rd sing. possessive suffix added to plural nouns, and thereby, automatically, *ū* in open syllables or in

---

[89] In comparing SH and TH forms we must assume that the underlying forms of *šiyyåd* had a *šəwa* between the first and the second consonant, i.e., in TH vocalization would be שְׁיִד. According to the pronunciation rules of the *šəwa* (1.3.3) it developed to a full vowel *ī*, thus forming a diphthong *iy*. On the interchange of segholate forms with the פָּעֵל pattern within the traditions of Hebrew, and between Hebrew and cognate languages see my "Observations," 19ff. To the examples cited there I wish to add MH סָיָג, "fence" (the usual vocalization) / סִיָג (MS Kaufmann *Avot* 1:1), SA *siyyaâgəm* סיאגים (*LOT* III/2, 59); קַיָם and קִיָם *The Bible in Aramaic*, ed. A. Sperber [Leiden, 1959], Gn 9:14]/ SA *qiyyåm* קיאם (Gn 9:14); SA טיאן (*LOT* II, 468b), *tiyyån* vs. Jewish Aramaic טִין, e.g., Ex 1:14. The phenomenon described here is attested in the tradition of the Tiberian vocalization as well, in the participle *Qal* with a strong III-y, e.g., כְּעֹטְיָה (Cant 1:7) / בֹּכִיָה (Lam 1:16). As is well known, there is no distinction between *īya* and *iyya*. Cf. n. 91.

[90] From the Arabic transcription I shall mention, e.g., Gn 18:8 عَالِيِّمْ *'ālīyyimma* עליהם, as against مِيْمُو *miyyimmu* מעמו (Gn 13:14).

[91] In spite of the assumption that *ī* = *iy* and *īy* = *iyy* (as mentioned in n. 89), I have chosen to express the unusual length of *ī* in the diphthong in question by "*īyy*."

1.4 Syllabic Structure and Stress

closed syllables following guttural consonants: *mot*, TH מֵת, *battok*, TH בְּתוֹךְ (Nu 35:5), *bâno* TH בָּנָיו, *'ā'o* TH אֶחָיו, *aftūkåkimma* TH בְּתוֹכְכֶם, *ūl* TH עֹל.

Note: *'ānu* TH עָנוּ, is apparently a passive participle stemming from **'anūw*; in *īšāb* TH עֵשָׂו, *w* became *v* (> *b*) before the contraction.

Historical *ay* became *i/e* in a closed syllable, and thereby, automatically, *ī* in an open syllable or a closed syllable following a guttural consonant: *bit/bet* בַּיִת, *zit* זַיִת, *deš* דַּיִשׁ, *bītu* ביתו, *zītåk* זיתך, *dīšū* דישו, *īl* אַיִל, חַיִל, *īn* אַיִן, עַיִן.

Historical *uy* may contract, as in *gâlo* TH גלוי. In SA *âbo* (< **'abūy* < **'abūhī*) אבוי "his father", but

(c) a diphthong containing an originally long vowel tends to split into two syllables:

ūy and *ōy* have become *uwwi*: *nåṭuwwi*, *råṣuwwi*, *guwwi*, TH נְטוּי, רְצוּי, גּוּי.

īw has become *iyyu*: *åbiyyu* אביו (cf. Aramaic אבוי above in b), *fiyyu* פיו, *šamtiyyu* שמתיו. Only in the (singular!) noun אחיו is there an *o* : *'ā'o* — since this form is equivalent also to אֶחָיו and Aramaic אחוי, one cannot decide if this is a contraction of *īw* to *o*, or perhaps it is the suffix which has been transferred from the other forms (see 4.6.5.2). At any rate, this is the only case where the 3rd sing. possessive suffix is the same with a singular and a plural noun. The form *iyyu* may develop directly from *īhū* (e.g., פיהו), and so it is impossible to rule definitively that in every case it results in the splitting of the diphthong, though spelling considerations would seem to support such an opinion.

It is similarly impossible to decide with such nouns as *nēquwwəm* (SP Gn 44:10 נקוים, TH נקיים), *åṣuwwəm* אצוים (SP Ex 5:13) if the base form is **åṣo* or **åṣuwwi*, etc., for their declension is the same.

Note: As to the shift *ūy* > *o* in western Aramaic dialects, see my article "Verdrängung," 16.

1.4.4.1 In conclusion, from the behavior of the descending diphthong the following rule results:

---

[92] The unequal development of the diphthong *ūy* in גלוי > *gâlo* and רצוי > *råṣuwwi* leads us to assume that the contraction of the diphthong *ūy* was at one time not an absolute requirement. However, it sometimes happens that alternations of pronunciation or of form that appear to us to be at a given time "free" — i.e., not contingent upon any *linguistic* conditions — are in fact not "free" as seen from another perspective: that of *social* conditions. This point is discussed in relation to Arabic dialects by D. Cohen, "Variante, variétés dialectales et contacts linguistiques en domaine arabe," *BSLP* 88 (1973), 215ff. For example, in Tunis the use of *aw* and *ay* or, alternatively, of *ū* and *ī*, is determined by sex and religion: women and Jews regularly pronounce the diphthongs, and this pronunciation is used to characterize those groups (pp. 218–219). Cohen cites other examples from other dialects. We have no way of knowing what the situation was in SH before the formation of the processes of contraction and splitting in the above-mentioned words and others like them. It seems, at least, that there were no clear, absolute *linguistic* conditions governing those situations.

The diphthong persists only when the consonantal element is geminated. If it is not geminated, the diphthong contracts. Yet, if a need is felt to maintain it[92] — whether because of an awareness of the length of the historical vowel, or because of an intention to prevent either the distortion of the word or a merging of forms — it can be maintained only by its splitting into two syllables or by geminating its consonantal element, as in the word *yayyən* (for the expected **yīn*). This diphthong split evidently began with a kind of expansion (see 1.4): **nāṭūyⁱ*, **gūyⁱ*,[93] an original auxiliary vowel created to prevent contraction becoming a full vowel (1.3.5), finally influencing the separation of the *yod* and its transformation into an *aleph* (1.5.3.2), thus forming *uwwi* (1.1.8b).

Note: (a) Three nominal forms maintain diphthongs in apparent contradiction to the rule: *'ay* חי, (but the verb וחי: *wī*!), *åydimma* אידם (Dt 32:35), *šē'tåy* < **שְׁתָיִ* (in TH שְׁתִי); in SA: *sē'gåy* סגאי (*LOT* III/2, 66, l. 26) "multitude." It is to be noted that in the articulation of these words I sensed an unusual prolongation of the *yod*, and my informant, who was asked to vocalize the words, also placed a *dageš* in the *yod* of these three words. Regarding the word שתי, the stress on the ultimate syllable reveals that this syllable is the result of the contraction of two syllables, such as **šētåyi* > **šē'tåy*. The SA gentilic suffix is also *ay*, as in *yi'dåy* יחידאי (*LOT* III/2, 44, l. 37), and it is almost impossible to distinguish between it and the plural *â'i* as in *zakkå'i* זכאי "righteous men") [Note the two reading versions *būrå'i/bū'råy* "creatures," *LOT* III/2, 211, l. 41 and the note there; in particular we must mention *yåy* יאי (= יאה) *ibid.* 166, l. 9]. Clear evidence for *ay* in medial position > *â'i* is represented by *â'īṭab* היטב (Gn 12:16), see 2.10.8. Note also that SH has *i*, as in *dēbåri* דברי, paralleling TH ־י as the 1st pl. pronominal suffix. (b) Also in the word *miyyā'īn* מאין, TH מֵאַיִן (the word does not appear in the Pentateuch without the מ) an original form with a diphthong preserved by consonant gemination must be assumed, such as **miyyayyin*, just like the word יין considered above. Only when the *miyy-* syllable (prepositional מ) was added, did **ayyin*

---

[93] In my article "Penultimate Stress," 159, I have cited parallels from Babylonian vocalization, such as נְטוּיִ, and, from Mishna MS Kaufmann, forms such as כְּרָאוּיִ and שָׁמַיִ. Contrary to those who argue that the dot under the *yod* in such words marks the consonantal value of the letter, similar to *mappiq he* (in some manuscripts) הּ instead of ה, (Bendavid, "Unusual Vocalisation," 257, and S. Morag, "Notes for a Description of the Vocalization System of the Worms Maḥzor," *Lĕšonénu* 11 [1964/5], 205) [Hebrew], I remain convinced that the *hireq* represents an actual *i* vowel, perhaps of minimal quantity, because those who vocalized these texts could not pronounce the diphthong without expressing the *yod*. [I find decisive evidence for my position in such spellings as נוֹאִי (for נוי), וְדַאִי, תְּנָאִי, and others, in which the *hireq* appears under א. See also M. Bar-Asher's introduction to his facsimile edition of MS Paris 328/9 [*Mishna-Codex Paris*, Jerusalem 1973], 34, especially section b, on the stress marker adjacent to *pataḥ*, and Tanḥum Yerushalmi's dictionary, ‏المرشد الكافي‎ s. v. נאה, attests to this pronunciation in his comparison of נוי to רואי, חולי, and יופי!]

contract to *īn* (דקק 1.5.3.4[4]). Without the diphthong, the final result would have been *mīn (see 1.4.4).

1.4.5 A syllable splitting into two is found in SH outside of the realm of the diphthong as well; in this case, too, the vowel involved was originally a long vowel. Though the process is indeed sporadic, it is, nevertheless, well attested: *rē'oš* ראש, *ṣē'on* צאן, *mē'od* מאד, *yā'ūkəl* יאכל, etc., *yā'ūmər* יאמר, etc. The sequences *ē'o*, *ā'o* result from the dissimilation of the original *ō'o* (1.5.3.2). The process apparently began as follows: *rōᵒš, *yōᵒkel, i.e., a dual-peaked syllable.[94] Finally, it split into two syllables: **ro'oš*, **yo'okel*. It is most interesting that these forms parallel such TH forms as בְּאֵר, מְאֹד. According to the rule, well attested in many forms, the *aleph*, which had closed the syllable in the earliest stages of Hebrew or even earlier (evidence ראש, יאמר), became silent, after which it was once more pronounced wherever necessary because of paradigmatic pressure. This is clearly sensed in the morphological doublets in TH, such as אספה/ וַיֶּאֱחֹז/ וַיִּאחֶז (Mic 4:6) but יֶאֱסֹף, and consequently in TH we might have expected בֵּאר* (like צֵאת), מֹאד*. The vocalization בְּאֵר, מְאֹד (the Masoretes pronounced it מְאֹד!) reflects an abnormal extension of the vowel (perhaps a syllable split?). The above mentioned forms in SH indicate that in such forms as TH מְאֹד, בְּאֵר the pronunciation is real and based on an ancient and reliable tradition.[95] Why the process under consideration took place in SH in only a few isolated forms is a question that can also be asked about the forms in TH. These forms may have been subject to some additional unknown condition which gave rise to

---

[94] For previous discussions and bibliographical references see Ben-Ḥayyim, *Studies*, 83. It should be noted here that the Aramaic plural endings -הֵתָא, -הָן in nouns such as אמהתתא, אמהו, and Syriac אידהתא have their origins in the common Semitic endings *-ān, -āt*. When the a vowel split into two — apparently due to extensive lengthening it had at first two peaks — the ending with this unusual form was created.

[95] *Pace* Bergsträsser, *Grammatik* I, §15–16), who denies the existence of this phenomenon of abnormal extension in the living language, although in the same work (§16c) he sees fit to say of something he viewed as similar that it dates from the Hasmonean period. In fact, the noun ῥοὺς" in LXX to 2 Sa 15:32, which so nicely parallels ראוש / רואש in the Dead Sea Scrolls (discussed in the literature cited above, n. 94), should be sufficient to establish the fact that underlying SH *rē'oš* is indeed *roᵒš > **ro'oš*. E. Y. Kutscher's statement (Kutscher, *Isaiah Scroll*, 169) that "Hebrew phonology ... indicates that it [= "the Samaritan form"] could not have arisen normally" is not born out by the data. No one has yet been able to define just what constitutes "normally" in matters of language. Kutscher argues that the explanation of the form's development offered in the present work is "entirely unfounded... in respect to the word זאת = *zê'ot* in Samar[itan]" (ibid., 170) because in this pronoun the א never had a consonantal value. This argument is fundamentally flawed, since the splitting in question is the result of an abnormally extended vowel, and it makes no difference what caused that extension (i.e., whether it was the elision of א). Furthermore, the assertion that the א in זאת was not consonantal has by no means been proved. After all, אז has been found in a Phoenician inscription from Cyprus (*KAI* 30:2), and Phoenician normally assigns a letter only to a consonant. Even if there was no glottal stop in this word in Proto-Semitic, one might be formed — and presumably was formed in Canaanite — in emphatic speech, just as in the negative particle לִי in spoken Arabic (see Ben-Ḥayyim, *Tradition*, 100, n. 1).

the results noted above. At any rate, the inconsistency of a phonetic shift or of any "law" cannot result in the discrediting of an old, living tradition.

> Note: On rare occasions one may hear in the reading of the Samaritans by a particular reader a syllable containing an extra-long vowel that splits into two, as in *kå'åqqåt*[96] (Nu 9:14) בחקת, *å'åšən* החשן contrasting with the regular *å:šən*. The same reader is quite able to utter one word two different ways. In such a case the process has returned to its starting point. In the words האחד, האחת, האחז (Nu 31:47) this has become routine with the words pronounced *å''åd*, *'a''åt*, *å''åz* respectively. Both the medial *'ayin* and the ultimate stress indicate that this is not the original situation, but rather the splitting mentioned above. Cf. *'åm* העם as opposed to **å''am*, *'å:bəd* העבד. In SA cf. *mimmēqa*, *mimmē'eqa* ממחקה (*LOT* III/2, 43, l. 32), i.e., "blotted out."

1.4.6 Stress. Biblical stress in the Jewish tradition is precisely given only in TH. Accordingly, one may say that it falls mainly on ultimate syllables, and less frequently on penultimate syllables, but the latter is in no sense rare. On the contrary, it is common in certain morphological groupings (such as "segholate" forms), in pausal forms, and in those phrases affected by *nasog 'aḥor* (i.e., the receding stress), such as קָרָא לָיְלָה (Gn 1:5), וַיֵּצֵא קַיִן (Gn 4:16) etc., as explained by the grammarians. SH is just the opposite: stress is usually on the penultimate syllable with ultimate stress existing as well. When studying words stressed on the ultima the conditions for such a development can be revealed and seen to maintain this rule.

Penultimate stress need not be demonstrated, but for ultimate stress, it is recommended to peruse the material gathered together in 4.4.1–2. The following is a summary of this material, according to the different groups:

a. *tū'lāt* תולעת, *ṭåb'bēt* טבעת, *ē'ṭåt* חטאת, *zuw'wā* זועה, *abbår'yī* הבריעי, *bå'līl* בליעל;

b. *må'rī* מראה, *gē'bāl* גבעל, *mē'bår* מבחר, *yå'ṣår* יצהר, *qē'nå* קנאה, *må'šā* משחה, *å'må* חמאה;

c. *må'nū* מנוח, *må'bū* מבוא, *å'lū* הלוא (see 6.3.12), *mē'lū* מלוא, *niy'yå* ניחוח, *sēfår'då* צפרדע;

d. *å''ū* ההוא, *å''ī* ההיא, *å''īš* האיש, *å''ūf* העוף, *å''īr* העיר, *wå''īr* והעיר (Nu 35:5; but *wīr* — Lv 25:33!), *lå''īr* לעיר (Gn 19:16), *bå''īr* בעיר (Dt 20:14), but *bīr* (Dt 22:23 as against בְּעִיר in TH);

e. *tiruw'wā* תרועה, *yēšuw'wā* ישועה, *tēmiy'yā* טמאה, *måliy'yā* מלאה, *månuw'wā* מנוחה, *šåluw'wā* שלוחה.

---

[96] Correct *kåqqåt* in *LOT* IV, 487 (ibid., 105).

1.4 Syllabic Structure and Stress

1.4.6.1. From group (a) one may conclude that the ultimate stress results from the reduction of two syllables to one: *tūlā'at*, *ētā'āt*, *bāliyi'l*. It is probable that this, too, is the stipulation for groups (b) and (c), except that in those groups a vowel glide evolved first, and then turned into a full vowel (1.3.4), something like *mar^a'i* > *mārī'i* > *mā'rī* מראה, *geb^a'al* > *gēba'al* > *ge'bāl* גבעל, *manū'uḥ* > *mānū'^{u}(ḥ)* > *mā'nū* מנוח, *ṣēfārda'^{a}(')* > *ṣēfārdā'a* > *ṣēfār'dā* צפרדע (see 1.3.6).

Similar to this is the ultimate stress on the diphthong *ay* in *šē'tåy* שתי and in the SA gentilic suffix discussed in 1.4.4.1. Nevertheless, group (c) is accompanied by many exceptions: *arqi* רקיע, *wyašbi* וישבי, etc., and also displays cases of vacillation: *zā'rū / zåru* זרוע, *mē'lū / mēlu* מלוא. But the final vowel when unstressed, tends to become longer, in comparison with the normal situation in other constructions. We, thus, learn that the vocalic off-glide (1.3.6) is not completely obligatory, having been a common custom, as is true with the formation of auxiliary verbs in general; or perhaps the fluctuation hints at the onset of a process of stress receding to the normal place for it in SH — on the penultimate syllable.

> Note: It is no wonder that the vocalic off-glide applies to final *aleph* as well (such as *mā'bū* מבוא), for by analogy the *aleph* in SH rejoined the ל"ה group in various phonological processes. At any rate, the SH development is typical (contrasting with מבוי in MH, where ל"א roots often behave like ל"י roots).

In group (d) the retraction of the stress from the word-final syllable (of monosyllabic words in the absolute state!) was prevented when the definite article was added, though it normally receded in words which do not begin with אהח"ע such as *bayyom* ביום, *akkål* הכל, *abbət* הבית, etc. The character of the initial consonant is what brought this about.

Yet the explanations provided with regard to groups (a)–(d) do not suffice to explain the ultimate stress in group (e), for, on the one hand, this group does not display reduction of two syllables to one while, on the other, whenever the forms occur in the construct state (final ת), stress is once again on the penultimate syllable, as usual: *tirruwwåt*, *yēšuwwåt*. Analogy would once again seem to have been active here, for ultimate stress occurs mainly in words whose last root consonant is אהח"ע and their disappearance in speech is what led to syllable reduction, this ultimate stress may even have been taken *a posteriori* to be compensation for the disappearance of the guttural consonant in this position, and the disappearance of the gutturals may have been responsible for group (e) forms without the original conditioning.

Occasionally, ultimate stress results from a mistaken etymological interpretation, such as *ṣa'bīn* צבען (*LOT* III/2, 138, l. 59) = "want," i.e., it was derived from חוץ instead of from צבה, while on other occasions, it results from the fact that while chanting the reading, one does not make a point of stressing words correctly, so in uncommon words the stress in this chanted reading becomes customary. This may be the case in the reading of *ayyå'lā* אילה (Gn 49:21), if this noun is indeed intended (see the note in *LOT* III/1, 35). These are all rare cases. Even if we add to them *fi'dwīm* פדוים (Nu 3:51), *ayyårīm* היארים (Ex 8:1), *måkå'ū'bū* (Ex 3:7), which is actually read with a double stress (see 1.4.10) and is spelled מכאו.בו as two words, and also *miyyå'īn* מאין (1.4.4 note b).

> Note: The chanted reading may also produce extra length of a vowel, as in *yå:nēnu* ינחנו (Dt 32:12), *yå:nīlu* ינחילו (SP Nu 34:17).

1.4.7 The SH stress system is, thus, simple and consistent, and the reduction of syllables which led to the deviations from the rule was apparently a much later development. I doubt if it had already taken place when the Samaritans spoke Aramaic. The transcription by Petermann, *Versuch*, who heard the reading of the Samaritans in 1853, consistently shows two equal vowels where we hear a single syllable, but he notes (on p. 161) that he was not successful in discerning clearly if he heard *a'areṣ* or *āreṣ*, and so he jotted down *aareṣ*. On the other hand, he makes no mention at all (on p. 10) of there being a finally stressed syllable in SH. For example, in the noun *wennaaš* והנחש (i.e., *wan'nāš*), he was under the impression he had heard two syllables. All in all, his testimony is not quite clear. In contrast, it should be mentioned that in the vocalized words in (the 14th-century) MS א,[97] one finds two vowel signs where today there exists only a single syllable, such as וּהֹלֹתִיןּ (*LOT* I, 191, l. 4) *wnå:låtən*, וּרֹחַ (*LOT* I, 195, l. 7 — in print the vowel signs have moved somewhat!) = *wrås*, מֹצֹרֹחת (*sic*, *LOT* I, 194, l. 12) = *amṣår'råt* מצרעת. This word displays two vowel signs in later manuscripts as well, and even הֹאֹ (*LOT* I, 189, l. 7); the vocalization is in striking agreement with Abū Sa'īd's eighth rule (*LOT* I, 155, and see above 1.3.6 for the vocalic off-glide), in which the word הוא figures as an example. In this vocalization system it is not possible to say that the two equivalent signs are intended to mark a single syllable! In contrast with the stress system in SH, the rules of stress in TH are very complex and, since, unlike SH, the location of the stressed syllable influences the vowel system in a decisive manner, even a descriptive grammatical presentation of it must not avoid attempting to interpret the given situation on the basis of the past. Since SH has been introduced into these attempts at interpretation, without justification, as shown below, we shall deal with the question in its entirety.

---

[97] See its description in *LOT* I, 84ff. Not all of the words vocalized in that manuscript are completely vocalized.

1.4 Syllabic Structure and Stress

1.4.8 Though the TH stress system is complex, there are a number of clear lines of development which come through when comparing TH with the assumed, but well-founded formulae known as Proto-Semitic:

a. The consonant-final forms have ultimate stress (except for the "segholate" forms);

b. Most of the vowel-final forms have penultimate stress, and even those which have ultimate stress take penultimate stress in pause, e.g., שְׁמַרְתֶּם, בְּנְכֶם, as opposed to שָׁמַרְתִּי, שָׁמַרְתָּ, שָׁמַרְנוּ, בְּנֵנוּ; שָׁמְרוּ, אָנֹכִי, אֲנִי, אַתָּה as opposed to the pausal forms שָׁמְרוּ, אָנֹכִי, אָנִי (not only in pause!), אָתָּה. As the consonant-final forms ended in short vowels in the earlier stage — *dabaru/a/i (> דָּבָר), *šamara (> שָׁמַר) — it would seem that in the earlier stage the forms listed in subsection (a), too, were originally stressed on their penultimate syllable. To this must be added that the feminine forms in ה- ended, at this early stage, in -at(u), so that their being of ultimate stress in TH does not contradict the assumption of general penultimate stress at the earlier stage of TH either. Indeed, all interpretations of the development of the stress in TH (see 1.4.9) assume a general penultimate stress at the stage immediately preceding the historical one, there being no interpretation capable of avoiding the use of analogy to explain away deviations from the rule — some doing so more frequently, others less so. It would seem at first glance to be possible to state that the SH penultimate stress preserves the stage prior to the TH shift to ultimate stress. In fact, the opposite is true: the position of the stress in SH results from stress recession from the ultimate to the penultimate syllable, as demonstrated[98] by (a) the existence of the šəwa in the previous stage of SH, and its various transformations and consequences in SH as described above (1.3); (b) the splitting of the diphthongs clearly demonstrating that the basic form of the split had ultimate stress, such as *nâtūy (= נטוי) > nâtuwwi (see 1.4.4); (c) a shift of vowels in the inflection of verbs known in TH as involving stress (Philippi's Law), which will be discussed below 1.5.1.2; 1.5.2.1.

It is, thus, evident that the SH stress system is built on the stress system known to us from TH. The SH stress on the penultimate syllable (i.e., at the stage prior to the one we hear at present) is a return to the situation which produced TH, after all the shifts which took place in the vowel system as a result of the stress.

1.4.9 The link between SH stress and that of TH, as demonstrated in the previous section, makes clear that SH is of no help in understanding the evolution of TH stress. With regard to TH stress, a few words must, *à propos*, be said, for the topic keeps cropping up. Since the publication of my article "Penulti-

---

[98] For more details see "Penultimate Stress."

mate Stress," which contained references to works on the subject that appeared after the grammars of Bauer-Leander and Bergsträsser and after the article by Brockelmann ("Neuere Theorien"), J. Blau published his article, "Changes in Accent." The large number of explanations and the constant need for new solutions testify to the uncertainty surrounding the question of the development of the stress in Tiberian Hebrew. Bauer-Leander (BL, 275 ff.) and Bergsträsser (*Grammatik* I, 116ff.) each assume two early stages preceding that of TH; similarly, they each assume that one of these two stages is identical with the stress in Literary Arabic — or rather, that attributed to Arabic. They differ from one another in that Bauer and Leander make considerable use of the force of analogy to explain away features which would seem to contradict their basic assumptions, whereas Bergsträsser prefers a consistent phonological reconstruction, thus creating an extremely complex structure focused around morphological distinctions: nouns and suffixed verbs take one form of stress, whereas unsuffixed verbs and construct nominal forms take other kinds. Brockelmann has correctly stated ("Neuere Theorien," 336) that this rule was derived in order to explain the difference between *pataḥ* and *qameṣ* in such words as גָּמָל/גְּמַל (ibid.). This means that Bergsträsser's reconstruction of the stage preceding TH is in reality a replacement of the situation by a formula of "Proto-Semitic," and not an acceptable explanation of the evolution of the stress in TH. Moreover, Bergsträsser seems not to have sensed the error affecting the main body of his theory in his assumption of *qataltúmu* in place of *qatáltumu* (a contradiction noted by A. Goetze, "Accent and Vocalism in Hebrew," *JAOS* 59 [1939], 441). Blau also consistently seeks a consistent phonological solution, going so far as to distinguish five consecutive stages, but he, too, is unable to do away completely with the use of analogy ("Changes in Accent," 32).

All explanations of stress are replete with contradictions, the most serious being, on the one hand, the fact that everything exact known of the stress system derives from the Tiberian stress system, while, on the other hand, scholars ignore the principles of that very system, claiming that the construct state of the noun is unstressed even when marked with an accent other than the *maqqef*, or claiming that that state has at best "a secondary stress," which is a justification for their ignoring it. This, of course, creates a vicious circle: all the changes are explained on the basis of the rules of stress derived from the system of biblical accents, yet whenever the changes do not suit the rules proposed (such as the construct state of the noun), one deduces from the changes that the accent does not indicate stress at all![99] In addition, the very assumption of a

---

[99] C. Sarauw, *Akzent*, 69, demands that we take into account the fact that the construct pair is accented with a primary accent.

1.4 Syllabic Structure and Stress

stage equivalent to the stress in Literary Arabic raises the following issue: the basis and reliability of the "accepted" stress in Arabic is uncertain or perhaps even disproved,[100] and it is evident that the Arabic stress has no phonological significance and that no distinctions are made on the basis of this stress, whereas in TH the very opposite is the case, vowel quantity being insignificant in TH, but stress decisive. The assumption that in Hebrew there was a stage similar to the "accepted" Arabic stress must be accompanied by an explanation of how this change in the phonological significance of the stress took place within the framework of TH development.[101] The proponents of the various theories do not seem to explain, by means of simple phonological process, how it is that a noun form such as *ṣadaqatu/a/i* gave rise to an absolute צְדָקָה and a construct צִדְקַת, and if the omission of final vowels in the construct state is assumed, i.e., a basis such as *ṣadaqat* (like that of the verb), how is one to interpret the difference between the aforesaid construct state and צְדָקָה.[102] Without applying a set of analogies, therefore, there would seem to be no explanation.

In my opinion, the nominal construct state is attracted to suffixed nouns: the construct state and a suffixed noun are syntactically equivalent and are grasped as a single feature. This is true, indeed, in the traditional grammar of the Arabs and with the medieval Hebrew grammarians. In a similar fashion (see my "Hebrew Grammar," col. 101, §F), I view the phonological relations within TH as so complex and beset by analogies, as befits languages with lengthy histories, that TH does not provide the possibility of deducing, with a reasonable degree of probability, any earlier stages — not even a single stage beyond that which is admitted by all to have preceded TH, the stage of general penultimate stress. This still survives in TH in a number of forms of regularly ultimate stress, but which, in pause, become penultimately stressed. Furthermore, the difference in stress between forms in context and forms in pause shows that it would not be judicious to explain the development of word stress in TH (and elsewhere) without relating to the sequence — to sentence stress. The function of sentence stress in the shaping of words can be sensed in such

---

[100] See J. Cantineau, *Études de linguistique arabe (Memorial Jean Cantineau)* (Paris, 1960), 119.

[101] H. B. Rosén, "La position descriptive et comparative de formes contextuelles en hébreu," *Actes du Premier Congrès International de Linguistique Sémitique et Chamito-Sémitique, Paris 16–19 juillet 1969* (The Hague and Paris, 1974), 246–255, deals with the origins of stress in Hebrew. This is not the place to discuss his theory, which addresses stages prior to the historical stage, but it should be noted that he, too, is of the opinion that the stress patterns of Hebrew and Arabic are not subject to direct comparison, as has been the practice until now in explaining stress in TH.

[102] Indeed, Sarauw, *Akzent*, on p. 13, does not see fit to explain this form by means of an intelligible phonological process, but instead thinks that this is in fact the ancient 3rd fem. pl. form that came to be used for 3rd fem. sing. His explanation is unlikely in and of itself, not to mention the dissociation of the form without pronominal suffixes from the form with pronominal suffixes, such as אֲכָלַתְנוּ!

features as נסוג אחור (stress recession), דחיק and its consequences, etc. (see 1.5.2.7).

1.4.10 In SH, as already noted, there are only long syllables, open and closed. *Auxiliary stress* assists in the preservation of the length of a vowel not adjacent to the stressed syllable, as sensed clearly in the Samaritan reading. This auxiliary stress appears in the second syllable before the stressed syllable if its vowel is long, and in the syllable adjacent to the stressed syllable if its vowel is extra-long, and this is yet another indication that a syllable with an extra-long vowel is actually equivalent to two (1.4.7). Examples: *lå,būtīkimma* לאבותיכם, *al,zērā'imma* לזרעם, *wå'ebtimma* ואהבתם, *tēllåtåk* תהלתך. On occasion, in emphasizing a word, this auxiliary stress is sounded as if it were the main stress, the word, thus, having two stresses, such as *''å'reš* חרש (Lv 19:14), *'kåbē'dåk* כבדך (Nu 22:37). In this way the main stress shifts to the final syllable in an exceptional fashion.

When reading regularly, and of course fluently, short words such as *al* אל, *am* אם, *kal* כל, *'al* על, may enter into a construct state with the next word, thus losing their own stress, e.g., *'al-å:bən* על האבן, *'al-ånnas* על הנס, *al-tå'bū* אל תבוא (Gn 49:6), *kī-am-'råṣ* כי אם רחץ (Lv 22:6), etc. On the other hand, short words may link up with the preceding word, thus influencing a stress shift to the ultimate syllable, e.g., *ab'yåm-sof* בים סוף, *wnār'ṣī-lū* ונרצה לו (Lv 1:4), in SA *amṣåd'dīn-lē* מצדין לה (= "frightening him," *LOT* III/2, 140, l. 79). This is especially felt with the *waw consecutive*, e.g., *wā'lā-u-må'nā* ועלה ומנחה (Ex 30:9) instead of the more usual *wāla; šå'nī-u-šeš* שני ושש (Ex 25:4) instead of the usual *šåni; mib'bēt-u-miyyoṣ* מבית ומחוץ (Ex 25:11) instead of *mibbət; naš'šēš-u-qalləl* נשיש וקליל (*LOT* III/2, 161, l. 31). In some cases a diphthong develops, as I heard in *alṣarro-wkåfər > alṣarrawkåfər* לצריו וכפר (Dt 32:43). However, in general, obscuring word junctures does not influence the forms of these words; in contrast, at the close of pericopes (קצין) it is the chanted reading which leads to the distortion of various word forms by means of extending sounds and making additions, as explained in *LOT* III/1, 26.

A singular instance of a kind of דחיק, as uttered by all readers, is found in the phrase *aniy'yē-lli* = הניחה לי (Ex 32:10). It is not certain that the ultimate stress results from the combination above, for this may be a case of inherent ultimate stress (1.4.6e), the TH parallel is evident from the gemination.

1.5 Sound Changes

1.5.0 There are two types of sound changes which take place in TH in the flexion of a Hebrew word: (a) certain *vowels* change or disappear, according to their position relative to the stress. These changes take place regularly, though

1.5 Sound Changes 75

not consistently, not even from a diachronic point of view. *Ḥireq/ṣere/šəwa* interchanges are as follows: שֵׁם/שְׁמוֹ, לֵב/לִבּ, עֵנֶב/עִנְבֵי, עֲנָבִים, נְבֵלָה/נִבְלָתוֹ (but נְבֵלָתִי in Isa 26:19!); *ḥireq/pataḥ* interchanges: פַּת/פִּתִּים, בַּת/בִּתּוֹ, (but עַל/וּגִלִּים!); *ḥolem/qibbuṣ* (or *qameṣ*)/*šəwa* interchanges like: גֻּלְגֹּלֶת/גֻּלְגָּלְתּוֹ/גֻּלְגְּלוֹתָם לְגֻלְגְּלֹתָם, etc. The explanation of a considerable portion of this lack of consistency is very clear from a diachronic standpoint. The interchanges almost always occur amongst originally short vowels,[103] and after the loss of the quantitative distinction, the original differentiations between vowels of similar quality became obscured, and the interchange or its absence became a matter of morphology by means of a set of analogies, not all of which are clear today. Thus, there exist forms which contain vowel interchanges while others maintain their vowels, as already noted, the difference in behavior between nouns and verbs being especially notable in this context: כָּבֵד/כְּבֵדִים with an unchanging *ṣere*, as against יִתֵּן/יִתְּנוּ with a *ṣere/šəwa* interchange. (b) shifts resulting from sounds in contact, such as *יִנְפֹּל > יִפֹּל (but יִנְקְפוּ in Isa 29:1), or תּוֹכוֹן > תִּיכוֹן, etc. (see 1.5.3).

1.5.1 Interchanges in the Vowel System

1.5.1.0 In SH the changes of the first type (a) are far fewer than in TH, for in SH, in its present stage, the reduction of a full vowel to *šəwa* is impossible (see 1.3.0).[104] All vowels in open syllables are long and maintain their length throughout the flexion of the words. Vowel reduction or vowel elision which do, nevertheless, take place in SH, result from the preceding stage, and because of their relative rarity they do not characterize word-formation.

In reviewing the vowel interchanges in SH, no distinction shall be made between originally short and originally long vowels, for vowel quantity in SH is automatic, depending upon the position of the vowel in the syllable (1.2.3). The order of the vowels in the interchanges adduced will be that of the vowel listing in 1.2, i.e., a matter of pure phonetics, with no elements indicating diachronic (see 1.5.2) or morphological considerations, namely, which vowel appears in the absolute form of the word or which vowel replaces it in the inflected forms of the word. In order to provide a foundation for a correct perception of the system of sound interchanges in SH in relation to TH and of the development of the SH system (taken up in 1.5.2), it is necessary to provide the following detailed synchronic description of the system of interchanges in SH.

---

[103] Instances such as קָרְבָּן / קָרְבְּנֵיהֶם or זָדוֹן / זְדוֹן and שָׂשׂוֹן / שְׂשׂוֹן, which are from עי״ו roots, are exceedingly rare.

[104] See also rare cases in which a *šəwa* in a previous stage of SH was completely reduced. See 1.2.1d, 1.3.5e.

1.5.1.1 i/ə/e: *i* in a closed stressed syllable, *ə* after the stress, *e* in an unstressed syllable, such as *dabbirtå, dabbər, dabbertimma, afdaberkimma* — TH דִּבַּרְתָּ, מַהֵר/דַּבֵּר, דַּבֵּר, דברתם, בדברכם; SH *mâ'ertimma, mâ'irtən, mâ'ər* — TH מְהַרְתֶּם, מְהַרְתֶּן/ מַהֵר; SH *wålbišta, wtalbəš* (Gn 27:15), *wålbeštimma* והלבשתם (Ex 29:8) — TH והלבשתם, ותלבש , והלבשת.

In words of a single syllable *i/e* sometimes interchange, even when stressed, such as *bet / bit* בית (see 4.1.2.1c), while in other cases only *e* appears in the absolute form, such as *qen* קן, whereas in the suffixed form: *qinnåk* קִנְּךָ (see 4.1.2.2).

i/ē: *ilmu*/חלמו/*ēlom* חלום, *idma* אדמה / *ēdom* אדום. It originates in two different patterns which merged forming a declension (see 4.1.3.12).

ī/ə or ē/ə: *tânīnəm* תנינים / *tânən* תנין, *fâtīləm* פתילים / *fâtəl* פתיל, *zâqīnəm* / זְקֵנִים *zâqən* זָקֵן, *ådēšəm* חֲדָשִׁים / *ådəš* חֹדֶשׁ. (This is not a real interchange, for *ə* includes something of both vowels [1.2], and historical differentiations do not interest us here).

ī/e: *dīšu* דישו / *deš* דיש, *īṣåk* עצך / *eṣ* עץ, *gīro* גרו / *ger* גר. However, *i* is also found in other words, such as *bīnu* בינו / *bin* בין / *binkimma* בינכם.

1.5.1.2 i/a(â): *immu* אמו / *am* אם, *itti* אתי / *at* את, *libbi* לבי / *lab* לב, *izəm* עזים / *az* עז, *šinnəm* שנים / *šan* שן, *šišša* ששה / *šaš* שש, *innåk* חנך / *ån* חן. (Gn 39:21). This relationship, e.g., בת, בתו / פת, פתים in TH is known as "Philippi's law" (see 1.5.2.1 note), and in SH, in this type, we find it even more consistently than in TH, just as it is more common in BH, e.g., לב, צל.

ə or ē/a: *bēni* בני / *ban* בן, *šēmåk* שמך / *šam* שם, *yēdu* ידו / *yad* יד, *ētimma* אתם/ *at* את, *ēšu* אשו / *aš* אש; when the vowel comes after the stress, it may even be *ə*, such as *miyyəd* מיד, *miyyət* מאת, *aššəm* השם, *'kal-əš* כל אש (LOT III/2, 242, l. 6) In these words, too, *a* survives if the syllable is stressed by virtue of chanted reading like *wab'yad* וביד (Nu 5:18 [LOT III/1, 74]). When the vowel is preceded by an *aleph*, *ē* is replaced by *ī*, e.g., *al* (אֶל)/*īli* אֵלִי etc.

The converging of such forms as *šam* שם and *lab* לב of different origins, led to the shift of the post-tonic vowel to *ə* in such words as לב when the stress shifted: *alləb* הלב, although the opposite occurs in the word בן, where the *a* remains: *abban* הבן.

Two forms of the word כן exist simultaneously: *kan, ken, alkən* לכן, and the grammarians attempt to define the use of each of them (LOT I, 281; III/1, 130, l. 14). The interchange *adkən/adkan* דכן in SA (LOT III/b, 286, l. 36) and the Pentateuchal reading fluctuations show that the grammarians' differentiations are not universally accepted. The word שם "name" shows a significant differentiation: *šam*, in its usual meaning; *šem* "reputation."

Note: Another example is the noun קץ pronounced in Gn 6:13 *qeṣ*, but

1.5 Sound Changes

with a derivational morpheme, an originally unstressed syllable has both *i* and *a* vowels: *qiṣṣa* קצה (Nu 22:41 and elsewhere) and *qåṣṣot* (Ex 25:18). To the best of my knowledge, this duality has not been exploited for any semantic differentiation.

1.5.1.3 a/å. As noted in 1.2.7.2, I view *å* as a parallel to Tiberian (and BH) *qameṣ*, but this does not signify that the *a/å* relationship in SH is equivalent to the *pataḥ/qameṣ* relationship in TH. Whether we hold that *pataḥ* and *qameṣ* in TH are two separate phonemes,[105] as seems to be the case, or that they are mutually complementary allophones of a single phoneme,[106] it is clear that in most linguistic situations the *pataḥ* cannot be substituted for the *qameṣ*, i.e., the distribution of these two vowels is severely limited, unlike SH. There is no phonological condition for such differences as *albaddimma* לְבַדָּם / *albådåkimma* לבדכם, *kallu* כֻּלוֹ / *kållå* כֻּלָּהּ, as well as *šāma* שמע / *šåmå* שמח and many more. Nevertheless, these phonemes replace each other frequently in verbal conjugation. In various cases, where no semantic difference depends on them, they interchange with each other even when not inflected, as read by different readers or by a single reader in different texts.[107] Indeed, most of the differences I became aware in Pentateuchal reading are of this type: *bâna* / *bånå* בנה (Gn 4:17), *åba* / *åbå* אבה (Gn 11:3,4), *åna* / *ånå* אנה, *ṣåda* / *ṣådå* צדה (both in Ex 21:13); *niššåba* / *niššāba* נשבה (Ex 22:9), *wyētåṣṣåb* / *wyētåṣṣåb* ויתעצב (Gn 6:6), *yåbbār* / *yābbār* יעבר (Gn 31:21), etc.[108] Were it not for all those places, and they are, indeed, numerous and decisive, where the differences are phonematic, it would be possible to compile a grammar using the sign *A* to include both vowels. The following are the interchanges found in flexion:

a. The usual interchange is *a* in a closed, stressed syllable / *å* in an open one, as in *ab* אב / *åbi* אבי, *dat* דת / *dåtu* דתו;

b. *a* in a closed unstressed syllable / *å* in a closed stressed one, as in *baddəm* בדים / *båd* בד, *kabbu* כפו / *kåf* כף, *salləm* סלים / *sål* סל. There are, however, words with an *a* in a closed, stressed syllable, just as there are words with an *å* in a closed, unstressed syllable, as in *kal* כל / *kallu* כלו, *tåfkimma* טפכם / *tåf* טף, *yåmməm* ימים / *yåm* יָם. Other examples can be found, e.g., in 4.1.2.7–8.

> Note: The *o/ū* interchange does not belong here, for it is not an interchange of phonemes, but rather of the allophones of a single phoneme, as noted in 1.2.4.

---

[105] This according to J. Cantineau, "Essai d'un phonologie de l'hébreu biblique," *BSLP* 40 (1930), 108, who noticed the opposition אֲהֲבָה / אֲהָבָה and גָּמֵל / גָּמָל.

[106] This according to I. Garbell, "Quelques observations sur les phonèmes de l'hébreu biblique et traditionnel," *BSLP* 50 (1954), 240, who does not give reasons for her assumption.

[107] E.g., מן is pronounced *man*, but למן (Dt 4:32, 9:7) is pronounced *almån*, even though the preposition ל does not normally influence the vowels of the noun.

[108] Similarly in SA; see *LOT* III/2, 29.

To sum up, in SH, too, there no longer exists the phonological conditioning which led to the development of all the above mentioned interchanges. It would seem that the interchanges themselves determine the nature of SH far less than TH. Regarding the *a/å* interchange, note that both vowels can appear in the same conditions, e.g., *an* הן, *ån* חן and possibly even within the boundaries of the very same form, such as לעמך, עמך: *'ammåk, lammåk/'åmmåk, låmmåk*. Indeed, there seems to be a certain tendency to vowel harmonization *a...a*, *å...å*, as in *'åla* עלה, *'ålūto* עלותיו — but *'ålåt* עלת, *'ålåtu* עלתו, *'am* עם, *'ammi* עמי etc., but *'åmmåk* (alongside *'ammåk*), *'ay* חי, *'ayyəm* חיים, but *'åyyå* החיה (cf. also 6.3.2). This tendency does not, however, under any circumstances become a rule or even a custom, for we have encountered *'ag* חג, *baggåk* בחגך; *az* עז, *bazzåk* בעזך; *'ay* חי, *'ayyåt* חית, or *bå'låm* בלעם.

Therefore, when SH adopts either of the vowels *a* or *å* within the boundaries of a word, and even more so, within the boundaries of a certain form or morpheme (e.g., *a* or *å* in the feminine suffix, but *åt* in its construct state!), SH has taken another step beyond TH in transferring an originally phonological interchange to the realm of morphology.

1.5.2 Diachronic Study

1.5.2.0 In order to grasp correctly the relationship between SH and TH, it is necessary to complement the description of the shifts taking place in the vowel system with a diachronic study: how did the vowels develop from the earliest stage common to both traditions (and this is not necessarily "Proto-Semitic"!) to what actually exists. Two points must not be overlooked: one, what is being compared is an apparently abstract average, i.e., there can never be complete certainty that a given word in the two traditions relates to the very same origin, e.g., a certain nominal pattern or a certain verb form, such as *yaqtulu* rather than *yiqtalu*, though this may be very probable; the other, the difference in stress between the two traditions was preceded by a period of equivalence (1.4.8). Nevertheless, this does not mean that the stress on each and every word was precisely the same.

Regarding the common stage, we assume the existence of three short vowels *i*, *a*, *u* and three long ones *ī*, *ā*, *ū*, and the existence of short vowels in word-final positions both with nouns and with verbs. There is no significance to the question under consideration whether all the qualities of the short vowels existed during the said period, and whether they still had the meanings of their functions in PS. In words of this stage the hyphen following them marks any short vowel.

1.5.2.1 *i*. Examples: *bin-, šim- libb-, bitt-, ṣila'-, libab-, ḥimār-, tihām-,*

1.5 Sound Changes

yittin-, yišib-, yittinū, yišibū, yudabbirū, ḥafiṣtā.

In TH the vowel *i (ḥireq)*:

a. remains in a closed, unstressed syllable such as יִתֵּן, בִּתּוֹ, לִבִּי, שִׁמְךָ, בִּנְךָ.

b. becomes *ṣere* [1] in a closed, stressed syllable, such as לֵב, יֵשֵׁב, יִתֵּן, שֵׁם; [2] in an open syllable adjacent to the stressed syllable, such as יֵשֵׁב, לֵבָב, צֵלָע; [3] in an open, stressed syllable, such as יִתֵּנוּ, יְדַבֵּרוּ.

c. becomes *pataḥ* in a closed, stressed syllable, such as בַּת, חָפַצְתָּ (and, in pause, *qameṣ*).

d. becomes *šəwa* in an open syllable (adjoining the stressed syllable), as in יְדַבְּרוּ, יֵשְׁבוּ, יִתְּנוּ, תְּהוֹם, חֲמוֹר.

Rule (a) is the only consistent one, i.e., only *ḥireq* will appear under these conditions. It is clear that during the common stage there was a difference between forms such as *šim-* (TH שֵׁם) and *batt-* (< *bitt* < *bint*). However, as time went on, flexional analogies in nouns and verbs resulted in the different traditions of Hebrew in forms unexpected according to these original rules, as for example TH חֲפַצְתֶּם (cf. שְׁאֵלְתִּיו 1Sa 1:20) or לֵב in TH. Analogies undoubtedly gave rise to it, though how they worked is not entirely clear. Questions of the unchangeable *ṣere* in Hebrew grammar are of this type.[109]

In SH an *i-* vowel in the common stage can (1) remain unchanged; (2) develop into any of the following: *e, a, å*, these reflexes being reflected in the vowel interchange described in 1.5.1.1 and 1.2.1.2; but (3) will not develop into a *šəwa*. As to the question if the four rules of TH are at the basis of the SH developments, the answer is that an independent study of SH structure demonstrates the existence of only rules (a), (c) and (d):

Rules (a) and (c) are clearly revealed in the *i/a(å)* interchange in such words as *lab / libbi* and, as already noted, in these cases the interchange has served as the basis for the analogous (!) shift of such words as TH שֵׁם (Rule b[1]) to *šam*.

Note: a. Only a single case is known where Philippi's Law does not apply, just as it does not apply in TH: *qen* קֵן / *qinnåk* קִנְךָ.

b. E. Qimron, "Did 'Phillippi's (sic) Law' Occur in Samaritan Hebrew?" (*Proceedings of the First International Congress of the Société des Études Samaritaines*, Tel Aviv 1988 [Tel Aviv, April 11–13 1991], 13*–17*), denies the existence of Philippi's Law in SH entirely. He does not even grant the traces of this law in a grammatical category which certainly fulfils the conditions for the application of this law: monosyllabic words such as *bat* בת / *bitti* בתי, *lab* לב / *libbu* לבו. As against this assumption, cf. my "Remarks on Philippi's Law," *Lěšonénu* 53 (1988/89), 13–19 [Hebrew]. I add here the statement of the thirteenth century gramarian,

---

[109] I have dealt with this in "Hebrew Grammar," col. 101, §G.

Abū Saʿīd, that the correct pronunciation of the pronominal suffix כם- is with *fatḥa*, i.e., *kamma*, not with *kasra*, i.e., *kimma*. See LOT I, 141, 143.

Rule (d), too, comes through clearly, though the words demonstrating its validity are extremely few, such as *tūm* תהום. There is no reasonable way to interpret such a form except as a result of **tū'um < *tᵘ'ūm* (1.3.3), with the original form certain and in accordance with Rule (d).

With regard to Rule (b), which clashes both with (d) (i.e., b[2]) and with (c) (i.e., b[1]), its existence in SH cannot be proved, since a form such as *lēbāb* may have developed in SH from לְבָב*, similar to חֲמוֹר — *ēmor*, and had rule (d) not been proven it would have been possible to derive *ēmor* from a base like TH חֲמוֹר*. Also, if we compare such forms as *yədabbəru*, *yittənu* (b[3]) with *yiššâbu* ישבו, *yiṣṣâ'u* יצאו, where the second radical is vocalized with *â*, they can easily be explained on the basis of Rule (d). In a similar fashion one should explain *ṣīla* צלע or *zâʿrū* זרעו on the basis of Rule (d)(1.3.1a). Similarly, in *tēlåd* תלד, *yēlåk* ילך the vowel of the prefix can be explained on the basis of Rule (d). It may be possible to view the *ə/a* interchange as an indication of the existence of Rule (b) in SH (1.5.1.2), for *ə* usually derives from *i/e* after a loss of stress; it may, however, develop in rare cases from vowels other than *i/e* as well (see LOT III/1, 23, n. 26). If, in fact, the rule that *i > ē* in an open syllable adjacent to the stress did not apply in the form of Hebrew which relates to SH, but rather *i > šəwa* (cf. *kâmtannəm* כמתאננים; see 2.2.1.5.2) — then that rule displays more phonological order than TH, and simultaneously shows an extremely interesting parallel to the development of the *u* vowel.

> Note: The conclusion that the *i > ē* shift did not take place in SH can be strengthened as follows: the noun גְּנֵבָה took the form *gēnība* (4.1.5.6), which, upon adding the 3rd sing. pronominal suffix, became *gânåbtu*, in accordance with the noun declension described in 4.1.5.7[4]. The suffixed form shows that the vowel following the נ was originally a short *i* — just as it was short in the TH form גנבה with the *ṣere* — and this *i* developed into *a* according to Philippi's Law and into a long *i* when it did not shorten to *šəwa*.

1.5.2.2 *a* Examples: *dabar-*, *kanaf-*, *katip-*, *gann-*, *maqra-*, *maqnay-*, *mattan-*, *maḥmad-*, *šamar-*, *šamartī*, *šamartīkā*, *šamarū*, *yišmur-*, *yilbaš-*, *yilbašū*, *yaḥmud-*.

In TH the vowel *a* split into two, *pataḥ* and *qameṣ* (which is a kind of A, see 1.2.7.2). Except for a few cases this vowel developed:

a. into *pataḥ* in a closed syllable [1] stressed, as in: גַּן; שָׁמַרְתִּי; [2] unstressed, as in: שְׁמַרְתִּיךָ, מַחֲמַדִּים, מַתָּן.

1.5 Sound Changes

b. into *qames* (I) in an open syllable [1] stressed, as in שָׁמְרוּ, יִלְבָּשׁוּ, מִקְרָא; [2] adjacent to the stress, as in דָּבָר, כְּנַף, כָּתֵף; (II) in a closed, stressed syllable in nouns (the abs. state), but not in verbs: דָּבָר, מַתָּן — but שָׁמַר, שָׁמַרְתִּי.

Note: In its pausal forms the verb behaves like a noun, as in שָׁמָר; in its construct state the noun behaves like a verb, as in מַחְמַד (1 Kgs 20:6).

c. into *hireq* in a closed, unstressed syllable. This is not a fixed rule, but rather a gradually spreading trend, and is not valid in syllables closed with a guttural consonant, a geminated consonant and, elsewhere as well; its consequences are not significant in BH, as in מִקְנֶה, כִּתְפוֹת vs. מַתָּן, מַחְמַד, and interchanges exist, such as מַלְכֵי / מַלְכָּם; גַּנַּת / גַּנָּה.

d. into *šəwa* in syllables adjacent to the stress in verb forms, such as שָׁמְרוּ, יִלְבְּשׁוּ.

Though there exists a choice between *patah* and *hireq* as well as between *patah* and *qames*, depending upon the parts of speech, it is clear that *patah* and *qames* originally developed as two allophones from a single phoneme, with supplementary distribution: *patah* in unstressed closed syllables, *qames* in open syllables and stressed closed syllables.

In SH, too, *a* split into two vowels, *a* and *å*, both of which developed into independent phonemes, their distribution not dependent upon syllable structure of any sort, as described above 1.5.1.3; only a faint trace of the TH relationship can be discerned in various words — see 4.1.2.8.

The trend of *a > i* mentioned in (c) occurs (1) in verbal forms, but (2) only occasionally in nouns. Examples: (1) in preformatives of the imperfect *Qal* like *yifqåd* יפקד < *yafqud*, TH יִפְקֹד; (b) with the *nun* of *Nifʿal* (Proto-Semitic *naqtal*) in imperfect and perfect, e.g., *tikkårət*, TH וְלֹא-תִכָּרֵת; *nikkårət*, TH וְנִכְרַת (Ex 30:38). However, the original *a* is maintained in *wnallaʾəm* (Ex 1:10) TH וְנִלְחַם, *allaʾəm* (Ex 17:9) TH imperative הִלָּחֵם, (as against infinitive *lēllaʾəm* [Ex 17:10], *lē* being a contraction of לְהִ). Cf. also *wnāʾēzu* ונאחזו 2.2.1.4.1. The difference in behavior in the noun formation in this respect between SH and TH may be best demonstrated by the prefixed pattern (see 4.2), e.g., *maqdaš* מקדש / TH מִקְדָּשׁ However, even here an exception exists: TH מִבְחָר (Dt 12:11) / SH *mēʿbār* (<*mibᵃhar*) as against *māʿnāl* (Dt 33:25) *mānāllək*, TH מִנְעָלֶיךָ.

The possibility of a shift *a > šəwa* (d) in verb forms cannot be proved: the *a*-vowel in the *šåmåru, yilbåšu* forms may stem from the *å* of the common stage of development, and may also develop from *šəwa* (see 1.3.2).

1.5.2.3 *u* Examples: *kull-, kullī, kullanū, qudš-, qumṣ-, qudqud-, qudqud(a)kā, gulgult-, gulgulāt-, yakul-, yakultī, yaqulū, wyaqum*.

In TH the vowel *u*

a. survives in a closed, unstressed syllable, as in קָמְצוֹ, גֻּלְגָּלְתּוֹ, כֻּלָּנוּ;

b. develops into *ḥolem* in a closed, stressed syllable, as in כֹּל, קָדְקֹד, יָכֹל, יָכֹלְתִּי, and also in an open (opened at a late stage), stressed syllable, as in קֹדֶשׁ, קֹמֶץ, גֻּלְגֹּלֶת;

c. develops into *qameṣ* in a closed, unstressed syllable, as in גֻּלְגָּלְתּוֹ, קָדְקֹד, קָדְשׁוֹ, וַיָּקָם, כָּל-;

d. develops into *šəwa* in an open syllable adjacent to the stress, as in קָדְקֳדוֹ, יָכְלוּ, גֻּלְגְּלוֹתָם.

(a) and (c) are rules of choice, and the survival of *u* is clearly preferred in syllables closed by a geminated consonant as, for example, in the verbal stem פֻּעַל; yet, under these precise conditions, too, we do find a *qameṣ*, as in עָזִּי (Ex 15:3). On the other hand, *u* is generally replaced by *qameṣ* in syllables closed by a simple consonant, e.g., in the verbal stem הָפְעַל, yet under these conditions we also encounter *u* as, e.g., הֻשְׁלַךְ, or אָמְנָם alongside אֻמְנָם.

The trend in TH is thus clear: elimination of *u* by replacing it with a *ḥolem* or even with a vowel lower than the *ḥolem* — the *qameṣ*. This is not so in BH, which preserves *u* in places where TH replaces it with *qameṣ* as, for example, in קרבן. The *u* > *i* shift is common throughout the ancient Semitic world, as well as in living Arabic dialects[110] and can apparently be seen in the relationship between the Hebrew and Arabic words: קפד / قُنْفُذ, שִׁבֹּלֶת / سُنْبُلَة. With regard, however, to a vowel *u* occurring in TH in one form of a word and being replaced by another vowel in another form of the same word, such an *u* would seem to develop no further than a *qameṣ*.

In SH the vowel *u* of the common stage vanishes completely.

1. It shifts to A (*a/å* as explained above in 1.5.2.2), as in *kal, kalli, kållånu, qådeši, qåmṣu, qådqåd, gilgålåt, gilgålūtimma, yåkål, yåkålti, wyåqåm, weråbbot* וארבות (Gn 7:11).

2. It shifts to *i*, as in *gilgålåt, fēqiddåt* פְּקֻדַּת, *lēnikkåt* לְהֻנַּכַת (Nu 7:11) *lēlimmåti* לַאֲלֻמָּתִי (Gn 37:7).

It does not seem possible to discover under what conditions the vowel shifts to *a/å* and when it shifts to *i*; the words with *i* may be relics from the earlier stage, parallel forms to שִׁבֹּלֶת, קפד.

One cannot prove on the basis of SH whether Rule (d) ever existed, for the *šəwa* has become a full vowel, so that even if *u* had developed into a *šəwa*, it would eventually have merged with the *a/å* reflex. It is, however, reasonable to suggest that Rule (d) affected SH early on, especially because of the strong link between the vowels *u* and i (see 1.5.2.1).

To sum up: the process discernible in TH, whereby the vowel *u* of the stage common to TH and SH is eliminated, culminates in SH. If *u* (not originating in *ū* !) is encountered in a few scattered words, such as *rubqå* רבקה, *mukkå* מֻכָּה,

---

[110] See *GvG* 1, 144ff., and Kutscher, *Isaiah Scroll*, 452ff.

1.5 Sound Changes

rummå רמה (Ex 16:24)(1.2), it did not stem from original *u*, but rather from sound proximity, and even as such these are only exceptional cases. The sole remnant of original *u* can still be found in the passive form *wtuqqa* וַתֻּקַּח (Gn 12:15); and see 2.10.7.

1.5.2.4 The long vowels *ī*, *ū* of the common stage survive without change in TH; in SH the only changes which affect them are those necessary because of the relationship between vowel quantity and syllable structure, i.e., they shorten in closed syllables (except, of course, in syllables beginning with a guttural consonant, which can take extra-long vowels, as noted in 1.2.3).

When *ī* shortens, it *may* shift to *e* in closed stressed syllables (unlike vowels derived from short *i*, see 1.5.1.1). Examples: *'ātīdot* עתידות, *rībot* ריבות, *rib* ריב, *den* דין, *ser* סיר, *šēbetkimma* שביתכם (SP Num. 31:19). This also applies to the vowel stemming from the contraction of the diphthong *ay*, as in *zītåk* זיתך, *zit* זית, *deš* דַּיִשׁ, *bit/bet* בַּיִת.

ū in a closed syllable shifts to *o*, as noted in 1.2.4, as in *wåṣūməm* וְעָצוּמִים: *wåṣom* וְעָצוּם, *'ammūdi* עַמּוּדִי: *'ammod* עַמּוּד.

Proto-Semitic *ā* had already shifted to *ō* during the stage common to SH and TH; each of these traditions contains, however, forms and words in which the shift did not take place. This fact gives rise to the following questions: under what conditions did the shift take place, and does the situation in SH contribute to our the understanding of the phenomenon?

1.5.2.5 *ā > ō*. Since the shift was a general one throughout the Canaanite area and is very common in both TH and SH, we shall note here those cases in which the shift does not take place in either tradition, where one encounters a *qameṣ* in TH (unless it is in the construct state, where a *pataḥ* replaces it) and *a* or *å* in SH, according to the rules of vowel quantity.

Verbal Forms:

a. *Qal* inf. abs.: שָׁמוֹר / *šåmår* (Dt 11:22), דָּרוֹשׁ / *dåråš* and others;

b. *Pi'el* verbal nouns: בַּקָּשָׁה, נֶחָמָה / -

c. *Hif'īl* verbal nouns: הַשְׁמָעוּת, הַכָּרָה / -

d. *Qal* part.: הרומש / *arrūməš*, שופט / *šūfåṭ*, etc. — but נותן / *nåtan* (alongside *nūtən*), הולך / *ålək*, חותן / *'åtən* and many more; ע"ו verbs: קָמָיו / *qāmo*, and in the later language as in SA צָם[111] *ṣåm*.

---

[111] Note the length of the vowel and what is stated below, 1.5.3.4. A form such as *ṣåm* or *qåm* can be explained on the basis of Aramaic, in which case the question of the presence of *ā (å)* instead of *ō* is not relevant.

Nominal Forms:

e. *qāl*: קוֹל / *qol*, דוֹר / *dor* — but also *dår*.
f. *qatāl*: שָׁלוֹם / *šålom*, כָּבוֹד / *kåbod*, לָשׁוֹן / *liššon*, אָתוֹן / *itton*, but שָׁלוֹשׁ / *šēlåš*.
g. *qi/utāl*: נְחֹשֶׁת / *nåššət*.
h. *qātal*: עוֹלָם / *ūlåm*, שׁוֹפָר / *šūfår*, חוֹתָם / *ūtåm*, but in Gn 38:18, 25: '*åtəm*, '*åtīmāk* (spelled with a *yod* in SP).
i. *qattāl*: גִּבּוֹר / *gibbor* but כִּנּוֹר / *kinnår*, גַּנָּב / *gånnåb*, חָרָשׁ / '*årråš* and corresponding to רוֹקֵם, חוֹשֵׁב, אוֹיֵב: *uyyåb*, '*aššåb*, *råqqåm*.
j. *maqāl*: מְנוּחָה / *månuw'wā*, מְנוּסַת / *månūsåt*, מְנוֹרָה / *mēnūra*, but בִּמְצֹלֹת / *båmåṣålot* (Ex 15:5) as against TH במצלות; cf. also TH מְצוּדָה as against וּמְצָד, if both words are to be derived from the root צוד.[112]

Formative Elements:

k. *ān*: רִאשׁוֹן / *rā'īšon*, זִכָּרוֹן / *zakron*, עֵרָבוֹן / '*årābon* but קָרְבָּן / *qåråbån*, שִׁלְחָן / *šā'lān*, כְּבָשָׂן / *kåbåšån*. Corresponding to אדוני אדון SH has *ådon*, pl. *ådūnəm* (Dt 10:17 האדונים) — on the one hand; *ådanni* (Gn 24:18), *ådāni* (Dt 9:26) — on the other. In proper nouns *å* is more frequent, such as *yiqšån* יָקְשָׁן etc.

l. Fem. suff. *āt*: this is generally *ot* in SH, but one does encounter *tūldåt* תּוֹלְדֹת, *yūmåt* יְמוֹת, *šēnåt* = שְׁנוֹת (Deut. 32:7; in SA السنوات), *mētåttək* מְטַטֶּיךָ (Ex 7:28; in SA اسرتك!), *far'rāt* פרעת (see 4.1.4.8). *tērūmåtīkimma* תְּרוּמֹתֵיכֶם (Dt 12:11), *zūnåtīkimma* (Nu 14:33) also belong here, where *åt* occurs instead of (historical) *ōt*, as the pronominal suffix indicates; see 3.2.4.

> Note: In certain cases, such as *miṭṭē'måt* מטמאת (Lv 16:19) or *tēbuwwåt* תבואת, it is impossible to determine if the noun is singular or plural, and the existing translations treat the nouns as singular in some cases and as plural in others.

m. Various words in which, according to comparative evidence there was an *å*, do not display *o/u* in SH: *ånåki* אנכי, *šēmål* שְׂמֹאל (cf. TH שְׂמָאלִי), *šåmåna* שמונה, *råšət* ראשית, *kå* כֹּה (cf. כָּכָה), *fā* פֹּה, *lå* לֹא, '*år'år* עֲרוֹעֵר.

1.5.2.6 From the standpoint of frequency, this presentation of the SH deviation from the phonetic shift under consideration makes no substantial change in what is already known from TH. The lack of the phenomenon in types (b) and (c) in SH, which are fairly common in TH, is balanced by the deviation occurring in such common words as אנכי or לא which are listed in (m). From the standpoint of the reliability of the comparison, in types (a) and (d) TH and SH cannot be compared, for it is extremely probable that the SH infinitive derives

---

[112] This derivation is presented in our common grammars and dictionaries. However the medieval Hebrew philologists, like their Arabic counterparts, derive מצד (scilicet مصد) from the root מצד; cf. my *Struggle*, 272, n. 15.

from a basic form parallel to the TH inf. const., i.e., פְּעֹל, whereas the SH participle with $\bar{a}/\hat{a}$ derives from a base parallel to that of TH פֹּעֵל. In other words, in both these forms $\bar{a}/\hat{a}$ is not the continuation of early $\bar{a}$. It is doubtful, too, whether several other words in SH and TH enjoy a common origin, e.g., טבו/*ṭâbu* or ראשית/*râšət*, where SH would seem to continue an ancient $\bar{a}$. Yet it would appear that the evidence from SH does support one of the explanations of the phenomenon in TH. There are three theories: (1) the $\bar{a} > \bar{o}$ shift always took place at a certain point in time, i.e., it is in no way a conditioned shift. The forms with $\bar{a}$ either originate in a short a or they derive from some other linguistic stratum after the shift took place.[113] (2) the shift is stress conditioned, i.e., only a stressed $\bar{a}$ shifted to $\bar{o}$. When the syllable lost its stress, the $\bar{o}$ vowel then remained. The survival of $\bar{a}$ in an originally stressed syllable means that the form belongs to the "Aramaic" stratum, insofar as Hebrew is the result of a mixture of Canaanite and Aramaic.[114] (3) the $\bar{a} > \bar{o}$ shift is stress conditioned. The lack of the shift in various words and forms results from inflexional analogies, which led to a generalization either in favor of $\bar{o}$ or in favor of $\bar{a}$ (as, e.g., in the *qaṭṭāl* pattern — see 1.5.2.5i).[115]

1.5.2.7 First of all, it should be emphasized that the reliability of the SH tradition in forms such as *ânåki* אנוכי, *šēlåš* שלוש, *fā* פה is not to be doubted or suspected of forgetfulness. Every in-depth study of this linguistic tradition reveals a zealous preservation of heritage, and forgetting the simplest and most common words in the Pentateuch is unthinkable.[116] For this reason, the words above suffice to undermine opinions (1) and (2) insofar as the words with the *a* in SH derive from the earliest Hebrew stratum and are unparalleled in Aramaic (אנכי, פה), or that the form contradicts the Aramaic (שלש with a *š*). With regard to שלש it should be noted, furthermore, that the pronunciation of the word in SH differs from that in SA: *tålåt*!

On the assumption that the shift is not conditioned by stress (1), there is no longer any way to understand the prevention of the shift, which nevertheless is common. We are forced to conclude that the shift affected only a stressed $\bar{a}$. And there coexisted within Hebrew forms with $\bar{a}$ and forms with $\bar{o}$ — of the

---

[113] This is the theory advanced by H. Birkeland in his *Akzent und Vocalismus im Althebräischen* (Oslo, 1940), 47, 128. C. Rabin, in his article on "The Hebrew Development of Proto-Semitic ā," *Tarbiz* 30 (1961), 100 [Hebrew], follows this path as well. He attempts to demonstrate that underlying such forms as גֶּנֶב, בִּקְשָׁה and others there is a short *a* vowel, i.e., they are of the *qaṭṭal*- and *qaṭṭalat*- patterns, but he failed to explain why this vowel is maintained in the inflected forms, unlike an original short vowel.

[114] See BL, 192. The mixture theory belongs to Bauer; he propounded it in his *Zur Frage der Sprachmischung im Hebräischen* (Halle, 1924).

[115] In the main, Brockelmann already expressed this opinion (*GvG* 1, 142), but the matter is presented more consistently in Bergsträsser, *Grammatik* 1, §25.

same word. Were this relationship caused only by inflexional analogy (3), it would be difficult to understand what led Hebrew to such leveling within the range of a word inflexion like גְּבוֹרִים - גִּבּוֹר as against גִּבֹּר - גִּבֹּרִים both being formed in the pattern *qattāl* in the early stage. For this reason, the assumption of analogy caused by flexion does not seem to suffice as an explanation.

As noted above (1.4.9), Hebrew in general had various degrees of stress in the sequence of words in the sentence. *ā* would seem to have shifted to *ō* only when fully stressed in such a sequence. In this way not only the inflected forms of a word, some displaying *ā* and others displaying *ō*, may clash (such as *maqōm-/ *maqāmōt-*), but the very same form itself had either *ā* or *ō*, depending upon **its position in the word sequence**. Very interesting evidence of this is provided by *aldår wdor* לדר ודור (Ex 3:15).[117] This means that a word like אנכי was sometimes pronounced *'ânâkī* and at other times *'anōkī*; פה sometimes *pā* and sometimes *pō*, לא *lā* or *lō*, just as words like אתי, אתה, הן were sometimes *'attī, *'attā, hinnā* and at other times *'at* (TH אַתְּ) for both masculine (cf. SP Nu 11:15, אתה) and feminine as usual in MH, *hin* by virtue of their stress in sequence (see 3.0). Fundamentally, this relationship is no different from that of the contextual and pausal forms in TH, such as שָׁמְרוּ/יִשְׁמְרוּ; שָׁמַע/שְׁמַע, upon which TH phonology is based.

When the differences in stress ceased to exist — this is clear by virtue of the disappearance of pausal forms in later Hebrew — there were many phonologically or morphologically unconditioned doublets. The forms with *ō* were generally chosen, and quite a number of words with original *ā* in both traditions remained, each in its own way. The difference between them would seem to indicate that in reality the ancient Hebrew tongue was more variegated than TH alone would show; a number of MH forms (such as לא = לְ or forms ending in -ִי) generally considered originally Aramaic may actually be alternate Hebrew forms. It is certain, for example, that such forms as רְבָעִי, שְׁלָשִׁי, (in Arabic: رباعي، ثلاثي) cannot be explained by Aramaic influence.

1.5.3 Changes Due to Proximity

1.5.3.0 Natural speech is such that sounds occurring in proximity, whether in contact, i.e., with no intervening sound, or at a distance, i.e., with some sound separating them, affect each other, whether with regard to the place or manner of articulation (or with regard to its nature). Most of their influence is assimilatory, for this entails a saving of effort. However, SH is a language of ritual

---

[116] This has already been noted above in 1.1.6.1.

[117] Notice that the same vowel interchange is found in an Akkadian text from Ras Shamra (!): *ana dāri dūri*, which means "forever" (see *CAD D*, 108). The Samaritan pronunciation of this phrase may be a very ancient tradition in Hebrew, independent of Hebrew phonological rules.

1.5 Sound Changes

whose purpose is for the reading of the sacred book. Carefully and precisely producing each and every sound according to tradition and to fixed principles is — in a sacred tongue — an ideal which everyone strives to realize. Thus, only those features of influence which have reached a level of accepted familiarity can be tolerated. Readers' slips of the tongue are revealing, as, e.g., *nētella* נתן לה (Lv 19:20 — *LOT* III/1, 66) or *šar'lā* < *šal'lā* שלחה (Nu 22:15 — ibid., 81), *sildu* in place of *sillu* סלוא (Nu 25:14 — ibid., 89).

The changes that took place in ancient Hebrew and became part of the written language as it appears in the Pentateuch, such as אחת < *'aḥadt*, יפל (*yippol* < *yinpol*), which SH and TH share equally, do not concern us in the following description. We are mainly interested in noting the changes gleaned from the pronunciation of SH as reflecting the spoken language revealed through the reading of the Pentateuch.

1.5.3.1 Assimilation. Wherever the process is clear, we see that assimilation takes place in environments where there is contact, and is regressive, and with consonants it results in complete mergers, i.e., it is total.

a. א, whether original or derived from ע/ה, assimilates, e.g., *māṣåtti* מצאתי, *lēqēttå* לקחת, *šāmánnu* שמענו, *yåmmåd* יעמד, *tēttiyya* תחתיה, *bīmma* בהמה, *yēllåm* יהלם, *yåddīfinnu* יהדפנו (? see *LOT* IV, 307). Hence, wherever assimilation does not take place, as in *yå:dål* יחדל, *yå:rågu* יהרגו, *yå:fåk* יהפך, a basic form similar to that in TH must be assumed — i.e., an intercalated element between the consonants (see 1.3.5d).

b. In the vernacular reflected in SH the ת of the *Hitpa'el* always assimilates to the following consonant; otherwise, one would not find in the Pentateuch *wniqqåddåšu* ונקדשו, *yibbårråd* יפרד, *iqqåbbåṣu* הקבצו — forms known as *Nif'al* with the second radical geminated (see 2.1.4.7) It must be assumed that in this vernacular there was no difference in pronunciation between ונברכו (Gn 12:3) and ונתברכו, both being pronounced *wnibbårråku*. This is especially noticeable in SA in alternate spellings such as מתנשי/מנשי ("forget"). In SA there is even a radical ת which assimilates, as in *אתכליה (= אשכלות, "bunches") > *akkålayyå* > *ankålayyå* אנכליה.[118] Thus, the pronunciation of ת in SH in forms such as *wetbårråku*/ והתברכו (Gn 22:18) or *yitqåddåšu*/יתקדשו (Ex 19:22), as against *wyiqqåddåšu* (Nu 17:3), should be recognized as a later innovation (a spelling pronunciation).

---

[118] See my "Palestinian Aramaic and Samaritan Poetry," 40. Regarding the word אנכהותי < אתכהותי, I can add the additional evidence of MS M (*LOT* I, קב), which renders the word חמס in Gn 49:5 as אכנהו and which undoubtedly should be אנכהו. The word is written as a gloss to the translation שקר in the text. (A most interesting case is to be found in MS M of ST to Gn 23:16. For the original Hebrew לסחר, there are variant translations: למגור, לתיגור. The word למגור is a *Qal* infinitive formed from למתגור. From this we note that the translator interpreted לסחר in the verse as an infinitive and not a participle).

c. ד may assimilate to ת, e.g., *wāgitti* והגדתי (Nu 23:3 — *LOT* III/1, 84), *wāfātta* ופחדת (Dt 28:66 — *LOT* III/1, 151). The rule, however, is to avoid such assimilation and to articulate the ד so clearly that a vowel is formed between them; hence, forms such as *wšādātå* וְשָׂדְתָּ (Dt 27:4), *mūlēdēti* מולדתי (Gn 20:13). Nevertheless, there is the form *wmūladtåk* (Gn 48:6). See also *LOT* III/2, 361, l. 1.

d. ל, ס, ת assimilate partially to the back vowel *a* and give rise to *ḷ, ṣ, ṭ* (see 1.1.7).

e. A short vowel *i* or *a(å)* assimilates to *w*, creating the sequence *uww-*, as in *yuwwåləd* יֻלַּד, *suwwåru* צֻוָּארוֹ, *tuwwu* טֻוּוּ (Pi'el) (Ex 35:26), *kåmṭuwwi* כמטחוי (Gn 21:16), *aššuwwåməm* (Nu 11:5) corresponding to TH הַשֻּׁומִים*,[119] *uwwålåt* — approx. *עֲוָלוֹת*, pl. of עוּל (Gn 33:13)[120] which in SH may be a plural form (1.5.2.5) of three words derived from the root עול: pass. part. (2.13.6) = TH עוּל, act. part. עוֹל (2.12.14) and עֻוָּל; as to the gemination of *l* see 1.5.3.3.

f. Progressive assimilation was uncommon in ancient Hebrew and not consistent, as can be seen from TH and SH. SH preserves it with greater consistency, however, as the following evidence attests:

1. In TH ה in the 3rd sing. object pronoun suffixes still occurs sometimes in its original full form -ֶנְהוּ, -ֶנְהָ, alongside the usual -ֶנּוּ, -ֶנָּה, but in SH always *-innu, -inna*. The same applies to אכלתהו (Gn 37: 20, 33), which is pronounced *åkålittu*, the ה absent in SP as well. Moreover, the gemination resulting from this assimilation was extended in SH, by analogy, to forms that do not display that phonetic precondition. Thus, we find the two forms side by side, e.g., *zåbådåni* זבדני (Gn 30:20) as against *lēqånni* לקחני (Gn 24:7) instead of **lēqåni* (< *lēqåḥåni*) or *yizbålinni* (Gn 30:20).

2. In verbs with a sibilant as first radical, the consonant ת as the reflexive marker total assimilates to the preceding consonant. In TH we find הִזַּכּוּ (Isa 1:16); in SH this is the common pattern, e.g., *wniššåmmådti* < *ונשתמדתי (Gn 34:30) or *wyiṣṣåmməd* < *ויצטמד (Nu 25:3). However, if the reflexive marker appears in the written text, it is pronounced in our day (see [b] above) *niṣtaddaq*/נצטדק (Gn 44:16). On the phenomenon of assimilation in Jewish Aramaic and CPA, see the evidence assembled in my article "Word Studies III," *Tarbiz* 50 (1980/1), 205–208 [Hebrew]: אשכח=אשתכח, אצלב = אצטלב, and to these may be added the variant readings אשבע / אשתבע in ST Gn 21:24 and איצר / אצטר in ST Ex 28:24 and elsewhere.

We see then that once the reflexive marker ת assimilated to the preceding consonant as it had to the following one (at least in the Aramaic vernacular of

---

[119] Notice that the difference in pl. of שׁוֹם between SH and TH is the same as in the pl. of דוד in TH: דּוֹדִים (2 Kgs 10:7)/ דְּוָדִים (2 Chr 35:13).

[120] This is one of the outstanding examples of *qəre* without *kətiv*. The spellings are עָאלת, אעלת, עלאת.

the Samaritans), its appearance in writing became a sort of *mater lectionis* indicating the gemination of the first radical. Thus, it must be assumed that a written form such as אשתלשל indicated the gemination of the first radical, just like אתשלשל.

A process precisely parallel to this can be found in the merger of the two spellings ־יי and ־וי to indicate an *o* vowel (at the end of words), as described in the introduction to *Tībåt Mårqe*, 17.

In a medieval Samaritan liturgical poem composed in LSH, the transposition of ת before a sibilant in the forms in question is standard practice, and the ת is pronounced today. This spelling eventually succeeded in eliminating *Nifʿal* from late poetic usage in the perfect as well.[121] (On the imperfect, see below 8.10.)

a. In such forms as *wābiṭṭå* והעבטת (Dt 15:6), *misṣår* מִצְעָר (Gn 19:20), examples of what is apparently progressive assimilation can be seen (the ת assimilated to the ט and the ע to the צ). This, however, is not so! The ת of והעבטת is pronounced ט in any case (see above [d]), while מצער is interpreted as meaning מן צער, as evident from SAV مـــن زغـر, similar to the reading of מתם (Dt 2:34; see *LOT* III/1, 95) *mittåm*, i.e., מן תם "entirely."[122] It would accordingly seem that the explanation to be provided below (2.4.7) on forms such as *wittīṣåbu* והתיצבו (Dt 31:14), *wyittīṣåbu* ויתצבו (Ex 19:17), namely, that they are forms of *Hittafʿal*, makes it necessary to assume the existence of early progressive assimilation.

b. With regard to the form *wqåbittu*, see 3.2.3.4.

g. When the preposition ב, regularly pronounced *af*, occurs before י or ל it is pronounced as a voiced labial plosive as in *abyom* ביום, *ablēbåbu* בלבבו. This prevents the loss of voicing of *av* (> *af*); in SH as it is realized today, only the plosive allophone of *v* exists.

h. The lack of assimilation in the words *wbintu* ובינתו (SP Gn 46:7), which has to be interpreted as sing. ובתו "and his daughter" and *lēbūnta* לבונתה (Lv 2:2) is noteworthy. In the noun לבונתה the long *ū* would seem to indicate the loss of a vowel after the נ, like the noun *tūldåt* תולדת (see 1.3.2c). The form *wbintu* is an example of an interpretive reading,[123] which ignores the fact that נ tends to assimilate in Hebrew; it is not the spelling, which obliges the Samaritan tradition to produce the נ.[124]

---

[121] Evidence of the inclusion of ת in spelling before a sibilant consonant and its pronunciation and of the elimination of *Nifʿal* from LSH is found in Florentin, *Shomronit*, 78, 215.

[122] See *LOT* III/1, 95.

[123] Indeed, SAV renders this بنته ("his daughter"). This reading frees the Samaritans from the need for an interpretation such as that of Abraham Ibn ʿEzra at Gn 46:7.

[124] See above n. 120.

1.5.3.2 Dissimilation

a. י becomes an א (1) usually in the combination yi whenever there is י in an adjacent syllable. For example, in the *Nif'al* of a verb I-guttural,[125] as in *yiyyâsâfu > iyyâsâfu יאספו, *yiyyāši > iyyāši יעשה, *yiyyâgår > iyyâgår יחגר (Lv 16:4), [*mi'iyyâbīkimma >] *miyyâyyībīkimma > mī'iyyâbīkimma מאיביכם (Nu 10:9), [*mihhay(y)ot >] *miyyāyyot > mī'ayyot מהיות (Ex 9:28); (2) in the combination yī after ā, as in *âyīti > â'īti הייתי, *âyītåb > â'ītåb הייטב (Lv 10:19) [but wyītåb וייטב (Lv 10:20)], *būrâyīn > būrâ'ən בוראין (*LOT* III/2, 100, l. 5); in SA in the gentilic suffix,[126] e.g., *qammâyīn > qåmmâ'ən. In this context, another development without any real dissimilation took place, common in Biblical Aramaic and in various MH traditions — the replacement of intervocalic י by א, as in *'annāyā(h) > *'annā'ā > 'an'nā ענהה (Dt 22:29 SP), and in SA: qammâyâ > *qammâ'â > qam'mâ. SH and SA, thus, show that the claim that this development is specifically characteristic of the Babylonian Aramaic and Babylonian Hebrew traditions is baseless. The change of י to א in the word miyyâ'åk מאחיך (Dt 15:7) from *miyyâyåk was only assisted by the trend to dissimilation (see above 1, 2).

b. The o/ū vowel preceding o/ū is tranformed into ē or into â. In this respect SH continues the ancient custom found in such forms as *ḥūṣon < ḥûṣon חוצון, *tūkon < תוכן תיכון and carefully maintains it, as in *kâmū'u > kâmē'u כמהו, tē'u תהו, bē'u בהו, rē'oš ראש, etc. (1.4.5), yā'ūkəl יאכל, yâbā'u יבאו. In this way the suffixes ūhū, ūnū lost their initial ū and the plural and singular forms merged, as in akkīrē'u הכירהו (SP Gn 42:8), wyištâmē'u וישטמהו (Gn 49:23), wyānnēnu ויעננו (Dt 26:6 SP) yisqâlånu יסקלנו (Ex 8:22). This is undoubtedly the reason for pronouncing ēdot אדות (Gn 20:3 SP; Nu 13:24), â:bētot העבתות (SP Ex 28:14) as against the sing. form 'abbot עבות.

Note: With regard to dissimilation in gemination see 1.5.3.3e–f.

1.5.3.3 Gemination.
A geminated consonant is a substantial morphological element in the Hebrew language, both in nominal and verbal forms. This is even more applicable to SH than to TH insofar as the ר in SH can be geminated, as in barrək = בֶּרֶךְ, šarra = שָׂרָה. In this regard SH preserves a situation prevalent as late as the period of the composition of the Septuagint, surviving in TH in rare traces and in traditions of MH.[127] The א (< אהח"ע), too, may

---

[125] It appears that dissimilation is not a hard and fast rule, since the *Pi'el* form yiyyâssår ייסר maintains the *yod*.

[126] The noun רתאי follows the *faqqåd* pattern, and the diphthong in the last syllable is not a gentilic suffix; nevertheless, we find the form with determination רתאה råt'tā < *råttâ'â < *råttâyyâ; for the *plural* form råttâyyâ see 1.5.3.4[4].

[127] Such as כָּרַת שָׁרֶךְ (Ezek 16:4), שְׂרָאשִׁי (Cant 5:2), and about ten other examples. On the

1.5 Sound Changes

develop into the geminated consonants -ww-, -yy- (see 1.1.8). In Hebrew, however, a geminated consonant may develop out of adjacent consonants or arise from rhythmic reasons, leading to the formation of a closed syllable with a short vowel instead of an open syllable with a long vowel, e.g., in TH: נִכְבְּדֵי / נִכְבָּדִים, and with regard to the relationship between SH and TH: *gâmâləm* / גְּמַלִּים, *šēlamməm* / שְׁלָמִים. Gemination and the loss of gemination shift nouns from one pattern to another and verbs from one stem to another; they are, thus, a considerable source of the differences in words or forms between one tradition and the other. One should be careful not to overexploit the geminated/ungeminated contrast in assigning various words or forms to a base common to TH and SH, e.g., *'āraš* / חֶרֶשׁ (see 4.1.3.14), especially in isolated phenomena such as *kâsa* / כִּסֵּא.[128] The phenomenon of gemination resulting from consonants in contact and syllable structure are dealt with here:

a. With regard to gemination as the result of assimilation see 1.5.3.1, and add words such as *uwwârəd* הוּרַד, if the form derives from *hitwârəd.

b. Examples of gemination deriving from rhythm: *kirrəm* / כִּרִים (Lv 11:35), *gēbirrâti* (< *gēbirra) / גבירה (Gn. 16:4), *yârišsât* ירשת (Nu 36:8), *ṣårri* צָרִי, *lallēdət* לָלֶדֶת, *mēgarrək* מֵגָרֵךְ (Gn 17:8) [but *bâmâṣâlot* במצולות !], *laššåd* לְשַׁד (Nu 11:8, constr.), *laššēlâšât* לשלשת (Ex 19:15, constr.), *lēqānni* לקחני (Gn 24:7), *mirrē'bāt*, מרבעת (SP Nu 23:10; TH אֶת רֹבַע), the gemination resembling that in nouns such as מִקְדָּשׁ (Ex 15:17), מְשׁוֹטָיִךְ (Ezek 27:6), in noun-patterns with prefixed ת, as in *tirruw'wā* / תרועה, *tinnuwwâti* / תנואתי (Nu 14:34),[129] contrasting with *tēnûfa*, תנופה; *mâdamməm* / מאדמים (Ex 25:5), *gâballot* / גבלות, *siddå* / צידה (Gn 42:25). Similarly in SA, as in *mittor*, the inf. of the verb תור alongside *mēšom* from שום (*LOT* III/2, 303 ll. 64, 65), *arṣimməm* ארצמים (= oppressed), variant *arṣiməm* (*LOT* III/2, 207 l. 66), *sēbarrīnån* סברינן ("our hope"), but *sēbârayyå* (*LOT* III/2, 92, l. 57, p. 93, l. 72).

c. By virtue of the principle above, sometimes nouns related to verbs geminating their second radical geminate their second radical themselves, such as (*mišlaḥ > **miš^alaḥ* > see 1.3.5) *mēšalla* / משלוח (Dt 12:7), in SA *låqqītən* לקיטין (*LOT* III/2, 222, l. 119), *fannəm* פנים (*LOT* III/2, 239 l. 11 = פנוים[130] "empty"),

---

Babylonian vocalization and especially MH, see Yeivin, *Babylonian Vocalization*, 351ff. See also S. Morag, "The Seven Doublets *BGD KPT*," *Tur-Sinai Festschrift* (Jerusalem, 1960), 207ff. [Hebrew].

[128] It is relevant to note that in the Sefire inscription (*KAI* 224:17) we read ישב על כהסאי. If this is not a scribal error, is it perhaps a parallel to the SH noun?

[129] The word מטוה in Ex 35:25 is pronounced *mittuwwå*, which may be derived from *mituwå*, with the change of the *šəwa*-like auxiliary vowel (1.4.4) into a full vowel with gemination of the ט; Samaritan tradition, however, perceives the word as a compound: מן טוה, as the translations attest: ST ואנדו מן עזלה, SAV احضروا من غزله. Apparently this is the noun *tuwwå*. The matter requires further inquiry. (In any case, note MH טוי.)

[130] As against *fåni* פני ("missing"), *LOT* III/2, 163, l. 65. A similar case of transferring a form from stem to stem can be found in the Ma'lūla dialect of Aramaic, in which there exist, on the

all these being originally simple, ungeminated forms.

d. Unusual geminations, whose etymological source is unclear, with long vowels are *abnēṭåtti* ובנטתי (Ex 7:5), *meṭåttək* מטתיך (SP Ex 7:28), *tēšūqåttək* תשוקתך (Gn 3:16), *tēšūqåttu* תשוקתו (Gn 4:7), *walkallūttimma* ולכלותם (Ex 32:12). Regarding the last example, see 3.2.3.4 n. 11.

e. In SH, as in TH, the gemination that has its origins in the element מן vanishes in the word *milmā:la* מלמעלה, but SH adds: *milmēṭå* מלמטה, *milfånək* מלפניך, *milbåd* מלבד, and similarly in SA *mibgēlål* מבגלל (*LOT* III/2, 184, l. 28). Since the word בגלל is pronounced *afgēlål*, the ב in the form מבגלל is evidently a trace of a geminated consonant; this gemination still survives in the form *millēbaddu* מלבדו (Dt 4:35). את ("with") geminates its ת in SH as well, yet not the form *ētimma* אתם. The word עני is pronounced *'anni*, but לעניך in Dt 15:11 is pronounced *lanyåk*; corresponding to וַאֲמִתּוֹ in Gn 24:27, SH has *wåmētu*. From this one learns that the loss of gemination does not depend on the consonant being vocalized with *šəwa*, as in the words מִלְמַעְלָה or הַמְבַקְשִׁים, which one encounters in TH. An especially interesting phenomenon is the loss of gemination in a few cases of determined nouns: *'arrəm* עָרִים/*'å:rəm* הערים (yet *'årrəm* — Gn 35:5!), *wåmma* ואמה (as in Ex 25:10) / *wåmå* והאמה (as in Ex 26:13) *'åbbot* עבות (Ex 28:14) / *å:bētot* העבותות. In addition to these and similar cases (see 2.2.3.4.1 n. 2; 2.5.13; 2.5.14), where the loss of gemination is sporadic;

f. one encounters permanent loss of gemination:

1. in the flexion of nouns in which a geminated consonant has lost its vowel (developing into *šəwa* in TH), as in *batkimma* = בְּתְכֶם contrasting with *bitti* = בִּתִּי; *tåfkimma* = טַפְּכֶם as against *tåbbimma* = טַפָּם, *atkimma* = אֶתְכֶם contrasting with *ittu* = אִתּוֹ, *damkimma* = דמכם contrasting with *dammu* = דמו, *kaltu* = כלתו as against *kallūtu* = כלותו; in TH — similar cases: חֻקְּכֶם, אֶשְׁכֶם.

2. in verbs: the formation of *Pi'el* and *Hitpa'el* forms "with simple second radical." In a number of verbs, such as אסף and כבד, the loss of the gemination has become so deeply rooted that Samaritan grammar recognized "heavy" stems with an ungeminated second radical.

> Note: In SA one encounters a substitution of gemination by replacing the first of the geminated consonants with ר as in דרשה (< דשה = the door), ארש (< אשש = the fundament, the root) pronounced *årəš*, in the plural *åråši* (constr.), and see *LOT* II, 484 b; III/2, 96, l. 26; 290, l. 40.

1.5.3.4. Syncope. The opposite of syllable splitting (1.4.2) — syncope — appears on occasion; yet in certain combinations it has become regular.

1. The pronominal suffix *-inna*, (*-imma*) הן-, (הם-) takes the form *kå'inna* כהן

---

model of *qtīl*, the passive participle of *Qal*, also participles of *Pa'el* (*qattīl*) and of *Af'el* (*aqtīl*). See A. Spitaler, *Grammatik*, 219, §187.

1.5 Sound Changes

when joining the preposition כ (כהן / כהנה Gn 41:19, a spelling found in SP), but when it joins the prepositions ב, ל the two syllables merge forming *bēnna, lēnna, bēmma, lēmma*, though both the ב and the ל take an *å* vowel with the other suffixes, as in *bånu, båkimma, låkimma, låmu* למו. The form *wmårēnna* ומראיהן (Lv 14:37) developed in this fashion, too. This phenomenon differs from that described in 1.4.6.1 and 1.4.7 in that the two vowels on either side of the א are different from one another. Thus, in SH the difference between בהם and בם is maintained, as follows: *bēmma/bimma*, as can be seen in Lv 22:25. Accordingly, the difference between *wēnna* והנה, and perhaps *wētbårråku* והתברכו as well, on the one hand, and *wimmu* ואמו or *winimma* והנם (Gn 47:1) on the other becomes comprehensible, for in the former pair *waw conjunctive* does not join the words directly, but rather by means of an intermediate vowel, originally *a*. This requires further study.

2. ונקית (Gn 24:8) is pronounced *wnēquttå*, which represents syncope in the combination of *wnēqo* (< *wnēquy*, cf. 1.4.4c) and *åttå* אתה, similar to MH מקדיש אתה > מקדישת (Epstein, *Introduction*, 1260). The reading of the transcription[131] ونيـقط, attests to the syncope in *wnēqi åttå*. Elision can also be found in *å:nūki* החנוכי (SP Nu 26:5) instead of **å'īnūki*, based on *īnok* חנוך.

3. The length of the vowel in the participial form of verbs II-w in SH and in SA, such as *ad'ṣåm* (*LOT* III/2, 240, l. 31, etc.), spelled דצעם, and also *qåm* (*LOT* III/2, 237, l. 155), spelled קעם, is puzzling, for both in the participial form and in the perfect a short vowel is to be expected, as evident, e.g., from *råm*, in Dt 2:10. Since the plural form is *ṣā'ēmən* צעמין (e.g., *LOT* III/2, 239, l. 12), and even in the language of the Pentateuch (Dt 28:7) one finds *aqqā'ēməm* (SP הק(א)מים), as of course in later SH and in SA, and alongside *qåm* there is also *qā'əm* — it seems reasonable to assume that *qåm* and similar forms are the result of syncope of two syllables into one, this also being the reason for the unusual vowel length. Clear evidence of such a process can be seen in **å'iliyyon* > *åliyyon* (Gn 40:17) העליון, **å'illən* > *ållən* האלין "these".[132] The very fact that SA displays two possible forms of the II-*w* participle (see *LOT* III/2, 181), one as in Hebrew and the other as usual in Aramaic, made the unusual syncope of *a'e* > *ā*[133] more common, and at any rate facilitated the introduction of this Aramaic participial form into the language of the Pentateuch.

---

[131] See *LOT* III/1, 12.

[132] Ben-Hayyim, *Studies*, 133 (= *LOT* III/2, 135, l. 26).

[133] The forms *qam* and *qā'əm*, spelled קעם, are equivalent in their use. This is evident not only from the interchange between versions cited in *LOT* III/2, 203, l. 8, but first of all from the fact that in the expression מן יכל קעם, which requires the participle, קעם is in one instance pronounced *qåm* (ibid., 177, l. 22) and in another *qā'əm* (ibid., 167, l. 20) with no disagreement about these readings, and also from the parallel דצעם בה ותהב (ibid., 240, l. 31), pronounced *adṣåm wtā'əb*. In translating the liturgical poems, I was not always able to employ the Hebrew form parallel to the Aramaic; see, e.g., ibid., 181, ll. 73, 75.

4. Whenever י, or the vowel *i* together with י, is repeated in a word, syncope takes place, as in *råttåyyå* רתאיה ("the merciful," *LOT* III/2, 109, l. 77) from **råttåyåyyå, måsāyyimma* מסעיהם from **måsā'īyyimma, fēšāyyimma* פשעיהם from **fēšā'īyyimma, anšiyyāyyimma* נשיאיהם from **anšiyyā'īyyimma, qaryā'i* קריאי from **qariyyā'i*. Hence, it is a simple matter to explain the form *råyyå* רָעָה (SP Gn 29:9 רע(י)ה) as often pronounced for *rā'iyya* (like TH בוכיה).[134] There is indication in Biblical Aramaic of a similar process in such words as מאניה from **ma'anayayyā*. This would appear to be the reason for such forms as *qaṭīl(at)* from III-*y* (and III-*y* roots declined like *qiṭl (qaṭl)* nouns, as in *nēbi* נביא: *nibyåk* נביאך, *wfidyu* ופדיו (SP Nu 18:16) from *fēdi < פדי;[135] in SA *biryå* בריה (< בְּרִיאָה; *LOT* III/2, 101, l. 20). This phenomenon is well known from MH traditions, as in קרית שמע = קריאת שמע. See also 4.3.7 note.

1.5.3.5 Metathesis of שמלה/שלמה is unknown in SP, which always[136] reads שמלה. SP does, however exhibit the metathesis of כשב / כבש, just as in the Masoretic text. In SH, however, it is not merely metathesis of consonants, but rather both words are equivalent in different patterns: כבש *kåbåš, kåbåša, kåbåšəm* / כשב *kēšəb, kišba, kišbəm*. The verb כבש in LSH and in SA appears in metathesis כשב (see "Book of Asaṭir," *Tarbiẓ* 14 (1943), 180 [Hebrew] and *Tībåt Mårqe*, 349, f. 272a).

The word *mēṭåṭṭək*, discussed in 1.5.3.3, may actually belong here with metathesis of gemination.

1.5.3.6 Neutralization of the distinction between final ם and ן has been demonstrated in Samaritan Aramaic literature, and this may possibly be the source of the SP spelling בנימים (= TH בנימין). At any rate this is the way in which the *usual* SA spelling of the plural suffix ־ים is to be interpreted. It is not a case of borrowing from Hebrew. Since there was no difference in pronunciation between ־ים and ־ין, spelling fluctuations occurred in SA, with ־ים eventually winning out, under the influence of the Pentateuchal spelling. Nowadays, of course, a distinction in pronunciation is made between –*n* (ין-) and –*m* (ים-).[137]

The contrast between voiced and unvoiced consonants is neutralized neither in SH nor in SA, but in the past such was the case in final position. Evi-

---

[134] 'Amram ben Isḥāq the High Priest and his brother צדקה ruled out the reading *råyyå* when I suggested it to them on November 25, 1969.

[135] Note: as against the nouns פדיון (פדיום) and פִּדְיָם in TH, there are three in SH: *fidyon, fi'dwīm*, and *fēdi (Nu 18:16) of the pattern of שבי.

[136] The word בשלמתו at Dt 24:13 in von Gall *(Pentateuch)* is surely a typographical error, since no variant of בשלמתו is found in any manuscript, and the latter alone is found in all other places.

[137] The fluctuation of אביו and אבוי in the spelling of the noun אב with the 3rd masc. sing. pronominal suffix in ST and other Samaritan Aramaic texts originates in the fact that both diphthongs *uy* and *aw* contract to *ō*. Cf. *Tībåt Mārqe*, 17.

dence of this is בלחוד = בלות in SA (*LOT* II, 458), יח — the name of the letter י (ibid., 478), תאף — the name of the letter ת (op. cit., 606), הב = אף ("give", *LOT* II, 606) לב = לף ("heart", *Tībåt Mårqe* 101, f. 53b).

In the last words cited above the older pronunciation was of a fricative ב (with which ו then merged); today a fricative פ is pronounced.

MORPHOLOGY

2. VERB

2.0 Preliminaries

2.0.1 The analysis of a Hebrew word into its basic structural components requires distinguishing between three of the smallest morphological units, i. e., three kinds of morphemes — the root, the base, and the formative.

The Root, in Hebrew, as in the other Semitic languages, is a sequence of consonants only, which maintains a semantic link, be it in the most general way, in a word family, e.g., תַּפְקִיד, מִפְקָדָה, פְּקֻדָּה, פּוֹקֵד, פְּקַד, פֶּקֶד, פָּקַד and so on, the common denominator of which being the consonantal sequence פק״ד. The usual, commonly found root in Hebrew consists of three consonants, though traces remain of roots of less than three consonants, as there are roots of four consonants — which are multiplying in modern Hebrew — and even a few of five consonants. The Hebrew verb cannot be derived from a root of less than three consonants; thus, if it is derived from a word of a single consonant (e.g., זה) or of two consonants (e.g., אָח, אָד), the language provides the missing consonants in various ways. זה״י is the root of זֶהֶה,¹ זִהָה; the sequence אח״י is the root of מְאַחֶה, אִחָה; אד״י or אי״ד are the roots of אָדָה, אִיֵּד, etc. The question of whether the roots of such verbs as קָם, דָּן are biradical or triradical, in which case one consonant "weakened," is irrelevant to a description of the Hebrew language in historical times.

Regarding Hebrew structure in general and the verb in particular, it is important to know whether the radicals are pronounced in all derived or declined forms, or whether some of them vanish in various forms without the consequent weakening of the link between those forms and the other words and forms derived from the same root. It is, thus, according to the nature of the structure of the root that all Hebrew roots are customarily divided into two groups known as classes: (a) the sound class and (b) the weak class.² In

---

[1] This new root which was created so as to serve a clearly technical purpose has already been used in poetry, where it has developed a new verbal stem *Hif'il*: נוֹפְךָ חֲרוּת בְּנוֹף הָאָרֶץ/בְּקַעְקַע עֲלֵי חֶזֶה/ שִׁבְעָים תַּחֲלִיף פְּנֵיהָ אָרֶץ/עֲלֵי גוּפָהּ אוֹתְךָ נַזְהֶה (Zerubavel Gilead, *Zemirot Yeruqot* (Tel-Aviv, 1972–3, 5 [Hebrew]).

[2] The traditional Hebrew term is עלולים (pl.) which means "weak," "sick." Yosef Qimḥi called

2.0 Preliminaries

accordance with the position of the weakness in the root, represented by the consonants פע"ל, it is customary to distinguish the following classes: פ"א, פ"י-פ"ו, פ"נ, ע"א, ע"י-ע"ו, ל"י, ל"א. In other words: a פ"א root means that the root has an initial א, whereas a ל"א root is one which has a final א — the א being "weakened," and in this way the names of the other subtypes are to be interpreted. A unique subtype — ע"ע — is made up of those roots whose second and third consonants are the same. These are positioned between the sound roots and the weak ones. This root classification fits Jewish Hebrew, whereas Samaritan Hebrew requires some additional distinctions. See also 2.15.

2.0.2 Base. A morphological analysis of Hebrew cannot, however, restrict itself to the concept of a root, for there are some words in Hebrew which, after a complete analysis, do not reveal a root as described in the previous paragraph, i.e., a sequence of consonants alone, but rather a sequence of consonants and vowels resembling the "root" in Indo-European linguistics. This phenomenon is rare in Biblical Hebrew, referring in it first and foremost to words borrowed from a non-Semitic language. Yet it is found also in authentic Hebrew words, especially those ending in the relative suffix or in ה *locale*. The words שאולי or המורשתי are, thus, not derived from the roots שא"ל or יר"ש respectively, but rather from the words שָׁאוּל, [גַּת] מוֹרֶשֶׁת. The element שָׁאוּל or מוֹרֶשֶׁת in the aforementioned words is to be called "a base."[3] The base can be (a) an independent word in the language, like those adduced *above*; (b) a sequence of consonants and vowels having no independent existence in the language, such as: יְמָן* in the word יְמִנִי, רָאשׁ* in the word רָאשִׁי, מִצְר* in the word מִצְרִי, or יְהוּד[4]* in the word יְהוּדִי; (c) an old, inherited element, as in the aforesaid examples; (d) borrowed elements, such as אַבְרֵךְ, הֵיכָל, or אַשָּׁף, which are incapable of further analysis. In Biblical Hebrew, the source of all the above examples, this system exists both theoretically and practically, yet the practice is scarce when compared with derivation from roots. In post-biblical and especially in modern Hebrew, words built up from a base have become common not only as a result of word borrowing, such as the word פִּנְקָס, from which פִּנְקְסָן, פִּנְקְסָנוּת, and פִּנְקָסוֹן are

---

them מְחֻלִּים (*Sefer Zikkaron*, 39), the opposite of שְׁלֵמִים, which is to be interpreted as "healthy," "strong."

[3] This term is used here as a translation of נטע, which I have adduced from the ancient grammatical literature of the Masoretes (see Baer–Strack, *Dikduke Ha-Teamim*, 35, §36). This concept of "root" is a very early one in Hebrew linguistics, even preceding the concept of a root as a sequence of consonants alone. Such a root is one of the fundamentals of Saʿadia Gaʾon's grammatical hypothesis (in his Arabic *ʾaṣl*), as I have already noted in my article "Theory of Vowels," 91 (The matter has been treated at length in Esther Goldenberg's profound research paper, "Studies in R. Saʿadia Gaʾon's Egron," *Lěšonénu* 37 [1972–73], 117ff., 275ff. [Hebrew]).

[4] This spelling is indeed found in Hebrew inscriptions and in the Aramaic part of the Bible; in the Hebrew part only וַיְהָד (Jos 19:45). In fact even in Biblical Hebrew יהודי is not related to the place name יהוד but to the the name of the tribe and land יהודה.

derived, but also from words derived from authentic Hebrew words, such as מְחִירוֹן which is to be analysed into the base מְחִיר and the formative וֹן-, for otherwise the meaning of מְחִיר "price" would not be maintained in the word מְחִירוֹן.

Living Hebrew has undergone shifts from root + formative derivation to base + formative derivation and *vice versa*. This can be detected in BH as well. Building words from base and formative is not possible within the framework of the Hebrew verb.[5] Therefore, in the case of the verb, the unique characteristic of Semitic language structure — (consonantal) root and formative — has been maintained strictly over the generations.

2.0.3 Formative. From our discussion it is clear that one cannot create a word from the root alone (a consonant is not able to serve as a syllable peak in Hebrew); one needs an element to turn the root into a form — a formative. A base, too, if it is not an independent word in Hebrew, has need of a formative to turn it into a word. The formatives which combine with roots to create real words are known as patterns, such as פֹּעַל, פָּעַל, פָּעוּל, פָּעִיל, and מִפְעָל, where the letters פע״ל represent any root. A pattern is thus (a phoneme or) a group of phonemes intermeshing with a root, i.e., the radicals and formative phonemes intermesh with one another. In contrast, the formatives which combine with bases consist always in a phoneme or a sequence of phonemes added on after the bases (suffixes) or before them (prefixes), but neither intermesh with them nor are inserted into them (infixes).

2.0.4 A group of interrelated patterns can be distinguished in Hebrew: if one of these patterns exists in the language, the others exist automatically as well, whenever the speaker needs them. For instance, when you say סֵפֶר, then סִפְרְךָ, סְפָרַי, etc., exist as well, and when you say פָּקַד, then פְּקַדְתִּי, אֶפְקֹד, etc., also exist. This dependence is called inflection (declension in the case of nouns; conjugation in the case of verbs). The lexical item is one of these patterns, and the others are included in it. On the other hand, there is a group of patterns not especially interrelated, though the link between them is completely clear, e.g., אֹכֶל, מַאֲכָל, מַאֲכֶלֶת, אָכְלָן or מַעֲבָר, תְּבוּרָה, עֲבֵרָה, — these are all words derived from the roots אכ״ל and עב״ר respectively; the existence of one of these in the language does not automatically guarantee the existence of another — it merely determines a certain, quite general, semantic link to the root. This dependence is generally called *derivation*. Yet, in fact, in a language like Hebrew the difference between inflection and derivation is not as sharp as is usually assumed.

---

[5] The proposal made many years ago to adopt "international" verbs into Hebrew in accordance with this principle, such as דִּיפְרֶנְצְיָה; סוּלְפוֹנֵן (N. Thun, "The Adaptation of International Loan-Word Verbs in Hebrew" [Hebrew], *Lĕšonénu* 3 [1931], 167–169), with the "international" verb serving as a base, was, not surprisingly, rejected.

On the contrary, there are stages of transition between these two types of dependence, which make the difference between inflection and derivation a relative one, similar to the relative nature of differences in other linguistic fields, such as the difference between consonants and vowels. This situation is particularly noticeable in the realm of the verb.

2.0.5 Verb patterns are known to be arranged in a number of comprehensive categories, each category of especially closely linked patterns being called a stem. Within the range of a derived stem, i.e., any verb stem other than the "ground stem" *(Qal)*, one encounters a dependence which may be termed a conjugation, viz., if one form is given, the other are predictable. As far as the *Qal* stem is concerned, this automatic nature is limited, viz., the vowel system of its constituents is no more interdependent. For instance: on the one hand, לִרְכֹּב / לוֹבֵשׁ – יִלְבַּשׁ – (לָבַשׁ) לָבֵשׁ yet also, גָּדֵל – יִגְדַּל – גָּדַל; on the other, שׁוֹמֵר – יִשְׁמֹר – שָׁמַר יִשְׁכַּב – לִשְׁכַּב / יִרְכַּב. Similarly, the relationship of *Pi'el* to *Pu'al* and of *Hof'al* to *Hif'il* is automatic, unlike the relationship of *Nif'al* to *Qal*. There exists a weaker link, though still of reasonable strength, between the *Hif'il* and *Qal* in many verbs. As for nominal forms: a similarly automatic relationship exists in patterns with possessive suffixes such as ראשך, ראשי, whereas there is only a high degree of probability in the dependence of number, for in many nominal forms the plural form is not automatically derivable from the singular or *vice versa*, though the dependence of singular and plural (including dual) patterns is customarily classified as a declension, despite this.

> Note: The original sense of the term בִּנְיָן (stem) was the equivalent of that of the term מִשְׁקָל (pattern), although with the passage of time בנין became associated with one specific pattern category, so that it is now possible to say, for example, that in the *Qal* stem there occur three patterns: פָּקַד, חָפֵץ, יָכֹל.

2.0.6 It is, thus, best to define the situation in Hebrew as follows: in word-formation, derivation is the general feature, while conjugation is but a subdivision of it. For this reason, not all types of behavior included in the concept of inflection as typical of the grammar of an Indo-European language may be applied to a language such as Hebrew. The distinction between derivation as against inflection is not one specifically between noun and verb forms or even between the patterns contained in the domain of a certain verbal stem and the verbal stems themselves. It should be noted that patterns including the expression of persons, whether nominal or verbal in nature, do relate to one another automatically, and within the realm of the verb this relationship goes even further. The verb, however, has a property the nominal form lacks: even where there is no real dependence of "conjugation" between verbal stems, their relationship to one another is strong, probably also because of the limited number of stems in comparison with the very large number of nominal patterns, so that with any given root, one may easily expect to encounter the existence and use of forms which may be derived from that root. Such ease is already not to be found outside the realm of the verb. Thus, the concept of root is often viewed as involving that of verb, as may be seen from the traditional terms: למ"ד הפעל, פ"א הפעל, and so on. All in all, it seems that from a morphological point of view, it would not be amiss but rather, on the contrary, it would be advantageous to include all the stems relevant to a given root and to ignore the fact that on occasion the semantic relationships between the stems are no longer valid (or, better yet, are no longer apparent to each and every speaker). This is what is properly done by a dictionary: it classifies, for example, the verb נכנס under the heading of כנס, though for many the semantic connection is obscure, and a more profound knowledge of the language is necessary in order to discern it.

This rigidity of the Hebrew verb and its adherence to the ancient structure it inherited from Proto-Semitic affect the relationships between the various Hebrew traditions as well. Indeed, in the verbal conjugation the affinity of SH to those of Tiberian Hebrew and other Hebrew traditions is more apparent than in other areas of word-formation.

2.0.7 Grammar. In Tiberian BH there are to be found seven common stems of the triradical verbal root, as well as at least eight rare stems considered to be vestiges of stems commonplace in very early times, such as: *Pōʿel*: לְמִשְׁפָּטִי, *Hitpāʿel*: הִתְפָּקְדוּ; *Nitpaʿel*: נִכַּפֵּר, passive of *Qal*. The seven common stems arranged in accordance with their interdependence are: *Qal-Nifʿal; Piʿel-Puʿal-Hitpaʿel; Hifʿil-Hofʿal*. Grammarians of MH or of an even later Hebrew omit almost all the rare Biblical stems, some omitting the perfect and imperfect tenses of *Puʿal* and adding to them the *Nufʿal, Pāʿel, Nitpāʿel, Nittafʿal*. The grammar of BH recognizes ten or eight root classes[6] in connection with the triradical verb and to them adds classes of four and five consonants. The grammar of MH preserves the same classes, whatever changes taking place in them concerning transfers from one class to another or mixing classes. As for tenses,[7] BH grammar distinguishes the perfect, the imperfect, the shortened imperfect, the lengthened imperfect, the converted perfect, the converted imperfect and also the imperative mood, while the grammar of MH recognizes only perfect,

---

[6] See above 2.0.1. To the classes mentioned there a mixture of types must be added; ten — if פ"י and פ"י, ע"ו and ע"י are listed separately.

[7] By "tenses" I refer to the morphological aspect without going at all into the question of the function of these forms, and so it also includes "moods" (jussive, cohortative, etc.) — i.e., the finite verb. See in detail 2.9.

imperfect and imperative. With regard to verbal nominal forms, BH grammar recognizes (a) two *Qal* participles (active and passive) and a single participle per stem for all the other stems; (b) two infinitives[8] per stem (absolute and construct). MH, too, which has no infinitive absolute, does possess two nominal forms denoting an action, such as: פָּעוּל - לְפָעַל - פְּעִילָה - לִפְעֹל. In all of these, SH has its own features.

2.0.8 Stem. Samaritan grammar recognizes[9]: (1) *light (=Qal)* of two types (a) with no vowel between the first and second radicals in the imperfect, (b) with a vowel between the first and second radicals in the imperfect; (2) *heavy (=Pi'el)* of four types: (a) with a geminated second radical; (b) with a simple second radical (which has a *sākin layin*, a quiescent "letter"); (c) a quadriradical root (such as כונן, כלכל); (d) with an added ה, i.e., *Hif'il*; (3) *Nif'al* of two types: (a) a simple form, (b) with a geminated second radical; (4) *Hitpa'el*. Counting each type separately, there are nine stems. While it is impossible to say that all verb features occurring in the Samaritan Pentateuchal reading can be completely classified in this set of verb stems, exceptions are indeed rare. It should be noted that no mention has been made of either *Pu'al* or *Hof'al*, Samaritan Hebrew having progressed a step beyond MH in this respect. It is also to be noted that in defining the concept of **heavy**, it has been said that **heavy** means those verbs which have more than three consonants, i.e., that a geminated consonant is considered two consonants, as is the compensation for a lack of such doubling, and that the quadriradical root type is not an independent linguistic division.

The SH verbal stems shall be named in accordance with the names customary in common Hebrew grammar, while those unique in SH will be denoted by means of attributes taken from Samaritan linguistics or by means of letters, for the sake of brevity, as follows: *Qal*; *Qal B* (with a vowel between the first and the second radical in the imperfect); *Hif'il*; *Pi'el*; *Pi'el B* ("with simple second radical"); *Nif'al*; *Nif'al B* ("with geminated second radical"); *Hitpa'el*; *Hitpa'el B* ("with simple second radical"). The quadriradical roots are included in *Pi'el* in all respects. This stem order will be maintained throughout our discussion of the verb; for the exception, see above 0.18.

2.0.9 Class. The phonetic merging of ע״הח with א in SH in most word positions raised the number of "weak roots" in SH. Samaritan grammar recognizes twelve

---

[8] I make no distinction between "infinitive" and "gerund" (=*nomen actionis*); such a distinction is valid neither in Biblical Hebrew nor, in my opinion, in modern Hebrew (see my "Sfire," 250, n. 12. By "two infinitives" I am deliberately ignoring features such as a third infinitive like למסע, ליראה, etc. in Biblical Hebrew, see 2.14.1. Similarly, it should be recalled that two separate infinitives are not morphologically distinguishable in every stem; see 2.14.2.

[9] See *LOT* I, 71, 85, 99, 101, 201, 205, 207, 209.

classes, as follows: the "sound" class, פ"א, פ"ה, פ"י, פנ"ל, ע"ו, ע"י, ע"ע, ל"א, ל"י. The quadriradical roots are not an independent root type, for they are included in the *heavy* stem (see above); the פ"י class includes פ"ו verbs as well, and there are instances where certain verbs in which the second radical is geminated, i.e., they behave like פ"נ (see 2.4.8). It should be noted that roots with ח or ע are not included in the weak root type, Samaritan grammar differentiating between א and ה, on the one hand, and ח and ע, on the other,[10] but their merging with א in most word positions has left an impression on word structure, and so the SH verb must be studied, with regard to the behavior of ח and ע, insofar as they occur in first, second, or third radical position.

2.0.10 Samaritan grammar distinguishes between tenses and time. Regarding the latter it recognizes the perfect, the present, the imperfect, and "perpetual" ("at all times"), yet the imperfect, and imperative have the same time, while the present, the imperfect, and the "perpetual" have the same form.[11] Regarding "tenses" Samaritan grammar recognizes the perfect, the imperfect, the converted perfect and the converted imperfect, as well as the imperative; the shortened and lengthened imperfect do not constitute separate and independent categories. In fact, from a morphological viewpoint there is no converted perfect in SH, but there is from a semantic viewpoint, for there is no difference between it and the regular perfect — neither in stress nor in vowel pattern. Wherever the converted imperfect exists, the difference between it and the regular imperfect is noticeable in a number of ways, yet not by the doubling of the preformatives ית"ן. For there is no difference whatsoever between *waw consecutive* and *waw conjunctive* in SH,[12] like the Hebrew of the Hexapla. The morphological realization of the shortened imperfect, too, is unlike its realization in TH because of the changes in the vowel system (see 2.9).

2.0.11 One of the most complex matters in the SH verb system is that of the participle. The *Hif'il* and *Hitpa'el* each have a single participial form; the *Pi'el* and *Nif'al* each have two participial forms; the *Qal* has six forms of the active participle, one of which is equivalent to the passive participle. Similarly, Samaritan Aramaic has two forms of the active participle and a single passive participial form.

---

[10] See, e.g., *LOT* I, 55 and also above 1.1.8.2.

[11] See *LOT* I, 65.

[12] This feature of SH is by no means an innovation of recent generations; it is early, a fact which may be deduced also from a 13th century transliteration such as *wtqb* (*LOT* II, 408, l. 7) — وتقوت, *wtmwt* (ibid. 411, l. 7) — وتردية, *wtrdymh* (ibid. 409, l. 3) — وتردية, in all of which the ת is plosive, though in the same source ת is generally fricative after vowels. A plosive ת in nominal forms is certainly not evidence of doubling, but rather the result of the addition of a consonantal conjuctive *waw* to the nominal form (and to the verb).

2.0.12 In contrast, the distinction between the form of the infinitive absolute and the infinitive construct has almost completely vanished in SH; this is evident from the Samaritan Pentateuch as well.[13] In places where the form was retained in SP, it is not always clear whether the Samaritan tradition viewed it as a true infinitive form. However, since the syntactic construction of infinitive + a finite verb form generally exists in SP as well, the awareness of the infinitive absolute was not lost in this tradition as demonstrated by the Aramaic and Arabic translations of various verses, which view one of the members of this construction as an infinitive. Abū Isḥāq, the grammarian, commenting on the form שמור in Dt 5:12, says that it is an imperative occurring in the form of an infinitive and adds: "And this applies as well to every one of the imperatives occurring in one of the forms of an infinitive,"[14] while Elʿazar ben Pinḥas, the Priest, who abridged Abū Isḥāq's grammar, writes explicitly that the infinitive "has a number of patterns, the most common of which — with all verbs — occurs in the form of the perfect,"[15] yet from the example בהפרידו (Dt 32:8) it would seem as if he did not distinguish between infinitive absolute and construct.

2.0.13 The verb in the perfect ends with the following afformatives:

	singular	plural
1st	ti	nu
2nd masc.	tå	timma
2nd fem.	ti	tən
3rd masc.	--	u
3rd fem.	a/å(åt)	u

There are two prominent differences between SH and TH and other Hebrew dialects: (a) the merging of the 1st sing. and 2nd fem. sing. afformatives and (b) the afformatives in the 2nd masc. pl.

There are known to be over twenty occurrences in the MT where the *kətiv* of the 2nd fem. sing. is תי, though the *qəre* is תְּ (such as זָכַרְתִּי in Ezek 16:22). Occasionally, the *qəre* does not differ from the *kətiv*, such as in Jud 5:7 שַׁקַּמְתִּי, שָׁבַרְתִּי in Jer 2:20, etc., as the traditional interpretation did not view them as 2nd fem. sing. forms. Such cases are more common in the Dead Sea Scrolls, as in 1QIsaᵃ, but there, too, this afformative is not the rule, as it is in SH and in SA.[16] The very fact that this afformative is found in Aramaic while forgotten in Jewish Hebrew raises the possibility that it may be the result of Aramaic influ-

---

[13] Instead of היו הלוך וחסור (Gn 8:5), the SP reads היו הלכו וחסרו, and similarly elsewhere; see Gesenius, *De Pentateuchi samaritanae origine*, 28.
[14] See *LOT* I, 8.
[15] See *LOT* I, 180.
[16] Kutscher, *Isaiah Scroll*, 142–143.

ence over SH. This, however, cannot be proved, the very opposite seeming more likely since the afformative תי in Tiberian Hebrew, both when merely written and also when read, is undoubtedly of early origin there, from before the shortening and eventual omission of final vowels, as whenever it occurred within the word — in forms with object afformatives like לִבַּבְתִּנִי in Cant 4:9, or וּנְתַתִּיהוּ in Ezek 16:19 — it was not omitted at all. The traces of תי in TH originate in early manuscripts reflecting the ancient pronunciation, which survived in SH. It seems likely that Aramaic, being the vernacular of the Samaritans, helped to maintain that which they had inherited from early Hebrew.

The gemination of the consonant in the 2nd. masc. pl. afformative, together with the lack of such doubling in the corresponding fem. form, parallels the treatment of independent personal pronouns and pronominal suffixes. Here, too, the form created by analogy (the masc. pl.) survives, while the form in which the doubling originated (the fem. pl.) eventually lost its doubling because of the omission of the final vowel of the ending.

Aramaic, such as that depicted by the vowel pointing in the Bible, in which there occurs a afformative ־ה to denote the 3rd fem. pl., makes it all the more likely that this afformative — a survival of Proto Semitic — exists in Hebrew in a few biblical verses, especially since the *qəre* would correct this and have us read the usual form, which is not differentiated from its masculine counterpart. For example, שפכה (Dt 21:7 — *kətiv*) — שָׁפְכוּ (*qəre*); נצתה (Jer 2:15 *kətiv*) — נִצְּתוּ (*qəre*); and, similarly, צעדה (Gn 49:22), קמה (1 Sa 4:15). This afformative is more common in the Dead Sea Scrolls than in TH,[17] and so it is somewhat surprising to find that SP ignores it in Gn 49:22, reading צעירי, and in Dt 21:7, reading שפכו with the *qəre*. Nevertheless, this afformative has been preserved in SH as well: *kåbåda* כבדה (Gn 48:10; the Jewish version is כבדו!), *kātta* כהתה (Dt 34:7). Note that in both of these verses the subject is dual (see 4.5.7 note). Modern Samaritans merely view this afformative as denoting the 3rd fem. sing., and the aforementioned verses, as lacking congruence between subject and predicate.

2.0.14 The preformatives of the verb in the imperfect are as follows:

	singular	plural
1st	*v*	*nv*
2nd masc.	*tv*	*tv…u*
2nd fem.	*tv…i,(ən)*	*tv…inna,(na)*
3rd masc.	*yv*	*yv…u*
3rd fem.	*tv*	*tv…inna,(na)*

---

[17] See Kutscher, *Isaiah Scroll*, 144. Bergsträsser (*Grammatik* II, 15) lists, I believe, all the places in the Bible where this afformative is considered a 3rd fem. pl. afformative, but also considers the possibility that these verses lack syntactical congruence.

2.0 Preliminaries

The symbol "v" represents the vowels u å a e i — long in open syllables, short in closed ones — the quality of which is linked to the root structure and to the verbal stem (e.g., yifqåd, yallən, yåšəm, yēqom, tūqåd), for which see the conjugations of the various root classes.

The 2nd and 3rd fem. pl. forms still show the same markers as those used in TH, e.g., תמצאנה (SP *plene* in Dt 31:21): *timṣåna*; ותקראנה (SP Nu 25:2): *wtiqrāna*, but the usual form resembles that in ותקרבנה *wtiqråbinna* (Nu 27:1). Since the 2nd and 3rd fem. pl. were generally expressed in post-BH by means of 2nd and 3rd masc. pl. forms, the feminine endings may have become somewhat obscure, the doubling of the *nun* resulted in this case from analogy to forms with object suffixes.

2.1 Strong Verb

2.1.1 Qal

2.1.1.0 In TH there are three clearly distinct verb types: (a) in vowel quality in the perfect and in the imperfect, (b) in the relationship of those vowels to one another, (c) and in the form of the participle. They are as follows: (1) qatal : yiqtol : qotel (like פָּקַד); (2) qatel : yiqtal : qatel (like גָּדֵל); (3) qatol : yiqtal : qatol (like קָטֹן). The system qatal : yiqtel : qotel has not been adequately preserved in the strong verb,[18] but is clearly visible in the verb נתן and in the פ״י class.

The rules of comparative grammar lead to the assumption that the original relationship of the perfect and imperfect in the above mentioned forms of Hebrew was: (1) qatala : yaqtulu (as in Arabic: قَتَلَ); (2) qatila : yiqtalu[19] (as in Arabic: فَرِحَ); (3) qatula : yaqtulu[20] (as in Arabic: حَسُنَ), and in the system which

---

[18] יֶאְטַם in Ps 58:5 and וְיַאֲמֵץ in Ps 27:14; 31:25 can be considered certain testimony to the existence of this type, since they have no *Hifʿil* perfect forms. J. Barth ("Vergleichende Studien: 3. Das i-Imperfect im Nordsemitischen," *ZDMG* 43[1889], 179ff.) listed additional cases which are less certain.

[19] The feature was first mentioned by J. Barth in his article in "Zur vergleichenden semitischen Grammatik," *ZDMG* 48 (1894), pp. 4–6, and therefore it is named after him: the Barth Rule. The originality of the [i] vowel in the preformatives of the verb with the [a] vowel following its second root consonant is well demonstrated in Hebrew by such forms as יֵבוֹשׁ < *yibāš* in contrast to יָקוּם *yaqūm*, and in Ugaritic (see H. L. Ginsberg, "Addenda to the Epic of בעל-אלאין," *Tarbiz* 4 [1933], 382 [Hebrew]), where one finds אֶשְׁאַל (=אֶשְׁאָל), אֶמְחַץ (= אֲמַחֵץ) on the one hand, and אֱמֶת (=אָמוּת), אֵרֵד (=אָרֵד), on the other. In Classical Arabic, the preformative vowel of imperfect forms with an [a] vowel following their second radical is the same as that of the other types. But both in grammatical literature and in various Arabic dialects, relics of the process *(taltala)* have been preserved; see C. Rabin, *Ancient West-Arabian* (London, 1951), 61–63, and also A. Bloch, "The Vowels of the Imperfect Preformatives in the Old Dialects of Arabic", *ZDMG* 117 (1967), 122ff., stressing that this feature is a very early heritage in Arabic, and not an innovation from external sources. This indeed seems to be so.

[20] Hebrew no longer has any trace of this mode, for the יִפְעַל form has attracted this type of

was not quite preserved: (4) qatala: yaqtilu (cf. the Arabic verb ضَرَبَ).

2.1.1.0.1 It is likely that the difference in vowel quality originally reflected a difference in meaning and in function, either active/stative or transitive/intransitive. In historical Hebrew, however, even in TH which maintains the differences between the aforesaid forms more than any other tradition, there is no longer any difference in meaning or in function linked with the quality of the vowel following the second radical. This is noticeable especially with regard to the possibility of a given verb having two different forms, such as לוֹבֵשׁ : יִלְבַּשׁ : לָבֵשׁ : or חָפֵץ : יַחְפֹּץ : יַחְפֵּץ. The verbs with *ṣere* or *ḥolem* following their second radical in the perfect originally expressed a state, rather than an action, as demonstrated in Hebrew by the fact that their participial forms are basically the same as the form of their perfect; see, e.g., the *Nif'al* stem or the ע״י class, which is made up mainly of stative verbs.

> Note: Since the difference in the vowel of the second radical is in historical Hebrew no longer linked with the function, the meaning, or the syntax of the verb, and the terms "transitive" and "intransitive," "action" and "state" no longer relate to the morphological difference between the verbs, it has become customary to designate the verbs with the *pataḥ* following the second radical "active" (*activa*) and those with *ṣere* or *ḥolem* following the second radical "stative" (*stativa*). When necessary, we shall use these terms.

2.1.1.0.2 In the Babylonian tradition of Hebrew, verbal forms not conforming to the pattern *qaṭal : yiqṭol* are few, even in the biblical language. In this tradition one encounters פָּעַל even where TH still has פָּעֵל.²¹ In early manuscripts of MH tradition vocalized in either the Babylonian or the Tiberian system, one finds no perfect pattern פָּעֵל, but rather פָּעַל; imperfect spellings such as ילמוד²² and participial למד, pl. למדים (i.e., לְמֵדִים) abound. These indicate that the series (1) and (2) (see 2.1.1) were no longer valid. Undeniable evidence of this in MH is the abundance of the participial form פָּעֵל, even in those verbs occurring in TH only in the פּוֹעֵל pattern.²³

2.1.1.0.3 The reasons that these verb types lost their unique meanings in historical Hebrew and their intermingling are phonological: (a) when stressed [i]

---

verb, too, the common denominator being the expression of intransitiveness or state, and so קָטֹנְתִּי exists alongside וַתִּקְטַן.

²¹ See Yeivin, *Babylonian Vocalization*, 435ff.: פָּעֵל exists only in pause. In contrast, in the imperfect (ibid., 450) there is no sharp trend towards יִפְעַל but rather vacillation.

²² Thus, already in the Dead Sea Scrolls. See Kutscher, *Isaiah Scroll*, 262.

²³ See Epstein, *Introduction*, 1256ff.

2.1 Strong Verb

in a closed syllable became [a] (Philippi's Law) and such forms as *labišti (cf. שְׁאֵלְתִּיהוּ, Jud 13:6) came to be pronounced לְבַשְׁתִּי, as did all the forms with *i* in such conditions — these forms, which were frequent, influenced others where those conditions did not apply, such as, e.g., *labištem > לְבַשְׁתֶּם or לְבַשׁ (alongside phonological לְבֵשׁ). For this reason, the strong verb imperfect pattern *yiqtel* (< *yaqtil*) ceased almost entirely to exist; (b) the pharyngeals הח"ע affected the short vowels [i, u] preceding them, turning them into [a], thus effecting the merger of all imperfect forms of verbs with a pharyngeal third radical — as יִפְעַל. In other words, in verbs with a pharyngeal third radical the difference between יִפְעַל : פָּעֵל and יִפְעַל : פָּעַל ceased to exist.

Once the morphological difference was obscured, the language found other means (verb stems) to render the necessary differences in function and in meaning. When it was no longer possible to link semantic differences to vocalic ones, the reason for maintaining the differences ceased to exist, and so the differences themselves became superfluous.

2.1.1.0.4 SH fits well into the withdrawal process of these verb types and their merger into a single type, as it — relative to the other Hebrew traditions — has an additional reason for the obscuring of the differences: the changing of the originally short *u* vowel into a front vowel, sometimes *ā/a* and at other times *i* (see 1.5.2.3). This led to the merger that produced results different from the general trend of the other traditions, for in SH there was no possibility of יִלְמַד being replaced by יִלְמֹד; on the contrary, *yifqod (< *yaqtul*) had to become *yifqåd*. Nevertheless, a trace of the early variety survived in SH as well, and the change of vowels following the second radical led to the creation of alternate types according to the vowel of the first radical as well — in the perfect. Thus, SH has the dominant type *fåqåd: yifqåd*, and with it in the perfect, though not in all persons, the types *fåqəd, fēqəd, fēqåd*. It must be recalled that also in verbs tending toward the dominant type in almost all their forms, sometimes *i/e* is found after the second radical in some form or another (see 2.1.1.2), and there is no way to decide whether *i/e* preserve an early state or were generated by the conditions of the Samaritan tradition (see, e.g., 2.10.10). At any rate, it is to be noted that SH may make use of the vocalic difference to vary the meaning of a given verb such as שרץ: when the subject is the water, the forms are *wšårås* (Ex 7:28), *šåråṣu* (Gn1:21), whereas when the subject is a living creature, the form *šērēṣu* (Gn 8:17) is used (but the imperfect of both is the same: *yišrēṣu*).

2.1.1.1 Perfect. The following is an example of the conjugation of the perfect:

	singular	plural
1st	fåqådti פקדתי	fåqådnu פקדנו
2nd masc.	fåqådtå פקדת	fåqådtimma פקדתם
2nd fem.	fåqådti פקדת	fåqådtən פקדתן
3rd masc.	fåqåd פקד	fåqådu פקדו
3rd fem.	fåqådå/a פקדה	fåqådu פקדו

2.1.1.2 Traces of the *fåqəd* type of strong verb appear mainly in the 3rd masc. sing.: *wdåbəq* ודבק, *šåkən* שכן (but *wšåkånti*!), *šåləm* שלם, *gånibtā* גנבת (Gn 31:30). These verbs are identical in form with *Pi'el B*, (see 2.1.3.5) and they may have been thought to be forms of that stem. On occasion it is impossible to decide whether such forms belong to the perfect or to the participle (a nominal form), as, e.g., *šåkəb* (Gn 26:10) שכב, *kåbəd* (Gn 12:10) כבד, for the common form of the latter takes the pattern *fåqåd*, and in this the translations disagree as well.

2.1.1.3 The active and passive 3rd masc. sing. forms of the *fēqəd* type, such as *qēṣəf* קצף, *wgēbər* וגבר, *gēbēru* גברו, *wšērēṣu* וישרצו, can only be distinguished from one another (see 2.10.10) by means of their context; the *e* vowel following the first radical may have been generated with the aid of the passive. At any rate, *fēqəd* should apparently be interpreted as a variant of *fåqəd*. Though the vowel of the first radical assimilated to that of the second radical, it is impossible to determine the conditions under which this assimilation took place because of the scarcity of vestiges: it may even have originally been sporadic. A similar case of assimilation in TH is the prefix vowel of the פ"י verb type; see 2.9.8.

2.1.1.4 Forms such as *wrēbåṣu* ורבצו, *wrēgåmē'u* ורגמהו are vestiges of the *fēqåd* type, as is perhaps also *rēbåṣ* in Gn 49:9. The latter has in fact been classified as a participle, as it undoubtedly is in Gn 49:14 and in Ex 23:5, and as the Arabic and Aramaic translations have it in Gn 49:9 as well. It must not be overlooked that verbs with *waw consecutive* are often semantically an imperative (like the ורגמהו above) and this vowel pattern matches that of the imperative.

2.1.1.5 The 3rd fem. sing. ending *āt* has been preserved in a few verbs, but the strong verb has no example of this; see 2.2.1.1.1.

2.1.1.6 Imperfect. The strong verb shows no sign of a morphological distinction between the regular imperfect and the "consecutive" imperfect, for the preformatives ית"ן are never geminated, the vowel of the *waw* swallows up the א and merges with its vowel, and the other signs visible in other verb types are not found in the strong verb. From paragraph 2.1.1.0.4 it would seem that in SH the three early kinds of imperfect have merged into one:

2.1 Strong Verb

	singular	plural
1st	*ifqåd* אפקד	*nifqåd* נפקד
2nd pers masc.	*tifqåd* תפקד	*tifqådu* תפקדו; *tifqådon* תפקדון
2nd fem.	*tifqådi* תפקדי	*tifqådinna* תפקדנה
3rd masc.	*yifqåd* יפקד	*yifqådu* יפקדו; *yifqådon* יפקדון
3rd fem.	*tifqåd* תפקד	*tifqådinna* תפקדנה

Similarly, for תִּשְׁמֹר in TH one finds *tišmår* in SH, just as for תִּקְצָר there is *tiqsår*, etc., in all cases.

2.1.1.7 Qal B. Nevertheless, in a number of cases SH recognizes another pattern that produces an *a* vowel between the first and second radicals, with a corresponding shift in the preformative vowel. For example: *tēzåkår* תזכר, *yēbåqår* יבקר, *yēdåqår* ידקר, *wyēfåsår* ויפצר, *wyēfåsål* ויפצל. This pattern resembles that of *Pi'el B* (see 2.1.3.5), and differs from it in the vowel of its second radical, which is *å(ā)* here but usually *ə(ē)* there. This difference could, at first glance, be ignored and verbs of this pattern classified as *Pi'el B*, except that the perfect tense of these verbs are conjugated according to that of *Qal*. For this reason it is best to adopt the position taken by those Samaritan grammarians who view this pattern as a variant mode of the *Qal* imperfect. Indeed, it even seems that this pattern results from the regular conjugation. In many forms of various verbs an auxiliary vowel first developed to break up the consonant clusters which were felt to be uncomfortable in pronunciation; in time, this vowel grew stronger, and the prefix syllable opened and its vowel changed in quality and quantity according to the accepted rules (1.3.4); thus: *yifsår > **yif^əsår* > *yēfåsår*.[24] The intermediate stage described here occurs here and there in TH as well: יְצָחָק or יִצְחָק with a *šəwa mobile* (Gn 21:6); הַתְמֲלֹךְ or הֲתִמְלֹךְ (Jer 22:15); the general rule, of course, in verbs whose first radical is guttural: יַעֲמֹד etc. This stage serves as the basis of common forms with the Babylonian vocalization: (**yiš^ər^əfu* >) יִשׂרפוּ, but in the Babylonian tradition the second *šəwa* quiesces, and does not develop into an independent vowel. The rare nature of this TH pattern in the strong verb and its frequency in "guttural" verbs (see 2.2.2.1.3) indicate that its origin was phonetic.

2.1.1.8 In isolated instances, the vowel of the preformative is *a*, and the forms resemble in this those of *Hif'il*, except that they have no *i* after their second radical, like *yatqā'u* (Nu 10:8) יתקעו, *yatqā'ē'u* (Ex 10:19) ויתקעהו, *wtalla* (Gn 47:13) ותלה, *wyåṭånē'u* (Ex 32:20) ויטחנהו, and perhaps even *wyårå:båk* (Dt 8:3) וירעבך (see 2.2.2.2.4). This feature is reminiscent of similar ones in TH, such as

---

[24] See Yeivin, *Babylonian Vocalization*, 33. I have already noted this in "Samaritan Hebrew," 125, where I referred to similar forms in Greek transcription.

וַיִּדְבְּקוּ, (1 Sa 14:22, etc.), וַיִּדְרְכוּ (Jer 9:2),²⁵ and in BH: יִדֹּחֲ (Lv 1:13 etc.).²⁶ See also 2.7.6 note.

2.1.2 *Hif'il*

2.1.2.1 The Perfect. A comparison of the perfect tense forms of the *Hif'il* in TH — 3rd masc. sing.: הִפְעִיל, 2nd masc. sing.: הִפְעַלְתָּ — with their counterparts in Biblical Aramaic — הַשְׁפֵּלְתְּ; הֵימַן, הַנְפֵּק — and in Arabic — اَفْعَلَ : اَفْعَلْتَ — makes it difficult to reconstruct clearly the TH original form. It is generally thought²⁷ that the TH original forms were, as in Arabic, in the perfect **haqtal*, and in the imperfect **yuhaqtil*, but the vowel following the second radical was apparently influenced by the vowel of ע"י verbs, for only in this manner is it possible to comprehend the length of the vowel following the second radical in an open syllable. It is, thus, impossible to determine whether such a form as הִפְעַלְתָּ preserves the short *a* vowel from an early period or it is the result of a shortening of the long *ī* in a closed syllable to *i/e* and subsequent shift to *a*, according to Philippi's Law (see 1.5.2.1).

2.1.2.2 A study of the paradigm of the Samaritan Hebrew perfect conjugation reveals the uniformity of the vowel of the second radical: *i* (when unstressed — *e*), and because the vowel quantity depends in the Samaritan tradition upon the nature of the syllable — long vowels in open syllables and short ones in closed syllables — it seems impossible to prove that the *i* in verbs not belonging to the ע"י class derives by analogy from the ע"י class, rather than from a lengthening of the short *i*, like the form in Biblical Aramaic (and in Syriac). There is, however, reason to assume that the basis of the SH form is the same as that of its TH counterpart, except that the *i* in the closed syllable did not become *a* by analogy to forms with open syllables, and perhaps with the addition of the influence of Aramaic, where the vowel *i/e*, rather than *a*, persists in a closed syllable. One must note that the lengthening of the *i/e* vowel in an open syllable in the *Af'el* of Samaritan Aramaic results in *e*, rather than *i*, e.g., אתב *attǝb* (= הושיב), אתבה *attēbe* (= הושיבו), תצריך *tāṣrǝk, tāṣrēkinnån*.

2.1.2.3 It should be noted that the marker of the *Hif'il* preserves its original vowel *a*, and does not turn it into an *i*, as is customary in other domains as well (see 1.5.2.2). The following is the relevant paradigm:

---

²⁵ The grammarians tend to assign these forms to the *Hif'il* stem (as Ibn Janāḥ did in his *Kitāb al-Luma'*, 81ff.) and to interpret them as a mixture of *Hif'il* and *Qal* (e.g., Bergsträsser, *Grammatik* II, 101), a less likely explanation. Note that *Qal* itself can be given the same meaning, and that הדריך קשת does not exist, but rather דרך קשת. Indeed, Babylonian Hebrew has in Jer 9:2 יִדְרֹכוּ, i.e., *Qal* (see Yeivin, *Babylonian Vocalization*, 451).

²⁶ See Yeivin, *Babylonian Vocalization*, 467.

²⁷ BL, 330; Bergsträsser, *Grammatik* II, 107.

2.1 Strong Verb

	singular	plural
1st	*afqīdti* הפקדתי	*afqīdnu* הפקדנו
2nd masc.	*afqīdå* הפקדת	*afqedtimma* הפקדתם
2nd fem.	*afqīdti* הפקדת	*afqīdtən* הפקדתן
3rd masc.	*afqəd* הפקיד	*afqīdu* הפקידו
3rd fem.	*afqīda* הפקידה	*afqīdu* הפקידו

2.1.2.4 It should be noted that when a verb bearing the marker of the *Hifʿil* — originally *ha* — is joined to *waw conjunctive*, its vowel is lengthened although it occurs in a closed syllable: *wâqrəb* והקריב, *wâbdīla* והבדילה, *wâlbeštimma* והלבשתם, *wâšlīku* והשליכו (see 2.1.2.6).

Note: In the forms *ēzåkårti* (Ex 20:21) אזכרתי (SP), *måzåkər* (Gn 41:9) מזכיר, the vowel of the first radical resembles that of imperfect *Qal B*.

2.1.2.5 Imperfect. The vowel of the preformative is as in TH, and the paradigm is as follows: *afqəd* אפקיד, *tafqəd* תפקיד — and similarly, all the other forms ending with a third radical; as for forms in which a vowel follows the third radical, the conjugation is *tafqīdu* תפקידו, *yafqīdu* יפקידו, etc. The following examples may illustrate this: *astər* אסתיר, *tabdəl* תבדיל, *yaqrəb* יקריב, *wnaqrəb* ונקריב, *taškīlu* תשכילו, *taqrībon* תקריבון, *yarkībēʾu* ירכיבהו, *yasgīrinnu* יסגירנו, *yašmīdimma* ישמידם.

2.1.2.6 Since א and ה are pronounced identically, there is no longer any distinction between the 3rd masc. sing. form of the perfect and the 1st sing. form of the imperfect, nor is there, in principle, any difference between the 3rd fem. sing. form of the perfect and the 1st sing. form of the cohortative imperfect. Thus *ašməd* is the equivalent of השמיד (e.g., Dt 31:4) and of השמֵד (Dt 33:27), which the Samaritans view as an imperfect form (אשמיד)[28] and which they pronounced *ašməd*; *abdəl* הבדיל (as, e.g., Dt 10:8) is indistinguishable from *(w)abdəl* (ו)אבדיל (Lv 20:26). When, however, *waw conjunctive* is added to these forms a difference develops: in the imperfect, it has no effect upon the quantity of the vowel of the preformative א (see 2.1.2.4), and so *wašlək* והשלך (Lv 1:16) / *wašlīkimma* ואשליכם (Dt 9:17). It is, thus, clearly proven that the difference in no way resembles that between *waw conjunctive* and *waw consecutive* in TH / BH; it depends on the original nature of the guttural consonant. Still, in this way a distinction was made between two forms which were in the process of merging. The possibility of the merging of the forms אפקידה/הפקידה is apparently theoretical only, for in practice אפקידה (1st sing.!) occurs only with *waw conjunctive* (see 2.9.11).

---

[28] ST: אשיצי; SAV: استاصل.

2.1.3 Pi'el

2.1.3.0 Samaritan grammar recognizes two types of *Pi'el*: the usual type, in which the second radical (excluding אהח"ע but including ר) is geminated, and the other type in which the second radical is never geminated. The first type is known as "with geminated second radical," the other as "lacking the second radical" or "with simple second radical,"[29] and this distinction applies to *Nif'al* as well and, to some extent, to *Hitpa'el*. (See 2.0.8)

With Geminated Second Radical

2.1.3.1 Perfect. In TH the vowel following the first radical is *i*, contrasting with the *a* in Aramaic in general and in Arabic, whereas the corresponding vowel in the imperfect is *a*, thus, establishing in TH an alternation פִּעֵל (or פִּעַל) / יְפַעֵל, unlike Aramaic פַּעֵל (or פַּעֵל) / יְפַעֵל (יְפַעֵל) and Arabic فَعَّلَ : يُفَعِّلُ. The accepted view is that the Arabic forms represent the origin of the TH and Aramaic forms — i.e., *qaṭṭala* — but that in TH and in Aramaic the vowel of the second radical in the perfect assimilated to that of the imperfect, forming the base form *qaṭṭil*. The TH paradigm led to an "attenuation" of the vowel *a* in an unstressed closed syllable, transforming it into *i* and reshaping the verb form. SH — with a less developed "attenuation" tendency — preserves the situation assumed to be that of TH in its previous stage: the perfect *qaṭṭil*. Aramaic may have helped SH to preserve the earlier situation, though one need not make this assumption. On the other hand, TH still clearly preserves the situation prior to the assimilation of the vowel of the second radical in the perfect to that of the imperfect, such as: אָבַד, גָּדַל, קָם, etc., while in ST only a few verbs with an *a* were preserved (see 2.1.3.2).

An example of the conjugation:

	singular		plural	
1st	*faqqidti*	פקדתי	*faqqidnu*	פקדנו
2nd masc.	*faqqidtå*	פקדת	*faqqedtimma*	פקדתם
2nd fem.	*faqqidti*	פקדת	*faqqidtən*	פקדתן
3rd masc.	*faqqəd*	פקד	*faqqēdu*	פקדו
3rd fem.	*faqqēda*	פקדה	*faqqēdu*	פקדו

2.1.3.2 One should note the difference between *Pi'el* and *Hif'il* regarding the vowel of the second radical in an open syllable — in *Hif'il* this vowel is *ī*, while here it is *ē*, as it is in the TH pausal form.

---

[29] See *LOT* I, 85, الخفيف العين/النقيل ibid., 57 للمحذوف العين. "With a missing '*ayin*" means "with a weakened second radical," rather than "without a second radical," i.e., the '*ayin* is weakened because it lacks duplication. I prefer, however, to use the term "with a simple second radical" in order to avoid any possible error as to the meaning of "missing." See my article "Some Problems," 236.

The *e* in the 2nd masc. pl. suffix replaces the *i* because this is not the stressed syllable (see 1.5.1.1), and so one finds *e* in *wgarreštiyyu* (Nu 22:11) וגרשתיו, but *i* in *wgarrišti* (Ex 33:2).

On occasion, the original *a* following the second radical is preserved: in the verb שבר — *šåbbårtå* שברת, *wšåbbårtimma* ושברתם; in the verb חלק *ållåq* (Dt 4:19), and also *makkår* מכר (Lv 25:27). See also below 2.2.1.3.2. regarding the verb עבר.

2.1.3.3 Imperfect. The preformative vowel is always *ē*, which is derived from the *šəwa*. The vowel of the preformative denoting the 1st sing. is, thus, the same as that handed down in the Babylonian tradition (like: אֹבַקֵּשׁ, אֲלַקֵּט, אֹדַבֵּר) and the regular paradigm is as follows: *ēfaqqəd*, *tēfaqqəd* and similarly the rest of the forms ending with a third radical. As usual, those forms which take a vowel after the third radical have an *e* (after the second radical): *tēfaqqēdu*, *yēfaqqēdu* and so on. Some examples: *ēdabbər* אדבר, *tēbarrek* תברך, *yēgarrəm* יגרם, *tēbaqqēšu* תבקשו, *yēlammēdu* ילמדו, *wēgarrēšinnu* ואגרשנו.

2.1.3.4 In only a few verbs one encounters the vowel *å* after the second radical, the vowel length depending upon the nature of the syllable; from שבר, for instance: *ēšåbbårimma* אשברם, *wēšåbbårā* ואשברה (in SP Lv 26:13), *tēšåbbår*, *tēšåbbåron*; from שקר: *tēšaqqår* (SP Gn 21:23!), *tēšaqqåru*. The verb דבר demonstrates that the ר as third radical is not the cause of these forms. It is likely that in SH the identity of the second radical in the perfect and the imperfect is considered an obligatory feature, and so the vowel characteristic of the perfect was transferred to the imperfect in the few verbs preserving the original *a*-vowel of the perfect.

With Simple Second Radical (Pi'el B)

2.1.3.5 This verbal stem differs from that "with geminated second radical" only in its lack of doubling, resembling it in its vowel pattern. In the perfect its form is *kåfər* כפר, *såfər* ספר, *wåsiftu* ואספתו (Dt 22:2); in the imperfect its form is: *wyēkåfər* ויכפר, *tēkåfər* תכפר, *ēkåbēdåk* אכבדך. In the perfect the forms of this stem are no different from those of *Qal* in the *fåqəd* pattern (see 2.1.1.2), and the assignment of a verb to *Qal* or to *Pi'el* "with simple second radical" depends upon forms of the verb other than the perfect: do they conjugate according to *Qal* or otherwise? The imperfect, too, resembles that of the second *Qal* (see 2.1.3.2), except that in the *Pi'el* "with simple second radical" the vowel following the second radical is qualitatively *ə/ē*. Because of a scarcity of examples, it is difficult to assemble a complete paradigm in the perfect and the imperfect, and so one cannot tell if the aforesaid difference is a decisive condition. Yet, the very fact that according to the grammarians this stem does not exist when the third root consonant is a guttural (see below n. 31) would seem to indicate that the vowel *a*, for example, after the second radical is not possible in verbs which do not end in a guttural consonant.

2.1.3.6 This stem has parallels confirming the independence of the forms of MH like מֹזְמִן, מֹשֵׁל, מֹשִׁיר and יֹחֹן, which appear in Targum Onqelos as[30] זֹמִין, מְלָחוֹך, בֹּוֹן. The aforementioned MH and Aramaic forms do not comprise a complete paradigm, neither in the perfect nor in the imperfect, and this is true, too, of the SH Pentateuchal forms — though Abū Isḥāq[31] taught that it is possible to form verbs freely in this stem (except for verbs whose second or third radicals are guttural). As examples he adduced למד *(*lāmǝd)*, קום *(*qåwǝm*, see *above* כוין), שים *(šåyǝm*, cf. מצץ). He was undoubtedly giving expression here to a distinct linguistic tradition, at least insofar as Palestinian Aramaic was concerned, in which this pattern was alive; however, only traces of this tradition were preserved in Hebrew and Aramaic, while in SH there is at least literary evidence of an independent stem.

2.1.3.7 Explaining the "simple second radical" stem is no simple matter. An attempt to fit the stem into the known early Semitic verbal stem system first encounters the Arabic فَاعَل stem. Morphologically, this can explain the forms cited above in Aramaic, but not in Hebrew, where the *ā > ō* shift normally requires an assumption that the *qameṣ* in them was originally a short vowel. True, TH does have forms that parallel the Arabic فَاعَل stem: מלושני (*kǝtiv* — Ps 101:5), לְמִשְׁפָּטִי (Job 9:15), יֹסֵר (Hos 13:3). Thus, the forms תְּרָצְחוּ (Ps 62:4), מְאַסְפָיו (Isa 62:9), מְלָשְׁנִי (*qǝre*), which undoubtedly resemble the SH "simple second radical" stem, cannot be reconciled with *fā'ala*. Though in SH there does exist an original *ā* which did not shift to *ō* (1.5.2.5), it seems unwise to relate the simple second radical stem to *qātala*, at least because of the forms in MH and in the Bible. It does, on the other hand, seem proper to assume that these forms originate in the *Pi'el* stem in which the doubling of the second radical is lost.[32]

---

[30] For MH forms, see Yeivin, *Babylonian Vocalization*, 582; for Aramaic forms, Dalman, *Grammatik*, 89; similarly in the Palestinian Targum (P. Kahle, *Masoreten des Westens* II [Stuttgart, 1930], 22, MS D) מְסָיַּיף. Since in SH the verb כפר is conjugated in the *Pi'el* stem, it should be noted that in the Babylonian tradition (Yeivin, *Babylonian Vocalization*, 515) forms of this verb lack the consonant doubling in the past and the infinitive as well: בִּיפֵּר, בִּיפּוֹרוֹ and also the *Hitpa'el* form מתכֹּפֵּר.

[31] *LOT* I, 95 (Hebrew translation, p. 94): "It may be that in the language (i.e., outside the Pentateuch!) all those types (i.e., other than the strong verb, those similar and those with a *nun* and a *pe*) serve in this part of the heavy stem except when its second or third radical is a guttural letter."

[32] *Pace* S. Morag in his article "On Some Lines of Similarity between Samaritan Hebrew and the Yemenite Tradition of Post-Biblical Hebrew," *Language Studies* 5–6 [Israel Yeivin Festschrift], 252–258 [Hebrew]. See now the English version of this article in *ScrHier* 37 (1998), 284–301. See

2.1 Strong Verb

This may have begun, as in TH, in forms with *šəwa*, such as TH מְבַקְשִׁים,³³ and then spread to other forms, as well. The phenomenon was originally a phonetic variant and this may explain why no entire paradigm has been found and why ע״י verbs following this pattern are especially numerous — for the simplification of the second radical doubling is quite understandable because of dissimilation, and even the simplification of the geminated *yod* vocalized with *šəwa* is well known. It should be mentioned that the verb צוה, whose conjugation today is that of *Pi'el* "with simple second radical," is ascribed by Abū Isḥāq, (*LOT* I, 49, 57) to the *Pi'el* "with geminated second radical." Both patterns may be assumed to have been customary in his time, the verb having been pronounced in various ways, while more recently the "simple second radical" form became more common. As evidence for this explanation one has an infinitive form such as זימון *zīmon* in SA (*LOT* III/2, 172). This pattern with a geminated second radical is the usual *nomen actionis* of *Pi'el* (see its counterpart in the Babylonian vocalization of Hebrew in n. 30 above).

2.1.4 *Nif'al*

2.1.4.0 As already noted (2.1.3.0), the Samaritan tradition makes a distinction between two *Nif'al* types: "with simple second radical" and "with geminated second radical," the first of these being the more regular and the original form, with parallels in the other Hebrew traditions.

With Simple Second Radical

2.1.4.1 Perfect. The main difference between SH and the other Hebrew traditions is in the regular doubling of the first radical, except for a few cases to be considered below. Thus, the paradigm of the perfect is as follows:

	singular	plural
1st	*niffåqådti* נפקדתי	*niffåqådnu* נפקדנו
2nd masc.	*niffåqådtå* נפקדת	*niffåqådtimma* נפקדתם
2nd fem.	*niffåqådti* נפקדת	*niffåqådtən* נפקדתן
3rd masc.	*niffåqåd (nifqåd)* נפקד	*niffåqådu* נפקדו
3rd fem.	*niffåqåda (nifqådå)* נפקדה	*niffåqådu* נפקדו

2.1.4.2 The doubling of the first radical is of course found in TH and outside it in the ע״י root type, as in נֱעוֹר, נָמוֹל, and it is a regular feature in the traditions of MH: נִדּוֹן. The explanation offered³⁴ with regard to these biblical forms is

---

also my article "Additional Elucidation," *Lěšonénu* 59 (1996), 93ff. [Hebrew] (see further 2.2.2.1.1).

³³ I already stated in "Medial *Šəwa*," 88 that this way was more common in Hebrew traditions than is apparent in TH.

³⁴ E.g., BL, 400.

that instead of a long vowel after the *nun* of the *Nifʻal* *nāmōl, there appears a short vowel followed by a geminated first radical: *nammōl > נִמּוֹל, i.e., what occurs here is the same phonological feature known from outside the category of verbs, such as גְּמַלִּים instead of *גְּמַלִּים. Such an explanation is certainly not valid for the SH conjugation, for the vowel following the *nun* of *Nifʻal* originally occurs in a closed syllable, and is thus short. On the contrary, the explanation applicable to the Samaritan form may prove valid for TH as well. Nöldeke[35] surmised that the doubling was the result of an analogy from forms of the imperfect, in which the first radical is properly geminated as a result of the assimilation of the *nun*. This explanation seems to me to be basically accurate, though it should be supplemented with the discussion below of the "geminated second radical" *Nifʻal* (2.1.4.7–8), thus making it easier to comprehend the doubling feature spreading to the entire verb paradigm.

2.1.4.3 It should be noted that in the 3rd sing. masc. and fem. forms we find *Nifʻal* as it occurs in TH, e.g., *nistārā* נסתרה, *nitfāša* נתפשה, *wnå:låmå* ונעלמה — all in Nu 5:13 — as well as *nårṣi* נרצה, *wnåmṣi* ונמצה (SP Lv 1:15). In all these places it is doubtful if they are understood in SH as perfect, rather than participial, forms. The form *nårṣi* in Lv 1:4 would seem to be participial, but this may well be impossible with such forms as נסתרה in Nu 5:13. However, from ST and SAV to that verse it seems quite clear that the forms were considered participial and were expressed either by participles or by impersonal forms, like נעלמה in ST: ותעלם (=ואתעלם) and in SAV: خفي. The form *nibnåtå* נבנתה (Nu 13:22), though ST and SAV consider this a perfect form, may be interpreted morphologically as a participle; see also 2.2.3.4.1.

> Note The forms *naksiftå* נכספת (Gn 31:30) and *nåʼibtå* נחבת (SP Gn 31:27) may be considered to be derived from the roots נחב, נכסף as indicated by the Aramaic and Arabic infinitive forms translating *naksəf* נכסף (Gn 31:30). See *LOT* II, 464, col. b; 525, col. b (however, see נאחזו 2.2.1.4.1).

2.1.4.4 Imperfect. One may discern two patterns: (a) verbs with an *ə(ē)* vowel following their second radical, such as *tiddåbəq* תדבק, *yiššåfək* ישפך, *yiššåraf* ישרף, *tiddåbēqu* תדבקו, *wyimmåtēqu* וימתקו; (b) verbs with a corresponding *å(å)* vowel, such as *yimmårāṭ* ימרט, *wyiqqåbår* ויקבר, *yiffåqåd* יפקד. These two patterns are, of course, known in both TH and BH, except that in TH the *pataḥ* is rare: it appears in a closed syllable, generally in pause (but תִּשָּׁבֵר in Ezek 32:28, not in pause!), whereas in BH the *pataḥ* is more common, as in יִמָּלֵט, יִשָּׁפֵךְ, יִנָּתֵן, תִּנָּצֵל, etc. The *pataḥ* is able to survive in open syllables as well, such as יֵעָצְמוּ (Ps

---

[35] Nöldeke, *Aussprache*, 499–500.

106:28).³⁶ In SH neither of the two patterns is clearly predominant.

2.1.4.5 The existence of the two patterns stemming from a common origin with an *i* vowel following the second radical, like **yanqatil(u)*, is likely in TH insofar as Philippi's Law applies to the shortened imperfect *(*yanqaṭil)*, turning *i* in a closed stressed syllable into *a*, for which reason forms with *pataḥ* are more common in the converted imperfect, like וַיִּגְמֹל, וַיִּנָּפַשׁ, etc., in a closed syllable. Otherwise the *i* predominates, having become a *sere*. Later the semantic distinction between these forms became obscure, and the *pataḥ* spread beyond the limits of the converted imperfect, such as תְּשָׁבֵר in Ezek 32:28 and the aforementioned Babylonian form, especially in MH. This way we can also interpret the SH forms with *å(å)*. It may, however, be possible that the tendency to adjust the vowel of the second radical to that in the perfect (see above 2.1.3.4) aided in the process.

With Geminated Second Radical

2.1.4.6 In SH there are a number of verbs which differ in pronunciation from the usual *Nifʿal* only in the doubling of their second root consonant; in the perfect, e.g., *nibbårrådu* נפרדו, *wnibbårråku* ונברכו, *wnissåmmådti* ונשמדתי, *wniqqåddåšti* ונקדשתי, *wniqqåddåšu* ונקדשו; in the imperfect, e.g., *yibbårråd* יפרד, *yimmakkår* ימכר, *yiqqåddåš* יקדש, *tikkåbbås* תכבס (Lv 13:58), *tiššåmmådon* תשמדון (Dt 4:26), *wyirråggåzu* וירגזו (SP Ex 15:14); in the imperative: *iqqåbbåṣu* הקבצו. The Samaritan grammarians found neither in Jewish Hebrew grammar nor in Arabic grammar a verb stem to which these forms could be ascribed; they thus assigned them to *Nifʿal*, attributing to it a special type: "with geminated second radical."

2.1.4.7 This *Nifʿal* type is not the main one in the Samaritan Pentateuchal reading; when Abū Isḥāq (*LOT* I, 103) deals with this category, hardly any of his examples are from the Pentateuch. Hence, this form was common outside the language of the Pentateuch, i.e., in the vernacular. The perfect forms have counterparts in TH in the verbs וְנִכַּפֵּר (Dt 21:8) and וְנֻסְּרוּ (Ezek 23:48), whose pointing is simply that of the *Nitpaʿel* forms common in MH. In other words: the Biblical spelling of these words relates to *Nifʿal* while the TH reading tradition of these verbs chooses the reflexive stem, linked with *Piʿel*, since *Piʿel*³⁷ is in

---

³⁶ Yeivin, *Babylonian Vocalization*, 507.

³⁷ This means that regarding Biblical Hebrew, and more specifically in the period of the writer of Deut 21:8, one must assume that כפר was used in *Qal* in the sense of "forgive," just as there still are cases in the Bible of יסר being vocalized in *Qal*: יֹסֵר (Prov 9:7; Ps 94:10), וְאֶסֳּרֵם (Hos 10:10). כפר was indeed still preserved in the Bible in the concrete sense of "cover:" וכפרת (Gen 6:14), but in the metaphorical sense of "cover:" forgiveness (cf. Prov. 10:12: ועל כל פשעים תכסה אהבה), the sense which became commonplace in the language, *Qal* shifted to *Piʿel* and for this reason נכפר is read נְכַפֵּר. In

TH their non-reflexive stem. SH was fertile ground for this phenomenon, for many verbs occurring in the *Qal* stem in TH appear in *Pi'el* [38] in SH, as is the case in MH, too. There are, accordingly, certain verbs occurring in the Pentateuch spelled like נפעל, but linked in SH with פיעל. Aramaic, too, helped this process along considerably. In Palestinian Aramaic, including Samaritan, the נ of אתפעל and of אתפעל regularly assimilated to the first radical, was often not written at all, and even if written was not pronounced.[39] In TH this assimilation occurred in forms such as הִנַּבְּאוּ (Jer 23:13), תִּכֹּנֵן (SP Nu 21:27: ותתכונן). It was, however, common in the Aramaic vernacular and may have been common in Pentateuchal reading as well. It may be assumed that a form like יתברך was usually pronounced *yibbårråk*, thus becoming a natural imperfect of *Nif'al B*. In fact, the only difference between the imperfect of *Nif'al B* and that of *Hitpa'el* is the pronunciation of the נ as opposed to the doubling of the first radical.

2.1.4.8 From the development of *Nif'al B* one can learn of the doubling of the first radical in the perfect forms of the general *Nif'al*. Just as in SH there existed harmony between the perfect and imperfect of the form with a geminated second radical: *niffåqqåd : yiffåqqåd*, so, too, there developed harmony between *niffåqåd : yiffåqål/əd*. The only difference is that in the usual *Nif'al* the doubling in the imperfect stems from the assimilation of the *nun*, whereas in *Nif'al B* it stems from the assimilation of the *taw* — a difference in origin, but not in the actual language.

The Samaritan grammarians may have retained an awareness of this process, for there is record of El'azar Ha-Kohen (*LOT* I, 185) deriving a *Nif'al* participle from נכרת: מכרת, whereas Ab Sakwa (*LOT* I, 253) interpreted הכרת (Nu 15:31) as if derived from *Hitpa'el*. The inability to distinguish between the two verbal stems is noticeable.

2.1.4.9 Note that this type of *Nif'al* differs from the usual one in the vowel of its second radical in the imperfect as well. In *Nif'al B* it is always *å(å)*, and this is another indication that this *Nif'al* was originally *Nitpa'el*, whose vowel of the second radical is *å(å)* in the imperfect. The identicalness of the imperfect forms of both SH *Nif'al* types with the SA אתפעל and אתפעל is worth noting: in both the forms are *yiffåqəd* (< *yinfåqəd*, *yitfåqəd*); *yiffåqqåd* (< *yitfåqqåd*).

SH, however, the *Nif'al* was retained without change, see 2.1.4.10. In SH, too, one finds the *Qal* in the sense of apostasy: *nikfår* (LOT III/2, 350, l. 5).

[38] See Ben-Ḥayyim, *Tradition*, 112–122.
[39] See my article "Palestinian Aramaic and Samaritan Poetry," 41.

2.1.4.10 Contrasting with וְנִכַּפֵּר (Dt 21:8) we find *wnikkåfər* in SH; SH grammar in its way can interpret this as a reflexive stem corresponding to "a heavy stem simple second radical," but it is clear that what has been preserved here is the *Nif'al* stem of כפ״ר which disappeared from TH — dating from the period when the verb כפ״ר also served in the *Qal* stem in the sense of "forgive." This is so of the forms אכבד *ikkåbəd*, *wikkåbēda* ואכבדה, found in *Nif'al* in TH in a sense equivalent to that of התכבד.

2.1.5 *Hitpa'el*

2.1.5.0 Two types of *Hitpa'el* are distinguishable: "with geminated second radical," i.e., the TH *Hitpa'el*, and "with simple second radical." It is surprising that the Samaritan grammarians did not discuss the second type, though it corresponds to the Aramaic אִתְפְּעֵל. The reason may be that its very existence is unusual.

With Geminated Second Radical

2.1.5.1 Of those forms found in the Pentateuch in the perfect, such as *wētqaddeštimma* והתקדשתם, *wētmakkertimma* והתמכרתם, *wētbårråk* והתברך, *wētbårråku* והתברכו, two basic forms may be isolated: (a) **itfåqqåd*, (b) **itfaqqəd* (והתקדשתם, והתממכרתם). The form with the *ə(e)* vowel is paralleled in TH, where it is dominant, whereas in Babylonian Hebrew the *pataḥ* is dominant. In the imperfect: *yitqåddåšu, niståddåq*.

2.1.5.2 A feature to be noted especially is the length of the vowel *ē* in the syllable *wēt-* in the perfect, for as a rule *waw conjunctive* attaches itself directly to the vowel of a word beginning with an original guttural consonant, such as ועשרון : *wišron*, ואת : *wit*. Thus, **wit-* and not *wēt*, is to be expected. This would seem to indicate that what we have here is a different origin, as if it were **wahit* > **wa'it* (1.5.3.4) > *wēt*, i.e., that the vowel *a* of the *waw conjunctive* was not elided here as in the other combinations, but see 1.3.3. At any rate it is quite clear (see 2.1.2.6) that this feature in no way depends on the fact that the aforementioned perfect forms have a *waw consecutive* in TH.

With Simple Second Radical

2.1.5.3 There is no doubt that this stem parallels the Aramaic אתפעל, i.e., it is the reflexive stem to *Qal*, and it appears in SH not only at Nu 1:47 *itfåqådu* התפקדו, but also in the root type, as *titgådēdu* תתגדדו (2.7.10), and when the first radical is a guttural, as in *bētåsēfu* בהתאספו. Of course, in forms such as אסף the Samaritan grammar can interpret it as the reflexive stem to the "heavy stem with simple second radical" (see 2.1.4.10).

2.2 Verbs with a אהח"ע Radical

2.2.0 The shift of הח"ע to א under various phonetic conditions on the one hand, and the retention of ע, which is a reflex of original ח or ע, in pronunciation under special conditions (see 1.1.8) on the other, make it necessary to study the verbs with a guttural as an independent category, according to the position in the root of the consonant under discussion. However, the class of verbs with א as its first radical is not automatically lost, and its special characteristics will be considered separately under the פ"א class. In contrast, there is no point in maintaining a separate ל"א class since the original ל"א verbs act like the original verbs with a guttural third radical — except for the verb חטא in almost all its forms, and another few forms which act as if derived from ל"י roots.

2.2.1 I-Guttural (הח"ע)
2.2.1.0 Verbs with an original ח or ע and the vowels *a* or *å,* long or short, in *Qal* or *Pi'el* are preceded by *'ayin* — except for חבל, חדל, חזק, חלה, חלץ, חלק, חמץ, חפש (passive), חרב, חרה, חרם such as *abbəl* (but *'âbål*), *âloṣ* (חלוץ), חפץ, חמץ, חנן, חנה, *âlåq, ållåq (Pi'el), âfiṣti, âfåša* — as against *'âkåmu* חכמו, *'âmådti* עמדתי.

2.2.1.1 Qal
2.2.1.1.1 Perfect. Most of the verbs conjugate like the strong verb in the *fåqåd* pattern. The vowel following the initial radical is usually *å, ā* being rare, e.g., *wāreltimma* וערלתם. This class preserves traces of the archaic 3rd fem. sing. not only in *åzålåt* אזלת (Dt 32:36), but also in *wåkålåt* (Dt 11:15), where TH reads וְאָכַלְתָּ.

2.2.1.1.2 In the *fåqəd* pattern we find the following forms: *wåliktå* והלכת, *ålək* (alongside *ålåk*) הלך, *åliknu* הלכנו; *årigtək* הרגתיך; *wāreltimma* וערלתם. As for similar forms derived from the verb אסף, it must not be concluded that it belongs here, for it is easily classified as *Pi'el* "with simple second radical," which coincides with the Samaritan tradition in this regard.

I do not know if the duality of the 3rd masc. sing. of the verb הלך was ever generally used to make a semantic distinction. We encounter it also in the verb אכל which, with the object suffix, is pronounced *wåkēla* ואכלה, the form morphologically and syntactically being the "converted perfect." Because of the merging of forms in their vowel patterns, such as the perfect and the participle in the *fåqåd* pattern (see 2.12.2), it is impossible to tell whether, for example, *ålåk* (Nu 22:22) is a perfect or a participial form; this is so, too, of the aforementioned *wåkēla* (Dt 14:21), while the verb *makkēra* (SP ibid.) would seem to be a perfect form (though *makkēra* can be interpreted as a *Pi'el* participle as well — see 2.12.9). The form *wēlåka* והלכה (Dt 24:2), the phonetic equivalent of ואלכה (Nu 23:3), is surprising in its *ē*-vowel after the first radical, instead of the expected *å*; that it is an old form one learns from the variant readings in SP וילכה, ואלכה, which accurately reflect the present-day pronunciation. Semantically it is a converted perfect form. The "future" sense it incorporates may have led to its vowel assimilating to that of the imperfect. See also 2.9.4.

2.2.1.1.3 The verb עבד has no complete paradigm in the *Qal* stem, it being mixed with that of *Pi'el*, i.e., the *Pi'el* replaces the *Qal*, leaving a few *Qal* forms. The shift from *Qal* to *Pi'el* in this verb is known from MH and the Dead Sea Scroll traditions as well.[40] Of the verb עשה, which also occurs in SH in most of its forms in *Pi'el*, only a few *Qal* forms remain (see 2.8.21–22).

2.2.1.1.4 Imperfect. There exist four conjugational patterns: the preformative vowel is *ē* (patterns a, d) or *å(ā)* (patterns b, c); the second radical is either simple (patterns c, d) or geminated (a, b). The following are a number of examples:

    a. *ellåq* אחלק, *tēssåm* תחסם, *tēmmād* תחמד, *tēbbåd* תעבד, *nēbbår* נעבר, *tērråṣon* תערצון, *wyērråd* ויחרד, *wnēbbårå* ונעברה.
    b. *tåzzåb* תעזב, *tåmmåd* תעמד, *tåbbåd* תעבד, *tåbbådu* תעבדו, *yåmmådu* יעמדו, *yårråfu* יערפו, *wtåmmådon* תעמדון, *wnåbbådå* ונעבדה.
    c. *tå:dål* תחדל, *tå:dår* תהדר, *yå:fåṣ* יחפץ, *tå:fåzu* תחפזו, *wyå:fåk* ויהפך, *wyålåk* וילך, *wtålåk* ותלך.
    d. הלך: *ēlåk*, *tēlåk*, *yēlåk*, *nēlåk*, *tēlåkon*.

2.2.1.1.5 The reason for the difference in the preformative vowel seems to originate in the old difference between the imperfect patterns *yaqtul* : *yiqtal*, as clearly discernible in BH in such forms as יֶחְמֹל vs. יֶחְדַּל, תַּעֲבֹד vs. תַּעֲשֹׂר[41] — unlike such TH forms as יֶעֱרַב : יַעֲמֹד, if the *segbol* is considered as an allophone of the *patah* (note: יַחְסְרוּ/יֶחְסַר!). Since original *u* shifted in SH to a front vowel, and very often to *å*, the difference in the vowel of the second radical was not preserved (see 2.1.1.0.4), the difference in the preformative vowel becoming predicated upon various distinctions, e.g., (1) between verbs differing in the original nature of their guttural consonants, such as *tēmmåd* from חמד as against *tåmmåd* from עמד (it is not the phonetic aspect of the guttural that makes the difference, as can be seen from such forms as *tēššåq* תעשק as against *yåssår* יחסר!); (2) between minor semantic variants of a given verb, such as *tēbbåd* תעבד (in the sense of "labor") as opposed to *tåbbåd* תעבד (in the sense of "worship"); (3) of this sort is the distinction between the regular imperfect and that imperfect which actually signifies past, such as *yēlåk* ילך, but *wyålåk* וילך. Samaritan

---

[40] For the Dead Sea Scrolls, see Ben-Ḥayyim, *Tradition*, 119.
[41] The examples are adduced from Yeivin, *Babylonian Vocalization*, 455, 457, 461, 464.

Hebrew is a language striving for harmony and uniformity; accordingly, it can be seen that one of the two possibilities, *ē* or *å*, tends to characterize a given verb and to persist in all its forms. This means that with verbs of two different preformative vowels, one of these characterizes a given meaning, as noted above with regard to עבד. This is probably the case even where it is difficult to appreciate the semantic distinction, such as *yēbbår* יעבר (Dt 3:28; 30:13) — *yåbbår* (Ex 15:16; Nu 6:5; Dt 24:5), but the semantic difference must be sought out in Samaritan exegesis; *inter alia*, the difference between a concrete meaning and an abstract or a borrowed one must be considered. Evidently, the distinction between imperfect denoting action yet to come and that denoting the past can exist only with verbs with preformative vowel *ē*.

2.2.1.1.6 The original relationship between the phonemes *a/i* has broken down in the preformative vowels in BH as well, the cause clearly being phonetic or paradigmatic in nature, such as יֶחֱזֹר / תֶּחֱזֹרְנָה, יֶחֱזֹר / אֶחֱבֹשׁ / יֶחֱבֹשׁ similar to the relationship between *seghol* and *patah* in TH: נֶחְמְדֵהוּ / תַּחְמֹד; יַאַסְרוּנִי / נֶאֱסָרְךָ, וַיֶּאֱסֹר; יַחְפֹּץ / יֶחְפַּץ; וַיַּחְדְּלוּ / וַיֶּחְדַּל, and the interchanges in both of these traditions have become so complex that there is no longer any possibility of determining the conditions for these interchanges (note that in TH a *seghol* occurs before a *holem* following the second radical not only when the consonant is an א, as in יֶהְדֹּף, וַיֶּחֱשֹׁף!). At first glance it is possible to compare the SH semantic distinction *yēbbåd* (יעבד) / *yåbbåd* with the commonplace Hebrew יַחֲלֹשׁ / יֶחֱלַשׁ, יַעֲרֹב / יֶעֱרַב (in the Bible: וַיַּחֲלֹשׁ / וַיֶּחֱלַשׁ), where the meaning is decisive, but this is not the case, for in TH and BH the difference depends also at least upon the difference in the vowel of the second radical, while in SH the difference depends entirely upon the preformative vowel.

2.2.1.1.7 Many verbs in this category have a geminated second radical in the imperfect, but this is not so of אגר, הדר, הפך, הרג, חבל, חגר, חדל, חמל, חפד (!) חפז, חפץ, עמס, חפר, while with some others, such as *yå:zåbåk* יעזבך (Dt 31:8), the doubling is omitted in some forms though the verb in general has a geminated second radical. It seems that the verbs and the forms displaying a geminated second radical reflect the basic pattern *yifqåd* with the guttural assimilating to the second radical; the verbs and forms without doubling reflect basic forms in which an auxiliary vowel developed between the first and second radicals (1.3.4, paralleling the *hatef* vowels in TH), and when the guttural consonant vanished, the two syllables contracted to one, as יעמד – *ya'mud* > *yåmmåd*; יהפך - *yahfuk* > *yah^{a}fuk* > *ya^{a}fåk* > *yå:fåk*.

2.2.1.1.8 The conjugation of the imperfect of הלך is, of course, that of the פ"י class, and there is no evidence from the I-guttural verbs of the existence of a form with an *ē*-preformative vowel and without doubling of the second radical.

2.2.1.2 *Hifʿil*

2.2.1.2.1 For the reason given above (2.2.1.1.7) one finds in SH: (a) verbs with doubling of the second radical in the perfect, such as *wāmmǝd* והעמיד (**wahaʿmid* > **waʾammǝd*), *wāzzīqa* והחזיקה, *wābbiṭṭå* והעבטת; in the imperfect, such as: *tānnǝq* תעניק (< **taʿnīq*), *yāllǝm* יעלם, *tārrǝš* תחריש, *tānnīnu* תעננו, *yānnīṭu* יחנטו, *tābbīṭinnu* תעביטנו; (b) verbs without doubling in the perfect, like *ʿå:tǝm* החתים, *ʿå:bǝd* העביד (Gn 47:21), *wå:riktå* והארכת, *wå:rimti* והחרמתי, *wå:zintå* והאזנת; in the imperfect: *yå:rǝm* יחרים, *tå:mǝn* תאמין, *wtå:na* ותענה (Gn 16:6[42]), *å:liqimma* אחלקם (Gn 49:7; there are readings of האחליקם, אחליקם). The base of forms of this sort resembles the TH יַחֲרִים, תַּאֲמִין, אֲחַלְּקֵם.

Note: The verb הלך is conjugated according to the פ״י class.

2.2.1.2.2 With verbs that geminate their second radical, the *Hifʿil* has merged with the *Piʿel* and, in general, no distinction can be made between the two verb stems; on occasion, the meaning of the verb is of no assistance either, for the causative sense can be expressed by both. A point of distinction may be found in the vowel of the second radical when it is in an open syllable: *ī* is to be expected in *Hifʿil*, *ē* in *Piʿel*, and indeed one finds *wāzzīqa* והחזיקה, *wāmmīda* והעמידה, *wnå:rīma* ונחרימה, *tå:rīmimma* תחרימם, *yå:mīṣēʾu* יאמיצהו (Dt 32:10, and in SP the spelling ימיצהו is not unknown), *tabbīdu* תאבידו (ST Nu 33:52), on the one hand; *yåkkēlu* יאכלו (Lv 22:8), *tābbēdon* תאבדון, *wyåzzēqu* ויחזיקו (SP Gn 19:16), on the other. With the verb חנך, however, *yānnīkinnu* (Dt 20:5; there exists a reading יחניכנו) as against *ʿannēku* חנכו in the very same verse. It would seem that the difference *ē*/*ī* was originally unique to the *Piʿel*/*Hifʿil* stems, but that here and there the similarity in forms with a closed syllable, e.g., *wāmmǝd* והעמיד (Lv 14:11) as against *wāmmīdu* והעמידו (Lv 27:8), may have undermined this distinction. (Nevertheless, one must not overlook the fact that *ī*, too, may have evolved from a *šǝwa*; in this case both forms in Dt 20:5 may present *Piʿel* [see also 2.11.5]).

2.2.1.2.3 Another point of distinction, applicable only to the perfect, is discernible, at least in certain forms, in the fact that the vowel preceding the doubling is long in *Hifʿil* (*haʾ* > *ā*) and short in *Piʿel*. It is, thus, a fairly safe assumption that *wåzziqti* (Ex 14:4), in SP sometimes והחזקתי, and *wåbbištå* (Ex 29:9) וחבשת are *Hifʿil* in SH (though in the SP there is no trace of the spelling והחבשת). This is true, too, of *wåbbǝd* (Nu 24:19) והאביד, but *wabbidtā* (SP Dt 7:24 ואבדת!) is *Piʿel*. It must be noted, however, that the form *abbīdok* (Dt

---

[42] The *Hifʿil* stem in this sense is found in TH in Ps 55:20 וְיַעֲנֵם, as interpreted by Abraham Ibn ʿEzra.

28:22: אֲבְדֶךָ) in SP is written האבידוך or הבידוך, and translated in ST יאבדונך, i.e., it is interpreted as a verb in the 3rd pl. perfect in the *Hif'il* stem, despite the fact that the vowel preceding the geminated consonant is short, while on the other hand *wyåzzēqu* (see 2.2.1.2.2) has both *ē* and a long *å*, and *wazzīqi* (Gn 21:18) a long *ī*, but short *a*! (perhaps these forms with the long *ī* are to be assigned to *Pi'el*; cf. above 2.2.1.2.2 concerning the verb חנך).

2.2.1.2.4 Therefore, it must be remembered that assigning verbs I-guttural to either *Hif'il* or *Pi'el* is done on occasion on the basis of inconclusive considerations, for SH cannot be judged according to TH convention, and it is not possible to rely on unique semantic uses in *Hif'il* or in *Pi'el* according to the SH tradition or that of Jewish Hebrew in general. The spelling of the Samaritan text, too, is sometimes confusing: *yåmēnu* is written in Ex 4:1 and elsewhere יאמנו, without a *yod*, a clear indication of an *ē*-vowel, yet in the perfect there is a ה: האמן (Gn 45:26) *å:mən*.

2.2.1.3 *Pi'el*
With Geminated Second Radical

2.2.1.3.1 In general, the perfect of verbs I-guttural is no different from that of the strong verb. In verbs with a geminated second radical, its vowel is almost always *ēli*, as in *'arrikti* ערכתי, *wamməṣ* ואמץ, *'annēku* חנכו, but a number of traces of *å* have been preserved: *ållåq* חלק, *'abbårnu* עברנו, *'abbårtimma* עברתם.

2.2.1.3.2 The imperfect is identical in certain forms with the *Hif'il* (see 2.2.1.2.2-3). It is unlikely that forms with *å* following their second radical, such as *tåbbåru* תעברו, *wyåbbåru* ויעברו, belong originally to *Pi'el*. Though the perfect is regularly in *Pi'el*, these are probably forms of *Qal* (2.2.1.1.5) which, from the point of view of their geminated second radical, are similar to *Pi'el*. This apparently applies also to *tåššår* (Dt 14:22) תעשר — *Qal* by virtue of the *å*. Cf. יְעַשֵׂר in 1 Sa 8:15. However, in the same verse the infinitive is *'aššår*, whose doubling seems to be *Pi'el*, yet in Gn 28:22 the very same infinitive is used alongside *'åššīrinnu* אעשרנו, which appears to reflect *Hif'il* (but see 2.2.1.2.2). The infinitive *låššår* (Dt 26:12) can easily be ascribed to *Qal*. It seems that the common denominator, i.e., the geminated second radical, in three separate verb stems — *Qal*, *Pi'el*, *Hif'il* — led to their serving in the very same function. This phenomenon was not limited to the verb עשר alone. Because of the infinitive *'aššår* it seems proper to assign *tåššår*, as well, to the *Pi'el* stem. Yet with the verb עבר, the imperfect with the preformative vowel *ē* was ascribed to *Qal*; the perfect with the geminated second radical, together with all forms with a geminated second radical phonetically unconditioned, was assigned to *Pi'el*. This, of course, is a decision made for grammatical purposes, yet in the aware-

2.2 Verbs with a אהח"ע Radical   125

ness of the Samaritan tradition, it is quite possible that the imperfect, too, is considered part of the *Pi'el* stem.

> Note: Concerning the vowel *a* following the second radical see also 2.1.3.4; it is, of course, impossible to classify the verbs listed there as *Qal*.

With Simple Second Radical
2.2.1.3.3 According to the Samaritan grammarians (*LOT* I 95, 205) the verb אסף occurs in the *Pi'el* "with simple second radical." It is conjugated in the perfect as *âsaf, âsiftā, wâsiftu* (Dt 22:2). Theoretically, this conjugation fits the *fâqəd* pattern of *Qal* (2.1.1.2), but the decision to assign such a verb form to the *Pi'el* stem comes both from the participle, which shows a preformative *m*, and from the imperfect, where the vowel of the second radical is *e*, the imperfect of אסף conjugating *tâsəf, wyâsəf*.

2.2.1.4 *Nif'al*
2.2.1.4.1 A clear sign of the *Nif'al*, whether the usual stem or *Nif'al B*, in the perfect is *niyyâ-* preceding the second radical, such as *niyyâsåf* נאסף, *niyyâfåk* נהפך, *niyyârâmu* נערמו. This, understandably, derives from *ni"a-*, i.e., from the type where the first radical is geminated in the perfect (2.1.4.6). This class included a number of verbs which do not geminate their first radical: *wnâ:lâmå* (Nu 5:13) ונעלמה or *wnâkkəl* (Ex 22:5) ונאכל, but it is doubtful whether these forms were ever considered perfect forms (2.12.10), and even where the Aramaic and Arabic versions translate them as perfect, as in the case of ונאכל, it may still be assumed that their pronunciation indicates a participle. It is, at any rate, possible to assume that even in certain cases, such as ונאכל, the *Nif'al* in its original form was used to make a semantic distinction, the meaning of ונאכל in the relevant verse being "and it was burnt." One cannot of course interpret *wnâ'ezu* ונאחזו (Nu 32:30) < **wna'hᵉzu* as a participle, like *nā'əz* in Gn 22:13; at best it can be considered a quadriradical verb.

> Note: The verb אסף is conjugated in the regular *Nif'al* and not in the *Nif'al* corresponding to *Pi'el* "with simple second radical" (2.1.4.10).

2.2.1.4.2 Imperfect. Its form, as expected, includes a geminated first radical: *tiyyâbåt* תעבט (Dt 15:6), *tiyyâšåb* תחשב, *wtiyyâṣår* ותעצר, *tiyyâzåqu* תחזקו (Dt 11:8), *niyyâlåṣ* נחלץ, *tiyyâfiyyinna* (< **tiyyâfi+inna*, see 2.0) תאפינה, except for the 3rd forms, singular and plural, where there is *iyyâ-* instead of *yiyyâ-* because of dissimilation, the 3rd sing., thus, merging with the first sing.: *iyyâsâfu* יאספו, *iyyâbår* יחבר (SP Ex 28:7), *iyyâbåd* יעבד, *iyyâgår* יחגר (Lv 16:4).

2.2.1.5 *Hitpa'el*
2.2.1.5.1 The guttural first radical vanishes, and though it seems originally to

have directly followed the *taw* of the *Hitpaʿel,* the *taw* is not geminated. In other words, the guttural did not assimilate to the *taw* as in Aramaic forms such as יתמר (> יתאמר); on the contrary, its traces are apparent in the length of its vowel.

With Geminated Second Radical
2.2.1.5.2 The forms of these verbs are as follows: in the perfect: *wētållåmtå* והתעלמת, *ētållak* התהלך, *wētåttånu* והתחתנו; in the imperfect: *tētåmmår* תתעמר, *tētåttån* תתחתן, *yētåššåb* יתחשב, *wyētåbbår* ויתעבר, *wyētånnåf* ויתאנף. Since one should assume basic perfect and imperfect forms of **(h)itfåqqåd* and **yitfåqqåd,* the length of the vowel following the first radical, which was originally in a closed syllable, must be explained. If we assume that an auxiliary vowel developed between the *taw* of the *Hitpaʿel* and the guttural first radical, similar to that found in Aramaic vocalized with Babylonian vowel signs such as תִּתנַשִּׂי, אִיתִ׳מְנֹעוּ,[43] the following process can be reconstructed: (התהלך) **ithallak > *it^ahallak > *ita'allak > *itāllak,* (יתחשב) **yithaššab > *yit^ahaššab > *yita'aššab > *yitaššab.* The short vowel *i* in the closed syllables -תִ, -יִ, when they became open, according to the rule, developed into long *ē* (1.5.2.1), hence *ētå-, yētå-*. Another possibility of development of this vowel, i.e., its shortening to *šəwa,* can be found in the participial *(k)åmtannēnəm* כמתאננים (Nu 11:1), where the syllables *(mit'an->) mitan-* first become *m^atan-* and then *amtan-*. (See also 1.5.3.4[1]).

With Simple Second Radical
2.2.1.5.3 Of this type of *Hitpaʿel* there exists the form *bētåsēfu* (Dt 33:5) בהתאספו (SP!). It is not at all clear if this reading refers to a perfect form with the preposition ב similar to the reading in Nu 14:3 *alnibbål* לנפל (see *LOT* III/1, 75) and to forms found in the medieval Hebrew poetical style, especially in liturgical poetry (such as כְּדִבֶּרְתָּ, כְּשָׁקַט),[44] or perhaps the form בהתאספו is an infinitive with a suffixed *waw* as in (בעור) בנו. SAV translates this UL ĩ w, and ST uses what is apparently a nominal form: בתכנש. To this stem belongs the form *iyyåsēfa* (Nu 12:15) האספה as well, which both ST and SAV translate with a past tense form: אתכנשת, إنحازت *inḥāzat.* They seem to have viewed the forms as *Hitpaʿel* with an assimilated *taw: *hit'åsēfa > *hi''åsēfa > iyyåsēfa.*

---

[43] Yeivin, *Babylonian Vocalization,* 393.

[44] The grammarians are known to have found great difficulty in dealing with biblical linguistic forms such as בַּהֲכִין (2 Chr 1:4), לְבָרָם (Eccl 3:18), בְּהַשַּׁמָּה (Lv 26:43). There is a tradition which the most important of the early grammarians relied upon, according to which these and similar forms are perfect forms (and not infinitives) with prepositions; see *Kitāb al-Lumaʿ* (cf. 2.1.1.8 n. 25), 35, 67 (concerning השמה!) and Abraham Ibn ʿEzra's commentary on the aforementioned verse in Ecclesiastes. On this basis Ibn Janāḥ allowed poets to use this mode of expression even "without poetic compulsion."

2.2.2. II-Guttural

2.2.2.0 The contrast between the "weak" guttural consonants א and ה and the "strong" ח and ע (*LOT* I, 54), expressed under certain conditions in the I-guttural consonant class, does not exist in the II-guttural consonant class, in which אהח"ע all behave similarly. In SH the inability to geminate אהח"ע as in TH, as well as the existence of *Qal B* (in the imperfect) and *Pi'el B*, i.e., "with simple second radical," even when the second radical is not one of אהח"ע, make it impossible to assign definitively many forms of verbs with a II-guttural radical to *Qal*, to *Pi'el*, or to the stems associated with them. It is, thus, not surprising that the Samaritan grammarians had difficulty with this, as can be seen from the writings of El'azar ben Pinḥas (*LOT* I, 205) in considering the *Pi'el* "with simple second radical": "A verb whose second radical is a guttural consonant does not display doubling, and it is different from its *Qal* in the addition of a *mem* in its *nomen agentis*, unlike *Qal*." In other words, he does not designate the nature of the verb's vowel system as a sign differentiating between *Qal* and *Pi'el*. Because of the greater use of the *Pi'el* stem in SH than in TH[45] and for the sake of appearances, it seems better for the verbs II-guttural that resemble *Pi'el B* morphologically to be assigned to *Pi'el* though they may have originally belonged to *Qal*, without making use of El'azar's sign: the existence of an initial *mem* in the participle of the *Pi'el*. In fact, a *Pi'el* participle without a *mem* is mentioned below (see 2.12.9) while, in contrast, the verb ארש is conjugated in *Qal* (in SH the ר can be geminated!) though its participle takes a *mem*; the SH pronunciation tradition and the SP text do not always match in linguistic matters.

2.2.2.1 *Qal*

2.2.2.1.1 Perfect. From the above it seems that in this class only the verb pattern *fāqåd* is to be considered *Qal*, because a verb in this class of the *fāqəd* pattern, such as *ṣā'ēqa* צעקה, will be considered *Pi'el B* (cf. מִצְעָק in 2 Kgs 2:12!), whereas a verb such as *wbārtå* ובערת (Dt 13:6) is to be considered *Qal*, though from the viewpoint of its origin, **wbā'artå*, it could be assigned to the *Pi'el* stem in the *wšåbbårtå* pattern. It should be noted how uncertain the Samaritan tradition itself is in this matter, to such an extent that the word וטהרה in Lv 12:7 pronounced *wtå'ēra*, is interpreted by ST as *Pi'el*: וידכינה "and he purified her," while the same word in the very next verse (12:8) is interpreted as if from *Qal* (ותדכי)! — unlike SAV, which translates both verses by the intransitive ותטהר. It should be assumed that the verb טהר in the *fåqåd* pattern, *wṭår* (Lv 13:6), and in the *fåqəd* pattern, *wtå'ēra* (ibid) is the same. This may indeed have originally been so, but there is nothing either morphological or semantic

---

[45] See below 2.15.5. For more details see Ben-Ḥayyim, *Tradition*, 112–123.

to prevent an analysis such as that above. This is true, too, of such a verb as *wmāla* (Nu 5:12) ומעלה — *Qal*, but *wmā'eltimma* (Dt 32:51) ומעלתם — *Pi'el B*.

2.2.2.1.2 Forms such as *wrå̄ṣtå̄* ורחצת, *wfātta* (< *wfadta*) ופחדת, *rå̄ṣ* רחץ, *šå̄t* שחת (*Qal!*), *nāg* נהג (*Qal!*) differ from ע"י verbs in that they have a long vowel. The reason for this length is to be found in the contraction of two syllables with the same vowel to one (see 1.1.8c). Surprising are the forms *wkånnu* וכהנו (*Qal!*), *wšāṭṭu* ושחטו, with a geminated third radical, as against *šå:tu* שחתו or *zā:mu* (SP Nu 23:8) זעמו. It would seem as if these forms reflect a development characteristic of SH, where, e.g., the *šəwa* of the basic form **šaḥᵃtū* (as in TH) was pronounced before the guttural consonant, thus, giving rise to such forms as **ša'aḥtū*, which, with the loss of the guttural and its assimilation to the following consonant, produced **ša'ṭṭu > šāṭṭu*. It must, however, be noted that the pronunciation of the *šəwa* before its consonant usually takes place in SH when the consonant occurs at the beginning of a word and not in its middle.

The following development may perhaps be considered: **šaḥᵃtu > *ša'ᵃtū*, followed by the quiescence of the *šəwa* and the development of the form **ša'tu* with the guttural assimilating to the third radical. The problem with this is the fact that the quiescence of a *šəwa* is an extremely rare phenomenon, occurring, for instance, in the form *qårbåt* (< **qarᵃbat*) קרבת.[46] It, thus, seems more likely that these forms result from analogy to the imperfect, where the doubling of the third radical is a normal occurrence (see 2.2.2.1.3).

Note: One should note *wbēš* (Ex 7:18) ובאש which seems to be in the *fēqəd* pattern. At any rate, it corresponds to the Aramaic בְּאֵשׁ.

2.2.2.1.3. Imperfect. The following are examples of the imperfect: *yē'ṭår* יטהר, *yē'rāq* ירחק, *yē'bār* יבחר, *tē'māl* תמעל, *tēšå̄ṭṭu* תשחטו, *yērå̄ṣṣu* ירחצו. The ultimate stressed forms indicate that they, at least, belong to the second imperfect type (2.1.1.7), for they originate in forms such as **yēṭā'år*; the doubling of the third radical in suffixed forms, too, however, should be interpreted from the stage where there was an auxiliary vowel similar to that found in BH יִרְחָצוּ and others[47]: *yērå̄ṣṣu* evolved from **yirḥᵃsū > *yirᵃḥᵃsū > yirāḥsū > *yiraṣṣū*.

2.2.2.2. Hif'il

2.2.2.2.1 The guttural consonant has vanished, its only trace perhaps being the retention of the ultimate stress, such as *å'šīr* השאיר, *yå'bīr* יבעיר, *bå'nīl* בהנחיל,

---

[46] In this way the Samaritan tradition interprets קרבת in Dt 2:37, as indicated, too, by AV (כל יד) دمت ما— from the reading تدن one can learn nothing. SH clearly has 3rd fem. sing. forms without the loss of the *šəwa*: אזלת *åzålåt*, ואכלת *wåkålåt* (see 2.1.1.1.1).

[47] See Yeivin, *Babylonian Vocalization*, 466.

for it is theoretically possible to assume the existence of basic forms such as *yab'ir > *yâbī'ir, etc., namely, making the šəwa vocalic before the guttural consonant, the way the Masoretes require with the words הִשְׁחִיתוּ, הִתְעִיבוּ when pronounced with certain accents.[48]

2.2.2.2.2 Of the perfect forms in the Pentateuch it is possible to compile a conjugation reflecting the varying second radical vowels (reconstructions are given in brackets):

Singular
1st   wårēbti והרחבתי
2 masc   wåqēltå והקהלת; wåzårtå והזהרת
2 fem.   <wårēbti> והרחבתי
3 masc.   å'rīb הרחיב; å'bēš הבאיש
3 fem.   wåmītå והמעיטה
Plural
1st   <åqēlnu> הקהלנו
2 pers masc.   åbēštimma הבאשתם; wåzårtimma והזהרתם
2 fem.   <åbēštən> הבאשתן
3rd   åqīlu הקהילו

2.2.2.2.3 This conjugation, which reveals the variations of the vowel of the second radical, would seem to reflect the fact that the basic vowel in the perfect of Hif'il in SH is i (as in the strong class). In a closed syllable this short i changed, under the influence of the guttural consonant, to either e or a (å), and with the disappearance of the guttural consonant the vowel lengthened in order to replace it; in an open syllable the long ī is maintained. In the 3rd masc. sing. the ī is maintained and the syllable is stressed, whether because it developed from a basic form such as *ar'ḥib > *ariḥib, or by virtue of analogy to the 3rd fem. sing. and 3rd pl. forms. At any rate, there is a certain vacillation in the vowel of the 3rd masc. sing. form: ē occurs there as well — å'bēš (the infinitive is formed like ע"י verbs, see 2.14.11). The form *wåkådēttiyyu והכחדתיו (Ex 23:23) is unusual. The expected form is either *wåkåttiyyu (< *wåkådtiyyu) or *wåkådētiyyu, i.e., with the addition of a vowel which arose in order to avoid the doubling, as in the word מולדתי: mūlēdēti (see 1.5.3.1). The presence of both an auxiliary vowel and a geminated taw is what makes the form surprising.

2.2.2.2.4 An i-vowel following the first radical in the imperfect is maintained in all forms, such as tå'šīt תשחית, yå'rīb ירחיב, yå'šīr ישאיר, tåšīttu תשחיתו, yåšīttåk

---

[48] See Baer-Strack, *Dikduke ha-Teamim*, 13, §11 and cf. Dotan, *Diqduqe Haṭṭē'amim*, 225.

ישחיתך, *yåkī:sē'u* יכעיסהו, *åkī:simma* אכעיסם. For this reason, the existence of a form such as *wyårå:båk* (Dt 8:3) וירעבך — where, according to the Jewish tradition, the *Hif'il* stem is required — is at first glance surprising. It would seem, however, that the Samaritan tradition makes use of a verb in the *Qal* stem paralleling the use of הרעיב in the Jewish tradition. Evidence of this, in addition to the grammatical form itself, is the fact that corresponding to TH *Qal* in Gn 41:55, SH has *Nif'al: wyir'rāb*. This indicates that the aforesaid form in Dt 8:3 is not to be classified as *Hif'il*. Furthermore, see 2.1.1.8.

Note that a non-final third radical is sometimes ungeminated and on other occasions geminated. This doubling seems to be the result of analogy from other stems, but the subject is in need of further study.

2.2.2.3 *Pi'el*

See 2.2.2.3.2 for what is attributed in this class to *Qal* and what is assigned to *Pi'el*.

2.2.2.3.1 The *ē/e/i/ə* vowel relationship of the second radical according to syllable structure and stress is reflected clearly in the paradigm of the perfect. Some examples are given here: *mā'iṣti* מחצתי, *nā'imti* נחמתי (Gn 6:7), *fā'iltå* פעלת, *šå'iltå* שאלת; *fā'əl* פעל, *'ā'əz* אחז; *så'ēqa* צעקה, *wtå'ēra* וטהרה; *wmå'ertimma* ומהרתם; *wmå'irtən* ומהרתם; *wtå'ēru* וטהרו.

2.2.2.3.2 In the imperfect, the forms are as expected: *tētā'əb* תתעב, *tēfå'ər* תפאר, *yērā'əf* ירחף, *yēmā'əṣ* ימחץ, *yēšā'əl* ישחל, *tēlā'əṭ* תלהט, *wtēlā'əṣ* ותלחץ, *tēkā'ēšu* תכחשו. Forms such as *tē'bār* (Dt 21:9) תבער have been assigned, according to the rule adopted, to the *Qal* stem (2.2.2.1.1); thus, *tētā:binnu* (Dt 7:26) תתעבנו is considered *Qal*, though the form without the suffix is *Pi'el*. In TH the *Qal* occurs only in the participle תועבה, but there is also a *Nif'al*, and MH also has תועב, and in poetry תֵעוּב as well. As to the origin, *tētā:binnu* < *tēta'abinnu*, may belong to the *Pi'el* stem.

> Note: The forms *yēlā'əm* (Dt 1:30) ילחם, *tēlā'ēmu* (Dt 1:42) תלחמו, of course, are not *Nif'al* but *Pi'el* forms (according to our rules). They may, of course, also be derived from *Qal*, as in TH. Thus, the form *wnēlā'imnu* (Dt 1:41) ונלחמנו cannot be interpreted as *Nif'al*, but rather as *Pi'el* with an appended 3rd masc sing. suffix[49] (Nonetheless, cf. *Nif'al* of נפקחו, 2.2.3.4.1 note b).

2.2.2.4 *Nif'al*

2.2.2.4.1 In the perfect its regular form is *nig'gål* נגאל, *wniš'šān* ונשען, *wniššårtimma* ונשארתם, *nibå:lu* נבהלו, which developed from a form like **niggå'al*.

---

[49] Cf. *tiqnā'ē'u* תקנהו (Lv 25:44 SP); the Targums ignore the suffix: תזבנן, תשתרון.

2.2 Verbs with a אהח"ע Radical

There does, however, exist a form in which the vowel of the second radical is *ə*, like that of the *Hitpaʻel B* of the strong verb: *wnallāʼəm* (Ex 1:10) ונלחם, which may have been influenced by the participle (see 2.12.10). At any rate, the *a*-vowel of the *nun* is unexpected.

Note: *nāʼimti* נחמתי in Gn 6:7 is interpreted as *Piʻel* (2.2.2.3.1).

2.2.2.4.2 The two imperfect patterns of the strong verb (2.1.4.4) exist in this class as well, e.g., (a) *yiggāʼəl* יגאל, *wyikkāʼēšu* ויכחשו, (b) *wyinʼnām* ינחם, *wyikʼkån* ויכהן, *tišʼšåton* תשחתון, *yiqqåtu* יקהתו (SP Gn 49:10).

Note: Morphologically, pattern (b) as it appears in *Nifʻal* II-guttural could just as well be attributed to the type "with geminated second radical" (see 2.1.4.6), which was originally נתפעל; accordingly, in contrast with יכהן in Dt 10:6(7), SP makes use of the reflexive conjugation *wyikʼkån*, which just might be expressing MH התכהן.

2.2.2.5 *Hitpaʻel*

2.2.2.5.1 Forms like *itnā:lu* התנחלו, *wētnåltimma* והתנחלתם, *yiʼtnām* יתנחם are *Hitpaʻel* forms according to the rules of SH; for the length of the vowel following the *waw* in the perfect, see *Hitpaʻel* of the strong verb. The form *wittāʼēru* והטהרו (Nu 8:7) has a short vowel following the *waw*, as in the imperative, a possible reason for this being its resemblance to the imperative and its meaning.

2.2.2.5.2 The SH form *wēššåttima* והשחתם (Dt 4:25) is *Hitpaʻel*, the *taw* having assimilated to the *šin*, the source of the assimilation being the original Pentateuchal form which is an intransitive *Hifʻil*, whereas in the later language such an intransitive *Hifʻil* was incompatible with the Samaritan tradition, and so the *Hitpaʻel* was adopted. It has already been noted (see 1.5.3.1b) that the assimilation of *taw* is always possible in SH and is the basis of *Nifʻal B*; see further *LOT* III/2, 156.

2.2.2.5.3 Of quadriradical roots there are the following forms: *itmā:månu* התמהמהנו (Gn 43:10), *wyitmā:må* ויתמהמה (Gn 19:16), without consonantal doubling to compensate for the missing guttural.

2.2.3 III-Guttural

2.2.3.0 The unique aspect of this class is that the guttural assimilates to suffixes beginning with a consonant, i.e., the 1st and 2nd forms (masculine and feminine, singular and plural) and the vowel of the second radical lengthens. This is true for א as well, the only difference between א and הח"ע being that in the case of final א the common vowel is *å*, whereas in other cases it is *ā*. As noted above in 2.2.0, in SH ל"א verbs are not a separate category, but rather a part of III-guttural verbs in general. Only the verbs קרא, קנא, מלא, טמא display forms reminiscent of ל"י verbs, whereas almost all the forms of the verb חטא are ל"י verb forms; as a result, חטא should perhaps be considered a ל"י verb.

2.2.3.1 Qal

2.2.3.1.1 Perfect. Almost all III-guttural verbs are of the *fåqåd* type; nevertheless, this class displays a number of verbs of the *fēqåd* type: *ṭēma* טמא, *zēba* זבח, *lēqa* לקח, *rēṣå* רצח, *rēṣå* רצע.

2.2.3.1.2 A sample of the perfect conjugation:
Singular
1st *šåkātti* שכחתי; *måṣåtti* מצאתי
2nd masc. *šāmåttå* שמעת; *wqåråtå* וקראת; *wnådåttå* ונדחת (Qal!)
3rd masc. *wšāba* ושבע; *kårå* כרע; *måṣå* מצא; *šåna* שנא
3rd fem. *wfā'tā* (< *wfātā'a*) ופתחה; *fā'rå* פרחה; *wmå'lå* ומעלה
Plural
1st *gåbānnu* גועני
2nd masc. *šāmåttimma* שמעתם; *wšåmåttimma* ושמחתם; *wnåṭåttimma* ונטעתם
3rd *šāmā'u* שמעו; *ṭåbā'u* טבעו; *wqåråu* וקראו.
The form *wqåråttå* וקראתה (SP Dt 31:29; TH וְקָרָאת) is especially noteworthy as it preserves traces of forms of both ל"א and final ל"י verbs. The Samaritan spelling and pronunciation of this word are confirmed by the reading in MS Kaufmann (*Yevamot* 12:3) וְקָרָאתָה and in MS Parma A (Haneman, *Morphology*, 397, n. 134) וְקָרָאתָה. A remarkable parallel in TH is נִפְלָאתָה in 2 Sa 1:26.

2.2.3.1.3 The conjugation of the verbs listed in 2.2.3.1.1 is no different from that of the other verbs, except insofar as the vowel *ē* follows the first radical, such as *wzēbåttå* וזבחת, *lēqånnu* לקחנו.

2.2.3.1.4 The Samaritans interpret ושבעת (Dt 11:15) as a 3rd fem. sing. perfect form referring to לבהמתך, and pronounce it *wšā'båt* (< *wšābā'at*), like *åzålåt* אזלת.

2.2.3.1.5 It should be noted that the difference between the 3rd fem. and masc. sing. forms in this verb class is in the stress and vowel length. This difference may disappear when a 3rd fem. sing. suffix is added to the 3rd masc. sing. verb form; accordingly, *wlē'qā* is ambiguous: וְלָקְחָה (Lv 12:8)/ וּלְקָחָהּ (Dt 25:5), just as *måṣåttå*, for instance, is ambiguous: מְצָאָתְ (Gn 31:37)/ מְצָאַתָּה (Gn 38:23), etc. — all according to the usual rules in SH. An apparently strange coincidence of forms in this class can be seen in *måṣåttānu*, which also is ambiguous: מְצָאַתְנוּ

(non-existent in the Pentateuch), מְצָאָתְנוּ (Nu 20:14), but this is understandable in the light of the Samaritan rules of pronunciation, as explained in 1.3.5.

2.2.3.1.6 Imperfect. In contrast with the two past tense patterns, the imperfect has only one: the *yifqåd* pattern. The following are representative examples of the conjugation of this verb type: *wiqa* ואקח; *wizbå* תזבח; *tirṣa* תרצח; *yišma* ישמע; *yirṣå* ירצה; *tifra* תפרח; *wniqqa* ונקח; *tigrā'u* תגרעו; *yizbā'u* יזבחו; *yiqṣā'u* יקצעו; *wigbā'u'wå* ויגבהה (Nu 32:35).⁵⁰

Note: The verb יבריא in Nu 16:30 is pronounced as a ל"י verb: *wyibri*; see *LOT* III/2, 321, l. 38.

2.2.3.1.7 Alongside the regular 2nd and 3rd masc. pl. forms, the Pentateuch often has such forms as תשמעון, ישמעון, pronounced *tišʼmūn, yišʼmūn* (rather than **tišmā'on*, etc.). One may, thus, apparently conclude that an original *ā(å)* following the second radical in the above forms (such as *yišmā'u*) was the old vowel (which was also not reduced to *šəwa* in TH in pause), whereas the forms considered here, such as *tišʼmūn*, originated in תשמעון with a *šəwa* — for, in accordance with the Palestinian rules of pronunciation, the *šəwa* assimilated to the vowel of the adjacent guttural consonant, i.e., תִּשְׁמְעוּן > **tišmᵘ'ūn* > **tišmū'ūn > tišʼmūn*. It suffices, however, to study the imperfect, for instance, of the *Pi'el* (such as *tēšallā'u* תשלחו), where *ā* is certainly not the basic vowel of the second radical, and yet in SH there is an *ā*. It must be concluded that both kinds of forms, with or without an *ā* following the second radical, originate in forms with a *šəwa*.

2.2.3.2 Hif'il

2.2.3.2.1 Like verbs with a II-guttural radical, the guttural consonant seems to have affected the change of the short *i* in the perfect of *Hif'il* to *a* (or to *å*) in a closed syllable, while not affecting the originally long *i*, i.e., the vowel in the opened or the originally open syllable. The lengthening of *a(å)* seems to have taken place after the omission of the guttural consonant in pronunciation. Thus, we find in SH *ībåtti* הבאתי, *wībåttå* והבאת, *ūṣåttå* הוצאת, *u'ūdåttimma* והודעתם and, etc., but *wåšbi* והשביע, *wåršiyyu* והרשיעו, etc.

2.2.3.2.2 One must note the tendency to stress the ultimate syllable (thus automatically lengthening the vowel of the second radical) in the imperfect, as in *tåṣ'lī* תצליח, *tåz'rī* תזריע, *tåṣ'mī* תצמיח, *wyaṣ'mī* ויצמיח, yet one also encounters *wyaṣbi* וישביע (SP Gn 50:25), *tirbi* תרביע (Lev 19:19). This inconsistency was apparently

---

⁵⁰ There are readings: ויגבחה, ויגבהוה — i.e., the perfect *Qal* of גבה, interpreted by the Targums: ורוממוה SAV, وعلوها.

known as early as the thirteenth century.⁵¹ In principle it is easy to derive such a form as *tāṣ'lī* from **taṣlī'a/iḥ*, i.e., from a form with a "furtive vowel" (see 1.3.6), be it a *pataḥ* or a vowel equivalent to the one before it, yet it is also possible to understand irregular stress as an attempt to retain the guttural consonant (1.4.6).

> Note: The (first) *i*- vowel in the form *tirbi* תרבי is unexpected. Nevertheless, it cannot be interpreted as *Qal* either semantically or by virtue of its spelling; cf. ירבה, which is imperfect *Hif'il*.

2.2.3.3 *Pi'el*
With Geminated Second Radical

2.2.3.3.1 The rules applying to *Hif'il* apply to the perfect of *Pi'el* as well. Since the vowel in 3rd forms (masculine and feminine, singular and plural) is originally short, too, the present form has an *a(å)* rather than an *ə(e)* as in the strong verb. The following is an example of the conjugation (reconstructions are given in brackets):

	Singular	Plural
1st	*šallātti* שלחתי	*šallānu* שלחנו
2nd masc.	*wšallattå* ושלחת	*šallāttimma* שלחתם
2nd fem.	<*šallatti*> שלחת	<*šallāttən*> שלחתן
3rd masc.	*šalla* שלח	*šallā'u* שלחו, *tāmmā'u* טמאו
3rd fem.	*wšal'lā* ושלחה	

2.2.3.3.2 The short vowel in the 2nd person singular — it is short with an added suffix: *šallattåni* (Gn 31:42; Ex 5:22), *šallattånu* (Nu 13:27) — is unexpected, just as the lack of doubling in the 1st pl. is unexpected. Regarding the 2nd sing., there is also a suffixed form: *wšallattå* (Dt 21:14). Cf. also *Pi'el B*. There probably exists an exegetical explanation for the irregularities, but their very existence indicates various possibilities in pronunciation. It should be noted that the form *šallānu* is regular, despite the lack of gemination of the *nun* (see 1.3.5[d]).

> Note: The verb *wnissåttimma* (Dt 28:63) ונסחתם would seem to be a *Pi'el* form, but instead of the vocalization of the first radical with *a*, there appears an *i*; yet see the פ"נ class, *Nif'al* (2.5.4).

2.2.3.3.3 The form of the imperfect is predictable: *ēšalla* אשלח; *tēnatta* תנתח; *yēgalla* יגלח; *tēšallā'u* תשלחו; *tēgad'dūn* תגדעון; *yēgallā'u* יגלחו. With regard to the form תגדעון appearing in pausal position in the reading of the Jewish Pentateuch (Dt 12:3), see 2.2.3.1.7.

---

⁵¹ See the eighth of Abū Sa'īd's "Reading Rules" (*LOT* I, 155), which is the addition of Pinḥas the Priest, ibid., 154, n. 3 and לה.

2.2 Verbs with a אהח"ע Radical

With Simple Second Radical

2.2.3.3.4 This stem type may exist in the verb מלא. Morphologically, the form cannot be distinguished from the *Qal* stem, for in the perfect the guttural causes a shift in the short *i*-vowel to *a* in this stem in the strong verb. Since *Qal* can be transitive, and since, especially in SH, *Pi'el* can be used in the same sense as *Qal*, there is no sure way of determining if there were originally two separate stems here, *Qal* and *Pi'el B* "with simple second radical," which then merged morphologically, or if there was only one original stem. Since both interpretations are legitimate, I have assigned all the forms resembling *Pi'el* (unlike the Samaritan grammarians; see 2.1.3.5) to *Pi'el B*, and so:

2.2.3.3.5 In the perfect: *mâlāttiyyu* (Ex 28:3) מלאתי from **mâli'tiyyu* (paralleling *wâsiftu*, 2.2.1.3.3) or from **mala'tiyyu* (regular *Qal*), *mâlāttå* (Dt 6:11) מלאת, *wmâla* (Lv 21:10) ומלא, *wmā'lā* (Lv 19:29) ומלאה. In the imperfect: *wyēmālā'u* (Gn 50:3) וימלאו, *yēmâlā'u* (Gn 50:3) ימלאו, *wtēfâqâna* ותפקחנה (Gn 3:7).

> Note: In principle, these imperfect forms may be assigned to *Qal B*. Forms belonging to *Qal* (the main type), at any rate, are *timlā:mu* (Ex 15:9) תמלאמו, *timla* (Ex 29:35) תמלא. The latter indicates that *wmala* in Lv 21:10, too, as well as the rest of the perfect forms in the Samaritan tradition, are originally *Qal* forms.

2.2.3.4 *Nif'al*

2.2.3.4.1 There exist two types of *Nif'al*, the one related to *Qal* (which is also the regular type), and the other which geminates its second radical: *Nif'al B*. *Nif'al* perfect forms are regular in accordance with the rules:
a. *niššābātti* נשבעתי, *niššābāttå* נשבעת, *niššāba* נשבע, *wnissâla* ונסלח, *wnizzā'râ* ונזרעה, *nimmâṣâ'u* נמצאו,
b. *niṭṭāmmātti* נטמאתי, *niṭṭām'mā* נטמאה.

> Note: (a) regarding the form *nūda* נודע, see 2.4.6. (b) *wnēfâqâ'u* (Gn 3:5) ונפקחו is unexpected; it should have been **wniffâqâ'u*, the imperfect of *Pi'el B wyēfâqa* (Gn 21:19) ויפקח having perhaps influenced it. (c) in the form *wniflânu* (SP Ex 33:16) ונפלאנו, the original *Nif'al* pattern has prevailed; see 2.4.6.

2.2.3.4.2 The imperfect, too, appears in two patterns:
a. *timmâna* תמנע, *tiššâka* תשכח; *wyiššāba* וישבע; *tiššâkā'u* תשכחו,
b. *yiqqarra* יקרע (Ex 28:32). The form *tirraggi* (Dt 28:65), which is spelled תרגיע in SP as well, is unexpected in that its final *i*-vowel does not suit a III-guttural verb. It is apparently a mixture of *Hif'il* and *Nif'al B (Nitpa'el)*, because the Samaritans found it difficult to read an intransitive verb in *Hif'il*.

The supposition that this form resembles that of verbs III-y, as is the case with *wtimmåli* (Ex 1:7) ותמלא, is a difficult one.

2.2.3.5 Hitpaʿel

In this class one finds *wētgalla* והתגלח (Lv 13:33) in the perfect, and in the imperfect *wyittamˈmāʾu* ויתמהו (Gn 43:33). Note that SH uses the *Hitpaʿel* of תמה to denote mutuality! Cf. also the infinitive form *itgallāʾu* התגלחו (Nu 6:19).

2.3 Verbs I-*Aleph* (פ״א)

2.3.1 The unique aspect of this class (פ״א) in TH, distinguishing it from other verbs I-guttural, is the few verbs (אפה, אמר, אכל, אבה, אבד) with their own imperfect conjugation in *Qal* and the isolated forms of the same conjugation in other verb stems: וַיִּחַר, יֹאכַל, יֹאבַד (apparently *Qal* of אחר), נֶאֱחָזוּ, אֲבִידָה. The verbs אסף, אחז, אהב behave similarly at times, but differently at other times. This unique initial *aleph* conjugation is ancient, deriving from an original form such as **yaʾkilu*, whereas the regular conjugation is the result of analogy to the strong verb (including verbs I-guttural). The early conjugation is unexpectedly found in a number of additional verbs in MH as preserved in old manuscripts, such as יוגדינו (= יֶאֶגְדֵנוּ) in *Sukka* 1:3 (MS Kaufmann) or שֹׁנוֹסֵר, נוֹסֵר (*Sifra* MS Assemani 66, 43) = נֶאֱסֹר(ש).

2.3.2 As noted above in 2.2.0, in SH all verbs I-guttural are virtually initial I-*aleph* verbs under most phonetic conditions, and the description given applies in general to original I-*aleph* verbs as well. Here we shall consider features unique to original I-*aleph* verbs, as well as forms of the verbs אמר, אכל insofar as they preserve the original initial *aleph* conjugation.

2.3.3 Perfect. The verb ארש appears in *Qal*: *åråš*, naturally wherever the Pentateuchal spelling does not require the *Piʿel* as it does, for example, in the form מארשה *mårråša*. *Piʿel*, however, exists without connection to this condition, as in *tårraš*, which because of the vowel of the second radical cannot be interpreted as *Qal*.[52] MH ארס is known to appear in *Qal* not only in the participial form ארוסה. The verb אהב *åʾəb* may belong to *Qal* in the *fåqəd* pattern (*LOT* III/1, 66), but because of its second guttural radical was attributed to *Piʿel* (see 2.2.2.1.1); the *Piʿel* of אהב is found in the Bible text in the participle only. The reading *wåʾibtå* ואהבת (as well as *wåʾibtimma, wåʾēbåk*) can be inter-

---

[52] This is learnt, too, from the words of Abū Isḥāq (*LOT* I, 89) to the effect that he uttered (?) the perfect in *Piʿel* as well.

2.3 Verbs I-*Aleph* (פ"א)

preted as *Pi'el*, but when reading *wåbtå* one undoubtedly preserves the *Qal*. The verb *ā'əz* אחז has also been attributed to *Pi'el*.

2.3.4 The only *Qal* form of the verb אסף is the infinitive *båsfåk* באספך, and the *Nif'al niyyåsåf*, which because of the vowel of its second radical must be considered a regular *Nif'al* form. The rest of its forms are *Pi'el B* ("simple second radical"), and just as the imperative *åsēfa* is *Pi'el B*, as indicated by the combination of its vowels, so are the perfect *åsiftå* and the imperfect *wyåsəf*. As to the infinitive *līsəf* (SP Lv 19:25, להסיף and להאסיף), see 2.14.13.

2.3.5 The forms *â:mårtå* האמרת, *â:måråk* TH האמירך (SP Dt 26:17, 18: האמרך!) were certainly not understood as forms of *Hif'il*, and so the vowel of the second radical is not *i*; they were considered compound *Qal* forms, i.e., הא (behold) + אמרת, הא אמרת. ST translates them אמרת, אמרך and SAV قايل لله قايلك ! The form *â:kålti* (Ex 16:32), however, can only be interpreted as *Hif'il* despite the *a*-vowel following the second radical (cf. שבר, perfect of *Pi'el*, 2.1.3.4).

2.3.6 The form *wåkålittu* ואכלתו (SP Dt 14:23) is not interpreted as derived directly from **wåkåltå + hū* (cf. וקדשתו *wqaddištu* 3.2.3.1). In contrast, *åkålittu* in Gn 37:20,33 אכלֻתו is derived directly from **akalat + hu*. The form in Deuteronomy parallels that in Palestinian Aramaic, such as CPA אכיריתה **akkiritte* (= הכרתו), while the form in Deuteronomy may conceal the Hebrew element *åkålt* instead of *åkåltå*, similar to CPA from *åkålt + hū > åkålittu* (see *LOT* III/1, 123). The form *wåmårinnu* ואמרנו (Gn 37:20) is very surprising, if we interpret it as first pl. perfect. Its pronunciation apparently indicates the interpretation "and we said of it," being a haplology from *wåmårnu + innu*, where *innu* is an object suffix.[53] I have not, however, found such an interpretation of the word amongst the Samaritans; see 2.8.5.

2.3.7 In the imperfect of *Qal* only the verbs אמר, אכל are distinct from other I-guttural verbs insofar as they stem from the older forms יֹאמַר, יֹאכַל. In this regard there is a big difference between SH and MH, as already noted above in 2.3.1. They are conjugated as follows: *ē'ūmər, ē'ūkəl; tā'ūmər, yā'ūkəl; tā'ūkəl; nā'ūmər; tā'ūkelu; yā'ūmēru; wtā'ūmērinna*. These forms are undoubtedly derived from יֹאכֵל and similar forms, and not directly from the original form **ya'kil*. The syllable with the *o* vowel in יאכל, which was at some time pronounced with two peaks, eventually split into two syllables, the first of which dissimilated (a firm rule in SH). And so the stages of the process are as follows: (יאכל) **yōkel > *yookel > *yō'ōkel > yā'ūkəl*. One should note the difference in

---

[53] Cf. already *LOT* IV, 306 under אמר, and in more detail in the author's article "Verdrängung," 11, n. 6.

dissimilated vowels: in the 1st sing. — *ē*, while in other persons — *a*. *ē* is common in other word types, such as **rōš* (ראש) > *rē'oš*; **kåmōhū* (כמהו) > *kåmē'u*. The dissimilating vowel *a* seems to have been considered analogous to the preformative vowels in the imperfect of I-guttural verbs.

Isolated forms in TH, such as תְּאָכְלֵהוּ, and in BH תֹּאבְלֵהוּ (Job 20:26) and similarly תְּאֶהָבוּ (Prov 1:22) and תֹּאהֲבוּ[54] are sister-forms to the Samaritan ones insofar as they, too, demonstrate the split of a vowel with a long vowel into two, the first of which develops into a *šəwa*. In SH, too, the first vowel may have originally had a *šəwa*.

Note: For the 3rd fem. pl. afformative *inna*, see 2.0.14.

2.3.8 The other III-*aleph* verbs are conjugated in the imperfect according to one of the patterns adopted by I-guttural verbs: (a) the regular pattern, doubling the first radical like *tåbbåd* תאבד, *yåbbåd* יאבד, *tåbbådon* תאבדון, *tåbbå* (Gn 24:5, 8) תאבה (3rd fem. sing.); (b) an ungeminated first radical like *tågår* תאגר, *tåbu* תאבו, *yåbå* יאבה, *tå:bå* (Dt 13:9) תאבה (2nd masc. sing.).

Note: *wtā'əz* ותאחז, *wyā'ēzu* (Gn 47:27) ויאחזו are *Pi'el* forms, to judge by the vowel of their second radical.

2.3.9 It is difficult to distinguish with any degree of certainty between the *Hif'il* and the *Pi'el* in their two patterns with regard to all the forms with a vowel of the second radical in a closed syllable, such as: (a) *tårraš* (TH תְּאָרֵשׁ); *tårrək* (TH תאריך); (b) *tā'ər* תאחר, *tåsəf* תאסף (*Pi'el* "with simple second radical," see 2.2.1.3.3); *tå:mən* תאמין. Yet *tåbbēdon* תאבדון relates to *Pi'el*, whereas *tårrīkon* תאריכון relates to *Hif'il*. In contrast, they are both distinct from *Qal* insofar as the vowel of their second radical is not *ā(å)*, and, thus, according to the vowel of the second radical it is possible to assign *tåbbådon* to *Qal*, *tåbbēdon* to *Pi'el*, **tåbbīdon* to *Hif'il*. It is, however, impossible to determine whether the verbs *tåwwå* תאוה, *tåbbå* תאבה belong to *Qal* or to *Pi'el*, for the tradition of SH is not the same as that of TH; for *a* in ל"י verbs, see 2.8.11.

2.3.10 In the *Nif'al* imperfect, the verbs אכל, אמר have an *ē/ə* vowel: *iyyåkəl* יאכל, *tiyyåkəl* תאכל, *iyyåmər* יאמר; in the others: *å*. See 2.2.1.4.2.

2.4 Verbs I-*Yod* (פ"י)

2.4.1 The unique quality of this class and the difference between it and the strong verb are noticeable only in those forms which do not begin with the

---

[54] Yeivin, *Babylonian Vocalization*, 587, 460 respectively.

2.4 Verbs I-Yod (פ״י)

first radical, such as the imperfect of *Qal*, the *Hifʿil*, and the *Nifʿal*. There is no difference at all between the perfect of *Qal* and the strong verb. It is naturally impossible to distinguish in the perfect between verbs in which the *yod* is original and those in which the *yod* derives from an original *waw*.

2.4.2 The following are examples of the perfect of *Qal*: *yâgårti* יגרתי, *yâṣåqtå* יצקת, *yåšåb* ישב, *yårås̆nu* ירשנו, *yåkålu* יכלו. The verb יסף seems to be conjugated in the perfect in the *qåṭǝl* pattern, e.g., *yåsǝf*, *yåsēfa*. These forms might theoretically have been assigned to *Piʿel* "with simple second radical," were it not for the fact that this root regularly produces a geminated second radical *Piʿel*.

2.4.3 Regarding the 3rd masc. singular and plural forms with *waw*, it is impossible to determine whether the SH tradition has preserved an authentic feature or whether they display a converted imperfect as, for example, *wyåråd* (Gn 15:11) וירד, etc. This is true, too, of *wyålåk* (Gn 12:4) וילך, for the root ילך is found in Ugaritic, and the Samaritan pronunciation may have preserved an early element. At any rate, the form of the imperfect is *yēlåk*; see below 2.9.8. The *ē* vowel of the second radical of *wyēlēdu* (Dt 21:15) is unexpected in the regular perfect, just as it is unexpected in the regular imperfect (consider תלד *tēlåd*), and is to be found in Gn 20:17 as well: *wyēlēdu*. This is apparently a perfect form in the *fēqǝd* pattern, cf. TH יְלִדְתָּנוּ (Jer 2:27). At any rate, it should be noted that in Aramaic the perfect form is not יָלַד, but rather יְלֵד, and the form here may be an Aramaic derivation.

2.4.4 In *Hifʿil* the difference between an original פ״ו verb and an original פ״י verb is evident: *ūlåd* הוליד, *u'ūfi* והופיע, *u'ūdåttimma* והודעתם, *ūšabti* הושבתי, etc., on the one hand, and *īṭību* היטיבו, *wītåbnu* והיטבנו, on the other; the *i* vowel is the result of the regular contraction of *hay* (> *hē*). The form *å'īṭåb* היטב in SP Gn 12:16, equivalent to the infinitive, should not be considered the past tense of *Hifʿil*, but rather a passive form as indicated by ST אתיטב (see 2.10.8), and the first *å*-vowel was considered a vocative element, i.e., (ה)+(א)ייטב = "it was done well." This also applies to *åyånåqå* הינקה (SP Gn 21:7), which is interpreted הא מינקת, i.e., a *Qal* participle in a causative sense, as demonstrated by ST המניקה.[55]

2.4.5 Alongside regular *Piʿel* forms such as *wyabbēma* ויבמה, *wyarrēqa* וירקה(!), *wyašs̆ēba* (Dt 21:13) וישבה, *yallǝd* ילד, one encounters an *å* vowel following the second radical in the form *wyåssåru* ויסרו, and since this occurs in a form requiring a *šǝwa* in TH, it is difficult to prove whether the *å* preserves the early form *qiṭṭal* or derives from the *šǝwa* (see 1.3.1–3), the form *wyåssårti* ויסרתי tending towards the former possibility.

---

[55] So, too, SAV to this verse: مرضعه.

Note:

a. With regard to the aforementioned form *yaššēba*, I have already noted in *LOT* III/1, 134 that this reading is unparalleled in the rest of the Pentateuch and was apparently adopted in order to express a certain view, i.e., the meaning of וישבת בביתך in the mentioned verse is "permanent dwelling" (in a house he uses, he encounters her upon entering and upon leaving").[56] But the idea suggested in *LOT* III/1, that the form reflects a TH noun יַשִּׁיב*, corresponding to יְתִיב, is unnecessary. Not only do the Targumim translate it by means of verbs, but also, and more importantly, the form suits the perfect of the *Pi'el* stem. This shows that here the meaning of this verb is that of the intransitive verb, which normally occurs in *Qal*, and although dictionaries do not carry this fact relating to the Jewish tradition, the verb וְיִשְּׁבוּ in Ezek 25:4 seems to be an intransitive verb, as it was considered in the Septuagint (κατασκηνώσουσιν) and the Peshitta (ונעמר בך חילהון); similarly, David Qimḥi's commentary to the relevant verse makes it clear that he considered this possibility ("as if the text had said וְיָשְׁבוּ בה"). The relationship between *Qal* and *Pi'el* in the verb ישב in TH, too, is the same as that of the verb הלך there.

b. Note that the verb ילד, when its subject is masculine as in Gn 4:18, is read in the *Pi'el yalləd*, for the later language cannot use ילד in *Qal*, which no longer indicates the formation of the embryo but rather its birth — unsuitable to a masculine subject. For this reason the Jewish Pentateuch has no יֵלֶד (imperfect) with a masculine subject, unless the verb is being used in a figurative sense (as in Prov 27:1); the preferred form is *Hif'il* (in the perfect, *Qal* is imposed by the letters of the text, which prevent it being read as *Hif'il*).

2.4.6 Forms such as *wnuwwā'idti* ונועדתי, *wnuwwāsåf* ונוסף are regular SH *Nif'al* forms, in which the first radical is geminated. Residues of the earliest form, as it is in TH, undoubtedly remain: *nūtår* (Ex 10:15; Nu 26:65) נותר; *wnūšåntimma* (Dt 4:25) ונושנתם, though it was possible to pronounce **wnuwwåšåntimma* etc. (cf. 2.1.4.3; 2.5.4), *wnūsīfa* ונוספה (SP Nu 36:3,4).

Note: On the passive form parallel to TH *Hof'al* such as *uwwårəd* (Gn 39:1) הורד (which in its imperfect forms is equivalent to *Nif'al*), see 2.10.4.

2.4.7 As against TH *Hitpa'el*, whether in the פ"י pattern such as בהתודע התודו, or in the פ"י pattern as in התיצבו, SH has three distinct types which apparently derive from different stems, as follows: (a) *wētbåddå* (Lv 16:21), *wētbaddu* (Nu 5:7); (b) *bēttūda* (Gn 45:1); (c) *wittīṣåbu* (Nu 11:16). Type (a) is entirely parallel to TH *Hitpa'el*. Type (b) can be interpreted reasonably, if we assume it

---

[56] *Sifre Deuteronomy*, ed. Finkelstein, 246.

derives from a *Hittaf'al* stem, originating in something like **ba'ithawda*; *Hittaf'al* forms are found sparingly in rabbinic literature. Type (c) strongly resembles Aramaic forms such as *wittīmən* ויתימן (ואתהימן) (*LOT* III/2, 236, l. 138), i.e., the *Hittaf'al* of הימן, though they differ in the vowel of their second radical. It is difficult to assume that type (c) is *Hitpə'el* (borrowed from the Aramaic), for in SA *Hitpə'el* has no geminated *taw*: *it'yēb* (< **ity^eheb*) אתיהב (*LOT* III/2, 230); it is also not *Hitpa'el*, for the *ṣade* is ungeminated, and *Hitpa'el* can be found in SA: *tityåqqår* (*LOT* III/2, 112) תתיקר. Accordingly, the stem of this form seems to be *Hittaf'al* ('*Ittaf'al*), but it preserves an initial *yod*, rather than a *waw*, while the opposite is common in Aramaic, e.g., אתותב, יתוסף, but Aramaic has similar forms in the *Af'el* stem (see n. 61 below).

2.4.8 Imperfect. In the conjugation of the imperfect *Qal* in TH there exist two distinct patterns, the difference between them related to their origin — פ״י verbs on the one hand and פ״ו verbs on the other: (a) like the type יִיטַב (פ״י); (b) the type יֵשֵׁב (פ״ו); there are, however, original פ״ו and פ״י verbs which mingle in conjugation, such as וַיִּיקַר in the פ״ו pattern (Ps 49:9) alongside וַיִּיקַר (1 Sa 18:30) in the פ״י pattern. (c) some verbs conjugate like פ״נ verbs, i.e., they geminate their second radical, like אֶצָּרְךָ (Jer 1:5); (d) the verb יכל is conjugated as יוּכַל (of the same type, perhaps, is תּוּקַד); (e) forms such as ויּר (2 Kgs 13:17), which may preserve its *waw*, the first radical, as *ō* as a result of contraction, i.e., **yawr > yōr*. Compare תּוֹסְףְּ (Prov 30:6).[57]

2.4.9 The four conjugational patterns (a) — (d) exist in SH as well, where they are joined by a fifth, (e), different from the TH (e). The following are examples:

a. *tīra* תירא, *yīṭåb*, *wyīṭåb* ייטב, *yīråš* ירש, *yīšår* יישר, *tīrā'u* תיראו, *tīråšon* תירשון; *wnīråm* ונירם (Nu 21:30)?[58]

b. *tēråd* תרד, *yēråd* ירד, *tēlåd* תלד, *yēlåk* ילך.

c. *iṣṣå* אצא, *wiššåb* וישב; *tiṣṣå* תצא, *tiššåb* תשב, *tidda* תדע; *wyiṣṣå* ויצא, *wyidda* ידע,

---

[57] This is certainly the way these forms were originally, but as they are in the language of the Bible it would seem that because of their similarity to *Hif'il* forms they were integrated into that paradigm; in fact, one finds הַמּוֹרִים together with הַיּוֹרִים in the very same verse in 1 Chr 10:3 (not in 1 Sa 31:3). The question of תוסף is a separate matter, the evidence from the Babylonian pointing being unclear; see Yeivin, *Babylonian Vocalization*, 611. In Arabic there exist parallels showing the existence of the *waw* in *Qal*; e.g., يوسخ "he is dirty," يوجل "he fears."

[58] The most common and accepted of the interpretations of this word is ונירה, with the 3rd pl. suffix, but this is not possible in SH, where the personal suffix is -*imma*, rather than -*am*. This means that the word was interpreted as if derived from the root ירם with a meaning similar to that of ירה, רמה. In the ST there appears וראמנן (MS Barberini) or וארמנן. SAV (MS Barberini) is problematic here, having ורשאקנהם (which should be ורשקנאהם = וירינום), in which there appears a suffix relating to the 3rd plural.

wiqqåṣ ויקץ; *nikkål* (Nu 13:30)⁵⁹ נוכל ; *yiṣṣå'u* יצאו, *wyiddā'u* וידעו; most of these are verbs whose second radical is a sibilant.

    d. יכל: *ūkål, tūkål, yūkål* (Nu 13:39).

    e. *wtåråd* ותרד, *wtåšåb* ותשב, *wtåqå* ותקע, *wtåṣå'inna* ותצאנה.

2.4.10 Pattern (b) differs from its counterpart in TH in the vowel of its second radical. In SH this is always *å(å)*. It is evident that the *å*-vowel spread over the entire paradigm from such forms as תֵּרֶד (Lam 3:48), וַיֵּלַךְ (in pausal position) or תֵּרַדְנָה. Pattern (c) is more common in SH than in TH; it encompasses a larger number of verbs. In TH, too, it is not limited to a sibilant second radical either, though there is no indication of this from the imperfect of *Qal*; such forms as הֻלֶּדֶת (Gn 40:20) provide relevant evidence. This phenomenon is obviously not to be attributed to Aramaic influence, though this is characteristic of פ"י verbs in Aramaic (יְתֵב, יְכַל), for the verb יצא does not occur in Aramaic the way it does in Hebrew. It should be noted that in SH the verb ישב is included in this pattern, though ישר is not, whereas in TH there are forms like וַיְשָׁרֵנָה (1 Sa 6:12), in accordance with the rule (1.2.3): a long vowel in an open syllable corresponds to a short vowel in a closed syllable.⁶⁰ Regarding pattern (d), it should be noted that in place of ותיקד (Dt 32:22), SP has ותוקד which is pronounced *wtūqəd*, the pronunciation and ST indicating that the form was interpreted as *Hif'il*. This applies also to Lv 6:2, i.e., where the *Hif'il* has the same function as *Qal*; this is also true of אוקד in Aramaic.⁶¹ Pattern (e) applies specifically to the converted imperfect; see 2.9.8. It does not seem appropriate to interpret *yåṣåq* יצק (Lv 14:26; Nu 5:15) as the imperfect in the ע"י pattern, though ST translates ירִיק and SAV يسكب, both with the imperfect. This is a case of the regular perfect form being used in the sense of the future (see *LOT* I, 67 on the discussion of ברכתני Gn 32:26), like *yåšåbu* in Gen 34:21, contrasting in form with *wtålåd* ותלד, a regular converted imperfect (2.9.8) used in Gn 30:3 (TH וְתֵלֶד) to denote the future.

> Note: For the reason above, it is sometimes impossible to decide on the basis of 3rd sing. and pl. forms of פ"י verbs whether they are to be attributed to the perfect or imperfect. For instance, *yåšåbu* in Ex 23:33 and *yåråd* in Ex 19:11 may be either perfect forms in a future sense or real

---

⁵⁹ *yūkål nikkål* in Nu 13:30 was translated in ST as נכול (יכלו/) יכל and in the SAV قــدره نــــقــــدر meaning יוכל (so the SP) interpreted as an infinitive (قدره). It is, thus, a noun in the פְּעָל pattern, cf. Aramaic יוכלא = ability; for interchanges of פְּעָל, פְּעוֹל/a segolate pattern, see my "Observations," 17ff.

⁶⁰ See Ben-Ḥayyim, "Penultimate Stress," 155.

⁶¹ See the Targum to Isa 10:16 — the reading being יוקדון, but the reading ייקדון, too, belongs to *'Af'el*; see my article , "Palestinian Aramaic and and Samaritan Poetry," 48.

2.4 Verbs I-Yod (פ"י)

imperfect forms (for the preformative vowel, see 2.9.8). In such cases the forms have generally been classified as perfect.

2.4.11 In *Hif'il* the originally פ"י pattern is dominant, as it is in TH, e.g., *tūləd* תוליד, *tūtər* תותיר, *yūrəš* יוריש, *tūki* תוכיח, *tūtīru* תותירו, *tūsīfon* תוסיפון, *yūrīdu* יורידו. In the פ"י pattern one finds *wtīnīqē'u* ותיניקהו (Ex 2:9; in TH in the ע"י pattern!), *tīṭəb* תיטיב.

> Note: (a) ויקץ (SP Gn 9:24) is read *wyāqåṣ*, i.e., perfect of *Qal*. (b) The Samaritans do not consider אימנה (Gn 13:9) a verb, but rather a nominal form (as indicated explicitly by ST), and so the reading is *ayyammīna*, i.e., הימין + postpositive article (see 7.2). (c) In various places one finds corresponding to TH יֹסֶף, וַיֹּסֶף *yāsəf* (e.g., Dt 1:11), *wyāsəf* (e.g., Nu 22:15). This form corresponds to the perfect of *Qal* or *Pi'el B*, see 2.2.1.3.3. An interchange of the roots אסף — יסף occurs in TH as well as in וַיֹּאסֶף in 1 Sa 18:29 / וַיֹּסֶף in 2 Sa 6:1, because of the merging of a number of their forms in the imperfect; it is, thus, no wonder that it exists in SH as well,[62] for it has no clear sign of being an converted imperfect, and so *wyāsəf* can be a perfect as well, the counterpart to TH וַיַּסֶף, and also the imperfect of אסף. Since *Qal* and *Hif'il* of the root יסף are equal in meaning, that which is not *Hif'il* may be considered *Qal*, though it can be derived from אסף as well. (d) Corresponding to הַיְצֵא (*qere*) in Gn 8:17 SP has הוציא, which is pronounced *ūṣi* as expected. (e) For ותוקד see 2.4.10.

2.4.12 In *Pi'el*, the form *yiyåṣṣår* (Dt 8:5) is to be noted, though the sequence *yiyy*- in I-guttural verbs becomes *iyy*- (see 2.2.1.4.2). The origin of this form is different in that the preformative vowel here was a *šəwa*: יְיַסֵּר;[63] cf. 1.5.3.2.

2.4.13 The imperfect *Nif'al* is attested only in original פ"י verbs, which appears in two patterns, such as (a) *uwwā'əd* אועד, *tuwwåqəš* תוקש, *yuwwåləd* יולד, *yuwwålēdu* יולדו; (b) *yuwwåtår* יותר (Dt 28:54 SP), *yuwwåṣåq* יוצק (Lev 21:10). For *uww* replacing *iww*, see 1.5.3.1e.

> Note: ירה יירה in Ex 19:13 appears in SP as ירא יראה and is pronounced *yårā yårā'i*. יראה was clearly not derived from the common verb ראה, which in *Nif'al* is pronounced *yirrā'i*. Neither was it interpreted as derived from ראה, but rather from ירא. There is no way to interpret it as *Nif'al* of ירה. See 2.10.7. This ראי is merely a metathesis of ירא; cf. Hebrew צוי vs. Arabic وصى.

2.4.14 The imperfect of *Hitpa'el*, as expected, developed from the perfect (on doubtful *Hitpa'el* see 2.4.7). Examples: *yittīṣåb* יתיצב, *wtittīṣåb* (SP Ex 2:4)

---

[62] See *LOT* III/1, 72.
[63] See my *"Penultimate Stress,"* 154.

ותיצב, *wyittīṣâbu*, ויתיצבו, *wyittīlâdu* ויתילדו. *tittīgår* תתגר (Dt 2:9), *tittīgåru* תתגרו (Dt 2:5) are derived by their pronunciation from the root יגר. For the לי"י/פ"י interchange, see above (2.4.9[1] and n. 48) for רמה/ירם, and in TH ספה/יסף and אבה/יאב.

> Note: The Samaritan reading *tittīrā'u* תתיראו in Gn 42:1, as against TH תִּֽירָאוּ, represents a *Hitpa'el* form of ירא "fear," which does not occur in the Jewish tradition of BH, but is found in the Book of Ben-Sira and is common in MH.

2.5 Verbs I-*Nun* (פ"נ)

2.5.1 A TH rule also applicable to the Samaritan version of the Pentateuch is that an initial *nun* assimilates to the adjacent consonant when nothing intervenes between them save before אהח"ע. There exist exceptions such as ינטר alongside יטר and נָחַם(<*ננחם) alongside ינחל. In addition, there are morphological categories in which the assimilation of the *nun* does not apply, such as כִּנְפֹּל, לִנְפֹּל, בִּנְפֹּל. The tendency to assimilate is stronger in MH, where one encounters לִטֹּל, לִפֹּל, etc.

2.5.2 Another feature characteristic of this class in TH is stem suppletion, i.e., in the imperfect *Qal* appears: יִגַּשׁ, יִדַּח, whereas in the perfect *Nif'al* is predominant: נִגַּשׁ, נִדַּח, and it is not difficult to comprehend that the *Nif'al* in these cases is merely the product of the vocalization; the orthography permits *Qal* to be read in the perfect as well. The vocalization represents a later stage than that inherent in the Biblical spelling, at least insofar as some פ"נ verbs are concerned.

2.5.3 The assimilation of *nun* takes place in SH and there is no stem suppletion (except for נתן; see 2.5.11). The verbs נגש and נדח appear in SH in *Qal* in the perfect e.g., *wnâgåš* ונגש, *wnâgåša* ונגשה, *wnâdåttå* ונדחת. In this, SH undoubtedly preserves an early feature, earlier than that reflected by the TH tradition, just as the use of נצב in *Qal*, e.g., *nâṣâbu* נצבו — contrasting with *Nif'al* in TH — is early, as indicated by both Aramaic and Arabic. Similarly, the use of *Qal* in the verbs נכל, נכה, נקה, נתך is probably original, e.g., *nåkålu* (Nu 25:18), *wnâqå* (Nu 5:31), *wnâqåtå* (Nu 5:28), *nåku* נכו (Ex 9:31,32), *nåtåk* (Ex 9:33). The SH *Nif'al* paradigm with its doubling of the first radical (*niffâqåd*) may well have led to the preservation of this early feature; the Pentateuchal orthography did not allow a reading like *ninnâgåš* (see also 2.5.6 below).

2.5.4 The form *nissåttimma* נסחתם (Dt 28:63) is apparently the only certain remnant in this class of a TH-patterned *Nif'al* (see also 2.4.6), and it need not be assumed that the form belongs to SH *Pi'el*, for the *i* vowel following the first radical is unlikely in *Pi'el*. The other residues are almost certain nominal forms (see 2.1.4.3).

2.5.5 The tendency to transform the *Nif'al* form of the II-*waw* (ע"ו) or the geminate (ע"ע) verb into an I-*nun* (פ"נ) root, like נפץ from פוץ in the Bible or נמיגה and נמיסה from מוג and מסס as found in MH, is prevalent in SH. Thus, one encounters in SH *nēmēgu* (Ex 15:15 contrasting with TH נָמֹגוּ, *nēməl* [Gn 17:26] and *nēmīlu* [Gn 17:27] in contrast with TH נִמֹּל, נִמֹּלוּ, respectively).

2.5.6 Since the passivity and intransitivity of the verb were not clearly expressed in the way mentioned above (2.5.3), and not every פ"נ verb could express intransitivity in *Qal* as the verbs נקה,נכה can, SH had to make use of the passive form of *Qal* where TH makes use of *Nif'al*, as is the case with *nēməl* or with *nētən* (Lv 19:20), in contrast with נִתַּן in TH. The 3rd masc. sing. passive is no different from its *Qal* active counterpart in the *fēqəd* pattern, yet from the context it seems best to assume that *nēsək* (Nu 21:9) is not a passive form, just as *nēmēgu* (contrasting with *nēmīlu*) is not a passive form (see 2.10.6).

2.5.7 One should note the changes in the vowel of the ה of the *Hif'il*, a short *a* in such forms as *abbəṭ* הביט, *abbīlu* הפילו, *aggitti* הגדתי, and a long *a* when a *waw* is added to the form; e.g., *wâggitti* והגדתי, *wâggəd* והגיד, *wâššīgok* והשיגוך. Is *wâ* a contraction of *waha > wa'a*? (See 1.5.3.4)

2.5.8 Alongside the regular *Pi'el*, such as *naššibtå* נשבת (SP Ex 15:10), i.e., *i* after the second radical, there are also forms with *a*: *wnåttåṣtimma* ונתצתם (Dt 12:3 in the same verse as *wšåbbårtimma*), *wnåttåṣu* (SP Lv 14:45).

2.5.9 The imperfect of *Qal* and *Hif'il* is usually the same as that of the strong verb (and of III-guttural), except insofar as the *nun* assimilates, as in *Qal*: *tiddår* תדר, *yiggåš* יגש, *yiqqåm* יקם (SP Dt 32:43), *tissåku* תסכו, *tittåṣon* תתצון (SP Dt 7:5), *yibbålu* יפלו. The verb לקח is inflected accordingly: *tiqqa, yiqqa, tiqqā'u*. In *Hif'il*: *aššəg* אשיג, *taggəš* תגיש, *yaggəd* יגד, *takkīru* תכירו. The form *wyånṣēru* וינצרו (Dt 33:9) may be *Hif'il*, but it is possible that it is actually *Qal*, according to 2.1.1.8; 2.5.11. With verbs III-guttural: *wyassa* ויסע, *wyaddiyyu* ויידיחו.

2.5.10 The imperfect of פ"נ verbs which are also II-guttural is like that of *Pi'el* B, and it is impossible to determine which of them was originally *Qal* and which *Pi'el* (see 2.2.2.1.1). Examples: *tēnā'əf* תנאף, *yēnā'əg* ינהג, *tēnā'ēšu* תנחשו. *Pi'el* B can be found in the verb *yēnåfəš* as well (Ex 31:17). The geminated *nun* in the forms *tin'nål* תנחל, *yin'nålu* ינחלו indicates that in SH these forms do not belong to *Qal* but rather to *Nif'al B* (i.e., to *Nitpā'el / Hitpa'el*),[64] and that they correspond in form to *yit'nām* יתנחם with the retention of *taw*. As for the II-guttural verbs, they are identical to the verb נצל: *wtinnåṣṣål*, *yinnåṣṣål* (cf. *wyitnåṣṣålu* in Ex 33:6) and נקש: *tinnåqqåš*. פ"נ verbs also occur in the regular *Nif'al*: *tinnågēfu* תנגפו, *yinnåzēru* ינזרו.

2.5.11 In the verb נתן the old *i* vowel following the second radical is realized in SH, as in TH, as an *e* : *ittən* אתן, *tittən* תתן, *yittēnu* יתנו, etc. For the forms paralleling יֵתֵן and יֵקַח see 2.10.6–7. In *Nif'al* the vowel following the second radical is regularly *å*, except for the verb נתן: *yinnētən* (Ex 5:18; Lv 24:20).

2.5.12 *tiṭṭor* תטור, *tiqqom* תקום (Lv 19:18) are not derived from the פ"נ class but rather from ע"ו (2.6.13).

2.5.13 In most of the forms of the verb נטה, which in TH generally require the gemination of the ט as compensation for the loss of *nun*, SH maintains a simple ט. Note that the distribution of the verbal stems in SH is not precisely the same as that in TH. The following forms are adduced according to the stems to which I have assigned them in SH. *Qal*: *ēṭi* אטה (SP Nu 21:22), *tēṭi* תטה (Ex 23:6; Dt 16:19; 24:17); *Hif'il*: *åṭi* הטי (Gn 24:14), *låṭṭot* להטות (Ex 23:2), *låṭṭūta* להטותה (Nu 22:23), *måṭi* מטה (Dt 27:19); *Pi'el*: *alnåṭṭot* לנטות (Ex 23:2; Nu 22:26). *abnēṭåtti* בנטתי (Ex 7:5) behaves as if the word were derived either from the root נטי (indeed, textual interchange of נטה and נטע in SP is not unknown, e.g., Gn 33:19) or from נתח, which is the Aramaic equivalent in ST of נטה (see *LOT* II, 525; III/2) both in the length of the vowel following the second radical and in the gemination of the *taw*, as if it were compensating for the guttural second radical. Gemination of the ט is absent from *mēṭā*, = TH מַטֶּה, מַטָּה, as well, unlike מַטֶּה (="rod") which is pronounced *måṭṭi*. Compensation for a lost *nun* is lacking also in TH, in תֵּשִׁי (Dt 32:18). This may have resulted from the influence of the very common shortened forms *wyåṭ* ויט, *wtåṭ* ותט, in which the loss of gemination is the rule. This reason does not, however, apply to the absence of compensation for the *nun* in the form *ēbåṭ* הבט (Gn 15:5), while the rest of its forms have a geminated ב. Can the form have been derived from בו"ט as common in the language of Jewish liturgical poetry (*piyyuṭ*)?

> Note: Since the characteristics of the פ"נ verbs do not appear in the verb נטה, its forms are dealt with under the rubric of the ל"ה verbs.

---

[64] This is definitely important with regard to syntax, since it proves that in the Samaritan tradition, too, a reflexive verb may govern direct objects, similar to TH תתנחל אתה (Nu 34:13, cf. also Nu 33:54).

2.5 Verbs I-Nun (פ"נ)

2.5.14 *wtådåd* ותדד in Gn 31:40 appears as if derived from a פ"י root; cf. the נצב/יצב root interchange. Similarly, *wyâṣårinnē'u* ויצרנהו (SP Dt 32:10) can be derived from the root יצר, though it is probably preferable to derive them all from II-*waw* roots. See 2.9.7 note 2.

2.6 II-*Waw* (and *Yod*) Verbs (ע"ו, ע"י)

2.6.1 Neither Hebrew nor any of its cognates supplies evidence capable of determining whether II-*waw* and II-*yod* verbs derive from a group of two consonants separated by one of the long vowels *ī, ā, ū*, or from three consonants, the middle one being one of the "semi-consonants" *waw* or *yod* — an assumption most grammarians have adhered to since the days of Yehuda Ḥayyūj (the end of the tenth century). Yet, it is evident that in historical Hebrew (and outside it as well),[65] the triradical root system is obligatory, and many II-*waw* verbs cannot be formed without postulating the existence of a *waw* or a *yod* between the initial and the final radicals (קָיַם), or without supplying a third consonant, by repeating the second (קוֹמֵם). Since we are interested in describing Hebrew the way it actually developed, we make the same assumption made by Yehuda Ḥayyūj, which is applicable to the other types of Hebrew and withstands the contrary claims made by Samuel Ibn Nagrela (= Ha-Nagid, 11th century) and by Abraham Ibn ʿEzra (12th century; in ספר צחות, the chapter on biradical verbs).

2.6.2 Furthermore, comparative grammar from the 19th century onwards distinguishes between two separate "hollow" classes: II-*waw* and II-*yod*, and tries to assign forms to one or another of the two and to explain their mixture of forms. This mixture is an unassailable fact. For example, a clear II-*waw* root such as קום produces a *Piʿel yod* form, קָיֵם, whereas such clear II-*yod* roots as בין, דין, ריב, generate not only מריבה or מדינה, but also תבונה (like תקומה) or יְרֻבַּעַל (Jud 6:32). Historical grammar is able to show how various forms of II-*waw* or *yod* roots evolved from different origins and resulted in similar forms by virtue of standard phonetic processes, such as, for instance, the infinitive absolute of קום and of שים: קוֹם, שׂוֹם (<*qāwāmu*, *śāyāmu* respectively), or the cause of the shift from II-*yod* to II-*waw* class and vice versa, i.e., the equivalence of the *Hifʿil* of II-*waw* verbs and the *Qal* (and *Hifʿil*) of II-*yod* verbs. As far as historical Hebrew is concerned, it is evident, however, that not a single II-*waw* or II-*yod* verb is conjugated in strict accordance with its original class. Ḥayyūj has already noted (*Kitāb al-'afʿāl dawāt Ḥurūf Allīn* [ed. M. Jastrow 1897], 87) that

---

[65] See Nöldeke, *Beiträge*, 46–47.

these classes are indistinguishable from one another. He went on to express his uncertainty in determining the *sākin lāyin* (= נח נעלם) and its place in these roots; accordingly, he chose *waw* or *yod* arbitrarily.[66] In this respect there is no difference between SH and TH and the other Hebrew traditions.

2.6.3 In TH one distinguishes three patterns in the *Qal* of this class differing in the vowel following the first radical. In the perfect: קָם, מֵת, בֹּשׁ; in the imperfect: יָקוּם, יָדִין, (יָבוֹא) יֵבוֹשׁ. This also separates the II-*waw* class from the strong verb, where these three types are characterized by the vowel of the second radical (see 2.1.1.0). Even those who assume that originally II-*waw* verbs were triradical have been unable to demonstrate any clear connection in the development of the three types between the II-*waw* and the strong verb. It is sufficient to mention that **qawama* should give rise to קוֹם; similarly, one may assume that **mawita* (> **mayita*) should produce after the loss of the final vowel **מֵי, and **bawuša* *בֵּשׁ. Even supposing that in the verbal forms, as against the nominal ones, the diphthong contracted to מֵת "die," it is puzzling that these verbs are never spelled with either *waw* or *yod*. Additional proof for the merging of י״ע and ו״ע roots into one class is the co-existence of doublets, such as גֵּר and גָּר, לָן and לִין in Biblical Hebrew. Obviously, the bases of the three ו״ע/י״ע types differ from those of the three types of the strong verb. Of the aforementioned types SH has almost only the type with the *a* vowel in the perfect, i.e., *qåm* קָם, *šab* שָׁב, though forms of the verb מת with an *e* vowel in open syllables also occur, e.g., *wmēta* וּמֵתָה, *wmētu* וּמֵתוּ, while in closed syllables an *a* vowel is characteristic: *mat, wmat*. The TH form with *o* does not exist in SH: in Nu 24:5 SH has *ṭåbu* vis-à-vis TH טֹבוּ. Only if it is assumed that this TH *ḥolem* reflects an original short *o*, can we conclude that the SH *å* or *ã* is related to it.

> Note: אוֹר (Gn 44:3) pronounced *or* may have been interpreted as a verb by ST and SAV, but its pronunciation does not support this classification.

2.6.4 Contact between the the י״ע class and the geminated second radical class (ע״ע), which is the result of the merging of several forms of the two classes, also exists in SH, where there are, consequently, true and imaginary י״ע roots (cf. 2.4), nonexistent elsewhere to the best of my knowledge, such as שׁוּ״ן (<שׁנ״י): *šanti* (SP Dt 32:41); תו״ם: *tåmu* (Dt 2:16); תו״ך: *tåku* (Dt 33:3) = תַּכּוּ, interpreted

---

[66] Hebrew grammar and lexicography should avoid arbitrarily assigning verbs to either ו״ע or י״ע, as Yehuda Ḥayyūj admits doing. Why should לי״ן be the accepted root and not לו״ן, or why דו״ן and not די״ן (and other examples)? A better approach, it appears, would be to establish one of the two patterns as the standard, and since ו״ע is more common, we represent the verbs in our grammatical classification not only with קו״ם but also with דו״ן and שו״ם.

2.6 II-*Waw* (and *Yod*) Verbs (ע״ו, ע״י)

in the Samaritan tradition as meaning "submission,"[67] מו״ס: *īmīsu* (Dt 1:28) = הַמַּסוּ (see 2.7.4).

2.6.5 The verb ושדת *wšådåtå* also belongs to this class, but, since a final ד tends to merge with the following suffixed ת (cf. ופחדת: *wfåttå*), in order to avoid such an assimilation, an epenthetic vowel was inserted between them, which eventually developed into a full one; cf. מולדתי *mūlēdēti*.

2.6.6 The TH vowel of the ה in the perfect of *Hifʻil* is known to be a reducible *sere*, as in הֵקִים, הֲקִימוֹתִי, הֱפִיצָם. This *sere* leads to the conclusion that the original *Hifʻil* form of ע״י was *hiqīm*. Aramaic cannot help to determine the nature of the early *Hifʻil* vowel, since according to the Aramaic rules such a vowel would become *šəwa*. Biblical Aramaic מְהָקִים does not provide evidence of an *a* vowel, for its *qames* does not support the assumption that it originated in a short *a* vowel. In SH there are two possibilities:

a. *i*, as in *wīqimtå* והקמת, *wīšībūtå* והשבת, *īšəb* השיב, *wīsīra* והסירה;

b. *å*, as in *wårəm* והרים, *wåremtimma* והרמתם, *wåʼīru* והאירו, *åqīṣu* הקיצו. The *å* vowel apparently penetrated the perfect from the imperfect (see 2.6.11). The *a* vowel occurs in those few forms in which the first radical is geminated: *allentimma* הלנתם (Nu 14:29) or *wanʼnī* והניח (Dt 12:10), *anni* הניא (Nu 30:6), *warråttimma* והרעתם (Nu 10:9).

2.6.7 The rule in SH, as in MH, is that the afformative beginning with a consonant (תן, תם, נו, ת, תי) is attached directly to the perfect *Hifʻil* base, i.e., only the type הֲקִמְתִּי exists, rather than הֲקִימוֹתִי, e.g., *wīšibti* והשבתי, *wīniftå* והנפת, *wīqimtå* והקמת, *wåremtimma* והרמתם. (See also 2.7.4.) The following forms are exceptions to this rule: *wīšībūtå* והשבות (Dt 4:39; 30:1); *wårēqåti* הרקתי (Lv 26:33), whose existence I cannot explain.[68] It is evident that SH regular forms preserve the old way, which Hebrew inherited from Proto-Semitic, while TH introduced innovations (according to ע״ע verbs), retaining only a few traces of the original forms: וְהֲמִתָּה (Nu 14:15), הֲבֵאתָ, etc. It should be noted that the vowel following the initial radical in these forms is *i*, which in SH was left unchanged by Philippi's Law.

Note: Concerning the passive that parallels TH הופעל, like *uwwåqåm* הוקם, see 2.10.4.

---

[67] A not far-fetched interpretation. Cf. Syriac תך = punishment, pressure *(Qal)*.

[68] Apparently, הרקתי conforms with הרחקתי (see 2.2.2.2.2), assuming that the vowel after ק developed from a vocalized *šəwa*. Indeed, such an orthography exists (see von Gall ad loc.), however, this explanation hardly looks tenable since אריק חרבי (Ex 15:9) is understood properly and pronounced in accordance with the ע״י verbs (*årəq*). Therefore, it seems reasonable to assume here, too, an ע״ו verb, whose *a* vowel originates from *šəwa*.

2.6.8 The *Pi'el* which has in TH a *yod* as the second radical and behaves like a strong verb, such as וְחִיַּבְתֶּם (Dan 1:10) or לְקַיֵּם (Ruth 4:7), is found neither in the Pentateuch nor in its Samaritan reading. When a Samaritan grammarian mentions the difference between *Qal* and *Pi'el* of the ע״י class, he does note that the *waw* and the *yod* are preserved in *Pi'el*,[69] but his examples for *waw* are קוה, צוה, *qawwīti* (Gn 49:18); for *yod*: איב (*wayyabti*—Ex 23:22) and צין, אים. Regarding the last verbs mentioned, he notes that they are unparalleled in the Pentateuch.[70] This means that the pattern did exist in SH outside of the Pentateuchal traditions, similar to the existence of ו and י in the *Pi'el* verbs "with simple second radical," **yēqåwəm* and **yēšåyəm*, as attested by that grammarian.[71] However, the verbs he cites are not among the defective ע״י class, and he derives a form such as *uwwalti* הואלתי (Gn 18:27) from אר״ל. The *Polel* stem, which takes the place and function of *Pi'el* in the strong verb, is viewed by the Samaritan grammarians as having a quadriradical root. From that pattern we have *kūnēnu* כוננו (Ex 15:17).[72] The form בשש in Ex 32:1 is pronounced *baššāš*, i.e., a verb of the ע״ע class, and indeed Abū Isḥāq categorizes that verb among the verbs with geminated second radical.[73]

2.6.9 The *Nif'al* form of ע״י verbs, such as מול, מוג, and בוך, were considered פ״נ verbs. It should be noted that the medieval Samaritan grammarians Abū Isḥāq and El'azar ben Pinḥas do not cite an example of a regular *Nif'al* verb in the ע״י class. Instead, they say that "the addition of -הו (e.g., הוקם) replaces *Nif'al*."[74] Abū Isḥāq, on the other hand, mentions "*Nif'al* with geminated second radical" of the ע״י class, such as נקים (i.e., **niqqåyyåm*), which is not attested in SP, but can be assumed to have been extant in later Hebrew. The original *Nif'al* has been preserved only in noun forms, such as *nåkūnəm* נכונים.

2.6.10 In the preformative of the imperfect of original ע״י verbs in *Qal*, two vowel patterns are at work: (a) the common pattern with *ē*; (b) the variant pattern with *å*. It need not be stated that (b) continues the ancient tradition. The following are some examples of the conjugation of verbs in these patterns:

a) *ēšob* אשוב, *ēmot* אמות, *tēgor* תגור, *tēqom* תקום, *yēqom* יקום, *tēsūru* תסורו, *yēnūsu* ינוסו.

b) *tå'bū* תבוא, *yå'bū* יבוא, *yåmol* ימול, *tå'os* תחוס, *yå'nu* ינוח, *nå'bu* נבוא, *åšūrinnu* אשורנו. The verb *yå'ol* יאהל (Gn 13:12) should be recalled: from the standpoint

---

[69] See *LOT* I, 87. Obviously, he means in writing, for the ו of צוה is pronounced [b]. See 12.14.15.
[70] See *LOT* I, 89 and also 88, n. 10.
[71] See *LOT* I, 95, n. 19.
[72] Note that the form is construed as imperative (as noted in *LOT* III/1, n. 17).
[73] *LOT* I, 89.
[74] *LOT*, I 101, 209.

of pronunciation, it would seem to be derived from the root או״ל, although it may well be that the source of the verb's vowels are in the noun *å'ol* אהל (see 4.1.3.20).

In some cases, the same verb is attested in both patterns, such as *ēmot* — *åmūta*/אמותה (but *ēšob* — *ēšūba* אשובה), *ånūsa* — *yēnos* from the root נו״ס, and others. It seems that the preformative *ē* originated in forms with *šəwa*, such as *tēṣūrimma* תצורם, and spread to other forms, perhaps under the influence of Aramaic, which has יְקוּם (in Biblical Aramaic) נִיקוּם, אִיתוּב, יִחוּס (see Dalman, *Grammatik*, 320). It is difficult to discern conditions governing the appearance of the *å* vowel, which is preserved from ancient use. On the ultimate stress in forms such as *yå'bū*, see 1.4.6.1.

2.6.11 The *Qal* imperfect of original ע״י verbs is the same as one of the *Hifʿil* imperfect patterns of hollow verbs (see below, 2.6.12), such as *åšəm* אשים, *tåšəm* תשים, *yådən* ידין, *tåšīmu* תשימו; *åqəm* אקים, *yå'ər* יאיר, *yårīmu* ירימו, *wyårībē'u* ויריבהו (SP Gn 49:23!). One cannot, therefore, distinguish between *Qal* and *Hifʿil* on the basis of morphology in such forms as *wyåbīnu* ויבינו, *yåriyyon* יריחון, or *wtåyyīnu* (Dt 1:41) < *wtå'īnu* ותהינו. This fact led — in SH no less than in TH, and perhaps even more so — to the blurring of original ע״י verbs and the creation of *Hifʿil* forms for no compelling reason, such as משים alongside שם, and in late SH[75] משיר from ישיר. As early as SP we find אשירו (Ex 15:1), a *Hifʿil* imperative. This is surprising in SH, given the possibility described in the following section.

2.6.12 In SH, one may distinguish between a *Qal* imperfect of the ע״י class and a *Hifʿil* imperfect, because the *Hifʿil* imperfect has an additional feature: preformative *i*, like the vowel of the perfect (2.6.6), is common: *īšəb* אשיב, *tīnəf* תניף, *tībi* תביא, *yīqəm* יקים, *tīqīmu* תקימו, *yīqīminna* יקימנה (Nu 23:19). There is no doubt that the *i* vowel, which a 13th century grammarian rejected,[76] entered the imperfect from the perfect. The original perfect and imperfect of קום were certainly *īqəm*:*yåqəm*, and those of רום **īrəm:yårəm*, after which the vowels of each pair became identical: the perfect of רום became *årəm*, and the perfect of קום became *yīqəm*.[77] We still find *yå'ər* יעיר (Dt 32:11), *wyå'əl* ויאל (SP Gn 13:18! TH וַיֶּאֱהַל), and *yåqīminnu* (SP Dt 33:11) as well as *yīqīminnu* (Gn 49:9). It appears that the original ע״י verbs were not affected by the analogy just described, so one may not eliminate such forms as *yåšəm* from the category of *Qal* imperfect in the Samaritan tradition, despite the blurring tendency de-

---

[75] See my article, "Samaritan Poems," 336.
[76] See Abū Saʿīd's seventh rule, *LOT* I, 153, and 152, n. 6.
[77] Perhaps this process elucidates the *ṣere* in some MH forms, such as וְהֹעֵידֹנִי (Yeivin, *Babylonian Vocalization*, 655), since in the perfect, the *ṣere* is attested as usual (ibid., 651).

scribed above. Had the process of *i* displacing *a* been completed in the ע"י class, leaving no exceptions, there would have been a sharp distinction between ע"ו and ע"י classes in SH.

> Note: The *ē* vowel in the verb קיא: *tēqi*, is an exception to both the *Hif'il* and *Qal* patterns, and has been assigned to *Qal* because of the perfect form *qā:* (Lv 18:28). Unexpectedly, we find *e* instead of *i* in the *Hif'il* form *wyårēma* וירמה (Gn 31:45).

2.6.13 As in TH, so too in SH do we occasionally find gemination of the first radical in the imperfect of *Hif'il*, instead of an open preformative syllable and a long vowel, but not necessarily in the same verbs as in TH, e.g., *takkən* תָּכִין, *yazzəd* יָזִיד, *wtazzīdu* וַתָּזִידוּ, *yassītåk* (Dt 13:7; TH יְסִיתְךָ), *yanni* יָנִיחַ (Dt 3:20), and (if it is a *Hif'il* form) *nallən* נָלִין. Unlike TH, the two verbs קום and טור have geminated first radicals in *Qal*: *tiqqom, tiṭṭor* (Lv 19:18). The Samaritan pronunciation certainly does not derive them from נקם and נטר, which we learn from the forms *yiqqåm* (see 2.5.9) and *yiṭṭår* in SA (see for example *LOT* III/2, 261), which do not contain the *o* (< *ō*) vowel. The *o* vowel would be anticipated only in forms derived from ע"י. While the Samaritan translations of this verse do not differ from the Jewish exegetical tradition, there is nothing to be learned from them about the traditions of pronunciation. We know from *Hammeliṣ* (*LOT* I, 477, n. 85) that תטור was derived from טור and not from נטר.[78]

2.6.14 Different from *tiṭṭor*, etc., are forms such as *wyiššåt* (Nu 24:1; TH וַיִּשֶׁת), *wyirråb* (Gn 31:36; וַיָּרֶב), and *wyiggåz* (Nu 11:31; וַיָּגָז), whose derivation follows the ע"ע pattern. See also 2.7.6.[79]

2.6.15 The converted imperfect differs from what is described above (2.6.10), having a form like *wyåqåm* (see 2.9.7), but even without *waw consecutive*, one finds *yåšår* ישר (SP Ex 15:1) in the sense of a perfect. With regard to *yåšåš* (Dt 28:63), which is supported by the infinitive *alšåš* (Dt 30:9), it would seem to belong to the ע"ע class, although it seems unlikely to assume such a root in which all three radicals are identical (but note the noun גג!); in any case, the

---

[78] If the Samaritan tradition did derive these verbs from נקם and נטר, the Samaritan scribes would not hesitate to write them without the *waw* as a *mater lectionis*. Instead, the scribes used *waw* generously in these verbs, because of their pronunciation and the class that pronunciation represents (see "Some Problems," 230–232, 254ff.). On the relationship between TH תִּקּוּן and SH *tiqqom* (< **taqqum*), cf. TH חַנּוּן: SH *ånon*, עַתּוּדִים: *'ātūdəm* (in Arabic عتر, without gemination). It may be that SH utilized this possibility, inherent in several areas of word formation, to draw semantic distinctions.

[79] See "Some Problems," 252, n.1, which mentions שַׁתּוּ (Ps 48:14) and וְרֹבּוּ (Gn 49:23).

tense of *yåšåš* is not perfect.⁸⁰ The forms *tâbā'u* and *yâbā'u* (as contrasted with *tāˈbū*, *yāˈbū*) are a separate matter. They are derived from **yâbū'u*, with dissimilation of the first *u*, as in the form *wyåˈūmər* וַיֹּאמֶר; see 1.5.3.2. The form *tāf* תעף (SP Dt 4:17) seems to belong to the ע"י class (2.7.7).

2.6.16 Strong *Pi'el* verbs in SH include *yåwwər* (< **yᵃ'awwir*) יעור. The verb צוה is among the *Pi'el* verbs "with simple second radical" (see 2.8.16). Quadriradical verb forms (i.e., *Polel* and *Hitpolel*) parallel the forms in TH: *wyēkūnēnåk* ויכוננך (SP Dt 32:6), *wtitkūnən* ותתכונן (SP Nu 21:27), *wērūmēminnē'u* וארוממנהו (SP Ex 15:2).

2.6.17 *Nif'al* imperfect verbs are attested only "with geminated second radical": *yiggåwwår* יגור⁸¹ (SP Lv 11:7), *yēwwåtu* יאותו (< **yē'uwwåtū* < **yi"awwatū*) (Gn 34:22), *nēwwåt* נאות (Gn 34:15, 23) (MS British Library Or 7652 and MS Barberini Vat Sam 2: יתשבן, נמתשבי, i.e., *Ettaf'al* of שוה — a passive form).

2.7 Geminate Verbs (ע"ע)

2.7.1 Verbs with geminated second radicals (ע"ע) are considered by Hebrew grammarians to be in a position between the strong verb and the verbs with weak radicals in that, while no radical consonant is "weakened" or left unpronounced, one radical consonant may assimilate to a neighboring consonant (as in the פ"נ class) and be doubled in pronunciation — and when that occurs, the original consonant is absent from the written form. As was noted of the ע"ו verbs (2.6), here, too, one cannot determine whether the verbs with geminated second radical have their origin in biradical roots that were expanded by gemination of the second radical or, alternatively, these verbs began with triradical roots and, in the course of time, lost the vowel between the second and third radicals, causing them to come into contact. It is, of course, possible to assume that a form such as *sababū might develop into *sabbū סַבּוּ. It is unlikely, however, that *yasbubū might develop into *yasubbū יָסֹבּוּ, so in this case we are forced to seek refuge in the assumption of a form antecedent to *yasbubū, such as *yasububū (cf. *GvG* I, 257), as the ancestor of יָסֹבּוּ.

---

⁸⁰ Since this verb has no cognate outside Hebrew, there is no way to tell whether there is any basis for the conjecture that its conjugation follows the pattern of خاف and نام in Arabic.

⁸¹ In a Geniza fragment, MS Oxford Heb. C 10, containing *Sifre Deuteronomy*, we find (cf. ed. Finkelstein, 342) "דרך ארץ הוא גוליורין מיתגורין במלחמה וגיבורים נוצחין"; other manuscripts read "מתגרין." The verb גור with the meaning "stir up" (usually assigned to גרה) is found, for example, in Ps 140:3 יגורו מלחמה. The form in the fragment above corresponds to the Samaritan *yiggåwwår*, although גו"ר in SH appears with another meaning, that of "drag," "pull" (גרר).

Whatever the origins of these verbs, their structure — not only in Hebrew, but also in Proto-Semitic — must be viewed as triradical,[82] since there is no difference between the geminated consonant in a given form of an ע"ע verb and any other geminated consonant generated in Hebrew by accidental contact. In other words, gemination such as that of the ב in סַבּוּ is no different in the surface form from the gemination of ת in כָּרַתִּי, despite their different origins.

2.7.2 In Tiberian Hebrew, a verb belonging to the ע"ע class may behave in any of five ways:

a. The second radical is geminated, unless, of course, it is at the end of the word, e.g., נָסַבּוּ, יֵקַלּוּ, יָסֹבּוּ, קַלּוּ, סַבּוֹת, בַּלּוֹתִי (but נָסַב), etc.

b. Both the first radical and the second radical are geminated, e.g., יִתֹּמּוּ, יִמַּקּוּ, וַיִּסֹּבּוּ, הִשַּׁמָּה; the *Qal* forms in this way are equivalent to the *Nif'al* forms. It is indeed difficult at times to decide with which to identify a given verb; we may generally distinguish them by past tense forms.

> Note: The form יִמַּס is usually identified by grammarians and lexicographers as *Nif'al*, even in Dt 20:8. It may be, however, that the form should be classified as *Qal*, and that its use in Dt 20:8 should be understood as a transitive verb, the object of which is את לבבם, in a fashion similar to the *Qal* verb סבב, which appears in both transitive and intransitive uses. In fact, this is the understanding of that verse in the Septuagint (which interprets: ἵνα μὴ δειλιάνῃ τὴν καρδίαν τοῦ ἀδελφοῦ αὐτοῦ) and the Vulgate (*ne pavere faciat*). The Samaritan pronunciation of the verb in that verse is *yīməs*, i.e., *Hif'il* of the verb מוס, similar to Dt 1:28. It has been suggested that the verb in Dt 20:8 should be vocalized יָמֵס, but there is no need to emend the text in order to make sense of the syntax.

c. The first radical alone is geminated, e.g., וַיִּקְּדוּ, יִדְּמוּ, וַיִּתְּמוּ, נִחַנְתָּ (< *niḥḥanta*). This type primarily, and to a lesser degree type (b), are known as "the Aramaic type," since Aramaic usually geminates the first radical in this root class.

d. No radical is geminated as a rule, but instead: (1) the verb follows the י"ע pattern, as in אֱמָשְׁךָ, בְּחָקְךָ, יְמִישׁוּן, כַּהֲתֹמְךָ (see 2.6.4 above); (2) an affix blends in, forming a new "root" as in נָזֹלוּ (from נָזֹלוּ [Isa 63:19]), נָבְקָה (from *נָבְלָה), *נָבְלָה (from נָבְלָה), and יָזֹמוּ (from *יָזֹמוּ); new roots have indeed been created from such forms in later Hebrew (v. 2.7.13 below), just as they have from other weak verbs, e.g., the later יִמֵּן, found in liturgical poetry and meaning "to order, prepare," generated from the Biblical וַיְמַן.

---

[82] Bauer and Leander (BL, 427) postulate that an ע"ע verb is composed of "a consonant + a vowel + a long consonant," which is nothing more than a variant formulation of "a geminated consonant."

2.7 Verbs with Geminated Second Radical (ע״ע)

e. The pattern of the strong verb is followed in every detail, such as סָבְבוּ, צָרוֹר, גָּנוֹן, הָרְנִינוּ, נָדֹד, לָגֹז, בָּזְזְנוּ, etc.

2.7.3 Patterns (a)-(d) above are not dictated by the orthography of the verbs in the Bible. This is not true of pattern (e). Thus, it happens only infrequently that the SP is distinguished from MT by the orthography of verbs of this class, such as the Samaritan לגוז (Gn 31:19) and לבז (Dt 1:39), as compared to לגז and לבז in MT. Differences between the patterns, such as יְמֻשֵּׁנִי (Gn 27:12)/יְמִישׁוּן (Ps 115:7) or סְבָבוּנִי/סַבּוּנִי both Ps 118:11) cannot be attributed to any semantic difference, not even slight shades of meaning, but must be seen to reflect different trends in the development of Hebrew during the period when it was spoken by Samaritans as well. It is well known that MH evinces a marked growth of the trend toward treating ע״ע verbs as originally belonging to the ע״י class, which is true of the Aramaic of that period as well.

2.7.4 With the exception of pattern (e), which is dictated by SP orthography, a widespread merger of ע״ע and ע״י forms is created in SH for two reasons. The first is that the distinction between *qameṣ* and *pataḥ* that makes us classify סַב among the ע״ע verbs and קָם among the ע״י verbs is not observed by SH, so that a form such as דק (Dt 9:21) is pronounced *dåq* in the same way that קם = *qåm*, and רע in Nu 11:1 is pronounced *rā* in the same way that שב is realized *šab* (with a front vowel!). The second reason for the merger is the absence in SH of an intercalated vowel between the base of the verb and the suffixes that begin with a consonant. Thus, one finds TH וְשַׂכֹּתִי (Ex 33:22): SH *wšakti*; וְסַכֹּת (Ex 40:3): *wsåktå*; וְקַצֹּתָה (Dt 25:12): *wqåstå*; וַחֲגֹּתֶם (Lv 23:41): *wā'egtimma* (< *wa'igtimma*); and וּמַדֹּתֶם (Nu 35:5): *wmådåtimma* (< *wmadtimma*) [as to the *å* vowel, see above 2.6.5]. This practice is, of course, common in MH.[83] These two phenomena caused several ע״ע verb forms in which the second radical or the first radical is geminated in TH, i.e., verbs that are inflected according to one of the patterns of ע״ע, to tend to follow the ע״י patterns in SH, such as קַבֹּה (Nu 23:8) *qåbu*; וְקַבֹּתוֹ (Nu 23:27) *wqåbittu*; יִמַּס (Dt 20:8) *yimas*; וַיִּקְּדוּ (Gn 43:28) *wyåqådu* (similar to :*wyåqåmu*); and in post-Biblical Hebrew קָד קידה; and possibly also וַיֵּצֶר (Gn 32:7) *wyåṣår*. These and others like them may be assigned to the ע״י class (see 2.6.4).

---

[83] I could not find an example of this in *Qal* that was similar to the Samaritan forms cited above, but only in *Hifʿil*. Note that MS Kaufmann at *m. Qiddushin* 4:14 is vocalized שֶׁהֲרִירַעְתִּי, as expected. In ע״י verbs, this form may occur in *Nifʿal* as well, e.g., (נ)ונתם in *t. Bava Batra* 8:18. In view of the fact that this form does not happen to appear in *Qal* verbs, we tend to assign verbs such as וְצַרְתִּי (את צרריך) (Ex 23:22) to the ע״י category. Is it right to so categorize verbs unattested in any form other than the one in question, which may be classified with ע״י, like the Samaritan forms above? See also 1.5.3.3f.

2.7.5 Nonetheless, a survey of the inflection of original ע"ע verbs in SH teaches us that of 65 verbs that can be found in the TH Pentateuch, only three or four (גרר, מסס, קדד, and perhaps נדד) consistently follow the י"ע pattern in SH. Thirteen follow both ע"ע and י"ע patterns: שכך, רבב, קלל, קבב, צרר, סבב, משש, מדד, גזז, בזז, and תמם. If we eliminate from consideration all those verbs for which the consonantal text dictates their classification as ע"ע forms, such as כמתאננים, מקשש, and others, there still remain in SH more than twenty verbs that follow the patterns unique to ע"ע verbs. We see, then, that the ע"ע conjugation pattern is firmly established in SH, and the transition from ע"ע to י"ע is not as common in SH as in Palestinian Aramaic. Furthermore, one can find in SH verbs of the ע"ע class that are unattested in TH, such as *dakku* for MT דַּכּוּ (Nu 11:8). See also 2.6.14.

2.7.6 The following patterns, then, are attested in SH:
  a. Gemination of the first radical. (This is the most common pattern.) In *Qal* imperfect — SH *wiqqåṣ* : TH וַיָּקֶץ (Lv 20:23), *wiqqål* : וַיֵּקֶל, *wiqqåd* : וַיִּקֹּד, *wikkåta* ואכתה (SP Dt 9:21), *tibbåz* : תָּבֹז (Dt 20:14), *tiggåz* : תָּגֹז (Dt 15:19), *wyillån* וילן (SP Ex 15:24), *yirråk* ירך, *tirra* תרע (Dt 28:56), *yiddåmu* : יִדְּמוּ, *wyikkåtu* : וַיַּכְּתוּ (Dt 1:44), *yittåmu* : יִתַּמּוּ (Nu 14:35), *wyirrånu* : וַיָּרֹנּוּ (Lv 9:24). In *Hif'il* perfect — SH *wåššimti* והשמתי (SP Lv 26:31): TH וַהֲשִׁמּוֹתִי, *wåṣṣår* : וְהֵצַר (Dt 28:52); in the imperative — SH *waqqəl* : TH וְהָקֵל; and in the imperfect — SH *yaggəd* : TH יַגֵּד (Gn 49:19), *yaggīdinnu* יגידנו (SP Gn 49:19), *wyarrəm*: TH וַיָּרֶם (Ex 16:20), *yarrēfåk* ירפך, *wyarriyyu* וירעו. With *Nif'al*, the perfect appears in such forms as SH *wniqqål* : TH וְנִקְלָה (SP Dt 25:3); we also see the gemination of both first and second radicals in SH: *wniššammu* (Lv 26:22) : TH וְנָשַׁמּוּ.

> Note: (1) As stated above (2.7.2), this pattern does not enable us to distinguish between the *Qal* imperfect and the regular *Nif'al* imperfect, and some verbs classified as *Qal* may be assigned to *Nif'al*. (2) The verbs *aqqåb* אקב (Nu 23:8), *yazza* יזח (Ex 28:28), *yarra* ירע (Dt 15:10), *tarra* תרע (Dt 28:54), and *wtalla* וַתֵּלַהּ (Gn 47:13), even though their preformative vowel is *a*, are assigned to *Qal*, because the vowel of their first radical is *a* and because of their form in TH. (On the preformative vowel, see also 2.1.1.8). With regard to the pronunciation *tarra*, it should be noted that in the parallel verse (Dt 28:56), the Samaritans read *tirra*. For the interchange of the forms *tarra* / *tirra* in Dt 28:54,56 תרע two explanations are possible: (1) both forms are variants of one verb in Qal, semantically indistinguishable, which function as predicates of the subject עינו/עינה; (2) the difference in form may reveal a different tradition underlying the analysis of v. 56, i.e., *tarra* is understood here as a *Hif'il*[84] form governing

---

[84] It is true that we have found the first radical with a vowel in *Hif'il* — in converted imperfect

2.7 Verbs with Geminated Second Radical (ע״ע)

the subject עינה. In this case the reading *tarra* in v. 54 results from a textual conflation of two passive constructions (see *LOT* III/1, 149). The first explanation seems to me more plausible.

b. Gemination of the second radical. This occurs in the *Qal* perfect: *qåṣṣå* (Nu 21:5); and in the imperfect: *wyēmaddu* וימדו, *wyēfazzu* ויפזו.

2.7.7 In I-guttural verbs, the preformative may take the following vowels: (1) *a* (as the original vowel), as in *tåg* תחג (< *ta'ag* < *tahug*), *yåm* יחם, *tåf* תעף.[85] (2) *e* (originally *i*): *tē'år* תאר, *tē'åt* תחת. Forms without suffixes cannot be classified according to the patterns mentioned in 2.7.6. The verbs *tåggu* תחגו and *tåggē'u* תחגהו (Ex 12:14) indicate Pattern (b); *wyå'ēnåk* ויחנך (Nu 6:25, Gn 43:29) and *tå'ēnimma* תחנם (Dt 7:2) indicate Pattern (a): *wyå'ēnåk* < *wyaḥḥᵉnak*. No clear disinction may, thus, be drawn between *Qal* and *Hif'il*: *wyå'əm* וַיָּהָם (Ex 14:24), *wyå'əl* ויחל (Nu 25:1), *wtå'ēlinna* ותחלנה (Gn 41:54). Therefore, I have chosen to arrange all such forms as *Hif'il*.[86]

2.7.8 The examples above clearly support the conclusion that SH does not inflect each verb in the same way as TH, whether in the gemination of the first or second radical or in following the ע״י pattern. Thus, for example: TH קוץ / SH קצץ, TH קדד / SH קוד,[87] or SH *wyēfazzu* ויפזו / TH וַיָפֹצוּ.

2.7.9 Note that the vowel of the preformative ה in *Hif'il* is always *a*, including those verbs that follow the ע״י pattern (see 2.6.6), e.g., *å'ilti* החלתי (Dt 2:31). Similarly, aformatives beginning with a consonant are always joined directly to the base of the verb. (See 2.6.7)

2.7.10 *Pi'el* (including *Polel*) and *Hitpa'el*, of course, act in the same way as strong verbs. *Pi'el*: *tēqallǝl* תקלל, *yēmaššǝš* ימשש, *yēbannē'u* יבננהו.[88] *Pi'el* with a quadriliteral root *(Polel)*: *tūlǝl* תעולל, *yēsūbēbinnē'u* יסובבנהו. *Hitpa'el*: *witfallåla* ואתפללה (Dt 9:20), *wetånnåna* ואתחננה (Dt 3:23). The verb *titgådēdu* תתגדדו (Dt

---

forms, such as *wyanna*/וינח (Nu 17:22) (as opposed to *yanni* [Lv 7:15], and in the imperfect of ל״ה verbs [see 2.8.11, 2.8.16]) — and one might assume a *Hif'il* use with the meaning of the *Qal* verb, particularly in the case of the verb וירץ (see *LOT* III/1, 149, n. 54). Nonetheless, *Hif'il* is inappropriate to the pronunciation of אקב, and I have preferred to list them all as *Qal*.

[85] From *yåffaf* יעפף (Gn 1:20) as against *tūlǝl* תעולל (see 2.7.10), it is evident that SH has the verb עפף in place of TH עוף. Note that *wyår* ויאר (SP Nu 22:6) is a passive form; see also 2.10.7.

[86] It seems likely according to Samaritan tradition that these forms are constructed from the *Hif'il*, just as it is customary to view יָגֵן as *Hif'il* ע״י, and not *Qal* (cf. וְגֻנּוֹתִי) with an original imperfect like יִתֵּן (cf. 2.1.1.0).

[87] A similar variation within TH can be found: אָקוּט: קטט/קוט (Ps 95:10), וְנָקֹטוּ (Ezek 6:9).

[88] Of course, the root is בנ״ן. Cf. Arabic تبنّى "adopt as a son" and indeed SAV (MS Barberini) at Dt 32:10 uses ובננה, where the ST reads ובניה/ובננה. See also 0.13 above.

14:1) is a *Hitpaʿel* form with a simple second radical, parallel to Aramaic *Itpeʿel*; see also 2.1.5.3.

2.7.11 It should be noted that in the conjugated forms of the *Piʿel* verb חלל — i.e., in open syllables — the imperfect is formed with *i* and not, as usual, with *e*: *talləl* תחלל; *tallīlu, yallīlu, tallīlinnu*; while in the perfect, the vowel is *e*: *ʿalləl* חלל, *wallīltå* חללת, *ʿallēlu* חללו. It is not inconceivable that the imperfect follows the *Hifʿil* construction (*yallīlu* < *yaḥlīlu*), but since the perfect forms are clearly *Piʿel*, the imperfect is presented here as *Piʿel* as well, and indeed we find *i*, and not necessarily *e*, in place of TH *šəwa*.[89] SH used the possibility of vocalizing the second radical with *a*, such as *wåṣṣår* והצר, *åra* הרע (SP Nu 22:32), to distinguish between *wållīltå* חללת (such as the use in Lv 19:12, in a sacral context) and *ʿallåltå* in Gn 49:4.

2.7.12 The form *zåməm* זמם (Dt 19:19) is not a *Qal* construction in the same pattern as *fåqəd*, but rather *Piʿel* "with simple second radical." It should be noted that ST translates this as יזמן, i.e., using a verb that occurs in the Yemenite tradition in the same construction: יְזַמֵּן, מְזַמֵּן. And indeed, for יָזְמוּ (Gn 11:6), SP reads יזמנו, pronounced as *yēzåmēnu*, i.e., a *Piʿel* "with simple second radical" of the root זמן.[90]

2.7.13 The forms נסבו *nåsåbu* נסבו (Gn 19:4) and *wnåmås* ונמס (Ex 16:21) parallel the TH practice mentioned in 2.7.2, Pattern (d) and may be assumed to be פ"נ verbs.

2.8 Verbs III-*Heh* (ל"ה)

2.8.1 Comparative grammar and several forms in TH, such as the spelling of נטוות (Isa 3:16) and עשווים (2 Kgs 23:4), along with other phenomena, can be used to demonstrate convincingly that the so-called ל"ה class includes verbs that originated as ל"י or ל"י,[91] but which, over time, became indistinguishable. In fact, all the forms of the verb of this class in historical Hebrew can be explained as derived from ל"י verbs. Given that such different, assumed original forms as *banaya* and *galawa* evolved into patterns identical to one an-

---

[89] See 2.2.1.2.2, 1.3.1; cf. 2.7.6.
[90] The variant pair זמם and זמן in SP indicates the antiquity of the phenomenon well known to us from ancient manuscripts of MH literature and from the Dead Sea Scrolls.
[91] Of course, such verbs as שָׁלוּ and forms such as חסיו and ירביון are to be classified as strong verbs.

other, such as בנה and גלה, the ל"י verbs have approached the ל"י class as the result of analogy, even where no identity of surface forms is anticipated, such as in the second person form: *qawwaytā* > קִוִּיתָ; but from *galawtā*, which should of necessity evolve into *galotā*, we have instead גָּלִיתָ. That entire process took place in the earliest stages of the development of Hebrew and appears fully-formed in the Masoretic text of the Bible, just as it does in SP.

2.8.2 On the other hand, SH preserves clear traces both of verbs with *a* as the vowel of the second radical and of those with *i* in the same position. In verbs with *a*, such as the reconstructed *banaya*, the diphthong *ay* contracted to ṣere, just as the rule would dictate, e.g., *nabnaytinna* > נִבְנֶיתֶן. In contrast, in verbs with the *i* vowel, such as *šatiy(a)*, the *iy* contracted to *i*: *šatiyta* > שָׁתִיתָ. The original meaning of the difference between ḥireq and ṣere as the vowel of the second radical was blurred over time with the loss of the distinction between active and stative verbs (see 2.1.1.0.2), and in TH, the vowels in question were distinguished according to fixed morphological patterns. In some patterns, both ṣere and ḥireq were used (e.g., קִוִּיתִי Isa 5:4, הֶעֱלִית Ex 32:7; קִוִּיתִי Gn 49:18, and הֶעֱלִית Ex 33:1). It must be assumed that in the same way, there was a difference at first between forms such as שָׁתוּ (< *šatiyū*) and forms such as *בָּנוּ (< *banayū*), until analogy blended the two patterns together. In Biblical Aramaic (but not only there), the forms with an *a* vowel in this aformative (בְּנוֹ) prevailed, while in Hebrew those with an *i* vowel prevailed.

2.8.3 At the stage displayed by SH, phonetic rules had caused a further streamlining of the conjugation of ל"ה verbs:

a. All *ay* diphthongs had become *i* vowels, and the distinction between forms such as קִוִּיתִי/קָוִיתִי was obliterated, with both becoming *qawwīti*;

b. The vowels *o* and *u* became one phoneme, and the occurrence of each vowel is determined by the structure of the syllable and not by its origin. In addition, SH took a path not taken by the Biblical Hebrew of the Jews, but one which is found in the traditions of MH: a consonantal י between vowels may become א, just as we find in MH שְׁאֵפָה and פְּדָאן alongside שְׁאֵפָיָה and פְּדָיִין, for example. Similarly, we find in SH: *anniglā'ot* הנגלאות (SP Dt 29:28), whose origin is undoubtedly *anniglāyot*, with the third radical י retained, similar to נְטָיוּ (Nu 24:6), מְמֻחָיִם (Isa 25:6), *'an'nā* (Dt 22:29) whose origin is ענאה (SP ענהה) < עניה = TH עָנָה, and perhaps also *qā'rāk* קראך (SP Dt 25:18), which, however, can be explained on the basis of ל"א roots, cognates to the ל"י class. These forms and others like them cause ל"י verbs sometimes to follow ל"א verb patterns (that is, III-guttural in SH). The phenomenon is ancient, as is evident from its spelling in SP. Nonetheless, the original method of conjugating ל"י verbs is preserved, for the most part.

2.8.4 The following are the conjugations of the imperfect *Qal*, employing the verbs ראה, קשה, קנה, בנה, and שתה:

šåtītī	rå'īnu
bånītā	šåtītimma
båna, qånå	bånu
qåšātā	

There are, though, several exceptions to this rule:

a. The verb שבה, whose 3rd pl. masc. form is properly *šåbu* (Gn 34:29), has an *ē* after the first radical in the 2nd masc. sing.: *wšēbītå* ושבית (Dt 21:10). Similarly, וחטאה (Lv 5:15) is pronounced with *ē*, as *wē'tå* (<*wētā'a*), in place of the *a* vowel in all other forms, e.g., *'åṭīti* חטאתי, *wfēru* ופרו (Gn 8:17), as against *fåru* (Ex 1:7). The origin of *ē* may lie in the *šəwa* of older forms, along the lines of שְׁבִיתֶם in TH, which later was extended to other forms. More plausible, though, is that the vowel of the imperative has been transferred here because of the meaning of these forms in the aforementioned verses, a hint, as it were, at the converted perfect (see 2.9.6).

b. בזה (Nu 15:31) was realized as *afzå*, and in ST there is a reading אבזה, which testifies to the antiquity of that pronunciation, which would otherwise seem to be an Aramaism: בזא.[92] But we can be nearly certain that the pronunciation reflects a Hebrew *Hif'il*, similar to that found in Est 1:17, although the *f*, instead of the *b*, is perplexing. (See 1.1.4).

c. The verb חסיו, a *hapax legomenon* in the Pentateuch (Dt 32:37, TH חָסָיוּ) forms in SH together with the following particle בו a single stress unit: *isyu-bū*. This fact caused the shift of its stress to the ultima and simultaneously the reduction of the *å/ā* vowel after the second radical (cf. 1.4.10). However, the *i* vowel after the first (originally *ḥ* or *'*) radical remains unexplained. The pronunciation of the verb in the given situation could be understood as an imperative (2.11.2), but this does not fit the context and disagrees with its translations in ST and SAV. It has been listed in *LOT* IV, 103 under *Qal* perfect.

> Note: the verbs היה, חיה, and עשה are dealt with separately, due to the complexity of their conjugation. See 2.8.18–20.

2.8.5 Alongside the *Hif'il*, which parallels TH so well (e.g., *aqså*/הקשה, *arbå*/הרבה, *wåšqīta*/והשקית), the verbs ראה and רבה display odd inflection. ראה geminates the initial radical ר in *Hif'il*, (and in *Hof'al*; see 2.10.8), e.g., *ar'rå* הראה, *ar'rånu* הראנו, *ārråttək* הראתיך (in Dt 34:4 and also in SP Ex 9:16!), *ar'råk* הראך.

---

[92] *afgåd* בגד (Gn 30:11) would seem to be a parallel form to בזה, but it is simpler to explain it there as גד with a prepositional ב, and indeed the LXX reading ἐν τύχῃ lends support to that assumption.

One cannot assume that א, occuring after ר, is assimilated to the ר. In any case, there are many forms of this verb without gemination. Reference to forms such as הִרְעִמָהּ (1 Sa 1:6) and הַצְּפִינוֹ (Ex 2:3) only serves to confirm the Samaritan tradition, but does not explain the phenomenon. The verb רבה is not found in SH in the recitation of the Pentateuch in *Pi'el*, but rather in *Hif'il*; however, in some of its forms, there seems to be an admixture of *Pi'el* (from the later liturgical SH, or from Aramaic?) forming hybrids: *wåråbbåk* הרבך (on this topic see 2.14.18). However, it is not inconceivable to derive such forms from ordinary *Hif'il*, i.e, **warbåk* > **warᵊbåk* > *wåråbbåk*, in accordance with what is stated in 1.3.5; this explanation appears to me to be preferable to the alternative. The form *wåšqinnu* in Gn 29:8 for וישקינו is surprising in its gemination of the *n* (see also 2.3.6), but the antiquity of this tradition is proved by SP's reading וישקין (alongside ותשקי), which seems to relate the verb to the shepherds mentioned in the verse.

2.8.6 The *i* vowel of the first radical of *Pi'el nissåta* נסתה (Dt 28:56) and *niššåni* נשני (Gn 41:51) is surprising (cf. *nåssitimma* נסיתם, *annåssa* הנסה), and I have not succeeded in discovering the reason for it. The forms appear as though they are formed from the *Nif'al* conjugation in TH.

2.8.7 The 3rd masc. sing. form in *Nif'al*, as in other constructions, ends in an *a* vowel, such as *niggåla* נגלה and *niššåba* נשבה (although the form of נראה in SH is *nirrå'i*). One should not conclude that SH has chosen a participial form, since both ST and SAV translate this form as a past tense verb. As we know, in texts with Babylonian vocalization, particularly those from MH sources, in the verb ראה and others, we find many 3rd masc. sing. forms such as נִרְאֹה, which parallels TH נִרְאָה, and alternately, participial forms vocalized with *qames*: וְנִקְלָה,[93] and in TH as well: נַעֲשָׂה (Eccl 8:11). This distribution of *seghol* in the participle / *qames* in the perfect is, therefore, not absolutely exact. The 3rd masc. sing. perfect and the participle have different origins. The origin of the 3rd masc. sing. form is **naglaya* > **naglā*, while the origin of the participle is **naglayu* > **naglae*, but the equivalence of the second radical vowel in the 3rd masc. sing. (in pausal forms in TH) to that of the participle in the other verb classes caused the ל״ה class to blur the original distinction. One form is found that acts like a normal TH verb: נבנתה; see also 2.1.4.3.

2.8.8 The various reflexes of the consonantal *waw* (with its preceding vowel) in *Pi'el* and *Hitpa'el* are worthy of note: *qawwīti* קויתי, *tuwwu* טוו (Ex 35:26), *wēštåbbīta* והשתחוית, *wēštåbbu* והשתחוו. (See also 2.8.16 below and 1.1.4.1.).

---

[93] See Yeivin, *Babylonian Vocalization*, 717ff. and Haneman, *Morphology*, 325.

2.8.9 The verb חטא, which is almost the only verb of the ל"א class conjugated in SH in the ל"ה pattern (see also 2.2.3.0), keeps alive in some forms its original verbal class characteristics (through the use of the *a* vowel): *wēʿtå* וחטאה (cf. 2.8.4), *ʾåṭåʾu* חטאו, and others.

2.8.10 The imperfect of *Qal* is variegated. The final vowel in the forms without afformatives is (1) *i* or (2) *a* (*å*); the vowel of the preformative is normally (3) *i*, or, *ē* in an open syllable or I-guttural verbs, but in some cases (sometimes even within the same verb) it is (4) *a*, and in I-guttural verbs, *å*. In addition, the (5) second way (*Qal B*) is common. Here are some examples:

1. בנה: *yibni, tibni*; זנה: *tizni*; פנה: *tifni, yifni*; רבה: *tirbi, yirbon*; שטה: *tišti*; שתה: *ništi*; מחה: *ēʾmi* (אמחה); עלה: *wēlli* (ואעל, SP Dt 10:3), *yēlli, nēlli*.

2. קנה: *wyiqnåʾēʾu* (Gn 39:1), *tiqnåʾēʾu* (Lv 25:44; SP v. 45); לוה: *tilwa(nnu)*, *yilwå(k)*; נכה: *yikkå(k)*; עטה: *yēṭṭå*; עלה: *tå:la* (Ex 20:23); the doubtful verb ויתא (Dt 33:21): *wyåttå* (see 2.8.14), and so נשה "claim a debt": *tišša, yišša* and נשה "forget": *tišša* (Dt 32:18); see also 2.8.13.

3. See 1.

4. קנה: *taqni, yaqni*; רדה: *wyardi* (Nu 24:19); שבה: *wyašbi* (Nu 21:1); עלה: *yålli, wtållu*; חזה: *yåzzi*; כלה: *yakli* (Gn 23:6); כרה: *yakri* (Ex 21:33); ענה: *tånna, wtånnu, wyånnu*; לאה: *wyallåʾu* (on the gemination of the ל, see 2.8.5).

5. פדה: *ēfēdi, tēfēdi*; ראה: *ērēʾi, tērēʾi, yērēʾi*; פשה: *tēfēši, yēfēši*; בכה: *(w)yēbēki, wyēbēku*; פנה: *wēfåna, wnēfåna* (both cohortative), *wyåfånu*; *wyåfådåk* (such as Dt 7:8).

Note: It is not inconceivable that the forms *yēʾbī* יבעה (Ex 22:4), *ēʾmī* אמחה, and *yēʾrū* ירעו belong to this group, being reflexes of **yēbīʾi, *ēmīʾi*.

2.8.11 The forms ending in an *i* vowel are as expected in SH, while the forms with *a* require explanation. They are not misreadings that have become established, for they are not at all rare, and there are verbs of which the two forms coexist (קנה). Furthermore, the antiquity of these forms is attested by the orthography of SH with א: יעטא, ישא. It is unreasonable to posit different underlying forms, such as that of *yibni* < **yibniy* as opposed to *yēṭṭå* < **yiʿtay*, since the contraction of the original diphthong to *ī (i)* (< *e*) is known in SH, and the contraction to *a* (similar to the forms in Targum Onqelos, such as גְּלִי < **galayin*) has not been demonstrated for SH from any parallel source.[94] It would seem that this is a fairly late phenomenon, caused most of all by analogy to the other verb classes, in which the vowel of the second radical is the same in the perfect and the imperfect. That analogy was particularly strengthened by the example

---

[94] Traces of the contraction of Proto-Semitic *ay* to *a* in TH are treated in my article, "More about the Seghol," 156.

of the III-guttural class (including לי״א). That is, just as we have šåmår:yišmår and måṣå:yimṣå, so, too, are formed qåna:*wyiqna and *'åna (cf. wånåtå, Dt 25:9): tånna. When the Samaritan tradition took shape, the analogy did not manage to spread far. This produced a situation similar to that found in TH where qameṣ occurs in place of seghol in the Nifʻal masc. participle, e.g., נִרְאָה (Nu 14:14), הַנִּרְאָה (1 Kgs 11:9), הַנִּלְוָה (Isa 56:3), נַעֲשָׂה (Lv 7:9), which are shaped by the equivalence of the participle and the perfect in other verb classes. It is also similar to what we find in BH, where pataḥ and qameṣ interchange in precisely this verb class.[95] Moreover, this is related to what we find in Targum Onqelos, where pataḥ occurs in such forms as ואתחזה (Gn 31:22) and דאתעדא (Lv 4:31).[96]

> Note: (1) One cannot reject out of hand the possibility that the a vowel in the imperfect has its origins in the afformative of the cohortative; see also 2.9.10. (2) As is stated above (2.8.3), there is contact between the לי״ה verbs and the III-guttural verbs in SH. Perhaps this can provide an explanation for the gemination of the ת in måššíttiyyu/משיתיו. (It may be that the gemination of the taw has its origin in Aramaic influence; see 3.2.3.4.)

2.8.12 The tendency mentioned above in 2.8.11 is what led to the a vowel in the preformative of the Qal imperfect (2.8.10[4]). The vowel combination a-i is characteristic of the Hifʻil imperfect, and, thus, the i of the middle radical brought about the introduction of a as the vowel of the preformative. In principle, one could assign the forms with a as the preformative vowel to the Hifʻil construction (see 2.1.1.8), and indeed in the case of certain verbs it may be that in SH the Hifʻil forms fulfilled the same semantic functions as the TH Qal. It should be noted that corresponding to וְיֵרְדְּ (Nu 24:19), we find יַרְדְּ (Isa 41:2) with the same meaning, and corresponding to TH יִכְלֶה (Gn 23:6) / SH yakli, we

---

[95] As for the forms in TH, David Qimḥi, too, explained them as participle forms (Mikhlol, ed. Rittenberg, 114b), and on the subject of the BH forms, many examples of perfect and participle forms from all the conjugations can be found in Yeivin, Babylonian Vocalization, 685ff. Note that this phenomenon is especially common in MH. This interchange of seghol and qameṣ between forms helped me to understand the differing vocalizations יְהָא/יְהֵא (Yeivin, Babylonian Vocalization, 898ff.). Neither the form יְהֵא nor the form יְהָא is likely to be explained by phonetic processes, i.e., as alternate versions of the Biblical יְהִי, not to mention that we do not find the jussive form in MH. The form יְהוּא (in Eccl 11:3) is derived from יִהְיֶה* (הוא is a Hebrew verb!), just as the Aramaic יהון is derived from יִהְיוּן*, in both of which, wū (wō) contracted to vowels. This is similar to the copulative particle wu (< *wi), which became a vowel. On the basis of יהו, etc., the singular form יְהָא is formed in Hebrew and יְהֵא in Aramaic. In יְהָא, the segol has been replaced by qameṣ, as explained above.
[96] See Dalman, Grammatik, 342, and also A. Dody, A Morphological Study of the Verb According to Targum Onqelos (M.A. thesis, Bar-Ilan University, 1970), 202 [Hebrew]. A related phenomenon is the use in contemporary spoken Hebrew of נַעֲשָׂה for past tense and even of נַעֲשֶׂה for present.

find in Onqelos (according to the Yemenite tradition as attested in old manuscripts of the *Taj*) an *Afʿel* form יַכְלִי; Nevertheless, it is not sensible to split the conjugation of one verb such as עלה: *yēlli/tāllu* or קנה: *yaqni/yiqnāʾēʾu* into two stems. It is difficult, too, to explain *wyašbi* as *Hifʿil* similar to דאשביתכון in the Peshiṭta, because the latter is a translation of אשר הדחתי in Jer 29:14; therefore, these forms have been understood here as *Qal*. One has the impression that the difference in vowels has been utilized to express a semantic difference, e.g., *yēlli* (Gn 2:12) "go up" but *yālli* (Dt 28:43) "prevail" — that is, "go up" in a transferred sense.[97]

Given this, it is not unlikely that a blurring might occur in the opposite direction, that is, *i* may occur as the vowel of the preformative in the *Hifʿil* imperfect. This seems to be clearly evident in these verbs: *išqi* (Gn 24:46) for TH אַשְׁקֶה, which must be *Hifʿil* in light of השקתה *ašqâtâ* in the same verse, even though in principle אשקה could be categorized as *Qal*, parallel to the Aramaic שקי or to the use of the verb in Arabic; *yirbi* ירבה (Dt 17:5,17) in place of *yarbi, the form expected on the basis of the participial form *marbi* מרבה, and so it is with object pronoun afformatives: *yirbåk* ירבך, *yifråk* יפרך. In any case ירבה in those verses is not originally *Qal*, unlike the word ירבה in Dt 8:13. The form *yikkåk* יככה (Dt 28:27,35) with the object suffix has no parallel in *Qal*, and indeed the other forms of this verb that require an object are in *Hifʿil*. Therefore, perhaps this, too, is a *Hifʿil* form with a preformative vowel *i* like *ikku* TH הִכּוּ (Gen 19:11). In any case, note that the *Qal* of נכה functions as an intransitive verb, as stated above (2.5.3).

2.8.13 The TH verb נשה, meaning "to lend," "to be a creditor," is spelled with final א in some cases in MT and in all cases in SH. And indeed it may be that it originated among the ל״א class, as the Arabic نسا indicates. Thus, the *a* vowel after the second radical in the imperfect (see 2.8.10[2]) is original, and the verb should not be categorized with the ל״ה class. However, נשה in the sense of "forget" is sometimes spelled with א in SH, as in נשאני (Gn 41:51) and always תשא (e.g., Dt 32:18), pronounced *tišša*, and it seems that נשה meaning "lend" influenced the orthography of נשה meaning "forget."[98]

2.8.14 The TH וַיֵּתֵא (Dt 33:21) is pronounced in SH *wyåttå*. *Prima facie* both forms are derived from the root את״י, meaning "to come." Indeed, so we are taught in the common grammars and dictionaries of Biblical Hebrew. As to

---

[97] The word *tā:la* (Ex 20:22), too, does not refer to literal ascent, but to a kind of drawing near, since Samaritan tradition explains במעלות as being from the verb מעל. (Cf. Ibn ʿEzra ad loc.!) In ST: ולא תסקון בשקרין, SAV: بغدر, but MS Barberini براق لا تصعد.

[98] From the SAV's translation of *tišša* תשא (SP Dt 32:18): ـطـرـح, as against *niššåni* נשאני (Gn 41:51): SAV نسـانـي, and ST אשפת (v.l. תשף) for Dt נשתי (< נשה+יתי), it is evident that the Samaritan tradition does not interpret תשא (Dt 32:18) as "forget."

the Samaritan tradition – although the form can easily be analyzed as a form of imperfect *Qal* (2.8.10[2]), with the possibility of *Hifʿil* not excluded either, it is not so, as the following facts attest: (a) The Samaritan tradition does not recognize the existence of a verb אתה in SH. Corresponding to TH וְאָתָה (Dt 33:2), it reads ואתו and pronounces *wittu* ("with him"), which is translated by ST as עמה and by SAV as معه. (b) On the other hand, אתה meaning "to come" is very common in SA and appears in Samaritan daily prayers with its regular inflections, e.g., perf. *wåtå* ואתה (*LOT* III/2, 106, l. 26), imperf. *yīti* ייתי (ibid., 77, l. 35), plur. *adyīton* דייתון (ibid., 280, l. 96). Had the Samaritan tradition intended to express the idea of coming or gathering (causing to come), it would use a regular form of the verb under discussion. (c) As to the meaning, the Samaritan tradition hesitates. In the oldest lexicographical work, *Hammeliṣ* (*LOT* III/2, 485), we find two explanations in Arabic: 1. زجر 2. جمع, i.e., "to rebuke." This led us to assume that another word underlies the pronunciation *wyåttå*, as is also the case with *yēšāʾəl* ישל (SP Dt 28:40, also ישעל); see Ben-Ḥayyim "Observations," 16. This in turn led us to suggest that the MH verb חתה[99] for the aforementioned pronunciation and to register it in *LOT* IV under both אתי and חתי, adopting the practice of *Hammeliṣ* in which ייתא is to be found under words beginning with י and those beginning with ת. This entire matter deserves further attention.[100]

2.8.15 The imperfect of *Hifʿil* is as expected: *takki* תכה, *yakki* יכה, *wtamru* ותמרו, *tūnu* תונו, etc. In the *Hifʿil* of ראה, the ר is geminated (cf. 2.8.5): *yarriyyåni* יראני, *wyarriyyēʾu* ויראהו. But, as stated above in 2.8.12, the preformative vowel of the imperfect is sometimes *i*, and even *a/i* in the same verb, as in *išqi* אשקה (Gn 24:14), *wtašqiyyēʾu* ותשקהו (Gn 24:18).

2.8.16 In addition to the normal, anticipated pattern of *Piʿel*, such as *ēkalli* אכלה, *tēṣabbi* תצפה, *yēnaqqi* ינקה, *yēnassu* ינסו, *wyēkassi* ויכס(ה), and *wyēgalli* ויגל(ה), one finds instead *a/å* as the vowel of the second radical: *tēkalla* תכלה, *wyēkalla* ויכלה, *tåwwå* תאוה[101] (see 2.8.11). The verb צוה in *Piʿel* always follows the pattern "with simple second radical": *ēṣåbi, tēṣåbi, yēṣåbi*. Note the difference in the

---

[99] As for "rebuke" = חתה, note that in some manuscripts of *m. Makkot* 3:15 it is a lexical variant of קצה in the common editions. On this problematic verb, see Moreshet, *Lexicon*, 159. As for the reading וכבע in ST and *Hammeliṣ*, there is a variant מבה in a fragment published by A. Tal, "The Samaritan Targumic Version of 'The Blessing of Moses' (Dt 33) According to an Unpublished Ancient Fragment," *AbrN* 24 (1986), 181. Cf. his discussion there.

[100] In considering this matter, the verb חות(?)/חתה in *m. Makkot* 3:15 must not be overlooked. This verb, found in manuscripts, is replaced in the printed editions by קצה (from קוץ), meaning "loathe."

[101] On the basis of the form, one could also identify *tåwwa* as *Qal*. I have followed the TH tradition: תאוה.

vowel of the second radical between *yēṣâbi* in the imperfect and *wyēṣâba*, *wyēṣâbânu* in the converted imperfect. However, in the additional section of SP to Ex 18:25 ויצו occurs twice, the first time pronounced *wyēṣâba*, the second *wyēṣâbi*, both expressing the past time in the Samaritan tradition, too, as ST ופקדת and SAV واوصيت demonstrate (so also *wēṣâbi* Dt 1:16, 18; 3:18). ואנוהו (Ex 15:2) is a *Pi'el* form "with simple second radical."[102]

2.8.17 The *Nif'al* of this class displays two patterns:

a. the usual pattern, such as *tibbâni* תבנה, *tirrâ'i* תראה, *yiqqāri* יקרה, *iyyāne* יענה (Nu 35:30),[103] *yirrâ'u* יראו;

b. "with geminated second radical," such as *ibbanni* אבנה (Gn16:2),[104] *tikkassi* תכסה (Dt 22:12), *tillawwi* תלוה (Dt 28:12), *yiqqašši* יקשה (Dt 1:17; 15:18). The form *yim'mī* ימחה (Dt 25:6) is not *Nif'al*, which should be **yimmâ'i*, but rather *Hitpa'el* "with simple second radical" (see 2.1.5.3 and 2.7.10). An example of regular *Hitpa'el* can be found in the quadriradical verb *tištâbbi* תשתחוה, *yištâbbi* ישתחוה, *wništâbbi* ונשתחוה (see also 2.8.8 above).

חיה, היה

2.8.18 The verbs היה and חיה, distinguishable in TH by the type of guttural consonant, could be expected to merge into one verb in SH in all their forms. But this did not occur, and they are almost always distinguishable. First, let us contrast the two, form for form (wherever these are attested):

Qal:	היה	חיה
Perfect:	*wā'īti* והייתי	
	â'ītå היית	*wā'ītå* וחיית
	ayya היה, *wēyya* והיה	*wī* וחי
	ayyåtå היתה, *wēyyåtå* והיתה	*wayyåtå* וחיתה
	â'īnu היינו	
	â'ītimma היתם	
	ayyu היו, *wåyyu* והיו	*'āyu* חיו,
Imperfect:	*ēyyi* אהיה	
		tiyya תחיה
	yēyyi יהיה	*yiyya* יחיה

---

[102] Note that while *Mekhilta de-R. Yishma'el* (ed. Horowitz-Rabin, 126) expounds the phrase זה אלי ואנוהו there by asking, "Is it possible for a person of flesh and blood to add glory (להנוות – *Hif'il*) to his Creator?" the parallel in *y. Peah* 1:1 15b reads לנאות (variant reading: לנוות), i.e, *Pi'el*.

[103] In ST: ילבט, i.e., from the sense of torment: "[the witness] will [not] be investigated;" SAV يستشهد.

[104] A *Pi'el* verb from this root can be found in MH מבונה and an "Amorite" personal name. See H. B. Huffmon, *Amorite Personal Names in the Mari Texts* (Baltimore, 1984), 82ff.

2.8 Verbs לי״ה

	tēyyi תהיה	*tiyya* תחיה
	tåyyu תהיו	*tiyyon* תחיון
	yåyyu יהיו	
	tåyyinna תהיינה	
Shortened impf.:	*wyå'i* ויהי	*yī* יחיה, *wyī* ויחי
	wtå'i ותהי	*wtī* ותחי
Infinitive:	*ayyot, låyyot*	*liyyot* (Gn 7:3)
Imperative:	*ayyu* היו (Ex 19:15)	*wāyyu* וחיו (Gn 42:18)
Participle:	*ayya* (Ex 9:3; ST הויה)	
Pi'el/Hif'il		*'ā'īti* החייתי
		'ā'ītånu החייתנו
		'ā'itimma החייתם
		āyu החיו
		wāyyi ואחיה
		tāyyi תחיה
		wnāyyi ונחיה
		tāyyon תחיון
		yāyyu יחיו
		wtāyyinna ותחינה
		liyyot להחיות (Gn 19:19)
		wliyyūtīnu ולהחיותנו (SP Dt 6:24)
Infinitive		
Nif'al	*nå'īta* נהית (SP Dt 27:9)	
	nēyyåta נהיתה (Ex 11:6)	

2.8.19 Note that in the perfect of היה the third person forms have a geminated second radical, as though they were inflected in *Pi'el* (see also עשה), but it may be that the gemination is secondary, i.e., it was transferred to those forms from the imperfect, in which *Qal* forms may have received gemination by the assimilation of ה to י or a similar extension from other forms, such as the imperative or the infinitive, which originally had a *šəwa* with the first radical (cf. 2.8.20); or perhaps the gemination is intended to prevent the elimination of the י, as explained in 1.4.3. It would seem that the form *å'īti* (and others like it) developed from *(h)āyīti* — that is, the י dropped out by a process of dissimilation — but it may well be that they developed from *hayyīti*, in the same way that *Nif'al nå'itå* developed from *nayyītå* (<*nahyītå*) or from *neyyīta*. The preformative vowels *a/e* are keyed to the number of the verb: singular or plural. The fact that in the shortened imperfect there is no gemination of the י may reflect the origin of this form in a form equivalent to that of TH — that is, forms with preformatives vocalized with *šəwa*: *tᵊhī* (תְּהִי) > *tåhī* > *tå'i*, as opposed to *tihyi(ae)* (= תהיה) > *tēyyi*.

Since the active participle may be identical in form with the perfect 3rd masc. sing., there is no way to decide whether *ayya*/היה in SH (SP Ex 9:3) is to be understood in the Samaritan tradition as a participle. Indeed, from the translation SAV كائن and ST היה, we assume that it is a participle. However, in *LOT* IV, 79, and in the Inventory of Forms at the end of this volume, I have included it among the perfect forms.

2.8.20 The 3rd masc. sing. form of חיה in the perfect, *wī*, is, of course, from the ע״ע class. Note that the perfect of חיה ends with an *a* vowel (see 2.8.10), which is not the case with היה. As for the imperfect, there is no way to determine whether what we have is *Pi'el* or *Hif'il*, since in the *Hif'il* form, too, the second radical would be geminated as a result of the assimilation of ה. The same is true of the infinitive. The alternation of forms such as להחיות/לחיות is also inconclusive, but they indicate the blending of *Pi'el* and *Hif'il* in the pronunciation of this verb. It would seem that the perfect forms such as *'ā'īti* represent *Hif'il*, but this alone is not enough to demonstrate that the reconstructed *Pi'el* *ayyīti is likely to develop into *'ā'īti*; see also 1.5.3.2. In any case, it is surprising that the infinitive of *Pi'el*/*Hif'il* has an *i* vowel, while the infinitive of *Qal* has *a (å)*. (cf. 2.14.18). Notice that an infinitive of היה does not occur in the Pentateuch.

עשה

2.8.21 The verb עשה appears in almost all forms of *Qal*:

Perfect:	*'aššīti*	*'aššīnu*
	'aššītå	*'aššītimma*
	'āša	*'aššītən*
	'āšåtå	*'āšu*
Imperfect:	*ēšši*	*nēšši*
	tēšši	*tēššon, tēššu*
	tēššən	
	yēšši	*yēššu*
	tēšši	*tēššiyyinna*
Converted Imperfect:	*wyāššu, wyāš*	
Imperative:	*ēši,*	*ēšu*
Infinitive:	*låššot*	
Participle:	*'āši*	
Nif'al forms:	*niyyåšåtå* נעשתה, *iyyāši* (<*yiyyāši) יעשה, *iyyāšu* יעשו

2.8.22 The forms without gemination of the second radical, in both *Qal* and *Nif'al*, show that in the forms with gemination in the perfect, an analogy with the imperfect has occurred, the rules of which are in conformity with SH (see also the verb היה). I do not understand why that analogy did not affect the third person forms. The assumption of an original *Pi'el* seems unlikely, even though the *Pi'el* and *Pu'al* forms of this verb appear in TH and MH. Note also the difference between the preformative vowels *e* and *a*. The *a* vowel is used in the converted imperfect, reflecting the vowel of the perfect. For the source of the difference, see 2.2.1.1.5. It is possible, of course, to assume that in forms like *'aššītimma*, the gemination is very early, since the basis for this form is something like עֲשִׂיתֶם, and the *šəwa* was pronounced before the first consonant, leading to contact between ע (the first radical) and שׂ (the second radical).

2.9 Tenses and Moods

2.9.1 In Biblical Hebrew, according to the tradition of the Tiberian Masoretes, one can distinguish six verbal forms (in addition to the imperative), some of which are known as tenses (1–4) and some (5–6) as moods. They are:
1. Perfect: e.g., שָׁמַרְתָּ
2. Converted Perfect: e.g., וְשָׁמַרְתָּ
3. Imperfect: e.g., יִשְׁמֹר, יָקוּם, יַעֲשֶׂה, יַקְרִיב
4. Converted Imperfect: e.g. וַיִּשְׁמֹר, וַיָּקׇם, וָאָקוּם, וָאַעַשׂ, וַיַּקְרֵב
5. Jussive (shortened imperfect): e.g., יָקֵם, יַעַשׂ, יַקְרֵב
6. Cohortative (lengthened imperfect): e.g., אֵלְכָה, נַחְפְּשָׂה

It can be stated generally that these forms have their individual characteristics in both syntactic usage and semantic distinctions, but these characteristics do not exist in their entirety throughout all the periods of Biblical literature and across the range of its genres and styles.

From the point of view of morphology, it can be said that this system of tenses and moods does not exist in every verb class and every stem, and in fact, at the stage reflected by the Bible, the system is undergoing continual decay. Clear evidence of this is to be found in the identical use of forms such as ישמעו and ישמעון, in very rare forms such as תִּדְבָּקִין and תִּשְׁתַּכְּרִין for 2nd fem. sing., which were originally regular imperfect forms; and even more so, forms such as וְיֵאָתָיוּן, וַתַּעַמְדוּן, וַתִּקְרְבוּן, and תִּבְכֶּה, whose afformatives belong with the regular imperfect and not the converted imperfect. The same is true for such forms as וָאֶצְאָה (Neh 2:13), וָאֶתְּנָה (Neh 2:6), which become more numerous as expressions of past time in the later books of the Bible, despite the fact that the ־ָה afformative was originally intended to express the cohortative mood. From the perspective of usage, it can be stated that the tenses expressed by the forms with *waw consecutive*, which are the reverse of those expressed by the same forms without the *waw consecutive*, can be expressed in the Bible — at certain periods and under certain syntactic conditions — by forms without *waw consecutive* as well. Thus, as is well known, perfect forms such as נָתַתִּי (Gn 15:18) and בֵּרֲכַתְנִי (Gn 32:27) refer to future events, while imperfect forms such as יָשִׁיר (Ex 15:1) and יָקֻם (Jos 10:13) express past time, and regular imperfect forms may express a jussive mood, such as יָקֻם (Gn 27:31).

2.9.2 Out of an ancient verbal system, presumably clear and consistent when it was in use — perhaps in the Hebrew just prior to that we have inherited — there developed the complex system of tenses and moods presented to us by TH, in which one can discern the tendency that led, at the end of the process, to the existence of just two verb forms, perfect and imperfect, and the elimination of the other four forms. In MH, the participle took on a greater role in the verbal system than it had in Biblical Hebrew. We note in MH the creation of analytic forms ("היה אומר" and the like), which came to express some of what had been expressed by those forms that fell into disuse at the end of the Second Temple period.

> Note: This is not the place to entertain the complex question of distinguishing tenses and moods in Biblical Hebrew according to the Tiberian tradition, on which much has already been written. A more detailed exposition can be found in my article, "Biblical Tenses and the Samaritan Tradition," *Sefer Dov Sadan* [Dov Sadan Festschrift], ed. S. Werses et al. (Tel Aviv, 1977), 66ff. [Hebrew].

2.9.3 The Hebrew reflected in the Samaritan tradition of recitation of the Pentateuch has its origins in the language of the late Second Temple period and the first generations thereafter. As far as we can ascertain from other sources, the converted perfect, the converted imperfect, and the lengthened and shortened forms of imperfect (cohortative and jussive) were not used in the living language of the time, and it can reasonably be assumed that awareness of these forms had disappeared even among educated speakers. Where no morphological difference remained, the Samaritans, reading the Pentateuch, understood the Biblical forms in accord with the usage of their own day — as long, of course, as those forms did not differ from what was common and accepted and as long as the apparent meaning of the verb form in question was not the opposite of what was required by the context of the Biblical verses. For example, the form וַיֵּשֶׁב could, in many contexts, be read as וְיֵשֵׁב, and was indeed read that way, just as would occur today if the average reader encountered the unvocalized form ויצא in a text from the *Haskalah* period: he would not read it as וַיֵּצֵא unless he had the same level of expertise in Biblical syntax as the *Haskalah* author (in which case he would realize that the syntax required וַיֵּצֵא). This is not true of forms such as וישמר or ותשב in contexts that imply past action, because the י or ת in each of these forms is unmistakably the preformative of the imperfect.

2.9 Tenses and Moods

2.9.4 The Samaritans were aware, then, that the reversal of the perfect and imperfect tenses of their own time appears in the Pentateuch mostly in forms with the conjunction ו. In their tradition, as in the tradition of the second column of Origen's Hexapla, there was no morphological distinction between what we know as *waw consecutive* and *waw conjunctive*. Neither of them caused gemination of the following consonant in the imperfect, just as they did not cause gemination in the perfect. Thus, the Samaritan grammarians stated that "in a minority of cases, the perfect forms indicate future time," (e.g., ברכתני), and the perfect with ו "normally indicates future time," while the imperfect form, "in a minority of cases, indicates past time" (such as *yēkassiyyåmu* יכסימו [Ex 15:5]), and as for imperfect with ו, "the ו shifts the meaning from the future to the past" (*LOT* I, 67). Nowhere is there any mention of a different vowel for *waw consecutive*.

> Note: It would be relevant to point out that the difference in time between the SH verbs *wšēmā'u* ושמעו (Nu 14:13) and *šāmā'u* שמעו (Nu 14:14) is achieved by a difference in pronunciation of the vowel following ש. The latter is the usual form for past time, and *wšēmā'u*, by reflecting the pronunciation of the imperative, indicates the future. It is possible, though, to take *wšēmā'u* as a perfect form of the *fēqad* pattern, as we have already noted (0.16d), of the form *nēdårå* (Nu 30:11).

2.9.5 Phonological processes caused originally distinct forms to be conflated in TH. Thus, in place of the forms *yaqtulu*, *yaqtula*, and *yaqtul*, Hebrew has the single form יפעל, which must bear all the shades of meaning and usage of the Arabic forms. Additional phonological processes acted on SH in later generations, bringing about further unification of forms that had been distinct in TH:

a. The standardization of stress on the penult caused the loss of the morphological distinction between perfect and converted perfect forms in all those forms in which there had been such a distinction in TH: וְשָׁמַ֫רְתִּי and וְשָׁמַרְתִּ֫י both become *wšåmårti*; וְשָׁמַ֫רְתָּ and וְשָׁמַרְתָּ֫ both become *wšåmårtå*.

b. The rule that a long *ī* vowel becomes *e (ə)* in a closed, unaccented syllable caused the loss of the morphological distinction in TH between such forms as וַיִּקְרַב and וְיִקְרַב: both become *wyaqrəb* when the stress moves back to the penult in SH. One sometimes finds *ṣere* in place of *ḥireq* in TH as well, e.g., וְתַגֵּיד (Ex 19:3) [SH *wtaggəd*], although in TH the waw distinguishes between imperfect and converted imperfect.

2.9.6 Notwithstanding what was stated above in 2.9.3–2.9.5, SH preserves a remnant of the verbal forms other than the perfect and imperfect. Such forms are attested not only in instances in which the consonantal text of the Pentateuch preserves them (such as the lengthened and shortened imperfect forms), but also in instances not dictated by spelling. Some of these are forms created in SH, without parallel elsewhere (see also 2.8.4 a):

In ל"ה verbs:

1. a few shortened forms are preserved, such as *wyāl* ויעל (*Qal*), *wyān* ויען, *wyāš* ויעש, *wtān* ותען, *wyåṭ* ויט, *wtåṭ* ותט, *wyår* ויחר [but cf. below, 2.9.9], *wyād* ויחד (Ex 18:9), *wyåʿaṣ* ויחץ (Gn 33:1), *wyēre* וירא (but *yērēʾi* יראה !), *wtēre* ותרא (but *tērēʾi* תראה). There are, however, other forms in which the Samaritan oral tradition employs regular perfect forms although the consonantal SP reflects shortened forms: *wēlli* ואעל (*Qal*), *wālli* ואעל (*Hifʿil*), *wyibni* ויבן, *wyiqna* ויקן, *wyēkalla* ויכל, *wyēṣåba* ויצו, *wyakki* ויך, *wnakki* ונך.

2. Among similar forms distinguishable only by vowel patterns, some are employed to distinguish the converted imperfect: *wyåššu* וַיַּעְשׂוּ : *wyeššu* וְיַעֲשׂוּ; *wyåfånu* וַיִּפְנוּ : *tifnu* תִּפְנוּ; *wyēṣåba* וַיְצַו : *yēṣåbi* יצוה; *wyåfådāk* ויפדך : *ēfēdi* אפדה.

> Note: The forms with geminated second radical, such as *yēkalla* (in which the gemination does not result from the assimilation of a guttural first radical), indicate that one should not see the vowel of the second radical as developing from a *šəwa mobile*, as can be assumed of a form such as *wyašbi* = וַיֵּשֶׁב. Instead, these forms originate in a normal imperfect.

2.9.7 In ו"ע verbs, too, the converted imperfect can sometimes be distinguished from the regular imperfect by vowel patterns alone, since both of them bear penultimate stress, which eliminates the criterion for distinguishing between them. For example: *wyåqåm* וַיָּקָם : *yēqom* יָקוּם; *wyåqåmu* וַיָּקוּמוּ : *yēqumu* יקומו; *wyåba* וַיָּבֹא : *yåʾbū* יבוא; *wyåqåd* וַיִּקֹּד (see 2.7.4); *wyåšåb* וַיָּשָׁב : *wyēšob* וְיֵשֵׁב (Nu 25:4, Dt 20:5, and other verses); *wtåšåbu* וַתָּשֻׁבוּ : *tēšūbu* תשובו. This possibility, however, was not realized in every instance: alongside *wyåba* וַיָּבֹא, we find *wnāʾbū* וַנָּבֹא in Dt 1:19, which is like *nāʾbu* נבוא in the regular imperfect. The basis for forms such as *wyåqåmu* and *wtåšåbu* is, of course, the forms without suffixes, such as *wyåqåm*, *wtåqåm*, which are equivalent to the parallel forms in TH, in which the *u* vowel, originally short, became *qameṣ*, which has its origins in an *a* vowel (a back vowel; see 1.2.7.2). The *å* vowel here spread by analogy to the forms in which it occurs in an open syllable and which originally had *u*.[105] The form *wnāʾbū* mentioned above teaches us that a sharp distinction cannot be drawn everywhere between the converted imperfect and

---

[105] On the basis of the form *wyētūru* ויתורו (Nu 13:21), one cannot conclude with certainty that it represents the *u* vowel in the converted imperfect, even though ST and SAV indicate that this verb was understood as representing past time, as fits the context of the verse. It can be understood as a regular imperfect, like the aforementioned ונבוא. The spelling, which can also be found without the first *waw* (i.e., ויתרו), might allow us to assume that an early reading was known, such as *wyåtåru, but was neglected under the influence of ויתורו in Nu 13:2, and this form does not occur elsewhere in the Pentateuch.

the regular imperfect, and it happens that the form with an *a* vowel occurs in the regular imperfect, as noted above (2.6.15).

> Note: (1) An interesting instance of converted imperfect in TH can be found in the verb *wyanna* וַיַּנַּח (Nu 17:22), as opposed to *yanni* יניח (Dt 3:20). (2) The verb *wyāṣârinnē'u* ויצרנהו (SP Dt 32:10) is derived according to Samaritan tradition from צור; see *LOT* III/1, 158.

2.9.8 In פ"י verbs, too, and in the verb הלך (but see 2.4.10), the converted imperfect can be distinguished from the regular imperfect by vowel pattern: *wtålåd* ותלד : *tēlåd* תלד; *wyålåku* וילכו : *yēlåku* ילכו; *wyålåk* וילך : *yēlåk* ילך. Of course, the forms with preformative yod, such as *wyårād* וירד and *wyåšåbu* וישבו, can be explained as the perfect with the addition of the conjunction ו.[106] But this understanding of the verbs is inappropriate to the imperfect with ת, א, or נ as the preformative vowel, such as *wtåšåbu* ותשבו (Dt 1:45, 46) or *wyåminna* ויחמנה (Gn 30:38). Thus, we can state with certainty that the preformative vowel *å* is derived from an ancient *a* vowel, as the Ugaritic verb *'ard* (equivalent to the Hebrew אֵרֵד) and Arabic verbs attest. Furthermore, the imperfect preformative vowel *e* — *ṣere* in TH — can be explained only as the product of assimilation to the vowel of the second radical. Originally, forms with *a* and forms with *i>e* coexisted at random in Hebrew; the Samaritan tradition utilized the two possibilities to create a semantic distinction. In some verbs, such as ישב, the converted imperfect differs from the regular imperfect not only in the vowels, but in the consonants as well: *wtåšåb* = TH וַתֵּשֶׁב : *tiššåb* תֵּשֵׁב; *wyåšåb* וַיֵּשֶׁב : *wyiššåb* וַיֵּשֶׁב (Lv 14:8!). This rule does not apply to the verb יצא, where we find *wyiṣṣå* וַיֵּצֵא : *yiṣṣå* יֵצֵא; *wyiṣṣå'u* וַיֵּצְאוּ, וְיָצְאוּ (Dt 21:2!); and *wtåṣå'inna* וַתֵּצֶאנָה. In the verb יקץ, the converted imperfect in the 3rd masc. sing. can be expressed simply, with the past time verb *wyaqås* וייקץ (SP ויקץ), but the 1st sing. is *wiqqås* ואיקץ, and we cannot tell whether איקץ is *îqås*, on the model of *tīra* תירא, or *iqqås*, on the model of *tidda* תדע — i.e., whether there is any distinction between the two tenses in question.

2.9.9 The shortened imperfect (jussive) in TH is equivalent in form to the converted imperfect without the prefix ו, and it is distinguishable from the regular imperfect. (See above, 2.9.1.) The difference, which depends on the relationship between *šureq* and *ḥolem* and between *ḥireq* and *ṣere*, cannot be maintained in SH because the vowels *ū/o* form one phoneme, and the presence of one allophone or the other is governed by the structure of the word and its stress and by the change of *i* to *e(ə)* when unstressed. In any case, it is under-

---

[106] For the sake of simplicity and for the reason discussed in 2.9.3, פ"י verbs with preformative י in TH have been classified as perfect, even though it is entirely plausible that they were originally converted imperfect.

stood that in SH, the existence of the shortened imperfect can be discerned almost solely in the ל"ה class. The merger of the several original forms of imperfect led to a conflation of the semantic variations into a single morphological type. While the boundary between the functions of the converted imperfect and those of the regular imperfect remains sharply distinguished — they represent different times — this boundary does not serve to distinguish the content of the original shortened imperfect, which represents the various shades of optative mood (implying future time), from the indicative mood of the regular imperfect form. Due to both morphological and semantic conditions, SH undergoes a greater conflation of the shortened imperfect and the regular imperfect than is evident in TH. The word יָקָם in Gn 27:31 undoubtedly bears a jussive sense, but its form is, nevertheless, that of the regular imperfect, and so it is in SH: *yēqom*, because of the usual vowel of the preformative in the SH imperfect.[107] In SH, one finds for יעל (Gn 44:33) — *yēlli*, and for ירא (Gen 41:33, Ex 5:21) — *yērē'i*, whose spelling in SP hints at the antiquity of the phenomenon. In fact, only a few isolated forms from the shortened imperfect were preserved, foremost among them those of the verb היה: *yā'i* (e.g., Gn 10:30); *wyā'i* ויהי (Dt 33:24),[108] *wtā'i* ותהי (Nu 23:10); those of the verb חיה: *yī* יחי (Dt 33:6); *tēfån* תפן (Dt 9:27), *yaṣṣəf* יצף[109] (Gn 31:49), and perhaps *yår* יחר. The last verb in that list may be derived from the root חר"ר, since the very same pronunciation appears in Ex 32:11 and Gn 6:15, where the shortened imperfect would be out of place.[110] The shortened imperfect deviates from the norm in the ל"ה class as well, as is proved by *tēyyi* (and not *tā'i*) in Gn 13:8, 26:28, 37:27; Nu 12:12; *wtēyyi* ותהי in Gn 24:51; *wtiyya* ותחי in Gn 19:20. In all of these, the jussive meaning is clear from context.

2.9.10 The lengthened imperfect, which originally bore a cohortative meaning, and which is found in the Bible primarily in the 1st person, singular and plural, is conflated with the shortened imperfect and the imperative to form a

---

[107] Thus, it seems unreasonable to derive *yaṣåq* יצק (Nu 5:15) from the root צוק and interpret it as a shortened imperfect. See also 2.4.10.

[108] While SAV (MS Barberini) reads ويكان مرضيا لاخونه the use of the perfect to express the jussive mood is quite standard. ST reads, properly, ויהי.

[109] This form belongs under the present rubric only if it is derived from צפ"י, as in the Masoretic tradition, and we attribute the gemination of the צ to an unusual phonetic factor. (Cf. 2.8.5.) It may be more reasonable, though, to posit its derivation from נצ"ף or צו"ף, in which case it is not a shortened imperfect. A derivation from צו"ף affords us a very interesting parallel to the form דמצטייפא in the Palestinian Targum to Nu 21:20, which appears in the marginal glosses in MS Neofiti as well. On the gemination of צ in the hollow verbs, see 2.6.13.

[110] If this is so, the basis for this form is something like **yaḥarr > *yā'år*. (See 2.7.7.) But note that the perfect form is *årå* (e.g., Gn 4:6), and the noun is *åri* חֲרִי. Similarly, we find that the verb רבה, normally part of the ל"ה class in SH as well, is read *wtirråb* ותרב in Gn 43:34 — a normal imperfect of the ע"ע class. (See also 2.6.14.)

fairly well defined unit: for the 1st person, lengthened imperfect; for the 2nd, imperative;[111] for the 3rd, shortened imperfect. It serves in the negated imperative as well. Beyond this familiar division, one finds the lengthened imperfect also used in an indicative sense. This is particularly blatant where the form does not express future time, as, for example, נגששה (Isa 59:10), אזכרה, ואהמיה, אשיחה, etc. (Ps 77), and even נשמחה in Ps 66:6, where the sense is undoubtedly past time. It has already been suggested[112] that particularly in the later books of the Bible one finds the (originally) cohortative suffix ־ָה in the converted imperfect as well — i.e., in past-time narrative (2.9.1). This occurs, of course, in forms other than 1st person, such as וַתַּעְגְּבָה (Ezek 23:20 and the *qəre* in v. 16). This trend in the later books to eliminate the unique semantic function of the lengthened imperfect (e.g., ואצאה in Neh 2:13), takes hold of the Samaritan tradition to such an extent that the latter tends to use the lengthened imperfect with a conjunction ו as a clear expression of past time. This seems to be the meaning of the differences in this realm between the Samaritan and Jewish versions. An examination of these differences in Deuteronomy turns up nearly 20 examples of regular imperfect forms in SP, such as ואשלחה, ואפנה, and וארדה, where the Jewish version has shortened imperfect forms. One finds the opposite as well: אסתיר and אשבית in SP (Dt 32:20, 26) where the Jewish version has lengthened imperfect forms; these forms refer to the future.[113] It is noteworthy, though, that in SH, these forms occur only in the first person. The form תבואתה (Dt 33:16) is not taken to be a verb; it is realized in the oral tradition as *tēbuwwātå* (i.e., תְּבוּאָתָה).[114]

2.9.11 The suffix ־ָה is usually pronounced *a* (in a stressed syllable *ā*), but it is sometimes *å*. Here are examples classified by stem and class:

Qal: *wiktābå* ואכתבה, *wēzåkårå* ואזכרה, *wnilkådå* ונלכסה, *wēlåka* ואלכה, *ēbbåra* אעברה, *wnēbbårå* ונעברה, *ē'ūkēla* אכלה, *we'ūmēra* ואמרה, *wid'då* ואדעה, *wērådå* וארדה, *wnis'så* ונסעה, *wåšīma* ואשימה, *wikkåta* ואכתה, *wēfåna* ואפנה, *wnēfåna* ונפנה
Hif'il: *waślīka* ואשליכה, *waggīda* ואגידה, *wå'īda* ואעידה, *wnårīma* ונרימה

---

[111] Of course, in certain verbs with a cohortative function, the cohortative ־ָה occurs in the imperative as well (i.e., 2nd person), such as לכה and קומה.
[112] Cf. Kutscher, *Isaiah Scroll*, 251ff. His hypothesis that the regular imperfect and the lengthened imperfect were in competition and that the form that expressed will or desire began to crowd out the regular form, as is evident in other languages, is contradicted by the data from SH, where that form was regularly used to indicate past time, as is noted in the present discussion.
[113] This is apparently the reason for the use in SP of אבוא in Gn 29:21 in place of the Jewish version אבואה. This is a distinct trend but not an absolute rule, as we learn from the variant pair אעברה (SP Dt 3:25): אעבר (SP Dt 2:29). Cf. also the variant pair ארדפה (2 Sa 22:38): ארדוף (Ps 18:38), both of which express past time.
[114] Thus, it seems inappropriate to explain the *a* vowel of *tā:la* תעלה (see n. 97 below) or of *tånna* תענה (see 2.8.10) or the like as a lengthened imperfect.

Pi'el: *ēdābbēra* אדברה, *wēdābbēra* ואדברה, *wēšalla* ואשלח
Hitpa'el: *witnābbǎla* ואתנפלה, *witfǎllǎla* ואתפללה

2.10 Passive Voice

2.10.1 It has become a well-established practice in the description of Biblical Hebrew grammar to assign a stem of its own to the passive voice, not only when it is distinguished from the active form in the consonantal text — i.e., *Nif'al* vs. *Qal* — but also when it is distinguished by a difference of vowels alone: *Pu'al* vs. *Pi'el*, *Hof'al* vs. *Hif'il*. This is not the situation in the grammar of Arabic, where each stem has two voices, an active and a passive: فَعَلَ versus فَعِلَ, فَعَّلَ versus فُعِّلَ, and so on for each tense and stem. Thus, Biblical Hebrew is seen to have only one participial form for each stem other than *Qal*, which has both active and passive participles, each morphologically distinct. The remnants of the passive form of *Qal* in Biblical Hebrew, such as לֻקַּח in the perfect and יֻקַּח and יֻתַּן in the imperfect, were recognized as early as the eleventh century by Samuel Ha-Nagid. Since these forms are morphologically equivalent to *Pu'al* and *Hof'al*, most of the medieval grammarians concurred with Ibn Janāḥ in classifying them as *Pu'al* or *Hof'al*, respectively.[115] Even in those days there were scholars who sided with Ha-Nagid, and their opinion is certainly the commonly-held view today. It seems, though, that both sides in this debate were correct. From a diachronic point of view, לֻקַּח and יֻקַּח are *Qal*'s passive voice, but from the perspective of the language state as presented in TH, those forms belong to *Pu'al* and *Hof'al* respectively, and the two stems complement one another in perfect and imperfect to the extent that they are to be viewed as one conjugation. It should be pointed out that this opinion is also reflected in the work of those who vocalized TH, as is attested by the form תְּאֻכְּלוּ (Isa 1:20) — created by analogy in *Pu'al* to אֻכְּלוּ (Nah 1:10), which was originally a passive form of *Qal*. (A normal imperfect passive of *Qal* would be expected to be *תְּאֻכְלוּ [< *תֻּאְכְלוּ].) Since the remnants of the passive voice *Qal* in their finite forms (i.e., perfect and imperfect) are identical to finite *Pu'al* and *Hof'al* forms in the perfect and imperfect, the participle, whose form is not like the perfect form[116] (i.e., following the *Pa'ul* pattern), became isolated from the rest of the system and classified, perforce, with the active-voice stem, i.e., with *Qal*.

---

[115] See Isḥāq Ibn Barūn's introduction to *Kitāb al-Muwāzana* (ed. Kokowzoff [1890], 12) in favor of Ha-Nagid, as against David Qimḥi in his *Mikhlol* (ed. Rittenberg), 62b; Ibn Janāḥ, *Kitāb al-Lumaʿ* (see n. 163), p. 161; Abraham Ibn 'Ezra, *Ṣaḥut* (ed. Lippmann), 68b. See also n. 137.

[116] E.g., אֻכַּל (Ex 3:2), לֻקַּח (2 Kgs 2:10), and others. As for the equivalence of participle and perfect forms, it should be noted that this is characteristic of both the passive verb and the intransitive verb; see active participle, 2.12.1.

2.10 Passive Voice

This practice, which emerged from the study of Biblical Hebrew and is intended to describe it, has been applied inappropriately to MH as well, even though the *Pu'al* stem occurs there almost exclusively in the participle[117] but not in a finite form. The stem *Pu'al* should be eliminated, then, from the description of MH, and its participle should be classified with *Pi'el*, parallel to the accepted practice in MH grammar with regard to *Qal*.

2.10.2 SH reflects a more advanced stage in the process of eliminating the "internal" passives, i.e., those forms distinct from the active voice in vowel pattern alone. Not only *Pu'al* is absent from SH; *Hof'al*, too, has also disappeared from the normal verb patterns. The loss of the *u* vowel and its replacement by *a (å)* (or *e/i*) undoubtedly contributed to the demise of the "internal" passive forms, even though in principle, the active/passive distinction could be maintained using the vowel of the second radical. In place of פָּקַדְתִּי : פֻּקַּדְתִּי and הִפְקַדְתִּי : הָפְקַדְתִּי, SH could have employed such forms as *faqqadti : *faqqidti* (<*fuqqidti) and *afqadti : *afqidti* (<*hufqidti). The Samaritan oral tradition undoubtedly reflects the state of the language as it was in the community during the last days of its use as a spoken vernacular. At that time, the passive voice was no longer expressed other than by external forms, i.e., *Nif'al* and *Hitpa'el* (as in MH). The Pentateuch, however, preserves verbs requiring a passive sense in context, but in which no sign of the external passive appears, forcing us to understand them as internal passive forms. In such instances, the Samaritan oral tradition employs a variety of methods for expressing the required sense, most of them substitutes for the original, ancient passive forms. These include:

2.10.3 Replacement of the passive voice by active in places where the spelling of the verb and the syntax of the verse allow. There are places in which the Samaritan reading originates in this trend. Thus, we find *u'ūta såbīti* ואתה צויתי[118] (Gn 45:19), *yēledu* = TH יֻלְּדוּ (Gn 6:1) (see 2.4.3), *yallǝd* יֻלַּד (Gn 10:21), *waggīdu* והגידו (Dt 17:4), *gånob* גֻּנֹּב (Gn 40:15), *å'ǝl* החל (SP Gn 4:26; TH הוּחַל), *yiqqa* יֻקַּח (Gn 18:4), *nåku* נִכּוּ (Ex 9:31, 32!). It is not inconceivable that the following forms, too, should be understood in this way: *baššēla* בַּשֵּׁלָה, *wmåråq* וּמֹרַק, *wšåtåf* וְשֻׁטַּף (all three Lv 6:21), *zåråq* זֹרַק (Nu 19:13, 20); but it is more likely that they should be seen as passive forms; see 2.10.6c and 2.10.9.

Note: (a) The trend to replace a passive form by an active one is found in the Qumran text of Psalms (1QPs^a), עניתני instead of TH עֻנֵּיתִי (J. A. Sand-

---

[117] Cf. Ben-Ḥayyim, *Tradition*, 89ff.
[118] ואתה (Gn 45:19), as ST ויתה, SAV وهذه, and the pronunciation *wūta* attest, is understood as the demonstrative pronoun "this." (See 3.3.1.3.)

ers, *DJD* IV [Oxford, 1965], 30); (b) The use of the passive form for an impersonal verb, such as the use of החל mentioned above, occurs from time to time in TH as well, e.g., קָרָא (Gn 11:9) and ויאמר (Gn 48:1).[119]

2.10.4 Replacement of the internal passive by an external form in places where the consonantal text allows.[120] In some instances, the reading in SP has its origin in this process and, thus, we find instead of TH גֻּנֹּבְתִּי (Gn 40:15) in SP: *niggånåbti* גגנבתי. It is a general rule that פ"י and ע"י verbs in *Hif'il* have as their passive counterparts forms such as *uwwårad* הורד, *uwwålēdu* הולדו (SP Lv 25:45), *uwwåmət* והומת, *uwwånəf* הונף, *wēwwåba* והובא, *uwwåråm* והורם, *yuwwåsåk* יוסך (SP Ex 30:32, in place of TH ייסך), *yuwwåšåt* יושת, *wyuwwåšåm* ויושם. The consonantal value of the ו is original only in the פ"י verbs, and it is, thus, certain that the ע"י verbs in this conjugation are built on analogy to פ"י (original פ"ו). It has been generally accepted that the *Hof'al* of ע"י verbs in TH can be explained this way.[121] As confirmation of this claim we may cite a parallel in Palestinian Aramaic, in which one sometimes encounters forms such as אתוקם alongside אתקם, the former modelled on the פ"י verb, such as אתוקד,[122] and this is common in the Aramaic of the Babylonian Talmud.[123]

Since the consonantal value of the ו is orginal in *Nif'al* of פ"י verbs, it is no wonder that Samaritan grammarians relate the forms in question to *Nif'al*,[124] but in fact they are derived from *Hitpa'el B*, with the ת elided in the following manner: **hitwared > *hiwwared > *(h)uwwared*. The *Hitpa'el* stem underlying this form may be the reflexive counterpart to *Qal* (cf. 2.1.5.3), or it may be the reflexive of *Pi'el* with the gemination eliminated; the first seems more likely, but no definitive answer may be given. In any event, there is a morphological similarity here to the *Hitpa'el* stem found quite commonly in Jewish liturgical

---

[119] The Samaritan tradition reads this as passive *(Nif'al)*: *wiyyåmər*.

[120] In TH, too, we find that if the consonantal text does not prevent it, the vocalized text sometimes uses a later stage of the language than the original text. (See my book *Struggle*, 69.) This provides a fine explanation for the phenomenon noted with surprise by D. Yellin ("Study of the Qal stem and its History," *Ha-Gan: Me'assef Le-Sifrut ul-Madda'* (St. Petersburg, 1899/1900), 34 [Hebrew]): that of 86 verbs that occur in the Bible in *Huf'al*, only 4 (שלך, קטר, עמד, חרם) occur in the imperfect. Yellin correctly hypothesized the reason for this, although he did not assign the responsibility explicitly to the tradition of vocalization.

[121] See, e.g., Bergsträsser, *Grammatik* II, 154. It is not impossible, however, that the *u* in such forms as הוקם replaces a short *u*, in order to prevent its reduction to *šəwa*, and for this reason — as is generally assumed — there is sometimes gemination, as in יֻלַּד (< **yulad*) or the exceptional form וְהֻנִּיחָה (Zech 5:11). Similar to the latter form, where the second radical is vocalized with *i*, is the form הֲקִימַת in Biblical Aramaic (Dan 7:5).

[122] See Dalman, *Grammatik*, 314, 326.

[123] See Epstein, *Grammar*, 92, 94.

[124] See *LOT* I, 101. The Samaritan grammarian does not claim that forms like הוקם are actually *Nif'al*, but that they are used in place of *Nif'al*.

2.10 Passive Voice

poetry.[125] In keeping with the substitution described above, we find that תבשל in Lv 6:21 is expressed by *Nif'al B* (= *Hitpa'el* with the ת assimilated to the first radical): *tibbåššål*; and similarly תֵּעָנֶה (Lv 23:29) in SP is *tiyyānne*, and יָחֳרַם in Lv 27:29 in SP is *iyyårråm*.

> Note: A specific case of mixing פ"י and ע"ו roots is *wēwwā'əd* (Ex 21:29) והועד. Indeed, it is impossible to determine in the given context whether the form derives from יע"ד (cf. Arabic وعد, "to warn"), as I have listed it in *LOT* IV, 123b, or from עו"ד. Another variation of this root is to be found in MH עד"י in the *Hif'il* verbal noun העדאה ("testimony").

2.10.5 Nonetheless, here and there, we do find the internal passive in SH, and not only in places where there was no other option. Alongside *wēwwåmət* והומת we find *yūmåt* יומת, *yūmåtu* יומתו (and not *yuwwåmət, etc.), *yūda/yiyyåḏa*, the participle *ammūšåb* המושב (Gn 43:12), *ūlēdət* הולדת (Gn 40:20).

The following are the passive forms that occur in SH, arranged according to stem:

2.10.6 *Qal* Perfect

a. *fēqəd*: *ēkəl* אכל (Ex 3:2), *ēmər* אמר (Ex 24:1), *yētən* יתן (Lv 11:38), *lēqi* לקח (Gn 3:23), *lēqīta* לקחת (Gn 3:19), *lēqiy'ya* לקחה (Gn 2:23), *yēlīdu* ילדו (Gn 10:25, 46:27, 50:23), *nēqību* נקבו (Nu 1:17), *wnūtettimma* ונתתם (Lv 26:25), *ū* is derived from the original *šəwa*. (See 1.3.1a, 2.5.6.)

b. *fåqəd*: *yåləd* ילד (Gn 4:26),[126] *tåṛəf* טרף (Gn 37:33), *'åbəd* עבד (Dt 21:3).

c. *fåqåd*: *wmåråq* ומרק (Lv 6:21), *wšåṭåf* ושטף (Lv 6:21), *zåråq* זרק (Nu 19:13,20), *kåfår* כפר (Ex 29:33),[127] *åråša* ארשה (Dt 22:28). Since their form is

---

[125] The Hebrew *Hippa'el*, too, originated from *Hitpa'el*, contrary to the view of David Yellin (see n. 120) This topic has been dealt with more recently by Yalon, *Studies*, 32ff., who mentions היוולד (= נולד) in Yannai's liturgical poetry (sect. 261), (among the strong verbs) היגזר (228), and other examples.

[126] SAV Gn 4:26 according to MS Or 7562: ولشم اف הוא ايضا هو اولد طرزوق and similarly ST ad loc.: אולד — *yåləd* ילד is understood as a transitive verb. Indeed, whenever the verb ילד in TH has a male subject, the Samaritan reading is *yalləd*, i.e., יִלֶד (meaning "fathered," "begat"). Perhaps the aforementioned translations (SAV and ST) read the text that way, just as the reading at Gn 10:21 is *yalləd*, ST אתילד (variant reading: אולד), but the reading today at Gn 4:26 is undoubtedly *yåləd*. The ל in ולשם (or, similarly, ולשם, Gn 10:21) does not prevent us from interpreting the form as an active verb, since the use of ל to introduce the subject is quite common, especially in the later books, e.g., לאבשלום in 1 Ch 3:2 vs אבשלום in 2 Sa 3:3, dealt with by A. Kropat in his book *Die Syntax des Autors der Chronik* (Gießen; 1909; *BZAW* 16), 4ff. This practice is attested in Aramaic as well. But note that at Gn 10:25, SP reads *yēlīdu* ילדו; could this mean that the author finds it implausible that ולעבר might be the subject?

[127] This verb in its active forms is a *Pi'el* with simple second radical. It would make sense to assume that the passive is of the same stem. Thus the form dealt with here, equivalent to the *Qal* forms, should perhaps belong below, 2.10.9, but unlike the imperfect forms described there, which may be understood as active voice, the form described here is undoubtedly passive, since the active voice is embodied in forms such as *kåfər*.

equivalent to that of the active *Qal*, it is not impossible to interpret them as such (see 2.10.3); however, it must be noted that ST and SAV translate them using passive verbs: ויתמרק (for ומרק), ויצטבע (for ושטף), אתרק (and the variant readings אזדריק, זריק, זרק) (for זרק), יִסְתַּגפר (for וכפר), and ST ארוסה and SAV تتزوج (for ארשה). This, it would seem, is the best way to understand *yå̄lå̄da* ילדה (Gn 24:15).

The forms in (a), (b) and (c) reveal two ways of expressing the passive voice in SH in its previous stage: (1) Forms (a) and (b), which are derived from פְּעִיל, the form common in Aramaic, with the difference between (a) and (b) being different developments from the original *šəwa* (see 1.3.3); (2) Form (c), derived from **qutal* — which takes the form *quttal* (with geminated second radical) in TH because of the impossibility there of maintaining the short *u* vowel in an open syllable. In SH, where every short *u* becomes a front vowel, the pattern first became **faqad*, and then, because of SH phonetic rules, *få̄qå̄d*. It would seem, on the face of it, that the first of these two categories, which is more common than the second, is influenced by Aramaic, although it should be recalled that a (short) *i* vowel of the second radical is typical of Arabic, and the *qatīl* pattern occurs in Hebrew as well with a passive meaning, as in שָׁלִיחַ and מָשִׁיחַ, and especially הַשְּׂנִיאָה (Dt 21:15), all of which indicate that there is not necessarily Aramaic influence at work here. Note that an *i* vowel occurs in TH in the passive forms of ע"ו (שִׂים alongside שׂוּמָה, וְהֻנִּיחָה (see n. 121).

> Note: The form *ēkəl* is categorized above as a perfect even though in the context of the verse where it occurs, it is a participle, as the predicate itself indicates. There is, we see, no morphological difference between the participle and perfect in the passive verb as in the intransitive verb (see 2.1.1.3.) The form *yētən* (Lv 11:38) cannot be understood as the imperfect of נתן, because the נ is always geminated in the imperfect of that verb. It is difficult to posit an error of analogy to the perfect in such a common verb, so we must conclude that SH has preserved a lone remnant of the root ית"ן that we know from Phoenician dialects, a cognate to the Hebrew נתן.[128] Note also that יתן in Nu 26:54 is pronounced *yittən*, which is a *Qal* imperfect[129] that appears in place of the TH passive, as noted above (2.10.3).

2.10.7 *Qal* and *Hifʿil* Imperfect

Given that these two stems share a common form in the imperfect, usually **yifqåd*, they will be discussed together. Undoubted passive forms from SP

---

[128] ST and SAV employ imperfect forms — יתיהב, يجعل — but this is no proof that the Samaritan pronunciation of *yētən* יתן is intended as imperfect. For the alternation of the two roots, cf. נצב/יצב, נכח/יכח, see Kister "Lexical Problems," 45–47.

[129] ST variants: יתיהב, יהב (MS Barberini: תתיהב).

are: *yiqqåm* יקם (Gn 4:24 TH יָקֻם), *wyimṣå* (Gn 44:12; TH וַיִּמָּצֵא), *yittåṣu* ויתצו (SP Lv 11:35), *wyiggåd* ויגד (Gn 38:24, 48:2; Ex 14:5), and *wtuqqa* ותקח (Gn 12:15).[130] Of course, the *i* vowel in the preformative is derived from *u*, and the *u* vowel in ותקח (Gn 12:15) is puzzling due to the lack of any phonological necessity. One can assume that an exegetical intent is behind this — perhaps a desire to eliminate the possibility of interpreting the verse to mean that Sarah went to Pharaoh's house of her own volition? On the basis of form, then, there is no need to state definitively that the form *yiqqa* in Gn 18:4 is not passive because it has an *i* vowel, not a *u*, since there is no need to assume here an exegetical impulse that would require an extraordinary *u* vowel. The form *wyårl* ויאר (SP Nu 22:6) is regular, derived from **yu'ar* (cf. TH יוֹאֶר) > **ya'ar*. The form *yårå'i* יראה (SP Ex 19:13, in place of TH יֵרָאֶה!), whatever the reliability of the verb or its etymology, is, morphologically, the passive imperfect of *Qal B* (see 2.1.1.7), i.e., it developed from the form **yara'i* > **yur^a'i*, which originally has a *šəwa* between the first and second radicals, similar to TH לֻקֳחָה (Gn 2:23) or רֻטֲפַשׁ (Job 33:25). In the passive *Hif'il* forms *yårṣi* (Lv 19:7, 22:23,27) and *yårṣu* (Lv 22:25), *u* became *å*. (Cf. 1.5.2.3.)

2.10.8 *Hif'il* Perfect

One clear passive form is *wå'rī* והראה (Lv 13:49; ST ויתחזי), since the *Hif'il* form is *ar'rå* הראה. (The participle is just the opposite; see 2.13.6c n. 2) It seems that the reading of הראה as *åri* in Gn 41:28 is intended as passive,[131] to avoid stating that the Lord showed Pharaoh, as is commonly done with Jacob and Moses. The difference in TH between active and passive voice, which depends on the *seghol/qameṣ* variation, cannot exist in SH, and therefore the possibilities for pronouncing the vowel of the second radical of ל״ה verbs (see 2.8.7, 2.8.11) were employed to make that distinction. No distinction could be made between the vowel of the second radical in afformative bearing forms, so that the realization of הראת in Ex 26:30 and Dt 4:35 is *arråttå*, similar to *arråtək* הראתיך (SP Ex 9:16). The form *å'ītåb* היטב (SP Gn 12:16) is passive, as ST form אתיטב indicates. A base form such as **haytåb* (similar to the Biblical Aramaic וְהֵיתָיִת, Dan 6:18) should become in SH **itåb*, so perhaps we may assume that the *a* preceding it (in *å'ītåb*) originates in an understanding that the ה prefix is added without meaning.[132] It is more likely in this instance, though,

---

[130] The sign for the *u* vowel (see 0.7–0.8) above the י of ויגד in some manuscripts is evidence that not so many generations ago (the 14th and 15th centuries) the *u* vowel was preserved in this word as well. See also below, 2.10.8.

[131] If the verb is meant to be passive, the intent is to avoid anthropomorphism. (See *LOT* III/2, 231, l. 33, n. 159). The vocalization אֻרִאֶ (Gn 41:28) in SAV according to Kuenen's edition attests to this interpretation.

[132] I know, however, only of a superfluous ה appended to nouns. See *LOT* I, 161.

that the diphthong of *hay* was not reduced, in order to prevent an identity of form with the infinitive *īṭåb*,[133] and finally, the diphthong *ay* was split into two syllables. (See also 1.4.4.) The *u* vowel is preserved in the verb *ukka* הכה (Nu 25:14).

2.10.9 *Pi'el*

a. According to the rules of SH, the passive base forms *quttal* or *quttil* become *faqqad* or *faqqəd*, fusing entirely with the active forms. Thus, it cannot be determined whether *baššēla* בשלה (Lv 6:21) really preserves the passive of *Pi'el* (=TH בָּשְׁלָה), as would be indicated by ST, which translates the verb אתבשלת, or whether it is an active verb, as would be indicated by the reading בשלה (SAV طبخها) and according to the possibility mentioned above, 2.10.3. The same is true of *šallā'u* שלחו (Gn 44:3), which is rendered in ST אשתלחו. The verb *'abbēdu* עבדו in Ex 1:14 is passive according to ST and SAV, contra TH עָבְדוּ.

b. The verb *yēkåfər* יכפר (Nu 35:33) is rendered in ST and SAV as the passive verbs יסתלח and يغتفر, but morphologically, it is equivalent to the *Pi'el* "with simple second radical" (i.e., the active stem). There is no way to determine whether we have here a form that was originally active used to express passive voice, or whether this form was originally passive **yekuppar* > **yekappar* > **yēkåfår*, and ultimately the vowel of the second radical assimilated to the *Pi'el* pattern. Similar to that is the form *tēqåṭər* תקטר (Lv 6:15; SP תקטיר!), which is translated in ST by the passive verb תתועד. On the form *kåfår*, see above, 2.10.6.

c. The form *ṣåbīti* צויתי (Lv 8:35, 10:13) is passive, as ST and SAV attest and as is required by the context, unlike the form mentioned in 2.10.3.

2.10.10 The identity of form between the *Qal* passive of the *fēqəd* pattern and the intransitive verb (2.1.1.3), where there is no vowel for the second radical in a closed syllable, along with the semantic contact between the passive and the intransitive, create a situation in which a form such as *ēfək* הפך (Lv 13:3,4 and others) could not be identified as one or the other were there not attested the feminine form *ēfīka* הפכה (Lv 13:10,25), in which the *i* vowel indicates that it is a passive form (cf. *yēledu* above, 2.10.3, vs. *yēlīdu* above, 2.10.6a). Along the way, we have, thus, learned an important fact: in SH the verb הפך, when it is transitive, is pronounced *åfåk*, while its intransitive sense, when not expressed by *Nif'al* as in Lv 13:17, is expressed by the passive form. There is, then, no finer evidence of the blurring of the boundary between intransitive and passive in SH.

---

[133] Like *īṭåb īṭəb* היטב איטיב (Gn 32:13) (ST איטבה, SAV احسانا).

2.10 Passive Voice

2.10.11 In summary, a consistent phonological process of eliminating short *u* on the one hand, and a shift in usage from reflexive to passive or the inclusion in usage of passive within the reflexive on the other — whether the second is dependent on the first or not — led to a nearly complete merger of the internal passive form into the active form. What remains of the former in the oral tradition of the Pentateuch attests to the fact that SH and TH passives, which develop differently, share a common origin.

2.11 Imperative

2.11.1 The imperative in TH generally has a simple structure: it is equivalent to the second person of the imperfect, both singular and plural, without the preformative ת. This is generally the case with the vowel of the second radical, at least (שְׁמֹר : תִּשְׁמֹר, פְּתַח : תִּפְתַּח, תֵּן : תִּתֵּן). The vowel of the first radical, though, may vary slightly in the imperative forms bearing suffixes. The first radical is sometimes vocalized with *ḥireq* (שִׁמְרוּ, מִכְרָה [Gn 25:31], sometimes with *qameṣ* (שָׁמְרֵנִי [Ps 86:2], שָׁמְרָה), sometimes with *šəwa* while the second radical has a full vowel even in a non-pausal position: פִּשְׁטָה, וַחֲגֹרָה (Isa 32:11), וּקְרָאֵנִי (Ps 50:15), רְפָאָה (Ps 41:5). In texts with Babylonian vocalization, the tendency toward the last pattern is particularly pronounced, especially the forms with object pronominal suffixes. (See Yeivin, *Babylonian Vocalization*, 480–481.) It is quite clear that the Hebrew imperative of *Qal* is derived from different base forms with different vowel patterns — something like *qutul, qatal, qitil* — but this difference cannot explain the behavior of the vowel of the first radical: why, for example, is the vowel reduced to *šəwa* in forms with penultimate stress from the *qatal* base (פְּעָלוּ and not פָּעֲלוּ), or why is that vowel *qameṣ* even in verbs not derived from the *qutul* base (e.g., קָרְבָה). This means that the imperative in TH was formed by analogies which have not yet been reconstructed in detail.

2.11.2 The imperative in SH is even more simple in its structure than its TH counterpart, and its connection with the imperfect, too, is more pronounced than in TH. In TH one finds, for example, רֵשׁ (Dt 1:21) alongside רַשׁ (Dt 2:24), but the SH form is consistently *rås*, parallel to *yīrås*. In the *Qal*, the vowel of the second radical is normally *a/å* (in an open syllable *ā/å*), since the historical short *u* is often expressed in SH as *a/å*, and in any case it is not expressed as *u* or, alternately, as *o*, although at times it becomes *ə(e)*, as in *šērēṣu* שרצו : *yišrēṣu* ישרצו. The first radical always has a full vowel, which, it can be assumed, is derived from *šəwa*; it would not be correct to assume that it preserves the situation as it was before Hebrew or in an ancient stratum of Hebrew. This is indicated by the fact that in place of the vowel that normally follows the first radical, one finds, if only as an exceptional case, a vowel preceding the first radical: *iktåb* כְּתֹב (Ex 17:14), *afsəl* פסל (Dt 10:1). This can only be explained by positing base forms with *šəwa*.[134] The original *šəwa* developed in SH into a full vowel of various qualities (see 1.3.0). The dominance of *e* may be due to the fact that the *e* vowel prevented the widespread merger of imperative forms with forms of the perfect. Indeed, Abū Isḥāq makes use of this criterion.[135] Nonetheless, there is *a/å*. This is the case with the form *šåmå* שמח: no morphological distinction can be found between the imperative in Dt 33:18 and the perfect form in Dt 24:5 (*Qal* in the Samaritan view!). The same is true of the verbs *rådåf* רדף, *fåtåt* פתת: the distinction can be made only on the basis of context. This does not aid us in the case of *šāma* שמע (Dt 33:7): context would seem to require an imperative, as indeed TH reads, but SAV perceives the verb as a perfect. Thus, we cannot prove that the form *šāma* exists in the imperative, since the usual form is *šēma*. In the form *šāmānni* שְׁמָעֵנִי (Gn 23:11,13), however, which is clearly an imperative, the first radical of שמעני is pronounced with *ā*, and, thus, *šāma* in Dt 33:7 may also be understood as an imperative.

2.11.3 The vowel of the second radical is maintained in all forms of the imperative, and thus, imperative forms with suffixes appear as though they were the pausal forms common in TH, e.g., *zēkåru* זכרו, *qēråbu* קרבו, *ēzåqu* חזקו, *zå:må* (< *z^a'āmā* זעמה (Nu 23:7, TH וְזֹעֲמָה), *šēmånnu* (< *šēmā'innu*) (Gn 23:6, TH שְׁמָעֵנוּ), *šēmā'ūni wfågā'u* (Gn 23:8, TH שְׁמָעוּנִי וּפִגְעוּ).

2.11.4 An unusual relationship can be found in the vowel of the second radical of the verb פסל between the imperfect *yifsål* and the imperative *afsəl*, and, it seems, between *yiktåb* and *kētəb* (Ex 34:27), which may not be an imperative.[136] The vowel *ə* is characteristic of *Hif'il* (*ī* in an open syllable) and *Pi'el* (*ē* in an open syllable); it is not found in *Qal* except in rare instances. Particularly noteworthy is the appearance of *o* as the vowel of the second radical in *Qal*: *šēmor* שמור, *zēkor* זכר. According to the assumption that the basis for the *holem* in TH imperative is a short *u* vowel and following the rule that TH does not allow for short *u*, we question if the *o* vowel here preserves the ancient impera-

---

[134] Cf. my article "Penultimate Stress," 153ff.

[135] *LOT* I, 72: "As for the imperative, its form differs from the perfect form in that the first vowel shifts from the 'great' *pataḥ* to the 'small' *pataḥ*."

[136] While the MS Barberini text of SAV here — واكتب — would lead us to assume that the word was taken to be an imperative, and ST כתב neither supports nor denies that assertion, the Kuenen edition of SAV translates كاتبٍ which would lead us to believe that *kētəb* was intended not as an imperative but as a participle! (On the imperative of כתב, see 2.11.2.) Furthermore, if this is true of כתב, the imperative form of פסל also raises doubts about whether the original interpretation differs from what we find in SAV and ST. It should be noted that in Samaritan Aramaic the participle may express an imperative sense. Cf. *LOT* III/2, 181, ll. 75, 80.

tive form. Indeed, the plural forms *šēmåru* שמרו and *zēkåru* זכרו support that doubt. It seems that these forms are remnants of the infinitive absolute form[137] with original *ō (< ā)*, which was generally lost in SH, as it is in MH.

2.11.5 As noted above, the vowel of the second radical in *Hifʿil* is *ī/ə*, e.g., *wåšlək* והשלך and *ašlīku* השליכו, while in *Piʿel* the vowel is *ē/ə*, e.g., *barrək* ברך and *barrēku* ברכו. In the other stems it is generally *å/å*, e.g., *Nifʿal*: *iššåmår* השמר, *iššåmåru* השמרו; *Nifʿal B*: *iqqåbbåṣu* הקבצו. However, *å/å* occurs in *Piʿel* as well in the verb עבר: *wåbbåru* ועברו. It should be noted that the vowels of *Piʿel* "with simple second radical" in the verbs כפר, כבה, and ספר are irregular; in the imperfect they are *yēkåbəd* and the like, while in the imperative, *kēbåd, kēfår, sēfåru*, reversing the usual order of vowels within the root and, thus, making the imperative look like that of *Qal*. (This is not the case with the verb אסף; see 2.11.7.)

> Note: The relationships between *ī/ə* and *ē/e* described above may guide us in analyzing imperatives, but not always with complete certainty. Thus, in the verb חזק, *åzzeq* (Dt 1:38) is classified as *Hifʿil*, and SP indeed reads החזק, but *wazzīqēʾu* (Dt 3:28) should perhaps be classified with *Piʿel* because of the short vowel after ו (on *ī* in *Piʿel* irregular forms, see 2.2.1.2.2), and indeed many manuscripts of SP read וחזקהו. The same is true of *wammīṣēʾu* (Dt 3:28): the vowel of its second radical is that common in *Hifʿil*, while the first vowel is short, and SP reads ואמיצאו, with the full vowel including י. There is no basis for a definitive decision between these two conflicting indicators in such instances.

2.11.6 Among the verbs with guttural radicals, the verb הלך deserves special note. Its vowel patterns lack coordination between the imperfect *yēlåk* and the imperative forms *lik, līku*, etc. The vowel of the imperative in this verb follows the pattern of original ע"י verbs. In *Hifʿil*, the first radical is sometimes geminated, as in *åzzeq* החזק, and sometimes not, as in *å:rəm* החרם.

2.11.7 Among the פ"א class, it should be noted that the vowel of the second radical of אמר and אכל is like that of the imperative of the strong verb, even though the vowel differs in the imperfect: *ēmår* אמר, *ēmåri* אמרי, *wēkåla* וְאֹכֵלָה (Gn 27:19), *wåkålu* ואכלו (Gn 45:18). Unlike the strong verb (see 2.11.5) is the imperative of the *Piʿel B* verb אסף: *åsēfa* אספה (SP Nu 11:16, Nu 21:16).

2.11.8 In the פ"י class, the vowel of the imperative, *å — råd* רד, *råš* רש, *ṣå* — צא generally retains its quality: *råda* רדה, *wråšu* ורשו, *ṣåʾu* צאו. Sometimes, though,

---

[137] See *LOT* I, 72, n. 7, and the section on the infinitive, 2.14.9.

it is replaced by *ē*: *šab* שב (SP Gn 29:19), *šēbå* שבה (Gn 27:19), *šēbi* שבי, *šēbu* שבו. (The relation is like that of *yad* יד to *yēdi* ידי, etc. The verb יהב is unattested in the second person in the Pentateuch, but in Samaritan liturgical poetry we have *ab*,[138] and in other forms, *â* and *ē* are interchangeable: *åbā* הבה, *wåbu* והבו (SP Dt 32:3), *ēbu* הבו (Dt 1:13). On the imperative *wittīgår* והתגר (Dt 2:24), see the discussion of *Hitpaʿel* in the פ"י class (2.4.14).

2.11.9 Among the verbs of the פ"נ class, it should be noted that the vowel of the second radical of נתן does not match that of its imperfect. Instead, it is similar to the vowel of the פ"י class, *å:tån* תן, *tåna* תנה.

2.11.10 The verbs of the ע"ו class retain the original distinction between ע"ו and ע"י: *qom* קום, *qūmu* קומו, *šim* שים, *šīma* שימה, *līnu* לינו. The vowel of the verb בוא is *å*, which apparently entered the singular form from the plural (see 2.6.15): from *bā'u* באו to *bā* בא. In *Hifʿil*, preformative ה takes either of two vowels — sometimes *ī*: *wīkən* והכן (Nu 23:1), sometimes *å*: *åšīru* אשירו (SP Ex 15:1). (Cf. discussion in 2.6.6.) The form הרם appears as *ērå̊m* (Ex 14:16), and הרמו as *ērå̊mu* (Nu 17:10), forms somewhat similar to the infinitive of the ע"ע class discussion in 2.14.15, but without gemination, and in fact, TH הָרֵמוּ is derived from that class. On the mixing of ע"ע and ע"י in this verb, the form *årēmi* הרימי (Gn 39:15,18) should be mentioned. It may be that *ēbåt* הבט, too, belongs to the ע"י class; see also 2.5.13.

2.11.11 Verbs of the ע"ע class that do not follow the conjugation patterns of the strong verb — such as *ṣårå̊ru* צררו (SP Nu 25:17) and *arnīnu* הרנינו (Dt 32:43) — do not geminate the second radical (see 2.7.4). Among the *Qal* forms are *ēra* ארה (Nu 22:6), *årå* ארה (Nu 23:7). We have not found an explanation for the alternation of *ē* and *å* vowels, but the same is true for the forms *qēba* קבה (Nu 22:11) vs. *wqåbinnu* וקבנו (Nu 23:13). Of course, forms ending in -ָה offer no evidence in regard to the gemination of the second radical in the other forms, since in TH, too, such forms do not have geminated second radicals, e.g., קָבָה (above), נָבְזָה (1 Sa 14:36), and the noun forms גִּתָּה (1 Kgs 2:40) and הַגְּגָה (Jos 2:6). Among *Hifʿil* forms we find a geminated first radical in *arrəf* הרף (Dt 9:14).[139]

2.11.12 In ל"ה verbs no distinction can be made between the 2nd masc. sing. and 2nd fem. sing., because both end in an *i* vowel, e.g., *ēli* עֲלֵה (Dt 1:21) vs. *ēli* עֲלִי (Nu 21:17). No shortened imperative exists in SH. Thus, for TH צֵא (e.g., Dt 2:4) we find in SH *ṣåbi* (SP צאי!), for TH הך (Ex 8:12) we find SH *wakki* (SP

---

[138] See, for example, *LOT* III/2, 91, l. 35.
[139] The Samaritan tradition derives הרף from רפ"ף. See *LOT* III/1, 101.

והכה!), and for TH והעל (Ex 8:1), we find *wålli* (SP והעלה). Note that the imperative of the verb קרא is *qēri* (Dt 31:14) (and קראן [Ex 2:20] is *qē'rīn*), and of מלי is *mēli* (Gn 44:1) or *mālli* (Gn 29:27), even though in all other forms they follow the patterns of other III-guttural verbs (see 2.2.3.0). That the form *qē'rīn* follows the ל"ה class is attested by the form *šē'mān* שמען (Gn 4:23). It should also be noted that הקרא (SP Gn 24:12), the written form indicating *Hif'il* imperative, is pronounced *iqra*. The form *'ānu*/ענו (Nu 21:17), by analogy to עלי, can be identified as an imperative, and one may find an *ā* vowel in the imperative (see 2.11.2), but SAV reads it as perfect: قالو.

2.12–2.14 Verbal Nouns

2.12 Active Participle

2.12.1 In TH, two types of active participles occur in *Qal*: one follows the פּוֹעֵל pattern, while the other shares the form of the 3rd. masc. sing. perfect, i.e., פָּעֵל or פָּעַל (infrequently), and in the ע"י class forms such as קָם and שָׂם. The type that takes the פּוֹעֵל pattern is a legacy from the Proto-Semitic *qātil*, found in Akkadian, Arabic, and Aramaic as the sole participial form. (Contrast Hebrew קָם with Aramaic קָאֵם and Arabic قائم). Despite the few deviant forms that may be found in Biblical Hebrew, an original division can be clearly recognized between active verbs on the one hand, which have participles of the פּוֹעֵל pattern, and stative verbs on the other, which have participles of the perfect 3rd masc. sing. form. This distinction is reflected neatly in the morphological distinction made in Biblical Hebrew between "active" and "stative" verbs (see 2.1.1.0.1). That consciousness of this distinction guided ancient speakers of Hebrew can be seen quite clearly in the example of the *Nif'al* participle. In cognate languages such as Akkadian and Arabic, the *Nif'al* stem takes the preformative *mu-*, similar to the other stems, e.g., Arabic (مُنْفَعِل), Akkadian *mupparsum* (< *munparisum* "cut off"). It is, thus, very reasonable to assume a Proto-Hebrew *Nif'al* participle with the preformative מ. The lack of this preformative in historical Hebrew already in ancient times can only be explained by the fact that the *Nif'al* became a pattern of intransitive or passive verbs. Thus, its participle took the form of the perfect, changing *pataḥ* to *qameṣ* according to the general rule; cf. the *Qal* verb חָכַם (Prov 23:15) as against the noun (participle/adjective) חָכָם. When the ability to distinguish active/passive and transitive/intransitive relationships through a vowel within the root (פָּעֵל vs. פָּעַל, etc.) became obscured, the reason for maintaining a distinction between participles was lost and, thus, doublets came into being, such as: לָבֵשׁ/לוֹבֵשׁ and שֹׁכֵחַ/שָׁכֵחַ. The פּוֹעֵל pattern came to dominate even stative verbs in Biblical Hebrew, such as שׁוֹכֵב (יִשְׁכַּב), while the opposite occured in MH, in which the פָּעֵל pattern came to dominate even active verbs (see 2.1.1.0.3).

2.12.2 The tendency described above became even stronger in SH and gave rise to a situation different from that of TH and of MH as attested in ancient vocalized manuscripts. In MH the פָּעֵל form is the widespread participial form, as has been noted, but "stative" verbs were eliminated from it,[140] that is, the פָּעֵל form is absent in the perfect, and so for this type of Hebrew, it cannot be said that the participle is equivalent in form to the perfect, except, of course, for the ע"י class and *Nifʿal*.

In SH, in contrast, the equivalence of form between participle and perfect became very widespread, leading to the collapse of the ancient פּוֹעֵל form of participle. This is so for all types of verbs and all classes. Given that the understanding of Scripture in the Samaritan tradition is not the same as the Jewish tradition's understanding in every case, it is difficult at times to state with certainty whether a particular form in the Qal stem in SH is to be construed as a perfect or participle.

2.12.3 The Samaritan grammarians are passing on a tradition — presumably a well-founded one — when they state that the *nomen agentis* [=participle] of the strong *Qal* verb whose second radical is not either of the guttural letters — I refer to ח and ע — has six patterns,[141] and they list them and describe their vocalization. The patterns that emerge from their descriptions are:[142] (1) *šāmer*, (2) *šēmir*, (3) *šūmir*, (4) *šūmer*, (5) *šūmar*, and (6) *šāmor*. However, not all of the Pentateuchal examples adduced for these forms are equivalent to those we hear today in the Samaritan reading of the Pentateuch. The example cited for (1) is today pronounced *šåmår* (Dt 7:9), and that cited for (4) is heard as *šåmēri* (Nu 31:47 and elsewhere). The primary difference between the situation

---

[140] From what is stated by M. H. Segal in his article, "Mishnaic Hebrew and its Relation to Biblical Hebrew and Aramaic," *JQR* 20 (1908–1909), 25, and in his *Grammar of the Language of Mišnaic Hebrew* (Jerusalem 1936), 113 [Hebrew], it would seem that he assumes the existence of פָּעֵל in the perfect as well. This assumption is not correct. Note that יָרֵא exists in the Mishna only as a participle, as is the case with יָכוֹל. This seems to be so in Tractate *Shabbat* 10:5 and 13:6, and in any case, there are no perfect forms in the Mishna from the verb ירא other than this, while in the Tosefta, where a perfect form does occur (יכלו) *t. Bikkurim* 2:2,5), we find that in situations where it would be possible to use third person singular forms in the perfect, the verb יכל occurs only in a compound tense, i.e., as a participle in the verb phrase היה יכול: "היה יכול לגנוב" (*t. Bava Qamma* 6:8). We find the same in the Mishna (e.g., *m. Avoda Zara* 1:4).

[141] *LOT* I, 49, 183.

[142] I employ the macron according to the pronunciation current today and certainly in the time of the sources in question, but they refer only to vowel quality, as is shown by the fact that "small *pataḥ*" designates something like *e* in contrast to the "great *pataḥ*," which is *ā/a*.

2.12 Active Participle

described by the grammarians and the contemporary situation is the lack of distinction now between *i* and *e* as the vowel of the middle radical, as a result of which patterns (3) and (4) are pronounced identically as *fūqəd*,[143] and the contemporary pattern *fâqåd* is absent from their list.

2.12.4 From an analysis of the Samaritan tradition of recitation of the Pentateuch today and from an examination of the Samaritans' understanding of that text based on a study of their translations and exegesis, wherever there is something to be learned on the topic, we find that we today, too, have six forms of the active participle, and they are: (1) *fâqəd*, (2) *fâqåd*,[144] (3) *fēqəd*, (4) *fēqåd*, (5) *fūqəd*, and (6) *fūqåd*. The participle *fâqod* is equivalent in form to the passive participle (see below, 2.13.2). Of course, not every form is free, that is, able to be derived from any verb.[145] Not every form listed above can be shown to exist for every class. The following are a few examples of these forms:[146]

(1) הלך: *ålək, ålēkəm*; זקן: *zâqən, azzâqīnəm*;

(2) דרש: *dârås̆*; שמע: *s̆āma*; שא'מִים: *yāda, yādā'i, yā'dīm*; משל: *ammâs̆ålǝm*; קרב: *qårâb, qārbəm*;

(3) נפל: *nēfəl, nēfīləm*; שבר: *s̆ēbīrəm* (Gn 47:14); כתב: *kētəb* (Ex 34:27);[147]

(4) רבץ: *rēbås̆, rēbīsåt, rēbīsəm*;

(5) רמש: *arrūməs̆, arrūmīs̆åt* (Lv 11:46); נכח: *wnū'kāt* (Gn 20:16); סכך: *sūkēkəm*; שגג: *as̆s̆ūgīgåt*;

(6) שפט: *as̆s̆ūfåṭ*; זלל: *zūlål*; שטר (SP Dt 21:2): *ws̆ūtårək*.

2.12.5 Because of the multiplicity of participial forms in the *Qal* stem, the original, exclusive connection of the participle to the conjugation of the verb in its finite forms was undermined, and we find many parallel forms of the participle in two ways:

---

[143] The literary evidence that distinguishes between *i* and *e* in this situation seems to be supported by the vocalization of MS א (from the 14th century; see *LOT* I, 30) in Form 1 שֹמֶר and in Form 2 שֹמִיר! The example of (2), however, is שמירים (SP Ex 12:42), so that it is possible to say that the form *s̆ēmir* reflected in the vocalization is only a backformation of *s̆ēmīrəm* in that verse. This argument cannot be made for Forms 3 and 4; Form 3 is written שׁמיר and Abū Isḥāq, author of *Kitāb al Tawṭi'a* (*LOT* I, 49) defines the last vowel explicitly as a *ḥireq* in the middle radical (وتكسر عينه), and Form 4 is vocalized שׁוֹמֵר, with the middle radical bearing a vowel (ibid., 182).

[144] For the sake of simplifying the issue, I have not made a distinction in marking between *â* and *ā*, e.g., *s̆āma* שמע as against *s̆åmå* שמח, both 3rd masc. sing perfect.

[145] The grammarian Abū Isḥāq (see *LOT* I, 53), in describing all forms in all classes, notes "some of them are attested in Scripture and some are postulated by analogy."

[146] Given that the vowels of every participle may not be exemplified by the strong verb, I have added examples from the hollow verb where the hollowness has no influence on the vowels.

[147] See n. 136.

a) forms existing side-by-side, such as נתן: *nâtən, nētən, nūtən*; ישב: *yēšəb, yūšəb*; זבח: *zēba, zāba*;

b) morphological suppletion, that is, different patterns in singular and plural or in masculine and feminine, e.g., רבץ: *rēbå̂s — rēbīsəm*; נפל: *nēfəl — nåfå̂låt*; שפט: *šūfå̂ṭəm — šå̂fåṭi* (construct state); נשא: *annūšå'əm — nå̂šå'i* (construct state); etc. This kind of inflection of the participle cannot be explained by phonological processes acting on one basic form, as is the case with *yā'dīm — yādā'i*; see 1.3.3. Parallel forms are found in TH as well, of course, but to a much smaller degree: לוֹבֵשׁ/לָבֵשׁ and לָמֵד/לוֹמֵד (the latter outside the biblical corpus).

Given the tendency of the Samaritan tradition to unify and harmonize, we may assume that this tradition made use of the variety of forms to express differences of meaning and exegesis, but this point is not sufficiently obvious and is in need of detailed investigation. Nonetheless, we note a certain tendency to use the *fūqəd* and *fūqåd* patterns to express a nominal function when a given verb has another pattern as well. Of the brook described in Dt 9:21, the Samaritan tradition realizes הירד (without ו!) as *ayyūrəd*, i.e., continually descending, while the descent of the angels of Gn 28:12 is pronounced *wyårēdəm*. For the expression "ישב הארץ" (or "בארץ..."), meaning a permanent resident,[148] the form *yūšəb* is employed (Gn 13:7, 50:11, Nu 14:14), and in each of those places ST is careful to render it as דיור or דיאר, while in all other places, ישב is pronounced *yūšəb* (or at times *yåšåb*; see below) and translated as דאר. Similarly, נתן with the definite article is *annūtən* (in Ex 16:29: *nūtən*), meaning "regularly, continually gives," while in all other appearances, the participle נתן is realized as *nâtən* (or *nētən* [Ex 5:10] or *nåtån*). Note also the difference between *lēqa* לקח (Dt 27:25) and *lūqā'i* לקחי (Gn 19:14). The distinction between nominal and verbal participles is well known from Palestinian Aramaic and SA: *qāṭēl* is verbal, *qāṭōl* is nominal. This distinction is to be found in MH as well.[149] However, it would seem that we are dealing here with a tendency alone, and in any case, our sources — the translations and exegesis — are not able to instruct us as to the exact function of each of the parallel forms, and the fact of morphological suppletion attests to the weakness of these distinctions

---

[148] It would be relevant to contrast יושב ארץ הכנעני (*yūšəb*!) (Gn 50:11) with ועפרון ישב בתוך בני חת (*yēšəb*!) (Gn 23:10), or with אשר אנכי יושב בקרבו (SP *yēšəb* ישב!) (Gn 24:3).

[149] This issue is discussed briefly in *LOT* III/2, 109, n. to lines 79-80. The distinction between nominal and verbal participles in SA is clearly evident from the ancient liturgical poetry, as noted there, e.g., יהוב *yā'ob* "a giver" : יהב *yā'əb* "giving"; זאון *zā'on* (from the root זון) "nourishes" : זאן *zā'ən* "nourishing," ibid., 168; עבוד *'åbod* "creator" : עבד *'åbəd* "creating," ibid., 89. An interesting parallel in MH is to be found in *Debarim Rabba* (ed. Lieberman, Jerusalem 1939/40), 22, where אתם עברים (Dt 2:4) is explained as אתם עבורים. [As to the semantic distinction between these two kinds of participles, see now M. Mishor, *The Tense System in Tannaitic Hebrew* (Ph.D. thesis, Hebrew University of Jerusalem, 1983], 170 [Hebrew].

and not their presence as established facts. So we find that *nåtən* appears alongside אני and אנכי — i.e., in a clearly participial use; while *nåtån* appears with a third-person subject, "אשר ד' נתן" — i.e., in a situation in which it could be understood as perfect (and similarly, *yåšåb*, e.g., Dt 1:4). However, the interchangeable Arabic translations اعطانا (perfect; e.g., MS Or 7562 at Dt 1:20) and معطينا (participle, e.g., Bloch edition at Dt 1:20, and both Bloch edtion and MS Barberini at Dt 2:29) demonstrate conclusively that the form *nåtån* serves as a participle as well. The tendency of Samaritans toward making a varied tradition uniform requires further clarification of the semantic relationships of the various forms of the participle.

2.12.6 If we follow the vowels of the first radicals among the six forms of the participle, and if we assume for the moment that the vowels of the second radicals are related to each other as phonetic variants, we arrive at three types:
  a. *fūqəd* (including patterns 5 and 6);
  b. *fåqəd* (patterns 1 and 2); and
  c. *fēqəd* (patterns 3 and 4).

The first two are parallel to TH's פּוֹעֵל and פָּעֵל forms, while in the case of the third we may posit a parallel to פְּעִיל, the Aramaic participle, the use of which to express active verbs is well known.[150] The hypothesis — that *fūqəd/fūqåd* and other, similar pairs among the other forms are differentiated only by interchangeable allophones — is difficult to support, since we have not found ə and å related as allophones even in a closed syllable after the stress,[151] and such an assumption is surely not accurate in regard to a stressed open syllable (שפט: *sūfåṭəm*, סכך: *sūkēkəm*) or even to an open syllable after the stress (קשה: *qåši* / פנה: *fåna*). There is, then, no way to avoid the conclusion that, apart from the inherited participle with ū as the vowel of its first radical, derived from *qātil* in Proto-Semitic, the other participial forms are modelled after the forms of the 3rd masc. sing. perfect (see 2.12.2). This is nicely illustrated in Nu 35:27: ורצח...הרצח / *wrēṣa*...*arrēṣa*. The *fēqəd* pattern, which has ī as the vowel of the second radical in its inflection, is originally related to the passive (see 2.10.6), while in the *fūqåd* pattern, the å vowel can be assumed to have resulted from analogy to the vowel of the inflected forms in which the original *šəwa* developed into a (see 1.3.3), e.g., singular *šūfåṭ* שופט and plural *šūfåṭəm* (< *šūfaṭīm*) שופטים.

2.12.7 Note: a. The following exceptions should be noted: *arråmšət* הרמשת (Gn

---

[150] This opinion is recorded in *LOT* I, 50, n. 7. On פעיל as active participle, cf. Blau, "Passive Participle," 68, n. 1. Cf. also רניניה ("those who complain") in *LOT* III/2, 135, n. 32.

[151] Those who tend to replace [å] with [ə] in that position [*šēlåšət* instead of *šēlåšåt* (Lv 12:4)] are a small minority. See *LOT* III/1, 22, n. 26.

1:28) and *qārbəm* קְרֵבִים, from which the vowel of the second radical has been eliminated (see 1.2.1). Note, too, that the vowel of the first radical in the plural of קרב is *ā*, while the singular form has *â* (*qâråb*). The form *fâtårâ* (Dt 23:5) should be understood as a participle bearing the definite article (see *LOT* I, 159).

b. The *fēqəd* participle is equivalent to the "segholate" noun pattern, and it may be that several of the participles are in fact nouns of that pattern. It is also possible that the participial forms are conjugated as though they were originally of the segholate noun pattern because of the merging of their forms, e.g., *rēkəb* רכב (Nu 22:22) as against *rikbu* רכבו (Gn 49:17) and *šēkən* שכן (Gn 14:13,TH שְׁכֵן) vs. *šēkīnu* שכני (Dt 1:7), on the one hand, as against *šēfək* שפך (Gn 9:6 TH שֹׁפֵךְ) vs. *šafku* שפכו (Nu 35:33) on the other. On *rēkəb*, cf. שני רכב סוסים (2 Kgs 7:14), translated in the Septuagint: ἐπιβάτας, "horsemen," "riders."[152]

2.12.8 The forms of the participle in the stems bearing a preformative מ are as would be expected from the phonetic rules of SH. *Hif'il*: קרב — *maqrəb*, *maqrībəm*; פרס — *måfrīsåt*, *måfrīsi* [plural construct form].

Pi'el: דבר — *amdabbər*; ברך — *ambarrək*; בקש — *måbaqqəš*; למד — *målamməd*; קדש — *amqaddēšimma*; רחץ — *amrā'ēšåt* (Lv 2:7 מרחשת!). There are no examples in the Pentateuch of *Pi'el B* in the strong verb,[153] but there is one example from the root אסף: *måsəf*.

Hitpa'el: הלך — *mētållåk*.

2.12.9 SH displays a participle without מ in *Pi'el*, too, as is common in Hebrew in the *Nif'al* stem.[154] It also is equivalent in form to the 3rd masc. sing. perfect. As examples, let us adduce דבר — *dabbər*, גרש — *garrəš*, מכר — *makkər*, חבל — *abbəl*, אבד — *abəd* (Dt 32:28), והאכל — *wåkkəl* (Lv 14:47),[155] שלח — *šalla*. One must distinguish between these forms and nouns of the פָּעֵל pattern in TH. (See *LOT* III/2, 166, on the difference between *'ayyåb* חַיָּב and the participle *'ayyəb*.) The preceding verbs and others like them function in SH as *Pi'el*, while in the consonantal text accepted by the Samaritans as well, the *Pi'el* stem is not dictated by the spelling. SH, therefore, makes the participle conform to the other

---

[152] G. R. Driver cites several examples in his article, "Hebrew and Arabic Collective and Broken Plural Forms" in *Dr. Zakir Husain Presentation Volume* (New Delhi, 1969), 202.

[153] But Abū Isḥāq (*LOT* I, 59) creates forms such as נפש **amnâfəš* and כעס - **amkā'əs*, and this is clearly the usual pattern in the II-guttural class.

[154] The form *mikkårət* מכרת cited by El'azar (*LOT* I, 185) has been categorized as *Nif'al* because of the vowel ə after the second radical.

[155] It is impossible to explain this form as a *Qal* participle because of the geminated כ, and the *Pi'el* is attested in the Jewish tradition as well (in the Bible, the *Pu'al* form is attested) with the same meaning as the *Qal*. See also *LOT* III/1, 69, n. 8.

verb forms that appear in *Pi'el* in that tradition by geminating the second radical of the *Qal* participle on the pattern of *fāqəd*. This is a phenomenon rooted in the Aramaic vernacular; see *LOT* III/2, 166, 222ff.

2.12.10 *Nif'al* has two participial forms:
   a. one equivalent to the perfect, such as *niddårəš* נדרש, *niṣṣåmēdəm* נצמדים; and
   b. the inherited form, such as *nikbåd* נכבד, *nišqåf* נשקף, *nårṣi* נרצה, *nā:zēləm* נאזלים (Ex 15:8), *wnā:mən* ונאמן, *wnā:mēnəm* ונאמנים, *nåbon* נבון, *nåkūnəm* נכונים (the *å*/*ə* alternation after the second radical is similar to the imperfect).

From contrasting pairs such as: אכל — *wnåkkəl* (Ex 22:5) : *anniyyåkēlåt* (Lv 11:47), and עלם — *wnā:låm* (Lv 5:2, etc.) : *wniyyållåm* (Lv 4:13, *Nif'al* B), we learn that the inherited participle form was considered nominal, similar to what we have seen in the *Qal* stem (see 2.12.5).[156] It should also be noted that in the participle following the perfect forms, the vowel of the second radical may be *ē*/*ə*, unlike the perfect forms themselves. There is no justification for claiming that the *å*/*ə* alternation represents allophones of one phoneme, since no such phenomenon is attested elsewhere in SH.[157] This may be seen from the

---

[156] See *LOT* III/1, 73, n. 13, and 2.1.4.3 above. The form ונוכחת (SP Gn 20:16), with its pronunciation *wnū'kāt*, is particularly difficult in regard to its derivation and it grammatical form, as is the case with וְנֹכַחַת as well.
   1. a. Sa'adia's Arabic version, which renders it جالك ("before you," "in front of you"), seems to derive the verb from the root נכה.
   b. Ibn 'Ezra takes issue with this, suggesting instead (following Ibn Janāḥ) a derivation from יכח, which has been the accepted opinion ever since.
The Samaritan tradition indicates that Sa'adia's opinion long predates him, since it is found in the oldest stratum of ST: ולקובל (variant: ודלקובל) and in SAV: فقابله (variant: في المقابله). But interpretation (b) is also represented in ST, by the word ו(א)תוכחן, if it is not the result of influence by Targum Onqelos.
Therefore, according to (a), the Samaritan form is a *Qal* participle, like *wsūba* (SP וסובה, Dt 21:20); according to (b) it is a *Nif'al* participle, nominal, unlike הנושע/*annuwwāša* (Dt 33:29).
   2. The results of this grammatical analysis provide us with no means for deciding between the two possibilities of derivation, not to mention means for preferring interpretation (b) to (a). We can learn only that, in light of the early appearance of interpretation (a), that the relationship of the roots נכח:יכח is like that of יצב : נצב or יקש : נקש or יתן : נתן in SH (see 2.10.6, note), in which each pair shares a common semantic core. In the verb הוכיח, the transferred sense of "standing opposite" became prevalent in speech. Kister, "Lexical Problems," 45 ff., provides a conclusive demonstration of the concrete meaning "stand opposite (one another)" for the verb מוכיחות (זו את זו) (*m. Para* 2:5). Add to this the term יוכיח and the like used in Halakhic discussion to introduce contrary evidence.
In light of the foregoing analysis, the categorization of *wnū'kāt* as *Nif'al* is not without some doubt.

[157] The *ə*/*å* alternation in this position can be heard in the pronunciation of certain readers, and Raṣon ben Binyamim Ṣadaqa tends to employ it sporadically. In his reading I sensed sometimes *i* instead of *å*, but these have no influence on the structure of the vowel system in SH as a whole. See *LOT* III/1, 22, n. 26.

difference in vowels when they are long as in II-guttural verbs: הנלחם/*anillā'əm* הנשאר/*aniš'šår* (< **annišša'ar*), or as in the form נאכלת cited above. Note that in the participial form of *Nif'al* "with geminated second radical," such as *wniyyållåm* (cited above) or נטמאה/*niṭṭåm'mā* (Nu 5:13; ST מסבה, SAV نجسة), or the forms cited below, in 2.12.12, we find important confirmation of the MH tradition that gives us such forms as נתאחין (*y. Kil'ayim* 1:1, 26a), נתרפין (*y. Berakhot* 1:1, 2c), הנשתנית (*b. Bava Qamma* 94b; but MS Hamburg המשתנת!) — i.e., participial forms of *Nitpa'el* without preformative מ!

2.12.11 As for the form of the participle in the other classes, we will point out unusual forms and those that complete the total picture. In the I-guttural class we note:

a. *å:tūrəm* האתורים (SP Nu 21:1) should be taken as an active participle of the *fåqod* pattern, given that the word is understood in the Samaritan tradition to mean "the scouts" — ST גשושיה, SAV الجـواسيــس; cf. Targum Onqelos מאלליא. Support for this understanding of the root את״ר can be found in the Arabic اثر. The form *šå'ūqəm* שחוקים (SP Dt 33:26) may also be an active participle in SH, even though the verb is at most intransitive (meaning "high"; SAV شواهيق). The form *ṭå'on* טחון (SP Dt 9:21) is a passive participle, as shown by ST טחין and SAV طحينا.

b. In the *Pi'el* participle of עבר, the vowel of the second radical is *å*: *'åbbår*. This is not due to the ר, as the form *dabbər* דבר demonstrates, but rather due to analogy to the perfect. (This is not so of the *å* in *amyåssåråk* מיסרך, which is derived from *šəwa*.)

c. Such forms as *måbbəd* (from אבד) cannot be conclusively categorized as either *Hif'il* or *Pi'el* (see 2.2.1.2.1). In the form *må:mēnəm* (Dt 1:32), *ē* is puzzling, since one would expect *ī* in *Hif'il*; perhaps this form is influenced by the *Nif'al* forms (see also 2.12.10). The form *måbbēdəm* מעבדים (Ex 6:5) would seem to be a *Pi'el* participle.

d. II-guttural: See (a) above. A form such as *zīfəm* זעפים (Gn 40:6) indicates clearly that the *fēqəd* pattern contains an original פְּעִיל pattern as well, since the form can only be explained by **zi'īfīm* > **zī'īfīm*. The same is true of *īf* עיף (Dt 25:18), whose origin is **'yīf* > **'īyif* (see 1.5.3.2).

e. III-guttural: The *fēqåd* pattern is more common in this class than in the other classes. It would seem we should assign הרוה (Dt 29:18) to this pattern, written in the Samaritan tradition also as הרואה, רוחה, and הרחה. These spellings hint at the pronunciation current today, *arrē'bå*, apparently a participle from the verb רוח, something like הָרְוֵחָה as current in Modern Hebrew.[158]

f. Forms such as *måli* מלא, *šēbi* שבע, *zå'rī* זרע, *ṭēmi* טמא, and *šēmi* שמח are

---

[158] See, however, 2.12.16e below.

conjugated like the verbs of the original ל״ה class. However, since there is no transition of verbs of the III-guttural verbs to the ל״ה class in SH, and even ל״א verbs do not generally become ל״ה verbs (see 2.2.0, 2.8.9), these forms and others like them are to be explained according to the assumption that their *i* vowel originates in the פעיל pattern and that it parallels the *ə* vowel of a closed syllable.

g. Forms such as *amsab'bēt* מספחת and *amgabbā'ot* מגבעות are easily explained as *Pi'el* participles (cf., e.g., *mam'rēt* ממראת = TH מַמְאֶרֶת, *Hif'il* participle of מרא!) or as *Pu'al*, in contrast with the Jewish tradition of these forms. They may be interpreted as nouns as well, though, exactly paralleling TH (see below 2.13.5).

2.12.12 The *Nif'al* participle of the פ״י class, such as *annuwwåləd* הנולד and *annuwwāša* הנושע, is of the type "with geminated first radical" (see 2.12.10). The form *mūṣā'i* מוצאי (Nu 14:37, defective spelling), as opposed to the regular *Hif'il* participle *mūṣi* with an *ī/i* vowel, may not be a participle, but instead a noun similar in form to מודע. In any case, it is difficult to classify it as a passive participle.

2.12.13 a. As we saw when dealing with the פ״נ class (2.5.3; 2.5.6), the regular TH *Nif'al* almost never appears in this class. This is clearly evident in the participle form. In place of such TH forms as נִצָּב, נִתָּן, and נִגָּשִׁים, we find in SH: *nēṣab*, *nētan*, and *nēgīšəm*, all of them active or passive *Qal* participles (see the end of 2.13.1).

b. The verb נטה, in which ט is not geminated in the finite forms in *Hif'il*, has as its *Hif'il* participle form *måṭi*, as if it were of the ל״ה class (unlike *makki* מכה). Similarly, *måšågåt* משגת (Lv 14:21, TH מַשֶּׂגֶת), even though that verb does geminate the שׂ in the perfect and imperfect.

2.12.14 The regular participle of the ע״י class in TH is employed not only in SH but in Samaritan Aramaic as well (see *LOT* III/2, 181, n. 85). For that reason, there is value in noting the participle form of קם: *aqqā'ēma* and *aqqā'ēmәm*, which are common in Aramaic alongside the Hebrew form: *qāmək* קמיך, *qāmo* קמיו. It appears that the form in the usual Aramaic pattern is intended to convey the verbal sense of the participle. This relationship obtains in the Aramaic verb מות: *mītan* (noun) versus *mā'ētan* (*LOT* III/2, 158, n. 70). In SH, the masc. sing. is *mat*, fem. sing. *mēta* (see part 2 of the note in the paragraph below), while the pl. form is *mītəm*, as in Aramaic. However, the forms of עד: *id*, *īdəm*, and גר: *ger*, *gīrəm* attest that the *i* vowel of *mītəm* מתים may be original in Hebrew. A form such as *almət*, with *šəwa*, also reflects the possibility **me/it* in the absolute state. The form *mat* should be compared with *kånəm* כֵּנִים, and the alternation of traditions in SH is like the interchange of לָנִים:לֵנִים. Cf. also גֵּר:גָּר,

which is reflected in SP as well: *ger:går*. Just as in the perfect, *Hif'il* participles have two forms, with *i* and *a* after the מ: *mībi* מביא, *må'ǝd* מעיד.

> Note: 1. The grammarians Abū Isḥāq (*LOT* I, 55) and El'azar (*LOT* I, 185) know of a participle זובה in Lv 15:19 (and there are manuscripts of SP which read this). We must, therefore, assume a pronunciation such as *zūba*, which is no longer known today, the contemporary realization being *zāba*. The medievals' pronunciation (or the one current in their time) has parallels in TH: קוֹמִים (2 Kgs 16:7),[159] בּוֹסִים (Zech 10:5), and in MH נח — נוחין, מולין (= מָלִים), בושין, חולות, and in SH *aṣṣod* הצוד (Gn 27:33).
> 2. מתי and other forms with pronominal suffixes were pronounced *mitti*, *mittåk*, *mittu*. Undoubtedly, the Samaritan tradition takes the noun to be feminine, and SAV does so as well (since the person described is Sarah). Thus, the opportunity is taken to read the feminine suffix *t* only: **mat+ti > mitti* (like *bitti* from בת); one can also posit **met+ti* with the same results. Thus, we have a very interesting parallel to Akkadian masc. *metu* ("dead") : fem. *mittu*; ("see") *CAD* M, Part II, 140.

2.12.15 In the ע״ע class, the following should be noted:

a. Relatively frequent use of the *fūqåd* pattern in the *Qal* participle, such as *ūbåb* חבב, *u'ūfåf* וחפף, and *zūlål* זלל.

b. Use of the regular *Pi'el* in place of TH *Polel* pattern[160] in the verb ענן: *månnǝn* (<*mᵃ'annǝn*).

c. The odd form *miqqēllå* מקלה (Dt 27:16) is a result of the *qǝre* of the verb קלל and the *kǝtiv* of the synonymous root קלה (*kǝtiv*). This seems to be the participle form in *Hif'il* from קלל, with an additional *å*. The *å* vowel (ה-) was understood by the Samaritans as either the definite article or "emphatic" (Arabic تفخيم) (see *LOT* I, 161, 253; III/1, 144, n. 16; 41, n. 19). While the *i* vowel is indeed surprising, there is no other way to interpret the word; the participle of *Hitpa'el* stem would require a form such as **miqqallēlå*. On the gemination of both the first and second radicals, see 2.7.2.b, and cf. הָעֲלוּ (Dan 5:15).

d. It is difficult to categorize the form *ammåråram* המאררים as a *Pi'el* participle because of the absence of gemination of the second radical ר. Perhaps it should be understood as a participle form of *Pi'el B*. But note that the vowel of the second radical is *å*, not *ē*, and that the verb exists in *Qal* in the form of *årårå* (Gn 5:29). On the possibility that we have here the pronunciation of המערערים as an interpretation of המאררים (Nu 5:18), see *LOT* III/1, 74, n. to v. 18; III/2, 141, n. to l. 86.

e. On *mūqåq* (< **mᵘ'ūqåq*) מחוקק, ST and SAV attest that it was understood

---

[159] But in SH this form is understood as an infinitive; see 2.14.15.
[160] On the other hand, we find the use of the *Polel* for *alsūbåb* (Nu 21:4) in place of לסבב.

2.12 Active Participle

as an active participle (see also *Hammeliṣ LOT* II, 517b), even though it has *å* instead of the expected *ǝ* (see 2.12.6).

2.12.16 The ל״ה class has barely absorbed any ל״א verbs, and even less so any other III-guttural verbs. On the other hand, it is not impossible that a SH verb of the ל״ה class belongs to the ע״י class in TH: the participle *zåka* זַכָּה (Ex 30:34); more likely, however, is that it represents an ע״ו verb, based on *zåk* זָךְ (Ex 27:20).

The following phenomena are worthy of note:

a. The participle רעה (Gn 29:9), which is pronounced differently from its usual spelling: *rā'iyya*, a form similar to בוֹכִיָה and others in TH (see 1.5.3.4). In *Pi'el* we find *amṣåbiyya* (SP Gn 27:8).

b. It is not certain that the verb שגע exists in the Samaritan oral tradition, even though it is found in SP in the forms שגעון (Dt 28:28) and משגע (Dt 28:34). The uncertainty stems from variant spellings: משגעה/משגה in Dt 27:18, and (in the opposite direction) משגה/משגיע/משגע in Dt 28:34). On this basis we may theorize that שגה replaced שגע in speech due to the semantic closeness between them. In any case, *amšaggi* in Dt 27:18 is, judging by its meaning, a *Pi'el* participle, while *amšaggi* in Dt 28:34 may be either an active participle (in *Pi'el*) or as in TH a passive participle (original *Pu'al*), because while the *i* vowel is uncharacteristic of the passive participle, we note that TH מַכֶּה is pronounced *makki*, while TH הַמֻּכָּה (Nu 25:14) is pronounced *ammukkå*. Thus, it seems likely to us that the form in Dt 28:34 is also an active participle, and here *Pi'el* is employed with the same meaning as *Qal*. An example of a verb that functions as both transitive and intransitive is TH שָׁנָה: we find both שנה את and שנה מן "deviated from" in MH).[161] There are other examples as well.

c. Note that there is no difference in SH between TH מְכַסֶּה and מְכֻסֶּה. Both are pronounced *mēkassi* (Ex 26:14), *ammēkassi* (Ex 29:13; Lv 3:4,9; and other verses). Only with the addition of the interrogative ה do we find the participle *åmkassi* (Gn 18:17). We find the same pattern in Isa 14:11, and this is the form of the MH words מִשְׁמֶרֶת, מְסֻנֶּנֶת, etc.

d. In place of משתאה (Gn 24:21), SP reads משתה, pronounced *mašti*. We would anticipate that the *Hitpa'el* participle from the verb שאה would take the form *mištā'i*, while *mašti* is appropriately derived from שתה. The standard interpretation of *mašti* among the Samaritans is no different from the standard Jewish interpretation of משתאה. ST translates the verb as שאם (referring to looking), and SAV employs متامل, and in *Hammeliṣ* (*LOT* II, 507b) there are additional synonyms: Aramaic מסתכל, מתאר. MS M of ST reads אשקה (לה) alongside glosses מ[סתכל],

---

[161] An interesting example of this is found in *Sifre Deuteronomy* (ed. Finkelstein, 330): ישראל קלקלו במקום והמקום לא שינה בהם וכן הוא אומר שינה בהם וכן הוא אומרכי אני ה' לא שָׁנִיתִי [citing Mal 3:6]. We have here the opposition TH *Qal* against MH *Pi'el* with the same meaning.

שאם/שהם, and in one manuscript, we even find (מנה) שתיו. This interpretation is an ancient tradition among the Jews as well. Demonstration of this can be found not only in the reading שתי in Targum Onqelos, but also in Saʿadia's Arabic translation مستــقــى and from the rejection by the medieval commentators Abraham Ibn ʿEzra and Shmu'el ben Meʾir of the interpretation based on a derivation from שתה. The Samaritan pronunciation *mašti*, then, provides decisive support for that tradition. The form could be understood as the noun משתה, but the context requires us to interpret it as a *Hifʿil* participle used in the sense of the *Qal*, a use absent from the Jewish tradition.[162]

e. The form *arrē'bå* (2.12.11) may, nonetheless, be a participle of the ל״ה class, having developed from *arrᵉwåyå* > **arrēbåyå* > **arrēbåʾå*.

f. The regular form of the active participle of the verb פרה is *fåri* (Dt 29:17). The word *fåråt* פרת (Gn 49:22) has to be analyzed as either (1) a participle with the quasi-feminine ending *at* (see 4.3.14) functioning as an adjective, similar to the personal name *āʾēzåt* אחזת (TH אֲחֻזַּת Gn 26:26 and TH גְּנֻבַת 1 Kgs 11:20), or (2) a substantive which is morphologically identical with the feminine participle, analogous to *fåʾråt* פרחת (Lv 13:57, TH פֹּרַחַת).[163] Explanation (1) underlies the Arabic translation مثمـــر ("bearing fruit, fruitful") in *Hammelis* (*LOT* II, 557) and SAV, while explanation (2), *fērūta* פרותה (*LOT* III/2, 144 "fruitfulness") is found in the ancient Samaritan Aramaic literature: ST Gn 49:22, *Hammelis* (ibid.), and *The Book of Wonders* (*Tībåt Mårqe* 101: ברה דפרותה יוסף).

2.13 Passive Participle

2.13.1 The accepted division of the verb into stems in Hebrew grammar sets out particular stems for passive verbs — *Puʿal* and *Hofʿal* — and does not consolidate them with the parallel active stems, *Piʿel* and *Hifʿil*. This division even delegates a place for the *Nifʿal* stem, which is not exclusively passive. (This is not so in Arabic grammar, in which active and passive voices are expressed by one stem.) An exception to the pattern in Hebrew is the *Qal* stem, which has a passive participle in addition to the active participle. The reason for this is that in Hebrew, there are no passive forms of *Qal* in the perfect or imperfect different from the participle. Those disappeared in ancient times,

---

[162] There is, however, a corresponding phenomenon in CPA. Although it is not recorded in Schulthess's *Grammatik*, it appears explicitly (so I learn from M. Bar Asher) in "אתקנותא דקודשא דנילוס," published by G. Margoliouth in "The Liturgy of the Nile," *JRAS* (1896), 677–730. The form appears there twice (705, 709) in the participle — דמשתין and ומשתן — as in SH. It seem that the perfect and imperfect forms, too, such as אשתו and שתן(א) can be understood as *Afʿel*.

[163] Other substantives of this formation have been quoted in Ben-Ḥayyim, *Struggle*, 431ff. It seems that the relationship between *fåʾråt* and *(k)åfʾråt* (Gn 40:10) is well explained there by the relationship of Biblical יותרת (*yūtårat* Ex 29:13) : MH יֶתֶרֶת.

2.13 Passive Participle

leaving only scattered remnants which are structurally equivalent[164] to *Pu'al* (in the perfect, such as לקח) and *Hof'al* (in the imperfect such as יתן), and which do not alone constitute a separate stem.

Thus, the passive participle known in the grammar of Biblical Hebrew as the *Pu'al* participle should be assigned in MH to *Pi'el*, since the perfect and imperfect forms of *Pu'al* have disappeared from MH,[165] with only the participial forms preserved. This is the standard practice in Aramaic grammar with respect to both *Pu'al* participle and *Hof'al* participle, even though in Biblical Aramaic there are still clear remnants of *Hof'al*.

In SH, the *Pu'al* and *Hof'al* stems have been consolidated in most forms of the perfect and imperfect with *Pi'el* and *Hif'il* because of phonetic shifts, and in some instances, the participles of *Pu'al* and *Hof'al* have become identical with *Pi'el* and *Hif'il* participles for the aforementioned reasons. A similar thing has occurred in Aramaic, in which מְבָרֵךְ and מְבָרַךְ are distinguished, while in the forms מְבָרְכָא and מְבָרְכִין, the active and passive are identical, and in מְגַלֵּא and מְגַלִּין, too, the active and passive are identical. It seems reasonable, then, to include the SH passive participles in *Pi'el* and *Hif'il* under the rubric of their respective active stems, just as this is self-evident for the passive participle in *Qal* (except for remnants of the passive forms, to which a separate chapter is devoted [2.10]). Henceforth, then, we shall not refer to *Pu'al* or *Hof'al* participles, but to the passive participles of *Pi'el* and *Hif'il*. Where the active and passive participles are equivalent (and in SH, they are equivalent even in *Qal*!), I shall follow the function of the form: if it describes the object of the action (passiveness), it is dealt with in the present chapter; if it expresses an action or situation (activeness), such as *yēšībåt* ישבת (Lv 15:23) or *šēmi* שמח (Dt 16:15), it is classified as an active participle. In various passages, there is room for doubt about how a given form is understood by the Samaritan tradition.

2.13.2 The *Qal* stem has three forms of the passive participle: (1) *fåqod*, (2) *fēqəd*, and (3) *fåqəd*, as exemplified by the following forms:

1. כתב: *kåtob, akkåtūbā, kåtūbəm*; גרש: *gårūša*; שרף: *šårof*; עשק: *'åšoq* (Dt 28:29); מרח: *må'rū* (Lv 21:20);[166] סרה: *sāru*; שלח: *šåluw'wā*.

2. בשל: *afšīla* (< **bᵃsīla*); שבה: *aššēbi* (Nu 31:26); גדל: *gēdəl* (Nu 6:5; SAV مظفور, ST מרבי)שרף: *šērīfa*; בעל: *bīlåt*.

3. משח: *ammåši, må'šīm*; בצר: *bāṣīrot*.

---

[164] Cf. above 2.10.1.

[165] In the Mishnah there are isolated *Pu'al* forms. Even if they preserve ancient traditions, they are mere remnants. See Yalon, *Vocalization*, 136ff.

[166] If, in fact, this word is derived from the root מרה, but see A. Tal, "Minuscula from the Hebrew Lexicon," *Sudies in Hebrew and Jewish Languages Presented to Shelomo Morag*, ed. M. Bar-Asher (Jerusalem, 1995), 95–104 [Hebrew]. Tal proposes a derivation from the root רוח.

2.13.3 When the *fâqod* form expresses a passive participle, it no doubt parallels the passive participle form in TH, but one should not ignore the observation of the Samaritan grammarians (see 2.12.3) that the *fâqod* pattern serves as an active participle form as well. On this point, they adduce evidence from the Pentateuch: וחנון *wânon* and רחום (today pronounced *rē'om*; both Ex 34:6).[167] Since in TH, both Biblical and MH, we find the passive (*pā'ūl*) participle form fulfilling the same semantic function as the active participle (contrast, e.g., אחוזי חרב : תופשי מלחמה and רכוב : רוכב[168]), one may say that the same situation obtains in SH. It should be noted, however, that in TH, the *pā'ōl* and *pā'ūl* forms coalesced because of phonetic processes; that in SH, *pā'ōl* regularly fulfills the same function as the active participle (*pō'ēl*) (*LOT* III/2, 109); and that in MH, *pā'ōl* quite commonly expresses what the *pō'ēl* form of active participle expresses. On this basis, it seems likely that the Samaritan *fâqod* form, when used as an active participle, is related to the *pa'ol* form. In any case, this phenomenon was in the mind of the Samaritan grammarians when they set down *fâqod* as one of the six forms of the active participle.

2.13.4 It is difficult to determine whether the *fâqəd* and *fēqəd* forms developed from one pattern, similar to the TH pattern *pā'īl*, i.e., that in the *fēqəd* pattern, the *e* vowel is the result of the *šəwa* in the inflected forms having penetrated by analogy into the base form as well, or whether we have two originally different forms of פעיל: Hebrew פָּעִיל and Aramaic פְּעִיל. As we know, in TH we can find פָּעִיל forms equivalent in meaning to פָּעוּל, and we even find occasional alternations, such as שנואה, שניאה, אסור, אסיר: משוח, משיח, and in MH, שלוח, שליח : שכיר, שכור, and in verbs of the ע״ו class, שום, שים : בּוּרָה ("fallow field"): נִירָה ("cultivated field").

> Note: It is worthwhile keeping in mind that *u*, too, may be a result of the *šəwa* (see 1.3.1). Thus, the SH pronunciation of הנשך (Nu 21:8) *annūšək* is a passive participle. Such a form is found particularly in SA and in later SH, e.g., סוכיל (*LOT* II, 537: "foolish"), זוכיר, סופיר ("Samaritan Poems" 346, 363).

2.13.5 The original *u* vowel in the passive participles of *Pi'el* and *Hif'il* (TH מְפֹעָל, מְפֹעַל/מְפָעָל) became *a* (sometimes *i*), and they may be distinguished from

---

[167] It would seem that we should conclude from this that Abū Isḥāq (*LOT* I, 51) considered ורחום to be like חנון, i.e., as having an *â* vowel after the first radical, but from the evidence of MS א (*LOT* I, 185, n. to l.1), which reads רֵחוֹם (it should be רֵחוּם!), we learn that at least in the 14th century the pronunciation was with *ē*, and presumably also in the pronunciation of Abū Isḥāq, whose description treats only the vowel of the second radical. The form *rē'om* reflects a base something like רְחוּם, and note the פְּעִיל/פָּעוּל alternation in SH and elsewhere (*LOT* III/2, 134, n. 18; 174, n. 40).

[168] See Blau, "Passive Participle," 67ff.

2.13 Passive Participle

the active stems first of all by their meaning, and also on the basis of the fact that the passive participles have as the vowel of the second radical *a/ā*. There is, thus, no doubt about *amšaqqådəm* מְשֻׁקָּדִים, *amšazzår* מְשֻׁזָּר, and *ammēṣårrå* המצרע, which are passive, just as there is no doubt about *mukkå* מֻכֶּה, *ammūšåb* המושב, or *mūsåbot* מוסבות (ע"ע following the ע"י pattern), which maintain the original vowel. The doubt arises when we consider a form such as *amšåbbēṣot* משבצות (Ex 38:11 and elsewhere), which appears to be *Pi'el*, but the context makes it difficult to undertand this form as a passive participle. But since the SH form of a noun such as תֶּשְׁבֵּץ — *tēšåbbəṣ* — is similar to that of the aforementioned משבצות, it is not inconceivable that underlying the Samaritan form is the same base, known from TH: מִשְׁבְּצוֹת (see 4.2.3.11). The forms *amgabbā'ot* מגבעות (Ex 29:9) and *amgåballot* מגבלות (Ex 28:14) may be seen as passive participles of either *Pi'el* or *Pi'el B*, with no way of knowing which of the two. The forms *alméqiṣṣå'ot* לְמְקֻצָּעוֹת (Ex 26:23) and *amméqiṣṣå'ot* הַמְקֻצָּעוֹת (Ex 36:29) may both be assumed to be passive participles.

> Note: We do not find passive participles in *Pi'el* without the preformative מ (as opposed to what was said of the active participle above, 2.12.8), i.e., there is no form attested such as **garrūša*, but rather *gårūša*, even though in all other forms, a *Pi'el* stem obtains. The same is true of *šåluw'wa*. It should be emphasized that SH did not utilize forms which geminate the second radical, like the TH form אֻכָּל, in order to integrate these forms into *Pi'el*.

2.13.6 Among the other verb classes, phenomena worthy of note are:

A. Roots with Guttural Consonants:

1. The forms *šēbi* שָׁבֵי and *wyāgi* וַיָּגֵי have been assigned to the active participle because they express a state (see 2.13.1), while *fåṣa* פצע (Dt 23:2) and *wšā'sa* ושסעה (SP Lv 11:26; ST פליגה, variant reading סדיקה; SAV مشقوقة) have been classified as passive participles solely on a semantic basis, since *a* after the second radical is unusual. This explanation does not apply to the case of *sårårot* (SP Ex 12:34, TH צְרֻרֹת), which ST and SAV translate by means of passive participles, צרירן, مصرورة, respectively, in contrast with the same pronunciation in Gn 42:35. It may be that what is expressed in TH by פצוע (note that ST reads פדי, פדיע, i.e., passive participle), SH expresses by means of a participle of a stative verb, something like *פָּצֵעַ* in the Jewish tradition. Cf. *wšåsa* (Lv 11:7) : TH וְשֹׁסַע, or the alternation אָבֻד : אָבוּד in Jewish sources.[169]

2. *mådamməm* מאדמים (Ex 25:5) can be assumed to be a passive participle of *Hif'il*, since the second radical is ungeminated, while the gemination of the

---

[169] E.g., the textual variants in the Mishna (*Ma'aser Sheni* 5:1): the common וְהַצְּנוּעִים (also MS Kaufmann) / והצניעים (MS Parma [De Rossi 138]). For other instances, see Hanemann, *Morphology*, 93.

third radical in place of a preceding long vowel is a well-known phenomenon in TH as well, as in נִכְבַּדֶּיהָ (Nah 3:10) and וְנִכְבָּדִים (SP Nu 22:15) (see also B below). An exact parallel to the form *mådamməm* מאדמים can be seen in the textual variant מְהַחְצְפָה (Dan 2:15).

B. The ע״י Class:

1. The form *uwwållåt* (Gn 33:13) is the realization of the SP spelling אעלת (variants: עאלת, עלאת), corresponding to the Masoretic form עֲלוֹת. This is the plural form of עוּל, similar to TH שׁוָקִים as the plural of שׁוֹק except in that the third radical is geminated. (See above A.2.) On the different possibilities of analyzing this word, see 1.5.3.1.

2. *īšəm* חשים (Nu 32:17), corresponding to TH חֲשִׂים.

C. The ל״ה Class:

The *Qal* participle of the *fåqod* pattern occurs in two singular forms, those like *nåṭuwwi* נטוי and those like *gålo* גלוי (see 1.4.4), both of which yield a lone plural form, such as *nēquwwəm* נקוים (SP Gn 44:10) and *åṣuwwəm* אצוים (SP Ex 5:13). The ו is not necessarily original in these forms, unlike the ו in נטווֹת (Isa 3:16) or that in עשווֹת (1 Sa 25:18), among other examples, but is rather a glide (see 1.5.3.2, 1.1.8 Rule B).

> Note: 1. אצוים is derived from a ל״י root; note also רצוא (Ez 1:14) in TH.
> 2. On the plural form of the participle in the *fåqod* pattern: *baryot* בריאות, *malyot* מלאות, see 1.5.3.4[4]. The form *aššēbi* השבי (Nu 31:26) is, according to the Samaritan version (המלקח השבי), a passive participle.
> 3. In the *Hifʿil* forms of ראה, there is a difference between the active and passive participles. The active participle appears as *måʾrī* (Ex 25:9) < *marīʾi* < *marʾi*, while the passive is *mirʾå* < *murāʾā* < *murᵈʾā*. On the last vowel, see also 2.8.11, and on the gemination of ר, see 2.8.5.

2.14 Infinitive

2.14.1 One of the unique features of the Hebrew verb is that there are in most stems two forms to express action without specifying the time and the person of the action. In traditional Hebrew grammar, this part of the verbal paradigm is termed מקור (really a translation of the Arabic مصدر "source") or שם הפעל (i.e., *nomen verbi* = *actionis*).[170] These two terms are entirely synonymous, although

---

[170] See, e.g., M. Wilensky's comment to ספר הרקמה (Yehuda Ibn Tibbon's Hebrew translation of *Kitāb al-Lumaʿ*), p. קפח l. 14; in the new notes edited by D. Tene in the 2nd ed. (Jerusalem, 1963/4), II, p. תרנט. In the Hebrew edition of the present work (*LOT* V), I distinguish between שם הפעל *nomen verbi*, which includes the non-finite forms of the verb paradigm (i.e., infinitives and participles), and שם הפעולה *nomen actionis*.

מקור ("source"), according to the theory predominant in the Middle Ages, indicates that the noun is the base of the verb,[171] while הפעל defines the character of this part of the verbal paradigm. Many grammarians writing Hebrew make a distinction between מקור = infinitive and שם הפעל = gerund or pseudo–infinitive (JM I, 145). We see no reason to maintain this distinction today, not only in treating Biblical Hebrew, MH and the style of Hebrew in the late Middle Ages, but even in the treatment of Modern Hebrew.[172]

In various periods in the development of the Hebrew language, different nominal patterns have been employed to fulfil the function of "infinitive," or in other words, have functioned syntactically[173] as finite verbs: just as the finite verb takes an object, so does the "infinitive," whatever its particular pattern, e.g., לַעֲבֹד אֶת ה' (Jos 24:15), רָגֹם אֹתוֹ בָאֲבָנִים כָּל הָעֵדָה (Nu 15:35), לְאַהֲבָה אֶת שֵׁם ה' (Isa 56:6), לְמַסַּע אֶת הַמַּחֲנוֹת (Nu 10:2), כְּמִצְוֹת דָּוִד שְׁלֹמֹה בְנוֹ (Neh 12:45), כְּמַהְפֵּכַת אֱלֹהִים אֶת סְדֹם (Isa 13:19 and elsewhere), and with other patterns. Similarly, in MH we find the פְּעִילָה pattern in Qal, the פָּעוּל pattern in Pi'el, etc., patterns which had not yet been established as infinitive forms in Biblical Hebrew. We can, thus, easily understand the SH version wafqâṣerkimma ובקצירכם (SP Lv 19:9) in place of TH וּבְקֻצְרְכֶם. We see here an alternation of two different nominal patterns in ancient Hebrew fulfilling the same task in the verbal paradigm. Distinguishing between them mechanically through terminology is useless; it would even lead to an error in categorizing one of them as a noun, the other as a verb.[174]

2.14.2 A multiplicity of infinitive forms is not unique to Hebrew.[175] In Arabic, for example, there are several forms functioning as مصدر in the Qal stem. The uniqueness of Hebrew is rather that there are normally two forms in use as the infinitive of a given verb, each with its own defined uses. In Biblical Hebrew, it has been the custom for generations to use the term מקור מוכרת (translated into Latin as *infinitivus absolutus*) for that form to which one cannot affix personal pronouns or prepositions, and the common use of which is accompanying a finite verb (before or after it), such as הָרֹג נָא הָרֹג, גָּנֹב גֻּנַּבְתִּי and נָתוֹן תִּתֵּן. The form

---

[171] See, e.g., Ibn Janāḥ, *Kitāb al-Lumaʿ*, 22 [*Ha-Riqma*], or Abraham Ibn ʿEzra's *Moznayim* (Offenbach, 1790), 48b. The point is well attested.

[172] This is not the place to engage in a dispute with those who see in Hebrew three forms of the verbal noun treated here. Cf. *LOT* V, 149, n. 143א.

[173] The criterion for distinguishing between the infinitive (مصدر) and the pure (محض) noun given by Ibn Janāḥ (*Kitāb al-Lumaʿ*, 158 = *Ha-Riqma*, קפא) [גמור שם/מקור] is essentially syntactic.

[174] H. Orlinsky, "*Qal* Infinitive Construct," 107ff., devotes a detailed study to the distinction between the infinitive construct form and the verbal noun, trying to prove, for example, that nouns such as כְּמַהְפֵּכַת (Isa 13:19) (p. 118) are not additional forms of the infinitive, but nouns used as infinitives.

[175] Ibn Janāḥ lists them in *Kitāb al-Lumaʿ*, 155ff. (=*Ha-Riqma*, קעה) and Abraham Ibn ʿEzra, *Moznayim*, 48b, says "and verbal nouns come in an infinite variety of forms."

to which personal pronouns may be affixed, on the other hand, is known as מקור סמוך (translated *infinitivus constructus*). It is even accepted practice to say that the infinitive absolute is more in the nature of a verb than its counterpart, and it may in fact occur in place of an inflected form not only in an imperative usage but also in the sense of the perfect verb (וְנָתֹן in Jer 37:21, ...שָׁתוֹ...אָכוֹל...וְהָבֵא) לְבוֹשׁ in Hag 1:6) or the imperfect (קָנֹה in Lv 25:14, הִשָּׁבַע in Nu 30:3). The infinitive construct is more in the nature of a noun than its counterpart, in that it takes a possessive pronoun.[176] While the differences between their respective usages are quite clear, a certain measure of inconsistency may be found even here, presumably from the end of the biblical period. One may find an infinitive construct used to intensify a verb, e.g. חֲבֹל חָבַלְנוּ (Neh 1:7) and הֱיוֹת אהיה (Ps 50:21), and an infinitive absolute preceded by a preposition, e.g., אחרי שתה (1 Sa 1:9), עד כלה (2 Kgs 13:17), עד לכלה (2 Chr 24:10), מהרבה (Jer 42:2), בהנחל (Dt 32:8). Thus, we find the infinitive construct employed in the function of the infinitive absolute, and vice versa. Greater than that, however, are the inconsistencies in form. In fact, the morphological distinction can be clearly observed only in the *Qal* stem, where we find פָּעֹל versus פְּעֹל (or, rarely, פְּעָל), and in the *Hif'il* stem: הַפְעֵל vs. הַפְעִיל. There is no morphological distinction in *Hitpa'el*, nor is there for most classes in *Pi'el* or *Nif'al*, although there are, nonetheless, in these stems some distinct forms, such as קַנֹּא and רַפֹּא (in *Pi'el*) [in *Pu'al* גֻּנֹּב] alongside the usual *Pa'el* form (like the מקור סמוך), *Nif'al* נִכְסֹף, נִלְחֹם, etc., and forms such as הָאֲכֹל and הִנָּתֹן alongside the usual הִפָּעֵל pattern (like the מקור סמוך). If Biblical Hebrew can display such forms as יָדֹעַ קָרָא (Isa 8:4) and אָבוֹא שָׁמוֹעַ (Isa 28:12) alongside אבוֹ...הָלוֹךְ (Isa 42:24), one cannot know how to categorize דַּבֵּר in לֹא יָדַעְתִּי דַּבֵּר (Jer 1:6). Such doubts may abound in SH, in which the morphological similarity is greater. In fact, in a situation in which there is no morphological difference, it is doubtful whether one may legitimately distinguish between two kinds of infinitive, and one may surely not assign a form to the category of infinitive absolute or infinitive construct in SH on the basis of its vocalization in TH.

2.14.3 In TH, the infinitive absolute is equivalent to the infinitive construct פָּעֹל in the vowel of the second radical *(ḥolem)*, but comparative grammar demonstrates that the two identical vowels have different origins. The vowel of the absolute is derived from a *qatāl* pattern (as in Akkadian), while the פְּעֹל form originates in *qutul*. The infinitive with *ā* as the original vowel of the second

---

[176] The oldest source for this distinction, which now appears regularly in grammar books, is apparently Samuel Ha-Nagid, as quoted in a composition attributed to Isḥāq Ibn Yašuš and published by Kokowzoff in his *Novyie Materiyaly*. .. 1916, 131: انه قسم المصدر قسمين مصدر فعليّ ومصدر اسميّ: فالفعليّ عنده ال قمّوْصْ الفا ، وما جاء مع فعله مثل שמוע שמע ע[בדך]. דבר ידברו... والاسميّ [عنده] ال שבא نيّ الفا ، وما ائصل بضمير وما دخل عليه [الحرف] בכלם...

radical is common in Old and Middle Aramaic other than in the *Qal* stem — הִתְפְּעָלָה, הִפְעָלָה, פְּעָלָה etc. — and in Late Aramaic in *Qal* as well: פְּעָל.[177] So, too, it is found in several stems in Arabic: فعال, افعال, انفعال, etc. Thus, it seems reasonable to assume that the Hebrew forms with *ḥolem* in *Pi'el* (including *Pu'al*) and *Nif'al* (see 2.14.12) are remnants of a system of infinitives with *ḥolem* in all the stems, and not late innovations, based on *Qal*, that failed to take root. In fact, we see a gradual disappearance of the infinitives with *ḥolem*, to the point that, in post-Biblical Hebrew, we witness the elimination of the infinitive absolute of *Qal*, a form of indisputed antiquity. This morphological deviation in TH is evident both in the vocalization of forms such as עָשֹׂה, רָאֹה, גָּלֹה, and in the presence of *ḥolem* in the infinitive construct of verbs with III-guttural. In the latter, if the vowel originates from *u*, there should be a shift to *pataḥ*, as indeed happens in some forms, such as בִּגְוַע (Nu 20:3), שְׁלֹחַ (Isa 58:9; cf. Targum: מֹרְמֹה); instead, what we see is a transference of the *ḥolem* from the infinitive absolute to the infinitive construct. In the stage reflected in MH, the duality of infinitive forms had not been entirely eliminated, but of the biblical pair, MH retained the infinitive construct only with prepositional ל, and in each stem a noun has been added of a particular pattern, which maintains what had been the nominal character of the infinitive (such as the addition of possessive pronoun suffixes). Only in the *Hif'il* stem does the biblical infinitive absolute continue to exist in MH, where its use is actually nominal; that is, the distinction in MH between הַפְעֵל and הַפְעָלָה is not the same as the distinction in Biblical Hebrew between הַפְעֵל and הַפְעִיל, and evidence for this can be found in the use in such expressions as לכלל הָפֵר and לכלל הָקֵם (*m. Nedarim* 10:7) or in forms with possessive pronoun suffixes, such as, הֶכְשֵׁרוֹ, הֶתֵּרָן "דבר שהוא בהכנו" (*y. Shabbat* 3:6).[178] Similarly, we find in SH *ā̊rēmi* (Gn 39:15,18), constructed like MH *הֲרֵמִי.

2.14.4 As can be seen from careful observation of other areas of SH, the Samaritan tradition of Hebrew is rooted in the language as it was used at the end of the Second Temple period and during the first generations thereafter. And it is well known that in that language, the biblical form of the infinitive absolute had fallen into disuse. We would, therefore, expect to find among the speakers of that language a weakened awareness of that form. The language of the Hebrew Bible is replete with forms such as נָתוֹן תִתֵּן and the like, whose syntactic construction is obvious and in which the status of the infinitive was under-

---

[177] This is found in SA as early as 1000 years ago, and perhaps even earlier. See *LOT* III/2, 289, l.13.

[178] Perhaps because of the foreignness of the form to Biblical Hebrew, forms such as הֲנֵץ (*m. Berakhot* 1:2, MS Kaufmann) or even הַנֵּץ, and הֶנֵּץ instead of הָנֵץ, came into being. See Yalon, *Vocalization*, 44, and my "Lexicographical Miscellanea," ed. S. Abramsky et al., *S. Yeivin Festschrift* (Jerusalem, 1970), 431 [Hebrew].

stood by the Samaritans. We can be nearly certain that in constructions such as that just mentioned, the infinitive was in use in their vernacular, whether Hebrew or Aramaic, just as the use of infinitive was widespread in languages other than those two.[179] Neither in Aramaic nor in other languages, though, is there a discrete form for this purpose, as there is in Biblical Hebrew. Apart from the phrases of which examples were given above, forms such as שָׁמוֹר (Dt 5:12, 16:1) and הָלוֹךְ וָשׁוֹב (Gn 8:3) can sometimes be understood in other ways, such as an imperative, or may be subject to adaptation to later norms, as we find in SP Gn 8:3: הלכו ושבו.[180] In addition, due to the phonological rules of SH and its morphological system, the infinitive became very similar to the 3rd masc. sing. perfect, and the distinction between infinitive absolute and infinitive construct has been completely blurred. Indeed, where TH displays contrasting forms such as: שׁוּב : שׁוֹב, or הִפְעִיל : הַפְעֵל or פָּעַל : פֵּעֵל, פָּעֹל : פָּעַל — contrasts which sustain the uniqueness of the infinitive and the distinction between infinitive absolute and infinitive construct — SH displays a single form: fâqåd (with lifqåd), faqqəd, afqəd for perfect and infinitive, šob for both infinitives. This is no doubt the factor that led to the blurring of the distinctiveness of the SH infinitive. Neverless, ST and SAV attest to an awareness of the existence of the infinitive, although it cannot be said that wherever TH has an infinitive, SH does as well, nor even that wherever SAV has an infinitive, ST does too.[181]

2.14.5 Furthermore, even where SH has two different forms of the infinitive, the distinctions drawn in TH between infinitive absolute and infinitive construct cannot be imposed on SH. For example, two infinitive forms are found for the verb בא: bā and bū(bâ). The former is found in the phrase בא יבא (bā yå'bū), i.e., where the infinitive absolute appears in TH; the second occurs

---

[179] See the many examples cited by G. Goldenberg, "Tautological Infinitive," *IOS* I (1973), 36-85.

[180] Another example: in place of שטוח להם וישטחו (Nu 11:32), SP reads שחוטה להם וישחטו; other substitutions are noted in Waltke, *Prolegomena*, 289-291. It may be that one of the most blatant adjustments to contemporary norms is to be found in SP Dt 28:56, הציגה *aṣṣīga* where the Jewish version reads הצג, as against the rendering in MS Barberini of SAV بوقوفها قدمها تفتح الم which indicates that the ה at the end of the word was understood as a 3rd fem. sing. pronominal suffix, nor is such an understanding reflected in ST's rendering הקעמה (but there is a variant reading מקמתה). Thus, we find that we have before us an infinitive following a הפעילה pattern, as we find here and there in manuscripts of rabbinic literature and in Ben Sira 14:13 יד השיגת (cf. N. Berggrün, *Studies in the Hebrew Language* [Jerusalem, 1995], 96 [Hebrew]). So in place of the Biblical Hebrew infinitive absolute, there is a MH (nominal) infinitive! The replacement of an infinitive construct by another form is quite common in 1QIsaª; see Kutscher, *Isaiah Scroll*, 361.

[181] E.g., עבור in Nu 22:26, pronounced as *'ābor*, ST (MS Barberini) renders as עבר, i.e., a participle (not למעבר!), while SAV uses the infinitive form عبورا.

with the prepositions ב, כ, and ל: *bā'bū*, etc. — that is, where the infinitive construct appears in TH. The infinitive form to which one affixes personal pronouns in SH, however, is the form whose use corresponds in TH with the infinitive absolute, *bā*: *bā*ʿ*bāk*, *bābā'imma*.[182]

In the light of this, it seems advisable to do away with any division of the infinitive into two kinds (a distinction based on TH), thus, avoiding the imposition of a foreign schema on SH rather than maintaining a distinction that would be both arbitrary and false. It is impossible to find support for this stance in ST or SAV, just as they may indeed be called on — exercising careful judgment[183] — for assistance in determining how the form was understood in a given passage, i.e., whether it was taken to be as an infinitive. The following sections survey the forms of the infinitive by verb class and stem, with special attention to irregular forms.

2.14.6 The usual infinitive form in *Qal* is *fåqåd*, and in verbs III-guttural there may be an *a (å)* vowel, e.g., *šåmår*, which is the pronunciation of both TH שָׁמוֹר (Dt 6:17) and שָׁמֹר (Dt 8:11); *dåråš* דרש; *åråg* הרג; *fårå* פרח; *šåka* שכח; and *šåma* שמע, which is the pronunciation of both שָׁמֹעַ (Ex 15:26) and שָׁמֹעַ (Dt 17:12). This form may be retained even with the addition of personal pronoun suffixes: *kåqåråbkimma* בקרבכם, *abråddåfimma* ברדפם, *afšåmā'u* בשמעו, *kåšåmåkkimma* כשמעכם, *qårånnu* קראנו, *båkålimma* באכלם. It may also be retained with the addition of a prepositional ב or כ: *kåšåma* כשמע, *kåbåla* כבלע (Nu 4:20), *afgåba* בגוע. With the addition of a prepositional ל, though, the vowel of

---

[182] The form *båbå'u* בבאו gives no evidence that it contains the infinitive *bā*, since an original u/o vowel preceding the personal pronoun suffix had to change; see 2.6.15 and 2.11.10.

[183] A systematic examination of how TH infinitive forms are expressed in ST and SAV to Genesis, undertaken by my former student Penina (Shatil) Hanani, supports the assumption we have made here in regard to the phrases combining the infinitive absolute and a finite verb form. ST regularly expresses the infinitive by use of an infinitive, and sometimes by means of a form usually used for substantives, e.g., Gn 26:28 חזון חזו, or Gn 43:3 אסיר סהדו. When the infinitive appears alone in TH, different approaches are taken, some of which are necessitated by SP ad loc. In SAV, though, TH phrases combining the infinitive absolute and a finite verb are sometimes rendered with an infinitive, as in ST, and sometimes without repetition of the root. For example, SAV to Gn 3:16 renders ארבה הרבה as كرو اكثر while MS Or 7562 ad loc. renders that phrase as اني لكثر. Similarly, Gn 22:17, where ST renders אברכך ברוך, SAV offers برکه اباركك while MS Or 7562 employs لاباركن نيك. Another of my students, Dr. Haseeb Shehadeh, investigating the versions of SAV, has pointed out this phenomenon and noted the similarity between certain versions of SAV, especially MS Or 7562 and Sa'adia Ga'on's Arabic version in the practice of eliminating the pleonasm of phrases combining the infinitive and a finite verb of the same root. Sa'adia's approach is based on an underlying linguistic conception, while the elimination of the phenomenon in SAV strays from the original Samaritan trend toward literalism in translation. It is, therefore, unwise to adduce the SAV mechanically in establishing the identity of a form in a given verse in SP. The question of the rendition of the infinitive in Samaritan translations has, nonetheless, given us an additional criterion for checking the adherence of a given version among the versions of SAV to the Samaritan linguistic and exegetical tradition.

the first radical disappears, and the form is equivalent (other than the vowel of the second radical) to the TH form: *lišmår* לשמר, *lišṭån* לשטן (Nu 22:22 לִשְׁטָן!), *lirgål* לרגל (Nu 21:32 לְרַגֵּל!), *lisfår* לספר, *lingåf* לנגף, *liktåb* לכתב, *liqṣår* לקצר, *lišma* לשמע, *ligba* לגוע, *lizba* לזבח, *låṭṭåb* (< **laḥṭåb*) לחטב, *lånnåṭ* (< **laḥnaṭ*) לחנט, *lå:båṛ* (< **la'abar* < **la'ᵃbar* < **la'bar*) לעבר, *lå:bådu* לעבדו, *lēmsål* להמשל (SP Gn 1:18). This pattern can be found when personal pronoun suffixes are added along with a preposition, which may be other than ל as well: *liškåni* לשכני, *lišṭånåk* לשטנך (SP Nu 22:32), *lētfåša* להתפשה (SP Dt 20:19; see 2.14.12), *lišmårå* לשמרה, *bingåfu* בנגפו, *baškåbåk* בשכבך. However, in verbs II-guttural the preposition ל is pronounced with a preceding vowel, as is the preposition ב: *al'mål* למעל, *al'bår* לבער, *al'kån* לכהן. (On the assignment of such forms to *Qal*, see 2.2.2.1.1.) On occasion, an infinitive with a personal pronominal suffix may take a form without a vowel following the second radical, such as *miššamru* משמרו (Dt 7:8) (in contrast with *lišmårå* לשמרה and *lišmåråk* לשמר), *båsfåk* באספך, *afšabri* בשברי (Lv 26:26).

2.14.7 The infinitive form under discussion is derived from פְּעָל (פָּעַל) in TH, except that in SH, the *šəwa* developed regularly into a full vowel, and, thus, this form came to be identical to the 3rd masc. sing. perfect. Unlike the participle (see 2.12.5), the infinitive is not linked necessarily to the perfect. The best evidence for this is provided by the phrases *šå'ål šå'əl* שָׁאֹל שָׁאַל, *åṣəm åṣåm* אָשֹׁם אָשַׁם (Lv 5:19), and *'åṣår åṣår* עָצֹר עָצַר, in which the infinitive and the perfect have different forms. The origin of *šəwa* as the vowel of the first radical can be discerned from the infinitive form with preposition ל, such as *lišmår*. One might say, at first glance, that this is an independent form derived by analogy to imperfect *yišmår*, just as we find in MH ליתן, לילך, etc., and in the vocalization of the Bible, *dageš* in בגדכפת when one of them is the second radical, such as לִזְבֹּחַ (unlike בְּזְבֹחַ) on the model of יִזְבַּח or לִשְׁכַּב (unlike כִּשְׁכַּב). However, forms such as *al'mål* למעל (Nu 5:6 — and not **le'mål*), where the imperfect is *tē'mål* תמעל, indicate that the original vowel of the prepositional ל is *šəwa*, similar to the vowel of prepositional ב and כ. The three bases of this infinitive — *fåqåd*, *fqåd* (with ל), and *faqd* (with pronominal suffixes) — correspond to the TH infinitive construct. As has been noted, this infinitive is also employed in situations where TH uses the infinitive absolute.

> Note: *årrås* הרס (Ex 23:24), even though it is equivalent in form to the *Pi'el* infinitive (see 2.14.11), seems to be *Qal*. Supporting this supposition is the form *tērråsimma* תהרסם.

2.14.8 Other than the *fåqåd* pattern and its variants, one finds the following patterns:

1. *fåqod* (*fåqod*), such as *'åbor* עבר (Nu 22:26), *gånob* גנוב (Gn 40:15), *'åbod*

2.14 Infinitive

עבד (Ex 14:12), *nåton* נתון (Dt 15:10 and elsewhere), *gådod* (Gn 49:19; ST בסור, which is a *Pa'el* infinitive). To this pattern may perhaps also be assigned the forms *wšåtu* ושתו (Ex 32:6) and, with the preposition ל, *låboṭ* לעבוט (Dt 24:10).

2. *fēqod*, such as *šēmor* שמור (Dt 5:12 and elsewhere), *zēkor* זכור (Dt 24:9 and elsewhere), *fēqūdi* פקדי (Ex 32:34). The form *līmor* לאמור (from *li'mor*) also seems to belong in this category.

3. *fūqåd*, such as *šūfåṭ* שופט (SP Gn 19:9), *åyūda* היודע (SP Gn 43:7), *åyūkål* היוכל (SP Nu 22:38), and *alnūga* לנגע (Gn 20:6).

4. *fåqəd*, such as *ṭårəf* טרף (Gn 37:33), *ålək* הלך (Nu 22:14), *lålək* להלך (Nu 22:13).

5. *fēqåd*, such as *miyyēlåk* מהלך (Nu 22:16), *ēråg* הרג (Nu 11:15), *afdēbåri* בדברי (Ex 19:9), *dēbåro* דברו (Gn 37:4)[184], *refa* רפא (Ex 21:19), *albēṭå* לבטא (Lv 5:4), *båbe'råk* בברחך (Gn 35:1) — and in particular verbs of the פ"נ class: *alnēdår* לנדר, *alnēdå* לנדח.

> Note: Feminine forms, such as משנאתו, ליראה, לטמאה (Dt 9:28), זקנתו (SP Gn 24:36), חרשת, יכלת, or forms with מ, such as למסע (Nu 10:2), מקבר (Gn 23:6) (which the Samaritans pronounce *måqbår*, i.e., something like מִקְבָּר), and others (for a detailed list, see Ibn Janāḥ, *Kitāb al-Luma'*, chap. 13) — these have not been included in the lists of infinitive forms.

2.14.9 The forms listed above may, for certain verbs and in certain contexts, be understood as something other than infinitives, primarily participle forms (as in TH, e.g., וילך...הלך in 1 Sa 17:41 or הלך...ובכה in Jer 41:6, ויצא in Jer 41:6). Since in other cases, however, an infinitive form must be posited, we have seen fit to include here the questionable instances as well. Thus, *'åbor* עבר (Nu 22:26) may be understood as a participle (thus ST MS Barberini: עבר, and not מעבר; as opposed to SAV عبورا), but *'åbod* עבד (Ex 14:12) may only be an infinitive (ST, SAV), and the same is certainly true of *låboṭ* לעבוט and *līmor* לאמור. The forms *šēmor* שמור and *zēkor* זכור cannot be classified as imperative forms, since *o* can only be derived from long *o/u* vowels, while in the infinitive, the vowel is originally short — the usual imperative form is *fēqåd*. These verbs have the regular imperative forms *zēkåru* זכרו (SP Dt 32:7) and *šēmåru* שמרו (SP Dt 27:1). The form *fēqūdi* פקדי is undoubtedly an infinitive. The form *šūfåṭ* may be understood as a participle, as perhaps it is by ST to Gn 19:9: דין (= MH דַּיָּן ?), just as the form *be'ūmər* באמר (Dt 4:10) can be understood without difficulty as a

---

[184] Since it was possible to read this as *dabbēru*, as in Ex 34:29 *afdabbēru*, we may conclude that the *Qal* form of דבר is preserved here, as it is in the noun *dēbīrūtək* (see 4.1.5.7), along with the forms דבר and דְּבוּר in TH. ST's rendition of this word as ממללה or מלולה and SAV's مخاطبته indicate that the word was taken to be an infinitive, even though it has the plural pronominal suffix, similar to the word בקומיהם (see below n. 192), but the reading דבריו may be a result of a scribal error under the influence of v. 8.

participle. In fact, ST has the form באמר alongside במימר. Even *yūkål* (Nu 22:38) can be interpreted as a participle; not so יוכל נבל (SP Nu 13:30), which, like *yūda* יודע, is of necessity an infinitive. (See n. 59.) The form *ålək* הלך (Nu 22:14) may be understood as a participle, and even *lålək* להלך (Nu 22:13) can be explained as a participle, but the Samaritan translations render them as infinitives: ST מיתה, SAV السير. Note also *baškən* בשכן (Gn 35:22), although it may be understood as a *Hif'il* form. The form *miyyēlåk* מהלך (Nu 22:16) should in principle be understood as a participle, just as *rēfa* רפא (Ex 21:19) is taken by ST to be a participle: ואסיה יאסי (in Leviticus there is another version, ואסו יאסי!); on the other hand, *albēṭå* לבטא (Lv 5:4) must be an infinitive. The same is true of *båšā'i* (SP Ex 36:8 בעשאי and בעשי; TH בְּעֲשִׂי), which is an infinitive form, according to the evidence in some manuscripts of ST.[185]

2.14.10 The data support this conclusion: in SH, the infinitive of *Qal* is *fåqåd* and its variants, which stem from a form like TH פְּעָל, and it alone of the two infinitives, construct and absolute, was in common use in SH in its last period as a living language. In SH too, though, other forms were preserved which cannot be read according to the common pattern of the infinitive. First of all, here and there remnants of the infinitive absolute form are preserved, and it can be discerned that while it was still in use, it influenced, with its original long *o* vowel, the infinitive construct in SH as in TH, creating such forms as *låboš* and *līmor*, which cannot be derived from the infinitive construct form alone. The form *fēqod* seems to have originally been a verb with a long *o* vowel, as mentioned, and since we have found it mostly in an imperative use, it may be that the imperative contributed to the *e* vowel of the first radical. The patterns *fēqād*, *fåqəd*, and *fūqād*, which serve to express the participle as well, are parallel to the segholate patterns in TH, and indeed in the understanding of these words in the Samaritan translations, one finds several paths taken: either a participle or a substantive, as above, 2.14.9, in the matter of עבר or היוכל in Nu 22:38: מכאל, יכל. Even though we find *lingåf* לנגף (see also 2.14.7), we see in פ"נ verbs a reluctance to maintain the נ instead of assimilating it to the second radical as in MH, e.g., לפל and לדר, and, therefore, the other forms were used: *alnēdår* נדר and *walnåfål* ולנפל (Nu 5:22) (translated in SAV as ولسقوط and in ST as ולמסאי),[186] and for this reason even finite forms of the verb have been

---

[185] The infinitive is reflected in the translations בעובדי and בעבאדי by their *matres lectionis*, while the reading בעבודי is a regular participle, and, thus, attests to a interpretation like that of TH. The quasi-plural ending of בעשאי (cf. 1.44.1 note) may be the source of the spelling of the aforementioned infinitive forms with *yod*; see also 2.14.15; 4.1.3.17, n. 19.

[186] The Samaritan tradition at Nu 5:22 does not employ a causative, but rather speaks of the thigh sagging and the belly being distended — in *Qal*. We have found in MH that even the *Pi'el* of נפל is used in the same way as the *Qal* to express the meaning in question in the expressions פת ניפולין, הפת ניפילת (*t. Ma'aser Sheni* 1:18), similar to the use of the verb in the phrase שבישלו ענבים.

employed: לנפל (Nu 14:3) is pronounced *alnibbål*, equivalent to לִנְפֹּל* in TH (i.e., "in order that we fall"). ST לנפל and SAV لسقط agree. The reading in ST, למפל, hints at a pronunciation different from that accepted today, i.e., an infinitive. The form *lēbbår* (Nu 24:13), with an *e* vowel, is a special case, to be compared with *lā:bår* (Dt 17:2). Its pronunciation would also seem to be an attempt to remain in keeping with the other reading, אעבר/*ēbbår*; see also 2.14.12 on *lēmšål*, etc.

2.14.11 The infinitive forms of the other stems generally behave as one would expect under the rules of SH. Examples are given below. Exceptions will be examined in 2.14.12. Note that in forms that follow the norm, the vowel of the second radical behaves like the vowel of the imperfect.

Hif'il: *afqəd*. In an open syllable and in verbs II-guttural, *ī* replaces *ə*, e.g., *askən* הסכן, *lāqrəb* להקריב, *låšməd* להשמיד, *'ānnəq* העניק, *â:rəm* החרם, *ašmīdimma* השמידם, *båfrīdu* בהפרידו, *lā'šīt* להשחית, *lā'kīsu* להכעיסו, *åšīrinnu* השאירנו (Dt 2:34!). [The form *lībīšåni* להבאישני (Gn 34:30), with *i* after *l*, follows the pattern of the ע"ו class; see 2.2.2.2.3].

Pi'el: *faqqəd*. There is also *faqqā/ad*, which is the general rule in verbs III-guttural, such as *dabbər* דבר, *makkər* מכר, *albarrək* לברך, *lillamməd* ללמד, *albåkkår* לבכר, *'åbbår* עבר, *'aššår* עשר, *bayyår* באר (SP DT 1:5 reads ביר and ביאר as well), *šalla* שלח, *låṭṭå* לחטא (Lv 14:49), *alqaddēšē'u* לקדשהו, *afdabberkimma* בדברכם, *båbbårkimma* בעברכם, *afšal'lāk* בשלחך, and *aftåmmåkkima* בטמאכם.

Pi'el B ("with simple second radical"): *kåbəd* כבד, *alkåfər* לכפר, *almåla* למלא, *kēlā'ək* כלאך, *båsefkimma* באספכם (Lv 23:39), *kåbēdåk* כבדך, *alṭā'ēru* לטהרו — but *sefər* (Ex 9:16), whose spelling ספיר already provides testimony as to the form.

Nif'al: *iffåqəd* or *iffåqåd*, such as *lēllā'əm* להלחם, *wlēddåbēqa* ולהדבקה (SP Dt 11:22, 30:20), *iš'šåt* השחת (Dt 31:29), *iššāba* השבע (Ex 13:19; in TH הִשָּׁבֵעַ!); there are some with geminated second radical: *iššåmmåd* השמד, *lēmmållåṭ* להמלט.

Hitpa'el: forms such as *lētållåm* להתעלם, *itgallā'u* התגלוחו, and "with simple second radical," perhaps *bētåsēfu* בהתאספו (but note carefully 2.2.1.5.3). It seems that *wlētfā'ērət* ולהתפארת (SP Ex 28:2), with a feminine suffix, similar to *Nif'al* להדבקה, belongs here.

2.14.12 Aside from the forms listed in the previous section, there are occasional uses of other forms with the function of the infinitive, and they have parallels in TH and MH:

1. In the phrase הסתר אסתיר (Dt 31:18), pronounced *istār astər*, the first word is no doubt a *Hif'il* infinitive, even though the vowel of the first radical is *i* (as in forms such as הרגיע Jer 50:34). Similarly we find הפצר (1 Sa 15:23) and הזכרכם (Ezek 21:29) with *pataḥ* as the vowel of the second radical. Perhaps we may similarly understand *lēmšål* (Gn 1:18) and *lētfåša* (Dt 20:19), spelled in SP

with ה: להמשל, להתפשה (but see also 2.14.18).

2. The Samaritan readings of *akbəs* הכבס (Lv 13:55) and *akbēsu* הַכַּבְּסוּ (SP Lv 13:56) reflect *Hif'il* infinitives, which may take pronominal suffixes in the same way that the MH infinitives do. (See above 2.14.3.)

3. The form הציגה (SP Dt 28:56) may be an infinitive found in MH. See above n. 180.

4. The forms *wbiššol* ובשול (SP Ex 12:9, TH בשל), *bittor* בתור (SP Gn 15:10, TH בשל), *birrok* ברוך (Nu 23:11 and elsewhere, TH ברך) are *Pi'el* infinitives in MH, and there is no morphological connection between them and the biblical infinitive of the type רפוא. This infinitive was adopted also by SA and CPA.[187]

5. The form *alqâdēšē'u* לקדשהו (SP Dt 5:12) would at first seem to be an infinitive of *Pi'el* "with simple second radical." Since, however, in all other forms, the verb appears as *Pi'el* with a geminated second radical, we should explain it here as a substantive. This is the view of Abū Isḥāq (*LOT* I, 21; see also *LOT* III/1, 103). Note, nevertheless, the variation in readings in ST: לקדשה (equivalent to Hebrew לקדשו "due to its sanctity") and לקדושה (infinitive form of the verb).

6. The forms *aššāba* (Nu 30:3) as against TH הִשָּׁבַע and *ammâši* המשיח (Lv 6:13), where TH reads הַמָּשַׁח, are not easily interpreted as infinitives; for the regular infinitive of נשבע in SH, see 2.14.11. By morphological criteria, the form *aššāba* could easily be a *Qal* participle, in which case SH may have an active participle alongside the passive participle represented by the noun שבועה. Note that these are rendered as perfect verbs in the ancient Samaritan translations (ST אשתבע, SAV اقسم). It is possible that the form in question is a perfect verb in an Aramaic pattern, i.e., with the ת of אתפעל assimilated.[188] SA does have some verbs in the *'Itpa'el* stem in which the vowel of the stem formative is *a* instead of *i*, such as *atfək* אתפך (= אתהפך) and *yatri* יתריח (= יתרעי). (See *LOT* III/2, 170, l. 79 and 321, l. 40.) It seems most likely, however, that the pronunciation in question reflects a *Qal* participle, and the syntax is entirely consistent with this. The form *ammâši* is more difficult. Morphologically, it appears to be a passive participle of *Qal* without irregularity, but the syntax of ביום המשח אתו hardly supports this understanding of the word. ST's rendering דאמשח יתה is open to two interpretations: "that anointed him" or "that he was annointed" (see 3.3.1.3). SAV's مسحه reads it as an infinitive. The form *mâši* may also be understood as an infinitive on the pattern of קציר (see 2.14.1), but in Lv 7:36

---

[187] See Ben-Ḥayyim, *Tradition*, 112. Now I find that M. Neumark, in his *Lexikalische Untersuchungen zur Sprache der jerusalemischen Pentateuch-Targume* (Berlin, 1905), 28, has already sensed that this pattern exists in Aramaic under the influence of Hebrew.

[188] If the Aramaic form is indeed reflected in the verb השבע as well as in the aforementioned המשח and in היסדה (2.14.14d), then SH offers additional support for the development in Hebrew of a *Hippa'el* stem, as suggested by D. Yellin in *Devir* I (1923), 22ff. [Hebrew], although it has to be derived from *Hitpa'el*. (See also n. 125 above.)

there is a regular infinitive from this verb, *māšā'u* משחו. Reading *ammāši* as an Aramaic verb may solve the difficulty, even though that word ends with *i*, not *a*; we find something similar with the verb רגז, as noted in 2.2.3.4.2b. Nonetheless, it seems to us more reasonable to define the form as a passive participle of *Qal*, and to interpret the verse as "on the day when they are anointed." On this use of את, cf. 3.3.1.3.

2.14.13 With regard to the other verb classes, only the unusual forms not included in the preceding description will be mentioned:

1. **Verbs I-guttural:** the usual form conforms with the *fāqåd* pattern, e.g., *āmår* אמר and *åbåd* אבד. The verb אסף is regularly conjugated in *Pi'el B*, including the infinitive (see 12.14.11) but the form *båsfåk* באספך (Ex 23:16) is an exception that must be understood as a remnant of the *Qal* stem in an earlier stage of SH, unlike the participle *å:səf* האסף (Nu 19:10), which may be classified as a *Pi'el B* form. The length of the *å* in *båsfåk* is due to paradigmatic analogy. For TH להוסיף (Lv 19:25), SP reads להסיף or להאסיף, and their equivalents in the Samaritan translations[189] indicate that this form is derived from אסף. Its pronunciation as *līsaf* is not in keeping with a פ"י verb in *Hif'il*, whose imperfect forms include, e.g., *tūsīfon* תוסיפון, but is instead entirely appropriate for an ע"י infinitive (see 2.14.15[2]). The mixing of אסף and יסף in SH as in TH, was mentioned above (2.4.11), but here we see the mixing of אסף and סוף, which is also known in TH: e.g., Jer 8:13 or Zeph 1:2. In the same way, we have *līdəf* and *bīdəf*, written in SP להדיך (Dt 6:19) and בהדיך (Dt 9:4), i.e., the verb is derived from the root דוך.[190]

2. **Verbs II-guttural:** The form *šā'ål* שאל (see 2.14.7), a *Qal* infinitive, is unusual in that it retains two syllables instead of one (*šål*), as we find in *tåb* תעב (Dt 7:26), following the rule explained in 1.4.6.1. The form *bayyår* באר (Dt 1:5) is intended as a *Pi'el* infinitive, as is indicated by ST מביארה. We have no other forms of this verb which might show us how it was transformed into an ע"י verb, as we have for SA ישול (< שאול), derived from שאל. In any case, this is a very interesting parallel to what occurred in MH with the verb שאר > שיר.

Note: For other forms of the infinitive of the verb אמר, see 2.14.9.

2.14.14

1. The unique feature of פ"י verbs and some פ"נ verbs is the *Qal* infinitive with the deletion of the first radical, alongside the usual form in the *fāqåd* pattern, which generally functions in TH in the role of infinitive absolute.

---

[189] ST למכנשה (variant: לכנוש); SAV ليضاعف does not translate it as does Sa'adia Ga'on with the verb زاد, which is the verb commonly used for expressing addition.

[190] Note that the tenth century grammarian Menaḥem ben Saruq derives להדך from the root דך (*Maḥberet,**130).

Some examples: *rēdət* רדת, *šēbət* שבת, *alrēšət* לרשת, *lallēkət* ללכת, *tat* תת, *al'qēt* לקחת. With the addition of pronoun suffixes, the vowel of the first radical is normally *i*: *šibtåk* שבתך, *alrišta* לרשתה, *liktåk* לכתך, *afgeštimma* בגשתם (on *i* in an stressed syllable, see 1.5.1.1), *altitti* תתי and *tatti*, but before the 3rd masc. sing. suffix, we find as the vowel of the first radical *a/å*: *šabtu* שבתו, *tattu* תתו, *gaštu* גשתו. The forms *rēdēta* רדתה (Dt 20:20) and *abrēdētu* ברדתו (Ex 34:29) are derived from something like **ridta*, initially by adding a semi-vowel after the *d* (see 1.5.3.1). The same is true of *ablēdēta* בלדתה (Gn 35:16 and elsewhere). In the III-guttural class the vowel is long: *al'qēt* לקחת, *alqēttu* לקחתו; *al'dāt* לדעת, *dāttu* דעתו, *šāt* שאת, *šāttu* שאתו. The forms *ṣiyyåt* צאת and *ṣiyyåtåk* צאתך appear to be derived from a base of *ṣåʾā* or *ṣåʾa*, as we find in מֶרְדָה (Gn 46:3; SP מרדת!), תִּנָה (Ps 8:2), or קְחַת (in construct state; 2 Kgs 12:9).[191] Similarly, we should interpret *afgiššåt* בגשת (Nu 8:19) and *miggiššåt* מגשת (Ex 34:30) as derived from a base with suffix *at* (not *t*), as we find with the forms דעה, לדה, and רדה in TH, with the difference that the ת is maintained in SH, and there is gemination (of ש) to compensate for the original short vowel.

2. In *Hifʿil*, SH, like TH, has two patterns: original פ״י verbs such as *lūraš* להוריש and *lūši* להושיע, and original פ״י verbs such as *līṭəb* להיטיב (SP Dt 28:67) and *bīṭību* בהיטיבו (SP Ex 30:7). The forms *būṣåʾu* בהוצאו (SP Dt 29:24) and *būṣåʾi* בהוצאי (SP Lv 23:43 and elsewhere) are puzzling because of the *å* vowel where the other forms have *ī*, such as *lūṣi* להוציא, *būṣiyyåk* בהוציאך, *lūṣiyyimma* להוציאם, *kåʾūṣyyimma* כהוציאם. Perhaps the noun *mūṣa* מוצא exerted some influence on the verb form. Note, too, however, the *å* in *īṭåb* היטב (Gn 32:13) and *istår* הסתר (Dt 31:18) (see 2.14.12).

3. In place of the TH *Nifʿal* form (Ex 9:18), SP reads *ayyåssåda* היסדה. On the basis of ST דאתיסדת (variant: אתרשת) and SAV اــــــــل, we would identify this as a perfect form, and the forms השבע and המשח were translated similarly; see 2.14.12[6]). If, indeed, these are *Nifʿal* perfect forms, see n. 188. It seems reasonable, though, to assume from the pronunciation that the form in question was intended to be a noun (and infinitive) originally of the פֻּעַל pattern. See also *LOT* III/2, 209, l. 6. The subject requires further inquiry. (Cf. also ברעה, 2.14.15.1c.) On the other hand, it is certain that *bēwwåʾēdåtimma* בהודעתם (SP Nu 26:9) is an infinitive parallel in structure to TH and similar to the standard pattern of infinitive in Biblical Aramaic.

> Note: On פ״נ verbs, see also 2.14.10. On the particularities of the verb נטה, see 2.5.13. The form *ūlēdət* הולדת is categorized easily in SP as a *Hifʿil* infinitive.

---

[191] It is surprising that the medieval grammarians encountered difficulty interpreting this form (see also Orlinsky "Qal Infinitive Construct," 120, n. 162), since קַחַת (absolute state *קחה) is related to תִּנָה as קַחַת is to תֵּת (תנת)!

2.14 Infinitive   215

2.14.15 The interaction between the ע"ו and ע"י classes are reflected in the forms of the infinitive as well.

1. In the ע"י class, there are three types of *Qal* infinitives:

a. Forms with *ū/o*, such as *šob* שוב, *alqom* לקום, *sob* סב (SP Dt 2:3), *algoz* לגוז (SP Gn 31:19), *alboz* לבז (SP Dt 1:39), *afqūmåk* בקומך, *afqūmīyyimma* בקומיהם (SP Ex 32:25; with plural suffix!),[192] and *båmūtimma* במותם. The form *åmol* המול (Gn 17:10,13), too, is a *Qal* infinitive, as indicated by ST המגזר and SAV ختنُ (variant: ختانه); the ה being interpreted as an exclamatory particle.[193]

b. Forms with *ī/ə* : *alšəm* לשים (so SH consistently), *afdīšu* בדישו.

c. Forms with *a/å*, such as *sar* סר (SP Dt 17:20), *råm* רם (SP Dt 17:20), *alšåš* לשש (SP Dt 30:9), *lå:mimma* להמם (Dt 2:15). It may be that with the verbs סר and רם, we could as easily assume that we have perfect forms, as we have in the case of *wšåb* ושב (Gn 8:7; the infinitive is *šob*), but with לשש and להמם, at least, we are obligated to interpret these as infinitives, and so it is with SAV for סר, רם and *zåb* (SP Lv 15:3). It appears certain, then, that these infinitive forms follow the ע"ע pattern, in which a short *u* vowel (> *a, å*) is original, and indeed we find *alqåb* לקב. The ע"י and ע"ע classes influence each other to such an extent that we find hybrids such as *tåmimma* תמם (Dt 31:24), in which the verb behaves as though derived from תום (absence of gemination in the מ), but the vowel of the infinitive is drawn from the ע"ע class. On the other hand, *bar'rā* ברעה (Ex 32:17) is not an infinitive in the Samaritan tradition, but the substantive ברעה.

2. In *Hif'il*, if the first radical is not geminated, the vowel of the morpheme is *ī*: *ībi* הביא, *līqəm* להקים, *līšåb* להשיב, *līmītimma* להמיתם, *lībiyyåk* להביאך. If the first radical is geminated, the vowel is *a*: *ban'nī* בהניח, *anni* (*yanni*) הניא (יניא) (SP Nu 30:6). But this sometimes occurs even without the gemination: *åmītu* המיתו (Ex 4:24),[194] and in verbs I-guttural such as *å'ād å'əd* העד העיד (Gn 43:3) and per-

---

[192] At first glance, one might classify the form as a participle because of the plural pronominal suffix (see 2.12.14 note), but as we see from ST אתריון and SAV نصايهم (both in MS Barberini), the Samaritans do not construe this form as a finite verb. (This is so unless we assume a reading نُصَّابهم, the plural of ناصب. This issue requires further investigation.)

[193] The form *mol* represents both the infinitive and the passive participle; see *LOT* I, אכff. and n. 13: the interpretation of ימול והמול to mean "one who is circumcised may be circumcised." Note also the liturgical poem of Ephraim b. Jacob of Bonn published in A. M. Haberman, "Liturgical Poems of Ephraim b. Jacob of Bonn," *Studies of the Research Institute for Hebrew Poetry* 7 (Jerusalem and Tel Aviv, 1958), 240: ימול המול גוי מלהולא לא אשה. The source we cited there as a Samaritan Pentateuchal commentary does not reflect Samaritan tradition, since it has been shown conclusively that it is a Karaite document; see A. Loewenstamm, "A Karaite Commentary on Genesis in a Samaritan Pseudomorphosis," *Sefunot* 8 [Itzhak Ben-Zvi Memorial Volume] (1964), סקff. [Hebrew].

[194] While it is true that the Samaritan exegesis known to us entirely rejects the derivation of this word from the root מות, deriving it instead from the root המם/הום or even from המי (so Munajja in his سائل الخلاف) and this is reflected in the translation in *Hammeliṣ* as well: למעצמתה (*LOT* II, 453, l.125); nonetheless, the pronunciation assigns the word to the root מות, as does ST: למקטלה. Cf.

haps *lā:mimma* להמם in Dt 2:15 (see above 1c), if it is understood as *Hifʿil* from the root הום. The form *līnēttimma* להנחתם (SP Ex 13:21) is derived from the root נו״ח, parallel root to נח״י, and it is a feminine infinitive form, akin to הנחה. This root alternation occurs in the Tiberian tradition as well, e.g., תניחנו instead of תנחנו (Isa 63:14). On the feminine infinitive form, we should recall בהודעתם (see 2.14.14) and הציגה (see n. 180). Its *ē* vowel hints at an original form TH *הניחה, and with pronominal suffix *hanihtimma*.

3. The form הטח (Lv 14:43,48), which is a *Nifʿal* infinitive in TH, either from the root טוח or from the root טחח (Isa 44:18), is pronounced *ʿatta* in SH, and is derived from טחח, but it is impossible to determine whether it is an infinitive in *Nifʿal* (despite the *ā* vowel in the *Nifʿal* formative [see 2.14.12]) or in *Hifʿil*.[195] In ST, both possibilities are embraced: דשטף, אשתתף. The *ayin* in the pronunciation of the beginning of the word, however, and the variant readings חטה and חטא, which provide support for that pronunciation, indicate that at a later period the word was taken to be derived from the root חטא. On the other hand, *lāʾlū* להחלו (Lv 21:4) is a *Nifʿal* infinitive of the ע״י class, *lahiḥḥālu*, with gemination only of the first radical. (Cf. 2.7.6a.)

4. The form *uwwâqåm* הוקם (SP Nu 9:15; TH הֻקַם) is understood by ST and SAV as the perfect, but it may also be regarded as the infinitive of the passive, i.e., inflected in *Hitpaʿel*. See also 2.10.4.

5. The infinitives of *Piʿel* quadriradicals (*Polel* verbs) and *Hitpaʿel* quadriradicals *(Hitpolel)* are as might be expected: *alsūbåb* לסובב (SP Nu 21:4), *ištūrår* השתרר (Nu 16:13). A single instance of an ע״י verb inflected on the pattern of the strong verb, like TH קִיֵּם, is *bayyår* (see 2.14.13[2]).

2.14.16 In the ל״ה class, the regular infinitive of all stems bears an *-ot* ending. In verbs I-guttural it is difficult to determine by morphology alone whether a given form is *Qal* or *Hifʿil*, *Hifʿil* or *Piʿel*. (See 2.2.1.2.2.) This is true of forms with prefixed ל or ב as well. To offer some examples:

Qal: *lištot* לשתות, *liznot* לזנות, *lā:lot* לעלות, *bāllūti* בעלותי, *lā:not* לענות, *alrāʾot* לראות, *alrāʾūta* לראותה.

Hifʿil: *arbot* הרבות, *lårbot* להרבות, *aqṣot* הקצות (Lv 14:43), *akkot* הכות, *lā:lot* להעלות, *bāllot* בהעלות, *akkūtu* הכותו, *lā:notkimma* לחנותכם (SP Dt 1:33; also להנחותכם), *bāllūtåk* בהעלותך.

Piʿel: *sabbot* ספות (Dt 29:18), *alnåṭṭot* לנטות (Nu 22:26), *alkassot* לכסות, *kåkallot* ככלות, *kallūtimma* כלותם (Dt 7:22), *walkallūttimma* ולכלותם (Ex 32:12).[196]

והמתי (Ex 23:27), pronounced, *wåmitti*, i.e., derived from מו״ת, a derivation supported by ST ואקטל, but not by SAV.

[195] It is also possible to understand this form as perfect *Hifʿil*, akin perhaps to *âʾūri rāʾīti* אחרי ראיתי (Gn 46:30), and certainly *akkīti* הכיתי (SP Nu 3:13). On ראיתי see 2.14.17.

[196] On gemination, see 1.5.3.3d and 3.2.3.4, n. 11.

Nifʿal: lērrâʾot להראות, apparently *arrâʾot* הראות (see 2.14.18), *lērrâʾotkimma* להראותכם (ibid.).

With the form *râʾu* ראו (Gn 26:28: ראו), it cannot be determined whether it represents TH רָאָה or רָאֹה, but the form *ayyu* היו (Gn 18:18) hints at a base of **aḥyu* הָיוּ > *ayyu*. In any event, this is how we understand the gemination in *lâyyot* להיות, *lâyyūtåk* להיותך, *miʾayyot* מהיות, *lâššot* לעשות, *lâššūtimma* לעשותם, which came to be similar to *Piʿel* or *Hifʿil*.

2.14.17 In addition to the regular infinitive, the infinitive form identical to the perfect — on the pattern of *fåqåd* — functions especially in *Qal*, of course, but not only there. It normally appears where TH has an infinitive absolute, such as *fåša* פשה (Lv 13:7), *må:* מחה (Ex 17:14), *râ:* ראה (Gn 48:11), *arbå* הרבה (Dt 3:5), *akkå* הכה (Dt 13:16), and *wåfådå* והפדה (Lv 19:20), which seems to be a *Hifʿil* infinitive in SH, with the vowel of the first consonant a reflex of *šǝwa*.

The *å/ā* vowel is found in the following forms as well: *alṣâbåt* לצבת (Nu 5:22), which is *Qal* according to Samaritan tradition; *dåbåtå* דותה (Lv 12:2); *abnētåtti* בנטתי (Ex 7:5);[197] *alṣâbåt* לצות (Gn 49:33); *ṣâbåtu* צותו (Lv 7:38), which is *Piʿel* "with simple second radical"; *abråttu* ברעתו (Gn 36:24); and *arråttu* הראתו (Lv 13:7), which appears to be *Hifʿil*. Underlying these forms may be a feminine infinitive pattern originally ending in *-āyā* (TH יָה־), which became *āʾā*. That is, a form such as *ṣâbâtu* is derived from **ṣâbâʾâtu < *ṣâbâyâtu*, and indeed this entire series of developments is outside the Samaritan tradition: צַוָּה, צַוָּאָה, צַוִּיָה. In SP Gn 46:30, where we find אחרי ראיתי, with the pronunciation *râʾīti*, the Samaritan translations treat this as an infinitive or a substantive: בתר חזותי, SAV بعد نظري, although in ST we also find the perfect form חזית (and דחזית). Note that in Eccl 5:10, the *kǝtiv* matches the Samaritan infinitive form. In addition, SP reads אחר בליתי in Gn 18:12, pronounced *bâlīti*; while the Samaritan translations understand it as an infinitive (ST בתר בליותי, SAV بعد بلاتي), there are versions with the perfect: ST בליתי, SAV ان بليت (like Saʿadia Gaʾon's translation!).

We occasionally find in SH a form parallel to the TH infinitive with *ṣere*, such as *arbi* הרבה (in that verse, Gn 16:10, TH הַרְבָּה) and *nakki* נכה (Nu 22:6; see Ibn ʿEzra ad. loc.)

2.14.18 There may be several compound forms, i.e., forms that combine elements of two stems. (See 2.8.5.) The form *lēznūta* להזנותה (Lv 19:29) is of this sort; *Hifʿil* would require an *a* vowel after the ל, *Qal* would require *i*, *Nifʿal* would require the gemination of ז. Note that ST and SAV do not employ causative verbs, but rather למזדנאה and עָנוֹ respectively. In the infinitive *arrâʾot* הראות

---

[197] On the infinitive form, cf. 2.14.8[5].

(Lv 13:14), we expect to find an *i* vowel in the *Nifʿal* formative (but see 2.14.6[6]; 2.14.14[3]). On the other hand, the form *lērrâʾotkima* להראותכם (Dt 1:33), while its meaning is appropriate to *Hifʿil*, and it is understood as such by the Samaritan translations, nonetheless, appears morphologically to be *Nifʿal*. To avoid anthropomorphism, the Samaritans sometimes opt for a passive form where an active form is usually used.[198] Note that in the infinitive of the root חי״י in *Hifʿil*, there is an *i* vowel: *liyyot* לחיות, *liyyūtīnu* ל(ה)חיותנו,[199] while in the *Qal* of the verb היה we find an *a* vowel. The opposite would be expected, and it may be that as the verbs היה and חיה merged due to the loss of the guttural phonemes in pronunciation, the infinitive forms exchanged places.

2.15 Mixture of Classes and Alternation of Stems

2.15.0 When the historical grammar of Biblical Hebrew according to the accepted vocalization treats the development of the conjugation of verbs with weak roots, it is sometimes unable to explain the development on the basis of phonetic processes that act on the strong verb or on some other field of Biblical Hebrew. It has recourse instead to the argument that a certain conjugation or a certain category in the conjugation of a given class is influenced by another of the defective verb classes. This is the path taken in explaining the *Hofʿal* of ע״ו verbs such as הוקם, יוקם as influenced by the פ״י class; the *Hifʿil* of ל״א, such as המצאתי, as influenced by the ל״ה class; and *Hifʿil* and *Nifʿal* of the ע״י class such as הקימותי and נסוגותי (with an auxiliary vowel before the afformative) as influenced by the ע״ע class; and there are many other examples. Such explanations are also common in the historical grammar of Aramaic, and against the background of the close similarity of word formation in Hebrew and Aramaic, some have labelled certain patterns in Hebrew "the Aramaic way." (See 2.7.2d.)

2.15.1 Beyond this interplay between verb classes, which led to the establishment of fixed rules of verb conjugation in the weak verbs, we find in Hebrew many forms in each class which do not conform to the rules that came to be established and which, upon analysis, display different roots from the other

---

[198] This phenomenon is known from the Jewish tradition as well, and this is the source of the TH reading מִדַּבֵּר in Nu 7:89. (Here the Samaritans actually read *amdabbər* — the active form מְדַבֵּר). Similarly in MH, the use of *Nifʿal* נדבר in place of דבר, as in *Mekhilta de R. Yišmaʿel*, section בא (ed. Horowitz-Rabin, 1): מפני מה לא נדבר עמו מפני כבודו של משה. Similarly *t. Berakhot* 1:14. We find the same phenomenon in a Samaritan liturgical poem, with the word אמלל (equivalent to אתמלל); see *LOT* III/2, 225, l. 19. See also n. 154.

[199] On the form of the pronominal suffix, which is that used with plural nouns, see 3.2.4.

2.15 Mixture of Classes and Alternation of Stems

forms of "the same verb." We shall briefly survey some well-known examples. The list below is representative:

a. פ"נ and פ"י: יצב/נצב, יקש/נקש
b. פ"נ and ע"ו: סוך/נסך, פוץ/נפץ, שוא/נשא
c. פ"נ and ע"ע נבל (mixed)/ע"ע בלל/נזל/נזל, and in MH נמס/מסס
d. פ"נ and ל"ה בלה/נבל, דחה/נדח
e. פ"י and ע"ו: (הוביש) בוש/יבש, גור/יגר, חול/יחל, טוב/יטב, עוף/יעף, קוץ/יקץ, צור/יצר
f. פ"י and ע"ע רקק/ירק
g. פ"י and ל"ה אבה/יאב
h. ע"ו and ע"ע: גרר/עור, משש/מוש, נדד/נוד (ריב), רבב/רוב, שגג/שוג
i. ע"ו and לה": ספה/סוף, ערה/עור, שגה/שוג
j. ע"ע and ל"ה: דמה/דמם, זכה/זכך, חפה/חפף, חקה/חקק, חרה/חרר, כלה/כלל, קלה/קלל, שסה/שסס
k. ל"א and ל"ה: חטא/ חטה (חטא), צמה/צמא (וצמית Ru 2:9), and many examples in MH.

To these we must add פ"א verbs in contact with other classes, such as אסף/ יסף/סוף/ספה and כפה/כפף/אכף, in which the interaction among verb classes is less obvious than in the examples listed above, but the example of זון/אזן in מזין (in Prov 17:4) is quite clear in light of וּמְחִיזִים (=ומאחיזים) in *m. Shabbat* 1:11 according to MS Kaufmann and MS Parma De Rossi 138.

2.15.2 The picture outlined above is enlarged when we compare Hebrew roots to their counterparts in cognate languages,[200] and the etymological connections between them are quickly confirmed by such an assumption. There are two reasons for the contact among various weak roots:

a. In the prehistoric process of the expansion of biradical roots into triradical roots, different methods were used,[201] similar to processes at work in Modern Hebrew, where biradical roots and nouns are expanded into triradical roots: e.g., from אט: אטה, הָאֵט; from אד: אָיֵד, אָדָה, from דם: דָּמֵם (also in SH דם is inflected *dammi*, etc.); but from עץ: עֵצָה. This model may explain the basic proximity in meaning of roots between which there is interplay of the sort described.

b. In periods accessible to history, phonological processes were at work that drew together and even united forms from originally distinct roots, and arising from those unified forms there was contact and intermingling of originally distinct roots. Thus, for example, *maṣaʾa* and *maṣaya* both yield *māṣā, but it is spelled different ways, according to the root from which the verb is derived, מצא or מצה. Out of this overlapping were created forms such as נִמְצֵאתִי

---

[200] Nöldeke, *Neue Beiträge*, 179–206.
[201] A survey of literature on the expansion of roots from Gesenius on, along with illustrations of reconstructed types of expansion in ancient times, can be found in G. J. Botterweck, *Der Triliterismus im Semitischen* (Bonn, 1952).

on the pattern of נִמְצֵיתִי, and in later Biblical Hebrew forms such as נְשׂוּי (Ps 32:1).

2.15.3 It will be self-evident that what is bequeathed to SH from ancient times maintains its existence there as in TH, while the contact engendered by the fusion of forms due to phonological processes exists also in SH as it does in TH. SH, however, is not identical to TH in all the particular ways that classes and forms interact in a given verb. In the description of the grammar of the verb to this point, we have found parallels to TH, such as the blending of ע"י and ע"ע, of פ"נ and פ"י, and others, as well as phenomena unique to SH, of course, due to the collapse of the ה, ח, and ע phonemes into א. The list of roots in the Inventory of Forms in this volume teaches us that there are some innovations in SH that do not appear in TH, such as the root אול as against TH יאל (in the form הואלתי), the root יתן alongside נתן, פול alongside נפל,[202] the root ירם (in ונירם Nu 21:30) alongside רמי, the root מוד alongside מדד, the root סוב alongside סבב, the root אצי (in אצוים Ex 5:13) as against TH אוץ, the root תוך as against TH תכך (in תֻּכּוּ), the root בנן alongside בון, a particular form of ל"ה on the pattern of ל"א (more precisely, along the model of verbs III-guttural) in the verb משה. Related to this is the reading *ūšabnu* הושבנו (SP Gn 44:8) instead of the anticipated **īšabnu*, mixing the roots שוב and ישב, similar to the form להוכיח in 1QIsaᵃ and other verbs in MH.[203] Note that the blending of the roots שוב and ישב can be found in Ezek 35:9 as well: *kətiv* תישבנה, *qəre* תֵּשַׁבְנָה; and in 2 Sa 19:33: בְּשִׁיבָתוֹ (in the sense of בישבתו "while he sat"); and in Jer 42:10: שׁוֹב תֵּשְׁבוּ; and one need not add וְהוֹשִׁבוֹתִים (Zech 10:6).

Although the basis for blending and contact between weak roots lies in phonological and morphological processes, (see 2.15.3.1), roots that became synonymous sometimes developed semantic distinctions,[204] such as those between the roots נבל and בלי, between כלי and כלל, between זכי and זכך, and between נסך and סוך. Where roots are not clearly distinct from one another, we have chosen not to separate them in the grammar, making of them two or more verbs on the basis of morphological criteria. Instead, we have categorized all the verb forms from merged roots under one root, usually the root

---

[202] Dr. Haseeb Shehadeh has pointed out to me that Abraham Alʻaya (in his commentary to Dt 32, British Museum MS Or 12257) translates פללים in Dt 32:31: ساقطين, i.e., "fall." This shows that the commentator saw no difficulty in relating פ"נ and ע"י etymologically. On פללים, see 0.13.

[203] See Kutscher, *Isaiah Scroll*, 345; H. Yalon, "The Stem Puʻal," *Lĕšonénu* 3 (1930/1), 347 [Hebrew].

[204] The process is similar to that which occurs in synonymous nouns and verbs in Modern Hebrew, which, over time, develop new shades of meaning, such as the distinctions between שמע (today, "hear"), האזין ("listen"), and הקשיב ("listen actively, pay attention") – verbs which did not bear such distinctions in, e.g., classical liturgical poetry.

2.15 Mixture of Classes and Alternation of Stems 221

with the most forms. This has been our practice in the case of doubly weak roots as well (such as נטה and יצא), where I have categorized every verb under one of the classes, as a rule the one in which the most significant features of the verb are evident.

> Note: 1. B. Landsberger, in his attempt to uncover the Semitic verb system in its prehistoric period, theorized that the different bases (*Themen*) of verbs, and particularly of those that were originally biradical, had distinct semantic qualities — that is, they belonged to different classes of meaning (*Bedeutungsklassen*) — and Hebrew, with its many weak roots, still preserved much of that situation. Thus, in his opinion, contact among classes in Hebrew has to do with that fact that roots such as דמם and דום were semantically close very early on.[205] This hypothesis has yet to be proven, and may not be subject to proof at all, but clearly, in historical times, the contact came about as a result of factors involving pronunciation and word formation. SH serves as evidence of this, since it is only by means of phonological and morphological processes that there came to be changes in SH in the system of verb classes as compared to TH and through contacts and interactions particular to SH.
>
> 2. A new and very interesting theory about the development of triradicalism in the Semitic languages from biradicalism has been propounded by J. Kuryłowicz.[206] According to his theory the enlargement came into existence in the prehistoric period and must be differentiated in accordance with the means by which the third radical was added: (a) petrified prefixes such as י and ת in the roots יאב, תאב, or נ and ש in the roots שפל, נפל. Such prefixes can be structurally explained from the data in the historical Semitic languages; (b) internal lengthening of vowels and consonants (=gemination) as in the ע"י and ע"ע roots; (c) old suffixes, the functions of which cannot be ascertained structurally (e.g., פרש-פרר-פרק-, פרץ-פרס-פרט-פרד), since no suffix like the third radical in the above mentioned roots is attested in Hebrew or in other Semitic languages.
>
> In conclusion, the similarities of meaning common to these types of roots stems from their common, biradical basis, and the expansions, more than just being the result of phonological processes, are the result of morphological processes.
>
> In connection with root enlargement, Kuryłowicz deals with the question of the incompatibility of consonants within a root. In this con-

---

[205] See "Die Eigenbegrififflichkeit der babylonischen Welt," *Islamica* 2 (1926), 355ff., especially 361-365.
[206] J. Kuryłowicz, *Studies in Semitic Grammar and Metrics* (Wroclaw, 1973), chap. 1, especially 12, sect. 10; 22, sect. 24.

text it might be worth mentioning that already in the tenth century Hebrew grammarians, especially Sa'adia Ga'on and Menaḥem ben Saruq (*Maḥberet*, 15*), dealt with this question in the language of the Bible.

2.15.4 A superficial survey of SH is sufficient to reveal many differences between SH and TH in the intermingling of root classes as is evident in the formation of nouns and in the conjugation of verbs. The basis for differences in nouns is usually in the area of phonology, with no discernable general trends. Note what is written about them in Chapter Four, under the various patterns. In contrast, the differences in verb formation are worth of inquiry; in some no linguistic trend can be discerned, while in others such a trend is entirely obvious.

2.15.5 As against TH *Qal*, we find in SH *Pi'el* as the standard stem in these verbs: שלח, רקח, רכס, קרע, קבץ, פרש, משח, מכר, לקט, יסף, גרש, בכה. Some of these verbs have no *Qal* form in SH, such as מכר, or only remnants of *Qal* remain, as in the verb שלח (the form שלוחה). Sometimes *Qal* and *Pi'el* occur with the same meaning and under the same conditions, such as *nâṣâbu* נצבו (Ex 15:8) and *naššibtå* נשבת (Ex 7:15), or *šåkålti šakkilti* שכלתי שכלתי (Gn 43:14), a usage similar to the expression בָּרוּךְ וּמְבֹרָךְ.[207] In the process *Qal*>*Pi'el*, SH has a partner in MH, and in the language of the Dead Sea Scrolls.[208] We see here the decline of the use of *Pi'el* to express "intensive action," or at least a vast reduction in this phenomenon, which itself dates from a very early period. Something of the semantic equivalence of *Qal* and *Pi'el* in this tradition is hinted at by something noted in MH: that sometimes a *Qal* verb in a given verse becomes a *Pi'el* in the hands of its interpreters, e.g., concerning יְעָדָהּ (Ex 21:8, SP — העידה *å'îda*), it is said in *Mekhilta de-R. Yishma'el* (ed. Horowitz-Rabin, 257): ר' עקיבא אומר מוכר הוא אם רצה ליעד מיעד; or concerning שניתי (Mal 3:6, it is said in *Sifre Deuteronomy* (ed. Finkelstein, 330): מי שינה במי? או המקום שינה בהם וכן הוא אומר כי אני לא שניתי.[209] Of course, The *Pi'el* stem may also be found in SH in place of *Qal* with a difference in meaning, such as a causative sense, e.g., וישמעו מצרים וישמעו בית פרעה *wyišmā'u*

---

[207] Samaritan exegetical literature has grappled with the difference in meaning between the two readings in the phrase in Gn 43:14. Mešalma Ha-Danafi (in a fragment published by G. L. Rosen, *The Joseph Cycle [Genesis 37–45] in the Samaritan-Arabic Commentary of Meshalma Ibn Murjan* [Ph.D. thesis, Columbia University, 1957], 60 in Arabic numerals) interprets the *Pi'el* with the word اتكل, i.e., as though it said that Pharaoh made me bereaved, while ST (MS Barberini) reads אמטיתי and SAV اتكلت, where the pronunciation today is in *Qal*. And Mešalma adds: "or the two meanings have become equivalent. ...and God knows which is correct."

[208] This was already pointed out in Ben-Ḥayyim, *Tradition*, 112–123, and see my "Word Studies," 50ff.

[209] The argument that in MH *Pi'el* may be used as *Qal* is in Biblical Hebrew with no difference in meaning, which we proposed in Ben-Ḥayyim, *Tradition*, we have now encountered in the brief remarks of D. Z. Baneth in *Lěšonénu La'am* 2:4 (1950), 27–28 in connection with the verb חנך.

2.15 Mixture of Classes and Alternation of Stems

miṣrəm wyēšammā'u bit fāru (SP Gn 45:2), where the second וישמעו is understood as causative (SAV واداعو). One also encounters *Qal* in SH where TH reads *Pi'el*, without the reason mentioned above, e.g., *'âqâru* עקרו as against TH עִקְּרוּ (Gn 49:6), *wšâkâla* ושכלה as against TH וְשִׁכְּלָה (Lv 26:22), and *wāšâb* וחשב as against TH וְחִשַּׁב (Lv 25:27).

2.15.6 The change discussed in the previous section caused the *Nif'al* of those verbs to become *Nif'al* "with geminated second radical," i.e., to become *Hitpa'el* with the ת originally assimilated (2.1.4.6–8). Thus, where TH reads וְנִבְרְכוּ (Gn 12:3 and elsewhere), which is still linked to the *Qal*, SH reads *wnibbârrâku* (related to ונתברכו). Thus, one finds *yimmakkâr* (=יִמָּכֵר), *wyissakkâru* (=וַיִּסָּכְרוּ), *niffattā'u* (= נפתח), *yiqqâddâš* (=יִקָּדֵשׁ), *yiqqarra* (=יִקָּרֵעַ), *iššâmmâd* (=הִשָּׁמֵד), and others. This *Nif'al* has absorbed TH *Pu'al*, of course, in the same way that in MH *Nitpa'el* becomes the passive of *Qal*, e.g., יְכֻבַּר (Lv 27:26) is pronounced *yibbakkâr*, and תְּעֻנֶּה (Lv 23:29) is pronounced *tiyyanna*, as described in 2.10.

2.15.7 In the Bible with Tiberian vocalization, we can discern a trend toward replacing *Qal* with *Nif'al* when the verb is intransitive or passive.[210] This, of course, occurs only where the consonantal texts makes such a change possible. Thus, we find "compensatory conjugation" such as נִגַּשׁ and נִדַּח in *Nif'al*, but the forms יִגַּשׁ and לִנְדֹּחַ in *Qal*. This tendency is evident in MH, and particularly in Talmud and Midrash, as in the substitution of נאבד for אָבַד or נתגבנו for גָּבְהוּ. This trend is quite evident in SH as well, e.g., *wiyyâzâq* וַיֶּחֱזַק (Ex 7:22), *iyyâgâr* יַחְגֹּר (Lv 16:4), *wtiyyâzâl* ותאזל (SP Dt 32:2), *tikkâbad* תִּכְבַּד (Ex 5:9), *wyiṣṣâbā'u* ויצבאו (Nu 31:7), *yiṣṣânaf* יִצְנֹף (Lv 16:4), and *yiqqāri* יקרא (Gn 49:1). In SH, too, of course, this substitution is limited by the consonantal text, so that in Dt 25:18, SP קראך is pronounced *qā'râk*.

Comparison of TH to SH, though, on this point, points up more clearly this trend in the Hebrew of the Second Temple period, since the difference in word formation in *Nif'al* between these two dialects of Hebrew (see 2.1.4.1.2) forces SH to maintain the ancient *Qal* in a place where TH was able to replace it with *Nif'al*; that place is the פ"נ class. Some examples: *nâgâš* נִגַּשׁ, *nâṣâbu* נִצְּבוּ, *nâtâk* נִתַּךְ (Ex 9:33), *wnâqâtâ* וְנִקְּתָה (Nu 5:28), *nēgəf* נִגַּף. The parallel *nâṣəm* נִצִּים (Ex 2:13) : *yēnâṣṣu* יִנָּצוּ (Dt 25:11), where *Pi'el* replaces *Qal* (see 2.15.5), is

---

[210] This phenomenon has been discussed in my monograph "An Ancient Language in a New Reality," *Lěšonénu La'am* 4 (1953) [Hebrew], included in *Struggle*, 36ff. It is regrettable that this phenomenon in TH, the existence of which is affirmed by SH, was not noticed by H. B. Rosén, "The Comparative Assignment of Certain Hebrew Tense Forms", *Proceedings of the International Conference on Semitic Studies*, (Jerusalem, 1969). Rosen derives יָנֻטָה and תְּנֻשַּׁנִי from *Qal*. The Targum תתנשיני (see my "Ha'azinu," 78) should suffice to demonstrate the error of this approach.

particularly instructive. But this trend does not eliminate the possibility that SH may preserve *Qal* as against TH *Nifʻal* outside the פ"נ class as well (see 7.0), as in *wyimla* (Nu 14:21) as against TH וַיִּמָּלֵא, or *tåzzåb* (Lv 26:43) as against TH תֵּעָזֵב, and their translations (ST תשתבק, SAV تخلو) indicate that no transitive verb is intended. Here, then, the root עזב is used in the same way as Arabic عزب. Similar to this is *yiṭmå* in *Qal*, as against TH יִטְמָא (e.g., Lv 21:1).

2.15.8 Other alternations between stems do not display general tendencies, but each individual verb must be explained separately, so that discussion of them belongs in a lexicon, not a grammar. Of this sort are the alternations *wyiškåm* (*Qal*):TH וַיַּשְׁכֵּם (*Hifʻil*); *tagmīlu* (*Hifʻil*):TH תגמלו (*Qal*, Dt 32:6); *taqdəš* (*Hifʻil*):TH תִּקְדָּשׁ (*Qal*, Dt 22:9; *Qal* in SP Nu 20:13); *wyannaʾimma* (*Qal*):TH וַיִּנְעָם (*Hifʻil*, Nu 32:13); and others. The form *wtūqad* ותוקד (SP Dt 32:22), too, as against TH ותיקד, is constructed in *Hifʻil*, as the vowel of the second radical demonstrates, and so it is consistently throughout SP.

3. PRONOUN

3.0 A comparison of the SH pronouns with their TH counterparts, category by category, will yield the following observations:

a. SH follows one consistent pattern, avoiding doublets.
b. Several rare pronominal forms in TH are actually the norm in SH. The Samaritan tradition chose from among the forms in the heritage common to both traditions. As for that common heritage, the basis for all traditions of Hebrew, it must be assumed that it contained independent pronominal forms ending in short vowels alongside forms ending in long vowels[1] (such as *'attā:*'atta, *'attī:*'atti, *hinnā:*hinna, etc., and in the pronominal suffixes as well), while the use of each form is conditioned by its status in a given sentence. Since the short vowels at the ends of these forms fell into disuse while the long vowels did not, historic Hebrew has forms that end with vowels and forms that do not. SH, which used only one form for each of the pronouns, does not display the variation of TH forms. At times it preserves what was rejected by TH. The orthography of the SH forms expresses the trend toward simplification of pronunciation, but pronunciation is an ancient, independent tradition that is not entirely identical with the written version.

3.1 Personal Pronouns

	ắni אני, ắnắki אנכי		
ắttå אתה		ắtti את (אתי)	
ū הוא		ī היא	
	ắnắnnu אנחנו		
attimma אתם		attən אתן	
imma הם		inna הנה (הן)[2]	

---

[1] This assumption fits the primitive forms in Hebrew and makes no pretence of describing the forms in Proto-Semitic. Opinion is divided on the latter; for contrasting views, see *GvG*, 298 [δ], 300 c[α] and Moscati, *Introduction*, 103ff.

[2] It should be noted that the form הן is unattested in the MT other than as a pronominal suffix. In SP Lv 18:10 הן appears in the written text of a single manuscript (see von Gall's edition) and in the edition of Avraham and Raṣon Sedaqa at Gn 21:29.

3.1.1 Regarding the second *å* in *ånåki* אנכי, instead of the anticipated *u*, see 1.5.2.6. There may be a parallel to the Samaritan form in Punic (according to Plautus): *anec(h)*. The Punic form can be understood if we assume that it originally had a short *a*. (On the development of short *a* to *e* in Punic, see J. Friedrich, *Phönizisch-Punische Grammatik* [Rome, 1970²] sect. 75b, 76b, 79c.) The SH form, however, is consistent with the assumption that *å* reflects an earlier *ā*; see 1.5.2.7.

3.1.2 It should be pointed out that there is no remnant of the masculine form אַתְּ in SP, which reads אתה also in Nu 11:15 and Dt 5:24, despite the fact that את is the standard form in MH,³ and in any case in Palestinian Aramaic. Furthermore, in SA, too, the form *åttå* predominates (not due to the influence of Hebrew!), and a form that does not end in a vowel appears almost exclusively in the contraction *dat* דת (< את + ד).⁴ And so the opposition between masculine and feminine forms of the second person sing. pronoun is different from that of TH, in that it contrasts *å:i* instead of TH *å:ø*.

3.1.3 The 2nd fem. sing. pronoun *åtti* is written with a י: אתי. The spelling את in Nu 5:20 is not interpreted as a 2nd fem. sing. pronoun; see demonstratives 3.3.1.3.

3.1.4 The pronunciation of the vowel of the 3rd fem. sing. personal pronoun is *i*, and the spelling is always היא, even where TH reads הִוּא (e.g., Gn 3:12). Similarly, in SH the 1st pl. pronoun appears always as אנחנו, even where TH reads נחנו (e.g., Gn 42:11).

3.1.5 In relating the 2nd plural pronouns to their original Proto-Semitic forms, it is agreed that that 2nd masc. pl. pronoun was **'antumŭ*, while with regard to the 2nd fem. pl., opinions differ: **'antin* (GvG I, 301), **'antina* (Moscati, *Introduction*, 105).

In TH, we do not find אתמה, although that form is found in DSS, and there is no tradition of pronunciation in accord with it. In אַתֵּנָה, on the other hand, there is no gemination of the נ in TH, although in Babylonian vocalization אׄתֹנה

---

³ See Kutscher, "Mishnaic Hebrew" in *Henoch Yalon Jubilee Volume*, ed. S. Lieberman et al. (Jerusalem 1963), 246-260 [Hebrew].

⁴ It is a common error to transcribe TH את as *'att* for etymological reasons: Hebrew does not tolerate gemination at the end of a word. The Samaritan tradition provides further evidence of this, since it — a tradition careful to preserve gemination — does not preserve it at the end of *at* את, the personal pronoun in SA, which is in use alongside *åttå* אתה. This pronunciation must be genuine, since it is attested in the old liturgical poetry (see *passim* in LOT III/2).

(Ezek 34:17) requires us to assume gemination. The gemination of the final ם of אתם in SH is certainly the product of analogy, probably from the 3rd pl. pronouns, or perhaps even from אתנה, which has meanwhile disappeared from SH. Particular mention should be made of the fact that the form of the 2nd fem. pl. pronoun bearing a final vowel disappeared from SH, and in SP the form used is consistently אתן.

3.1.6 The pronunciation of הם as *imma* led to the complete elimination of the spelling המה in SP, and it happens that the spelling הן replaces TH הנה. We learn from the 13th century grammarian Abū Saʿīd that in the past, an *a* vowel served in place of the *i* used today before geminated מ or נ throughout the system of pronouns,[5] and in this SH was identical to the Babylonian tradition.

3.2 Pronominal Suffixes

3.2.0 The differences between the various pronominal forms that are joined to nouns, particles, and verbs in TH (other than first person singular) originate not in differences between base forms of the pronoun, but in different ways in which the same base form of the pronoun attach to the various parts of speech, as well as the phonological rules governing the manners of attachment. The base form of the pronoun may attach immediately to the uninflected form of a word, or it may be attached with the aid of a vowel of a specific quality, or with the aid of a syllable including a consonant. The inserted element may be an etymological element from an earlier period in the development of the word, or at may be derived by analogy to another form; for historical Hebrew there is no difference, for in it the intercalated element along with the base form of the pronoun constitute the pronominal form.

SH sometimes differs from TH in pronominal forms, particularly because of the difference in the phonological rules that governed the joining of elements in the formative period of SH, but also due to different choices of inserted elements. It can be shown, however, that no SH pronominal form is entirely unattested in TH. It should be pointed out that in SH no difference developed between pronominal suffixes attached to nouns and those attached to particles. Now we shall survey the SH pronominal suffixes in detail.

3.2.1 1st singular. With forms other than verbs, the pronominal suffix is *i*, whether joined to a singular noun or to a plural noun: *ʿammi*/עַמִּי, *ʿimmi*/עַמִּי,

---

[5] See *LOT* I, 37, and my article, "Penultimate Stress," 150–160.

bēnī/בְּנֵי, bånī/בָּנַי (see 1.4.4b). With the verb, its form is ni after a vowel, åni after a consonant, and sometimes also inni (with the imperfect), e.g., yårāgūnī/יַהְרְגוּנִי, yårågånī/יַהַרְגֵנִי, åkēlånī/אֲכָלָנִי, tiqbårinnī/תִּקְבְּרֵנִי, wtērē'innī/וְתִרְאֵנִי. Note that the mediating element, where it is needed, is a, used with the imperfect and the imperative as well, as in ašqiyyånī [TH הַשְׁקִינִי] (Gn 24:43,45). This can be found in TH as well, as in תְּדַבְּקֵנִי (Gn 19:19).

3.2.2 2nd singular.
The pronominal suffixes, both masculine and feminine, are without final vowels — the opposite of their independent pronominal counterparts (see above, 3.1.2) — and so in SH such spellings as ידכה (Ex 13:16) and רעתכי (Jer 11:15) are nowhere to be found, except in the word באכה, which is pronounced båka. In this word, the pronominal suffix parallel to TH ךָ- (כה-) is preserved. Samaritan tradition, however, fails to analyze this clearly, and some ancient translations do not see in the suffix ka a 2nd sing. pronoun, and interpret באכה as an infinitive.[6] In fact, the usual distinction between the masculine and feminine forms of the pronominal suffix in SH is maintained by the vowel before ך, and in the plural forms and other forms following this paradigm, the distinction is largely erased, as we shall soon see.

3.2.2.0
The masculine pronominal suffix is simply k after a form ending in a vowel, such as åbək אביך, barriktək ברכתיך, wåbådok ועבדוך. (The vowels ə , o replace i, u.) Its form is åk following a consonant, as in yēdåk ידך, ūtåk אותך, bak בך, wyismåråk וישמרך. If the vowel of the suffix encounters a form originally ending with a guttural consonant preceded by an a vowel, it combines with that vowel, forming a long, stressed vowel. At times it forms a front vowel ā (if the front vowel appears with the guttural, as usual), e.g., zē'råk (< *zēra(') + åk) זרעך, yiq'qåk (< *yiqqa(ḥ) + åk) יקחך — as opposed to zåruwwåk זרועך. The form that is joined to a plural noun (or to other words that take suffixes of that paradigm), is, of course, ək (<-ayk), e.g., yēdək ידיך, 'ålək עליך. If it occurs with the plural form of a noun originally ending in a guttural, the vowel of the pronominal suffix joins with the vowel before the guttural to form a long, stressed ī, as in mim'mīk (< *mim'mī'ək < *mimmī'ēk(a) < *mimmi'ayk(a) ממעיך (Gn 15:4). SH bears no trace of the occasional gemination of the pronominal suffix ך found in TH (e.g., יִשְׁמָרֶךָ); if it once maintained

---

[6] This is an interesting example of a pronominal suffix losing its meaning due to infrequent appearance. A similar process occured with ערכך (e.g., Lv 27:2), where Onqelos translates בפורסן and ST translates בשיאם, both of them ignoring the pronominal suffix! Not all memory of the fact that באכה contains a 2nd sing. pronominal suffix was lost, however, for we find in ST Gn 19:22 מיעלך, and in SAV حصولك (variant reading: دخولك). See Ben-Ḥayyim, Studies, 60, n. 72. See also 6.3.7 below, on אֵיכָה.

that phenomenon, it could not continue to do so because SH does not allow gemination at the end of a word.

3.2.2.1 The 2nd fem. pronominal suffix (with a singular noun) is *ək* after any consonant other than a guttural. (Its form after a vowel is unattested in the Pentateuch.) When the suffix is stressed, its vowel is explicitly *e*, e.g., *yēdək* [TH יָדֵךְ], *bek* [TH בָּךְ]. After a guttural, its form is *īk* and it is stressed, e.g., *zē'rīk* זרעך. It is fairly certain that the origin of this suffix is not like that of TH ־ֵךְ; that is, it is not *ĭk(i)*, but rather *īk(i)*. The vowel of this suffix is, thus, like its vowel in Aramaic in general and in SA in particular, and in MH as well. This can be seen in the full spellings, including י, in SP, e.g., in Gn 3:16: עצבוניך, תשוקתיך, והריוניך, ביך in various manuscripts, and it is demonstrated by the formation of a form such as *zē'rīk*, in which the quality of the short vowel before the ע is assimilated into the long *i* vowel: **zēra(') + īk*. When joined with a plural noun (and words following that paradigm) as well, the form of the pronominal suffix is *ək* or *īk*, according to the conditions noted above, e.g., *bīnək* בעיניך, *mim'mīk* [TH מִמֵּךְ] (Gn 25:23).

> Note: In Gn 21:17 a pronominal suffix form is preserved that has a final vowel: *līki*, and it, too, finds support in the spelling of SP: מליכי, מלכי (variant: מה ליך).

3.2.3 3rd singular. The masculine pronominal suffix as it is attached to a singular noun is *ū* (< *hū*), and as attached to a plural noun (and to other words following that paradigm) is *o* (< *aw* < *ayhu*). For instance, *yēdu* = יָדוֹ (Gn 3:22 etc.) : *yēdo* = יָדָיו (Gn 27:23, etc.); *ašfāttu* = שִׁפְחָתוֹ (Gn 29:24): *ašfātto* = שְׁפָחֹתָיו (Gn 32:23); *'ālo* = עָלָיו : *īlo* = אֵלָיו. It should be noted that the pronominal suffix is the only instance in SH in which a difference in meaning hinges on the difference in quality between *u* and *o*, for in every other instance they are allophones of one phoneme.

The rule distinguishing the use of the suffix with plurality (in form!) and singularity is very rigorous. Thus, we find in SH, too, the *o* suffix in words like *âdanno*/אדניו (Gn 24:9; "his master"), *bālo*/בְּעָלָיו (Ex 21:29 "his owner," the semantic singularity of which is clearly expressed by the predicate). However, when there is an exegetical need to avoid any misunderstanding with regard to the singularity of such a noun, the *u* suffix is used, as in *ēluwiyyu* = אלהיו, instead of the expected **ēluwwo*. The same reasoning has shaped **ēluwwåk*, instead of *ēluwwək*.

In the light of this phenomenon we should understand *kallūtu* (in accordance with SP Gn 11:31 שרי ואת מלכה כלותיו as a dual form,[7] for if the noun is

---

[7] It appears that for this reason the Samaritan pronunciation in Gn 19:15 is *(šitti) bånūtåk* and

construed as plural, the form would be *kallūto (the singular of which is *kaltu* in Gn 38:11, like the form *bintu* in Gn 46:7, which SAV renders as بنته (sic! see A. Tal, review of H. Shehadeh, *The Arabic Translation of the Samaritan Pentateuch*, in *BiOr* [1993], 460–464). The pronominal suffix changes form according to the type of noun to which it is attached, as follows:

3.2.3.1 After a consonant, it is regularly *u*, as in *yēdu* ידו, *ūtu* אותו, *bū* בו, *wtå'ēru* וטהרו, *wtåmmå'u* וטמאו. With regard to the form *wqaddištu* וְקִדַּשְׁתּוֹ, it may be assumed that the pronominal suffix has been attached directly to the base *qaddišt-*, or perhaps that an *o* vowel (*qaddištāhū > *qaddištaw > *qaddišto) has been changed to *u* in line with what was stated above (3.2.3) about the the use of pronouns with singular and plural noun forms.

3.2.3.2 After a vowel, it is regularly *ē'u*, as in *qiṣṣā'ē'u* קצהו, *kåmē'u* כמהו, *såbē'u* צוהו, *nassītē'u* נסיתהו, *nåssā'ē'u* נסהו, *wqārā'ē'u* וקר(א)הו (Gn 42:38), *wyallē'u* ויעלהו, *wyiqqā'ē'u* ויקחהו, *wyiqnā'ē'u* ויקנהו (Gn 39:1), *akkīrē'u* הכירהו, *wyistāmē'u* וישטמהו, *yā'ūkēlē'u* יאכלהו, *wīnīqē'u* והניקהו (Ex 2:9). The pronominal suffix in this form may appear after a consonant as well: *almīnē'u* למינהו (alongside *almīnu* למינו), *barrēkē'u* ברכהו (SP Gn 27:27). From these examples it may be seen that this form of the pronoun has many sources:

1. original *ēhū*, which occurs in TH as the usual form with verbs in the imperfect and the imperative but not in the perfect, whereas in SH it has penetrated from the imperative into the perfect as well;

2. *ē'u* formed by dissimilation from the sequence *ūhū* (see 1.5.3.2), and that this is an ancient process can be seen from the spellings in SP: וישטמה, יאכלה, and other such forms without ו,[8] even though the Samaritans are generous in their use of ו as a mater lectionis. In this process, the 3rd masc. singular and plural forms have overlapped, so that the form *yāllē'u*, for example, may correspond to TH יעלהו or יעלהו;

3. in forms such as *nassītē'u* נסיתו and *wīnīqē'u* והניקהו, it seems self-evident that the vowels of the verbal endings have been elided in the verbs *nassītā+ē'u* and *wīnīqi+ē'u*, or perhaps it is preferable to assume that because the pronominal suffix *ē'u* is so common, the suffix הו was read that way in several places, even though a vowel precedes it. On פיהו, see n. 9 below.

---

not -*ək*, although we are unable to determine why it occurs precisely in these places. The reading *wbintu* in Gn 46:7, even though Hebrew does not normally preserve the נ in the singular, is intended as singular, referring to Dinah, since no other daughter is known from the Bible to have been born to Jacob.

[8] This appears to be the pronunciation in the Dead Sea Scrolls as well. See G. B. Sarfatti, "The Forms יפעלהו, פעלהו and the Expression of Impersonal Subject in the Manual of Discipline (1Q5, 1Q5a, 1Q5b),", *Lěšonénu* 32 (1967/8), 63ff. [Hebrew].

3.2 Pronominal Suffixes

3.2.3.3 In forms ending with an *i* vowel, the suffix appears as *iyyu*, as in *abiyyu* אביו, *fiyyu* פיו,[9] *wgarreštiyyu* וגרשתיו, *šamtiyyu* שמתיו, *wånniyyu* והניחו (Dt 6:24). It cannot be determined whether the form of the pronominal suffix is derived from *īhū* or from *īw*, since the diphthong *iw* is likely to split into two syllables, restoring the original situation.[10]

3.2.3.4 There may be forms in which the pronominal suffix element includes gemination of (a) the נ or (b) the ת, such as (a) *tēbarrēkinni* תברכני, *wqåbinnu* וקבנו (Nu 23:13), and with the suffix *ē'u*: *yåṣårinnē'u* יצרנהו, *yēsūbēbinnē'u* יסובבנהו, *yåšīminnē'u* ישימנהו; (b) *wåkålittu* וְאָכְלַתּוּ (SP Dt 14:23), *åkålittu* אָכְלַתּוּ (SP Gn 37:20), *wqåbittu* וקבתו (SP Nu 23:27), *måšīttiyyu* משיתיו (Ex 2:10), *wīnēttu* והנחתו (SP Dt 14:28). By geminating the נ, SH differs from TH in extending this phenomenon from the imperfect to the perfect and the imperative. The gemination of ת in והנחתו may be explained as a product of the assimilation of the guttural to the ת of the morpheme (i.e., the underlying form is **whiniḥtāhū*), but this does not apply to the other instances cited above, where we must instead assume one of two possibilities:

1. In these verbs, the pronominal suffix *hū* is attached directly to *t* (even for the 2nd masc. sing.!) with its vowel elided, as it is added in אכלתו in SP Gn 37:20; or
2. This pronominal suffix form was influenced by SA, in which *itte* is the regular form, and the antiquity of this form is demonstrated by CPA (see 2.3.6, 2.8.11). The second explanation more easily explains the vowel *i* in both the 2nd masc. sing. and 3rd fem. sing.[11]

> Note: *wåmårinnu* ואמרנו (Gn 37:20) departs from the rule if we interpret it as וְאָמַרְנוּ. The form seems morphologically to include a 3rd masc. sing. pronoun that is without meaning, a frozen form like the 2nd masc. sing. pronominal suffix in the form הערכך (Lv 27:23, etc.), and the same is true of *wnēlā'imnu* ונלחמנו. (See 2.2.2.3.2.)

3.2.3.5 The spelling of the pronoun with ה occurs in SP in the word לחה (Dt 34:7) (and perhaps in the word *ayye* איה in SP Ex 2:20), and it is pronounced *e*:

---

[9] In Nu 27:21, however, the reading is (twice) *fiyyē'u* פיהו (SP), and this other form of the pronominal suffix (*ēhū*, not יהו-!) has been used to create a semantic distinction: it means "according to His word."

[10] See 1.4.4c and my "Penultimate Stress."

[11] Indeed, the spelling of the vowel in CPA in forms such as אכירתה, from something like אָכֶרֶת + ה-ַ, meaning "I knew him," and קבילתה from קַבְּלַת + ה-ַ, meaning "I received him/it" (Schulthess, *Grammaik*, 78, §153, sect. 3; the transcriptions are mine) hints at *i*, yielding forms such as **akkīritte* and **qabbēlitte*. It may be that the tendency to geminate the ת in the pronominal suffix (in Aramaic, the source of the ת is in the word ית in its declension!) is found in the form *walkallūttimma* ולכתותם (Ex 32:12), as opposed to the absence of gemination in Dt 7:22.

lā'e. The pronunciation no doubt represents the Aramaic 3rd masc. sing. pronominal suffix.

3.2.3.6 Corresponding to the two forms of the pronominal suffix in TH, ־ָהּ and ־ֹה, SH has only *a* (at times, *å*), whether short — the usual form — or long, in a stressed syllable. This *a* may be derived from either *ah* or *hā*. The form of this pronominal suffix, too, changes according to the type of form to which it is attached. Following a consonant it is normally *a*, as in *bīta* ביתה, *lā* לה, *wammīda* והעמידה, and *kåruw'wā* כרוח, but note also: *dåbåtå* דוותה (Lv 12:2), *šēnåtå* שנתה (Lv 14:10), *qåbbåtå* קבתה (Nu 25:8). Its form is *iyya* when attached to a plural noun (or similar morphological form), or, of course, following an *i* (*ī*) vowel, e.g., *fåniyya* פניה, *nīrūtiyya* נרותיה, *måriyya* מַרְאֶהָ, *'åliyya* עליה, *åbiyya* אביה, *wyībiyya* ויביאה (Gn 24:67). In the verb, its form may even be *inna*, as in *yīqīminna* יקימנה, *īšībinna* אשיבנה.

3.2.4 1st plural. The pronominal suffix attached to a singular noun, a particle, or a verb takes the following forms: (1) after a consonant, *ånu*; (2) after a vowel, *nu*; but if the vowel is *u*, (3) it changes before the pronominal suffix to *a*, which leads to a fusion of forms. Examples: (1) *nafšånu* נפשנו, *yēdånu* יָדֵנוּ, *tå'ūkēlånu* תאכלנו (Dt 5:22); (2-3) *åbīnu* אבינו, *ūṣåttånu* הוצאתנו (SP Nu 21:5) and הוצאתנו, *'allītånu* העליתנו (Nu 20:5) and העליתנו, *yisqålånu* יסקלנו (Ex 8:22) and יִסְקְלֻנוּ. The relationship between ־נוּ and ־נֻ in TH, in which the latter is attached only to particles and the noun כל (which follows the same pattern), is not in effect in SH, which has made the two forms identical.

The form that is attached to a plural noun and other forms that follow the same pattern is always *īnu*, e.g., *åbūtīnu* אבותינו, *'ålīnu* עלינו. The infinitive forms ולהחיותנו (SP Dt 6:24) and חנתינו (Nu 10:31) are pronounced with the pronominal suffix of plural nouns — *wliyyūtīnu, ånūtīnu* — by attraction to forms ending in the plural marker *ot*, in the same way that in Ezek 16:31 we find בִּבְנוֹתַיִךְ instead of בבנותך. See also 3.2.5.

3.2.5 2nd plural. The masculine pronominal suffix is *kimma*, and after an original guttural consonant it is *kkimma*, since the final consonant assimilates to the initial consonant of the pronominal suffix, a phenomenon similar to the gemination of an initial consonant after מן, e.g., *åbīkimma* אביכם, *åreṣkimma* ארצכם, *dūrūtīkimma* דורותיכם; *zērākkimma* זרעכם, *zēbåkkimma* זבחיכם, *wmåråkkimma* ומוראכם. In the word זונתיכם (Nu 14:33), we find the plural suffix: *zūnåtīkimma*; see 3.2.4.

3.2.5.1 The feminine pronominal suffix is *kən*, as in *wåbīkən* ואביכן. The relationship between the two forms of the pronominal suffix is entirely the same as the relationship between the parallel personal pronouns אתם and אתן — gemination of מ and the absence of gemination in the ן.[12] In this pronominal suffix, too, the vowel was once pronounced *a* (see 3.1.6).

3.2.6 3rd plural. The masculine pronominal suffix has two forms, one common, *imma*, and one rare, *(â)mu*, which occurs only with verbs. The *imma* form as attached to plural nouns (or after an *i* vowel) becomes *īyyimma* (from *ayhimma > *ēhimma, *īhimma), and with the prepositions ב or ל its form may be *ēmma*. With the prepositions, the two possibilities are distinguished by spelling: בהם is pronounced *bēmma* (< *bali + *himma*), while בם is pronounced *bimma* (< *b* + *himma*). In a verb, after the vowels *i*, *a*, or *u*, it is *mma* (with the *i* elided), e.g., *yēdimma* ידם, *riglimma* רגלם, *tērūmåtimma* תרומתם, *miyyimma* מהם (<**mī'imma* < *mīhimma <*mihhimma), *ålīqimma* אחליקם (SP Gn 49:7), *åbīyyimma* אביהם, *yēdīyyimma* ידיהם, *båbīyyimma* וביהם, *'ålīyyimma* עליהם, *šāmāttimma* שמעתם[13] (Gn 37:17), *wyårǻstimma* וירשתם (Dt 19:1), *wsåqåltimma* וסקלתם (Dt 17:5), *såtåmumma* סתמום; *kassåmu* כסמו, *yēkassiyyåmu* יכסימו (cf. above 3.2.4 on הוצאתנו), *tibyåmu* תביאמו.

Note: In the forms וירשתם and וסקלתם above, the vowel after ת is that of the 2nd masc. singular. See n. 13.

3.2.6.1 Note: On the basis of ST and SAV to תורישמו = *tūrišmu* (!) and תמלאמו = *timlāmu* (both Ex 15:9), it seems that מו- is understood there (although not at 15:17!) as a 3rd masc. singular pronominal suffix. If this is so, it provides support for those commentators and grammarians (see Sa'adia Ga'on and David Qimḥi ad loc.) who interpret פנימו (Ps 11:7) and עלימו (Job 20:23) as "his face" and "upon him."

3.2.6.2 The 3rd fem. pl. pronominal suffix also has two forms: *inna* and *ən*. After the vowel *i* and in plural nouns, *inna* takes the form *īyyinna*;[14] with the prepositions ב and ל, and occasionally with other words, its form is *enna*, e.g., *libbinna* לבן, *qirbinna* קרבהן (Gn 41:21), *albaddinna* לבדהן (Gn 21:28), *miyyinna*

---

[12] The 2nd fem. pl. pronominal suffix is rare in the Pentateuch, and the grammarian Abū Isḥāq (*LOT* I, 32) finds the need to use an example from outside the Pentateuch. Therefore, it is no surprise that one Samaritan reader read in our presence: *makkerkinna, šāmårkinna* (see *LOT* I, 32). These forms should not be relied on as additional support for such TH forms as וַמְתֻכֶנָה (Ezek 23:48) and כְּסְתוֹתֵיכֶנָה (Ezek 13:20).

[13] In an earlier period, a distinction was made between the pronunciation of the 2nd masc. sing. verb *-tamma* and the 3rd masc. *-timma*; *-tamma* paralleled תֶּם- and תָּם- in TH, but over time the differences between the vowels were blurred, and indeed we find manuscripts of SP which read שמעתם at Gn 37:17 instead of the common שמעתים. On this matter, see Abū Sa'īd's criticism, *LOT* I, 133, 144ff.

[14] אתהן (SP Ex 35:26) is pronounced according to the plural paradigm: *utiyyinna*.

מֵהֶן (SP Lv 4:2), *bēnna* בְהֵן, *wmiyyēlåbīyyinna* וּמֵחֲלָבֵיהֶן, *nā̊:låtən* נַחֲלָתָן. It should be noted that the 3rd masc. and fem. pl. pronominal suffixes do not stand in the same relation to one another as the corresponding personal pronouns, and in the 3rd fem. pl. the form without a final vowel is preserved.

3.2.7 Below are comparative tables of the pronominal suffixes in SH and TH. But first we offer a survey of the **reconstructed** core forms in the stage of Hebrew common to both traditions, from which the SH and TH pronominal suffixes are derived.

Singular		Plural	
1st	*ī*; pl. noun *ayya*, *nī* (verb)	1st	*nū*
2nd masc.	*ka/ā*	2nd masc.	*kimma/ā*
2nd fem.	*ki/ī*	2nd fem.	*kinna/ā*
3rd masc.	*hu/ū*	3rd masc.	*himma/ā*
3rd fem.	*ha/ā*	3rd fem.	*hinna/ā*

3.2.7.1 It should be noted that the reconstructed forms above are not identical to the reconstructed forms in Proto-Semitic. The forms presented here are based on the following assumptions: (a) that long and short versions of the final vowels originally coexisted under defined conditions, and (b) that in this early common stage, the influence of analogies brought about changes leading to the equality of vowel and gemination patterns in the 2nd and 3rd pl. pronominal suffixes. It is, of course, possible to assume that this standardization took place at later stages in each of the two traditions, but the assumption that it took place in the stage of shared development seems preferable. In that stage, there were case endings before the basic pronominal suffixes, as well as the dual form *ay*, and from the attachment of those endings to the basic pronominal suffixes we may explain the development of the historical forms of those suffixes.

Possessive Suffixes

3.2.8.0 SH is unaware of the difference in TH between nouns and "particles" (see 6.0) in regard to the quality of the "inserted element" (see 3.2.0), such as עִמְּךָ vs. עֲתֶךָ; אִתְּךָ vs. לִבְּךָ; כָּלָנוּ vs. עָוֹנוּ. The following table presents a comparison of SH and TH:

[The forms in square brackets are pausal forms, and those in parentheses are unusual or rare. The superscript numbers refer to the following section]

3.2 Pronominal Suffixes

Singular Suffixes

	After consonant		After vowel		Plural noun	
	SH	TH	SH	TH	SH	TH
1	i	ִי-	i	ִי-	i	ַי-[ִי-]
2m	åk, 'āk	ךָ- [ךֶ-], ךְ- [ךְ-]¹	k	ךָ-	ǝk, īk	ֶיךָ-, ֶיךְ-
2f	'īk, 'ek, ǝk ik	ךֵ-, ךְ-, ךִ- (-ךִי², -כִי³, -כֵי⁴)		ךְ-	ǝk, 'īk	ַיִךְ- [ֵיִךְ-] (-ֵכֶה⁵, -ֵכִי⁶)
3m	u (e, ē'u)	וֹ (-הוּ), (-יוּ⁷)	ē'u iyyu	הוּ, וּ	o	ָיו-, -ֵהוּ), (-ֵימוֹ-), (-ֹהִי?⁸)
3f	a, (å)'ā	ה- ָ, ֶהָ- (-ֶיהָ-)?	iyya	הָ	iyya	ֶיהָ-

Plural Suffixes

	After consonant		After vowel		Plural noun	
	SH	TH	SH	TH	SH	TH
1	ånu	נוּ-, ֵנוּ-	nu	נוּ	īnu	ֵינוּ-
2m	kimma īkimma	ְכֶם-, ֶכֶם-	kimma	כֶם (-ֵיכֶם⁹, כֶם¹⁰)	īkimma	ֵיכֶם- (-ֵיכֶם-¹¹)
2f		ְכֶן-, ֶכֶן-, (-כֶנָה⁹)¹²	kǝn	כֶן		ֵיכֶן- (-ֵיכֶנָה¹³)
3m	imma (ēmma) (īyyimma)	ְהֶם-, הֶם-, ָהֵמָּה- (-מוֹ¹⁴, -הָם¹⁵)	īyyimma	הֶם	īyyimma	ֵיהֶם- ֵיהֵמָּה¹⁶ (-ֵימוֹ)
3f	inna ēnna (īyyinna) ǝn	ְהֵן-, הֵן-, ָהֵנָּה-, (-הֵן¹⁷, ֶהֵן¹⁸, -ָנָה¹⁹, -ֶנָה²⁰, -ֶנָּה²¹, -ָנָּה²²)	īyyinna	הֵן	īyyinna	ֵיהֶן- (-ֵיהֵנָה)

3.2.8.1 The following are examples of the rare forms of possessive suffixes in the table above: (1) e.g., דֵּיֵךְ, אַיֵּכָּה; (2) e.g., אַלְמְנוּתַיִךְ (Isa 54:4), עֲצָתָיִךְ (Isa 47:13), בִּבְנוֹתַיִךְ (Ezek 16:31). (3) שְׁלִשְׁתֵּיךְ (Ezek 5:12); אַשְׁרֵיךְ; (4) e.g., רָעָתֵכִי, (Jer 11:15); (5) e.g., מְנוּחָיְכִי (Ps 116:7); (6) מַלְאֲכֵכֶה (Na 2:14); (7) וַחֲמִשְׁתָיו (Lv 5:24): (8) according to those (Sa'adia Ga'on, David Qimḥi) who interpret פָּנֵימוֹ (Ps 11:7), עָלֵימוֹ (Job 20:23), and other such forms as "his face," "upon him," etc.; (9) in the word מִן: מִכֶּם, מִכֶּן. (10) e.g., בְּהִזָּרוֹתֵיכֶם (Ezek 6:8), זְנוּתֵיכֶם (Nu 14:33), and once in SH: zūnātīkimma (SP Nu 14:33 זונתיכם); (11) תִּפְוֹצוֹתֵיכֶם (Jer 25:34) as understood by the traditional commentators; (12) זַמַּתְכֶנָה (כָּ)פִסְתוֹתֵיכֶנָה; (13) כְּסָתוֹתֵיכֶנָה (Ezek 13:20); (14) כֻּלָּהָם (2 Sa 23:6); (15) חֶלְבָּמוֹ (Ps 17:10), פְּרִימוֹ (Ps 21:11); (16) אֲלֵיהֵמָה (Ezek 40:16); (17) פִּתְהֵן (Isa 3:17); (18) מִלִּבְהֵן (Ezek 13:17); לְבַדְּהֶן (Gn 21:28); (19) לְכָלְהֵנָה (1 Kgs 7:37), בְּתוֹכְהֵנָה (Ezek 16:53); (20) לְבַדָּנָה (Gn 21:29), כֻּלָּנָה (Gn 42:36), and others; (21) קִרְבֶּנָּה (Gn 41:21); (22) לְיַחְמֵנָּה (Gn 30:41); since it is an infinitive, the נ may have been geminated following the verbal paradigm.

236   Pronoun

Object Suffixes
3.2.9 Singular objects

	Perfect		After consonant Imperfect		After vowel	
	SH	TH	SH	TH	SH	TH
1	âni	־ִנִי (־ְנִ־)	inni, âni	־ֵנִ־	ni	נִי¹
2m	åk, 'āk	־ְךָ [־ֶךָ], ־ָךְ (־ֶךָ²)	åk, 'āk	־ֶךָּ [־ֶךָ] (־ֶךָ), (ךָ)³	ək, k	(ךָ) ךְ
2f		־ָךְ ־ֵךְ־, (־ֶךָ)			k	ךְ
3m	u (iyyu) â(mu)?	־ֵהוּ ו (ה), מוֹ	ē'u, innu (nnu)	־ֶנּוּ ־ֵ־הוּ (־ֶנְהוּ)⁴ (־ֶנּוּ־)	ē'u	הוּ, ו
3f	a	־ָה	(iyya) inna	־ֶנָּה ־ָ־הָ (־ֶנְהָ־)	(uww)a (iyy)a	הָ

Plural objects

	Perfect		After consonant Imperfect		After vowel	
	SH	TH	SH	TH	SH	TH
1	ânu	־ָנוּ	ânu	־ֵנוּ, (נוּ)	nu	נוּ⁵
2m masc.		־ְכֶם	kimma	־ְכֶם		כֶם
3m masc. imma		־ָם, (ת־)ם	imma âmu	־ֵם ־ֵמוֹ	mma âmu	ם מוֹ־, ־מוֹ⁶
3f fem.		־ֵ־ן, ־ֵ־ן				־ן

3.2.9.1 The following are examples of the forms of object suffixes in the table above: (1) e.g., רְמִיתֻנִי (1 Sa 19:17), or צָמְתֻנִי (Zech 7:5); without the object suffix, the verb ends with a consonant: רָמִית, צמתם; (2) וּבֵרֲכֶךָ (Dt 24:13 wbarrēkåk); (3) אֶתְּקֶנְךָ (Jer 22:24); (4) e.g., וְקָבְנוֹ (Nu 23:13); (5) including such forms as הֶעֱלִיתָנוּ (Nu 21:5); regarding the vowel before the suffix in SH, see 6.3.2.4; (6) כִּסָּמוֹ, תְּבִאֵמוֹ (Ex 15:10,17), יְכַסְיֻמוֹ (Ex 15:5).

3.3 Other Pronouns

3.3.1 Demonstratives
3.3.1.1 The Samaritan grammarians distinguish, too, between the demonstrative of near reference and the demonstrative of distant reference.[15] Not all that is in TH is found in SH, though, and not everything considered a demonstra-

---

[15] See *LOT* I, 15ff., 191ff.

3.2 Pronominal Suffixes

tive in TH is similarly understood in SH, and vice versa. These, then, are the demonstratives:

Demonstratives of Near Reference: זה *zē*, זאת *zē'ot* (see 1.5.3.2), אלה *illa*, and with the addition of the definite article: *azze, azzē'ot, â'illa*.

Demonstratives of Distant Reference: ההוא *â'ū*, ההיא *â'ī*, ההם *â'imma*. The form ההן is unattested in the Pentateuch, but the grammarian Abū Yisḥaq has no qualms about including it (*LOT* I, 17) among the demonstratives, and he presumably pronounced it *â'inna*.

3.3.1.2 It is noteworthy that SH does not have the form זו (זֹה), which does not appear in the Pentateuch, and the form זו is also unattested, זה appearing in its place (Ex 15:13,16). The form הלז (thus SP Gn 24:65, 37:19 in place of הלזה), pronounced *allåz*, is not a demonstrative. The Samaritan tradition understands it as: "radiant, happy."[16] Thus, the form of the demonstrative has been preserved precisely, but its original meaning has been replaced.[17] In the form הלז, SH chose the path of shortening the form (from *hallåze*), while it did not do so with the demonstrative (ה)אלה; indeed, SP consistently reads האלה in place of האל. The 3rd masc. sing. personal pronoun without a preceding ה does not serve in SP as an attribute with a demonstrative function. Instead, it always appears preceded by the definite article ה, and, thus, one finds in SP בלילה ההוא (Gn 19:33, etc.), הקדשה ההיא (Gn 38:21). It does serve as a demonstrative when it appears as a predicate, e.g., in Gn 41:28 הוא הדבר, which one reading of ST renders הא ממלל(ה). It should also be noted that in the pronominal forms ההוא and ההיא, the first syllable (with ה) did not cause a shift of stress to the penult, and that unlike the process of בהם > *bēmma*, the form does not become **ēmma* or **åmma*, but instead the *i* vowel is maintained.

3.3.1.3 The reading ואת כי שטית (SP Nu 5:20) *wit ki šåṭīti* provides evidence that SH is aware of the use of את as a demonstrative, as in Zech 7:7, where את הדברים

---

[16] In ST הלז is rendered זעיה (or זהיה), and in SAV it is usually translated as بهي or مسنبشر.

[17] We have already pointed out in our commentary to *Hammeliṣ* (*LOT* II, 499, note to l. 77) that notwithstanding the above, the Samaritan tradition does preserve a remnant of the demonstrative meaning of the word הלז, whether one accepts our interpretation of the word אכית as a compound formed from אך ית (on ית, see 3.3.1.3) or whether another interpretation is preferred. In any case, it seems to us necessary to add that the word אכית, which we have not located elsewhere in SH, apparently has a counterpart in the language of the Palestinian Talmud in the expression כותי פשיטא (or כתי פשיטא). S. Lieberman, in his commentary on the Palestinian Talmud, *On the Yerushalmi* [Jerusalem, 1929], 80ff. [Hebrew], and J. N. Epstein, *Introduction to the Amoraitic Literature* (Jerusalem, 1963), 391, [Hebrew], have shown how this word has been corrupted in the sources, both in printed editions and in manuscripts, due to its being rare and exceptional. The form כותי is undoubtedly a corruption of כיתי, a form close to the Samaritan אכית, and it is easier to understand לית (פשיטא) in y. *Ma'asrot* 54a (3:1) as being a corruption of כית, with י after the כ. The meaning "this is..." fits well with the context there.

means "these are the words," and according to common use in MH (e.g., *m. Berakhot* 3:2), although ST reads וית (and not וֹאתי!), and an Arabic translation renders this phrase بذا (see *LOT* III/1, 74). The forms אותו *ūtu* and אתהן *u'ūtiyyinna* in Lv 20:14 are demonstrative pronouns, since the verb ישרפו is read as *Nif'al* (cf. ST יתוקדן). The same is true of the reading *ūtimma* in Lv 26:39 (אֹתָם יִמְקּוּ), which is intended as a demonstrative, and, indeed, SAV renders وهم يخشعون and ST renders יתון ישתנקון (יתון is a demonstrative!).

3.3.2 The Definite Article -ה

Since the definite article originated as a demonstrative, it will be dealt with in this chapter.

1. The definite article -ה is pronounced as a short *a* (on rare occasions, *å*) before a noun whose first consonant is not א, ה, ח, or ע, and the first consonant is geminated. The vowel *a* is replaced by *i* in only two nouns: *willåṭå* והלטאה, *wikkå > *wukkå* הכח, both in Lv 11:30; ST and SAV attest, in fact, that ה has been understood as the definite article.

2. Before a noun beginning with א, ה, ח, or ע, the definite article is generally pronounced as a long *å*.

3. If the vowel of the initial א, ה, ח, or ע is a form of A (i.e., *a* or *å*), the vowel of the definite article combines with it and takes on its shape.

4. If the initial consonant of the noun is a pronounced ע, the ע remains in its initial position even once it is made definite, with few exceptions.

Examples:

1. *addēbår* הדבר, *ayyårdån* הירדן, *attūra* התורה, *arrē'os* הראש;
2. *å''īš* האיש, *å'or* האור, *a''ū* ההוא, *å'ibbi* החיי, *å''ūr* העור;
3. *å:raṣ* הארץ, *å:dəš* החדש, *årqi* הרקיע (<**å'arqi*);
4. *å:bad* העבד, *'åm* העם (עַם, too, is pronounced *åm*), *'āyyəm* החיים (חיים also is pronounced *'āyyəm*); but *å''åd* האחד, *å''ay* החי.

The prepositions ב, ל, and כ, as well as the copulative ו, take on the vowel of the definite article, e.g., *bå:dəš* בחדש, *wå'ibbi* והחיי.

The definite article sometimes causes a loss of gemination in a particular noun, e.g., *'årəm* ההרים (*'arrəm* ערים!), *wåmå* והאמה (*åmmå* אמה).

> Note: As to the reason for the difference between *amdåbbər* = TH מְדַבֵּר and *ammådåbbər* = TH הַמְדַבֵּר (Gn 45:12), see 1.3.2 and also 7.1.

3.3.3 Interrogative, Indefinite, and Relative Pronouns

3.3.3.1 The interrogative pronoun *mī* מי refers to humans, *må* מה to all else. The question in Gn 33:8, מי לך המתנה, causes a problem for SAV, which renders it as مِن لك and not, with ST, as مِن لك In Nu 22:9 SP reads מה האנשים האלה, and SAV and ST translate as "what." All the peculiarities of מה in TH — the gemination of a following consonant, the variation of its vowel as מָה and מֶה — are unknown in SH, and even with the addition of the preposition ב or ל, the form of the interrogative pronoun itself remains unchanged: *bâmå* במה, *lēmå* למה. The difference of vowels between במה and למה is noteworthy. The preposition ל with possessive pronoun suffixes takes the form *lå-*, as in *lånu* לנו and *låkimma* לכם. Thus, the form *lēma* is parallel to לְמָה and is unrelated to לָמָּה. The word מן in Ex 16:15 is not regarded by the Samaritans as a Hebrew pronoun, while the word מי in מי יקימנו (SP Dt 33:11) is not interpreted by them as an interrogative: ST translates ית, and SAV حتى لا.

3.3.3.2 As is well known, the interrogative pronouns mentioned serve also to introduce indirect questions, to indicate indefiniteness, as a correlative (in an expression such as מי אשר in Ex 32:33), and they may serve alone as relative pronouns, as for example, למי זהב התפרקו (Ex 32:24) or מה אקב... ומה אזעם (Nu 23:8), as well as the Samaritan reading in Nu 23:3 *wdabbər må yarriyyåni*, which makes מה into a relative pronoun and not a correlative particle as in the Tiberian reading וּדְבַר מָה. However, it should be recalled that SAV to Nu 23:8 understands מה as a negative particle: لا العن ولا اشتم.

Note: on מה and its collocations, see 6.3.15.

3.3.3.3 Demonstratives and the definite article may, of course, introduce relative clauses. It should be borne in mind that SH employs the demonstrative pronoun זה precisely for that function (see 3.3.1.2). As we know, the subordinating conjunction ש does not appear in the Pentateuch, but instead, אשר fulfills that function. Nonetheless, the existence of ש- as a relative clause marker is not entirely absent from the traditions of the Samaritans or their grammarians, on which see 6.3.18.

4. NOUN

4.0 Preliminaries

4.0.1 On the formation of Hebrew words and the analysis of their structural components, see above 2.0.1–4.

The primary manner of noun formation in Biblical Hebrew, including SH, is by means of a noun pattern (משקל) — a combination of root and infixed formative. Far less common is a combination of base and suffix formative — the latter a suffix such as י, ה, ת, or ים. In classifying nouns one should distinguish between nouns in compound patterns bearing endings, such as דלקת, יבשה, בתולים, קהלת, and צהרים, and nouns in which the same endings indicate feminine forms as distinct from masculine, or plural forms as distinct from singular, such as: אילה, שומרת, and שומרים. Examples of the first type are categorized as a matter of word formation, while examples of the second must be categorized according to the masculine singular form — the absolute form. Certain nouns, such as עֲרָבַּיִם, may be variously considered in either of the two categories. Since not all nouns occur in their absolute form in the Pentateuch, and the full declension does not appear for all the nouns whose absolute form does appear, there is no alternative to listing reconstructed forms. A reconstructed absolute form is given where no such form appears in SP. This is so even where it does appear in the Tiberian Biblical text, because we cannot draw conclusions about SH on the basis of evidence from TH. Instead, our knowledge of extra-Biblical Samaritan Hebrew has provided the basis for reconstructed noun forms in the language of SP. In reconstructed forms, there is considerable doubt regarding the short vowels a — $â$, especially when they appear in an unaccented syllable, since in the declension of certain nouns, those vowels tend to be interchangeable. In particular, a in a closed syllable may be replaced by $â$ in an open syllable.

4.0.2 The character of the root and Hebrew phonological rules cause a particular noun pattern formative to apply to several forms different in appearance (surface forms); for example, the ֶ‑ֶ pattern in TH includes from the root מל"ך, the noun מֶלֶךְ; from the root מל"ח, the noun מֶלַח; from the root מע"ל, the noun מַעַל; from the root בכ"י, the noun בֶּכִי (pausal form) and בְּכִי (absolute and construct); from the root בי״ת, the noun בַּיִת. The diachronic study of TH generally maintains the morphological unity of such disparate forms by establishing the common formula behind them in the historical stage preceding their different development in TH. Thus, the formula common to all the forms listed above is, according to the system of historical grammar, *qatl*. That unity is still quite evident in the declension of these nouns in TH, the common feature being the monosyllabic base form occurring with the possessive suffix: -מַלְכּ, -מִלְח, -מֵעֲל, -בֵּית, -בְּכִי. This is not so, however, of other nouns, such as גִּבּוֹר and דַּיָּן, which are combined by diachronic grammar under the rubric *qattāl*, or the nouns חֲמוֹר and אֱסָר, combined under the rubric *qitāl*. In the observable state of TH, these pairs have nothing in common — neither in their absolute forms nor in their declined forms. Establishing a common formula in TH, therefore, requires that one, first of all, distinguish between the surface form of a noun and the noun pattern to which it belongs. These two are related to one another in a way similar to the relationship between a phone and a phoneme. Just as a phoneme may be realized in various phones, so a noun pattern may be realized by nouns of different appearances according to the characteristics of the roots of those nouns and according to the character of the vowels and the rules for their substitution or elimination in particular structures in TH or SH. For example, the nouns גִּבּוֹר and דַּיָּן, which belong to different noun patterns in TH, may be assigned to one pattern in the earlier stage — *qattāl*. Similarly, the nouns שָׁלוֹם and עָנָן, are assigned to one earlier pattern, *qatāl*, while the nouns אֱנוֹשׁ, חֲמוֹר, זְרוֹעַ, and בְּרוֹשׁ, which belong to the same pattern in TH, belong to different patterns in the earlier stage: *qitāl* (the first two) and *qutāl* (the latter two). This sort of change occurred in Hebrew not only in the shift from the pre-historic (or PS) stage to the historical stage, but between various types of the language as well. For instance, in TH גִּבּוֹר and צִפּוֹר are assigned to different patterns, due to their different declensions — גִּבּוֹרִים vs. צִפֳּרִים; while in SH they must be assigned to the same pattern: *gibbor* and *ṣibbor*, *gibbūrəm* and *ṣibbūrəm*. Alternatively, we find that in TH אָדוֹן, אָתוֹן, and כָּבוֹד all belong to the same pattern, while in SH they all differ from one another: *ādon* : *ādanni*; *kābod* : *kābūdi*; *itton* : *ittūni*.

4.0.3 In TH, where changes occur in the vowels of a word during declension in proportion to the distance of the vowel from the stress, the question is: which of the many forms in one paradigm should serve as the representative of that pattern? The question arises in the synchronic description of TH and not in its diachronic analysis, where the Proto-Hebrew or PS form defines the pattern. Thus, of the forms מֶלֶךְ, מַלְכּוֹ, מְלָכִים, מַלְכֵי, etc., diachronic grammar states without difficulty that the pattern is *qatl*, while synchronic grammar could choose, instead of the absolute form, the form מַלְכּ, which appears in declension, to stand for the pattern. In fact, it would be wise to do so, since this would mean choosing a form from which one may generate the other forms according to the phonological rules of that language. From among the forms תֹּם, תֻּמּוֹ, תֻּמִּים, etc., it would do well to build the pattern on -תֻּם, and not תֹּם, since the latter form can be explained on the basis of TH phonological rules operating on the former — *qibbuṣ* becomes *ḥolem* in an accented syllable, and gemination is eliminated in a final consonant — but not vice versa, since there is the phenomenon of *ḥolem* retaining its value and a final consonant is not always doubled when it appears in the middle of a declined form. It would appear advisable to construct SH noun patterns, too, according to this principle,[1] such as assigning *dērək* דרך and *nēdår* נדר to one pattern due to their similarity in declension: *dirku, nidru*, etc., or distinguishing, for example, between *målək* מלך and *qådəš* קדש on the basis of their different declensions: *malkåk, qådēšåk*. In the following description, though, this principle has not been followed consistently. Instead, in the simple patterns (4.1), the noun, as it appears in the absolute form, has been employed to represent the pattern. Thus, nouns such as *dērək* and *nēdår* are taken to belong to different patterns, while *målək* and *qådəš* belong to one pattern. The reason for this is as follows:

4.0.4 SH is markedly different from TH and from non-Samaritan Aramaic in that the vowels of a word tend to be maintained throughout its declension (because of the difference in stress and the absence of a *šəwa*), and even some originally monosyllabic nouns in PS ("segholates" in TH) have been affected by this process. In this way, SH resembles classical Arabic. Unlike the situation in TH, one finds that vowels are retained (with changes in their quality, of course, according to the rules of SH) in such words as *gåmål* גמל: *gåmåli, gåmålåk, gåmåliyyimma*; *rå'oq* רחוק: *rå'uqot*; *kåbåš* כבש: *kåbåšəm*; *låbən* לבן: *låbēna, låbēnot*; *qådəš* קדש: *qådēšåk, qådēši* (plural construct form); and others. Thus, it seems self-evident that the form with no pronominal or other suffix should serve as the base form, and it would not be wise to diverge from this practice for the sake of upholding principle alone, even with those nouns in which changes take place in their declension according to TH, such as *kåsəf* כסף: *kasfu*. We did not see fit, therefore, to employ a *faqd* pattern for this purpose, especially since the phenomenon under consideration can be considered a remnant of an earlier state of the language, as is stated in 4.6.4.2.

Restricting the application of the principle (4.0.3) is intended to exclude those nouns in SH whose absolute form ends with a vowel and those derived from III-guttural roots or III-*y*. This is due to the fact that the effect of the original consonant on the structure of the word or on its declension is still

---

[1] This is described and examples are given in my article "Hebrew Grammar," col. 108ff.

evident, and it is, therefore, still present. Nouns such as *zēra* זרע, *mēṣå* מצח, *qåmå* קמח, and *yēra* ירח do not behave in declension as feminine nouns with *a/å*, but instead: *zē'rāk* (< **zēra'åk*) זרעך, *mēṣå'u* מצחו, *yē'rīm* (< **yērī'im*) ירחים, *gådi* גדי : *gadyi* = גְּדְיֵ. Therefore, they are classified with noun patterns ending with a consonant: *fēqad*, *fēqåd*, etc. In these nouns, as in the prefixed patterns (4.2), the distinction between the surface form and pattern is appropriate for SH as well.

The method adopted in the present work for classifying nouns according to patterns seems to us to be appropriate for SH in the state in which it appears, since the method takes into account the transition from pattern to pattern (from the "original" to the present one) — this applies to the simple patterns — and makes it easier to establish the place of SH in word formation vis-à-vis TH and vis-à-vis their common Proto-Hebrew heritage. This last point seems to us important, since it is immeasurably more difficult to demonstrate the close similarity of the two traditions, TH and SH, in the word formation of nouns than of verbs. This is true not only of these two traditions but of two cognate Semitic languages, because, in fact, it is not two forms alone that are compared — i.e., the two combinations of phonemes that constitute the forms — but the forms in relation to their contents, the concepts they embody, such as tense, person, gender, number, the verbal noun, the infinitive, etc. It is according to these that we measure the relations between the two traditions, or even between two morphological groups (verbal classes) within the same language. When we are dealing with nouns, though, in their given state in historical languages, we are not able to establish criteria for comparison that are as clear as with verbs (with the possible exception of a few noun patterns). Thus, we are forced to compare external form to external form without their necessarily having a common content.[2] The cause of this difference is to be found in the evident fact that nouns undergo a greater degree of lexicalization, with consequent damage to the grammatical uniqueness of their morphemes, especially of the type known as "noun patterns."

4.0.5 Unlike the verb (see 2.0.1), the noun displays forms with roots of fewer than three consonants, such as פה, יד, דם, בן, אמה, and שפה.[3] Some have had their roots expanded to three radicals, whether in order to generate a verb root, as

---

[2] Barth, *Nominalbildung*, 1ff., bemoans this, and as a consequence he constructs his comparative approach (in the diachronic plane) on the basis of the contents of the forms as he defines them. As a result, the same pattern may be treated in several places according to the characteristics attributed to it. The "contents" of nouns, however, unlike verbs, may be defined in different ways, and perhaps for this reason, Barth's taxonomy has not been generally accepted in comparative grammar.

[3] This is discussed by Nöldeke in his *Neue Beiträge*, 109–178.

with אֶחָה,⁴ שִׁשָּׁה in MH, or in the declension of the noun, as with אֵשׁ : אִשּׁוֹ and גַּג : גַּגּוֹ. Such nouns should be treated as having been generated from triradical roots, and in any case, structurally that is how they are in historical Hebrew.

Such expansions, however, are not always indentical in TH and SH. For example, דם in TH has a biradical root, just like יד, while in SH the root has been expanded to דמ"ם: the forms דמים and דמי are pronounced *dammәm* and *dammi* in SH. In classifying the nouns and noun patterns, we have employed the root form that is necessary or most likely according to the linguistic tradition of SH. Therefore, for example, the root of ע is biradical despite the existence in Aramaic of איתי, the root of עת is עת"ת without regard to the various etymological derivations from ענ"ת or from וע"ד, and the root of *šišša* ששה in SH is שש"ש and not שד"ש (not to mention PS *šdṯ*). The SH counterpart of TH שר"ר is שו"ר, and TH סר"ר has as its SH equivalent סו"ר. Wherever this classification is inconsistent with regard to Proto-Hebrew (or to what is accepted in the historical grammar of TH), this reflects the historical development of SH.

4.0.6. In patterns in which changes occur in the declension of their nouns, the changes have been mentioned in detail according to their type, but quantitative changes in vowels have not been considered changes, since they are automatic: a short vowel appears in a closed syllable, a long one in an open syllable. This is not so of qualitative changes, which cannot be predicted by general rules, but each is a type unto itself.

4.0.7 Three different sets of letters will be used here to indicate the noun roots in patterns, in order to avoid confusion among the historical stages and various versions of Hebrew: *fqd* for SH, פע"ל for TH, and *qtl* for Proto-Hebrew. Just as in the treatment of verbs the quadriradical roots were treated belonging to the stems in which the second radical is geminated, so in the nouns patterns as well, the quadriradicals will be listed among the patterns with gemination of one consonant, as long as, from the perspective of the noun, there is no difference between the two. For patterns based on two consonants (from "weak" roots), the first two of the three representative consonants (e.g., *f* and *q* of *fqd*) will be employed to describe the pattern, without regard to the location of the weakness (4.1.2). In patterns of four and five consonants, the third and, if necessary, also the second of the three consonant symbols will be repeated (4.1.4.11–12), without regard to their gemination in the root.

---

⁴ If the vocalization וְשִׁשִּׁיתֶם in Ezek 45:13 is an authentic tradition, the verb ששה was born when Biblical Hebrew was still a spoken language. In any case, it exists in later Hebrew, e.g., מְשֻׁשֶּׁה meaning "hexagon."

4.1 Simple Noun Patterns

4.1.0 The term "simple patterns" refers to all those patterns which are a combination of a root with a vowel or with a discontinuous sequence of vowels, as distinguished from "compound patterns," which have, in addition to these vowels, consonants added before the first radical or after the last radical (other than feminine suffixes).

4.1.1 Forms with One Consonant

4.1.1.1 At first glance, it would seem that in SH there are many patterns of only one consonant with a vowel after it (long or extra long), since alongside the few nouns originating in this category there are also nouns in which a guttural consonant ceased to be pronounced, such as *rī* ריח, *rē* רע, *'ā* אח, *rā* רע, *dā*: ראה, *fā* פאה, *kū* כח, and *rū* רוח. Since these words, though, belong to patterns that end with a consonant — as stated above, 4.0.4 — SH is left with only the following single-consonant nouns: *fī* פי (construct state), *šī* שה, *dī* די, *fā* פה (TH פֶּה), and *šū* שוא. The word צי is unattested in SH, and where TH reads צים (Nu 24:24), SH reads יוציאם, and from the form *ayyi* איי (Gn 10:5) one cannot infer the singular form *ī*, especially since we find that *fī* is declined as *fiyyåk* (< *fī* + *åk*) פיך, *fiyyu* פיו, and similarly *šiyyu* שיו, maintaining the *i* vowel before the pronominal suffix. The word דים (TH דָּיָּם, Ex 36:7) is pronounced *dem*; in SH it does not contain a pronominal suffix, but a plural ending of *dī* > *dī'īm* > *dīm* > *dem*, as ST and SAV also attest, while *mådi* (Ex 36:5 TH מִדֵּי) is understood to be derived from the root מד״ד = מו״ד (see 4.1.2.8[4] note).

4.1.2 Forms with Two Consonants

4.1.2.1 *fiq, feq.* These two forms are two aspects of one pattern in SH, not only because several nouns appear in both, but also because each is a product of the very same historical processes. If the vowel were not accented and thus expressly enunciated as *i* or *e*, its place would be taken by *ə*; indeed, in certain instances the syllable is pronounced with *ə* even in an accented syllable such as *məm* מים. See *LOT* III/1, 113.

    a. Those with an *i* vowel are *bin* בין, *zit* זית, *rib* ריב, *riq* ריק; *zir* זר.

    b. Those with an *e* vowel are *den* דין, *deš* דיש, *ser* סיר, *ṣeṣ* ציץ, *qer* קיר, *qen* קן, *šeš* שש (meaning "linen fabric").

    c. Those with both *i* and *e* are *il/el* אל, *bit/bet* בית, *bir/ber* באר, *gir/ger* גר, *id/ed* עד, *iṣ/eṣ* עץ. A Samaritan grammarian (*LOT* I, 283ff.) proposed general rules for a few words, but his rules do not always agree with the pronunciation currrent in our time. It can be discerned that the forms with *e* were pausal forms, but not in every situation that warrants a pausal form do we find an *e* vowel today, and vice versa. Different readers sometimes differ on this point.

In any case, it should be pointed out that in the phrase גר יתום (Dt 24:17, 27:19), the pronunciation is *gir*, and in Dt 27:19, a *maqqef* joins the two words in the Jewish Pentateuch.

4.1.2.2 Two types can be discerned in the declension:
1. those that maintain a simple second radical, such as *bin* בן: *bīni, bīnåk, binkimma; zit* זית: *zītåk, zītəm; ser* סיר: *sīrot, sīrūto; deš* דיש: *dīšu; i/es* עץ: *īṣåk, īṣa, īṣəm, īṣo; be/ir* באר: *bīrot; ger* גר: *gīrəm*;
2. those that geminate the second radical: *zir* זר: *zirru; qen* קן: *qinnåk, qinnu*.

4.1.2.3 For a number of nouns that appear in SH only in declension, such as *giggu* גגו, *iṣṣəm* חצים, *kirrəm* כרים, *siddo* צדיו, *šiddəm* שָׂדִים, *šīdəm* שֵׂדִים, and *bīṣəm* ביצים, it cannot be determined whether the absolute form has an *i* or an *e* vowel, and some of them could even be assigned to the *faq* or *fåq* patterns (see 4.1.2.7).

Note 1. On nouns that have an *e* vowel in declension, such as *dēgi* = דְּגֵי (*dēga* = דְּגָה) or *mēti* = מְתֵי, but no attested absolute form, see *faq* (4.1.2.8 [4]).

2. *be/ir*: even though spelled באר, its pronunciation implies a form parallel to TH בֵּיר (Jer 6:7). The pronunciation of זאב in SH (4.1.2.5) supports this assumption.

4.1.2.4 Thus, in SH some PS noun patterns have merged: *qil* (עץ) and *qatl/qitl* of the ע"י class (רִיב, בַּיִת) and of the ע"ע class (כַּר, קֵן).

4.1.2.5 *fīq*. The length of the vowel is a result of contact with a guttural consonant:
1. those with a guttural first consonant are *īl* = אַיִל, חַיִל, חֵיל; *īš* = אִישׁ; *īn* = אַיִן, עַיִן; *īr* = עִיר; *rī* = רִיחַ.
2. those with a guttural second consonant are *zīb* זאב, *ṣīr* צעיר, and *šīr* שעיר, to which we may add *rīm* רחים and *mīm* מעים (*bå'mīk* במעיך). These two types have different origins: the first began as a monosyllable of the *qatl/qitl* pattern (see 4.1.2.4), and the second is derived from a two-syllable pattern that contracted to a monosyllable. It seems that the first syllable is not derived directly from PS, i.e., *ṣīr* is not a direct derivative of *ṣuġair* (cf. TH צָעִיר), but is instead derived from *ṣeʿīr* > *ṣiʿīr*. Similarly, *zīb* is derived from *ziʾib*, i.e., a form parallel to TH זְאֵב, and *šīr* originates from שָׂעִיר. In this pattern, several PS patterns have merged: *qitl/qatl, qutail* (?), *qatīl*, and *qital* (רֵחַיִם).

4.1.2.6 *fēq*. This pattern appears where the second radical is a guttural, and it is always a derivative of a bisyllabic word, e.g., *bēd* בעד, *lēm* לחם, *nēl* נחל, *rēm* רחם, *rēd* רעד, and *tēt* תחת. In declension, the third radical is geminated, e.g., *bēddåk*

4.1 Simple Noun Patterns

בעדך, *rēmma* רחמה, *tēttək* תחתיך, *tēttiyya* תחתיה, and *ṣērrəm* צהרים. From לחם we find, alongside *lēmmu* לחמו, also *lē:mu*. Its origin is a PS monosyllabic pattern, the same as the one underlying *fāq*. The difference in the realization of the vowel in SH may be illustrated as follows: PS *ṭa'm*, TH טַעַם, Syriac *ṭ'em* [Biblical Aramaic both טְעֵם and טַעַם], SH *ṭēm* — as against PS *ba'l*, TH בַּעַל, Aramaic בְּעֵל, SH *bāl*. For the *fēq* form, we must assume an intermediate stage within SH: פְּעֵל.

4.1.2.7 *faq, fåq*. Even though the relationship between *a* and *å* is not similar to the relationship between *i* and *e*, we must treat these two patterns, too, as one, because of the identical types of declension of the nouns in these patterns. It is even clear that these two are the result of the same historical processes and at a relatively late stage, their absolute forms diverged.

a. Those with an *a* vowel are: *ab* אב, *'ā* אח, *al* אֶל, *am* = אֶם, *af* אף, *aš* אש, *at* את (the preposition), *ban* בן, *bat* בת, *dat* דת, *an* הן, *'ag* חג, *'ay* חי, *yad* יד, *yaš* יש, *kal* כל, *kan* כן, *lab* לב, *lā* = לָח, לָח, *man* = מן, *nad* נד, *'ad* עד, *az* עז, *'az* עז, *iy*, *'al* על, *am* = עם, *'am* = עם, *at* עת, *rā* רע, רַע, *šam* שם, *šan* שן.

b. Those containing an *å* vowel are: *båd* בד, *gåz* גז, *gån* גן, *dål* דל, *dåm* דם, *dåq* דק, *dår* דר, *år* הר, *båb* וו, *zåg* זג, *zåk* זך, *zår* זר, *ån* חן, *åq* חק, *tål* טל, *tåf* טף, *yåm* ים, *kåf* כף, *låg* לג, *mån* מן, *nås* נס, *nåṣ* נץ, *sål* סל, *får* פר, *ṣår* צר, *qåš* קש, *råb* רב, *råk* רך, *šår* שר, *tål* תל, *tåm* תם, *går* תר.

4.1.2.8 The following types may be discerned in declension:

1. Nouns which maintain a simple second radical, in which case: (a) *faq* generally blends with *fåq* through the substitution of *å* for *a*, as in כן, דת, אב, and ש׳: *åbi, åbūtimma, dåtu, kånəm,* and *yåšak*, on the model of שׂ, זך: *šårəm, zåka*; (b) when the second radical is guttural, the *faq* pattern retains its vowel, e.g., *lā'əm* לחים, *lā'e* לֶחֹה, *rā'əm* רעים, *'ā'o* אחיו, and in the prepositions על and עד as well: *'ålək, 'ådi*; (c) in the nouns אש, בן (singular), יד, and שם, the *a* vowel is replaced by *ē*, as in *yēdi, yēdak, ēšu, bēni* (equivalent to TH בְּנֵי, but the form equivalent to TH בְּנֵי is pronounced *båni*); and the substitution of *ī* for *a* in *al* אל: *īli, īlək*.

Note: *yåšat* (SP Gn 23:8 יש(א)ת; TH יֵשׁ אֶת) is a compound word understood as a *Qal* 3rd person perfect, as attested by ST אתרעית, SAV هـوېـت. There exists also a (later?) interpretation identical with the Jewish tradition: ST אית ית, SAV كانـت في

2. Nouns in which the second radical is geminated: (a) those with an *å* vowel in the absolute form generally replace *å* with *a*, as in בד, כף, פר, and סל: *baddəm, kabbu, farrəm, farra, salləm*; (b) in the nouns טף, ים, יצר, and רב (= רַב, רֹב), the *å* vowel is maintained: *tåbbånu, tåfkimma, yåmməm, ṣårro, råbbot, råbbək*; (c) those with an *a* vowel generally replace *a* with *i*, as for example בת,

עֹז, לֵב, הֵן: *bitti, bittåk, libbi, libbu, innåk, izzəm*; (d) but the vowel is maintained in these nouns: אַף, חַג, חִי, יֵשׁ, כֹּל, עֹז, עַז, and עַם: *abbi, abbu,'aggåk,'ayyot, yašnu, yaškimma, kallu,'azzi,'ammi,'ammu*; (e) אָן חֵן is declined with an *i* vowel: *innåm* חֻנָּם.

3. The multiplicity of types of declension leads to the declining of some nouns in more than one way. Thus, we find: (a) *å* in place of anticipated *a*, e.g., *'ammåk* עִמָּךְ (although there is also *'ammåk*), and with the noun *kal* כֹּל: *kållåk, kållå, kållånu, kållåkimma*, and even *kåkål*, but *kallu* and also *albådkimma* לְבַדְּכֶם; (b) *a* and *e* in place of *i*: at אֵת: *itti, atkimma, ētimma*; at עֵת: *bēttu* (**be'ittu*), but among the words derived from עֵת are *'atta* עַתָּה and *'āti* עִתִּי (Lv 16:21, understood to mean "designated"); *aš* אֵשׁ: *ēši* and *bēš* (**be'eš*).

4. Because of the situation described in the previous paragraphs, it is impossible to determine with certainty the absolute forms of some nouns which only appear in SH declined, such as *sammən* סַמִּים, *tammən* תַּמִּים, and *ayyi* אַיֵּי, which appear to belong to the *fåq* pattern, but see 2(d) above, or such as *iṣṣəm* חִצִּים, *kirrəm* כָּרִים, and *ṣiddo* צִדִּיו, which appear to belong to the *faq* pattern, but see 2(e) above and 4.1.2.3.

> Note: The same is true of some other plural forms as well, such as *'arrəm* עָרִים and *battəm* בָּתִּים; *yåməm* יָמִים and *šåqəm* (TH שׁוֹקַיִם); and *mådi* = מַדִּי (SP Lv 6:3), which is understood to refer to measurement,[5] as ST attests.

4.1.2.9 The SH noun patterns discussed above continue the PS noun patterns *qal* and *qil*, and also the patterns *qitl* and *qatl* in the ע״ע class. These two have become intertwined in SH, but not so much so that the earlier situation in SH cannot be discerned through the thicket of mutual influences. The earlier situation is very similar to that found in TH:

a. In nouns in which the second radical is not geminated, the vowel in a closed syllable was presumably *a* (i.e., *faq*), whether that vowel was original or derived from *i* (e.g., **šim > šam*); and in an open syllable, *å* (or *ē*, if the original vowel was *i*). An *å* vowel in a closed syllable (i.e., *fåq*) was used only for special situations, perhaps as a pause marker. The general rule, then, was *faq: fåq-* or *fēq-*.

b. In nouns in which the second radical is geminated, *a* appears in stressed syllables and *a* or *i* in unstressed syllables, and the division between these two vowels was according to the original pattern: *qatl* or *qitl* — that is, *faq: faqq-* or *fiqq-*. In this type as well, an *å* vowel may appear in place of *a* in special

---

[5] I.e., the singular form is something like **mad*, and the noun is formed from a root of the ע״י class. Note the verb מָדוֹן in 2 Sa 21:20, which appears as the counterpart to מִדָּה in 1 Chr 20:6, and the Targum דמשחן at 2 Sa 21:20. See also David Qimḥi, *Sefer Ha-Shorashim, s.v.* מדד. As to the word *mådi* in Ex 36:5, while there are manuscripts of ST that render it as "measurement" (משחי), the reading ספוק and SAV كفو indicate that this term is parallel to TH מַדַּי(?) (2 Chr 30:3).

situations (proximity of certain sounds, pausal forms), in a manner similar to that known from TH: הָעָם/עַם, הָרֵעַ/רֵעַ, חָג/חַג, etc. The elimination of the conditioning factors governing the previous system led to a certain confusion in the fluctuations.

4.1.2.10 *fåq, fāq*. These forms apply only to nouns II-guttural, which are originally bisyllabic nouns that were reduced to one syllable with the disappearance of the guttural and the elimination of the division between two equal syllables. This process certainly occurred at a very late stage. It is doubtful whether it occurred when the language was still spoken (see 1.4.7). This would explain the lack of reduction of the vowel in a closed syllable.

a. Those with an *ā* vowel are: *bāl* בעל, **yād* יחד, *yār* יער, *mār* מחר, *māt* מעט, *māl* מעל, *nāš* נָחָשׁ, *nār* נער, *fām* פעם, *qāl* קהל, *rāb* רעב, *šāf* שחף, *šār = שַׁעַר*, שֵׁעָר, *tāš* תחש, *tār* תער.

b. Those with an *å* vowel are: *båq* בהק, *zåb* זהב, *tår* טהר, *lås* לחץ, *nåm* נאום, *fåd* פחד, *sår* צהר, *råm* ראם, *råb = רְחָב*, רֹחַב, *råq* רחק, *šåm* שהם, *šår = שְׁאָר*, שְׁאֵר, שָׁחוֹר, *tår* תאר, *tåt* תחת.[6]

4.1.2.11 In the declined forms, the following two patterns may be discerned:
1. One maintains a simple third radical, e.g., נעל: *nā:lu, nā:līkimma*; נער: *nā:ri, nā:ro*; קהל: *qā:limma*; פחד: *få:dåk, fådkimma*.
2. The other features gemination of the third radical, e.g., יחד: *yāddu*; תחש: *tāššam*; נחש: *nāššəm*; רחב: *råbbu, råbba*; לחץ: *låssånu*.

The noun בעל *bal* follows both of these patterns: *bålli (בעלי), bā:la, bā:lo*. The noun מעל *māl* is sometimes declined according to the *fāqəd* pattern: *båmā'elimma*. The noun מעט *måt* replaces *ā* with *å* after the exclamatory ה: *å'måt*.

4.1.2.12 The reason for the difference in gemination of the third radical in these forms may only be understood against their background in PS and their history within Hebrew. It is evident that in SH the PS monosyllabic patterns *qa/i/utl* (in TH the "segholate" nouns) merged with the PS bisyllabic patterns *qatal, qi/utal, qatul, qitāl* (in TH, e.g., שְׁאָר, שָׁחוֹר, מְעַט, נָחָשׁ). In some of the original monosyllabic noun forms, the second radical came into contact with the third, and during the time when gutturals were still pronounced in SH, the second radical assimilated to the third: **pa'maym > *pāmmēm > fāmmam* פעמים; other forms (in the plural) followed the gemination pattern, such as *tāššam* (*< *tāšəm < *tahašīm*) תחשים. The opposite also occurs: in certain words the

---

[6] Note that תחת appears as *fåq* meaning "instead of," while in its primary sense of "under" it appears as *fēq*. In addition, צהר in the sense of "window" or the like appears as *fåq*, but צהרים follows the *fēq* pattern.

gemination is cancelled, in keeping with the forms without gemination, even when these are originally monosyllabic words, such as *nā:lu* נעלו and *fā:du* פחדו, and obviously when the words are originally bisyllabic, such as *šā:ru* = שָׂעֲרוֹ. The merger of absolute forms brought about a disruption in the original patterns of declension (and of derivation). See also 1.3.4ff.

4.1.2.13 *fūq, foq.*

1. The *o* vowel, which is replaced by *ū* in declension (and in an open syllable) appears in this pattern in nouns with no guttural consonant, such as *dor* דור: *dūrūtimma*; *mot* מות: *mūti, mūtu*; *qol* קול: *qūlånu*.

2. The *ū* vowel appears if one of the radicals is an original guttural, such as *ūt* אות: *ūtot*; *ūd* עוד: *ūdinni*; *ūf* חוף; *ūl* עול: *olkimma*; *būr* בחור; *tūm* תהום: *tūmot*; *kū* כה; *rū* רוח: *ruwwåk*. Exceptions to this rule are *or* אור (plural: *ūrot*), and **oṣ* חוץ when combined with the preposition מן: *miyyoṣ* (Gn 14:23); otherwise *ūṣ, būṣ* (e.g., Gn 9:22; Lv 18:9).[7]

4.1.2.14 The vowel in this pattern is clearly long, whether as an inheritance from an earlier form (e.g., *būr* בחור, *ūr* עור) or as a result of the contraction of a diphthong (e.g., *tok* = TH תָּוֶךְ, *ūn* = TH עָוֹן). One should not posit an original short *u* in the noun *or* אור,[8] because short *u* was not retained in SH (1.5.2.3); see also 4.1.2.10 *båq*: בהק, and it is certainly not an original short vowel in the word **oṣ* (unstressed). SH here merges monosyllabic PS nouns of the ע"י class (segholates and contracted diphthongs in TH) and bisyllabic patterns with an original guttural second radical: *būr* בחור < **bā'ūr*, *tūm* תהום < **t"ōm* < **tihām*. With original bisyllabic words, we must posit that a vowel different from the original *ū*, whether derived from *šəwa* or not, assimilated to *ū* before the reduction of the two syllables into one; thus, **bā'ūr* (or *bᵃ'ūr* in declension) > **bu'ūr*.

> Note: a. SH *qor* קר is derived from the root קו"ר, closely related to קר"ר, and in fact the spellling in SP Gn 8:22 is קור, while a feminine form occurs in SP, *wqū'rå* at Gn 31:40, where the written text reads וקרחה and the translations employs words meaning "cold" (קור).
>
> b. Note that the plural of רוח is not **ruwwot* but **ruwwå'ot* - i.e., it is derived from a form something like TH *רְוָחוֹת, similar to the relationship between MH לְוָחִין and TH לוּחוֹת.

4.1.3 Forms with Three Consonants

4.1.3.1 *fīqvd*. Nouns with *ī* as the first vowel are very few in number. We list

---

[7] But in Dt 23:13,14, SP reads החוצה, as is common.
[8] *Pace* Macuch, *Grammatik*, 382.

4.1 Simple Noun Patterns

them here grouped according to the second vowel: *šīməš* שמש, *kīli* כלי, *fīri* פרי, *sīla* סלע, *ṣīla* צלע; *dīgån* דגן, *tiyyåməm* (< **tī'aməm*) תאומים.

The *ī* vowel in these words is not derived directly from PS *i* - that vowel developed under these conditions into *e* (cf. *šēkår* שֵׁכָר) - even though in some nouns (e.g., כלי) an *i* vowel may be posited at an early stage. In all the cases listed above, the origin of *ī* may be assumed to be a *šəwa* (see 1.3.1), e.g., *שְׁמֶשׁ, *סְלַע, and certainly also תְּאָם* ("twin").

4.1.3.2 The originally monosyllabic nouns — that is, the "segholates" — also became bisyllabic in SH even in declension: *ṣilā'u* צלע, *ṣīlā'ūto* צלעותיו. In the form *kīlək* כליך, the singular and plural have been conflated, and in the word פרי only the plural forms exist: *fīro* פריו (and not **fīriyyu*), *fīriyya* פריה.

4.1.3.3 *fēqəd*. There are more than seventy SH nouns of this type, whose form in III-guttural and III-*y* classes is, of course, *fēqi*. The following patterns of declension may be discerned:

1. In the singular: (a) the vowel of the second radical is deleted, as in: *nigdi* נגדי, *isdåk* חסדך, *fidyu* פדיו, *nibyåk* נביאך (see 1.5.3.4[4]), *dirku* דרכו, *iṣyu* חציו, *isla* אצלה, *šibya* שביה; in some *a* or *å* appear as the vowel of the first radical, such as *båṭnåk* בטנך, *zakrimma* זכרם. This is the usual way in nouns declined in the Pentateuch; (b) the vowel of the second radical is *i*, as in *šēkīnu* שכנו, *tēmiyya* טמאה, *qēdīša* קדשה.

2. In the plural (including "dual" forms), the vowel of the second radical is: (a) *ī*, as in *ēlīləm* אלילים, *gē'bīm* (< **gebī'īm*) גביעים, *qēlīm* (< **qēlī'īm*) = TH קְלָעִים, *nē'tīm* (< **nētī'īm*) נתחים, *šēlīšo* שלישיו; (b) *ē*, as in *dērēkəm* דרכים, *yērēkəm* ירכים, *ēzēnəm* אזנים, *yētēdot* יתדות, *yētēdūto* יתדותיו; (c) *å/ā*, and the vowel of the first radical is sometimes *ē*, sometimes *ā/å*, as in *tēmā'əm* טמאים, *feqå'əm* פקחים (singular: *fēqi* פקח), *wmiyyēlåbīyyinna* ומחלביהן, *'åqåbi* עקבי, *dålåtəm* דלתים; (d) deleted, as in *kišbəm* כשבים, *katfot* כתפות, *katfūto* כתפותיו, *dirkīkimma* דרכיכם, *irbəm* ערבים.

4.1.3.4 The various ways of declining *fēqəd* may be easily understood on the basis of the assumption that in SH (according to its phonological rules) different PS patterns have been conflated. This is evident by contrasting the SH form with the TH forms of the same nouns: פָּעֵל (אזן), פָּעֵל (נגד, אצל), פָּעֵל/פָּעַל (קדש, ירך), פָּעִיל (נדיב), פְּעִיל (אליל), and even פָּעֵל (ירק) and פָּעֵל (ספיר). The originally monosyllabic nouns of the patterns *qaṭl*, etc., of which there are many, had no vowel after the second radical in their declensions in the singular, and they attracted other, originally bisyllabic, nouns as well, such as *iznåk* (Dt 23:14), equivalent to TH אָזְנֶךָ (unless we have here originally a relationship like that between יָרֵךְ and יֶרֶךְ), and *nibyåk* נביאך. They did not, however, make an impact on the declension in the plural, and the number of those with *â* (e.g., *dēgâlo* דגליו in SP Nu 2:2) is small. The nouns of the *qatīl* pattern, on the other hand, not only maintained their vowel but also attracted some nouns of the *qatil* pattern as well, such as *šēkīnu*, and of the *qatl* pattern as well, such as *qē'līm* קליעים. (Cf. TH נְטִיעִים/נֶטַע!) The *qatil* pattern is maintained in the plural not only in words such as *yērēkəm* ירכים, but also attracted words from the segholate patterns, such as *dērēko*; the words טמא and פקח, however, follow the *qatl* pattern. The interplay of these originally distinct patterns brings about two phenomena:

a. surprising forms with no vowel after the second radical in the plural, such as *katfot* כתפות (not in the construct state) and *kišbəm* כשבים — and it may well be that even the "dual" form, such as *irbəm* עֲרָבִּים, has contributed to this development; and

b. declension of nouns in more than one way: *tēmiyya* טמאה but *tēmā'əm* טמאים; *ēzēnəm* אזנים but *bēzniyyimma* באזניהם; *nē'tīm* (< *nētī'īm) נתחים but *nēto* נתחיו, based on *nētəm (< *nithīm), similar to *nibyəm* נביאים.

4.1.3.5 In addition to what is noted in the previous section, we see that the *fēqəd* pattern sometimes merges with another pattern in declension. Thus, the absolute form of יתד is *yâtâd*, and in declension *yētəd*; in the singular *nēqi* נקי but *nēqo in the plural: *nēquwwəm* נקויים. The noun ספיר has two forms: *sēfər* is the name of the precious stone, but *sâfər* in the phrase לבנת ספיר.[9] One should mention here the plural ("dual") form of *regəl* רגל: *rēgâləm* (Lv 11:23, TH רַגְלַיִם) and *argâlem* (Ex 23:14, TH רְגָלִים).

4.1.3.6 From the above, it clearly emerges that the *ē* vowel of the first radical in the absolute form is sometimes a development from an *i* vowel in PS or early Hebrew and sometimes derived from *šəwa* in the stage before that of SH. Originally *šəwa* arose in the declined forms. On the basis of such forms as *nēdībi* נדיבי and *nēzīrâk* there came into being *nēdəb* and *nēzər*, which displaced *nâdəb* and *nâzər* because of SH's characteristic tendency to make the declension uniform. In the word ספיר, though, there are still two forms (4.1.3.5), and the two forms of רגלים provide clear evidence of the different possibilities for converting *šəwa* into a full vowel.

Note: It is relevant to point out that even though *šəwa* may develop into *â* (see *dâlâtəm* דלתים), the *â* is not maintained in the construct form of *šâni* = שָׁנִי, but instead we find *ē*: *šēni*. One surprising form is the construct

---

[9] Among the translations of the word ספיר given in *Hammeliṣ* (*LOT* II, 539a, l. 145) we find חכם meaning "black" (= אָכָם in common Aramaic). This tradition, of course, found it difficult to agree with the fact that ספיר in the phrase לבנת ספיר (with לבנת translated in the Arabic column of BL Or 7562 as بياض, meaning "white!") should be pronounced in the same way as "sapphire stone."

yēfət instead of *yefåt יְפַת corresponding to the absolute state *yēfa* for both genders. It seems that the Samaritan tradition derives this form from the root יפ״ת and interprets its meaning as synonymous to יפ״ה.[10]

4.1.3.7 *fēqad*, *fēqåd*. These two forms are considered together because in this situation, it is possible that *a* and *å* were not distinguished in certain words, independent of the kind of melody used in the recitation of the Pentateuch and prayers. A survey of the nouns reveals that *a* occurs almost exclusively before a guttural third radical, such as *dēša* דשא, *ēla* (equivalent to TH אֱלֹהַּ), *zēba* זבח, and *rēša* רשע, while *å* normally appears before all other consonants: *nēdår* נדר, *qēråš* קרש, *fēråṭ* פרט. Note, however, these exceptions: *bēqar* on the one hand, and *bēṭå* בטח and *ēṭå* חטא (because of the ט?) on the other.

4.1.3.8 A comparison of the nouns in these forms with their forms in TH teaches us that most have segholate nouns as their TH counterparts (many of the *qitl/qatl* origin, but some *qutl*) and a minority are divided between *qatal* (דבר, נקם, רשע, etc.) and *qital* (שכר, ענב, לבב), and even *qitāl* (*ēla* אלה, *šēmål* שמאל). One might think that of those nouns which have segholate parallels in TH that the *fēqad/fēqåd* pattern (especially the former!) is a variant of *fēqəd* under the influence of the guttural third radical, but since such a rule cannot be applied to nouns in which the third radical is not a guttural, we should instead view these nouns as belonging to two independent patterns. Fluctuation between segholates and פְּעָל is quite common in the Jewish traditions of Hebrew (e.g., שֶׁבַח/שְׁבָח) and between Hebrew and Aramaic (e.g., עֲקַר/עִקָּר (> יְעָקָר*), בְּרִי/כִּי, etc.[11]). This is also the case here: in these nouns, the vowel of the first radical originates in *šəwa*, if not in all instances then in many of them, and it makes no difference whether the *šəwa* in the absolute form in the stage previous to SH is the result of phonological processes in Hebrew or is formed by analogy to the declension. In other words, the relationship between TH דְּבַר and SH *dēbår* (<*דְּבָר*) is like that of נְשַׁר and נְשָׁר in various traditions of *m. Sukka* 1:3 and like λαρεσα (Ps 36:2 in Col. II of the Hexapla) as against λαρασα (ibid. 36:10) TH לְרֶשַׁע.[12] As was stated above, forms such as *דְּבָר, etc. came into being by analogy to דְּבָרִי, etc., while TH עֲנָק SH *ēnåq* may have developed from PS *qitāl* in light of הָעֲנוֹק (Jos 21:11). Certainly it holds true in the case of *šēmål* (TH שְׂמֹאל).

---

[10] And indeed in Gn 9:27, the verb יַפְתְּ is rendered in SAV as يحسن, and there is a reading of the personal name יפת (Japheth), too, as حسن. Thus, we find the personal name ابو الحسن translated into Hebrew as יפת.

[11] See my "Observations," 18ff.

[12] I do not agree with Brønno's view of λαρεσα as a corruption (Brønno, *Studien*, 154), even though we find λαρασα in Ps 32:10. The same is true of λαμεσα in Ps 49:5, which is not sufficiently certain — it does not seem to me to be a scribal error.

As for their behavior in SH, nouns of this type decline the same way regardless of their different origins.

4.1.3.9 What is stated in the previous section provides a simple explanation for why the vowel of the second radical of most nouns that are segholate in TH is maintained even in the declension of the singular, such as *lēqā'i* לקחי, *nēgā'u* נגעו, *nēkā'u* נכחו, and *ēṭā'u* חטאו, alongside the original segholate pattern: *nidru* נדרו, *nizru* נזרו, *sitra* סתרה (from *sētår* סתר), *ibriyyimma* עבריהם (from *ēbår* עבר), *šikmu* שכמו and *šikma* שכמה (from *šēkåm* שכם).

4.1.3.10 Special Instances

1. Several of the nouns in these patterns, such as פרס, שלך, שלל, and קטף (SP Dt 32:24), have no cognates outside Hebrew, and several are without declension in the Pentateuch, making it difficult to assess the relationship between the SH and TH forms and to determine whether the SH nouns reflect originally different forms. It is clear, however, that *gådalləm* גדילם (without י in the MT) is not formed from **gadīl*, and that the relationship of SH and TH here is like that of TH נְגָעִים and the Qumran form נגיעים (e.g., 1QS 4:12), or נֵזֶק, נְזָקִים appears in Est 7:4) and נזיקים, or, within TH, נְטָעַי and כִּנְטִיעִים (Ps 144:12). Also to be noted in this context are the variants in manuscripts to *m. Miqwa'ot* 9:2: וְגֶלֶד in MS Kaufmann, וְגֶלֶד in MS Parma B, וגליד in MS Antonin 262.

2. SH distinguishes between פללים (Ex 21:22), pronounced *fēlåləm*, and פלילים (Dt 32:31; SP without י), pronounced *fallåləm*. The former is an abstract noun, the second a *nomen agentis*, both being derived from the same root.[13]

3. The plural form *lē'būt* לוחות requires us to assume a consonantal ו as the second radical and an absolute form something like **lēba*, making the relationship of SH to TH in this noun like that of רֶוַח/רוּחַ, and indeed a consonantal ו can be found in MH as well in the form לווחין, and in SA *lē'bīn* לוחין (*LOT* III/2, 97, l. 45), *lēbāyyå* לוחיה (ibid., 220, l. 82). The plural form *lē'būt* in SH (!) reflects something like *לְוָחוֹת (see 4.1.3.3[2d]), which developed: **libḥot* > **libᵉḥot*, which, through the rule of the assimilation of *šəwa* and the disappearance of ח, became **lēbū'ot*, from which the present form developed. (See also 4.1.2.14 n. b)

4. The term *kēwås* כוס ("little owl") is undoubtedly derived from a form such as **כְּוָס* (in accordance with what is stated in 4.1.3.8), as distinct from

---

[13] The word בפללים in Ex 21:22 is rendered as בשדלין or בצלואן by ST, which has, thus, ascribed to the word a meaning related to prayer. Note also that the root חנ״ן bears two meanings, "prayer" (תְחִנָּה) and "gift," and perhaps the meaning of "giving fairly" is intended by SAV (and Sa'adia): بانــصــاف (Or. 7562). The word פללים in Dt 32:31, too, is translated by ST as שדלין, but in the aforementioned manuscript by the word סכיאין (read סכאין?), i.e, Qal participle meaning "seeing," "hoping." פללתי in Gn 48:11: ST סכית, SAV ت رجـــو) Note that ST nowhere translates פללים as "judges," and that it derives all these shades of meanings from one "Grundbedeutung."

"cup": *kuwwås* (see below 4.1.4.10). Since כוס ("little owl") has no cognate outside Hebrew, no conclusions may be drawn about the originality of the ו in the SH form.

5. The form of the noun *ētå* חטא follows the pattern of the strong roots, similar to דשא and פרא in TH.

4.1.3.11 *fēqod*. The nouns of this pattern are few in number, and most parallel TH פְּעוֹל or פעול. One cannot tell from SH or from TH whether a given noun has its origins in *qutāl* or *qitāl* on the one hand, or *qitūl* or *qutūl* on the other, because of the reduction of the first vowel to *šəwa*. Only parallels in cognate languages may hint at the origins of these forms in PS. Thus, the form *lubūšu* in Akkadian, and not the Arabic لِبَاس, is congruent with TH לְבוּשׁ; حِمَار with TH חֲמוֹר; أُنَاث with TH אֱנוֹשׁ. If the noun *yētom* (= TH יָתוֹם) is not a backformation from the plural *yētūməm* but the original form, then it is not cognate to TH יָתוֹם, but instead has its base in a form such as יְתוֹם, which is indeed found with Babylonian vocalization: זִיתוֹם (MS Assemani 66 of *Sifra*, 438). The basis for *rē'om* is apparently רְחוּם, which is attested in TH as a personal name (see 2.13.2). Apparently, also belonging to this pattern is *åšqot* השקות (SP Gn 24:20), cognate to TH הַשְׁקֵת (without the definite article **ašqot* < **š*qot*; on the change in pattern see 4.1.3.8). The nouns *rē'oš* ראש, *ṣē'on* צאן, and *mē'od*, which all originate in *qa/utl*, became part of this pattern due to special conditions of pronunciation (see 1.5.3.2).

4.1.3.12 It is relevant to point out the similarity in the relationship between the absolute form and the declined form in the nouns *ēlom* חלום / *ilmu* חלמו (in Biblical Aramaic חֵלֶם; plural *â'ēlåmot* הַחֲלוֹמוֹת); *ēdom* = TH אָדָם / *idma* = TH אֲדָמָה. Within TH this relationship is attested in the פָּעֵל form, e.g., עָמֹק/אָרֹךְ/אֲרֻכָּה, יָרֹק/יְרַקְרַק, עָמְקֵי. As for *ēdom*, structurally it does not seem to parallel TH אָדָם. Its origin may be from *qutāl* (as is that of חלום ?), and in ancient Arabic this is a common pattern for color words,[14] and similarly in Aramaic אוּכָּם (black), יוֹרָק (green), סוּמָק (red),[15] and חִוָּר (< חֲוַר*, حُوَار); note also the parallel صُحَار — Syriac צוּחֳר — TH צְחֹרוֹת.

> Note: 1. In its understanding of כפורים, SH distinguishes between *kefūrəm* (atonement in general) and *kibbūrəm* (in the context of the Day of Atonement). The former is an abstract noun of the *qatūl* pattern, like בתולים and זקונים. The verb כפר occurs in SH in *Pi'el* "with simple second radical" (see 2.1.3.5).

[14] See W. Fischer, *Farb- und Formbezeichnungen in der Sprache der altarabischen Dichtung* (Wiesbaden, 1965).

[15] In 1QapGen 21:17–18, its form is שמוקא! The term ימא שמוקא refers to the Red Sea, and this is another development from the same Proto-Semitic pattern that parallels חֲשׁוֹכָא and נְהוֹרָא.

2. From ēnoš אנוש there is a plural form ēnūšəm אנושים (Gn 18:2), which is employed differently from ēnâšəm אנשים. This parallels Phoenecian אדמם, from אדם, as in the inscription of Eshmun'azar of Sidon (*KAI* 14:6).

4.1.3.13 *fāqəd, fâqəd.* Of all the nouns occurring in this form, nearly one quarter have an *ā* vowel (in an open syllable), and these have either (1) an original ח or ע as the first radical (both pronounced as y) or, on occasion, ק; or (2) ח or ע as the second radical, or, in one noun, א. The other group consists of those with an *â* vowel, in which, if there is an original guttural, it is א or ה as the first radical (not pronounced as y) or ה as the second radical. Examples: *'ārəš* = TH חֶרֶשׁ, חֲרֵשׁ; *'ākəm* חכם, **'ātəm* (*'ātīmåk* חתמך, Gn 38:18), *'ābəd* עבד, *'ārəl* ערל, *qāšət* קשת, *qāši* קשה, *nā'əš* נחש, *mā'ər* מחיר, *kā'əs* כעס, *mā'əl* מעיל, *tā'i* תאי (= תאו); *nâfəš* נפש, *kårəm* כרם, *mâlək* מלך, *gâdi* גדי, *årək* ארך, *årəb* חרב, *åšən* חשן, *åzi* חזה, *kå'ən* כהן, *så'əb* צהב.

> Note: It is to this form that we should assign the pronunciation of the noun אבטיחים (in most manuscripts of SP without א) *abbā'ṭīm* (Nu 11:5), on the basis of which we should posit the absolute form **bâṭi* without prosthetic א, as in Arabic and Aramaic. The gemination of ב together with the absence of lengthening in the preceding vowel prevent us from reconstructing **abbâṭi* with prosthetic א as the absolute form.

4.1.3.14 Most of the nouns listed above have segholate parallels in TH, and for those with non-segholate TH parallels, an underlying form of the *qatl* or *qutl* type can easily be assumed. E.g., the form *âmən*, paralleled by אָמֵן and אֹמֶן in TH, may originally have been a cognate of אָמֵן; *tâmērəm* תמרים may be derived from something like TH תֹּמֶר; the Aramaic counterpart of SH *'ārəb* and TH עוֹרֵב is עוֹרְבָא. On the other hand, there is no doubt that at least some of the nouns entered these patterns from others, following rules of morphophonemic development in SH. The following are the PS patterns underlying the nouns in question, with the nouns listed according to their TH forms:

qatil: e.g., זקן, כבד, חצר; *qatīl*: סביב, תמיד, שעיר (= hairy); *qitīl* (?) > פְּעִיל, such as פתיל, מעיל; *qatal*: שפל, לבן, כנף, חכם; *qatul*: צהב, טהר; *qātal*: חותם; *qātil*: כהן, עורב; (*qattil?*) > *qittil*: חֵרֵשׁ. The first three groups listed are clearly the sources for SH *fâqəd* (*zâqən, sâbəb, fâtəl*)/ *fāqəd* (*mā'əl, šā'ər*) following SH rules, and it would seem reasonable to assume in all the other instances as well an *ī/i* vowel with the second radical, unlike TH. Evidence for this may be found in Aramaic חַכִּים (on the gemination see 1.5.3.3), Arabic لَبِن (לבן)[16] خَاتَم alongside خَاتِم. The noun

---

[16] Meaning "one who likes milk." Of relevance here is the Ashkenazi reading in such passages as *m. Beṣa* 1:4 זימן שחורים ומצא לבנים. See also D. Sadan, *Avnei Safah* (Tel-Aviv 1956), 207ff. [Hebrew]. Similar to this is the relationship between absolute חָלָב and construct חֲלֵב. On the relationship of קָצֵר and קְצַר, see S. Sharvit, "Notes on the Vocalization of נייר and קצר," *Lěšonénu* 38 (1974), 238–240 [Hebrew].

4.1 Simple Noun Patterns

form פֵּעֵל in TH (indicating persons disabled in various ways) is specific to TH and has no SH cognate (see *LOT* III/1, 59, 103, and 183; and below 4.1.4.4); thus, the origin of *'āraš* חֶרֶשׁ is clearly *qatil*. Similarly, there is no gemination in *måqəl* = TH מַקֵּל. This points up the fact that if we disregard the shift in pattern of a few nouns between TH and SH, the development in SH appears rather uniform and conforms to accepted rules.

4.1.3.15 The different origins of *fāqəd/fåqəd* are reflected in their declension, with, as expected, some blurring of original distinctions:

1. Singular: (a) no vowel after the second radical, such as: *arbi* חרבי, *karmåk* כרמך, *maryåk* מריך, *'anyåk* עניך, *'aršu* חרשו, *šamna* שמנה (Lv 2:2,16), *nafša* נפשה; *girnåk* גרנך, *siltå* סלתה, and similarly *ifši* חפשי; (b) *ē* after the second radical: *qådēšåk* קדשך, *fā'ēlu* פעלו, *šādē'u* שדהו (absolute state *šådi*), *låbēna* לבנה, *šåmēna* שמנה,[17] *å'ērət* אחרת, *åmēnimma* אמנם; (c) *ī* after the second radical: *åsīmåk* אסמך, *'åtīmåk* חותמך, *måqīli* מקלי, *qåṣīråk* קצירך, *šåkīråk* שכירך, *tåmīda* תמידה.

> Note: העלמה (Gn 24:23) is pronounced *å:līma*; the masculine form is unattested in the Pentateuch, but it seems to be pronounced *åləm* and is, therefore, formed in this pattern. The *ī* vowel apparently has its origins in a diphthong found in Syriac and underlying the Jewish Aramaic form עוּלֵימְתָא, עוּלֵימָא (see 1.1.8.3).

2. Plural: (a) *ī* after the second radical: *ådīrəm* אדירים, *fātīləm* פתילים, *sådīqəm* צדיקים, *tånīnəm* תנינים, *zåqīnəm* זקנים, *yåšīrəm* ישרים; (b) *ē* after the second radical: *ådēnəm* = TH אֲדָנִים, *målēkəm* = TH מְלָכִים, *qārēno* קרניו, *qārēnūto* קרנותיו, *kårēməm* כרמים, *mātēni* = TH מְתֵנִי, *åmēri* = MT אִמְרֵי, *ådēšəm* חֲדָשִׁים; (c) *å* after the second radical: *kånåfəm* כנפים, *åbånəm* אבנים, *ålåfəm* אלפים, *qåråni* קרני; (d) the form *gadyi* = גְּדָיִ necessitates a plural form **gadyīm* (see כשבים, 4.1.3.3), but *åli* חלי (TH חֳלִי Dt 7:15) has as its plural form *(w)åləm* (Dt 28:59), parallel to the plural of כלי (4.1.3.2).

It is quite clear that the *ī* of *qatīl* penetrated *qatil* by analogy, which usually requires *ē*, while *ē* and *å* may be seen as separate developments from the *šəwa* in various forms, but it is also possible to see them as the product of a mutual analogy to forms such as TH פְּעָלִים and פְּעָלִים. Evidence of this is provided by such mixed declensions as *åzēqa* חזקה vs. *åzåq* חזק, *šåfəl* שפל vs. *šåfåla* שפלה, *qārēno* קרניו and *qåråni* קרני,[18] *šamna/šåmēna* שמנה. Indeed, *malku* מלכו / *målēkəm* מלכים stand in the same relation as כְּתָף/כְּתֵף and the like. Note also that the Arabic cognate to TH מֶלֶךְ is مَلَك.

---

[17] Nu 4:9, unlike the other occurrences, and we have not discerned the reason for this pronunciation.

[18] Note that the twofold declension of קרן occurs in the same verse, Dt 33:17, and that the pronunciation of קרני is best elucidated from the variant קראני.

4.1.3.16 Special Instances

1. From the noun *yåləd* and its declension *yālīdəm*, etc., it is evident that the two TH forms יֶלֶד and יָלִיד have merged into one; however, corresponding to *yåšīrəm* in SH (SP ישירים) we do not find ישיר (= Modern Hebrew יָשִׁיר) in its absolute state, but only ישר as in TH.

2. The noun *mirri* מרי (Nu 17:25), as opposed to *maryåk* מריך, can be derived from *marri < *mari. It seems, though, the distinction between the roots מר"י and מר"ר has been blurred, evidence for which can be mustered from מרי שיחי (Job 23:2) rendered by the Aramaic version as מריר מימרי. This may be the origin of the *i* vowel after the מ, since מרת (Gn 26:35) is pronounced properly as *mirråt*.

3. The word *lā:mət* לעמת indicates to us that it is derived from the root עמ"ם, and not, as is commonly stated, from עמ"ם. The form parallels something like *עֹמֶת.

4.1.3.17 *fāqad, fâqad, fâqåd.*

Since the nouns in the first two of these patterns end in an original guttural, one might consider them to be merely variants of *fāqəd/fâqəd*, e.g., *qāma* (TH קֶמַח) like *'ābəd* עבד, *šāsa* שסע like *mâlək* מלך, *qāra* (TH קֶרַח, but קֶרַח personal name in 2 Kgs 25:23) and *gâba* (TH גֶּבַח) like *'arəš* (TH חֶרֶשׁ), *gâba* (TH גֹּבַהּ) like *sâ'əb* צֹהַב, and so on, while *šāma* שמע can also be understood as an infinitive absolute. Because nouns III-guttural may also be found in the *fâqåd* pattern, however — *fårå* (TH פֶּרַע, פָּרַח), *sårå* (TH סָרַח), *tåråkkimma* טרחכם — we cannot posit a substitution of *a* for *ə* as the second radical, leaving us no choice but to regard these as independent patterns. A considerable portion of these nouns are segholate in TH. The rest are derived from other PS patterns: *qatal*, such as: *yåtåd* יתד (Arabic وَتَد), *yåtår* יתר (Arabic وَتَر), *gâbån* גבן, *'âqåš* עקש, *gâba* גבח (in Syriac we find קְרַחָא and גְּבְחָא); *qvtāl* (= פְּעָל), such as: *bâšā'i* בעשאי (Ex 36:8), akin to a TH *בַּעֲשִׂי form;[19] and *qatul*, such as: *gâba* (TH גֹּבַהּ) and perhaps *šâtåm* שתם. The developments within SH may be explained on the basis of this assumption.

4.1.3.18

It is relevant to know that the auxiliary vowel that developed in the monosyllabic patterns — the TH segholates — is *å* here, which is unusual, since we would assume that the origin of *åkål* is the same as that of TH אֹכֶל because of *aklimma* אכלם, that *qâbår* is the cognate of קֶבֶר because of *qabri* and *qabru*, and even that *šåkår* may be the cognate of שֵׁכָר (Pr 11:18) and, therefore, its declension is *šakru*. We need not add that *gådål* is TH גָּדֵל, as is evident from

---

[19] The use of the *fēqqåd* pattern in the function of the infinitive in SA — and not only in SA— is clearly attested by the interchange of פצוי/פצאי in ST Ex 5:23 to express *wåṣṣəl* (TH וְהַצֵּל). This pattern is also common in MH with ל"י roots, e.g., דמאי ("doubt whether the tithe was [properly] taken"), גלאי ("an open place"), פנאי ("vacancy," "emptiness").

gådlåk and *gadlu*, nor that *dåšån* is דֶּשֶׁן because of *dišnu*. It is surprising that TH בָּקָר and עָקָר behave like the segholates in SH: *baqråk* בקרך, *'åqrå* (TH עֲקָרָה).

4.1.3.19 Special Instances

1. Note that SH has no יָגֵעַ form, but instead *yåga*, *yå'gāk*, cognate to either יָגֵעַ (Job 20:18) or יָגֵעַ, which is not found in the Bible.

2. The noun כסא, formed along the lines of גֵּב and the like in TH, also does not geminate the second radical in SH: *kåsa*. It is evident that the source of gemination in כסא is not the same as in גבח, etc. We should consider whether the SH form is in any way connected with כס (which appears in SP Ex 17:16 as כסא) and/or כהסאי (= כסאי) in the Sefire inscription (KAI 224:17).

3. The noun טנא is pronounced *tåna*, but טנאך is *tånåk*, and that pronunciation is hinted at in the variant reading טאנך. This is a metathesis similar to בצנאכם in Nu 32:24.

4. The noun *tåma* טמא (Dt 26:14) is presumably a masculine form of טֻמְאָה. (See *LOT* III/1, 122).

5. There is undoubtedly a noun **qåsåm* meaning "magic" (TH קֶסֶם), as we learn from *qåsåmīyyimma* (SP Nu 22:7), but that is the participle form as well, and they both occur in Dt 18:10 *qåsåm qåsåmǝm*. The word *qåssåm* in Nu 23:23 is translated "magic," even though its form is more appropriate to something like קַסָּם*, and perhaps that is in fact the intended meaning.

6. Note the lack of gemination in the second radical of גָּמָל: *gåmålo* גמליו, etc., while זָקֵן has such gemination in *zåqannu* זקנו and not in *zåqånimma*.

7. The noun *šåbā'ot* (TH שְׁבֻעוֹת) is the plural of *šå'bā* (TH שְׁבֻעָה) or of שְׁבֻעָה*. (See 5.6.1.)

4.1.3.20 *fåqod, fåqod.*

The nouns occurring in these forms are generally found in TH as פָּעוּל (the passive participle of *Qal*), פָּעוֹל < *qatāl* (שָׁלוֹם, etc.), פָּעוֹל < *qutul* (שְׁבוּ, בְּכוֹר, Akkadian *šubu*) or *qitāl* (תְּמוֹל). All this is necessitated by the accepted rules. In some of them, though, there is a difference between SH and TH in the gemination of the second radical (see 1.5.3.3) and what is related to it: SH — *ålof, åqu, wåšūqīyyimma, 'åtūdǝm* (in Arabic عَتُود, without gemination of the ת); in TH — אַלּוּף, אַקּוֹ, חֲשׁוּקֵיהֶם, עַתּוּדִים. The relationship of the SH nouns *å'ol, bå'on, kå'os* (alongside *kå'ǝs*), *wåṣom* (Dt 8:17; some manuscripts of SP read ועצום) and the TH nouns אֹהֶל, בֹּהֶן, כַּעַס, and עֹצֶם can be found even within TH in the relationship between בֹּהֶן and בְּהוֹנוֹת, or between TH and Aramaic: חֲלֹם / חֲלוֹם / בכור / בוכרא (Arabic حُلْم) or בוכרא.[20]

4.1.3.21
SH does not provide support for the opinion that nouns such as גדול,

---

[20] See my "Observations," 18–20.

טהור, and קרוב in TH are derived from *qatul*. Instead, by maintaining *o/u*, it supports the assumption that their basis is actually *qatāl*, since original short *u* is not maintained in SH. But the relationship between the absolute form and the declined forms in such instances as *gādol* גדול : *gādalləm*, *ādon* אדון : *ādanni* (*ādūnəm* is also attested), *ṭā'or* טהור : *ṭā'ēra*, and *'ākom* חכם alongside *'ākəm* and *'ākēməm* attest to the suppletion of patterns.

4.1.3.22 Special Instances

1. *gāballot* גבלות (Ex 28:22) may be understood as the plural of **gābol* (like גדול, 4.1.3.21), but see below 4.3.14.

2. The gemination of נ in the noun אדון is paralleled by the Punic *donni* (Poenulus ll. 998, 1001). Note that אֲדוֹנִי is pronounced *ādāni* (like *ānāki* אנכי). The retention of the *ū* vowel — that is, the lack of gemination of נ — is found in the plural form *ādūnəm*. That form, of course, in the Pentateuch is a divine appellation, but such a form is found in the language of the later liturgical poetry and in SH for a human as well: *ādūnån* אדונן = "our lord."

4.1.3.23 *fūqəd, fūqad, fūqåd*.

All three appear in the *Qal* participle (6.12.4–6). There are other nouns as well in this pattern, especially with *a/å* vowels, such as *ūṣår* אוצר, *gūzål* גוזל, *šūfår* שופר, *ūtåm* חותם,[21] and *ūlåm* עולם, which are derived from *qātal* or *qūtal* (< *qawtal*), and similarly *kūkåb* כוכב follows the פּוֹעָל form in TH. In some nouns, *ū* is derived from *šəwa* (see 1.3.1), e.g., *ūmår* עמר (TH עֹמֶר), *(miyy)ūdåni* מ(עודני) (Gn 49:20) based on עֶדֶן (TH עֵדֶן), *kūfår* (TH כֹּפֶר) (meaning both "pitch" and "ransom"), *kūrā'əm* = TH כְּרָעַיִם (some manuscripts read כורעים at Lv 11:21; note Arabic كُرَاع). The plural nouns *dūbērəm* דבורים (whether the singular is **dūbər* or **dūbēra*) and *tū'līm* תולעים seem to indicate absolute forms on the model of participles, something like *תּוֹלְעִים and not, as in TH, תּוֹלָעִים. The singular would seem to be **tūla*, and the relationship of the forms is like that of *yāda* ידע and *yā'dīm* יודעים in SH. Morphologically, one could assign *guwwi* < **gū'i* to this pattern, which was formed from גוי by splitting the diphthong (see 1.4.4c).

4.1.4 Forms with Four or More Consonants

4.1.4.0 This chapter includes — following the rule adopted and explained in the chapter on the verb (2.0.8) — roots with geminated second radicals, since the gemination increases the number of radicals and no distinction in declension may be made between roots in which no two radicals are the same and roots with a repeated radical in any position.

---

[21] Cf. 4.1.3.14–15.

4.1 Simple Noun Patterns

A. Forms with Geminated Second Radicals and Similar Forms

Note: *fiqqəd* — see 4.1.4.4 note.

4.1.4.1 *fiqqåd.* This form is used for only a few words. It is sometimes a) an alternate form of *faqqåd* and *fåqqåd* in which the original *a* became *i* in a departure from the norm: *riggåz* = TH רְגֻּז, *illåm* < **allåm* (and not **illəm*, see 4.1.3.14) אִלֵּם; **iyyåb*, declined as *iyyåbåk* אוֹיִבָךְ, *iyyåbək* אוֹיְבֵיךָ, *iyyåbo* אוֹיְבָיו, as against the absolute form *uyyåb* (see 4.1.4.10); *šiddi* < **šidday* שדי; *kirkåb* כרכב; and it is sometimes b) the result of the gemination of *y* in the transition from *i* to another vowel, such as *šiyyåd* = TH שִׂיד, from שִׂיד* (see 1.3.3);[22] *tiyyåməm* (< **tī'åməm*) תאומים. Thus, SH preserves, in the spelling איב and the aforementioned pronunciation, an earlier noun of the *qattāl* type, as indeed in Akkadian we find *ajjābu(m)*.[23] The u vowel in the absolute form *uyyåb* may have been influenced by the participle as it appears in TH, i.e., it is a hybrid form.[24]

4.1.4.2 *fiqqod.* As expected according to the rules of SH, this form unites nouns differentiated in TH by *ḥolem* and *šureq*, such as רמון *rimmon*, *rimmūni*; שקוציהם *šiqqūṣīyyimma*; גלוליכם *gillūlīkimma*. In addition, however, there are SH nouns of this form whose TH cognates have simple second radicals. Those of the פָּעוֹל form include לשון *liššon*, *liššūnu*; אתון *itton*, *ittūnåk*; צפונה *ṣibbūna*. Those of the פָּעוּל form include שבועיים *šibbuwwå'əm*. Those of the פָּעוֹל form include בכור *bikkor*, אזוב *izzob*, אפוד *ibbod*, שאול *šiyyol*. This SH form represents several (hypothetical) PS patterns, e.g., *qatāl* (אתון), *qatūl* (שָׁבוּעַ), *qattāl* (גִּבּוֹר), *quttāl* (רמון), *qutul* (צפור), and perhaps also *qitāl* (e.g., אפוד). The development of *šəwa* into a full vowel caused צִפֳּרִים and גִּבּוֹרִים to take the same form: *ṣibbūrəm*, *gibbūrəm*. In contrast, the *ū* vowel of *wiškūli* ואשכלי (thus SP Dt 32:32) is not derived from *šəwa*, but instead from PS *ā*, as attested by the Arabic اشكال (عثكال) and Aramaic אתכלא (Onqelos to Gn 40:10).

---

[22] Similar to the relationship of שִׂיד / שִׂיד* is the SA pair טיאן/טין = **tiyyån* in *Hammelis* (*LOT* II, 468b, l. 311), and in MS M to Gn 14:10 the word appears: טעים, i.e, both spellings, טעים and טען, are proposed. These spellings, too, provide support for טִין*.

[23] The double "j" is the spelling used by W. von Soden in his *AHw*, I, 23ff., while *CAD* A Part I, 222, has a simple "j." Both, however, certainly intend the same form. This form and not the participle is reflected in a letter from Byblos in El Amarna tablet 102, l. 27 (J. A. Knudtzon, *Die El-Amarna-Tafeln* [Aalen, 1964], 456): *ḫa-ia-b[i-i]a*, in which the letter ḫ takes the place of a pronounced Western Semitic א.

[24] It is true that the noun איב appears in the Pentateuch without ו when it is not in its absolute state, but one cannot infer from the orthography that the vowel *u* exists in the absolute state and is absent in declension. In fact, it may be that the orthography follows the pronunciation. The word איב in Hebrew, then, has two different traditions: אוֹיֵב and אָיָב* (in SH), and a development of the latter form is reflected in the personal name אִיּוֹב (like גִּבּוֹר).

4.1.4.3 Special Instances

1. Alongside the forms *birrūki* ברכי and *birrūko* ברכיו, there is *båråkəm* ברכים, which corresponds to the TH form. The form in question, **birrok*, is identical to the *Pi'el* infinitive of בר"ך, and has even been interpreted as "blessing."[25] Its pattern in PS is *qutl* or *qutul* (in TH לִפְעֹל), as we find in Syriac: ברוך, בורכא. In TH, however, the vowel of the first radical, whether original or derived from *šəwa*, became *i* because of the gemination of the second radical, thus, uniting the *Pi'el* infinitive and this form. A derivation from *qutl* is seen in the noun בֻּרְךְ in MH and 1QIsaᵃ 45:23.

2. Concerning *šibbuwwå'əm*, it has been stated (see 4.1.4.2) that it is derived from *qatūl*, which is most probably correct and in this it is similar to TH, but it may originate in a *qittūl* form, like the numerals of this form in Palestinian Aramaic.[26]

3. Note that in SH there are two different developments of **bukur* (TH בְּכֹר): *båkor* (4.1.3.20) for the firstborn of humans or animals (e.g., Ex 13:15) and *bikkor* for the first fruits and animals if appropriate for sacrificial offering.

4.1.4.4 *faqqəd*.

The nouns with triradical roots are almost all derived from *qattīl*, with a few derived from *qattil*, the *Pi'el* infinitive pattern. Those with original *ī* sometimes have a geminated second radical, unlike what is found in TH: *yammən* ימין (but the proper noun "Yemen" is *yāmən*!), *'ammət* עמית, *assīdåk* חסידך, and *'anni* עני; and *yabbīšəm* יבשים and *qaddīšəm*, the plural of קדוש (*qādoš*!), are of this form, as their Aramaic parallels attest. The words *dabbər* דבר (Gn 15:1,4) and *šalləm* שלם are certainly *Pi'el* infinitives. The gemination in the noun *'awwər* עור is apparently secondary, intended to prevent *w* from becoming *b* (4.1.3.14, on חרש). The gemination of י in the noun *yayyən* יין is secondary [and intentional?] to the retention of the diphthong, because otherwise the form of the noun would be something like **in* or **yin*, but once the gemination occurs the noun takes on the pattern discussed, as witnessed by *yayyēnu* יינו, *yayyēnimma* יינם. For the noun **azzər* חזיר (with the definite article *åzzər*)[27] it cannot be determined whether the source of the gemination is the preservation of a form parallel to Ugaritic חנזר and Arabic حِنْزِر or a derivation from **aḥzīr < חֲזִיר*. In the SH form *'anni*, two nouns have merged, which remain distinct in TH: עֲנִי and עָנִי. The element parallel to TH עֲנִי appears in the declension: *'anyi* עניי, *'anyək* עניך (fem. sing.), and even *lanyåk* לעניך (Dt 15:11), although not so for *'annīnu* עָנֵינוּ (Dt 26:7).

---

[25] SAV to Gn 30:3 renders this as تلد على بركتي!

[26] See my "Palestinian Aramaic and Samaritan Poetry," 72. See also A. Tal, "Concerning the Formation of Nouns in Samaritan Aramaic: The קטול Pattern," *Te'uda* 9 (1995), 93ff. [Hebrew].

[27] Cf. *årbi* הארבה, *arbi* ארבה.

4.1 Simple Noun Patterns

Note: It is apparently to this form that we should assign the nouns *qiddəm* קדים (Gn 41:23), *ṣinnīmot* צנימות (SP Gn 41:23), in which the *i* after the first radical is exceptional, and one should not construct a special pattern *fiqqəd*.

4.1.4.5 In nouns with quadriradical roots, the last vowel is originally short. This is so for the nouns רענן: *rā:nən* and חרצן: *miyyårṣinnəm* מחרצנים. In the proper noun תרשיש, there is, of course, no certainty that the ת is a radical.

4.1.4.6 *faqqad, faqqåd, fåqqåd.* Two groups of nouns occur in these forms:

1. among those with triradical roots, those formed in TH according to the פָּעָל pattern (maintaining the *qameṣ* in the declension, < *qattāl*; or eliminating it, < *qattal*), e.g., *gånnåb* גנב, *'arrås* = TH חָרָשׁ, *šåbbåt* שבת, *ayyål* איל;

2. among those with quadriradical roots, such nouns as *qarqa* קרקע and *qå:qå* קעקע, as well as nouns in whose TH cognates the last vowel is not necessarily *a/å*, such as *kaftår* כפתר, *qådqåd* קדקד, and a few whose TH forms do not entirely correspond to the corresponding SH forms, such as *qålqål* = TH קִלְקֵל, *ṣålṣål* = TH צִלְצָל (in the construct state צִלְצַל!), and *ṣåfṣåf* = TH אספסף (see 4.1.4.12 note). The final *a* vowel occurs only before a guttural, such as קרקע (mentioned above), *šanna* שנא, and *farra* פרע (see 4.1.4.7[7]); but this is not an absolute condition, as is demonstrated by קעקע.

4.1.4.7 SH is consistent in forming nouns denoting persons of professions (*nomina opificum*) or of permanent characteristics, while TH sometimes uses the participle form, sometimes other forms, e.g., *råqqåm* : רֹקֵם, *'aššåb* : חֹשֵׁב, *šanna* : שנא, *mī'åṭṭåb* : מֵחטֵב, *råkkåb* : רֹכֵב, *'annåtəm* : הַחֲנֻטִים (Gn 50:3), *wånnåg* : והעֲנֻג, *wånnåga* והענגה, *fallåləm* פלילים (see 4.1.3.10), *såqqår* : שקר (Dt 19:18).[28]

4.1.4.8 Special Instances

1. The *u* vowel in the noun *ṣuwwår* צואר is a result of assimilation to ו.

2. The *ē* in the declined forms *šabbētot* שבתות and *šabbētūti* שבתותי reflects an older *šəwa*, and they are the source of the absolute form *šabbētot*.

3. The nouns כפתר and חרטם geminate the last consonant in declension:

---

[28] The phrase שקר ענה, then, is interpreted: "[as] a liar he has testified against his companion," since the form meaning "falsehood" [TH שֶׁקֶר] is pronounced *ašqår* in SH. Against this reading, SAV, which is able to distinguish between the two nouns spelled שקר, translates עד שקר as وان شاهد كذوبا ذلك شاهد .بالكذب شهد, i.e., (עֵד שָׁקֶר) and שקר ענה as שקר ענה. No clear conclusion can be reached on the basis of ST's שקר(ה) סוד and לבט שקר(ה). Is it possible that things have been reversed in the reading current in our own times? One should also bear in mind the midrash on עד חמס (Dt 19:16): אין חמס [=חָמָס?] אלא גזול (*Sifre Deuteronomy* 189, ed. Finkelstein, 229), and the similar midrash in *Mekhilta de R. Yishma'el* (ed. Horowitz-Rabin, 322): עד [=חָמָס?] חמס תשת אל - ידך תשת "אל.

kaftarriyya כפתריה, *kaftarrīyyimma* כפתריהם, *årṭåmməm* החרטמים, and *årṭåmmi* חרטמי (similar to עקרבים "scorpion" in TH).

4. In the TH noun אריה, the final ה is no doubt a suffix attached to ארי. In SH we find אריה and not ארי, and it is pronounced *aryå*, like Aramaic אריא. It cannot be determined whether this noun is determined[29] (parallel to *kallibyå* כלביה, which is determined). In any case, it should be recalled that ארבה is pronounced *arbi!*

5. Given the fact that nouns that do not indicate permanent characteristics can also be found in this form (e.g., *ayyål* איל, *kakkår* ככר talent (weight),[30] we cannot determine whether the SH form *qåssåm* (Nu 23:3) is equivalent to TH קֶסֶם ("magic") or קֹסֵם ("magician," see 4.1.3.19).

6. The form *'ånnåṭəm* certainly refers to the members of a profession, and this is how ST חני/וטיה is to be understood. The word חנוטיא appears in the Palestinian Syriac Targum[31] as the translation of הרפאים (Gn 50:2), which LXX renders ἐνταφιασταῖς.

7. The form *far'rāt* פרעה (Dt 32:42) is the plural of a form such as **farra*, i.e., it was formed from **farrā'āt*. (On *-āt* as plural suffix, see 1.5.2.5.) The word was understood to mean "leaders," as attested by SAV قواد. This is also Sa'adia Ga'on's understanding, as reflected in his Arabic translation (Dt 32:42) فرعانه and LXX ἀρχόντων.

4.1.4.9 *faqqod.* Other than the word *'ammod* עמוד, which has the same form as its TH counterpart, there is also *'abbot* עבות, which loses its gemination with the definite article: *'ā:bētot* העבותות[32] (see 1.5.3.3e). The פָּעוּל form is uncommon in TH other than in proper nouns, and it is considered an intensive form of the passive participle פָּעוּל, and so it is in SH with the nouns אלוף and עתוד (see 4.1.3.20), and even with proper nouns such as *zåkor* : זַכּוּר and *åšor* : אַשּׁוּר (but *fillu* : פַּלּוּא!).

> Note: The *ē* vowel in the plural form עבתות may possibly be explained as the product of dissimilation, but it seems more likely that there were two originally distinct forms in complementary distribution in the declension, similar to the noun חזק (see 4.1.3.15).

4.1.4.10 *fuqqad, fuqqåd.* Since original short *u* is not maintained in SH except in rare instances that cannot be included in a single phonological rule, it is

---

[29] On final ה as a marker of determination, see *LOT* I, 159.

[30] But in its geographical sense: *kēkår*.

[31] So according to the emendation offered by Schulthess (*Lexicon*, 57), but in the manuscript חטוניא and the verbal forms (ibid.) חטנו and יחטנון. SA, a dialect very close to CPA, supports this very plausible emendation.

[32] Having said this, we must add that in the phrase *'a:bētot az'zåb* (עבתות הזהב) in Ex 28:24, the first word is determined, as in Ex 39:17, and there are manuscripts of SP that read העבתות there.

clear that in the nouns *uyyåb* אויב (see 4.1.4.1) and *dukka* דֻּכָּא, *u* is a substitute for older *a*, while in the noun *kuwwås* כוס, it is a derivative of *šəwa*, i.e., it comes from כְּס < *kuwwas*, a form similar to שִׂיד (=) *šiyyåd* (for a parallel development, see 4.1.3.10).

B. Quadriradicals
4.1.4.11

fēqådəd: *ēlåməš* חלמיש.

fåqådəd: *åbånət* אבנט (plural *åbånītəm*), *sånåfər* סנפיר, *'åṭåləf* עטלף, and perhaps *rā:nən* רענן (< **ra'anən*, like TH רַעֲנָן). Note that SH differs from TH in the absence of gemination of the third consonant. The vowel after the ב in אבנט can be interpreted as the result of a *šəwa* developing into a full vowel, but it may also be that the *a* vowel is original; in any case it is old, as attested by Josephus, *Antiquities* III 7:2.[33]

fåqådəd: *wbåruwwår* = TH וּבְחַרְחַר. SH here provides a form akin to TH קִלְקֵל (see 4.1.4.6), i.e., something like *חַרְחַר or *חֲרְחַר in TH. The term חרחר in Ben Sira 40:9 with its "defective" spelling provides no decisive support for either SH or TH. (The gemination of the third consonant in the word, following SH pronunciation, is not inherent in the pattern, but is instead a function of a rule related to the pronunciation of gutturals, as explained in 1.1.8 Rule 2.)

C. Quinqueradicals
4.1.4.12 *fēlåqådqåd*: *yēråqråq* ירקרק, *yēråqråqot* ירקרקות; *ådåmdåm* אדמדם, *ådåmdåmət* אדמדמת, *ådåmdåmot* אדמדמות; *fåtåltål* = TH פְּתַלְתֹּל; *šåqå:rårot* שקערורות.

The absence of gemination in the declension of the nouns אדמדם, ירקרק, and שקערורות is noteworthy. Whether we assume that in the noun שקערורות the שׁ is a formative and the root is ער״ע or that the noun was formed by a blend of שק״ע and קע״ר (as appears most likely to us), this noun must be classified synchronically as belonging to this pattern.

> Note: a. The noun האספסף (Nu 11:4) is regularly written in SH as הספסף, and its pronunciation as *assåfsåf* attests that in SH this is not a quinqueradical noun, but is rather treated as if derived from the root ספס״ף, like the Arabic noun سفساف, and so it would seem from the translations as well. See also 4.1.3.13.
>
> b. For the sake of thoroughness we must mention the nouns *šåṭnəz* שעטנז and *qinnåmon* קנמון, each of which follows its own unique model.

---

[33] In translation: "Moses called it ἀβανηθ. We, however, have learned from the Babylonians to call it ἔμιαν." The last word is, of course, identical with הֲמָיָן in Targum Onqelos.

D. Compounds

4.1.4.13 Unlike TH, one finds in SH two separate words combined into one:

a. *kå'ēnån* (Gn 41:45 and elsewhere), normally written in SH as one word: כהנאן. From the wording of ST, which renders this as כהנה רבה, we learn that אן was not taken to be a toponym, but rather a noun corresponding in meaning to און ("strength"). This not the only version of ST. SAV renders the term as امام اه سكندريه

b. As to *yåšåt* (Gn 23:8), which appears in many SP manuscripts as one word, see 4.1.2.8 note.

> Note: In contrast to ישת, it should be noted that the TH compound word לולא is usually written as two words in SH; see also 6.3.14.

4.1.5 Feminine Patterns

4.1.5.1 The feminine endings in SH, *a* or *å* (written ה-) and *åt* or *ət* (written ת-) are, as in TH, elements that appear not only in the declension of nouns and distinguish feminine from masculine, such as שָׂמֵחַ vs. שְׂמֵחָה and פּוֹעֵל vs. פּוֹעֶלֶת, but they constitute formatives in word formation. There they do not function as markers of feminine gender: the nouns שירה, חֻקָּה, יותרת, and שמחה (SH *šå'må*) are not actually the feminine forms of שיר, חק, יותר, and שָׂמַח (*šåmå* שמח in SH), not to mention such nouns as ביצה, אימה, and דלקת, which have no counterparts without the feminine marker. Where there are masculine forms alongside feminine ones, the latter, as is widely known, express the single unit *(nomen unitatis)* and the former functions as the collective noun, e.g., שַׂעֲרָה (MH: "one strand of hair") vs. שֵׂעָר ("hair") Occasionally the opposite is true, e.g., גּוֹלָה ("a community of exiled individuals") vs. the individual גּוֹלֶה, the collective דגה versus the individual דג. Sometimes the "feminine" form conveys a meaning not dependent (any longer?) on the meaning of a masculine form, but instead reflects a parallel development from the same source, e.g., קצירה, הליכה, and חרישה (verbal nouns beginning in MH) vs. קציר, הליך, and חריש, or להבה vs. להב, נקמה vs. נקם. In a number of nouns — such as the last pair, or מַשְׁעֵן vs. משענה, or שבי vs. שביה — the "feminine" form is only a stylistic variant of the "masculine" form.[34]

4.1.5.2 Thus, even though from a diachronic perspective it is quite clear that the feminine forms were generated from a base (the masculine form) with an added morpheme (the feminine ending),[35] the type of noun mentioned at the end of the previous section teaches us that much of this kind of word forma-

---

[34] In the past — that is, even in early Biblical Hebrew — the variation was not merely stylistic, since there are passages in which the choice of masculine or feminine forms seems to be governed by the gender of what they describe, as was noted by U. Cassuto in "Parallel Words in Hebrew and Ugaritic," *Lěšonénu* 15 (1947), 101ff. [Hebrew], in relation to both Biblical Hebrew and Ugaritic, and see also idem, *The Goddess Anath* (trans. I. Abrahams; Jerusalem, 1971), 45.

[35] See 4.0.1.

tion, from a synchronic point of view, deserves to be considered independent patterns not directly linked to the masculine noun patterns, and in some instances there is no masculine form at all in the language. In SH there is an additional factor dictating the separation of feminine forms from masculine forms. Phonological rules of SH brought about a blurring of the morphological connection between feminine and masculine nouns over a wide range, and certainty about matching feminine to masculine forms is undermined, e.g., שֵׂיבָה, שִׂיבָה, and לַיְלָה in TH are easily assigned to different PS patterns. Not so in SH, where *šība* (= שֵׂיבָה and שִׂיבָה) and *līla* לילה either developed into the same pattern or originated in the same pattern, and we are unable to determine which is the case. The same is true for TH קְדְמָה and קֵדְמָה, both of which are *qidma* in SH. The difference between stressed ־ָה and unstressed ־ָה (locative) is not observed in SH because of the practice in SH of regularly stressing the penult. Thus, *līla* could, in principle, be a cognate to the Arabic ليلة (in Akkadian and Geʻez, too, there are feminine forms) and not bear the locative ה- suffix. Similarly, it may be noted that in TH as well, nouns such as מוּתָה and ישׁוּעָתָה should not be analyzed as noun-with-locative-ה, but rather as nouns expanded by means of a formative ה-, the historical origins of which are a locative. Of course, in TH, one must distinguish between that ה- formative and the feminine ending; in SH there is no distinction beween the two.

This logical conclusion of the preceding analysis leads us to classify *abbākīra* הבכירה in Gn 19:31 together with בכיר, within the scope of the masculine patterns, but to list *kābākīrātu* כבכירתו in SP Gn 43:33 as a separate item, i.e., with the feminine noun patterns.

We shall now survey the feminine noun patterns, discussing only those nouns in need of additional clarification, whether due to their difference from TH or for other reasons.

4.1.5.3

1. *fiqalå*, e.g., *īda* עדה, *īdātåk* עדתך, *īfa* איפה, *īma* אימה, *gīrå* גרה (the unit of money), *tīna* תאנה.

2. *fēqalå*, e.g., *šēna* שנה ("year"), *šēnəm* שנים ("years"), *gēbot* גבות ("[eye]brows"), *yēfa* (masc. and fem. forms of יפה; see 4.1.3.6 note). The absence of gemination in *gēbot* indicates that it is not derived from a root of the ע״ע class but from a root of the ו״י class or the like, and note that TH גֵּבִים in 1 Kgs 6:9 has been interpreted (e.g., by David Qimḥi) as a variant of גֵּב. There is room to speculate that in the form *mētå*, which represents both TH מִטָּה and TH מַטֶּה, the מ is not a part of the formative but a radical in the root מט״י, known to us from MH.[36]

---

[36] *Sifre Numbers* (ed. Horovitz, 94) includes the phrase ומתמטים על מיטותיהם, and we find מיטוי in

3. *fāqa, fâqalå*, e.g., *'āla* (TH עָלָה), *qāba* (TH קֵבָה), *āla* אלה, *mâda* מדה; *åmå* (TH אָמָה and חֵמָה), *zåmå* (TH זִמָּה), *qålåt* קהלת. It may seem at first that *zåmå* is the same word as its TH equivalent with the loss of gemination (cf. 1.5.3.3), or that it is derived from the root *זו"ם*, but it seems to us that the SH term is identical to זהמה (post-Biblical זֻהֲמָה, which also bore the meaning "harlotry").[37] Similarly, the form *qå:låt* does not appear to be cognate with TH קְהִלַּת (see 4.1.5.5 below, on כהנה), but rather a feminine form of קהל. On the derivation of מדה from ע"י, see 4.1.2.8[4], n. 3. The construct state of חמה appears both as *åmåt* and *åmət* (Dt 32:24, 33).[38]

Note: In principle, nouns such as *dāt* דעת, *qāt* קאת, and *šāt* שאת belong here as well, in accordance with the rule that a syllable with an extra-long vowel functions as two syllables (1.2.3).

4. *fâqålət*, e.g., *'åtåt* חטאת (< *ḥata't*) — parallel to TH חֲטָאָה and not TH חַטָּאָה, *fåtåt* (< *paḥtat*)[39] = TH פֶּחֶתֶת, *åmət* אמת. [The word *fåråt* in Gn 49:22 is a participial form of the verb פרה].

5. *fūqå*, e.g., *ūma* חומה, *tūba* טובה, *qūma* קומה, *šūbåtåk* שובתך, *zūlāti* זולתי.

4.1.5.4

1. *fiqdalå*, e.g., *kišba* כשבה, *sitra* סתרה, *fišta* פשתה; *ikmå* חכמה, *irbå* ערוה, *libyå* לביאה (SP לביה); in the ע"ע class, *iššā* אשה, *iššat* אשת, *ištu* אשתו,[40] *mirra* (TH מְרָה), *niddå* נדה, *siddå* (TH צֵדָה),[41] *girrå* גרה (the cud; the coin, see 4.1.5.3). In nouns II-guttural, the preceding vowel is lengthened whether or not the consonant after it is geminated: *bīmma* בהמה (< *bihma*; cf. TH בְּהֵמַת), *bi:måtåk* (< *bihimåtåk*) בהמתך, *bīmtu* בהמתו,[40] *nēmma* נעמה (TH נָעֲמָה Gn 49:15).

Jewish liturgical poetry (see Ben Yehuda, *Thesaurus*, 2947). This is not a verb derived from the noun מְטָה, but an original root found also in Arabic.

[37] Cf. the midrash in *Sifra* (ed. Finkelstein 406, l. 16): תלי' לוי' זמה זה מה, which reflects the SH pronunciation. (Prof. Y. Yeivin pointed out to me the vocalization הַזְהֻמָה in MS Kaufmann to *m. Terumot* 10:1, which is close to the SH form under discussion.) See also *Shir Ha-Shirim Rabba* 1:9: לפי שישראל נדמו לסוסים נקבות והמצריים הרשעים לזכרים מזוהמים (the last word equivalent to TH מיוזנים), which in fact underlies the Septuagint at Jer 5:8. See E. S. Rosenthal, "A Contribution to the Talmudic Lexicon — Elucidation of Words Based on Textual Variants," *Tarbiz* 40 (1970–71), 178ff. [Hebrew].

[38] Some read *åmət* in v.14 for [בקר] חמאת. Note that there are textual variants חמאת/חמת, but the pronunciation of חמאה is *å'må*.

[39] The origin of the TH form פֶּחֶתֶת, is of course, the "masculine" pattern with the "feminine" ending *t* (see *GvG* I, 40), like מְלֶכֶת < *malakt*; the SH form *fåtåt* developed from the same "masculine" pattern with the "feminine" ending *-at*. The BH form פֹּחֵת (Yeivin, *Babylonian Vocalization*, 1062) strengthens this assumption.

[40] On the elimination of the vowel in the feminine suffix, see 4.1.5.7[4].

[41] Note that לְצָדִים in Jud 2:3 has been interpreted (by Ibn Janāḥ and David Qimḥi) as a derivation from the root צו"ד. On the variation צֵידָה/*sidda*, see also 1.5.3.3.

4.1 Simple Noun Patterns   269

Note: The noun *qiṣṣa* קצה may appear to be derived in SH from קצ״ץ and to belong to this noun form, but the retention of *a* in the declension, e.g., *miqqiṣṣa årəṣ miṣrəm 'ad qiṣṣå'ē'u* (Gn 47:21), demonstrates that something else is represented here; see 4.3.4.

2. *fiqdåt*. Perhaps the form *kitbåt* כתבת exists only in the construct state and there is no absolute form at all. (See שִׁכְבַת 4.2.1.4[4], קְטֹרֶת (4.1.5.10).) It seems appropriate to mention here *bēkītu* בכיתו (Gn 50:4) and *bēkət* בכית (SP Gn 35:8, corresponding to TH בָּכוּת), forms whose origin is *bikyt > *bikyit > *bikīt.

4.1.5.5

1. *faqdalå, fåqdalå*, e.g., *šalma* שלמה, *qaryå* קריה, *anyot* אניות, *kalyot* כליות, *fårså* פרסה, *ålqat* חלקת. Among the ע״ע class (i.e., *falåqqå*): *aqqå* חקה, *'ayyå* חיה, *åyyå* האיה, *sakkot* סכות, *fannūto* פנותיו, *gannot* גנות, *'allå* חלה, *qåbbå* (TH קֻבָּה), *åmmå* אמה (but *ammot* אמות, and there is *ammåtå'əm* אמתים), *måddå* מדה, *måssåt* מסת, *qåṣṣot* קצות, *qåṣṣūto* קצותיו, *sårrot* צרות. Among the III-guttural class: *šā:ra* שערה, *qā:ra* קערה, *nā:ra* נערה, *nå:la* נחלה, *rå:må* (TH רָחֲמָה), *åzza* אחזה, *kånna* כהנה, *ṭårråtu* טהרתו.

With regard to the III-guttural class, it is not at all certain that they are derived from the PS *qatlat* pattern, since *kånna* or *åzza* may be explained as derived from **kå'anna* < *kahunna, **å'azza* < *ahuzza. Furthermore, there is nothing that compels us to assume that *ṭårråtu* טהרתו is built on the same base as the parallel TH form. The same is true for those without gemination, such as *qā:ra*, which may be assigned to either *qatla* (the Arabic cognate is قَعْرَة or *qatala*, as in TH, but with regard to SH, assigning nouns such as these to our pattern is based on the assumption that the open syllable with an extra-long vowel is of the same value as the closed syllable with a regular vowel.

Special instances: (a) Alongside *aqqå* חקה one hears *åqqå* as well. (b) The word *šalma* is a feminine form, and *šalməm* a plural form of *šålom*, which is semantically equivalent to both TH שֶׁלֶם and TH שָׁלוֹם; TH שלמם (Dt 23:7) is pronounced *šalmimma* in SH; see *LOT* III/2, 153, l. 83. (c) Corresponding to TH צָרָה, there are in SH three forms: (1) *wṣårrot* (Dt 31:17) וצרות, which is derived from the ע״ע root; this derivation also fits *sårti* צרתי (Gn 35:3) as stated in 1.5.3.3, (2) *afṣåråt* בצרת (Gn 42:21), derived from the י״ר root. The pronunciation with ultimate stress *aṣṣå'rå* (Gn 42:21) mixes the two roots צרר and צרע. Indeed, we also find in SP Gen 42:21 the orthography הצרעה and the translations ST עקתה, SAV الضوائق in Ex 23:28. (d) The TH noun אָמָה is formed in SH according to the pattern under discussion, but we find in the Pentateuch only two occurrences: one as expected, *låmmåtimma* לאמתם (Gn 25:16), but the singular construct form is *ammət* (Nu 25:15). (e) The form *anyot* אניות must be explained as derived from *anyå, which is the feminine form of TH אֳנִי, and it stands in relation to TH אֲנִיוֹת in the same way that BH גְּדִיֹתֶיךָ is related to TH גְּדִיּוֹתָיךָ.

2. *faqdət*. Forms originally II-guttural: *naššət* (< *naḥšət*) נחשת, *râ:šət* ראשית.

3. *fuqdå̄*. The preservation of the *u* vowel in this situation is unusual, and in fact there are only two nouns of this form: *šurṭå̄* (in place of TH שֶׁרֶט, שָׂרֶטֶת in Lv 19:28, 21:5)⁴² and *uwwåt* = TH אַוַּת. In the latter, the vowel *u* is a product of assimilation to the adjacent semi-consonant ו.

4.1.5.6

1. *fēqīdalå̄*, e.g., *gēnība* גנבה, *tērīfa* טרפה, *nēbīla* נבלה (*nēbiltək* נבלתך, *nēbeltimma* נבלתם), *ēfīla* אפלה, *ēbīda* = TH עֲבוֹדָה, *šērīqa* = TH שְׁרֵקָה, *ēmirâtək* אמירתך (SP Dt 33:9), *ēmīrti* אמירתי (thus SP Dt 32:2 as against TH אִמְרָתִי), *šēfīla* שפלה. In *middēbīrūtək* מדברתך (Dt 33:3) we find preserved *דְּבִירָה, a form found in MH as a verbal noun from the *Qal* verb, although this root is not commonly found in *Qal* in SH (see 2.14.18, n. 15). Alongside *ēfīkot* הפכת (thus SP as against the Masoretic תהפכות at Dt 32:20) in SH we find *âfīka* in Gn 19:29. In the plural form *millīlåt* (Dt 23;26) the second radical has been geminated in place of a preceding long vowel.

2. *fēqēdalå̄*. We find in this form *gēbēra* גברה (Ex 32:18). Since no other form exists, it is difficult to assume an underlying form such as *גְּבֵרָה (words of this form in TH are of the form *fēqīdala* in SH), and the form appears to be a participle. Indeed, ST translates it as מתגברה, and SAV as قاهر, as opposed to *wkâgēbūrūtək* וכגבורתיך (SP Dt 3:24), which ST translates as וכגבורתך and SAV as وكجبروتك.

> Note: ST and SAV translate *yēbēšåt* (Gn 8:7, TH יָבֵשָׁת) by means of a perfect form, Qal 3rd fem.: אתיבשת, قلة. But the SH form is in fact a noun used as infinitive (gerund), the underlying form of which is identical to the TH form. Compare *yâkålåt* (Nu 14:16) / TH יְכֹלֶת; *afqåråt* (Lv 19:20) / TH בְּקֹרֶת > *בְּקֶרֶת in connection with the change of the original short *u*; see 1.5.2.3.

3. *fēqūdalå̄*, e.g., *bētūla* בתולה, *lēbūna* לבונה, *sēgūla* סגולה, and *gēbūra, as discussed in the previous paragraph (see also 4.1.5.7 *fåqūdå̄*).

4.1.5.7

1. *fāqīdalå̄, fâqīdalå̄*, e.g., *'ālīlåt* עלילת, *'ātīdot* עתידות; *ṣādīqa* צדקה, *ṣādīqat* צדקת, *yâriyya* (< *yârī'a*) יריעה, *yârīyyot* יריעות, *â:sīda* החסידה; *fâliyya* פליאה (SP Ex

---

⁴² Cognate to this are סִירְטָה in MS Kaufmann of the Mishnah and שירטה (*Makkot* 3:5) in MS Lowe, 131a, as against the traditional reading שריטה, and also BH סירטה and סירטה, as documented by Yeivin, *Babylonian Vocalization*, 863.

15:11 as against TH פֶּלֶא), sâbībåt סביבת, sâbībūti סביבותי, åšīrīyyimma אשריהם (but TH אֲשֵׁרָה is åšårå in SH!).

2. **fâqēdalå, fâqēdalå**, e.g., qâ'ēma קמה (also spelled קאמה) — certainly a participle on the Aramaic model; fā'ēlåt (TH פָּעֳלָת; cf. fā'ēlu = TH פָּעֳלוּ); lā'ēba להבה, lā'ēbåt להבת (in Ex 3:2 we find in place of TH בלבת: בלהבת), nåšēmåt נשמת, å'ēba אהבה[43] (infinitive absolute form), åfēdåtu = TH אֲפֵדָתוֹ.

3. **fâqēdət.** In this form we find fårēkət פרכת; and perhaps mā'ērət מחרת, in which the מ appears to be originally part of the pattern. The latter SH form in fact still presents the original form מאחרת; the issue is in need of further study (see 4.3.7).

4. **fâqådalå**, e.g., bårāka ברכה, kåbāša כבשה, nåbāla נבלה, nåqāba נקבה, qålāla קללה, ådåmå אדמה, åšåmå אשמה, åšårå אשרה, 'årābå ערבה, šådåmot שדמות, wåbårātimma ועברתם, altåtåfot לטטפות. Many of the nouns are declined like פְּעָלָה in TH, i.e., without the vowel of the feminine suffix (like יִבְמְתּוֹ), such as šåmåltu שמלתו, šåmåltåk שמלתך, šågågtu שגגתו, šågågtimma שגגתם, bårāktu ברכתו, åšåmtu אשמתו — as against nådåbåtimma נדבתם, ådåmåtåk אדמתך, ådåmåtimma אדמתם.

Note: Cf. nådåba to TH חֲלָלָה and SH wålåla.

5. **fâqådåt.** dålåqåt. The relationship between SH forms and TH forms is like that of בָּרֶקֶת to בָּרֶקֶת within TH itself. As for yåkålåt יכלת, it cannot be determined whether ת is present in the singular absolute form in the Samaritan tradition, since in the Pentateuch the noun appears in its construct state, while in SA and late Samaritan Hebrew there are different noun forms corresponding to TH יכלת: yåkålūtåk (LOT III/2, 201, l. 52; 346, l. 10) — something like יְכָלוּת*; plural: yåkålot (ibid., 306, l. 37), from *yåkålå or from *yåkålat?; yēkiltåk (ibid., 324, l. 15) similar to Aramaic יְכַלְתָּא; and yåkūlå (ibid., 123, l. 18).

6. **fâqūdalå**, e.g., åmūna אמונה, båkūrå בכורה, båkūråti בכורתי.

4.1.5.8

1. **fūqīdåt.** In reality, this is not a noun-class but the loanword dūgīfåt דוגיפת (SP!).]

2. **fūqēdalå.** This is the feminine form of the Qal participle and is found in the nouns tuwwēba תועבה, tuwwēbot תועבות, kåtuwwēfot כתועפות (if this is not derived from the root יע"ף). If there was in fact a form *dūbērå דבורה (based on addūbērəm Dt 1:44, SP Nu 14:45, and there is a reading הדוברים), its u vowel is derived from šəwa and the ē vowel is the product of dissimilation: *dᵉbūrå > *dubūrå > *dūbērå (see 1.5.3.2), which is also preserved in the personal name

---

[43] This form is found in the Pentateuch only in the infinitive absolute, and so, too, å'ēbåttu with gemination when it occurs with the personal pronoun suffix.

dibbūrå דבורה (the gemination of ב is found also in Aramaic and in Arabic دبّور.).

3. **fūqådət,** e.g., ūfårət עופרת, yūtårət יותרת. This the feminine form of the Qal participle parallel to פועלת.

4.1.5.9

1. **fiqqēda.** ilmēna אלמנה, ilmēnot אלמנות, and ilmēnūta אלמנותה. There is no masculine form corresponding to this feminine form (see 4.1.4.4 note). It is difficult to posit that the basis for the SH form is the same as that of TH אַלְמָנָה, and it seems that the origin of the e vowel is in o, i.e., that the base form is אַלְמֹן (וְאַלְמֹן Isa 47:9), which appears in Talmudic literature אלמון meaning "widow." Note that even MS Kaufmann, which includes the form אַלְמְנֻתוֹ, which is derived from אלמנה as expected, also has the form אַלְמְנַת, with šəwa following מ, which would not occur in a form bearing a double qames in the absolute form.

2. **fiqqådå/fiqqådət.** Geminated second radical: qiṭṭårå קטרה (SP Dt 33:10), qiṭṭårət קטרת, kittårət כתנת, kibbårət כפרת. Quadriradical roots: širšårət שרשרת. The gemination of a consonant in the nouns קטרה and קטרת is certainly secondary, as it is in the TH form כָּתֳנָת as against TH כְּתֹנֶת. It appears that the same is true of the noun כפרת in SH, in which the second radical of the verb כפ"ר is not geminated (see 2.1.3.5). The early date of the gemination in such forms as קטורה is perhaps hinted at in the LXX form of the name קטורה: χεττουρα. (However, SH qīṭūrå, SP ק(י)טורה.) The noun *ištårrot underlying weštårrot ועשתרות (צאן) is surprising for the combination of the geminated ר and the long vowel å. The length of that vowel seems to be hinted at in the manuscript orthography spelling ועשתארות; the toponym עשתרות bears no gemination: bištårot.

3. **fiqqūdå/å.** The noun bikkūrot בכורות (e.g., Dt 12:6,17) may be the plural form of בְּכוּרָה or בַּכּוּרָה, unattested in the Pentateuch, or it may be a (second) plural form of bikkur בכור (see 4.1.4.3[3]).

4. **faqqēda/faqqēdət, fåqqēdət.** Geminated second radical: barrēqət ברקת, takkēlət תכלת, yabbēlət יבלת, yallēfət ילפת, ṣårrēbət צרבת, 'awwērət עורת, bå'ērət בהרת. Quadriradical roots: qašqašət קשקשת, arnēbət ארנבת. It should be pointed out that despite the fact that in SH the faqqəd noun pattern does not especially denote a person with a disability (see 4.1.3.14), the corresponding feminine noun pattern usually does, as in Jewish Aramaic (see, e.g., Dalman, Grammatik, 160: קִדְחָתָא, etc.).

The lack of gemination in the noun å:lēma אחלמה indicates that some element turned the šəwa of the ח into a šəwa mobile: a form such as אַחֲלָמָה*. Its ē vowel is not from the same origin as the ē vowel in the other forms cited here, and the vowels of this noun outside Hebrew are unknown.

5. **falåqqåda.** yåbbåša יבשה. This noun form and faqqēdət are originally variants of qattalat / qattalt, and an example of this relationship in TH is לֶהָבָה

/ לְהָבָת, but this is not so in SH. The construct form is *yåbbåšåt*.

6. **fēqiddalå, fålåqiddalå.** These forms combine patterns which are represented in TH by פְּעֻלָּה and פְּעֻלָּה, and in the TH forms it is evident that the gemination sometimes replaces a short vowel, i.e., they originate in PS *qatilat* and *qatulat*, which are the source of the variants פְּעִילָה / פְּעֵלָה / פְּעָלָה, such as אֲבֵדָה, שְׁמִטָּה, חֲלִיקָה, and the (rare) variants פְּעוּלָה / פְּעֻלָּה, such as אֲגֻדָּה, קְבוּצָה. The differences in development are evident also in the relationship between TH and SH, such as *šĕmittå* = שְׁמִטָּה but *ēbidda* : אֲבֵדָה, *gēbirråti* גברתי as against גבירה, *qēbirråtu* קְבָרָתוּ (and not *קְבָרְתוּ!), *qēbirråta* קְבָרְתָה, *yårišša* = TH יְרֻשָּׁה and יְרֻשָּׁה. In SH we also find in this pattern *fēṭidda* פטדה and *'årilla* ערלה (Akkadian pl. *urullāti, urūlāti*). Is there in fact reflected in the word *yērakkētu* ירכתו something like TH יְרֵכִית?

4.2–4.3 Compound Patterns

4.2 Prefixed Patterns

4.2.1 With א-.

4.2.1.1 From a diachronic perspective it is not easy, and in fact it is sometimes impossible, to distinguish between two group of nouns: (a) those in which initial א is a part of the root (radical) in Hebrew (or even in PS), such as (we may assume) אלמנה, אבנט, אביון, ארבה, and אריה; and (b) those in which the א is a component in the formative, as is clear, for example, in אזרוע and אצעדה. How we classify nouns such as אכזר, איתן, ארגז, and אשכול depends on the etymologies we assign them, which do not constitute a sufficient basis for a decision. From a descriptive, synchronic perspective, however, it is possible in most instances to determine whether, in a given stage or tradition of Hebrew, the א in a particular word is a radical or part of the pattern. The decision is made this way: א is part of the pattern if (1) parallel to the form with א there is a form without it, e.g., זרוע, צעדה, and תמול alongside אזרוע, אצעדה, and אתמול; or (2) if the language has a root (whether in a verb or a noun) without the א that is related in meaning to the noun in question, such as the verb הצביע (MH) in relation to the noun אצבע, רביעי in relation to ארבע, or אזקים in relation to the verb זקק in *Qal* or *Nif'al* in MH; or (3) if the particular noun is formed in such a way as to prevent א from being part of the root or make it difficult to do so, as is the case, for example, with איתן, because there is usually no spelling with י that is not a radical, or with *abbā'ṭīm* = האבטיחים in TH as against SH (see 4.1.3.13 note). If none of these conditions is met, it is advisable not to consider the א a formative component of the word, even if the same root is known in a cognate language. Thus אבטיח in TH (as against SH) and אזוב are nouns in which א is treated as a radical, even though we find זוּפָא in Syriac and *zupu* in Akkadian.

4.2.1.2 It is not certain that there exists in Hebrew a prefix pattern with initial א like the elative pattern أَفْعَل in Arabic, but it is clear that we find א as a carrier of an auxiliary vowel created when splitting a consonant cluster at the beginning of a word, such as אזרוע < *zroʿ. Of course, splitting a cluster by means of a vowel **before** the first consonant of the cluster is not the normal manner of splitting the cluster in TH; creating an auxiliary vowel after the first consonant of the cluster (šəwa mobile) is the rule. Once the phenomenon occurred in ancient times, it was expressed in the orthography with א. TH preserved this ancient stage; however, in the oral tradition of SH and of SA, the other way is very common, though without changing the ancient spelling tradition (without א).[44] In any case, the pattern with prefixed א is more common in SH than in TH. Of course, this does not include the instances of א resulting from the weakening of gutturals, e.g., הרבה arbå (cf. Gn 3:16), which cannot be considered to belong to a pattern containing א.

4.2.1.3 The vowel of the prefixed א in nouns written with א in SH is either a or i, and the difference does not parallel that between אַ and אֶ in TH; the i vowel is more common. In nouns written without א in SP, a is prevalent, although i can also be found. Of those written with א we shall mention (with the proviso cited above in 4.2.1.1): ifrå'əm אפרוחים, iṣbaʿ אצבע, itnån אתנן, iškol אשכול (?), ēṣidda (< *iṣʿidda) אצעדה, and obviously ītan איתן, arba ארבע, am'tāt אמתחת, *azra אזרח (attested only with prepositions: bâzra, kâzra, etc.).

> Note: From ak zarri in Dt 32:33, there is no way to know whether SH has a single noun or whether the spelling as two words אכ זרי indicates that the latter word is derived from זר ("stranger") in SH, from the root זר״ר, as ST ברן בראי attests. On the other hand, SAV according to MS Barberini and MS 6 of the Shekhem synagogue (מע סם אלרקש אלחקדה) considers it a single word. If this latter tradition is authentic, it presents a derivation from the root כז״ר (found in Syriac) parallel to אכוב from כז״ב.

4.2.1.4 From this point on, we shall mention only nouns belonging to this category and not spelled with א in SP. They are:
  1. In the **afqad** form: afsəl פסל, afsīli פסילי, ašqaṣ שקץ, irrəf (< *iḥrəf) חרף, irraš (< *iḥraš) = TH חֶרֶשׁ; amgən מגן, asfī שפי, anši נשיא, anšiyyā'i נשיאי, anšiyyāyyimma (< *anšiyyā'iyyimma, see 1.5.3.4[4]) נשיאיהם, inšəm נשים, asfīkot שפכות (SP Dt 23:2, TH שפכה; cf. 4.3.14 note). It would seem that this category should include âzzəq החזק (Nu 13:18) and bâzzəq בחזק (Ex 13:3); by assuming a basic

---

[44] The phenomenon of א with an a vowel at the beginning of a word remaining unexpressed in writing in SH led to the absence here and there of this letter even where it was originally written, as, for example, in azmintå, the Afʿel form of זמן, which can be found spelled זמנת in an Aramaic liturgical poem (see LOT III/2, 325, l. 25).

4.2 Prefixed Patterns

form *'aḥzaq > *azzaq we can easily explain the gemination of ז in this word (see 1.5.3.1). The noun 'aššər = TH הֶעָשֵׁר should also be assigned to this category.

It appears that the basis for forms such as פסל, שקץ, and others in SH is not the PS *qatl* pattern underlying the TH forms, but instead the pattern that yields the TH form פְּעָל. The independent forms with original *šəwa* may have been derived by analogy from the declined forms. This seems to be a likely explanation, and in any case the necessary one with regard to words such as *anši* < *נשיא and *amgən* < *מָגֵן.

2. In the **afqåd** form: *alšåm* לשם, *(k)anšår* כנשר, *asfår* = TH סֵפֶר, *miyyasfåri* מספרי, *asfåråk* ספרך, *afsa* פסח, *asfåm* שפם, *asfån* שפן, *asqår* שקר, and *irrås* < *ihrås* (only *bērrås* = TH בְּחֶרֶס is attested). With the exception of שפם and שפן, it may be assumed that the original relationship between SH and TH in these words is an alternation of the forms פְּעָל/segholates (see 4.1.3.8); and indeed in TH we find סֵפֶר, but its meaning is different from that of סֵפֶר. Along with *anšår* we find in SH *nēšår* as well, which may be understood as a segholate. As for שפם and שפן, see the discussion in 4.1.3.8.

3. Feminine nouns: *asfa* = TH שָׂפָה, *asfåt* שפת, *asfåtu* שפתו, *asfåtək* שפתיך; *aš'få* שפחה, *asfåttu* שפחתו, *asfåtta* שפחתה, *asfå'ot* השפחות; *ēzåkårå* אזכרה, *lēzåkårå* לאזכרה, *ēzåkårta* אזכרתה. Also: *aškåbåt* שכבת, *aškåbtu* שכבתו, *afqåråt* בקרת (akin to TH *בְּקֹרֶת), *atkånåt* תכנת (*wbatkantu* בתכנתו SP Ex 30:32). The first two nouns reflect the following underlying forms: *שָׂפָה, paralleling *må* < מְאָה = TH מֵאָה; *שִׁפְחָה, declined on the model of עֲטֶרֶת and עֲטֶרֶת, from עטרה and עשרה. In *ēzåkårta* אזכרתה, the א may not be a formative component of *Hif'il*,[45] i.e., a variant of ה, even though it is precisely in SH that we would expect such an occurrence, but it is instead an independent morphological element. Thus, we may compare the Samaritan form to TH אבטיח, which has an א with a *šəwa*.

4.2.2 With -י

As anticipated on the basis of the rules of TH, יחמור and ינשוף are realized as *yå:mor* and *yanšof*, and יקום is *yēqom*. From *yēllåm* יהלם we can learn that TH and SH share the same pattern and the final vowel is originally short, but, alternatively, it may be fair to assume that the SH form takes a shape similar to that of TH יִפְעָל; cf. *yå'ṣår* יצהר.

---

[45] At Ex 20:20, SP reads אזכרתי where the Jewish Pentateuch reads אזכיר, but from the pronunciation, which is *ēzåkårti* and not something like *azkirti* (cf. *wazkirtåni* והזכרתני Gn 40:14), it appears that this word was not interpreted as *Hif'il*. The reading אזכרתי as it is pronounced appears to indicate that the Samaritan tradition could not interpret the word אזכיר as a perfect verb as in the Jewish tradition, and from a morphological perspective it did not understand אזכרתי as equivalent to הזכרתי. Further study, however, leads us to interpet *ēzåkårti* as a perfect *Hif'il* verb; see 2.1.2.4 note.

4.2.3 With -מ

4.2.3.1 We do not include among the forms with מ the participle (including those like *mēkassi* מכסה = TH מְכַסֶּה!) in the various verbal stems. The noun patterns with מ in TH are fewer in number than those thought to have existed in PS because of phonological developments in TH. For example, the original distinction between the components *ma* and *mi* has been blurred in TH: מַ has become the common mode and מִ is reserved for special circumstances such as following a guttural, in the פ״נ class, or the like. The inherited forms were even further limited in SH by the phonological changes that took place in that tradition of Hebrew, and, thus, the derivatives of *maqtul* merged with the derivatives of *maqtal*, but new patterns were created on the basis of distinctions created within SH. The table below exemplifies the relations among the three linguistic traditions as they are reflected in the strong roots. It should be stressed that only the patterns are compared, and one should not derive any conclusions about certain synonyms in the various Semitic languages since they may actually relate to different forms and patterns in the different linguistic traditions, as for example מַפְתֵּחַ: מִפְתָּח or مِفْتَاح, and the same is true of the relations between TH and SH.

	PS	TH	SH
1.	*maqtil*	מִפְעָל (or מַפְעֵל)	*mafqəd*
2.	*miqtīl*		
	(in Arabic, e.g., مِنْطِيق = "very eloquent")		
3.	*maqtal* ⎫	מִפְעָל (or מַפְעָל)	*mafqad*
4.	*miqtal* ⎭		(with *a/å* variation)
5.	*maqtāl* ⎫		
6.	*miqtāl* ⎬	מִפְעוֹל (or מַפְעוֹל)	*mafqod*
7.	*maqtul* ⎭		
8.	*maqtūl*	מַפְעוּל	

It is apparent, then, that the eight PS patterns were reduced to four in TH, most of which have מַ/מִ variants, and in SH to three. In addition to these inherited patterns SH developed new forms, some of which due to the splitting of the single phoneme /a/ into two phonemes /a,å/. The following are the SH forms:

4.2.3.2 *mafqəd, måfqad,* e.g., *mamzər* ממזר, *mazrəq* מזרק, *mamkər* ממכר, *mazrēqúto* מזרקותיו, *mamkēru* ממכרו, *mållēlək* מעלליך, *maknēsi* מכנסי, *makrētīyyimma* מכרתיהם (Gn 49:5).

In the ל״ה class: *måšši* מעשה, *maqni* מקנה, *mâ:ni* מחנה; *måzzi* מחזה; *måššē'u* (< *måšši + ē'u*) מעשהו, *mâ:nək* מחניך, *maqnīyyimma* מקניהם. The construct form *maduwwi* = TH מַדְוֵי was created when the *šəwa* of the ד became *mobile*, and the same is true for in *måšå'əl* = TH מִשְׁאֵל (< *mašª'el* < *maš'el*).

In the פ״י (פ״ו) class, the surface form is *mūqaš* מוקשים, *muwwəd* (< *mū'əd*) מועד (in the sense of "gathering, coming together"), plural *muwwēdəm*.

4.2.3.3 *mafqåd, måfqåd*, e.g., *madbår* מדבר, *madråk* מדרך, *makbår* מכבר, *masfår* מספר, *maqdåš* מקדש, *masfåṭ* משפט, *maškån* משכן; *mayyån* מעין. The vowel of מ, when lengthened, may become *å*: *måssaru* מחסרו, *måššår* (some read *māššår*) מעשר, *mā:kål* מאכל, *mā'nål* מנעל (< *man^a'al*). And of course, the vowel of the second radical in an open syllable is *å* as well, e.g., *masfåṭəm* משפטים and *målqåyyå* (*malqā'iyya*) מלקחיה.

In the פ״י (פ״ו) class, the surface form is: (1) *mūsår* מוסר, *mūfåt* מופת, *mūṣå* מוצא, *mūšåb* מושב, and *muwwad* מועד (in the sense of a fixed time), plural *muwwādəm* מועדים; (2) *mīṭåb* מיטב; (3) see below, under the פ״נ class.

In the פ״נ class, the gemination of the second radical is sometimes eliminated: *måsa* מסע, *måša* = both TH מַשָּׂא and TH מַשָּׁא, plural *måsåkkimma* משאכם. Gemination is also absent from the noun in *måråkkimma* = TH מַרְאֲכֶם and *båmårå'əm* במראים, from the root יר״א,[46] as against the gemination in the noun מַדָּע from יד״ע in TH, and it should be noted that SH actually tends to geminate the second radical in פ״י verbs more than does TH; see 2.4.9c.

In the ע״י class, the surface form is *måqom* מקום, *mā'or* מאור, *måṣoq* מצוק, *måqūmu* מקומו, *mā'ūrot* מאורות.

It might appear that *mirråk* מרך (Lv 26:36) is a noun of this form from the ע״ע class, but take note of the fact that SAV treats this word as רך with a prepositional מ, and so, too, ST in the reading מרכיך,מרוכה.

In the ל״ה class, we cannot distinguish between מפעל and מפעל in TH, since both bear the ending ־ָה. In SH, nouns ending in *i* have been classified with the *mafqəd* form; under this rubric we should classify *maquwå* מקוה as well, because the ending *å* is not the feminine ending here, since the construct state form of the word is identical. This form resembles the ל״ה verbs ending in an *a/å* vowel (see 2.8.10[2]; 2.8.11).

4.2.3.4 *mafqod*. *makšol* מכשול, *malqoš* מלקוש, *mašqol* משקול; and in the פ״י class *mīšor* מישור.

4.2.3.5 We learn from the preceding that the shift $a > i$ in a closed syllable, common in TH and found in SH as well, as for example in the vowel of the preformative of the imperfect (א, י, נ, ת), does not occur with the prefix מ of these noun forms, just as it does not regularly occur in these noun forms in BH

---

[46] In place of TH ובמרא (Dt 26:8) and המורא (Dt 34:12), SH reads ובמראה and המראה, and the noun is in fact pronounced *mā'ri* — i.e., מראי — and the Samaritan translations, too, interpret this as referring to sight: ST חזי, מחזב; SAV مناظر. It is possible that מרא according to its SH pronunciation is to be identified with Aramaic מרע; see *LOT* III/2, 248, l. 17.

or in the Hebrew of the Hexapla. In a noun such as *mē'bār* מבחר, however, *mē* may not be explained directly from *ma*. If its original form was not actually *mibᵃḥar, it may have been *mᵉbār (< **mᵉbā'ar* < *mabᵃḥar*), similar to what is described in 4.2.3.6.

4.2.3.6 SH sometimes requires a noun form for a given verbal stem. For example, the nouns מכסה and משלח, the roots of which usually appear in *Pi'el*, take the following shape: *mēšalla* משלח, *mēkassi* מכסה (and similarly *mēṣāba* מצוה, whose verbal form is conjugated in the *Pi'el* "with simple second radical"). The origin of the *ē* vowel presumably lies in *šəwa*, and the form is the same is that of the participle; in fact, this noun form may be the participle.

4.2.3.7 Feminine Patterns (4.2.3.7–4.2.3.11)

The feminine patterns below, which are derived from the masculine patterns (4.2.3.2, 4.2.3.3), have three forms of feminine endings: *å/a*, *åt*, and *ət*. The vowel of the מ in a closed syllable is normally *a*; in an open syllable, *å*. An *ā* vowel will sometimes occur before a guttural consonant. The masculine pattern ending in *ə* has as its feminine equivalents patterns ending in *ī* and in *ē*. The distinction between the two latter forms does not precisely match that between מִפְעָל and מַפְעִיל; it is instead the result of analogies within SH. In addition, there are SH nouns in feminine patterns with מ that, due to particular processes, have come to resemble the participle to the point that the two cannot be distinguished with certainty. The evidence for this follows.

4.2.3.8 Forms originating in **mafqəd** and **måfqəd**: (1) *mårrēka* מערכה, *masgērət* מסגרת, *masgirtu* מסגרתו, *maskēnət* = TH מִסְכֵּנֶת; *måṣnēfət* מצנפת, *mā:gērət* מעגרת (=מגערת), *måkkēlət* מאכלת, *mā:bērət* מחברת, *mā:båṛtu* מחברתו; *mamkēråt* ממכרת; (2) *maggīfa* מגפה, *maggīfūti* מגפותי; *massīka* מסכה, *massīkūtīyyimma* מסכותיהם, *måṣṣība* מצבה, *måṣṣībūtīyyimma* מצבותיהם, *måzåkīråt* מזכרת (Nu 5:15; the *â* vowel after the ז originated in the *šəwa* becoming *mobile*).

4.2.3.9 Forms originating in **mafqåd** and **måfqåd**: *mamlåkåt* ממלכת, *mamlåkot* ממלכות, *mamlåktu* ממלכתו; *mamšālåt* ממשלת, *markåbåt* מרכבת, *markåbtu* מרכבתו, *mašmårət* משמרת, *mašmårtu* משמרתו, *mašmårti* משמרתי, *maškåråti* משכרתי, *maškåråti* משכרתי, *maškåråtåk* משכרתך, *målā:ka* מלאכה, *målåktåk* מלאכתך, *målā:mot* מלחמות, *måsā:nūtimma* משענותם. In verbs II-guttural we sometimes find gemination of the third radical: *målåmma* מלחמה, the product of contact between a guttural second radical and the third radical: *malahma < *malᵃhama after the *šəwa* developing into an actual vowel (see 1.5.3.1; 1.3.5e), which is clearly evident in the declension: *målā'imtu* מלחמתו, *måsā'intu* משענתו.

4.2.3.10 With the weak roots, these patterns take on the following forms: (1) in the פ"י class: *mūråša* מורשה; (2) in the פ"נ class, the gemination of the second radical is sometimes eliminated, and, thus, alongside *måttåna* מתנה, *måttånot* מתנות, *massot* מסות, *mukka* מכה (< *makka), *makkot* מכות, and *makkūtåk* מכותך, we find *meta* = TH מַטֶּה, מַטֶה; (3) in the ע"י class: *måšūra* משורה, *mū:na* מעונה (< *m‛ūnā), *menūra* מנורה, *mårība* מריבה, *båmåṣålot* במצלות, *båmå:lot* במהלות, *må:må* מהומה (cf. מְצוּדָה/מְצָדָה); (4) in the ל"ה class: *makwå* מכוה (TH מִכְוָה), *måqqå* = TH מֶעֲקֶה, *må:la* = TH מַחֲלָה, *mā:la* מעלה, *meṣåba* מצוה, *måqåša* מקשה (the vowel after the first radical is derived from *šewa*). The pronunciation *mā'ət* מחית (Lv 13:24) corresponds to TH מִחְיַת*, i.e., it is, formed with the vowelless feminine ending -*t* (*maliḥyt) whereas *miyya* (Gn 45:5) is formed with the feminine ending -*at* as in TH מִחְיָה.

4.2.3.11 With nouns such as *amgåballot* מגבלות (SP Ex 28:14), *amgabbā'ot* מגבעות, *amsab'bēt* מספחת, and *amšåbbēsot* משבצות, it cannot be determined whether (a) they are formed according to the *mafqad* or *mafqəd* pattern and have undergone the process described above (4.2.3.9–10) in reference to מקשה and מלחמה (sect. 4) with the addition of gemination in place of a long vowel (i.e., *mašbēsot > *maš‹bēsot > m‹šåbbēsot > amšåbbēsot; *magbalot > *mag‹bal(l)ot > *amgåballot) or (b) they are originally participles (see 2.13.5), similar to *amnaqqiyyūto* מנקיותיו, *mīnqåt* מינקת, *mīniqta* מינקתה, and *mīnqot* מינקות (SP Gn 32:16). It appears that *kåmīfkåt* כמהפכת (Dt 29:22) is also a *Hifʿil* participle, akin to TH מַהְפֶּכֶת*. The elimination of the *i* vowel after the נ in *mīnqot* may have been the result of Aramaic influence and the same influence may be responsible for treating כמהפכת (Dt 29:22) as if it were פ"י (= פ"א in Aramaic: מיפך, ניפוך). The word *mīnqot* in Ex 2:7 is singular, and, thus, its base is something like מינקות, and we find in y. Nidda 1:5 (49a) מינקותה and in t. Kelim II 4:5 מיניקות שעשאה.

4.2.4 With ת-

4.2.4.1 The noun patterns with initial ת correspond in form and development to the noun patterns with מ. Before a guttural first radical, the *i* (< *ē*) vowel is more common than *å/a*, and we also find gemination of the first radical in place of a long vowel following the ת. Thus, we find in SH:

4.2.4.2 Masculine Forms: *tafqad*: perhaps the nouns *taršaš* תרשיש, *tešåbbaṣ* תשבץ (see 4.2.3.11 משבצות); *tafqalåd*: *tånnåg* תענג (SP Dt 28:56), *tīråš* תירוש, *tīmåna*[47]

---

[47] The form תימן with the meaning "south wind" is unattested in the Pentateuch. We find only the personal name (e.g., Gn 36:11). There is no distinction in SH between a masculine noun with a locative ה and a feminine noun. Both have penultimate stress. The noun תימנה (e.g., Ex 26:18) has been assigned to the masculine form on the basis of its TH cognate.

תחמוס *tā:mos*; תחלאיה *tēllā'iyya* (originating from *taqtāl*), תושב *tūšab*, תימנה (Lv 11:16, SP Dt 14:15). Also the noun *tiballāl* (Lv 21:20, TH תִּבַלָּל).

4.2.4.3 Feminine Forms: Based on *tafqəd*: *tånšēmət* תנשמת, *tardīmma* תרדימה(!). Based on *tafqaldd*: *tērra* תחרה, *tāwwå* תאוה, *tēwwåt* תאות, *wbattēllålot* ובתהללות (SP Dt 32:10) [for which a TH form such as *תְּהִלָּה*[48] would be appropriate], *tēbā:ra* תבערה (< *tib'ara*); in the פ"י class: *tūra* תורה, *tūda* תודה; in the ע"י class: *tēbūna* תבונה, *tēmūna* תמונה, *tēbuwwåtåk* תבואתך, *tirruwwa* תרועה, *tinnuwwåti* תנואתי; in the ע"ע class: *tēllå* (< *t^ehilla*) תהלה, *tēlla* תחלה (in liturgical poetry, LOT III/2, 75); in the ל"ה class: *tēliy'yå* תלאה (if not derived from תל"א), *tibnət* תבנית, *tirbət* תרבית (Lv 25:36 and in v. 37 in place of מרבית), and *tirbot* תרבות.

> Note: (1) In the noun forms *tūldåt*(!) תולדות and *tūldūtimma* תולדותם, the vowel of the second radical has disappeared, and it is, therefore, difficult to assign that noun to a pattern in SH. However, from the name of a chronicle *tūlīda* תולידה, which is written partially in Aramaic we learn that the noun belongs to the *tafqəd* form. (2) The word *kåtuwwēfot* כתועפות, if derived from יע"ף, belongs to the *tafqəd* form as well. (The noun *tuwwēba* תועבה is a participle from תע"ב.)

4.3 Suffixed Patterns and Nouns with Suffixes

4.3.0 As we stated above (4.0.1), we must be cognizant of the distinction between two types of noun formation: (1) compound patterns bearing endings, by which we mean syllables following the last radical, often referred to imprecisely as suffixes, and (2) bases (see 2.0.2) bearing endings, by which we mean syllables after the base, which are properly termed suffixes. An example of (1) is זִכָּרוֹן. An example of (2) is the Modern Hebrew noun מְחִירוֹן ("price list"), formed by expanding the base מְחִיר (and not combining directly with the root מח"ר) by means of the suffix ןֹ-. A pattern bearing an ending is a morphological unity in which the ending is not independent, or, to put it differently, the ending cannot be transferred to another pattern; while a suffix may attach freely to all sorts of bases. Type (2) is more rare in classical Hebrew than in Modern Hebrew, and by the same token it is rare in SH. The elements that generally serve in the compound patterns serve as suffixes to bases, which occasionally engenders difficulties in the morphological analysis of nouns. In addition, we can see how the compound patterns developed from bases with suffixes, not

---

[48] This is understood as "praise" (TH תְּהִלָּה); ST renders it ובתשבחן, SAV وبالمدايح. It is found used in this sense in liturgical poetry; see LOT III/2, 131, l. 219, and 331, l. 11. As to the reconstructed vocalization, cf. תִּבַלָּל above (4.2.4.2).

only in the instance of the "feminine" forms (4.1.5) but also occasionally in other categories. For example, we see that the origin in Hebrew of the noun רְעָבוֹן is from רָעָב with the addition of וֹן-, which is not true of TH צִמָּאוֹן. The latter does, in fact, derive from: צמא + ון; this origin, was obscured by a phonological process in TH, but remains apparent in SH ṣåmå'on.

4.3.1 The suffixed formatives, as they appear in SH, are:
   a. the vowels *i*, *e*, *a/å*, and *u*;
   b. a combination of a vowel followed by a consonant: *əm/'īm*, *ən/'īn*; *ət/'īt*; *åy/a'ī*; *åm/'åm* ('*ām*), *om*; *an/'ån*; *on/ūn*; *(i)nn*; *åt — ot*. In these, the original vowel quantity is generally long, but in SH the length depends on the syllable rules that apply;
   c. a consonant not originally preceded by a vowel, but one that developed in Hebrew to serve as a bridge between the final radical and the suffixed formative, as is clear especially with ן-. By this we mean such elements as ל in כרמל (as against כרם) and ל in ספל (as against סך), ם in שפם (as against שפה) and פתאום (as against פתע?), and ן in כנען and צפרן. It is very doubtful whether in this type of word the formative is perceived as something separate and not part of the root. Those with ם and ן are classified here with this form, since ם and ן are clearly components of other suffix forms. The nouns with a final ל, on the other hand — *gē'bāl* גבעל, *karməl* כרמל, *(w)arfəl* (ו)ערפל — are classified with the simple patterns.

Since the suffixed patterns are few in number, and since some of the suffixed elements are rare in compound patterns and they appear as well in base + suffix forms, we include in the following description the patterns with endings along with the base + suffix forms. Thus, we pay due attention to proper names, among which suffixed forms are common.

4.3.2 *i.* SH combines originally distinct forms still distinguishable in TH:
   a. ִי- as in שֵׁשִׁי; אָחֳזִי, כֵּלִי, גּוּבִי — and in SH: *šalwi* שלוי (TH שְׁלָו, Syriac ܣܠܘܝ, Arabic سَلْوَى), *šarri* שָׂרִי, *šīšī* שֵׁשִׁי;
   b. ֶה-, ָה- as in ארבה, אִשָּׁה, אריה, עשרה — and in SH: *arbi* ארבה, *ēši* אשה. There is, of course, no exact parallel between words in SH and TH; e.g., *aryå* (as in Aramaic) = אַרְיֵה, *libna* לבנה; עשרה does not exist in SH (see 5.2.1);
   c. ִי-, i.e., the gentilic suffix as in *karmi* כרמי, *libni* לבני, *madyåni* מדיני, *nikri* נכרי, *ifši* חפשי, *'åti* עתי (derived from *at* עת);
   d. a paragogic ִי- as in *åsūri* אסורי (SP Gn 49:11, where TH has אסיר), *bēni* בְּנִי (Gn 49:11), *nå:dåri* נאדרי (Ex 15:6), *rå:mi* (SP Dt 33:17 ראמי).[49]

---

[49] The Samaritan tradition leaves the nature of this paragogic י unclear. Sometimes it is absent from their version, as in שכן (Dt 33:16): *šåkən* and גנובת (Gn 31:39): *gēnūbåt*. At other times, it is translated in different ways, as with אסורי: ST אסירי (see also *LOT* II, 537, l. 109) or אסירי — that is,

4.3.3 e. This vowel does not have the same origin as *seghol* and *ṣere* in TH, as we noted in the previous section, especially since *seghol* and *ṣere* usually parallel an *i* vowel in SH, e.g., *mašši* מעשה, *šādi* = TH שָׂדֶה, and others. We find the *e* vowel in SH in instances where TH has *qameṣ*: *yašbe* : יִשְׁוֶה, *yamne* : יִמְנֶה, *ilqāne* : אלקנה, *mizze* : מִזֶּה, *ʿalwe* : עֹלָה, *ʾāne* : עֲנֵה, *ʿayyåre* : חִירָה, *mākke* : מֶכָה. It appears as though this vowel represents a slight shift of the feminine suffix *a/å*, perhaps because the things represented by these nouns are masculine and, thus, a feminine ending seemed inappropriate for them. Such slight shifts of vowel are known in Arabic dialects (إمالة).[50] Other than in proper nouns, this vowel is found in the nouns *yašfe* : יָשְׁפֶה, *lā:ne* : לֵנָה, *yā:ne* : יֵנָה, *iyyåbe* : אִיבָה, *māne* : מִנָּה, *nåbe* : נוה. In the last two nouns, it seems that, etymologically, the vowel is not a suffixed formative but rather a replacement for a radical consonant. However, since an *i* vowel is to be anticipated, as in שָׂדֶה (mentioned previously), but is not present, we may assume that the last syllable was thought to be the suffix under discussion.

> Note: In the toponym that appears in TH as אֶלְעָלֵה, SH reads *ālēla*, even though there are toponyms that end with *e* — not just *nīnåbe* נינוה, but *mīdåbe* מידבא as well.

4.3.4 a/å. This refers, of course, to the locative ה, the original function of which was blurred and which became a fixed element in various nouns, as in *līla* לילה or the adverbs *almēṭå* לְמַטָּה, *milmēṭå* מלמטה, *almā:la* למעלה. In addition to what is common in TH, we find in SH *ṣibbūna* צפונה, which is always spelled this way in SP, and *šamma* even when the spelling is שם and not just when it is שמה. On the other hand, we find in Ex 15:12 *īma* אימה, and not (as in the Masoretic text) אימתה. In these examples, there is no essential difference between SH and TH except for the suffixed formative. In the noun *qiṣṣå* קצה (see 4.1.5.4 note), the vowel remains in declension as well, as in *qiṣṣåʾēʾu* קצהו, and in the construct form: *qiṣṣå* (Nu 22:41) — a phenomenon that occurs only in nouns with an original guttural third radical. Given that the root קצ״ץ is close to the root קצ״ע, it is not impossible to assume that the pronunciation (*qəre*) of this word is derived from the latter, but it is a more likely assumption that a new suffix has been created and even sustained in declension. It is not impossible to take the same approach with *yēfa* = TH יָפֶה (!); that is, *a* is the suffix under discussion and, thus, the masculine and feminine forms (4.1.5.3.) became equivalent.

---

with a 1st pronominal suffix — but there exist also אסורה and the verb יסטי (MS Barberini) and SAV يربط [MS Barberini] يـغـبـط. Similarly, בני: ST ברי, בני (MS Barberini), and SAV בני all point to a construct plural (=TH בְּנֵי), but the pronunciation *bēni* (and not *båni*!) is inappropriate for a construct plural. The first word in the phrase צפינתי פענה (SP Gn 41:45) is rendered in ST as טמירתי.

[50] The إمالة phenomenon in the feminine suffix is ancient in Arabic, and the comments of the earliest grammarians attest to it. On this, see A. Levin, *The Imala in the Arabic Dialects* (Ph.D. thesis, The Hebrew University of Jerusalem, 1971), 30ff. [Hebrew].

4.3 Suffixed Patterns and Nouns with Suffixes

4.3.5 u. The suffix וֹ-, found in TH in personal names (e.g., שְׁלֹמֹה, עֵדוֹ) and toponyms (e.g., מְגִדּוֹ, יְרִיחוֹ), occurs in SH only in the proper noun יריחו pronounced *yăriyyu*, while שלה is pronounced *šīlå*, i.e., like the name שֵׁלָה.[51] The suffix וֹ- in the noun חיתו — the origin of which is not the same — is not found in SP. Instead we find חית, but בנו is retained in Nu 23:18 and 24:15, and SAV يا بن would seem to indicate the suffix is a vocative particle. In place of TH מדּוֹ in Lv 6:3, in which וֹ- can be understood as a paragogic element, SP reads מדי, pronounced *mådi*. On the other hand, where TH reads חכלילי (Gn 49:12), SP reads חכלילו, pronounced *iklīlu*. Similarly, יחדו is pronounced *yāddu* and understood to be without pronominal suffix, as is evident from ST כחדה and SAV جميعا. This word in SH, therefore, does not include an וֹ- suffix like that found in TH, but instead וֹ- or ו-. This suffix may also be present in the word *bêtåsêfu* בהתאספו; see also 2.2.1.2.5.3.

4.3.6. īm/əm, ən. By this is meant first of all:

a. common nouns whose base form is a plural or dual, such as *'ayyəm* חיים, *fånəm* פנים, *mallā'əm* = TH מְלֵאִים, *rēmməm* רחמים, *bašməm* בשמים (is not its singular form; see *LOT* III/1, 40, l. 6), *wbåfåləm* ובעפלים, *bētūləm* בתולים, *alzånəm* לונים (SP Gn 38:24, where the Masoretic text reads לזונים), *nā:rəm* = TH נְעָרִים, *zåqīnəm*, **zåqannəm* (*alzåqanno*) = TH זְקֵנִים,[52] *rīqəm* ריקם (sometimes spelled ריקים, e.g., Gn 31:42), *mem* מים, *sērrəm* צהרים, *mīm* מעים, *fid'wīm* פדוים;

b. proper nouns, such as *qaryåtəm* קריתים and *dūtən* דותין (SP Gn 37:17). Note that *īnəm* עינים (Gn 38:14, 21) is understood as "eyes," and according to the tradition expressed in ST and SAV, the phrase בפתח עינים means "in a visible (public) place."

Note: 1. Corresponding to ולשנינה (Dt 28:37), SP also reads ולשנאינה, pronounced *walšănā'īna*. ST ולסנה and SAV وبغضة also attest that the word is derived from שנ"א, and there is apparently a suffix *īna* here, as in the noun *dūtīna* דותינה, although it may be that this word is a conflation of שנאה and שנינה;

2. where TH reads הזוזים (Gn 14:5), SP reads הזוזאים, pronounced *azzūzâ'əm*, which may appear to display the dual form, but see 4.3.8 below.

4.3.7 īt/ət. The nouns ending with this syllable are of two types: (a) nouns III-y to which a feminine ending has been added, such as *bēkət* בכית; (b) nouns in

---

[51] Perhaps this can assist us in understanding the variation between TH הַשֵּׁלָנִי (Nu 26:20; SH *asšīlāni*) and הַשֵּׁלָנִי (Neh 11:5), הַשִּׁילֹנִי (1 Chr 9:5).

[52] The word *zåqīnəm* is the plural of *zåqən* זקן, but came to be understood as an abstract noun functioning adverbially in the sentence: *wyūlad zåqīnəm qåtån*. The Samaritan translations bring this to the fore: in Gn 44:20 ST translates בזבן סיבותה and SAV translates في حال كبره The word *zånəm*, too, is a participle understood as an abstract noun: ST זנו, SAV زنا.

which the feminine ending has been added after the gentilic suffix *i*, as in *yammīnət* (< **yammī'nīt*), spelled in SP ימינת or ימינית, but is no longer limited to expressing the feminine gender, having merged with the ending *i* to become an independent suffix fulfilling other functions as well. This is the case with the nouns *gifrət* גפרית, *rāšət* ראשית, *å'ērət* אחרית, *å'ērītåk* אחריתך, *å'ērītu* אחריתו, *tēttət* תחתית, *å'ērinnət* אחרנית, *kērītət* כריתת (Dt 24:1,3), *alṣēmītət* לצמיתת (Lv 25:30), and perhaps also *mimmå'ērət* ממחרת (without the ת: *mār* מחר!) (see, however, 4.1.5.7 [3]), *rē'bīt* רביעית, *kaṣṣē'fīt* כצפחית (SP Ex 16:31). The etymology of the noun *bērət* ברית is unclear, and therefore no determination can be made as to its classification with (a) or (b). Probably the noun *gizzət* גזית (Ex 20:22, TH גָּזִית) belongs with category (b), and in SH the noun is derived from the root גז״ז and not from גז״י. It should be noted that the form גְּזִית is attested (in Babylonian vocalization!) in Jewish sources as well (see S. Pinsker, *Einleitung in das Babylonisch-Hebräische Punktationssystem* [Vienna, 1863], 17 [Hebrew]), and the possibility of a derivation from גז״ז was considered by as early a scholar as David Qimḥi, in his *Mikhlol* (ed. Rittenberg, 162b). In the light of the SH form, the questioning of the reliability of the BH form (Yeivin, *Babylonian Vocalization*, 1053) should be reconsidered. Cf. also 5.1.2 note.

Note: In the noun *åzniyya* העזוניה the feminine suffix appears in the form of -יה (TH -יָּה) < **iyyat*. In the noun *albinya* חלבניה (SP Ex 30:34) < **albiniyya* (cf. Syriac חֶלְבָּנִיתָא) we see the process described above, 1.5.3.4[4].

4.3.8 *åy, ǻy / å'i, ǻ'i*. This is in Aramaic the gentilic suffix, equivalent to the Hebrew relative suffix *ī*. It can be found in MH — seldom in Tannaitic sources — and is apparently absent from the Jewish traditions of Biblical Hebrew.[53] In any case it is absent from the TH vocalization of the Pentateuch. However, in SH it occurs in such words as *šēlīšǻ'əm* שלישים (Gn 6:16 and Ex 20:5, etc.; TH שְׁלִשִׁים), *rēbiyyǻ'əm* רביעים (SP Ex 20:5; TH רְבֵעִים), *anṣiyyǻ'əm* נשיאים, *qaryā'i* קריאי (Nu 26:9 *qare*). In the latter two nouns there is an addition of the suffix *å/åy* to the forms קריא, נשיא (**qārī'āy* > **qariyyāy* > **qaryāy*, following the pattern described in 1.5.3.4[4]). Built in the same way is *riggålā'i* רגלאי (SP Ex 12:37; Nu 11:21), expressing the meaning of the *agens* both by means of the pattern and through the suffix. This suffix may also be preserved in הזוזאים; cf. 4.3.6, n. 2.

It should be pointed out that original *ay* in the ultimate syllable is reduced to *i* in SH (4.3.2), whereas when functioning as a gentilic suffix it maintains its

---

[53] Unless the -ִי in אַחֲרַי (Pr 28:23) is to be understood, as it is by Ibn Janāḥ (*Kitāb al-Lumaʿ*, 108) and his followers, as a formative component cognate in form with MH אחראי ("responsible"), and not as the first person pronominal suffix, which is the common opinion of the exegetes, in accordance with Saʿadia's translation (לטאעתי). Ibn Janāḥ interprets the word as an adjective meaning "(a man) who deviates from the right way" [i.e., keeping "another way"].

4.3 Suffixed Patterns and Nouns with Suffixes

diphthongal character by splitting into two syllables, as is customary in SA.⁵⁴

Note: The double expression of relationship in SH *riggālā'i* supports the authenticity and antiquity of the singular form זהבי "goldsmith" (found in Tannaitic souces in the plural only, e.g., *m. Kelim* 29:4) in the later stratum of MH (e.g., *Pesikta de Rav Kahana*, ed. Mandelbaum, 248) and its common pronunciation זְהָבִי, in Yemenite vocalization זַהֲבִי (*b. Shabbat* 128a). This last piece of information I owe to Dr. Mishor of the Historical Dictionary Project of the Hebrew Language Academy; additional variant spellings are listed there.

4.3.9 ǻm / 'ǻm ('ām), om. In the SH suffix *ǻm* we see the merger of originally distinct suffixes: *am* and *um*. This suffix is found (a) in proper nouns such as *ūnǻm* אונם, *gēttǻm* געתם, *maryǻm* מרים, *giršǻm* גרשם, *bā'lām* בלעם, and others; (b) in some words such as *innǻm* חנם, *yūmǻm* יומם, *fē'tǻm* פתאם. However, the use of this suffix in SH does not exactly parallel the use in TH; sometimes one finds the plural, such as *rīqəm* = ריקם (see 4.3.6) and *kinnəm* (Ex 8:13, 14) = TH כִּנָּם, and sometimes even a fossilized use of 3rd pl.: *āmēnimma* אמנם (= אמן+ם), in the same way that the suffix in ערכך is fossilized (see 3.2.3.4 note). This suffix has become part of the root in the nouns *asfǻm* שפם, *'arom* = עירם, *'arēməm* עירמים. The *om* form appears in the noun *šalšom* שלשום. In place of TH הפדיום (Nu 3:49, 51), SP reads הפדוים, and the pronunciation *affid'wīm* (! < *affidwiyyīm*) indicates that it is a substantive and not a plural participle. The ancient translations render it פרקניה (ST) and الفدا (SAV).

4.3.10 ǻn/ 'ǻn, on/ 'ūn and related forms. The origin of these elements in noun patterns and words is the same in TH as well as in SH — namely, PS *ān*. The rules of Hebrew require that its form in Hebrew be ון-, and that is indeed its common shape in TH, as in אחרון, זכרון, רעבון, and the proper noun חצרון, but the ן- form, nonetheless, also occurs in TH: כבשן, שלחן, קרבן, and especially in personal names such as חֶמְדָּן, עֵינָן, and others. One of the explanations⁵⁵ for the existence of ן- in words like קרבן is that the *ān* > ון- process was prevented from occurring in noun patterns in which the ending is preceded by *u*, and in fact such variants as אֲבַדּוֹן — אֲבַדּוֹן in Biblical Hebrew, פֶּרְעוֹן — פֻּרְעָנוּת, or שִׁלְטוֹן — שִׁלְטָן would seem to support this assumption, but it is incapable of explaining the existence of דְּרְבָן — דָּרְבוֹנוֹת, כִּבְשָׁן — כִּבְשׁוֹן (MH), *fitrǻnəm* — *kǻfitron* in SH,⁵⁶ nor

---

⁵⁴ The transcription *ǻy* in SA, as in *yī'dǻy* יחידאי (*LOT* III/2, 178, l. 71), and the transcription *ǻ'i* are two aspects of the same thing. See 1.4.4.1 note.

⁵⁵ Barth, *Nominalbildung*, XXIX, nn. 1, 318.

⁵⁶ It will be recalled that ון-/ן- is found in Aramaic as well, not only in areas where Canaanite dialects prevailed earlier or in proximity, but even in Mandaic; see Nöldeke, *Grammatik*, 140. From SA we may mention רחצן (*LOT* III/2, 155, l. 17; as against the general Aramaic form רוחצן),

does it explain the frequent occurrence of וֹ֯ן in proper names. The division between *ån* and *on* in SH is not identical with the division in TH, and it is obvious that the reconstructed conditions for TH — that the presence of *u* makes *ån* obligatory — does not apply to SH, because original *u* changes in SH to *a*, etc. (see 1.5.2.5).

4.3.11 The three noun forms with an וֹן- ending in TH — פְּעָלוֹן, פִּעָלוֹן, and פְּעָלוֹן — are derived from two PS patterns *qi/utlān* and *qatalān*, the latter being represented in TH by two alternate forms: רְעָבוֹן / צִמְאוֹן (< *צָמְאוֹן). Following the rule that short vowels either become *šəwa* or are maintained with gemination of the following consonant (see 1.5.3.3), the פִּעָלוֹן form became prevalent in TH, leaving only a few nouns in the פְּעָלוֹן form, mostly of the ל״ה class, such as חָזוֹן and the like. SH has hardly used the פִּעָלוֹן form preferring פְּעָלוֹן and developing forms of its own. These, then, are the SH forms derived from the PS noun patterns with *ān* ending:

a. **faqdon, fiqdon**: *zakron* זכרון, *fåmmon* פעמון, *ibyon* אביון, *išron* עשרון; and from the ע״י class: *zīdon* זידון, *tīkon* תיכון, and *qīṣūna* קיצונה, as well as *wdībon* ודיבון (SP Dt 28:65; TH וְדִיאֲבוֹן), *å'ēron* (< *aḥeron*) אחרון.

b. **fåqådon (fēqådon)**: *'årabon* ערבון, *såmå'on* צמאון, *sådåfon* שדפון, *šåfåfon* שפפון (SP Gn 49:17), *yērāqon* ירקון. The *e* vowel in the last item teaches us that the origin of this SH form is not directly from PS *qatalān* but from forms like פְּעָלוֹן, and the *šəwa* developed into *å* or *ē* according to the rules. Were this noun to parallel TH יֵרָקוֹן, its form in SH would be *yirrāqon*. As noted above, historically this is where one should classify nouns derived from ל״ה roots: *'åron* חרון and *råṣon* רצון, which resemble the *faqdon* form, and *ūn* = TH עֲוֹן (< *'awayān*). The SH form seems originally to have been in the construct state form (*ᵃwōn* > *ᶜᵘwōn* > *ūwon* > *ūn*), which is its most common form in the Pentateuch.

c. **faqqådon, fiqqådon**. Clearly *såbbåton* שבתון belongs to this group, although one may question whether the gemination is accidental, reflecting the influence of *såbbåt* שבת, i.e., *on* is a suffix appended to שבת. As for the nouns *bēbbåzon* בחפזון and *bēwwåron* בעורון, the gemination in them is easily explained on the basis of *ḥᵃfazōn* (= TH חִפָּזוֹן*; > *iḥpazōn* > *ippazōn*) and *'awarōn* (= TH עֲוָרוֹן*; > *i'warōn* > *uwwarōn*), and this explanation is preferable, since the pattern of רְעָבוֹן is common in SH.

d. **faqqīdon, fiqqīdon**. Some of the nouns that appear with these forms have gemination in TH and some do not: *kalliyyon* כליון, *šaggiyyon* שגעון (Dt 28:28; SP has בשגיעון as well), *tammiyyon* תמהון, *arriyyūnǝk* הריונך (SP Gn 3:16), פשרון (LOT II, 562 ב, l. 164; 600 ב, l. 181), פקדון אמסרון (LOT II, 560 א, l. 98), ערבון (ST Gn 38:17), and similar words.

illiyyon עליון. They would appear to be cognates to the פַּעֲלוֹן form with a change of vowel of the second radical, but this difference is what demonstrates that the two forms and TH פַּעֲלוֹן do not have a common origin. We would like to see in them a parallel to a certain very rare form in TH represented by the nouns קִמְּשׂנִים, קִלְּשׂוֹן (Pr 24:31), זֵרְעֹנִים (Dan 1:16), יִדְּעֹנִי, and the personal name גֵּרְשׁוֹן, in which the second radical is geminated and vocalized with *šəwa*.[57] TH cognates of the aforementioned SH forms, then, would be: *כִּלְּיוֹן, *שִׁגְּעוֹן, etc. The shift of *šəwa* to *i* before י is the rule (see 1.3.3) and even happens elsewhere, as, for example, in *sīla* צלי and *šīməš* from such base forms as *צְלָי and *שְׁמֵשׁ (see 1.5.2.1), and the same is true of the forms *yiddūni* ידעוני and *wbanqiyyon* ובנקיון. The origin of *yiddūni* can be explained thus: *yidd^u'ūni* (< יִדְּעוּנִי) > *yiddu'ūni*; the origin of *ạnqiyyon* is: *nåqiyyon [on the vocalization of *šəwa* see (e) immediately below] > *n^aqiyyon > *ạnqiyyon. This last form has no connection to the gemination of the second radical as seen in TH זִכָּרוֹן or נִקָּיוֹן.

> Note: *ạnqiyyon (= *ạnqīyon!) is, therefore, similar to nouns such as *yåšīmon* ישימון and *rå'īšon* ראשון, in that one must reconstruct an original *šəwa* after the first radical, although in each case the reason for the *šəwa* is different.

e. **faqdån, fiqdån.** The process of vocalizing the second radical discussed immediately above (d) is evident in this group in the words *qåråbån* (< *qar^aban*), *kåbåšån* כבשן, and *šå'lān* שלחן, but there are examples without this phenomenon: *qinyån* קנין, *īšån* אישון. Note the parallel between the former examples and TH הַקָּרְבָּן (Ezek 40:43), הַדָּרְבָן (1 Sa 13:21), כַּדָּרְבֹנוֹת (Eccl 12:11). In SH, this form is common among personal names as well, such as *'akrån* עכרן, *kislån* כסלן, *yiqtån* יקטן, and *yiqšån* יקשן, here, too, because a *u* vowel has been replaced by *a*, *i*. The suffix *ån*, though, sometimes occurs in SH even where TH has וֹן-, such as in the name *zēbūlån* זבולון.

4.3.12 Suffixes with Geminated *n*. The nouns with suffixed formatives *ån* and *on*, when declined in the plural or with a personal pronoun or gentilic suffix, (a) appear with lengthened vowels, as a rule: *ån-*, *ūn-*, as, e.g., *qåråbånu* קרבנו, *qåråbåna* קרבנה, *qåråbånīyyimma* קרבניהם, *išrūnəm* עשרונים, *fåmmūni* פעמוני,

---

[57] Not all the nouns listed here are equivalent from a historical perspective. For example, in the noun קמשונים, the syllable וֹן- is derived from the ancient plural marker that occurs in Hebrew plant names (alongside ־ִין, as in נִצָּנִים and in סַמְּנִים, from סם), according to this process: קִמּוֹשׂ (sing.) — *קִמּוֹשׁוֹן (pl.) — קִמּוֹשׁוֹנִים with the addition of the usual plural marker and the reduction of the first *o* to *šəwa*. However, from a synchronic perspective all these nouns represent a single form, in which the second radical is geminated and vocalized with *šəwa*. Perhaps we may learn from Syriac זַרְעוּנָא that the (potential) gemination in זֵרְעֹנִים was not originally present. SH and Syriac support the tradition of MS Kaufmann, which offers us (*m. Kil'ayim* 3:1 and elsewhere): זַרְעוּנִים. In other words, this vocalization and that found in the Bible are variants of the same form.

wlibyūnåk ולאביונך, and *ådåmūni* אדמוני; but (b) *on* is sometimes replaced instead by *inn*-, as, e.g., *å'ēron* אחרון, *å'erinnəm* אחרונים, *båī'ērinna* באחרונה, *lå'ērinna* לאחרונה; *šē'mūn* שמעון, *šēmuwwinni* שמעוני; *gåduwwinni* גדעוני, *zifrinna* = TH וְפִרְנָה as against *aššimrūni* השמרוני, *'åṣåmūna* עצמונה, etc.; and from the noun אחרון we even find *å'ērūnəm* אחרונים outside the Pentateuch (*LOT* III/2, 130, l. 195). Given that a geminated נ appears in TH in a few nouns: אֲחֹרַנִּית (SH *å'ērinnət*), קַדְרַנִּית, and perhaps also חַשְׁמַנִּים and מְחַרְצַנִּים (SH *miyyårṣinnəm*) — if the נ is not a radical — it clear that this formative is the one that appears in the declension of the nouns above bearing an *on* ending. This is a rare formative, both in and outside of Hebrew,[58] and its semantic and etymological connection to *on* has not yet been clarified. The gemination could have come into being in SH in accordance with the rule, applicable in both TH and SH, in which a short vowel followed by a geminated consonant is replaced by a long vowel followed by a simple consonant (see 1.5.3.3.1); i.e., instead of *-ūni* we might find *unni* which develops in SH into *inni* (cf. 4.1.5.9[6]). In any case, it appears that *inni* (*on* with gentilic suffix) became an independent form, as demonstrated by the form *šēmuwwinni* שמעוני, where the *u* following the מ is derived from a *šəwa mobile* that has assimilated to the vowel of the formative *'ūn-/on* in accordance with the rule described in 1.1.8. These are the reconstructed stages of development that the SH rules would indicate: שִׁמְעוּנִי > *šim"unni* > *šim"'inni* > *šimu'inni* > *šēmuwwinni*. Had the formative been attached directly to שְׁמַע or to גֶּדַע — like the nouns זפרנה or אחרנית — their forms would be *šēminni* and *gådinni*. What occurred in SH in the relationship between *on* and *inn*- occurred in TH in the relationship between the personal name גרשון and גֵּרְשֻׁנִּי (SH *giršūni*!). Note that in the transcription of the Septuagint, זפרנה sometimes appears as [Σ]εφρωννα.

4.3.13 Suffix ן not Preceded by Vowel. Two TH words definitely bear this suffix:[59] צִפֹּרֶן (Aramaic טַפְרָא, Arabic ظُفْر) and כְּנַעַן (see כִּנְעָתֵךְ Jer 10:17). This is true in SH as well, although there the basis for צפרן is a form akin to צְפֹּרֶן, a pronunciation attested in MH in both the Babylonian and Tiberian vocalizations.[60] In SH one finds, then, *sēferniyya* צפרניה (Dt 21:12). Note that the relationship of the SH form (and צִפֹּרֶן in Jewish Hebrew) to צִפֹּרֶן is like that of *ṣåmå'on* to TH צִמָּאוֹן with regard to the gemination of the second radical (see 4.3.11b). Here we must analyze the ending in *ēbirna* (Nu 33:34) עברנה: *n + a* as against TH עָבְרֹנָה: *on + å*.

---

[58] See Barth, *Nominalbildung*, 344.

[59] BL, 504, erred in including in this category גָּרְזֶן with its ultimate stress. In fact, גרזנו is regularly vocalized גַּרְזֻנּוֹ, etc., with geminated נ, similar to חַרְצַנִּים.

[60] This form is found in Mishna MS Parma B (De Rossi 497); see also M. Bar-Asher's introduction to the facsimile edition (Jerusalem 1970/1), 16. See Yeivin, *Babylonian Vocalization*, 1069.

4.3 Suffixed Patterns and Nouns with Suffixes

4.3.14 *åt — ot*. The suffixes ־ָת (־ַת) and וֹת in TH occur in personal names such as בְּכוֹרַת, בָּשְׂמַת, שִׁמְרָת, שִׁמְעָת, לַפִּידוֹת, and יְרִיעוֹת, and in toponyms such as אֵילַת, דִּבְרָת; רְחוֹבוֹת, and קְדֵמוֹת. These suffixes are identical with the feminine suffix — one singular (without ה having become ת as in the 3rd fem. sing. form אָזְלַת) and one plural. Even if it may still be assumed that וֹת- in toponyms was originally the fem. pl. ending and perhaps even that ־ַת is the fem. sing. ending with the original ת retained, such assumptions do not apply to the personal names with these suffixes, since there are males whose names end in ת, such as בכורת and שמרת. We must instead view these as independent suffixes used in forming proper nouns,[61] which just happen to be identical with the grammatical suffixes. In addition, Hebrew has abstract nouns with the suffix וֹת-, i.e., words whose base form appear in the plural, such as ידידות, חכמות, and in SH *zūnåtīkimma* (Nu 14:33; SP זונתיכם); cf. 4.3.6 and n. 47.

Since in SH *åt* occurs as a plural ending in common nouns such as *tūldåt* תולדות and *yūmåt* ימות, we cannot dismiss the idea that this noun formation ending in SH has another origin in addition to that of TH ־ַת. It may be, then, that a noun such as *fī ā'īråt* פי החירת should be considered in light of the relationship between תולדת in SH and TH. We see, therefore, that with nouns such as *båšåmåt* בשמת or *ayyålåt* אילת, it is not at all certain that the TH and SH forms are cognate (cf. also מאילות 2 Kgs 16:6), just as there is no exact congruence between *ēsēnət* and אָסְנַת, where the ending of the SH form resembles that of TH תַּנְחֻמֶת.[62]

The SH suffix *ot* is a merger of וֹת- and ־וּת in TH. If it is permissible to use TH to distinguish the different origins of SH forms, e.g., *målåkot* מלכות, *målåkūtu* מלכותו, *kassot* כסות, *kassūtåk* כסותך, *ilmēnūta* אלמנותה, but *țåțåfot* טטפות — then we cannot draw any inferences from TH about the nature of SH words, such as *asfīkot* שפכות (Dt 23:2, where TH reads שפכה) and *ēfīkot* (Dt 32:20; TH תהפכות, SH הפכות or הפיכות); TH may support either שפיכות or שפיכות, and either הפיכות or הפיכות. ST understands שפכ(ו)ת as plural, rendering it שפי(כ)ן, while it takes הפי(כ)ות to be singular, translating it תפוך (plural אפיכן). The noun *gåballot* גבלות (SP Ex 28:22) is understood by the Samaritan translations as plural: ST מתחמן, SAV منعطه (*Hammeliṣ*, *LOT* II, 441, l. 55: مقلده), taking it to be the plural of גבל (see 4.1.3.22); nonetheless, the original suffix may actually be ־וּת, with the ל geminated in accordance with what is described in 1.5.3.3. The noun *maksot* מכסות (SP Ex 12:4) appears in the Samaritan translations in the singular. The noun *ṣåråfot* צררות (Gn 42:35) is translated in MS Barberini as a singular noun

---

[61] This has been noted by M. Lidzbarski, *Ephemeris für semitische Epigraphik*, II (Giessen 1902–15), 29.

[62] As to the interchange of *seghol/pataḥ* in TH and its phonemic state, see my "Reflections," 78ff.; a more detailed discussion can be found in "More About the Seghol," 153–158. As to the different feminine endings, see 4.5.1.

צררות (צְרָרוּת* or the like), but in MS M₁ as a plural: צוררת. We find in SH ṣåror in the same verse.

> Note: Corresponding to TH שָׁפְכָה (Dt 23:2), reliable manuscripts of SP present two different readings, שפכת and שפכות, both pronounced in the same way: *asfikot*. A parallel to שפכת is now to be found in *MMT* B 39, and is discussed there on p. 101. The antiquity of the orally transmitted form in ST שפכ(י)ן and שפכין is demonstrated in their plural endings and by the orthography with י after פ. As to the relationship between TH שָׁפְכָה and SH *asfikot*, note that in MH the פְּעִילוֹת form is used also to express verbal nouns of *Qal* (gerunds), as does פְּעִילָה, e.g., שפיכת דמים / שפיכות דמים (*m. Avot* 5:9). A pattern usually denoting abstracta may — especially euphemistically — denote concreta; cf. in the same semantic field as SP שפכות: MH זַכְרוּת "male genitals" and נַקְבוּת "female genitals." This explanation may be applied to שפכת in MMT as well.

4.4 Ultimately-Stressed Nominal Forms

4.4.0 In our discussion of noun morphology, we have until now excluded from our sample all those nouns stressed on the ultimate syllable in the absolute form (other than those in which a suffixed formative received ultimate stress; see 4.3), even though they may be classified with the patterns discussed above, since these nouns are worthy of separate attention. Unlike penultimately-stressed nouns in TH, which can be described by the single category "segholates," the SH forms with ultimate stress belong to a variety of patterns. It is advisable, therefore, to group them here according to the combinations of vowels in their absolute forms. First we shall survey them, masculine and feminine forms listed separately.

4.4.1 Masculine forms

$\bar{\imath} - \mathring{a}$:	*niy'yå* ניחוח.
$\bar{\imath}(i) - \bar{u}$:	*šib'bū* שבוע.
$\bar{e} - \bar{a}$:	*gē'bāl* גבעול, *mē'bār* מבחר.
$\bar{e} - \mathring{a}$:	*šē'tåy* שתי.
$\bar{e} - \bar{u}$:	*mē'lū* מלוא (but in SA, *mēlu*; cf. *LOT* III/2, 152).
$\mathring{a} - \bar{\imath}$:	*mā'rī* מראה (as against *måzzi* מחזה!), *bā'līl* בליעל.
$\mathring{a} - \bar{a}$:	*mā'nāl* מנעל, *šā'lān* שלחן.
$\mathring{a} - \mathring{a}$:	*yå'såṛ* יצהר, *mā'låk* מלאך.
$\mathring{a} - \bar{u}$:	*zā'rū* זרוע, *mā'nū* מנוח, *mā'bū* מבוא.
$\bar{e} - \mathring{a} - \bar{a}$:	*ṣēfår'dā* צפרדע (plural *ṣēfårdā'əm*).

4.4.2 Feminine Forms

$\bar{e} — \bar{\imath}$:	*rē'bīt* רביעית.
$\bar{e} — \bar{a}$:	*bē'qā* בקעה.
$\bar{e} — \hat{a}$:	*qē'nâ* קנאה, *šē'bâ* שבעה, *ē'tâ* חטאה, *ē'tât* חטאת (in the sense of "sin," but the sacrifice known as חטאת is *'âṭât*), *alqē'rât* לקראת.
$a/\bar{a} — \bar{e}$:	*qā'dēt* קדחת, *šā'fēt* שפחת (=שחפת), *sab'bēt* ספחת.
$a/\bar{a} — \bar{a}$:	*qā'rāt* קרחת, *aš'fā* שפחה.
$(a)\mathring{a} — \bar{e}$:	*ṭåb'bēt* טבעת, *såṛ'rēt* צרעת.
$\hat{a} — \bar{a}$:	*gâ'bā* גבעה, *šâ'nā* שנאה, *mâ'nā* מנחה, *mâ'šā* משחה, *mâ'šāt* = TH מִשְׁאֵת (as well as = TH מִשְׁחַת).
$\hat{a} — \hat{a}$:	*â'mâ* חמאה, *šâ'mâ* שמחה, *sâ'râ* צרעה, *yâ'rât* יראת.
$\bar{u} — \bar{a}$:	*zuw'wā* זועה, *tū'lāt* תולעת.
$\bar{u} — \hat{a}$:	*qū'râ* קרחה.
$\bar{\imath} — \bar{e} — \bar{a}$:	*mirrē'bāt* מרבעת (SP Nu 23:10 רְבַע) = TH *מְרֻבַּעַת (1.5.3.3b).
$\bar{\imath} — \bar{u} — \bar{a}$:[63]	*tirruw'wā* תרועה (but *tirruwwâ* תרועה!).
$\bar{e} — \bar{u} — \bar{a}$:[64]	*yēšuw'wā* ישועה, *šēbuw'wā* שבועה (but *šēbuwwât* שבועת!).
$\hat{a} — \bar{\imath} — \bar{a}$:[65]	*mâliy'yā* מלאה (this is the feminine form of *mâli* מלא, just as *ṭēmiy'yā* is the feminine form of *ṭēmi* טמא).
$a — \hat{a} — \bar{a}$:	*ayyâ'lā* אילה.

4.4.3 The common factor in all but a few of these nouns in their various patterns is that they are derived from roots in which the second or third radical is a guttural. In some types of nouns, mostly feminine forms, such as *rē'bīt* רביעית, *qā'rāt* קרחת, and *zuw'wā* זועה, it is evident that the stressed ultimate syllable results from the reduction of the last two syllables into one through the elimination of the consonant separating their vowels (see 1.4.6.1) at a previous stage of development. The extra syllable at the earlier period may have been original, as in the nouns listed previously, or it may even have been created within SH by the transformation of an auxiliary vowel (or even *šəwa*) into a full vowel. The latter possibility entails a process of the sort *yā'sar* < *yasᵃhar* יצהר, *mā'låk* < *malᵃ'ak* מלאך, *mē'bār* < *mibᵃhar* מבחר, *šâ'nā* < *šanᵃ'a(t)* שנאה, *qū'râ* < *qurᵃha(t)* קרחה, *mā'rī* < *mar'ī* < *mar'ay* מראה. However, given that the SH noun need not parallel the form of the same noun in TH, we cannot state with certainty whether such nouns as *šâ'nā*, *gâ'bā*, and *bē'qā* are derived

---

[63] It should be pointed out that *uwwa* and *iyya* are equivalent in their pronunciation value to *ūwa* and *īya*.

[64] Yeivin, *Babylonian Vocalization*, 326.

[65] The origin of the term ניחוח in TH is uncertain. BL, 475, derive it from *נוּחֹחַ, a *Polel*-stem infinitive. Barth, *Nominalbildung*, 213, derives it from the form *נִיוֹחַ. In either case, in the given language situation it is a quadriradical from נח"ח, and the relationship of the TH form to the SH form is like that of נְהֲלוּל to נָהֲלָל within TH, and particularly similar to forms with a מ preformative: מִשְׁלָח/מִשְׁלוֹחַ, מִבְחָר/מִבְחוֹר, מִשְׁקָל/מִשְׁקוֹל, and others.

from precursors similar to TH שְׂנָאָה, גְּבָעָה, and בִּקְעָה, or whether they are instead derived from forms that in TH would give us שְׂנָאָה*, גְּבָעָה*, and בִּקְעָה*. The latter type of derivation is clear in the case of *asʿfā*, which is derived from שְׂפָחָה* and not from TH שִׁפְחָה, since only שׁ with *šəwa* could yield the syllable *aš-*. Such alternate pairs can be found in TH: שָׂמָּה/שִׂמְחָה, רָנָּה/רְנָנָה, זַעֲוָה/זְוָעָה, and חֲטָאָה versus חֵטְא, and we need not resort to analogy to the plural, such as בִּקְעָה: בְּקָעוֹת.

4.4.4 It is quite clear that in the masculine forms as well we must posit an extra syllable in the stage previous to that recorded, meaning that, e.g., *šibʿbū* שבוע is derived from **šibbuʾu*. That is, at one time a noun that ended with a guttural consonant, which was pronounced, developed a glide between that consonant and the preceding (long) vowel. This phenomenon is akin to the development of the *furtive pataḥ* in TH, except that in SH the quality of the glide is not limited to *a* and occurs after any vowel, including *a*. In BH the *furtive pataḥ* is very rare, but as in SH it occurs also after *a*. In the same way *šētåy* (TH שְׁתֵּי) became ultimately stressed (see 1.4.6.1). The reason for the development of the ultimate stress in SH is evident in the contrast between *mazba* (TH מִזְבֵּחַ) and *ammazʿbā* with locative ה (TH הַמִּזְבֵּחָה). As was stated in section 1.4.6.1, *māʿbū* מבוא, in which the א quiesced at the earliest of stages, must be assumed to have ultimate stress by analogy to *māʿnū* מנוח, *madʿdū* מדוע and others. In the same way, we cannot assume the reduction of two vowels to one in such words as *yešuwʿwā* ישועה, *tirruwʿwā* תרועה, or *måliyʿyā* מלאה, because there was no condition for a furtive vowel between the vowel (*u* or *i*) and the guttural consonant in medial position; instead, we must assume an analogy to many forms with guttural radicals, perhaps with support from the declension. Clear evidence that the ultimate stress is a secondary development in such words is provided by the existence of the parallel forms *šēbuwʿwā* שבועה / *šēbuwwåt* שבועת and *tirruwʿwā* תרועה / *tirruwwåt* תרועת, where ultimate stress and penultimate stress exist side-by-side (which is not the case with, e.g., *tišʿšā* תשעה / *tišʿšāt* תשעת). It may even be that the furtive vowel phenomenon does not apply consistently and under all conditions, which would explain these variations: *zåʿrū/zåru* זרוע, *mēʿlu/mēlu* מלוא.

4.4.5 It should be pointed out that when the ultimately-stressed nouns are declined (with pronoun suffixes or in plural), the final consonant is geminated: *qēʿnå* קנאה: *qēnåtti, qēnåttu*; **rēʿšā* רשעה: *rēšåttu*; *ēʿtå* חטאה: *ētåttu*; and similarly *yaråttåk* יראתך, *månnåttu* מנחתו, *alqēråttåk* לקראתך, *alqēråttu* לקראתו, *tåbēttu* טבעתו, *gåbēttu* גבחתו, *målåkkəm* מלאכים. In each of these, we must assume the loss of the vowel before the final consonant when the suffixes were added, in a process similar to **qinaʾati > *qinaʾti > qēnåtti* (cf. also the *fåqådalå* form, 4.1.5.7 [4]), or **malaʾkīm > *malaʾkim > målåkkəm*. This common phenomenon

4.4 Ultimately Stressed Nominal Forms

also yields *yēšuwwåttåk* ישועתך, *yēšuwwåttu* ישועתו. That this is not an unbreakable rule we learn from *forms* such as *yâṣârâk* (< **yâṣâ'ârâk*, or perhaps directly from *yaṣharak) יצהרך.

4.4.6 Special Instances

a. The difference in vowels between such ultimately-stressed forms as *qā'rāt* קרחת and *gā'bāt* גבחת on the one hand, and *qā'dēt* קדחת (cognate to what would be *קָדַחַת in TH) and *sab'bēt* ספחת on the other, derives from an earlier difference between vowels: *ē*, which developed from either *i* or *u* in PS. Thus, *qā'dēt* can be explained on the basis of either *qadiḥt or *qaduḥt, *šab'bēt* on the basis of either *sappiḥt or *sappuḥt. Cf. the coexisting TH forms בַּצֹּרֶה and בַּצֹּרֶת.

b. The word *šā'fēt* שחפת teaches us that the alternation שחפת/ספחת is not just an orthographical variation, but that the word in its given pronunciation is derived from שפ״ח, a cognate of שח״ף in a fashion similar to כבש/כשב and שלמה/שמלה.

c. The noun *ayyā'lā* אילה has none of the characteristic causes of ultimate stress surveyed above, unless we say that the melody in one mode of recitation gave the word this stress (as noted in *LOT* III/2, 140, l. 79), or unless we say the word is derived from something like *אִילָאָה (meaning "in the image of a ram"), as we find in Targum Pseudo-Jonathan to Gn 49:21: דמי איילא (see *LOT* III/1, 35, at l. 21). The latter possibility requires further inquiry.

d. From *šēbuw'wā* שבועה we have the form *miššēbūtti* משבועתי (Gn 24:8). The gemination can be explained on the basis of a form like **šēbū'ti* with the vowelless feminine suffix *t*, perhaps by analogy to what appears in 4.4.5.

e. Further evidence of the alternation of stress between ultimate and penultimate syllables noted above in 4.4.4 is provided by the relationship between *ē'tåt* חטאת and *'åtåt* חטאת (the sacrifice), which exists even though the base conditions were identical: something like **ḥᵃta'at*. (See also *LOT* III/1, 52, at l. 14.)

f. The word *niy'yā* is apparently derived from **nīḥᵃ'aḥ* < **nayḥᵃ'aḥ*, with a short *a* vowel like the one in TH פִּרְחָח.⁶⁵

g. The form *bā'līl* בליעל in composed of two words, but the compounding is no longer transparent. The SH form is derived from **bali+yi'l*.

4.5 Gender and Number

4.5.1 Nouns, like verbs and pronouns, have two genders: masculine and feminine. Masculine nouns bear no special suffix marking gender, while feminine nouns are for the most part formed from a masculine noun with the addition of one of the suffixes written in SP (as in MT): -ה, -ת (MT -ֶת, -ַת), -ית, and -ות

(MT ת-‎), which are pronounced in SH: a/å, åt, ət, and ot. In ultimately-stressed nouns, the vowels are long and stressed: ā/â, āt/ât, it, and ūt. Many examples are provided above in the discussion of "feminine" patterns in sections 4.1.5.1–0, 4.2.1.4[3], 4.2.3.7–11, and 4.2.4.3; 4.4.2–5 (ultimate stress), since there is no phonological difference between those suffixes as used in declension and as used in word formation.

It should be pointed out that nouns ending in the suffix ת־‎ in TH do not necessarily have as their counterparts in SH nouns ending in ət, but instead we find the suffix ât. It will suffice to mention the numbers šēlåšåt שלשת and šiššåt ששת (see 5.1) or the nouns iššåt אשת and nūšånåt נושנת (as against wannūtårət והנותרת). It might appear that in SH the suffix of those nouns and others like them is related to PS -at and not to TH -t, but in fact, their -åt suffix developed by analogy to the form of the suffix in the construct state, while PS -at dropped the t in SH as well, as attested by SP.

4.5.2 There are, of course, in SP and, therefore, in SH, nouns that do not bear any feminine suffix but whose grammatical gender is nonetheless feminine, such as באר, גפן, חצר, שמש, and others. Particularly surprising are the names for uniquely feminine parts of the body, such as שָׁדַיִם and רחם, along with the names of female animals, such as אתון, לביא,[66] עז, and רחל. This fact demonstrates that the division of nouns into masculine and feminine is not original to Hebrew, nor even to ancient Semitic.[67] This helps explain why we find "feminine" nouns without feminine suffixes, even though the trend in Hebrew, which increases as we come to later periods, is to add feminine suffixes to such nouns. This is particularly widespread in Modern Hebrew, where we find such neologisms as חתולה, דֻּבָּה, זאבה and many others, in keeping with the trend represented by חֲמוֹרָה, לְבִיאָה, and רְחֵלָה in MH and in the vocalization of Biblical forms.

4.5.3 Nouns which regularly appear in one gender and on rare occasions in the other display a tendency toward uniformity in SP. Thus we find in SP at Gn 32:9 המחנה האחד ('ad, not 'at), Gn 49:6 יחר (yår) instead of תחד as predicate of כבודי, Gn 49:20 שמן לחמו (šåmən), Gn 38:24 כמשלשת חדשים (kåmiššēlåšåt),[68] Gn 48:22 שכם אחת ('at), Gn 46:22 נפש ארבע עשרה (arba 'åšårå). An anomaly such as

---

[66] It has been stated elsewhere (LOT III, 85) that in Biblical Hebrew, לביא is the term for a female lion, corresponding to the masculine ארי or אריה, just as אתון is the female corresponding to חמור, and that only in MH (b. Sanhedrin 106a) do we find the expanded form לביאה for the female, similar to MH חמורה (alongside חמור for the female, as in "הלכה חמורך"). The vocalization לְבִיא in Ezek 19:2 is a qəre in keeping with late usage. This indicates that the SP form כלביה (Nu 23:24), along with its pronunciation kallibyå, represents a later form than that of the Masoretic version.

[67] See GvG I, 404.

[68] See 5.1.3, n. 4.

4.5 Gender and Number

עמדיו אדניה (Ex 35:17) is clearly not in keeping with SP's harmonizing tendency,[69] and SP reads עמודיה there and, similarly, את מיתריה ואת יתדותיה in Ex 39:40. This is presumably the reason SP reads כזבית בת צור (Nu 25:15; TH כָּזְבִּי), בחצרותם (Gn 25:16; TH בְּחַצְרֵיהֶם), מיד כל חי (Gn 9:5; TH מִיַּד כָּל־חַיָּה, but the use of חיה does not normally include humans). All these tendencies are indicative of language usage later than that underlying TH, just as the Samaritan spelling נערה (Dt 22:23 and elsewhere) matches the *qəre* of TH נַעֲרָ, as opposed to the *kətiv*, which reflects the ancient epicene use of נַעַר.

> Note: Since the letters ד and ר are significantly different from each other in the Samaritan script, it is almost impossible to assume that the SP reading יחר (Gn 49:6) יחר is a result of a scribal error. Indeed, the Septuagint translation of the verb reflects a different verb from that in the MT: ἐρείσαι/ ἐρίσαι. The SH verb is derived from the root חר"י. As to the variants of the Greek text, and their meanings in the above mentioned verse, cf. J. Barr's thorough discussion, "ἐρίζω and ἐρείδω in the Septuagint. A Note Principally on Gen XLIX 6," *JSS* 19 (1974), 198–215.

4.5.4 Nevertheless, it can be assumed that some of the differences in gender do not stem from linguistic or literary harmonization in the redaction of SP, but reflect instead the natural choice of one of two versions of speech that were (and are still) current in Hebrew, such as לטוב in SP Dt 28:11 as against TH לטובה, ברעה אשר תמצא in SP Gn 44:34 as against TH ברע אשר ימצא, ושביתכם in SP Nu 31:19 as against ושביכם, תליתך in SP Gn 27:3 as against TH תליך. The relationship between תליך and תליתך is like that of בכי / בכית and שבי / שבית within the Jewish biblical tradition.

In notable contrast to the harmonization tendency is the use of שַׁעַר as feminine: *bāt šārək* באחת שעריך (SP Dt 15:7, 16:5, and elsewhere), also found in TH: הילילי שער (Isa 14:31). Similarly בדרך אחת (SP Dt 28:7,25; SH *āt*) alongside ובשבעה דרכים (*wafšā'bā*) in the same verses. We should also point out the treatment of שדה as feminine in later Samaritan Hebrew,[70] as we find in MH as well. Note that SP Lv 25:34 reads לא ימכרו where TH reads לֹא יִמָּכֵר, taking שדה as the object of the verb and using the pronoun היא to stand for it in the second part of the verse; the same is not done in Lv 27:20ff. and Gn 27:27.

4.5.5 There are three forms of grammatical number: singular, dual, and plural. The singular bears no particular number marker. The dual form is marked by the suffix -ַיִם added generally to the singular form, as in רַגְלַיִם, קַרְנַיִם, and

---

[69] Earlier scholars have dealt with the harmonization evident in the redaction of SP. See Gesenius, *De Pentateuchi samaritanae origine*, 26ff., especially 45. A more recent treatment is in Waltke, *Prolegomena*, especially 302ff.

[70] See Ben-Ḥayyim, *Tradition*, 108.

אֲמָתַיִם, although on occasion it occurs with the base form of the plural, as in קְרָנַיִם, חוֹמֹתַיִם, and לוּחוֹתַיִם. The masculine plural carries the suffix ־ִים and the feminine plural וֹת, although it must be recalled that the ־וֹת suffix is not infrequently used for masculine nouns as well (such as דּוֹרוֹת, קוֹלוֹת, אָבוֹת, and מִזְבְּחוֹת) and also that ־ִים appears, although less often, as the plural marker for feminine nouns (such as שָׁנִים, עִתִּים, and חִטִּים). There are even nouns in which both plural suffixes occur, such as קֶבֶר, שָׁנָה, יוֹם, and דּוֹר, and in post-Biblical Hebrew the choice of ־וֹת/־ִים becomes solely a matter of style: סְגֻנּוֹת/סִגְנוֹנִים, מִדְרָשׁוֹת/מִדְרָשִׁים.

4.5.6 The dual form is usually only a matter of morphology, and no longer bears the semantic function of expressing duality. However, one may still discern from its use in Biblical Hebrew that its orginal function in Hebrew (or perhaps only in the stage previous to Hebrew) was to express duality. It commonly appears with paired body parts, such as כְּנָפַיִם, נְחִירַיִם, עֵינַיִם, רַגְלַיִם, יָדַיִם, etc., although its use with a number of items greater than two (שָׁלוֹשׁ כְּנָפַיִם, שֵׁשׁ כְּנָפַיִם, רַגְלַיִם, etc.) indicates that the semantic function of the suffix fell into disuse. Despite this, many examples remain of a dual/plural distinction in Hebrew using the dual suffix: פְּעָמִים/פַּעֲמַיִם, שָׁנִים/שְׁנָתַיִם, אֲלָפִים/אַלְפַּיִם, אַמּוֹת/אֲמָתַיִם, *šibbuwwâ'əm* שבועיים (SP Lv 12:5), etc. It it significant that all these are nouns denoting measurements of time and space.[71] Modern Hebrew commonly makes use of the dual suffix in naming instruments that are by nature pairs: אוֹפַנַּיִם (bicycle), מֶלְקָחַיִם (vise), גַּלְגִּלַּיִם (scooter), and many others.

4.5.7 The orthography of SP spelling does not differ in this respect from the Jewish Pentateuch, but the Samaritan pronunciation reflects a stage of Hebrew that has taken a further step toward the elimination of the dual form, blurring its morphological distinctiveness as well. As noted in 1.4.4b above, the dual and plural suffixes *aym* and *īm* have been united through the reduction of the diphthong, and both have become *əm* (or *īm* where there is ultimate stress). Nevertheless, a few remnants of the original dual suffix still remain in the suffix form *â'əm*: *âlâfâ'əm* = TH אַלְפַּיִם (but *âlâfəm* אֲלָפִים), *yūmâ'əm* יומים, *fāmmâ'əm* פַּעֲמַיִם (but *fāmməm* פְּעָמִים), *ammâtâ'əm* אֲמָתַיִם (and not **ammâtəm*, like *mâttəm* מָאתַיִם), *šēnâtâ'əm* שְׁנָתַיִם, *šibbuwwâ'əm* שבועים (SP Lv 12:5; TH שְׁבֻעַיִם), *šibbuwwâtâ'əm* שבעתים.[72] All these are nouns denoting measurements of time and space.

In their treatment of number, the medieval Samaritan grammarians list the

---

[71] G. Hanemann, in his address to the Fifth World Congress of Jewish Studies, Jerusalem, 1973 (never published), pointed out that the dual form was retained in MH in conditions similar to those stated here.

[72] The pronunciation presents a *forma mixta*, a contamination of שבוע and שבעה. For the meaning of this word, see 5.6.1.

dual form, noting that it is indicated by the number שתים/שנים and by "the addition of a soft letter between the י of the plural and the letter preceding it" and providing the examples אלפים and שנתים.[73] We may assume that their pronunciation of these words was similar to that attested in our time.

> Note: a. Eliminating the unique pronunciation of the dual suffix made the Samaritans choose a different way of distinguishing dual from plural where they felt comprehension of a passage required such a distinction: the use of the pronominal suffix normally affixed to the singular instead of that normally affixed to the plural: $bânūtåk$ בנותיך, $kallūtu$ כלותי. See 2.0.13 and 3.2.3, n. 7.
>
> b. Note that some SH words ending in $\mathring{a}$'∂m do not contain the dual marker, but rather the plural ending -∂m attached to a singular noun ending in $\mathring{a}$'i (< $\mathring{a}y$) (see 4.3.8), e.g., $šēlīšā$'∂m שליש(א)ים (SP Dt 5:9), $anšiyyā$'∂m נשיאים. It may be that $wallā$'∂m והלחים (SP Dt 18:3; TH וְהַלְּחָיַיִם), too, does not include the dual suffix but the plural suffix ∂m affixed to a base of *$lā$'i לְחִי. On the possibility that the $š\partial wa$ developed into $\bar{a}$, if the base form was לְחִי, see 1.3.3.

4.5.8 The question of whether in SH the original dual suffix is attached to the noun only in its singular form or whether it also attaches to the plural form cannot be answered decisively, for two reasons:

a. in nouns such as $\mathring{a}lāfā$'∂m אלפים, $rēgål\partial m$ רגלים, $kånåf\partial m$ כנפים, $wqårāni$ וקרני (Dt 33:17), $qårēno$ קרניו (Dt 33:17), $mâtēn\partial m$ מתנים, and even $layyērēkūt\partial m$ לירכתים (Ex 26:27; some manuscripts read ולירכותים), in which there is a vowel between the first and second radicals, the vowel need not be explained on the basis of a plural base form, since it can be explained as derived from $š\partial wa$ (see 1.3.4–6). The form קרנים in the toponym עשתרות קרנים is pronounced $qarn\partial m$, with no vowel between ר and נ, and it is well known that names tend to preserve their early form — in this case, before the creation of a $š\partial wa$ mobile in this position;

b. the suffix $\mathring{a}tā$'∂m or $\mathring{a}t\partial m$ in feminine nouns such as אמתים and מאתים may be attached to the singular form, according to the rule and parallel to the corresponding nouns in TH, or they may be attached to the plural form of the noun, since SH has a suffix $\mathring{a}t$ ($åt$ with ultimate stress) for the feminine plural (see 1.5.2.5[1]; 4.3.14). In the latter instance, they parallel TH forms such as חוֹמוֹתַיִם.

> Note: Two forms of SH $ēz\partial n$ אזן occur in the plural/dual: (a) the organ of hearing, "ear" (Ex 32:2), (b) the abstract sense of hearing as in the phrase דבר באזני (Nu 14:28).

---

[73] See *LOT* I, 13, 181.

4.5.9 In SH, too, there are nouns that have no singular form but only a plural form (including the dual form), such as *šåməm* שמים, *məm* מים, *dūdəm* דודים (SP Gn 30:14; TH דודאים), and in addition *affid'wīm* הפדויים as against הפדיום at Nu 3:49 and הפדים Nu 3:51. Such nouns are more numerous in SH than in TH, because of nouns whose singular form does not happen to occur in the Pentateuch, e.g., *sīm* סאים occurs at Gn 18:6 but there is no סאה in the Pentateuch, and לחיים occurs but not לחי, etc. Where the singular form does occur in later Samaritan Hebrew, its tradition of pronunciation does not have the same reliability as a Pentateuchal form.

4.6 Construct State and Pronominal State

4.6.1 The term for the "construct state" (in Hebrew סְמִיכוּת, סְמִיכָה; in Arabic إضافة) was employed by the medieval Hebrew grammarians[74] to describe the condition of the noun when it does not stand in the absolute state, that is, when it is joined to what follows it, whether what follows is (a) a noun or (b) a pronoun. In the Jewish traditions of Hebrew vocalization, these two types have something in common morphologically inasmuch as the changes that occur in the noun when it is not in the absolute state apply equally to (a) and (b), with the exception of the segholate nouns and those that follow the segholate model, where vowel shifts apply only in the declension. Feminine nouns ending in ה- and nouns whose dual and plural forms end in ־ים are always different in the absolute state from their appearance in the construct or pronominal states, and the difference is expressed even in orthography, which demonstrates its antiquity. Even though these are commonly observed phenomena, we may note some examples for the sake of thoroughness: דָּבָר -:דְּבַר, דִּבְרֵי, דְּבָרָיו; גֻּלְגֹּלֶת -:גֻּלְגֹּלַת or מִלְכֵי, מַלְכִּי, מַלְכָּיו, מֶלֶךְ -:מֶלֶךְ as against — אֲדָמוֹת֫, אַדְמָתִי, אַדְמַת אֲדָמָה, גֻּלְגְּלוֹתָם, גֻּלְגַּלְתִּי. The reason for the vowel shifts is stress, which brings about the reduction of a historical short vowel in certain circumstances to a semivowel (*šəwa*), as explained in 1.5.1–1.5.2.3. Thus was formed the situation in TH, where in most noun patterns the situation of the noun in the construct and prepositional state finds expression in morphology (which is not the case, for example, in literary Arabic), and the declension of the noun is divided into several subgroups according to common behavior in vowel shifts.

4.6.2 SH is unlike TH in this respect. SH maintains the distinction between the construct and pronominal states of the noun on the one hand, and the absolute

---

[74] See, e.g., Ibn Janāḥ, *Kitāb al-Lumaʿ*, chap. 19; L. Prijs, *Die grammatikalische Terminologie des Abraham Ibn Ezra* (Basel, 1950), 85. This was still the usage in Yehuda Leib ben Zeʾev, *Talmud Lašon ʿIvri* (Vienna, 1883/4), 104, §112, [Hebrew].

4.6 Construct State and Pronominal State

state on the other, which exists in TH and is reflected in the orthography, such as אדמה; דבריו: דברים; etc., but SH does not thoroughly maintain the system of vowel shifts, which is so characteristic of the declension of nouns in Jewish Hebrew. In SH, the vowels are generally stable in declension, those of the declined form being identical with those of the absolute. Here, too, the reason is obvious: there is no *šəwa* in SH (see 1.3), and even an original *šəwa quiescens* may become a full vowel (1.3.4). This means that even if the stated stability is not original in every pattern and every noun but is instead derived from *šəwa*, the absolute and declined forms have, nevertheless, become identical. It appears correct to assign the origin of the phenomenon to the point in time when the transition occurred between *šəwa* and a full vowel, for as we have seen (1.3.3), the *šəwa* tended to vary qualitatively in words according to their phonetic environment and, to a lesser extent, in analogy to the vocalism in the declension (paradigmatic analogy). Thus, we find, for example, *ē* in the plural, e.g., *qâdēši* TH (קָדְשֵׁי, קָדְשִׁי) *dērēko* דרכיו [but: *dirkīkimma* in Lv 26:22 as in TH!], *mâlēkəm* מלכים,[75] and in dual form (originally): *ēzēnəm* אזנים; or *â* in the singular, e.g., *gâdâl* (TH גְּדָל) and *kâbâš* (TH כֶּבֶשׂ), the latter perhaps not only under the influence of the plural form *kâbâšəm* (TH כְּבָשִׂים) but also due to the process **kabšåk* > **kabᵃšåk* > *kâbâšåk* כבשך. Clear evidence for this kind of analogy is certainly to be found in forms such as *kišbəm* (TH כשבים) according to the singular *kēšəb*, fem. *kišba*; *niskəm* (TH נְסָכִים) of the singular *nēsək* נסך in accordance with the vowel in the declension *nisku* (sing.); *nisko* (pl., SP ונסכיו; TH וְנִסְכֹּה Lv 23:13); and *katfot* כתפות (not in construct state!).[76]

It must be pointed out that even in the nouns in which vowel shifts do occur when pronominal suffixes (or feminine or plural endings) are appended, these vowel shifts do not occur in the construct state. This means, then, that in SH the construct form and the pronominal form are **not** identical in their morphological behavior.

4.6.2.0 The inventory of SH nouns can be classified according to their behavior in declension (with pronominal suffix and feminine and plural endings) into four categories: (A) nouns that do not vary from the absolute form; (B) nouns in which changes occur in their consonants (with or without vowel changes);

---

[75] The noun מלך in SH may contain an original *ē* vowel, i.e., its basis may be **malik* (as in Arabic) and not **malk* as in Hebrew and Aramaic. See also 4.1.3.15[2b]. TH מַלְכַּת (Jer 44:17) can be explained in the same way.

[76] Note that corresponding to TH עֲדָשִׁים (Gn 25:34), manuscripts of SP read two separate words: עד שים, understood as עד שים (ST: סעד שוי, SAV حتّى شبع), but the pronunciation **adsəm* may reflect the single word עדשים in a form akin to **עֲדָשִׁים, parallel to TH בְּטָנִים, שְׁקֵמִים. This seems to me quite likely. The word was divided into two solely for homiletic purposes, and the midrashic reading was projected onto the written text.

(C) nouns in which changes occur in their vowels; and (D) nouns that are special instances.

Note: On the pronominal suffixes themselves and the changes that occur in them over time, see Chap. 3.

4.6.2.1 Category (A): nouns that do not differ from the absolute form. The declension of this category is simple and can serve as a model for the other categories, with the exception of the changes specific to each of those categories. Not every form of the noun chosen as an example is attested in the Pentateuch, but its declension occurs more clearly than that of other nouns.

SH	TH	SH	TH
dēbår	דְּבָר	dēbårəm	דְּבָרִים
dēbåri	דְּבָרִי	dēbåri	דְּבָרִי
dēbåråk	דְּבָרְךָ	dēbårək	דְּבָרֶיךָ
dēbårək	דְּבָרֵךְ	dēbårək	דְּבָרַיִךְ
dēbåru	דְּבָרוֹ	dēbåro	דְּבָרָיו
dēbårå/a	דְּבָרָהּ	dēbåriyya	דְּבָרֶיהָ
dēbårånu	דְּבָרֵנוּ	dēbårīnu	דְּבָרֵינוּ
(båšårnu	בְּשָׂרֵנוּ)		
dēbårkimma	דְּבַרְכֶם	dēbårīkimma	דְּבָרֵיכֶם
dēbarkən	דְּבַרְכֶן	dēbårīkən	דְּבָרֵיכֶן
dēbårimma	דְּבָרָם	dēbårīyyimma	דְּבָרֵיהֶם
dēbårinna	דְּבָרָן	dēbårīyyinna	דְּבָרֵיהֶן
(nå:låtən	נַחֲלָתָן)		

4.6.2.2 Nouns with a feminine ending are also declined in this way, e.g., båkūra בכורה: båkūråti בכורתי; nå:la נחלה: nå:låtåk נחלתך, nå:låtu נחלתו; ådåmå אדמה: ådåmūtīnu אדמותינו (SP Gn 47:19).

4.6.2.3 In nouns III-guttural, changes occur in consonants and vowels as dictated by the rules governing gutturals and stress. For example, fåṣa פצע and zēra זרע are declined as follows: fåṣå'i פצעי, zē'råk (< *zērå'åk < *zirᵃ'åk) זרעך, zē'rīk (< *zērī'ik < *zirⁱ'ik < *zir'īk) זרעך (see the rules in 1.3.5d, zērånnu זרענו, zēråkkimma זרעכם (see 1.1.8g), *zēråkkən זרעכן, zērå'imma זרעם, *zērå'inna זרען.

4.6.3 Category (B) includes: (1) nouns with two consonants in the absolute form, derived from roots with repeated second radical; (2) nouns in which the last consonant doubles before pronominal and other suffixes, whether due to the original noun pattern or due to the tendency to replace open syllables with closed syllables; (3) nouns in which the last consonant is doubled as compensation for the loss of a guttural consonant.

4.6 Construct State and Pronominal State

Examples:

1. *zir* זור: *zirru* זרו, *qen* קן: *qinnåk* קנך, *'am* עם: *'ammi* עמי, *kal* כל: *kallu* כלו, *kållåk* כלך, *kaf* כף: *kabbu* כפו, *yåm* ים: *yåmməm* ימים, *lab* לב: *libbåk* לבך, as well as *šiddəm* (TH שָׁדַיִם Gn 49:25), *şiddo* צדיו, and *işşəm* חצים, whose respective singular forms are unattested in the Pentateuch. Additional examples may be found in the patterns *fiq* and *feq* (4.1.2.2) and *faq* and *fåq* (4.1.2.8).

> Note: When not declined, nouns of this group with derivational suffixes may not double their last consonant before the attached suffix, such as *wyåmå* (e.g., Gn 28:14; TH יָמָּה) and *'āti* (Lv 16:21; TH עִתִּי) as against *'atta* (TH עַתָּה). This phenomenon occurs in TH as well, e.g., כְּרְמֶלָה as against כַּרְמְלוֹ, and גִּתָּה (1 Kgs 2:40) as against גִּתָּה (Jos 19:13) and גִּתִּי.

2. No clear distinction can be made between Categories (A) and (B): *gådol* גדול: *gådalla* = גדולה,[77] *gådalləm* = גדולים, *ådon* אדון: *ådanno* = אדוניו (we also find *ådūnəm* אדונים), *zåqån* זקן: *zåqannu* זקנו (we also find *zåqånimma* זקנם), *kaftår* כפתר: *kaftarrəm* כפתרים. To this group we must also assign *šelamməm* שלמים, whose singular form is unattested in the Pentateuch. Relevant to this group is the gemination of the נ in *on*; see 4.3.12. The phenomenon described here can be found in the noun patterns *fåqåd* (4.1.3.19), *fåqod* (4.1.3.21), *faqqəd* (4.1.4.5), and *faqqod* and the like (4.1.4.9).

3. *råb* (TH רֹחַב and רָחָב): *råbbu* (TH רָחְבּוֹ), *råbbå* (TH רָחְבָה, רָחְבָה); *lås̄* לחץ: *lås̄s̄ånu* לחצנו; *tåššəm* תחשים; *tåššəm* תחשים; *fåm* פעם: *fåmməm* פעמים; *bål* בעל: *bålli* בעלי (but *ba:lo* בעליו). This phenomenon is common in the noun patterns *fåq* and *fåq* (4.1.2.11) and in ultimately-stressed nouns in all patterns, such as *må'låk* מלאך: *målåkku* מלאכו, *målåkkəm* מלאכים, *målåkkək* = TH מַלְאָכֶיךָ; *qē'nå* קנאה: *qenåtti* קנאתי; *må'nå* מנחה: *månåttimma* מנחתם; see also 4.4.5.

4.6.4 In Category (C) we shall classify nouns in whose declensions either (1) a vowel existing in the absolute form is eliminated or (2) such a vowel is changed.

4.6.4.1 Elimination of the vowel occurs in these noun patterns:

i. *fēqəd* (4.1.3.3), e.g., *nēgəd* נגד: *nigdi* נגדי; *ēsəd* חסד: *isdåk* חסדך; *dērək* דרך: *dirku* דרכו; etc.

ii. *fēqåd* (4.1.3.9), e.g., *nēdår* נדר: *nidru* נדריו; *šēkåm* שכם: *šikma* שכמה.

iii. *fåqəd/fåqəd* (4.1.3.15), e.g., *kårəm* כרם: *karmåk* כרמך; *nåfēš* נפש: *nafši* נפשי, *nåfeškimma* נפשכם (see 1.3.5e); *målək* מלך: *malku* מלכו; *'åbəd* עבד: *'abdi* עבדי, *'åbdåk* עבדך.

iv. *fåqåd* (4.1.3.18), e.g., *åkål* אכל: *aklimma* אכלם; *qåbår* קבר: *qabru* קברו, as well as *dirkīkimma* דרכיכם, which is exceptional; see 4.6.2.

---

[77] The form *gådalla* corresponds to the TH form גְּדֻלָּה as well, and indeed in LSH we find *gådallot* (LOT III/2, 314, l. 10) corresponding to the TH forms גְּדֻלּוֹת and גְּדֻלּוֹת.

It is clear that these forms and others like them preserve the original monosyllabic form (the segholate patterns in TH), while others of identical origin have been converted entirely (i.e., in declension as well) into bisyllabic nouns. E.g., *qådəš* קדש: *qådešåk* קדשך; or *fā'əl* פעל: *fā'ēlåk* פעלך, *fā'ēlu* פעלו. Sometimes the elimination of the vowel occurs as a result of analogy, e.g., *båqår* = TH בְּקָר: *baqråk* where TH has בְּקָרְךָ; see the patterns listed above.

The elimination of the vowel also takes places in SH in nouns ending in the feminine suffix, originally *at*, such as *nēbīla* נבלה: *nēbiltåk* נבלתך, *nēbiltu* נבלתו, *nēbeltimma* נבלתם; *bårāka* ברכה: *bårākti* ברכתי, *bårāktåk* ברכתך, *bårāktu* ברכתו; *šåmåla* שמלה: *šåmåltu* שמלתו; *målåka* מלאכה: *målåktåk* מלאכתך; *šågåga* שגגה: *šågågtimma* שגגתם (see 4.1.5.7[4]). It also occurs in nouns ending with the suffix *ət*, such as *masgērət* מסגרת: *masgirtu* מסגרתו; *mašmårət* משמרת: *mašmårti* משמרתי; *må:bēråt* מחברת: *må:bårtu* מחברתו. However, we also find *ådåmåtåk* אדמתך and *maškåråti* משכרתי as well. We even find both types associated with the same word: *ēmīrti* אמירתי and *ēmīråtåk* אמירתך.

Note: The noun כלה occurs in the Pentateuch only with pronominal suffixes: *kaltåk* כלתך, *kaltu* כלתו. Its declension may be influenced by the noun בת, which is declined *bittåk*, etc. As for the elimination of the gemination of the third radical, see 1.5.3.3f[1].

4.6.4.2 Vowel shifts that are automatic in SH — such as *ə* in a closed syllable after the stress, *ī* or *ē* in a syllable that becomes open (see 1.5.1.1), or *o/ū* (1.2.4), which are conditioned allophones of one phoneme, and also the alternation *a* in a closed syllable / *å* in an open syllable — as far as they occur in the declension are not the subject of this category. The following alternations are of concern here:

a. *a* in the absolute form, *i* in all others. This applies to nouns derived from roots with doubled consonants, such as *lab* לב: *libbi* לבי, *libbåk* לבך; *šan* שן: *šinnəm* שנים; *at* את: *ittu* אתו, etc., including *bat* בת: *bitti* בתי, *bittåk* בתך, etc. As is stated in 1.5.2.1, *a* (and in the word חן, *å*) is derived from PS *i* (Philippi's Law); only in one instance is the alternation *e/i* as in TH: *qen* קן (see 1.5.2.1 note).

b. *a* in the absolute form, *ē* in declension. This is a variant of type (a) above, with *ē* in place of *i* because of the openness of the syllable. This applies to the nouns *aš* אש, *ban* בן, *yad* יד, *šam* שם, declined in such forms as *yēdi*, *yēdåk*, *ēšu*, *bēnu*, *šēmu*, *šēmå* שמא (the pronuciation of the Tetragrammaton). The noun בן in the plural has *å*, which in SH implies a base form *ban*, following a familiar subsitution (4.1.2.8, 1.5.1.3); thus *ban* בן: *bånəm* בנים, *båno* בניו, similar to *ab* אב: *åbot* אבות, *åbūtīnu* אבותינו. The phenomenon of vowel shifts in declension is limited to nouns of the patterns *faq* and *fåq* (4.1.2.7).

To sum up: the declension rules of this category do not apply to all nouns of the same structure, nor to all nouns of similar origin (cf., for example, *šam*

שם < *šim, as against iṣ or eṣ עץ < *'iḍ), and even the vowel elimination rule that appears stronger has many exceptions. From this we may conclude that we are dealing here with the remnants of an earlier language situation, as opposed to the clear and obvious tendency to maintain the vowel pattern of the noun in the declension as in the absolute form, which distinguishes SH from TH (and, of course, from BH).

4.6.5 Category (D) includes (i) nouns in which some or all of the declined forms follow different patterns from the absolute form, i.e., in which there is suppletion in the declension; and (ii) nouns with some irregularity in their declension.

4.6.5.1 Type (i) includes nouns such as ēlom חלום — but ilmu חלמו and ēlāmot חלמות, forms based on something like חֲלֶם (as in Biblical Aramaic); ēdom = אָדָם — but idma = TH אֲדָמָה (see 4.1.3.12); qādoš קדוש — but qaddīšəm קדושים (in later Samaritan Hebrew qadūšəm! — LOT III/2 362, l. 7); 'anni עני (= TH עֱנִי, עֲנִי) — but 'anyåk, etc. (see 4.1.4.4); yåtåd יתד — but yētēdot יתדות (4.1.3.17; 4.1.3.3); nēqi נקי — but nēquuwəm נקוים; gådol גדול, ådon אדון but gådalləm, ådanni, etc., and we find gådūlå ("the great") as an Aramaized Hebrew epithet for God (LOT III/2, 204) and ådūnəm (see 4.1.3.21 and 4.6.3[2]); bet/bit בית — but battəm בתים, etc.; īr עיר — but 'arrəm ערים, etc.; šåbbåt שבת — but šabbētot שבתות (see 4.1.4.8-9); rē'os ראש, rē'ūši ראשי, etc. — but råšəm ראשים, råšīkimma ראשיכם, etc.; īš איש — but ēnåšəm אנשים; iššå אשה — inšəm נשים (see 4.2.1.4); bat בת — but bånot בנות, etc.; mem מים, construct state mī מֵי — but also mīmi מימי, mīmək מימיך, etc.; yom יום — but yåməm ימים, etc. (and we find yūmåt יומת, SP Dt 32:7; TH ימות); ēla אֱלָהּ — but ēluwwəm אלוהים, ēluwwåk (!) אלוהיך, ēluwwiyyu אלהיו (3.2.3), etc.; åmå אמה - but åmå'ūto אמהותיו; and others like these.

4.6.5.2 Under type (ii) we classify: (a) nouns which, although their absolute form is singular, take the pronominal suffixes associated with plural nouns, such as ab אב: åbək = אָבִיךָ, אֲבִיךָ (however, åbiyyu אביו and not *åbo), etc.; *am חם: åmək, åmiyya חמיך; 'al על: 'ålək עליך, 'ålo עליו, 'ålīnu עלינו, etc.; al אֶל: īli אלי, īlək אליך, īlo אליו, īlīyyimma אליהם, etc.; tåt תחת: tåttīyyimma תחתיהם (so in SP at Dt. 2:12 and everywhere else); (b) the noun få פה, which, even though it ends in a vowel, takes pronominal suffixes like those of nouns ending in a consonant: fī in construct state, fiyyi with the 1st pronominal suffix (SP Nu 20:24 פִּי, TH פִּי), fiyyåk (< *fī'åk), fiyyu פיו, fiyyē'u פיהו, fiyyånu פינו (LOT III/2, 122, l. 1), fiyyimma פיהם. The same is true of the noun ši שה: šiyyu שיו.

> Note: fiyyi is to be understood as derived from *fī'ī, but the resulting diphthong has not been contracted (see 1.4.4), apparently due to analogy to the other forms or in order to remain distinct from the construct form.

In the noun אח, phonological rules (see 1.5.3.4[4]) acted to unite the different forms of the singular and the plural, and it may be that analogies, too, contributed their share to this, forming the following declension pattern:

'ā̊	אָח
'ā̊'i (< *'aḥī)	אָחִי
'å̄yå̄k (< *'ā̊'iyyå̄k < *'aḥī'å̄k)	אָחִיךָ (also אָחִיךְ)
'ā̊'o (by analogy to the plural)[78]	אָחִיו
'å̄yyå̄ (<'a'iyya < *'aḥīhā)	אָחִיהָ
'å̄yå̄nu (< *'a'iyyå̄nu < *'aḥī'å̄nu)	אָחִינוּ
'å̄yå̄kimma (analogy to 3 m. pl.)	אֲחִיכֶם
?	אֲחִיהֶם, אֲחִיהֶן
'ā̊'əm	אַחִים
'ā̊'i (< *'aḥay)	אַחַי
'ā̊'ək (< *'aḥayk)	אָחִיךָ (also אַחֶיךָ)
'ā̊'o (< *'aḥayw)	אֶחָיו
'å̄yyå̄ (< *'a'ayha < *'aḥayhā)	אָחֶיהָ
'ā̊'īnu (< *'aḥaynū)	אַחֵינוּ
'ā̊'īkimma (< *'aḥīkimma < *'aḥaykimma)	אֲחֵיכֶם
'å̄yyimma (< *'ā̊'iyyimma < *'aḥihimma < aḥayhimma)	אֲחֵיהֶם

---

[78] In "Samaritan Vowel System," 518, n. 15, I explained 'ā̊'o, the singular form on the basis of Aramaic: *'aḥō < *'aḥūy אחוהי (according to the rule explained in section 1.4.4b). In other words, an Aramaic form has penetrated into the Hebrew declension, which is not the case with אבי: å̄biyyu, not å̄bo < אבוי (< אבוהי) as in SA (4.6.5.2). Each person may prefer the explanation he finds convincing.

5. NUMERALS

5.0 Cardinal Numbers

5.0.1 The pronunciation of some of the following numerals is not attested in the recitation of the Pentateuch but in the reading of other Samaritan texts. After taking into consideration the unique features of the vowel and stress pattern of SH, the elements common to SH and TH in most numerals will be obvious. In some forms, SH has followed a different path. Below are listed the cardinal numbers in SH alongside their TH counterparts and the forms representing their conjectured common origin.[1]

5.1 From 1 to 10

	For Counting Masculine Nouns			For Counting Feminine Nouns		
	SH	PS	TH	SH	PS	TH
1	'ād; 'ādem	'aḥad-; 'aḥadīm	אֶחָד; אַחַד אֲחָדִים	'āt	'aḥadt	אַחַת
2	šēnəm; šēni	tinay(m-)	שְׁנֵי; שְׁנַיִם	šittəm; šitti	tintay(m-)	שְׁתֵּי; שְׁתַּיִם
3	šēlåša;-åt[2]	talātat-	שְׁלוֹשָׁה; שְׁלוֹשֶׁת	šēlås[2]	talāt-	שָׁלוֹשׁ
4	ar'bā; -āt	'arba'at-	אַרְבָּעָה; אַרְבַּעַת	arba	arba'-	אַרְבַּע
5	ēmišša; 'amšåt	ḥamišat-	חֲמִשָּׁה; חֲמֵשֶׁת	'amməš	ḥamiš	חָמֵשׁ
6	šišša; -åt	(šidtat >) šiššat	שִׁשָּׁה; שֵׁשֶׁת	šaš	(šidt- >) šišš-	שֵׁשׁ
7	šå'bā; -āt	šab'at-	שִׁבְעָה; שִׁבְעַת	šåba	šab'-	שֶׁבַע
8	šåmåna;-åt	tamāniyat-	שְׁמוֹנָה; שְׁמוֹנַת	šåmåna	tamāniy-	שְׁמוֹנֶה
9	tiš'šā; -āt	tiš'at-	תִּשְׁעָה; תִּשְׁעַת	tišša	tiš'-	תֵּשַׁע
10	'åšårå; -åt	'aśarat-	עֲשָׂרָה; עֲשֶׂרֶת	'åšår	'aśr-	עֶשֶׂר

---

[1] The "original" forms are not necessarily the PS forms (even though the heading PS is used); they are the formulae that represent forms in the historical development of Hebrew that are closest to the stage represented in Hebrew (TH, for the most part) according to commonly recognized rules, such as the rule that ṣere is derived from *i* under certain conditions and from *ay* under other conditions. These forms of origin sometimes end with a hyphen, indicating that one of the case vowels *u, i, a* is to be expected; for our purposes it does not matter which one is reconstructed.

[2] As is well known, the numbers 3–10 in the masculine form are used with feminine nouns and vice versa.

5.1.1 One might have explained the ע in the SH numeral *ʿād* אחד on the assumption that this pronunciation presents the numeral in its Aramaic form, where the word also begins with ח: חד, חדה (see 1.1.8). However, the length of the *a* vowel does not support such an assumption; instead, it can be explained on the basis of a ח that divides the two vowels *aḥa* > *ā* (see 1.4.6.1; 1.5.3.4). In any case, it is unlikely that *ʿāt* should be explained on the basis of Aramaic. It, therefore, seems that the pronunciation of חד in SA, *ʿād*, has actually been influenced by Hebrew (SA חדה is pronounced **ʿåddå* < *ʿaḥda*; see *LOT* III/2, 244, l. 25). Bauer and Leander posit *aḥḥad* as the form underlying אֶחָד, אַחַד, and אַחַת, but this assumption is not necessary, since the shift of *qameṣ* to *seghol* also occurs in circumstances other than before an originally geminated ח, such as דֵּעָה חָכְמָה and אֲנָה וָאָנָה, and a full vowel can be found in place of a *ḥatef* after א in TH as well and certainly in BH (although in אֲחָדִים there is a *ḥatef*).

5.1.2 In TH, the anticipated feminine form of שְׁנַיִם, i.e., **šintaym* > **šittayim* (1.5.3.1), was lost. The form שְׁתַּיִם was formed by analogy to שְׁנַיִם. The Samaritan tradition, though, preserved the ancient form.[3]

5.1.3 Regarding the numeral שלוש(ה), it is worth noting that SH has *ē* where TH has *šəwa*, while SA has *å* in place of the *šəwa*: *tålåt(å)* תלת(ה) (see *LOT* III/2, 361, l. 1), and the same is true of the declined forms of שלוש.[4]

5.1.4 The gemination of the מ in חמש can be found in SA, Syriac, and in the Neo-Aramaic dialect of Maʿlūla, but there is no need to make the Hebrew form dependent on the Aramaic, since gemination often occurs in place of vowel lengthening (see 1.5.3.3, and see also *LOT* III/1, note to 47, l. 1, where it is suggested that *ʿamməš* is a reflex of the construct form *aḥməš*). The gemination of ש in חמשה is like that of ט in שְׂמָטָה and ל in קְהִלָּה; analogy to שִׁשָּׁה may also have contributed. The construct form *ʿamšåt* resembles the SA numeral *ʿamša* (*LOT* III/2, 217, l. 41) and the pattern of this numeral in Arabic خَمْسَة < **ḥamišat*.

5.1.5 Regarding the construct form of ששה, note that, as with the noun אשת, in ששת SH does not eliminate the *a* vowel in the feminine ending *-at*.

---

[3] As is well known, the forms שְׁתַּיִם, שְׁתֵּי are attested in a number of manuscripts with Babylonian vocalization. (See Yeivin, *Babylonian Vocalization*, 1108). The assumption that its existence is due to falsification (ibid.) must, in the light of the Samaritan tradition, be reconsidered, first of all by comparison to the manuscripts that are now accessible.

[4] The form מִשְּׁלֹשׁ (Gn 38:24) does not exist in SH; SP reads כמשלשת, which is interpreted as including the particle מִן: *kåmiššēlåšåt*.

5.1.6 The noun שבע in Lv 26:18 is pronounced *šēbå*, and השבעה in Dt 15:9 is pronounced *aššēʿbå*. However, these are not variants of the numerals שבע and שבעה, but words derived from the root שבח, which does not occur in Biblical Hebrew, but is very common in MH and in Aramaic meaning "praise," "advantage," "surplus." Thus, the Samaritan tradition interprets שָׁבַע and שִׁבְעָה in the above verses as MH שָׁבַח, שִׁבְחָה.[5] The phonological background of such an interpretation is the shift of ח > ע, (see 1.1.8), whose antiquity is attested in the reading ἐξομολογήσεται (= תְּשַׁבַּח) of the Septuagint in Isa 45:23.

5.1.7 It is surprising that the distinction between masculine and feminine nouns in the absolute forms of שמונה has been eliminated in SH. It is difficult to posit that a contraction of the diphthong *īy-*, *īya(t)* led to identical results, as the participle form of ל"ה verbs shows. It seems likely that the source of the merger of those forms is syntactic: the partial dissolution of the distinction between masculine and feminine forms in the the usage of numerals in LSH. On the maintenance of the ancient *ā* vowel after the מ, see 1.5.2.7.

5.1.8 In the SH numerals for nine, the reason for the gemination might appear to be the assimilation of the ע to what precedes it, but this is not a common phenomenon (see 1.5.3.1[1]). Perhaps there is some influence here of the SA numeral, where the gemination in the number nine may be easily explained: תִּשַׁע > *atšaʿ* > *aššaʿ* > *ašša* (sometimes written אשע). This phenomenon is known also from the Mandaic עתשא.[6] From *ašša* (< תִּשַׁע) are derived SA *ašša* = תשעה (written also אשעה) and *asʾšīm* = תשעים (אשעים), which do not fulfill the phonetic condition — ת in contact with ש — that leads to gemination.[7] In SH, too, the form *ašša* could have come into being as well, as it did in SA, independent of Aramaic influence but instead as a derivation from the construct state of תשע, but it did not because the other forms, without *šəwa*, prevented this. Therefore, it appears that the gemination of ש in SH should be explained from within SH: (*itša* [< TH תִּשַׁע] > *tišša*; see 1.5.3.3), and perhaps the existence of gemination in SA contributed to its preservation in SH.

5.1.9 The form *ʿåšår* עשר may represent a merger of two originally different forms distinct in TH: עֶשֶׂר and עָשָׂר (which is used in the numbers 11–19). It may also be that עָשָׂר was originally absent from SH; as is well-known, it has no parallel outside TH, despite being the basis for the feminine form עֲשָׂרָה.

---

[5] See my "Palestinian Aramaic and Samaritan Poetry," 42.
[6] See *LOT* II, 607, where the Mandaic forms עתשא and עתשין are treated.
[7] The Maʿlūla forms preserve the stage preceding SA and preceding Mandaic: *etšaʿ* = תשע as against *tēšʿa* תשעה, *tišʿ* = תשעים.

5.2 From 11 to 20

For counting masculine nouns		For counting feminine nouns	
11	'ād 'åšår — אחד עשר	'āt 'åšārā — אחת עשרה
	<'ašti> 'åšår — עשתי עשר	'ašti 'åšårå — עשתי עשרה
12	šēnəm 'åšår — שנים עשר	šittəm 'åšårå — שתים עשרה
13	šēlåša 'åšår — שלושה עשר	šēlåš 'åšårå — שלוש עשרה
14	ar'bā 'åšår — ארבעה עשר	arba 'åšårå — ארבע עשרה
15	ēmišša 'åšår — חמשה עשר	'amməš 'åšårå — חמש עשרה
16	šišša 'åšår — ששה עשר	šaš 'åšårå — שש עשרה
17	<šå'bā 'åšår> — שבעה עשר	šåba 'åšårå — שבע עשרה
18	šåmåna 'åsår — שמונה עשר	<šåmåna 'åšårå> — שמונה עשרה
19	<tiš'šā 'åšår> — תשעה עשר	<tišša 'åšårå> — תשע עשרה

5.2.1 SH makes no distinction between עֲשָׂרָה and עֶשְׂרֵה. In the numerals from 11 to 19, it employs the form parallel to עֲשָׂרָה. The TH form עֶשְׂרֵה has a cognate only in Aramaic, including SA: עסרי (עסרה).[8] Therefore, it cannot be assumed that the absence of a distinction between עֲשָׂרָה and עֶשְׂרֵה in SH is the result of a lapse of memory. It is not yet known whether Ugaritic עשרה parallels TH עֶשְׂרֵה, since ה does not usually serve as a *mater lectionis* in Ugaritic.[9]

5.2.2 Compounds such as TH חמשת עָשָׂר (Jud 8:10) or שמנת עשר (Jud 20:25) are unattested in the Pentateuch and unknown in SH.

5.3 Remaining Cardinal Numbers

20	išrəm — עשרים	60	šiššəm — ששים
30	šēlåšəm — שלושים	70	šå'bīm — שבעים
40	ar'bīm — ארבעים	80	šåmånəm — שמונים
50	ēmiššəm — חמשים	90	tiš'šīm — תשעים

100 *må* — מאה; 200 *måttəm* — מאתים; *må'ot* — מאות.
1000 *åləf* — אלף; 2000 *ålåfå'əm* — אלפים; pl. *ålåfəm* — אלפים; const. *ålåfi* — אלפי.
10,000 *råbåbå* — רבבה; pl. *råbåbot* — רבבות.

Note: The form of the numeral for 40 is, it appears, formed by analogy to that for 70, because otherwise it should be **arba'əm*. Perhaps the Ara-

---

[8] Mr. Raṣon Ṣadaqa informed me that he had not encountered the form עסרי in Samaritan liturgy, but upon inquiry he pronounced it *'åsåri*.

[9] On this cf. E. Y. Kutscher, "Marginal Notes to the Mishnaic Lexicon and a Grammatical Note," *Lěšonénu* 31 (1967), 33–36 [Hebrew]; J. Blau, "'Esre < 'Israyh Followed by a Short Vowel," *Lěšonénu* 32 (1968), 267–268 [Hebrew]; and S. Loewenstamm, "The Numerals in Ugaritic," *Proceedings of the International Conference on Semitic Studies* held in Jerusalem, 19–23 July 1965 (Jerusalem, 1969), 6.

maic numeral *ar'bīn* < אַרְבְּעִין (see 1.3.3) contributed to the formation of SH *ar'bīm* as well.

5.3.1 Examples of compound numerals: *ā:ləf wšăba ammā'ot ēmišša wšābīm* (Ex 38:28) — 1775; *'amməš wšănāməm šēna wšăba mā'ot sēna* (SP Gn 5:19) — 785; *ālāfā'əm wšăba mā'ot wēmiššəm* (SP Nu 4:36) — 2750; *alšaš mā'ot āləf wšēlāšāt ālāfəm wamməš mā'ot wēmiššəm* (Ex 38:26) — 603,550.

5.3.2 The form of the numeral 100 is the same in SH and SA, and was apparently borrowed by SH from SA, since the normal development in SH would be either **mē'a* or *miyya (< **mi'a*), while in SA *mā* is derived quite properly from מְאָה.

The gemination of ת in the dual form מאתים hints that the א in this word was originally pronounced in a form something like **ma'taym*. The tendency toward renewing the pronunciation of א, which, according to the rules, should disappear — and certainly had disappeared — is attested in this numeral in the Neo-Aramaic dialect of Ma'lūla, where it has even been exaggerated into an ע: *em'a* (< **m'a*). This may have been brought about by the need to distinguish the numeral from the interrogative מה, pronounced *mā*; thus, the pronunciation of מאתים is a remnant of a pronunciation in which (a secondary) א was produced in SA (and SH?) : **mā'*–. [Cf. the common pronunciation of Arabic لا *lā'* ("no").]

The *a* vowel in מאות is derived by analogy to the singular, since the form cannot be Aramaic. (In SA the plural is מואן, pronounced *mā'bān*.)

5.3.3 The dual ending ־ִים is preserved in only a few nouns (see 4.5.7), among them the numeral אַלְפַּיִם. It was not necessary to preserve it in the numeral מאתים, because that form is in any case quite different from the plural מאות. The necessity of distinguishing dual אלפים from plural אלפים prevented the usual contraction *ayim* > *ēm* > *əm*; the vowel after the ל apparently hints at forming the dual on the basis of the plural, like TH קְרָנַיִם, דְּלָתַיִם, etc., but see 4.5.8.

5.3.4 The form רבוא is unattested in the Pentateuch and does not appear in Samaritan usage.

5.4 Ordinal Numbers

	A. Masculine forms		B. Feminine forms	
1	*rā'īšon*	ראשון	*rā'īšūna*	ראשונה
	rā'īšūnəm	ראשונים	*rā'īšūnot*	ראשונות
2	*šēni*	שני	*šēnət*	שנית

	šēnəm	שְׁנַיִם		
3	šēliši	שלישי	šēlišət	שלישית
4	rē'bī	רביעי	rē'bīt	רביעית
5	ēmīši	חמישי	ēmīšət	חמישית
6	šišši	ששי	šiššət	ששית
7	šē'bī	שביעי	šē'bīt	שביעית
8	šemīni	שמיני	šemīnət	שמינית
9	tiš'šī	תשיעי	tiššīt	תשיעית
10	ēsīri	עשירי	ēsīrət	עשירית

5.4.1 It cannot be determined whether הראישן (Job 15:7) and ריאשונה (some manuscripts of Jos 21:10) with an extra י reflect the Samaritan pronunciation. In any case, the pronunciation is derived from the pronunciation of the long *ī* with two peaks — i.e., **rīšōn > *riišon* — which caused the splitting of that syllable in two, ultimately changing the first *ī* into *å* analogically to the development of *yå'ūmər* יאמר and *rē'oš* ראש. (See 2.3.7.)

5.4.2 The identity of the plural form *šēnəm* (SP שנים Gn 6:16, Nu 2:16; TH שְׁנַיִם) with the cardinal numeral two has been caused by the contraction of the diphthong *iyyi* into *ī* (see 1.4.4[2]), which has become in SH, under the given conditions, *ə*.

5.4.3 The ordinal numerals 3–10 follow the *qatīl* pattern with the addition of a relative pronoun, similar to Aramaic, although in Aramaic, of course, the usual Aramaic relative suffix is used, as in תְּלִיתִי. The Aramaic mode appears in Samaritan Hebrew in the words *šēlīšā'əm* (SP שלישים, TH שְׁלֵשִׁים) and *rēbiyyā'əm* (SP רביעים, TH רְבֵעִים).

5.5 Fractions

The fractions that occur in the Pentateuch are:

1/2	*ēṣi* חצי; *mēṣṣå* מחצה; *må'ēṣət* מחצית; *(kå)ēṣət* כ(ח)צית (SP Ex 11:4).
1/3	*šilšət*
1/4	*rē'bīt*
1/5	*ēmīšåt* חמישת (SP Gn 47:24); *(l)åmoš* ל(ח)מוש (SP Gn 47:26)
1/10	*ēsīråt* עשירית; *išron* עשרון; *måššår* (some read: *måššår*) מעשר.

5.5.1 Originally, there was no one system for expressing fractions, and remnants of various types exist in Hebrew. Of the type beginning with מ, common in Ugaritic, there remain מחצה, מחצית, and מעשר. Over time, though, a system developed for expressing fractions: the ordinal number (from 1/3 up) in its feminine form. In TH, the words שְׁלִישִׁית, etc., have two meanings. That system may be reflected in SH in the noun rēʾbīt, and it is employed analogically in the SH numeral ēṣət חצית as well, but SH is characterized by its own way of distinguishing between the feminine ordinal number and the fraction. Thus, one does not find in SP the *plene* spellings חמישית, etc., with a י preceding the ת in the fractional form of the numeral. That omission reflects the pronunciation preserved even now.

5.5.2 The different development of מחצה and מחצית merits discussion. The form mēṣṣå is derived from *meḥṣā, while in מחצית, the ח did not come into contact with the צ. It is not impossible that the form without gemination חצית exerted influence on the form מחצית.

5.5.3 The form šilšət is like a TH segholate noun with the addition of ת-. The Aramaic form תַּלְתָא (Syriac תולתא) and the Arabic ثُلث, too, which represent 1/3, are "segholate" nouns. TH preserves the forms שֶׁלֶשׁ and שְׁלֹשָׁה as personal names (1 Chr 7:36ff.), and their original meaning may be "third (child)." The type represented in TH by רֶבַע, רֹבַע, and חֹמֶשׁ is not used for these numbers in SH; SP consistently reads רביעית and, in place of חֹמֶשׁ, חמוש. The forms שליש and רביע are unknown in SH. While the form שלישי (Ex 15:4) is translated by ST as תליתאה ("third") and the pronounciation šēlīšo would be appropriate as the pronunciation of an ordinal numeral, a true numeral in this pattern does not exist.

5.5.4 Were it not for the pronunciation ʿāmoš, it would be possible to view the written form as built on the model of MH תישוע 1/9 and עישור 1/10 (whence in Jewish Aramaic עישוראה, עישורין), with the second radical geminated. Indeed, we find in the Mishna עישור alongside עשירית and מעשר. The pronunciation of חמוש follows the passive participle pattern, and in SH עשור, too (see 5.6), may be understood as belonging to this pattern. The pattern of the passive participle expresses multiples in Jewish traditions of Hebrew (משולש, מרובע, רָבוּעַ), but in the Samaritan tradition, the form חמוש in Gn 47:26 means 1/5. The opposite of this is noted below (5.6.1) regarding שבוע. It may be, however, that the relationship of SH חמוש to TH חֹמֶשׁ is like that of כָּבֵד to "כבוד" as treated in my "Observations," 18.

> Note: SA חמוש (e.g., Gn 47:24), however, is a fraction, like תישוע above. Remember that *חָמוּשׁ 1/5 is indirectly attested in MH in the interpretation of וַחֲמֻשִׁים (Ex 13:18; SP וחמישים) אחד מחמישה (*Mekhilta de R. Yišmʿael*, ed. Horowitz-Rabin, 77). It is worthwhile noting that in Hebrew the same pattern may express a fraction and multiplication, as through addition of

a feminine ending to an ordinal number, e.g., עשירית "1/10" — עשיריה "a group of 10" (1 x 10). Only the context can establish the intended meaning.

5.6 Multiplicatives

Forms: *mašni* משנה, meaning both "double" and "second";[10] *šibbu* שבע (Gn 29:27) and the dual form *šibbuwwā'əm* (Lv 12:5); *'āšor* עשור.

> Note: It is not certain whether the noun עשור as pronounced means "tenfold"; in Gn 24:55 SP reads חדש where the Jewish Pentateuch reads עשור, and in other verses SAV translates עשור as عاشر = "tenth."

5.6.1 The form *šibbu* is undoubtedly intended to mean "sevenfold," like words of this pattern in Aramaic and MH עישור. Its source may be *šabo* (< שבע) and the gemination secondary (see 1.5.3.3[2]). Note that the name of the festival שבעות is pronounced *šăbā'ot*, which is a plural form of the number seven (i.e., seven weeks), an interesting parallel to a non-existent TH plural שְׁבָעוֹת*. The form שבעתים (Gn 4:15,24) is pronounced *šibbuwwåtā'əm*, and it has already been noted (see n. 5 below) that the word is not to be taken as a number but as meaning "surplus" or "even more so," derived from the root שב"ח, and there is consequently no evidence for expressing a multiple by the ending ־ים.

5.6.2 Worthy of special note is the expression of the multiple by means of the numeral אחד in SP Ex 22:6,8: אחד שנים, as in Aramaic usage, such as חד שבעה in Dan 3:19, and the MH expression על אחת כמה (וכמה).

---

[10] In *Hammeliṣ*, *LOT* II, 512, it as translated as מצאעף ("double") and as וזיר "second;" and in Ab Isda's *Turjuman* (*LOT* I, קף and קט) there is also the translation תאני.

6. PARTICLES

6.0 The traditional classification of Hebrew words into three categories — noun, verb, and particle — is based on close observation of the meanings of the words and their function in the sentence. In this view, the particles are distinguished by their use as "instruments and connectives for discourse,"[1] meaning that they express grammatical relations and have no independent existence. If the test of classification is meaning and function, it is clear that the part of speech known as "particle" requires, or admits of, a more detailed classification: a particle indicating relations among nouns ("preposition"); a particle modifying an action or situation ("adverb"), which may itself be divided into subcategories of time, place, manner, etc.; a particle joining clauses; a particle joining words, and others. In this way it became common for textbooks of Hebrew — under the influence of the linguistic treatment of Indo-European languages[2] — to classify parts of speech in Hebrew into nine categories. The most well-founded objections made by grammarians of the structural school against the methods and approaches of their predecessors in linguistic analysis is undoubtedly the division of parts of speech. Their refusal to mix considerations of meaning, function, and form and their insistence on criteria of form alone[3] should guide us as well. Form, after all, gives us the most objective criterion for categorizing the vocabulary of a language, as it stems from the structure of the language under analysis and helps the grammarian to free himself from the background of his own language (which is sometimes quite different in structure from the language he analyzes) and the terminology forged in it and for it.

6.1 The classification adopted in this grammar is based principally on considerations of form; in fact, this leads to a tripartite division of all the words in

---

[1] This outlook is most clearly formulated in the first chapter of Ibn Janāḥ's *Kitāb al-Lumaʿ*, 23.

[2] The extent of this influence is apparent from the following detail: the Hebrew term for "adverb," תאר הפעל ("verb modifier"), in contrast to תאר השם ("noun modifier") is a product of Hebrew in its later stage being in continued contact with the European languages, in which the predicate of a sentence is almost always a verb. In Hebrew, however, the predicate is very often a noun (without copula) — e.g., אין יוסף בבור (Gn 37:29), פה אלישע בן שפט (2 Kgs 3:11), עוֹד אָכְלָם בְּפִיהֶם (Ps 78:30). Nevertheless, אין, פה, and עוד are, strangely enough, usually listed under the rubric of "adverb."

[3] E. Sapir (*Language* [New York, 1929], 119): "Each language has its own scheme. Everything depends on the formal demarcations which it recognizes."

Hebrew. Noun and verb are so distinct in formal phenomena that no difficulty is involved in identifying them and their functions in a sentence. The logic of the division requires us to classify the infinitives and participles as nouns ("verbal nouns"), because they do not differ from "pure" nouns in declension, i.e., in regard to the construct state and the connection with *possessive* pronominal suffixes. However, as they are also able to govern objects and to be connected with *object* pronominal suffixes, as, e.g., לְדָרְשֵׁנִי (Jer 37:7) and הַמְאַזְּרֵנִי (Ps 18:33), they are treated, as is common, together with the finite forms of the verb (2.12–2.14).

6.2 A definition of particles based solely on formal criteria will be more complicated because the term "particle" in the grammar of Hebrew (and other Semitic languages) is a blanket term. It includes words of different kinds and structures, which have in common that they have neither the characteristics of a noun nor those of a verb.

It may be argued that a strict application of the aforementioned principle requires us to classify personal and demonstrative pronouns with the particles, but we have, nonetheless, dedicated a separate chapter to them (Chap. 3), as is customary due to their peculiar characteristics: they are declined (by way of suppletion) in regard to gender and number. To this we add their function in a sentence as substitutes for real nouns.[4]

From the descriptive, synchronic perspective we have to distinguish in Hebrew between (A) indeclinable particles and (B) declinable particles. The particles listed below are not arranged according to their meaning or the function they fulfill in a sentence. In that area, they present no departure from TH usage. Instead they are presented alphabetically as they are spelled in SP.

A. Indeclinable Particles

a. Without specific endings: *åbəl* אבל, *ū* או, *az* אז, *ik* איך, *īka* איכה, *ak* אך, *åkən* אכן, *am* = TH אם, *åna* = TH אנה and אנה, *af* אף, *ēšår* אשר, *båli* בלי, *gam* גם, *åba* הבה and *åbu* הבו (imperative forms of the verb יהב), *åki* הכי, *ēlåm* הלם, *åna* = TH הנה, *yån* יען, *kā* כה, *kī* כי, *kan/ken* כן (*alkən* לכן), *lå* לא (*ablå* בלא), *lū* לו, *lēbi* לוי (SP Gn 17:18; MH לְוִי), *mē'ūmå* מאומה, *miyyå'īn* מאין, *mēti* = TH מתי, *nå* נא, *få* פה, *fan* פן.

b. Originally inflected words, which were lexicalized together with their

---

[4] It should be noted that the prominent 13th century grammarian David Qimḥi, who recognized the tripartite division (*Mikhlol*, ed. Rittenberg, 190ff.), did not hesitate to include אתה, אנכי, זה, אנחנו, etc. in the chapter on particles. For this he was criticized by the 14th century philosopher and grammarian Profiat Duran ("Efodi") in his *Ma'aseh Efod*, (ed. J. Friedlander and J. Kohn [Vienna,1865], 32) on the basis of semantics and function.

Particles   315

flexional elements and became particles bearing different endings: *wå'lā* והלאה, *ålīla* חלילה, *lēṭṭå* לאטה (SP Gn 33:14; in other versions לחטא), *milmēṭå* מלמטה, *milmā:la* מלמעלה, *šamma* שם; *bilti* בלתי, *zūlåti* זולתי, *we'ūlåm* ואולם, *innåm* חנם, *yūmåm* יומם, *fē'tåm* פתאם, *rīqəm* ריקם (see 4.3.9), *yåddu* יחדו, *åmēnimma* אמנם = TH אָמְנָם, *qūmåmət* קוממית (SP Lv 26:13), *mittåm* מתם (Dt 2:34; TH מְתִם) "completely."

Note: The endings of *åmēnimma* אמנם and *yaddu* = TH יַחְדָּו are in fact pronominal suffixes.

B. Declinable Particles

These are mostly prepositions and adverbs. From a historical perspective they are nouns, and morphologically they continue to behave as nouns in regard to the construct state and the connection with pronominal suffixes, e.g., אצל, אל ("beside," "at"), מפני, עד, על, תמול ("yesterday").

According to a strict formal criterion, the *literae serviles* belong to this category as well.[5] They were, in fact, listed in *LOT* IV and the Inventory of Forms in this volume under the respective nouns, e.g., בעבור, למען under עבור, מען. The diachronic perspective neither supports nor contradicts this procedure.

6.2.1 Note (a) In accordance with the conception above of the nominal character of a declinable particle, the construct state in phrases like כְּשִׂמְחַת בַּקָּצִיר (Isa 9:2) or חוֹכֵי לוֹ (Isa 30:18) and others (which is also to be found in Modern Hebrew poetry) does not present an exception to the rule that the *rectum* must be a noun. (b) Further evidence is to be found in the substitution made for the construct state (i.e., the expression of the genitive by a circumlocution): a proleptic personal pronoun attached to the particle being *regens*. Examples: (1) MH עליו של הרופא (= על הרופא; *y. Nedarim* 38c); (2) עליו של האדם (*t. Ḥagiga* 2:5, ed. Lieberman, 387); (3) ממנו של אבימי (*Hilkhot Re'u*, ed. Schlossberg, 92); (4) לכמותן שלדברים (L. Ginzberg, *Geonica* II [New York, 1909], 270).[6] As is well known, this phenomenon is common in Eastern Aramaic: in Jewish Aramaic, e.g., עליה דאיניש (*b. Shevu'ot* 34b), כוותיה דרב.... (passim); in Mandaic, e.g., in an

---

[5] The principles of division applied here have for many years guided my work in teaching Hebrew and can be found in my article "Hebrew Grammar," col. 168, but only much later did it come to my attention that Efodi (see n. 4 above), "after careful consideration" applied (p. 145) the criterion of form (!) in deciding that particles such as בעבור, etc., are in fact nouns. For some reason this criterion escaped him when criticizing Qimḥi.

[6] Reference (2) was brought to my attention by Dr. M. Mishor, and reference (4) by Prof. S. Abramson.

"Amulet with Four Incantations":⁷ עלאיחון ד׳ דייא (98, l. 19), מראיחון ד׳ עלה (99, l. 26). One might explain the examples from the ancient Hebrew texts as loan translations; can one do the same for the neologisms in Modern Hebrew: לפניהן של ארצות מפותחות "before developed countries," לקראתם של הפלשתינאיים "toward the Palestinians"? (See *LOT* V, 267, n. to 238)

Thus, the declinable particles in Hebrew are not only originally nouns, but are still felt to be nouns.

6.3 The particles are treated here to the extent that they have qualities setting them apart from their TH counterparts in addition to their pronunciation. These, too, are arranged alphabetically:

6.3.1 The original vowel of the particles -ב, -כ, and -ל in both SH and TH was *a*, as forms with pronominal suffixes attest: *bânu* בנו, *kâkimma* ככם, *lânu* לנו. In accordance with the phonological rules, that vowel was reduced to *šəwa*. In a later stage of SH, the *šəwa* developed into a full vowel (see 1.3.2) with -ב and -ל before the consonant of the particle, but with -כ after the consonant, e.g., *abyom* = בְּיוֹם, *alyom* = לְיוֹם, *kâyâmi* = כימי, *kēlā'ək* כלחך. When the particle -ב precedes a noun beginning with one of the labial consonants ב, מ, and פ, an *â* vowel follows the consonant, e.g., *bâbâṭnək* בבטנך, *bâmâqom* במקום, *bâfâno* בפניו. When -ל precedes a noun that itself begins with ל, the -ל of the particle normally takes the *a* vowel and the first consonant of the noun is, as a rule, geminated: *lalliyyâ* לְלֵאָה, *lallâbân* לְלָבָן, *lalloṭ* ללוט, *lallēkət* ללכת. The vowel after the particle -ל under these conditions may also be *i*: *lillamməd* ללמד. Other consonants, too, in addition to ל, sometimes are geminated after the particle -ל, as in *laššēlâšət* לשלשת (Ex 19:15, in construct state!), *larrē'oš* לראש (Gn 49:26 Dt 33:16 construct state), and perhaps *laššad* according to some translations of לְשָׁד (Nu 11:8 construct state); see 1.5.3.3b. Before a word beginning with a guttural consonant, the vowel of -ב and -ל fuses with the vowel of the consonant, e.g., *bēšår* באשר, *bisdâk* בחסדך, *lēšår* לאשר, *lūlâm* לעולם, etc. (Note, however: *kâ'ēšår* כאשר.) In the particle -ב, the shift from plosive to fricative (1.1.4) has been preserved in the form *af*-, which precedes every word beginning with any consonant other than י, ל, or ר: *afdor* בדור, *afgēlâlək* בגללך, *afgåd* בגד (Gn 30:11), and the like as contrasted with *abyəd* ביד, *ablēbâbu* בלבבו, *abrē'ušu* בראשו, etc. In two instances, -ב occurs with a form that is explicitly a verb — as is found in Jewish Hebrew from ancient liturgical poetry on:⁸ *bētâsēfu* בהתאספו (2.2.1.5.3), *alnibbâl* לנפל (2.14.10).

---

⁷ J. C. Greenfield and J. Naveh, "A Mandaic Lead Amulet with Four Incantations," *EI* 18 (1985), 97–107 [Hebrew].

⁸ Cf. לנולדו על ברכיו in M. Zulay, ed., *Piyyuṭe Yannai* (Berlin, 1938), 71 [Hebrew]; לשלחו לו in a *piyyut* of Qalir in D. Goldschmidt, *Maḥzor la-Yamim ha-Nora'im* I (Jerusalem, 1970), 53 [Hebrew]. The Masoretic vocalization of לְתִּתֶּן (1 Kgs 6:19) would seem to put that word in this

Particles   317

6.3.2 The exclamatory *â* (-ה) is present in SH, and unlike in TH, does not require the gemination of the following consonant: *â'qâl* הקהל (Nu 15:15; as distinct from *aq'qāl* in Nu 22:4), *â'māṭ* המעט (see 6.3.3, as distinct from *am'māṭ* המעט in Nu 35:8).

SH reads *â* in Gn 47:23 where TH reads הֵא. This is undoubtedly the same word as הָא occurring in MH in such phrases as הא למדת and written sometimes joined with the following word, as in הכיצד. It is found in SH; for an example, see *LOT* III/2, 199, l. 17, where more examples may be found as well; see also the index there. It appears that the Samaritan tradition includes exclamatory -ה in these words as well: *â'îṭâb* הייטב (Dt 9:21), *â'lū* הלוא (see 6.3.12), *āna* in the sense of אָנָא, *âmol* המול (Gn 17:12,13; see 2.14.15), and perhaps *âyânâqâ* הינקה (SP Gn 21:7; see 2.4.4). If *akku* הכו (SP Gn 27:36) is derived from ה and כו (see 6.3.11), then perhaps this serves as an example of an exclamatory -ה that does cause gemination.

In the word *ēgåm* הגם (Gn 16:13), the ה is understood as an exclamation and not an interrogative, as the Samaritan translations attest, and the particle *ē* is known in SA, usually written אה, whose meaning is akin to TH הוי (English "O...!"). For an example, see *LOT* III/2, 44, l. 8; 60, ll. 11,19.

6.3.3 The interrogative -ה occurs in SH in two forms: (1) without gemination of the following consonant, e.g., *åšāma* השמע (Dt 4:33), *â'māṭ* המעט (Gn 30:15 and elsewhere); (2) with gemination, e.g., *annåsså* הנסה (Dt 4:34), *anniššāma* הנשמע, as is found in TH: הַכְּצַעֲקָתָהּ (Gn 18:21; in SH two words: *ik ṣâ'iqtâ*), הַלְבֶן (Gn 17:17; SH *âlban*). In the first category, it is sometimes difficult to determine whether the ה is exclamatory or interrogative in the Samaritan tradition. The grammarian Abū Saʿīd's commentary on הֲשֹׁפֵט (Gn 18:25) assumes that the prefix is exclamatory (see *LOT* I, 161).

6.3.4 Conjunctive -ו includes *waw consecutive* because in SH there is no difference in form between them, just as there is no such difference in Origen's Hexapla[9] and just as there was originally no difference between them, the distinction having been created in Jewish Hebrew from among different phonological options.[10] From the descriptive perspective it seems that, unlike the particles -ב, -כ, and -ל, the -ו lost its original vowel and attached directly to the

---

category, but the occurrence of תתן as the *kətiv* in 1 Kgs 17:14 as well requires us to explain לתתן differently.

[9] For example: ουσαμθι ושמתי (Ps 89:30), ουθεθθεν ותתן (Ps 18:36). Brønno (*Studien*, 231) is of the opinion that conjunctive -ו in the Hexapla's transcription was almost certainly not vocalic. Was its situation not like that of conjunctive -ו in SH?

[10] I.e., a long vowel in an open syllable and a short vowel in a closed syllable, with gemination of the following consonant as necessary for closing the syllable (see 1.5.3.3). Lack of gemination after the ו in SH is paralleled in the words במה and כמה; see also below 6.3.15.

noun, e.g., *wyom* ויום, *wtūṣi* ותוצא, and *wšēmå* ויהוה (read as Aramaic שמא). In a slow reading, the semi-vowel may be lengthened to *u* — that is, to the homorganic vowel. Thus, other transcribers render it as the full vowel *u*. For phonological reasons, both synchronic and diachronic, we render *w*. The reasons are:

1. a vowel in an unclosed syllable must normally be long, while this is always short, even when produced as *u* and not *w*;

2. in a bisyllabic word, it will never receive the stress — והוא is pronounced *u'’ū*, in which the first syllable is not only not long but unstressed, and so it is in such phrases as מבית ומחוץ, pronounced *mib'bēt-u-miyyoṣ*, and others, discussed in 1.4.10 — which is not the case with -ב, -כ, and -ל, the interrogative -ה, and the definite article -ה, which do receive the stress under certain circumstances;

3. in Arabic transcriptions of the thirteenth century, which are careful about the fricative pronunciations of ב, פ, ד, and ת, one always finds ת transcribed as a plosive in a word such as ותקרא وتقرا (see 1.1.4);

4. before a guttural consonant that disappears after -ו, the vowel of the -ו reflects the vowel of the consonant in question (see 1.3.3), e.g., *wåmår* ואמר, *wišron* ועשרון, *wukka* והכה (Lv 11:30).[11]

> Note: The vowel *ē* in *wēlåka* והלכה (Dt 24:2) does not indicate the existence of an *waw consecutive* in SH, but it is caused by the loss of the 1st guttural radical (cf. 2.2.1.1.2).

The existence of *w* in SH outside of the sequence *uww-* is a problem, because normally ו (> *v* >) becomes *b*, as in *mēṣåba* מצוה and *båb* = TH וָו. Perhaps we may conjecture that *w* of the conjunctive ו is what remains of the glide formed between the vowel *u* and the vowel after a lost guttural; that is, originally there was *u* (< *wu* < *wa*), as is reflected in the Hexapla,[12] and from forms like **ū'åmår*, **uwwåmår* developed according to the usual rules (see 1.1.8b). Perhaps the original vowel of the particle -ו is reflected in the length of the vowel in such forms as *wēnna* (= TH וְהִנֵּה) and *wē'ūlåm* ואולם and *Hitpa'el* forms such as *wētbårråku* והתברכו. In all these the vowel remains long.

6.3.5 *uwwi* או. This seems at first to be related to וי, with the semi-consonant ו maintained, but it is not so, having been formed instead from אוי as in TH, just as *guwwi* is formed from גוי (1.4.4c). See also 6.3.8.

---

[11] In the last example, the *u* vowel for the definite article ה is more perplexing. Does this pronunciation perhaps reflect a noun, different from that of TH, matching the Arabic noun حكى (as mentioned in KB³, s.v. II כה; or its variant, see *Lisān al-'Arab* s. v. حكى)? For further discussion and identification of the reptile, see D. Talshir, *The Nomenclature of the Fauna in the Samaritan Targum* (Jerusalem, 1981), 65–67 [Hebrew].

[12] But see also the opinion of Brønno, n. 9 above.

6.3.6 אחור(י) / אחור(י). In SH there is no distinction like that in TH between אַחַר and אַחֲרֵ; both are âʼər (e.g., Lv 14:8,42). SH frequently has אחור(י) where TH has אחר(י), e.g., âʼūro (Nu 25:13) for TH אַחֲרָיו. Similar fluctuations are found in MH as well, e.g., *m. Rosh Ha-Shanah* 3:7 עובר אחורי בית הכנסת (see also in the same Mishna in MS Lowe, 62a); MS Kaufmann: אחר.

6.3.7 *ayye* איה. The word איכה in Gn 3:9 (TH אַיֶּכָּה) is pronounced *īka*, just as in Dt 1:12. The translations of ST איכה (MS J), איך (MS A) indicate that the word was understood as an exclamatory particle, not an interrogative one. We may assume that the Samaritan translators had difficulty with the 2nd masc. ending *ka*, although the pronunciation maintains it in the word באכה (3.2.2). Where TH reads וְאַיּוֹ (Ex 2:20), SH reads ואיה, pronounced *wayye*; the Samaritan translations understand it as bearing a 3rd masc. suffix: ST ואין הוא or והאנו, SAV واين هو indicate a reading of *ē* as a 3rd masc. ending (3.2.3.5).

6.3.8 *âfu* = TH אפוא. It appears that the SH pronunciation reflects a reading of this word as equivalent to the phrase אף הוא. Note that the Septuagint at 2 Kgs 2:14 renders אף הוא ἀφφώ; also 2 Kgs 10:10 אפוא. The Greek word is obviously a transcription of the Hebrew. Note as well that Targum Onqelos translates אפוא at Gn 27:33 as דיכי and at Gn 43:11 simply as הוא (and in a variant reading as הכא as in other verses), and MS C of ST at Gn 23:33 has explicitly אף הוא (MS Or 7562 אפו). The word אפו is found in the *Words of Aḥiqar* from Elephantine, l. 52 and especially l. 140: מן אפו (= מי אפוא). At Elephantine we also find the word אפם with a similar meaning; most derive it from אף מה.

6.3.9 אשרי. There is undoubtedly a semantic connection between אֲשֶׁר and אַשְׁרֵי (cf. אָמְרֵי/אֹמֶר), but the latter, the form of which appears to be plural, is subject to differing interpretations. It should be pointed out that SH does not recognize any apparently plural form for this word: at Dt 33:29, the word is pronounced *âšârak*, which is akin to a TH form *אַשְׁרְךָ.

6.3.10 את / אֶת in TH marking the direct object has as its usual SH equivalent *it*,[13] and as a preposition ("with") its SH pronunciation is *at*. The former (*it*) is declined *ūti*, etc., while *at* is declined *itti*, etc., although with 2nd and 3rd person pl. pronominal suffixes the ת of *at* is not geminated: *atkimma* אתכם, *miyyetkimma* מאתכם, *ētimma* אִתָּם. On the form with the 2nd pl. ending, see 1.5.3.3f.

6.3.11 *akku* הכו appears in SP Gn 27:36, where TH reads הכי, and is understood

---

[13] It also functions as a demonstrative; see 3.3.1.3.

in the Samaritan tradition as "fitting, proper" (cf. in *Hammeliṣ* under ה: *LOT* II, 452b, ll. 112ff.). Both the meaning ascribed to this word and its appearance under ה — while הכי appears under כ (ibid., 486b, l. 37) — indicate that the two words are not etymologically related according to the Samaritan tradition. It would seem that הכו is the TH כֹּה (cf. the spelling מְפוֹ in Ezek 40:12!) with the addition of an exclamatory -ה (see 6.3.2).

6.3.12 *å'lū* הלוא. It is generally accepted that הלא is a combination of two forms: לא and the interrogative -ה. This interpretation, however, is not in harmony with the tradition of SH, where the negative particle is always pronounced *lå* (as occurs in MH as well[14]), while the word in question is always spelled with ו and its pronunciation is different from that of the negative particle (see 1.5.2.5m, 1.5.2.6). It is more likely that this is an exclamation that shares a common origin not with the negative particle but with Old Aramaic הלו and Biblical Aramaic אֲלוּ (akin to אֲרוּ). It may be that TH הלא as well should be explained this way.

> Note: (a) In Gn 27:36, SH reads הלא and indeed realizes it as *ålå*. (b) The Yemenite pronunciation of MH ואילו (meaning "whereas") as וַאֲלוּ corroborates our interpretation of this Samaritan pronunciation.

6.3.13 *innā* הִנֵּה. The a vowel here is not only parallel to Arabic اِنَّ, but is also the form underlying TH הִנּוּ < *hinnahū*.

6.3.14 *lūlå* לולא. SP consistently reads this as two separate words: לו לא. The pronunciation obviously would not support the spelling לולי. The TH form, of course, is understood as resulting from the dissimilation of לו and לא, a process that could not occur in SH because of its pronunciation of לא as *lå*. I suspect the *ṣere* in the Aramaic forms (and the spelling with י) of אלולי and אילולִיפון — alongside אלו לא פון and אלו לפון — of Hebrew influence.[15]

6.3.15 *må* מה. There is no gemination of the initial consonant in SH in combination with -ב, -כ and -ל: *båmå*, *kåmå*, *lēmå*. The last of these clearly indicates an original form *לְמָה. It is not clear whether this shares a common origin with מו in such forms as *kåmūni* כמוני and *kåmē'u* כמהו (see 1.5.3.2b, but note also

---

[14] E.g., שלהנץ (= שלא הנץ), S. Lieberman, *Tosefta Ki-feshuta, Zeraʿim* (New York, 1955), 502, ll. 22ff. in the commentary). Lieberman notes that "this is a common spelling in the Tosefta." It is difficult to assume that, without pronouncing the word as *lā*, the copyists would join it to the following word.

[15] אלולי appears in SA as well, e.g., ST to Gn 31:42, and the liturgical poem אזל שלם לננה (*LOT* III/2, 264, l. 7): *willūli*, and in Targum Neophyti. However, in Palestinian Syriac it is spelled as two words: אלו לא, and in the Peshitta it is vocalized אֶלוּלָא.

kåmūnu כמונו!). The Samaritan tradition might well spell the word מה with a מ alone, joined to the following word, like TH מַלְּכֶם (Isa 3:15) or מַדּוּעַ *mad'dū*. Also explicable in this way are מאשור (Nu 24:22; variant reading מהאשור), rendered in SH as *måšor* (ST MS Barberini: מה משבחה "How splendid!"), and מאשר (Gn 49:20), pronounced *måšər* (see *LOT* III/1, 35). See also 3.3.3.1–2.

6.3.16 *man* מִן. With prefix -ל: *almån*.[16] There is a distinction in SH between the form bearing a 3rd masc. sing. ending, *mimminnu* ממנו, and that bearing the 1st pl. ending, *mimmånu* ממנו. (In TH both are מִמֶּנּוּ.) Of course, Eastern Masoretes distinguish between מִמֶּנּוּ (3rd masc. pl.) and מִמֶּנּוּ (1st pl.). On the loss of gemination after מ, see 1.5.3.3. On a combination such as *mīl* מֵאַיִל, see 1.4.4. On the possibility that *am-* is derived from מ (< מן), see 0.13c. A reduplication of מן appears in ממעל (Gn 22:9 and elsewhere), which the Samaritans pronounce *mimmiyyal* — equivalent to TH *מִמַּעַל. A combination of מן and a noun can function as an adverb, e.g., *mittåm* (Dt 2:34) מתם and *miṣ'ṣår* (Gn 19:20) מצער. (See 1.5.3.1f.)

6.3.17 *lā:mət* לעמת = TH לְעֻמַּת. The SH particle is derived from the root עמ"ת (as is the noun *'ammət* = TH עמית) and not from עמ"ם. If the final ת were a feminine ending, as the TH form might seem to indicate, the word should end in *åt*. The Samaritan tradition, then, agrees with the view of important medieval Jewish grammarians and lexicographers (see, e.g., Ibn Janāḥ, *Kitāb al-Uṣūl*, col. 535). However, the derivation from the root עמ"ם (as is common in the dictionaries of the Bible) is also very old, as forms with pronominal suffixes such as (1) לְעֻמָּם and (2) לְעֻמּוֹ indicate.[17]

6.3.18 *ši* -ש. Although this relative pronoun does not appear in the Pentateuch (see "Note" below), it is known in the Samaritan tradition and underlies the reading of some words, including שניר (TH שְׂנִיר), pronounced *šinnər* and understood as "of the yoke," and שדי, pronounced *šiddi* and understood as "[the One] who is sufficient" (see *LOT* III/2, 314). The grammarian Abū Isḥāq mentions this particle in *Kitāb al-Tawṭi'a* and cites as an example שיעשה (*LOT* I, 125), and El'azar the High Priest, in his *Mukhtaṣar al-Tawṭi'a*, includes it in the mnemonic אלום כבשתון כבש יתון or אלהים כבשתון (*LOT* I, 215). This use stands in con-

---

[16] The vowel of מן in SH has a parallel in the Aramaic of the Palestinian Talmud and sources linguisticallly close to it, as is witnessed by the occasional spelling with א: מאן (see Lieberman, *Ha-Yerushalmi kiphshuto* [Jerusalem, 1934/5], 23; and Yalon, *Studies*, 102–104 [Hebrew].

[17] Example (1) is taken from *The Pizmonim of the Anonymus*, ed. Ezra Fleischer (Jerusalem, 1974) [Hebrew]. Example (2) is taken from Benjamin Klar, *Megillat Aḥima'aṣ* [Jerusalem, 1974], 20 [Hebrew]. In the materials for the Historical Dictionary of the Hebrew Language (of the Academy of the Hebrew Language), many other attestations are to be found.

trast to the LSH usage, where Aramaic -ד appears (alongside אשר). The *i* vowel in *ši* has a parallel in the Copper Scroll (*DJD* III, 1962): שיבצפון (9:14), שיבית הכרם (10:5), as well as in the oral traditions of Hebrew among the Jews of Iraq and Djerba (Ktzia Katz, *Mishna Tractate Shevi'it in the Reading of Three Communities* [Jerusalem, 1993], passim [Hebrew]).

> Note: The word בשגם (Gn 6:3) is pronounced in SH without gemination after the ש: *afšågåm*, and it was not interpreted as including the relative pronoun -ש. Instead, it is taken to be related to the root שג and explained as "because of" (see *Hammeliṣ*, LOT II, 603, l. 227).

6.3.19 *tåt / tēt* תחת. The word when pronounced with *ē* means "underneath," and when pronounced with *å* means "instead of." SH, thus, takes advantage of the existence of two developments of the same primitive "segholate" pattern *qa/itl* (see 4.12.9) to distinguish between the two meanings, in the same way that Biblical Aramaic distinguished between טַעַם and טְעֵם, using the former in relation to God. The form with *ē* may have a parallel in the Hexapla at Ps 18:39,40 θεθ, θεθαι, and it seems unlikely to relate this form to an underlying *tiḥt* form in Hebrew, as Brønno (*Studien*, 246) has suggested, because of the guttural nature of the 2nd radical, and, in fact the reconstructed form appears in no other Semitic language. It cannot be determined whether the Syriac form תְּחֵית is cognate with tēt (תְּחֵת*) or instead parallels זְעֵיר. On the gemination of the 3rd radical in declension — *tētti* תחתי, *tētto* תחתו, *tåtto* תחתיו, etc. — see 4.6.3 and 1.5.3.1.

7. SOME POINTS OF SYNTAX

7.0 General Remarks

Among the thousands of textual variations between SP and the Masoretic version, there are quite a few syntactic differences between the two versions of the Hebrew Bible. One salient feature of SP, which has long been noticed, is its tendency to harmonize parallel passages so that they are precisely alike in content and language, including number and gender agreement between a noun and its complement and between the subject and predicate of a sentence.[1] In this area, as is widely known, the Hebrew Bible — particularly the Pentateuch in its Masoretic form — is replete with many "exceptions" that in fact embody some quite ancient syntactic usages that antedate the language of the later biblical books and of MH. The manner of grammatical agreement in SP generally reflects the usages of later Hebrew, in which the lack of agreement in question is a violation of established rules and patterns, and, thus, we find in SP such instances as:

1. Gn 49:20 — *šāmən* (SP שמן; TH שְׁמֵנָה) *lēmmu* לחמו
2. Gn 49:15 — *mānuw'wā kī ṭūba* (SP טובה; TH טוֹב)
3. Gn 46:27 — *wbāni yusəf...yēlīdu* (SP ילדו; TH יֻלַּד) *lu*; see also Gn 10:25
4. Ex 39:1–3 — *'ašu* (SP עשו)... *wyāšu wqåṣṣåṣu* (SP וקצצו; TH וְקִצֵּץ)
5. Lv 19:27 — *wlā tāšittu it fāt zāqånkimma* (SP וזקנכם; TH זְקָנֶךָ)

and many others. If we add to these SH's common replacement of infinitive absolute forms by other verb forms (2.14.4ff.), its changes in verb tense and usage (2.9.3ff.), its replacement of passive forms by active ones or by changes in sentence structure (2.10.2ff.), and other isolated phenomena, such as the marking of the subject with ל- (see 2.10.6b, n. 52), we find ourselves with a syntactic portrait of the written form of SP that differs in many individual verses from the syntax of the Masoretic version of the Pentateuch. But as regards the language itself, beyond the range of this or that particular verse, it cannot be said that SP in its written form displays any new syntactic phenomenon unknown to us from the Masoretic text.

---

[1] Cf. Gesenius, *De Pentateuchi samaritanae origine*, especially sect. 4, 45; Waltke, *Prolegomena*, 294ff.

Given that the subject of the present work is the description of SH as it emerges from the recitation of the Pentateuch, our concern here will be limited solely to syntactic phenomena that are revealed by the Samaritan pronunciation, while those based on the written text of SP need no description since they come under the categories of syntax included in standard grammars of Biblical Hebrew. It was necessary to deal with some of those standard phenomena in the morphology section of the present work, because it sometimes happens that the morphological distinction between SH and TH is connected with the different syntactic treatments accorded a given form. Here, then, we will deal with items not treated in the chapter on morphology.

> Note: It should be pointed out that just as there is not complete consistency in the trend of variations within SP, in the same way a search for complete consistency in linguistic trends reflected in SH will prove fruitless. SH is certainly anchored in the Hebrew of the Second Temple period and of the first few generations after its destruction (see 2.9.3), while the Pentateuch is far more ancient than SP, and even in the form in which it has been preserved by the Samaritans (whose approach to the text allowed greater latitude than that of the Masoretes), one cannot bridge the gap between the written source and the language as it was current in those times. Furthermore, the occasional inconsistencies within that tradition have their origins in separate and varied traditions of exegesis and language within the Samaritan community itself. There may also be minor instances of simple forgetfulness or ignorance, characteristics which have been all too lightly ascribed to the Samaritans due to unfamiliarity with their traditions and ways.

7.1 Determination

There are very many textual variations between TH and SH in the determination of nouns. Those in which the definite article is indicated by ה- are evident.[2] Those in which the definite article is combined with the preposition ב-

---

[2] A rather lengthy list of variants involving the definite article ה- can be found in Macuch, *Grammatik*, 482–490. Given that ה is not pronounced, when it appears as the definite article preceding a noun that begins with אהח"ע, the ה is sometimes eliminated without any impact on the word's pronunciation, and, therefore, in such instances we find disagreement among manuscripts of SP. It is not at all a simple task, then, to compile a comprehensive list of such variants that have some linguistic substance. Only on the basis of the pronunciation of such words can we expect to reveal whether there is any difference between the two traditions. E.g., in Gn 19:9 we find in SP the spelling אחד alongside that of the Masoretic text האחד. This might appear to be nothing more than a spelling variation were it not that the pronunciation *'ad* (and not *â''ād*) indicates that the traditions differ over the presence or absence of the definite article.

7.1 Determination

or -ל, however, are revealed only in pronunciation. We can contrast, for example, these Masoretic and Samaritan readings: כִּשְׂעִירִים... וְכִרְבִיבִים / *kaššī:rəm... wkarrēbībəm* (Dt 32:2), בְּזָרִים וּבְתוֹעֵבוֹת / *bazzarrəm wbattuuwēbot* (Dt 32:16), לַשֵּׁדִים / *alšīdəm* (Dt 32:17), בַּמְּעָרָה / *bāmā:ra* (Gn 19:30), and others. It might appear at first that SH does not observe the same rules as TH in marking determination, but the congruence between the two traditions in this matter is actually quite extensive. Of course, nouns beginning with אהח"ע in SH cannot be compared with their TH counterparts because of the development of the *šəwa* into a full vowel in SH, which must be long in an open syllable.[3] In fact, the only basis for comparison of nouns with the preposition -ב, -כ, or -ל between SH and TH are those in which the first consonant after the preposition is not geminated, since it may be that gemination in SH is secondary (see 1.1.5.3.3), such as after -ל (see 6.3.1): the gemination in a form such as *laššēlåšåt* לשלשת in Ex 19:15 (in the construct state!) is not at all the result of the presence of the definite article.[4] Accordingly, there is no need whatsoever to assume that there is a syntactic variation between the two traditions in the examples כשעירי, כרביבם, etc., but we are forced to posit a difference in the syntax of determination in the cases of לשדים and במערה.

The question of determination in SH should be explored not only vis-à-vis TH, with the aforementioned caveats, but also in relation to the practice in the Mishna as reflected in ancient manuscripts, which differ from one another significantly in spelling and no less so in vocalization.

Phrases such as פני הארון יהוה (SP Ex 34:23) and ואכלתם מן התבואתה ישן (SP Lv 25:22) have aroused controversy among grammarians. Abū Isḥāq is of the opinion that the force of these nouns is like that of undetermined nouns (*LOT* I, 43), while El'azar the High Priest admits the possibility that the *rectum* is marked as definite (*LOT* I, 197; see n. 8). According to the latter, then, *attēbuwwåtå* comes under the same rubric as, say, המוציאך (Dt 8:14). Abū Sa'īd (*LOT* I, 161) views the final ה in התבואתה as "superfluous" or as the "ה of emphasis" (in Arabic تفخيم). (The two terms are essentially synonymous.) I have

---

[3] Abū Sa'īd's ninth rule (*LOT* I, 155ff.) ascribes an indication of determination to nouns beginning with a guttural consonant that are preceded by the prepositions -ב, -כ, or -ל, that indication being the length of the vowel. This rule is applicable only to a small number of nouns, though, because the difference in vowel length can occur only in a closed syllable such as *bår* בהר in Gn 31:23 or Ex 15:17, as opposed to *bar* בהר in Ex 25:40 and elsewhere. In a noun beginning with a guttural consonant in an open syllable, in which the vowel is long even without the affixed -ב, -כ, or -ל, or if the vowel there is long for some other reason, there is no disinction in vowel length between the definite and indefinite forms. Both בחדש in the construct state (as in Dt 16:1) and בחדש with the definite article but not in the construct state (as in Ex 19:1) are pronounced *bådəš*.

[4] In the expression *laššēlåš aššānəm* לשלש השנים in Lv 25:21, SAV makes the number definite: ללתלאת, which means that the gemination was understood, mistakenly, as an indication of determination.

not succeeded in clarifying the grammarians' opinion of המשכבה (SP Lv 15:23); their translations do not render the 3rd fem. sing. pronominal suffix at all, so perhaps they construe משכבה to be the absolute form of the noun. [However, note the rendering of British Library MS Or 7562: مضجعها].

7.2 He Locale

In TH, the distinction between the feminine ending ־ה and the same ending indicating direction toward a goal (this being the original, primary function of that ending in Biblical Hebrew) is marked by the placement of stress. If the ending is accented, it is a feminine marker. If it is unaccented, it is *he locale* (including paragogic ה). Of course, this distinction is inappropriate to SH, where stress is always on the penult. Thus, there are nouns in which one may encounter some doubt about the nature of the *-a* ending as understood by the Samaritans. For example, *līla* לילה, whose plural in the Bible is לילות (in some non-Pentateuchal passages) and its Arabic cognate is ليل. On the basis of morphology alone, it may defined as a feminine noun in SH. In such instances, the grammarian can come to a conclusion only on the basis of syntax (e.g., *ballīla azze* in Ex 12:8) or by semantic considerations according to the rule that "anything that needs a prefixed -ל but does not get one receives instead a ה- ending, as for example חוצה — לחוץ" (*y. Yevamot* 1: 6).

From the debate there on the legal implications of the word חוצה in Dt 25:5 we learn that the Samaritan interpretation of חוצה as meaning "external" is not foreign to the Jewish tradition, since it fits the opinion of Bet Shammai: כאילין כותיא...דאינן דרשין חוצה החיצונה (*y. Yevamot* 1:6) — analyzing חוצה as an adjective with the feminine ending *-a*.

While ST translates החוצה in Dt 25:5 as בראיתה ("external"), the Samaritans are not unaware of the use of *he locale* as a "substitute for ל," as is evident in *LOT* I, 253, where ה in *šamma* שמה is explained in Arabic اى الى (i.e., "to"). In various forms they ignore it (as "superfluous"), for example, in a word such as *šamma* (the consistent pronunciation), where no distinction is made in pronunciation between the two spellings שם and שמה. There are also words in which the Samaritans construe it as the definite article, as in Aramaic (*LOT* I, 159), and indeed their translations render מעונה in Dt 33:27 as if it were מעון marked with the definite article: ST מעונה, SAV الموطن.

In the light of the above, it is easy to understand that the reading וישליכו אתו הבור (SP Gn 37:24) presents no problem within the Samaritan tradition, and it is translated by ST as לגובה and by SAV as الجوب, since the final ה may be deleted (*LOT* I, 161).

7.3 את

The choice of one or the other of the two modes of pronouncing the particle את may determine the form of verbal predicate in a given sentence and thus even influence the meaning of the verse, as we see in the verb שמח in the last example in 7.4 below.

1. Something similar occurs in TH with the verb שפט. The *nota accusativi* את joins the verb in *Qal* to express (a) "judge," while the *Nif'al* of the same root is joined by the preposition את to express (b) "enter into controversy." Biblical dictionaries and ancient translations make this distinction consistently; they even include Jer 2:35 and Ezek 20:36, despite the fact that these two verses express the same idea using different particles. As for the verb שפט in SH, it appears only in the *Qal* stem, governing the prepositional את, as in *wšåfåṭu at 'ām* ושפטו את העם (Ex 18:22) or *tišfåṭ at 'ammītåk* תשפט את עמיתך (Lv 19:15).

An interesting parallel to the use of שפט governing the preposition עם for meaning (b) above is to be found in the Aramaic *Words of Aḥiqar* from Elephantine, l. 104: למ[ה] ישפטון עקן עם אשה בשר עם סכין "Why should trees contend with fire, flesh with a knife?" The verb ישפטון must be a form of *Qal*, since *Nif'al* does not exist in Aramaic.

2. In SH, the verb ירא, too, is followed by a prepositional את, as can be learned from examples such as *at å'ēluwwəm åni yåri* את האלהים אני ירא (Gn 42:18) or *yåri ånåki ittu* ירא אנכי אתו (Gn 32:12). Since the preposition את is understood to be synonymous with מן (see *LOT* I, 271), the phrase ירא את in the Samaritan tradition is not syntactically different from ירא מן, and this is reflected in their understanding of phrases such us *yåṣå'u at å''īr* יצאו את העיר (Gn 44:4), *kåṣiyyati at å''īr* כצאתי את העיר (Ex 9:29), or *wtimmåli å:rəṣ ētimma* ותמלא הארץ אתם (Ex 1:7), where ST translates the preposition by מן.

From the above we learn that SH indicates clearly where it employs את as an object marker and where it uses it as a preposition in places where TH leaves the decision to the grammarian. E.g., את פני (such as in Gn 19:13; Lv 4:6) is pronounced *at fåni*, and יראה פני כל זכורך את פני הארון יהוה (Ex 23:17, SP 34:23) is pronounced as *yirrå'i kal zēkūrak at fåni å:ron šēma*, with the preposition understood as "with" or "at" and with ST rendering it as יתחזי כל דכ(ו)רך עם קדם/לקמי. The Samaritans have no difficulty with their reading of את הזהב ואת התכלת and the other ואת phrases there (Ex 28:5); they vocalize them *at az'zåb wat attakkēlət*, etc., and understand them as "from the gold and from the תכלת..." Likewise, the reading *at 'anyi wat yåga kabbi* את עניי ואת יגע כפי (SP Gn 31:42) enables us to explain שלחתני ריקם...ראה אלהים והוכיח ("You sent me away empty in exchange for my affliction and for the labor of my palms, [but] the Lord saw and was opposed" [SAV واجة]; as for the root נכח/יכח, see 2.12.10, n. 82). That this is not the only understanding of the verse in the Samaritan tradition is demonstrated by the variant renderings of את in ST: מן עמלי ומן ליחות כפי and ית....ית. Another example can be found in Lv 10:18 and 16:27 regarding the phrase it *damma* את דמה or *it dammimma* את דמם. There we find in the substitution a hint at a reading different from that currently in use; the same is true of Lv 27:22 with respect to the phrase *at šādi* את שרה.

> Note: 1. A special case is the pronunciation of the particle in the phrase *liznot at bit âbiyya* לזנות את בית אביה (Dt 22:21; MT without את), since the verb disagrees with the written form in SP, להזנות, which underlies the Septuagint translation. We would expect here a *Hif'il* infinitive **lēznot*, which is attested in *lēznuta* להזנותה (Lv 19:29); cf. also 2.14.18. The present-day pronunciation of this phrase cannot be an innovation of a recent generation is shown by ST למזני ית/מן בית אבוה, with the *Qal* infinitive and variant reading מן, and by SAV (according to MS Or 7562) فى بيت ابيها The textual problem needs further investigation, but that is not a matter for grammarians.
>
> 2. On the syntactic change resulting from reading עם as a preposition, see the comment at 7.7 about Ex 34:10.

7.4 In the Realm of Sentence Structure

The syntactic relations among the basic elements of the sentence — subject, predicate, object — according to the Samaritan version of the Pentateuch differ at times from the syntax of the vocalized Masoretic version. In some cases, the difference can be traced to differences in interpretation of a verse, but it may also be that the different readings are what gave birth to the variation in interpretation. For a grammatical understanding of the existing differences, though, the underlying cause is insignificant. The following are but a few examples:

1. In the phrase אִשָּׁה כִּי תַזְרִיעַ (Lv 12:2), the verbal predicate indicates that the subject אשה performs some action. This view is explicitly corroborated in *b. Nidda* 31a: ....אשה מזרעת תחילה ("A women emits seed first..."), in which the *Hif'il* form cannot be understood as intransitive: "to be pregnant," as BDB (232a) and KB³ (271a) suppose. However, in the Samaritan reading *iššå kī tizzårå*, the subject is the passive recipient of the action — as the two versions agree in their respective readings of Nu 5:28, TH וְנִזְרְעָה, SH *wnizzå'rå* The present Samaritan reading is indeed ancient as attested by ST (ad loc.) תזדרע.

2. The SP counterpart of the Masoretic וְגַם־דָּמוֹ הִנֵּה נִדְרָשׁ (Gn 42:22) is *wgam dammu ånå* [= MT הִנֵּה] *niddaraš*. The verb in SH may be understood morphologically as a *Nif'al* participle; if so, the syntactic relations within the sentence

are the same in the two versions. If the verb in question is instead construed as 1st plural of the imperfect, the word דָּמוֹ is no longer the subject but instead an object, the subject of which is contained in the verb: "we will be called to account for his blood." This is in fact what is intended by the Samaritan translations: ST נבעי/בבעי (>נתבעי), SAV نطالب.[5] According to this analysis, the reflexive form of the verb governs a direct object, but this is a phenomenon that has already been noticed and documented in Biblical Hebrew, e.g., *itgallā'u it nizru* TH הִתְגַּלְּחוּ אֶת נִזְרוֹ (Nu 6:19), *wyitnakkălu ūtu* TH וַיִּתְנַכְּלוּ אֹתוֹ (Gn 37:18).

3. In the reading *å'īni ā'enåšəm ā'imma tinnåqqår* (TH הַעֵינֵי הָאֲנָשִׁים הָהֵם תְּנַקֵּר) (Nu 16:14), עיני — which in the Tiberian tradition is the object — becomes the subject: "will the eyes... be gouged out?" SAV confirms that in fact the verse was understood this way: انعورت اعين اوليك الرجل, as does the Aramaic translation of תנקר in Hammeliṣ (*LOT* II, 528b, l. 261): סמין, which is an adjective modifying the subject העינים. (ST provides no conclusive evidence.) There might seem to be disagreement between subject and verb here that is uncharacteristic of SP and SH, but in fact in SH a predicate or complement in the singular may occur with a noun in dual form without it being thought irregular, as shown in 4.5.7 note.[6]

4. In the reading *ik nūda it addēbår* איך נודע את הדבר (SP Dt 18:21; TH אֵיךְ נֵדַע אֶת־הַדָּבָר) as well, the Masoretic text's object, הדבר, is the subject of the verb: "How shall/does this matter become known?" This reading is attested by ST: איך חכים ית ממללה, and by SAV: كيف يعلم الخطاب (Both את and ית may be used as demonstratives; see 3.3.1.3.)

5. What TH renders as וְשִׂמַּח אֶת־אִשְׁתּוֹ (Dt 24:5), the Samaritans pronounce *wšåmå at ištu*, i.e., "he shall have happiness [וְשָׂמַח*] **with** his wife." (Note that the Peshitta and Fragment Targums read עם). The TH causative verb bearing a direct object becomes in SH a simple active verb with an object introduced by a preposition. See also 7.7 on Dt 2:37.

> Note: Even though the differences between the two versions of the Pentateuch — those previously enumerated and others — do not teach us anything that we did not already know from the syntax of Biblical Hebrew,

---

[5] It is quite surprising that Sa'adia Ga'on, too, chose to translate similarly in his Arabic version of the Pentateuch: פהודה נחן מטאלבון דמה, and not in accordance with the Masoretic vocalization and traditional Jewish interpretation.

[6] We should mention in this context H. Blanc's observation in his article "Dual and Pseudo-Dual in the Arabic Dialects," *Language* 46 (1970), 49ff., that "the true dual form" (i.e., a form that refers to something of which there are in fact two) is distinguished from the "pseudo-dual" in number agreement as well. According to the rules of those dialects, number agreement with the "pseudo-dual" requires relating to it as a plural noun, while the "true dual" form acts otherwise. Of course, there is no exact similarity between this and the practice in SH, but only a general trend of keeping the true dual form distinct from the plural — the two forms no longer being morphologically distinct — by means of special agreement rules for the true dual form.

the differences, nonetheless, deserve to be systematically examined across the entire corpus using the Samaritan **oral** tradition, because hidden within those differences are useful data for the study of the Samaritan faith and behavior that are not accessible on the basis of the written Samaritan text alone.

7.5 Sentence Types (Verbal/Nominal)

It is customary to divide all Hebrew sentences into two categories according to the type of predicate they display: (a) verbal sentences, that is, those in which the predicate is a finite verb, and (b) those in which the predicate is any other part of speech, including verbal nouns, i.e., participles and infinitives. (The latter type is known as a nominal or verbless sentence.) By means of this morphological criterion, we may easily place every sentence in the vocalized Masoretic Pentateuch in one or the other category. The same is not true of the Pentateuch of the Samaritan oral tradition. The reason for this is that is in SH certain verbs have undergone a process in which their verbal nouns have become identical with certain finite forms, as described above in the Morphology section (2.12.2; 2.14.9). This sometimes enables the Samaritan tradition to interpret a Pentateuchal verse differently from the Jewish tradition, and it may also be that the different interpretation is what gave rise to the grammatical/syntactic difference. The grammarian has only the data in the text with which to work.

Here are but a few examples:

1. The structure and precise meaning of the sentence וְחָטָאת עַמֶּךָ (Ex 5:16) are a matter of debate among medieval Jewish exegetes and grammarians (see my note in "Rashbam's Explanation to *Weḥaṭ'at ʿAmmekah* (וחטאת עמך — Ex. 5:16)," *Tarbiẓ* 47 [1977], 247–8 [Hebrew]), but there is no doubt that from the perspective of the Masoretic vocalization, the word is a verb. In contrast, the same sentence in the Samaritan oral tradition, *wēʾtåt immåk*, presents a well-formed nominal sentence whose meaning agrees with the reader's expectation in the context. This is so by virtue of the fact that SH has preserved the noun חטאת from the historical pattern *qaṭal(a)t*, as is evident from Gn 4:7, Nu 12:1, and other verses, while the same noun has disappeared from TH, where its cognate form would be *חֲטָאת/חֲטָאָה*.

2. In the Samaritan reading הנה הוא יצא המים (SP Ex 7:15; TH הִנֵּה יֹצֵא הַמָּיְמָה), pronounced *inna ū yiṣṣå ammǝm*, the predicate is quite clearly a verb in the imperfect (perhaps because it refers to an event about to happen), a reading facilitated by the defective spelling of יצא. This reading may be the product of late exegesis, since ST נפק and SAV خارج reflect the same tradition as TH.

3. Where the Masoretic version reads כִּי־הֲרִימֹתִי קוֹלִי וָאֶקְרָא (Gn 39:15), the Samaritan version has *kī ā̊rēmi qūli wiqra*. The Samaritan predicate is an infinitive construct with a pronominal suffix, as in כהרמי *kå̄rēmi* (SP Gn 39:18). The use of the infinitive as syntactically equivalent to a finite verb is known in Biblical Hebrew.

7.6 The differences between the versions in their understanding of the meaning of the Hebrew Bible and in their perceptions of its syntactic structure is not as evident everywhere as in the verses mentioned above, because many SH forms may legitimately be interpreted in either of two ways (see 0.16–17), and in such instances we must admit that there is no certainty about the syntax of the passage. For example, it is difficult to say whether the clauses ונרצה לו לכפר אותו (Lv 1:4) and ונמצא דמו על קיר מזבח (Lv 1:15) are verbal or nominal, since *nårṣi* and *wnåmṣi* may be participial or perfect. Even the Samaritan translations, which are generally literal, cannot always save us from uncertainty. One very interesting example should be cited here, since it may be illustrative of a more extensive phenomenon. It has been widely remarked that in TH nominal clauses, the subject precedes the predicate, whereas in TH verbal clauses the opposite is true. This is the case with subordinate clauses, where there is no special emphasis and, therefore, no inversion of word order to indicate emphasis (except in rare instances).[7] Take, for example, אשר נָתַן לך ה' אלהיך (Dt 20:14) as contrasted with אשר ה' אלהיך נֹתֵן לך (Dt 20:16). The Samaritans pronounce נתן *nåtån* in both verses, and that may be either a perfect verb or a participle (see 2.12.15). Nonetheless, SAV draws a distinction, rendering the form in v. 14 as perfect اعطاك and that in v. 16 as participial معطيك. This would seem to indicate a sensitivity to word order in SH. (ST, which translates both forms as יהב, provides no insight into this question.) In any case, the issue of word order in SH in those verses containing words of indeterminate grammatical status is worthy of further research, because it may yield a test by which all those words may be more precisely defined on the basis of their function and place in the various sentences.

7.7 It is noteworthy that the borders between verses and the borders between sentences within verses in SH are sometimes different from those in TH. It has already been noted (in *LOT* III/1, 140) that in contrast to the Masoretic version of Dt 25:2–3: ...וְהִכָּהוּ לְפָנָיו וְהִכָּה לְפָנָיו כְּדֵי רִשְׁעָתוֹ בְּמִסְפָּר. אַרְבָּעִים יַכֶּנּוּ לֹא יֹסִיף... the Samaritans divide the SP equivalent as follows: והכה לפניו כדי רשעתו. במספר ארבעים יכנו לא יסף... A reading such as the latter underlies *m. Makkot* 3:10: "Forty lashes

---

[7] This is easily observable in F. I. Andersen, *The Hebrew Verbless Clause in the Pentateuch* (Nashville/New York, 1970), where the entire corpus of nominal clauses is cited and sorted by type.

less one, as it is written במספר ארבעים." It seems that the prefix -ב in במספר was understood like -כ, to mean "approximately." At Nu 17: 2–3, where the Masoretic version has ...וְאֵת הָאֵשׁ זְרֵה־הָלְאָה כִּי קָדֵשׁוּ. אֵת מַחְתּוֹת הַחַטָּאִים... the Samaritan oral tradition divides it differently: ...זרה הלאה כי קדשו את מחתות החטאי [Pi'el: qaddēšu] and whereas the Masoretic version divides Ex 22:12 as follows: אִם טָרֹף יִטָּרֵף, יְבִאֵהוּ עֵד; הַטְּרֵפָה לֹא יְשַׁלֵּם the Samaritans divide its SP equivalent thus: אם טרף יטרף יביא עד הטרפה, ולא ישלם. In the latter, the ו in ולא hints at a pause in the syntax, but in Ex 34:10 only the Samaritan oral tradition indicates that instead of the Masoretic understanding of נגד כל עמך אעשה נפלאות, the Samaritan version is divided thus: *nēgəd kal, immåk ēšši niflå'ot*. At Dt 2:37 the Masoretic version reads: רַק אֶל־אֶרֶץ בְּנֵי־עַמּוֹן לֹא קָרָבְתָּ; כָּל־יָד... while the Samaritan tradition has *lå qarbåt kal yad*, in which קרבת, taken to be 3rd fem. sing. (like אזלת in Dt 32:36), becomes the predicate of כל יד, which is joined to it syntactically.

8. EPILOGUE

8.1 A summary evaluating the type of Hebrew presented in the contemporary Samaritan reading of the Pentateuch, especially in the field of phonology and morphology, is called for. To what extent is contemporary SH an authentic reflection of the language when it was a living reality, i.e., when it was a vernacular, and what is the status of this Hebrew in relation to other types of Hebrew already known to us? In the process of describing and discussing the development of SH under various grammatical rubrics, we have already sketched, here and there, some items contributing to that evaluation. It is, therefore, necessary now only to assemble them into a comprehensive picture.

8.2 From an examination of the work of the Samaritan grammarians of the Middle Ages (*LOT* I, II), it is clear that the language which they describe is exactly the same Hebrew that can be heard today in the Samaritan reading of the Torah. It is self-evident, therefore, that while we cannot learn all the phonological details and morphological rules from a grammar book that was written in earlier times, what can be learned is adequate to establish their essential identity.

1. In the field of phonology it will be remembered that:

a. The *šəwa* does not exist in this dialect. Although the grammar of Jewish Hebrew was known to the Samaritan grammarians, and the *šəwa* has an important place in Jewish Hebrew grammar, there is no trace of this in Samaritan grammar.

b. The vowels *u* (certainly *ū*) and *o* form a phonological unity.

c. There is only one ש, pronounced *š* like the same letter in Jewish Hebrew. This is established from transcriptions into Arabic in the works of Samaritan commentators and grammarians.

d. The consonants אהח"ע behave in a special way. Verbs with these consonants are considered defective verbs. Even so, there is a difference between א and ה on the one hand, and ח and ע on the other, the former being described as "defective guttural letters" and the latter as "sound guttural letters." From this we learn that ה and א on the one hand, and ח and ע on the other, were similar before the time of these authors. Yet, the same grammatical sources say nothing about the pronunciation of the ע. However, in some manuscripts from the period of the grammarians or from nearly the same period there is a mark indicating the pronunciation of ע under special conditions, including an etymological ח.

Despite the equivalence in pronunciation between former times and the present, it is necessary to point out the differences in the pronunciation of בפד"ת (1.1.4). According to what the Samaritan grammarians taught, there were two sets of pronunciation for these consonants: hard and soft, whereas today בדו"ת are always hard and the פ is always soft. This rule does not contradict the fact that an original plosive פ can be produced like the ב (plosive). It just testifies to the fact that the plosive פ is no longer in existence. It should also be noted that with the loss of the fricative pronunciation of ו (identical with the fricative pronunciation of ב [=v]), what the grammarians called "the third articulation" has not been lost, i.e., the semi-consonant w that appears today under limited, defined conditions.

2. In morphology it will be recalled that the noun gives an inadequate basis for comparison, but the verb, with its stems and classes, demonstrates in a general way the same forms which are used today. We will cite only a few of them here.

a. the two forms of the *Pi'el*, geminated and ungeminated (2.1.3).

b. two forms of the *Nif'al*, geminated and ungeminated (2.1.4).

c. six forms of the participle in the *Qal*.

d. the morphemic convergence of the infinitive and the perfect in the 3rd masc. and the lack of distinction between the two forms of the infinitive as they are presented in TH (2.14.4).

e. A form behaves today in a way that was rejected by one of the grammarians (2.6.12), but the essential point about his rejection of the form is that it testifies to its existence in his day.

The characteristics noted above — and these are not all the characteristics which indicate the equivalence — are fundamental and give SH its special nature.

8.3 The Samaritan grammarians were speakers of Arabic, their writings were in Arabic, and their teachings relied on their knowledge of contemporary Arabic both in their method of analysis and in terminology.[1] It is obvious that they

---

[1] In general, however, we find them using terminology taken from Jewish grammarians: *dageš* and *raphe* in Arabic guise (*LOT* I, 123, 213), and also terms which have no foundation in Arabic linguistics and which cannot be explained from the Arabic language. I refer to the names of the three *pataḥs*: *fatḥa* of exclamation (نب), of indication (لي), and of brotherhood (اخ, i.e., from the noun اخ) (see *LOT* II, 309, 323, and above 0.7). These indicate the vowels (even though they are short). I have already explained that the name *fatḥu-'iḫā* was created to hint at the vowel as it is in the noun אא ['*ā*] in SH and SA. Here I shall add that in SA, but not in Arabic, there exist an exclamatory particle *ē* and a deictic particle *ā* that are spelled אא or הא (*LOT* III/2, 44 l.9, and see above 6.3.2). This detail is a faithful witness to the tradition of the study of the language, at least

held up as an ideal that the reading of the Pentateuch should be extremely precise, just as this was the objective of the Jewish Masoretes, and just as this was the objective of the Arabic grammarians with regard to the reading of the Qur'an. In spite of this, we are not aware of even a single complaint about "neglecting" the articulation of the gutturals, even though not one of the consonants אהח"ע was uttered properly, in the manner in which it was uttered in Arabic. On the contrary, the grammarians saw these letters as models for shaping **vowel signs** (*LOT* I, 309). Thus, a non-consonantal pronunciation of the gutturals in SH was to them a datum from ancient times, as if it were transmitted by Moses from the mouth of God. This fact alone is sufficient to testify to a continuous tradition of SH that reached back not merely to the end of the first millennium CE (some of their linguistic writings go back to that time) but to some period previous to that, to the time when they spoke Aramaic.

Indeed, there is no doubt that already in an earlier period of Palestinian Aramaic there had taken place a certain weakening in the pronunciation of the gutturals, and with regard to this process, at least in the earlier period, we are able to make accurate inferences from the Samaritan tradition. Today, with the evidence of the Dead Sea Scrolls, we are able to assume that a certain weakening in the pronunciation of the gutturals also occurred in Hebrew, which was spoken — perhaps only in a few places — in the generations just prior to the destruction of the Second Temple. We should not, therefore, attribute the changes in the pronunciation of אהח"ע that occur occasionally in SP to the influence of late Medieval Aramaic. They are common occurrences in SH from older times when Hebrew speech was common among the Samaritans. In fact it is surprising that I have not found any interchange of the letters ע (or ח) with א (or ה) in a place where ע is pronounced today.

If to this we add all the other morphological data — some of which is attested in ST in its method of translation — we reach the clear, general conclusion that the Hebrew heard today in the Samaritan reading of the Pentateuch — and on its authority every Hebrew word that was written thereafter — derives its unbroken tradition from a very old source in the period when they spoke Hebrew. Logically we are obliged to conclude that SH represents a certain type of Hebrew which was spoken at the end of the period prior to its fossilization as strictly a "sacred tongue."

8.4 We are accustomed to viewing Hebrew, from the time it began to be used as a spoken language in ancient times to the time it ceased being so, as being divided into two distinct entities, Biblical Hebrew and Mishnaic Hebrew, on

---

when the Samaritans spoke Aramaic, if not before, and this is further internal evidence of the continuity of the tradition of SH.

the basis of R. Yoḥanan's statement (*b. 'Avoda Zara* 58b): "the language of the Pentateuch is one thing, and the language of the Sages another." Even though R. Yoḥanan does not use the word לשון to denote a linguistic entity, even less so does he intend to draw a distinction between the grammatical characteristics of one variety of Hebrew and the other.[2]

This division into two takes into account a number of conspicuous and common characteristics of both, characteristics which were fashioned in the course of time either through the pointing of the Hebrew Bible or in current editions of rabbinic literature. But it has been clear for quite a while that Biblical Hebrew is not one single, consolidated and uniform system, certainly not from the grammatical point of view, even though the pointing, a language system in itself, obscures the time-bound and place-bound lines of distinction in Biblical Hebrew.

The problem of the deviations from the rules of pointing is well known or, as Nöldeke's nomenclature would have it, "inconsistency" in the pointing.[3] "Scientific" grammarians of recent generations who do not attach much importance to the different Jewish traditions so far as the Hebrew language is concerned, or who have not given much thought as to how these traditions can be properly recognized, consider all the exceptions to the rules as resulting from the errors and forgetfulness of the Masoretes. The grammar books simply discard them under the label of "errors." It has already been possible to demonstrate that numerous exceptions to the rules are regular phenomena of the Samaritan tradition.[4] We certainly cannot continue to maintain the supposition that there is an error in pointing or forgetfulness — in particular if the exception appears in one of the books outside the Pentateuch and is a regular form in Samaritan Hebrew preserved in their Pentateuch, which is regularly read and studied.

We learn that even the pointing of the Hebrew Bible, which so successfully makes the whole of Biblical Hebrew uniform, is not a consolidated system, entirely closed, but rather that different Hebrew traditions are interwoven within it — living traditions requiring historical understanding and interpretation. The matter needs no explanation. For generation after generation, before the fixing of the biblical language by means of the pointing, the language was transmitted orally and it was apparently learned from persons with excellent memories, expert in the reading of different books or different groupings of biblical literature, just as in later times the Oral Law was learned from the mouths of the "Tannaim," who taught and transmitted it orally, or just as

---

[2] See Ben-Ḥayyim, *Tradition*, 123, n.1.
[3] Cf. Nöldeke, "Inkonsequenzen der hebräischen Punktation," *ZA* 26 (1912), 1–15.
[4] For example, with regard to הַגִּידָה in Zech 5:11, see 2.10.4, n. 47, or with regard to the *dageš* that seemingly does not imply gemination, as for example in הָרְצָמָה, see 2.8.5.

ancient Arabic poetry was transmitted orally by expert transmitters (رواة) before it was set down in writing. In this respect it is natural that there are recorded in the reading of the Torah — and ultimately fixed for future generations — a number of linguistic phenomena which do not belong to the general stream, but are products of specific spoken Hebrew dialects.

8.5 As for MH, it is clear in our day that it, too, was not monolithic. We learn this first of all from research into Talmudic literature that assigns it to periods and strata and to schools in which it was formed, and we have learned a considerable amount from older manuscripts about the linguistic traditions of this literature. All of this has been confirmed by sources which have been discovered in the last decades — the Dead Sea Scrolls, both from copies of the Pentateuch and especially from works which were composed after the redaction of the Hebrew Bible, during the period when some of the rabbinic literature was written. The sources which are now in our hands from the end of the Second Temple period, especially from close to the time of its destruction, point to a Hebrew which was rich in variety and character.

Whoever examines the language of works composed in those days using the criterion of distinguishing between Biblical and Mishnaic Hebrew will find various mixtures containing elements of both types. Phenomena whose forms do not exist at all in the Hebrew Bible as we have them today, or in rabbinic literature, tend to be regarded as imitations of Biblical Hebrew that did not turn out well.[5] Thus, the idea arose that the language presented in a number of the compositions among the Dead Sea Scrolls is substandard, whereas the standard language is considered to be that of the Hebrew Bible as it is reflected in the accepted pointing. This theory necessarily posits the existence of a single standard for all users of Hebrew in that period. We have no knowledge of the existence of such a thing. What we do in fact know is that the society which spoke Hebrew at the end of the Second Temple period was varied and divided concerning belief and religion, and there is no reason for us to suppose that only one set of rules prevailed in the use of the language: in deciding what to

---

[5] From this perspective, linguistic literature is full of statements arbitrarily evaluating certain specific words and forms: unsuccessful imitations of biblical language, slips of the pen under the influence of MH, hypercorrections, and similar labeling (cf. C. Rabin, "Historical Background of Qumran Hebrew," *ScrHier* 4 [1958], 141–161), which flow from the belief that we have within our grasp knowledge of what constituted the standard language in the society of that period. It is a desire of linguists to classify phenomena the likes of which are not found (or which are rare and, therefore, not known) either in the Scriptures or in rabbinic literature, according to those two types. From such assumptions gross blunders have arisen, e.g., the denial of the "Biblicicity" of למה in the sense of "lest" (D. Barthélemy and T. J. Milik, *Qumran Cave I [DJD,* I] (Oxford: Clarendon, 1955), 93, l. 4; 102, paragraph 1, l. 5), seeing it as a calque of שמא even though this usage is attested in Genesis 27:45 and elsewhere.

accept from the ancient inheritance and what to reject from it, and how far one should add, renew, and introduce.

It is best, therefore, to desist from evaluations which attribute different status to various dialects of Hebrew and one should be satisfied with establishing the fact that the Hebrew of those days was multifaceted and diverse. As in every period of the language, the new and the old were intertwined with one another. The degree of preservation of old, inherited elements that had, in the meantime, disappeared from daily speech and the degree of penetration of new elements originating in colloquial speech — which were already in existence though they had not yet won a place in the written language — were not at all equal among the diverse groups of Hebrew speakers. But experience and strict logic oblige us to say that the reading of the Pentateuch that was continued from earlier generations was also likely to be influenced by the forms of Hebrew that were in everyday use. It seems to follow, therefore, that since there was no single standard against which the correctness of language could be gauged — such a suggestion in regard to those times would be an anachronism — and, of course, one cannot properly measure the Samaritan tradition against that of the Jews, for the former is centered on the "Holy Mountain," Mount Gerizim, and the latter is centered on Jerusalem and the Temple.

However, if the expressions "language of the Torah" and "language of the Sages" (MH) are taken merely as signposts, we are entitled to say, after detailed observation of SH, that the "language of the Torah" of the Samaritans has a closer relationship to MH than it has to the "language of the Torah" of the Jews — yet, it is a language in its own right, as the following will show.

8.6 First, let it be said that the difference between the biblical and the mishnaic language is almost unrecognizable in phonology and, with the exception of certain patterns, almost unrecognizable in the formation of the noun as well. However, a difference is recognizable in the formation of the verb and the pronouns.

1. **Verbal Stems:** In SH, a *Nif'al* is found with a geminated second radical. This is the *Nitpa'el* in regular use. It occurs in place of the *Nif'al* of Masoretic Hebrew, i.e., in *wnibbårāku* TH וְנִבְרְכוּ, *nibbårrådu* TH נִפְרְדוּ, *tiššåmmådon* TH תִּשָּׁמְדוּן; in place of the *Pu'al*, e.g., *tibbaššål* TH תְּבֻשַּׁל, *tiyyanna* TH תֻּעֲנֶה. There are two reasons for this. The first is that the *Pu'al* has no living use in SH, just as it has no active use in MH. In SH the process of exchanging the internal passive for an external passive was completed, thus, causing the reflexive of the *Pi'el* to be used as a passive, rather like what happened to the *Nif'al* in Biblical Hebrew in the Jewish tradition.

Second, the massive shift of verbs from the *Qal* to the *Pi'el* — which was taking place at the same time in SH and MH — required a passive that was a suitable match for the *Pi'el*, and this was the *Nif'al* with a geminated second radical. Nonetheless, a number of traces of the internal passive were preserved in SH, and these are the forms that appear in the Pentateuch and could not be read according to the principles of Hebrew as reflected in the usual recitation of the Pentateuch.

2. **Tenses**: The system of converted tenses as presented to us in TH has completely collapsed. There are no longer any structural differences between the two forms of the perfect, and even the difference between the simple imperfect and the imperfect with *waw consecutive* or the shortened imperfect is considerably reduced and is found only in the פ"י and ע"ו verbs (2.9). These, however, inconsistently maintain the double conjugation system, such as *wtēlåk* TH וְתֵלֵךְ / *wtålåk* TH וַתֵּלֶךְ, *wyēqom* TH וְיָקוּם, *wyēmot* TH וְיָמוּת / *wyåqåm* TH וַיָּקָם, *wyåmåtu* TH וַיָּמוּתוּ. In regard to the form of the 3rd masc. sing. and pl. in פ"י verbs such as *wyåšåb* = וישב, *wyåšåbu* = וישבו, I am reasonably sure that the regular perfect was read instead, where וַיֵּשֶׁב, וַיֵּשְׁבוּ are normally found in the Masoretic text, just as the imperfect *wyiddā'u* is read instead of TH וְיָדְעוּ (Ex 7:5). A few remnants of the shortened form of the imperfect are preserved in ל"ה verbs.

Samaritan neologisms in the converted imperfect should not be seen as continual mistakes by modern Samaritans just because the form is no longer used. It is rather the result of a different development according to the principles governing SH at a later stage (cf. 2.9.7).

3. **Infinitive**: The morphemic loss of the infinitive absolute and its merger with the infinitive construct eliminated the difference in the use of the infinitives, which is characteristic of the biblical language according to the Jewish tradition. Since the originally long *ū/o* was preserved in SH, whereas the short *u* changed into another vowel, the widespread infinitive of the *fåqåd* pattern must be derived from an original form that is reflected in the Jewish tradition by פָּקֹד and not פָּקַד, even in the living and common combination *fåqåd yifqåd* פקד יפקד. It is true that in the Jewish tradition the morphemic boundary between the infinitive absolute and the infinitive construct blurs, but the complete loss of the form of the infinitive absolute in SH is a characteristic which is common only to it and to MH. Moreover, we find the formation of the infinitive in the *qittūl* pattern in the *Pi'el* such as *birrok* / ברוך contrasting with בָּרֵךְ as is the situation in MH.

4. **Pronouns**: There is an abundance of pronominal forms in the Bible. Some have final vowels while others do not, such as אַתָּה and אַתְּ, הֵמָּה and הֵם, and even -ךָ (כה) and -ךְ. Already in ancient times the distinction between variant forms

ceased to have grammatical significance and became a stylistic indicator. In different types of Hebrew at the end of the Second Temple period, one or the other of the pronominal doublets was selected. This applies to SH as well. SH, however, almost always chose — as against MH — the forms ending in vowels, such as *attimma* / אתם; *imma* / הם, המה. These are the forms read in the Pentateuch, for SP is no different from the Jewish version in this respect. It is also worth noting that the word את, which normally indicates the object, serves in SH to indicate the demonstrative pronoun, too, like אותו in MH. This certainly does not occur in the Jewish Pentateuch, and it is doubtful whether it occurs in the Hebrew Bible at all.

8.7 We learned from the pronouns that the characterisitics of SH developed in the wake of the linguistic trends that became prominent in the period of the Second Temple, though SH selects only what is in keeping with its own elements, and it is this which makes it a dialect in its own right. This can best be seen in those prominent features of SH where it contrasts with TH — in the infinitive and the participle. What SH and MH have in common is the loss of the infinitive absolute, but SH produced various alternate forms in its place, unlike MH. This is most noticeable in the formation of the *Qal* participle in SH. As in MH, in SH too, the original relationship between the forms of the participle, perfect, and imperfect יִפְעַל — פָּעַל — פָּעֵל; יִפְעַל—פּוֹעֵל — פָּעַל was severed, and in its place a series of active participles instead came into being. (2.12.13). These and many other phenomena in the morphology of the noun, e.g., the reading of גמא (Ex 2:3; TH גֹּמֶא) as *gāmi* (cf. MH גְּמִי); of בעשי (Ex 36:8; SP בעשאי/בעשי; TH בְּעָשִׁי) as *bāšā'i*, which corresponds to TH עֲשִׂי*/עֲשִׂי* (cf. דְּוִי/דְוַי) (cf. 2.14.9) — and even more so in phonology make SH a dialect in its own right, with its own history, and its own links to the earlier stage of Hebrew.

Since we have no knowledge whatsoever about local differences in the Hebrew language either in the First or Second Temple periods, with the exception of rare hints such as the interchange ס/שׁ in the Ephraimite tongue (and even then this is given different explanations) or the complete loss of the diphthongs *aw* and *ay* in the north of Palestine, we have no way of knowing what was preserved in the Samaritan tradition from the language that was commonly spoken in the hill country of Ephraim, the spiritual and residential center of the Samaritans. Common sense suggests that some of the local characteristics were preserved in SH, but what were they? On the other hand, we are able to say that signs of a later period are evident in SH. More precisely, SH preserves one of the language types that were spoken among the last generations of Hebrew speakers before Hebrew was displaced by Aramaic.

8.8 It is appropriate now to comment on the connection between SH and

Aramaic, especially since our investigation of SA (*LOT* III/2) clearly revealed that the rules of phonology suggested in the present work are the same for the two languages, and there are also many similarities between them in morphology.⁶ It is generally accepted that Aramaic has left its impression on MH, the language of the Dead Sea Scrolls, and even in a number of phenomena in the later biblical works. The gist of the argument is that these are phenomena like those common in the Aramaic of the generations when Hebrew stopped being used as the vernacular. I have already had the opportunity to argue that various characteristics common in Palestinian Aramaic — whether Samaritan, Jewish, or Christian, but without parallels in Eastern Aramaic — are suspected of being borrowed from Hebrew.⁷ There is no way of glossing over the fact that, from the very beginning, the substratum underlying Aramaic in Palestine was Hebrew. The core of the issue is that we cannot ignore the close contact between the two languages while Hebrew was still spoken, and we should now recognize what is common to the two living languages as well as the differences between them in order to understand the relationship of the two languages.

It is common knowledge that languages of a common origin, which border closely upon one another, will find, in the region of closest proximity, a congruence of characteristics, so much so that it is nigh impossible even for a researcher to decide to which language one should ascribe the spoken idiom.⁸ There is no difference in this matter whether the congruence is original or is formed in the course of the period of proximity. It will be even less clear to the simple speaker which of the two languages he is speaking. This situation pertained in various places in Palestine at the time when Hebrew and Aramaic were in use concurrently, one alongside the other, or even at the moment when Aramaic began to replace Hebrew. The transition stage from Hebrew to Aramaic persisted to different degrees in different places and among different groups of Hebrew speakers. If we want to describe for ourselves "moments" in the

---

⁶ It is generally accepted that there are substantial Hebrew elements in CPA, and we learn from M. Bar-Asher, *Palestinian Syriac Studies* (Ph.D. thesis, The Hebrew University of Jerusalem, 1977 [Hebrew]) that there are quite a few grammatical links between CPA and SA. There is no doubt that some of these were forged through their link with the Palestinian Aramaic substratum, which is Hebrew. J. A. Fitzmyer, "The Languages of Palestine in the First Century AD," *CBQ* 32 (1970), 501–531, did not pay attention to the role of spoken Hebrew in Palestinian Aramaic when he evaluated the linguistic situation of the period.

⁷ Cf. my "Contribution," 162–174.

⁸ See, e.g., L. Bloomfield, *Language* (New York, 1933), 44: "Dutch and German actually form only one speech-community" in the border region, and ibid., 314, on the lack of real borders between the various Romance languages and the existence of "gradual transitions." An absorbing description of the actual transitions from Italian in French — "French forms in Italian" — is found in H. Schechardt-Brevier, *Ein Vademekum der allgemeinen Sprachwissenschaft*, ed. Leo Spitzer (Niemeyer, 1922), 144–147.

drawn-out process of the replacement of Hebrew by Aramaic, it seems to me that the Samaritan tradition of both Hebrew and Aramaic provides some data for the description of this process and may, shed new light on something that has surprised many scholars: that the term ἑβραϊστι in the writings of Josephus and in the Gospels (John 19:13, 20) sometimes denotes Aramaic and at other times Hebrew. (A detailed description of the Greek term in both sources is given in the commentary to John 5:2 in H. Strack and P. Billerbeck, *Kommentar zum Neuen Testament aus Talmud und Midrasch*, II [München, 1924], 442ff., where the underlying Hebrew words are vocalized in accordance with TH).

8.9 Of the numerous data presented in the preceding pages, we will concentrate here on some of the more prominent.

1. The principal grammatical factor distinguishing Aramaic from Hebrew in the vowel system, based on the pointing of the Bible (and in Aramaic also according to the Syriac tradition), is the place of the *šəwa* with regard to stressed syllables and, in some cases, also the differences in their accentuation, such as גְּמַל vs. גָּמָל, כָּתַב vs. כְּתָב, כְּתָבוּ vs. כָּתְבוּ (both derived from *katabū*), יְמוֹת vs. יָמוּת, יָדַיִן vs. יָדִין, and many other similar examples. It is clear, therefore, that the shift of the *šəwa* to a full vowel and the development of penultimate stress (with automatic change in the vowel quantity) yielded a common form in Hebrew and Aramaic, which is *gåmål, kåtåb, kåtåbu, yēmot, yådən*.

An interesting consequence of parallel developments in Hebrew and Aramaic due to the loss of the *šəwa* is the emergence of the preposition אל in SA, which developed from the preposition ל (which was pronounced *al* in both SH and SA). Thus, the spelling of אל in a verse such as וזעק יהוה אל משה (alongside למשה) in ST Ex 19:20, is, of course, a result of the metanalysis of למשה = *almūši*, which parallels the formation of the prepositions כד, מד and מי (<מן), כי (<כ) in Jewish Aramaic or של in Hebrew, and also כל in the combinations כָּל קֳבֵל and כָּל עֻמַּת, which merged the two prepositions -כ and -ל into a single word.

2. The passive of the *Qal* in Hebrew is the *Nifʿal*, which has no Aramaic cognate, and the passive of *Qal* in Aramaic is the *Itpəʿel*, which has no regular cognate in Hebrew, and certainly not in the Hebrew of the Second Temple period. There are many common roots in Hebrew and Aramaic without any phonological differences, and there are verbs which have the same meaning in both languages. Let us see, therefore, the appearance of specific forms common to the two languages in these stems.

a. כתב

Hebrew: **yankatib* > יִכָּתֵב > *yikkåtəb*

Aramaic: יִתְכְּתֵב > *yitkateb* > *yikkåtəb*

Epilogue

b. גלה

Hebrew: *yangali(y) > יִגְלֶה > yiggāli

Aramaic: יִתְגְּלִי, יִתְגְּלֶה > *yitgali > yiggāli.

3. The masculine plural ending in Hebrew is -ים, and in Aramaic, -ין. Because of the neutralization of the phonemes /m/ and /n/ in word-final position (1.5.3.6), Aramaic and Hebrew forms converged to a considerable extent, and this factor caused the spelling -ים to appear routinely in SA not only in words that were common to the two languages, such as בנים, טבים, זכאים, חיבים (*LOT* III/2, 144, ll. 110ff.; 137, l. 48), but also in words which were unique to Aramaic, such as מנירים ("shedding light"), קדישים (ibid., 80, ll. 4ff.), קרבנים (ibid., 81, l. 22), עלאים וארעים (ibid., 290, l. 37), זבנים (ibid., 86, l. 17), and many more.

4. The relative particle -ש is not found in the Pentateuch.[9] It was known, however, in SH. Were it not for this, the Samaritans would not be able to explain *šiddi* (TH שַׁדַּי) as שֶׁדַּי or *šinnər* (TH שָׂנִיר) as שֶׁנִּיר (6.3.18). These explanations are ancient and were not influenced by the works of the Jewish grammarians. In SH we see that -ש causes the gemination of the following consonant. The same phenomenon occurs in SA with regard to the ד (if it is not pronounced with a prosthetic *a*, i.e., *ad*), such as דמה *dimme* = TH שֶׁמָּא (there is also the pointing שְׁמָא!) and דילי realized as *dilli*, etc., as a parallel to שֶׁלִּי. Apparently the gemination in Aramaic of *dilli* is the result of an internal Aramaic process, parallel to that of Hebrew (see 1.5.3. and *LOT* II, 102, l. 36), and it is unreasonable to suggest Hebrew morphological influence, particularly since the particle -ש does not appear in the Pentateuch. We see here a convergence, certainly not phonological but rather morphological, of two particles of entirely different origin but with identical function.

This is the position regarding forms which *a priori* belong to either one or the other of the unique core stocks of the two neighboring languages — how much more so with forms common to both languages. Under this condition, it is no wonder that Palestinian Aramaic, expecially the Samaritan, Christian, and Jewish dialects, borrowed from the Hebrew language the infinitive of *Pi'el* — *qittūl*, the like of which was not to be found in Eastern Aramaic or in Official Aramaic and its later offshoots.

8.10 It is known that many developments appeared in Aramaic (and so, too, in other Semitic languages, e.g., the different dialects of Modern Arabic) in the course of generations, which paralleled the developments which occurred — sometimes earlier — in Hebrew, such as the loss of the internal passive and the use of reflexive conjugations in its stead, the simplification of "tenses," and

---

[9] The word בשגם in Gn 6:3 is neither explained nor read as if it were constructed from -ש and גם. See 6.3.18.

the like. In the course of time the structure of late Second Temple Hebrew drew closer to the structure of its Aramaic contemporary. We find the same situation when comparing the relationship of Biblical Hebrew with Old Aramaic (as revealed in inscriptions) in the realm of grammar — as far as it is possible to know from unpointed sources — and even more with regard to vocabulary.

In the light of all that has been said, it seems to me that one should assume that SH is the result of inner Hebrew developments, which were supported by what it had in common with Aramaic. Because SH was strengthened and crystallized in Aramaic-speaking circles, it was able to survive even at a time when it found itself faced by an entirely new and different situation — at least from a phonological standpoint — when Arabic became the vernacular. The "sacred tongue" was already definite and clear in its character in all its minutiae.

If one maintains, for example, that the 2nd fem. sing. pronoun אתי in SH (pronounced *atti*) has penetrated Hebrew from the Aramaic form, one should say that the Aramaic form of the 2nd masc. sing. pronoun in Samaritan liturgical poetry, אתה (pronounced *'åttå*) has entered SA from Hebrew — that is, from the dead language to the living one! — and so on *ad infinitum*.[10]

In making this point, I do not mean to exclude the possibility of Aramaic influence here, such as the preference of a form or word in common use in Aramaic. Nevertheless, it is by no means right to regard SH as a Hebrew language read by speakers of Aramaic, just as it is not logical to consider MH a Hebrew written by speakers of Aramaic.

---

[10] Nöldeke, "Texte," 214, has rightly explained *hači* (= *hačči*) in the Aramaic dialect of Maʿlūla as an offshoot of Old Aramaic *'attā*.

USER'S GUIDE TO THE INVENTORY OF FORMS

In order that the reader have a clear picture of the purpose of the Inventory of Forms, its structure, and the way in which one can locate a form, I offer the following prefatory remarks:

a. The Inventory of Forms is intended as a supplement to the grammatical description (see 0.18 above) by presenting all the *morphological patterns* that nouns and verbs follow in SH, and alongside these all the roots (in the verb) and lexical entries (in the noun) in which these patterns are realized. It will, of course, be understood that this inventory makes it superfluous to present the tables of noun declensions and verb conjugations that are standard appendices to grammar books.

> Note: I use here the term "pattern" in a broader sense, including "appearance" (surface form; see 4.0.2).

b. The preparation of this Inventory was undertaken during the preparation of *LOT* IV: *The Words of the Pentateuch* (see *LOT* IV, יג). Using a specially-prepared program, a computer performed the basic work of compiling the data according to the grammatical categories I had established. After abstracting the morphological patterns from the actual words (see *LOT* IV, יח), I arranged the Inventory so as to present the structure of the entire range of the types of words, regardless of their semantic value or syntactical use. The data are organized to form a sort of skeletal grammar book, fleshed out by the foregoing description.

c. It might seem that the simplest approach would be to list the actual forms under taxonomic rubrics without having to coin artificial terms. For example, under the rubric "the strong verb, *Qal* perfect, 1st person" one would list the forms פָּגַשְׁתִּי, כָּתַבְתִּי, זָכַרְתִּי, and the like, and under the rubric "פ״נ verbs, *Qal* imperfect, 3rd masc.," the forms יִסַּע, יִפֹּל, יִנְחַל, יִנְהַג, etc. This approach is possible, however, only with the verb (see 4.0.4 above), and only at the expense of a certain number of morphological distinctions, such as that between יִסַּע, יִנְחַל, יִנְהַג, etc., on the one hand, and יִפֹּל, יָקֹם, etc., on the other. It is not possible to present the noun in the same way, and one is forced to resort to an abstraction to provide a rubric under which one may list all the nouns with similar features and declensions. For example, only by creating such rubrics as "מִפְעָל" for nouns like מַזְלֵג, מַכְבֵּשׁ, and מַסְמֵר can the nouns be listed together and their declension be described.

Indeed, such has been the path taken by Hebrew grammarians for many centuries, and their approach is entirely justified when the goal is to present linguistic forms according to their orthography and vocalization.

d. The presentation of the words in the Pentateuch solely according to their pronunciation in an oral tradition such as that of the Samaritans, however, presents a particular and quite complex challenge. Noticeable changes, sometimes quite marked, occur in certain consonants in SH. First and foremost, the gutturals (א, ה, ח, ע) merge with each other or fluctuate with other consonants, generally in accordance with fixed rules, but not always so. Thus, even a reader familiar with SH will be unable to recognize with ease and certainty the word written in the Pentateuch on the basis of its pronounced form alone. Four examples will suffice to illustrate this point: (1) the pronunciation *īn* is common to אֵין, הִין, and עִין, just as (2) the pronunciation *šår* is common to שְׁאָר, שָׁאַר, and שָׁחֹר; (3) the pronounced forms *yēmmad* and *yåmmåd* alone are insufficient even for someone who is familiar with the principles of Samaritan pronunciation to know which is derived from עמ״ד and which from חמ״ד, just as (4) one cannot establish on the basis of the pronunciation rules alone that both *tåbbåd* and *tēbbåd* are derived from עב״ד. The student new to SH will certainly be unable to make such distinctions and inferences.

For that reason, I have found it necessary in this grammar to provide, alongside each pronounced Samaritan form, the corresponding written form. This is not the case in the Inventory of Forms. By abstracting the morphological patterns from the actual realized words, which was done in order to emphasize the structural element and unify the data, a reduction in presentation was, in fact, accomplished: in the verb, only the root is cited alongside a given pattern, and in the noun, only the lexical entry is cited (in Hebrew letters) and not the particular written form corresponding to the pronounced form.

e. The difference in nature between the structures of nouns and those of verbs makes it necessary to employ different strategies of morphological abstraction for the two categories.

Verb forms have been sorted, using the symbol *fqd* (see 4.0.7 above), according to categories in which everything is equal but the radicals. Alongside the common pattern created in this way is a list in Hebrew letters of the roots of the actual words occurring in that pattern. In the strong verb, there can be no difficulty or doubt how the actual SH verb will be formed, given the particular root. In forms derived from "weak" roots — that is, roots in which one or more radicals do not appear in some forms, such as the *Qal* imperfect of פ״נ verbs or the *Hifʿil* of פ״י verbs, or roots in which a radical never appears, such as the י״ע class — there could be some doubt about what shift occurs if the point at which there is a change or deletion is not marked with some sign. Indeed, there are grammarians who insist on creating a single rubric for such groups of nouns, such as פֵּעָה to represent מֵאָה, פֵּאָה, etc., or עֵלָה to represent לֵדָה, שֵׁנָה, and the like. Similarly, מַפָּל represents מַשָּׁק (from שׁק"ק; see Isa 33:4), while מַעַל represents מַשָּׁק ("joint," from the root נש"ק "kiss"), מַגָּשׁ, and מַצָּע. This method, which pays attention to the derivation of a word from its root (a derivation that may at times be questionable) — and which is somewhat inconsistent, conflating פ"נ and פ"י — entirely ignores aspects of actual words that are certainly equivalent and also ignores similarity in declension among them. The words שֵׁנָה, פֵּאָה, and מֵאָה, e.g., while stemming from different origins, are all declined in the same way. This is true of the infinitive forms (which are nominal forms in Hebrew) גֶּשֶׁת, שֶׁבֶת (from יש"ב), and שֶׁבֶת (from שב"ת). It is just such commonalities, though, that declension tables are intended to present.

f. In light of the preceding dilemma, it is obvious why it has become the prevailing practice among grammarians, when they take up nouns derived from weak roots, to choose from among the three representative consonants (פע"ל, קט"ל, or פק"ד) two consonants to express the model of the actual nouns without carefully coordinating them with the placement of consonants in the triradical root (such as פָּל or קָל to represent nouns such as יָד and דָּג), assuming that even the beginner will be able to rely on his own good sense in relating the realized form to its root. Recognizing the wisdom of that approach, I have concluded that it is unnecessary to spell out the principles underlying my choice of representative consonants for the nouns and verbs, respectively. Rather, in each instance where one of the consonants in the root is not realized in SH as pronounced, I have chosen consistently to drop the *d* from the representative consonant triad *fqd*, and not to insist that in *fq* the letter "*f*" represents the first consonant of the root and *q* the second. Thus, just as the *faq* pattern might stand for *nad* derived from נו"ד, *ban* derived from בנ"י, and *lab* derived from לב"ב — it being unwise to label one as *faq* and the other as *fad* — so might *yēfoq*, e.g., stand for *yēqom*, derived from קו"מ, and *yâffåq* might stand for *yåmmåd*, derived from עמ"ד. Following this method, all the realized forms of the SH noun and verb respectively that share completely identical structures have been grouped together. Once that grouping was accomplished, I saw fit to dispense with the artificial labels, which are at times odd and irregular, such as *ūfīqu* vis-à-vis the root יר"ד, or *åfåq* vis-à-vis חב"ר as opposed to *fåqåd* vis-à-vis עב"ר, where the intent is to describe *ūrīdu*, *åbår*, and *'åbår*, respectively. To serve as rubrics, which are necessary for the clustering of the forms, **realized word forms** are used, the first member of each group (marked in the noun by large type) serving as the rubric for the others.

g. The forms have been divided into two categories: (1) those without the consonants א, ה, ח, or ע in the root, and (2) those with one or more of those consonants in the root. It became clear that in this way, the phenomena unique to the Samaritan tradition are grouped together, enabling the similarities between the Samaritan and Jewish traditions of Hebrew to stand out more clearly than would otherwise be possible. Only in the presentation of pronominal suffixes of the verb have the forms been divided into three categories: (1) most verbs, (2) ל"ה verbs, and (3) III-guttural verbs. This tripartite division exists because the purpose is to present the ways in which pronominal suffixes attach to the verb, and in categories (2) and (3) the elements that attach to the suffix are likely to be different from those of other verbs.

h. In the **verb**, the form with initial ו and its counterpart without initial ו have been considered separate entities. Each of these appears consistently in its own group, whether the perfect or the imperfect is intended, because the Samaritan tradition does not have those indicators, such as differences in the vocalization of the initial ו or differences in the position of stress, which in TH indicate the semantic distinctions of tense. In this way, the user is presented with all the morphologically similar forms for consideration in drawing a grammatical conclusion. In the imperative, where no distinctions of tense apply, and in the lists of pronominal suffixes of the verb, where the focus is on the suffix and less importance is assigned to the form to which tense applies, the forms with and without initial ו have been considered and listed as one form. (As to the order of stems and vowels, see 2.0.8 above and 1.2.0, and [j] below.)

In the **noun**, the form without conjunctive ו or prefixed preposition and the form with either or both of those additions have been considered the same form. Thus, while a listing such as רגל *rēgålīkimma* may appear in the Inventory, one may not infer than only רגליכם occurs in the Pentateuch; instead, there may be a form with both the 2 masc. pl. suffix and a prepositional prefix, and the opposite may be true when a form with a prepositional prefix is listed in the inventory. Readers in search of such data are referred to the listing under the appropriate root in *LOT* IV, Part I. The present Inventory is intended only to gather and present the pure *grammatical* forms.

i. The presentation of the **noun** encounters great problems.[1] To the best of my knowledge, no single approach has yet been found which makes it possible to categorize all noun forms. Usually, the main patterns alone are presented and the rest left to the reader's diligence. The Inventory of Forms, however, must present *all* noun forms and may not refrain from listing any morphological pattern under which one or more of the realized forms may be described. A number of sortings were attempted, each of which took into consideration twenty-two factors, before the system used in the present Inventory was adopted. In truth, all such arrangements are possible and justifiable, but each treats certain structural criteria as primary and others as secondary. My goal was to arrive at a listing of all the *pronounced* forms written in *phonetic* transcription

---

[1] On the definition of a noun and what falls under that heading in the Inventory, see 6.1 above.

according to criteria acceptable to the grammarian of Hebrew accustomed to Hebrew letters and the TH vocalization system. It seems to me that this has basically been achieved in the method used for grouping nouns in the present Inventory.

j. The following are the rules by which the order of presenting of morphological types is determined in each section of the Inventory:

1. The alphabetization of the phonetic transcriptions follows the order of the Hebrew alphabet. Thus, ירק *yēraq* precedes כליל *kēlal*.

2. The order of vowels, too, does not follow the order of the Latin alphabet, but rather agrees with the order I have introduced in Hebrew for the Historical Dictionary of the Hebrew Language (with regard to the TH vowel signs):[2] x (x̱, x̣, x̤) x x̱ x̣ x̤ x̱ ix x̣ ix. A vowel with a colon follows the corresponding vowel without a colon, e.g., *â* precedes *â*:.

3. Under each rubric within the noun (see [g] above), the forms have been listed in order of the number of radicals they include.

4. Within each group organized by the number of radicals, the nouns have been divided into: (a) those of simple structure; (b) those with prefixes, with the prefixes listed alphabetically; (c) those with suffixes, with the suffixes listed thus: first those that begin with vowels (following the order of the vowels), and then those that begin with consonants, in alphabetical order; (d) those with both prefixes and suffixes, listed as in (b) and (c).

5. In sorting the morphological patterns, the following factors have been taken into consideration: (a) the number of consonants, those with fewer consonants preceding those with more (note: initial א is not recorded and is, therefore, not treated as a consonant); (b) where the number of consonants is the same, forms without a geminated consonant are listed before those with a geminated consonant, so that, for example, *fiqda* and *fiqdå* are listed before *fiqqa* and *fiqqå*; (c) when the number of consonants (geminated or not) is equal, the number of vowels in the pattern (according to their rank as listed above) determines the order: thus, e.g., מחמצת *māmmēṣət* comes before מאכלת *mākkēlət*, even though the root אכ"ל is prior to חמ"צ alphabetically, because these nouns are equivalent in both the number of consonants and the number of vowels; (d) a pattern with penultimate stress will precede a pattern with ultimate stress, e.g., *fēqåd* comes before *fe'qåd*.

6. Within each pattern, the forms that occur in the Pentateuch have been listed according to the following order: absolute state (equivalent to the entry; see [k] below); construct state, if different from the absolute; feminine; singular with pronominal suffixes; absolute plural; construct plural, if different from

---

[2] See *Sefer Ha-Meqorot*[2], I (Jerusalem, 1969–70), 34 [Hebrew]. The order of the vowel signs in Hebrew was treated by the Jewish grammarians in the Middle Ages; see my paper "Theory of Vowels."

the absolute; plural with pronominal suffixes. In a number of nouns there are doubles (that is, changes in form), and these, too, are listed in the Inventory, but an alternate form not equivalent to that of the entry is listed only after all the absolute forms that are equivalent to the entry. The noun with locative ה- suffix is placed before the forms with pronominal suffixes; if that form is itself a separate entry; however, it does not appear under the entry without the suffix, so that לילה, for example, does not appear as a form under the entry for ליל.

Given a particular noun as pronounced in the Samaritan tradition, a search in the Inventory for related forms or for its declension would require first an analysis according to the factors listed above, after which the desired forms could easily be located.

k. In certain instances, there was no way to avoid constructing noun entries by inference from the actual forms in the Pentateuch, as is stated in *LOT* IV, 4, sect. ו. Here it is important to note that since the Inventory is not cross-referenced to the Pentateuchal text, it will not be evident whether a given entry (the absolute state of the noun) has been inferred from other forms appearing in the Pentateuch or not. For that reason, the **entries** that have been abstracted from one or more declined forms are marked with a circle. An asterisk following a particular **form** indicates that there is some doubt about some component of the form as analyzed, but not about its pronunciation. The nature of the doubt is generally explained in this Grammar; see also *LOT* IV, 306ff.

l. The abbreviations are to be understood as follows:

א — 1st sing.	ו — 1st pers. pl.
ב — 2nd masc. sing.	ז — 2nd masc. pl.
ג — 2nd fem. sing.	ח — 2nd fem. pl.
ד — 3rd masc. sing.	ט — 3rd. masc. pl.
ה — 3rd fem. sing.	י — 3rd. fem. pl.
נ — feminine; ס — construct state; ר — plural	

Where combinations such as א+ב occur with verbs, the first element (to the right of the "+") indicates the person, number, and gender of the subject, while the second element (to the left of the "+") indicates the person, number, and gender of the object, so that א+ב describes a verb with a 1st sing. **subject** and a 2nd masc. sing. **object**. Combinations such as ר+ס indicate, e.g., a noun that is in the construct state of the plural.

m. Note that a noun with a 1st sing. pronominal suffix -*ī* that is identical in sing. and pl. will be marked with א and listed according to the singular, even if it occurs in the Pentateuch only in the plural form. Any noun with the pronominal suffix -*ək* (-'*īk*) is defined as having a 2nd fem. sing. suffix (ג), even though that suffix form is also appropriate for the 2nd fem. sing. with a plural noun. When a noun marked with a ג is identical in singular and plural forms, it appears among the singular nouns, even if it appears in the Pentateuch in the plural. Thus, "(ג) *gămālək*" might represent גְּמַלֵּךְ, גְּמָלַיִךְ, or גְּמָלַיִךְ in the Pentateuch, and "(ב) *battək*" might represent בָּתַּיִךְ or בָּתַּיִךְ, while *bītək* may only stand for בֵּיתֵךְ. The reason for this is explained in *LOT* IV, טו.

Contents of the Inventory

The Verb
א. Roots of the Verbs 353

ב. Verbs Formed from Non-Guttural Roots 362
    Strong Verbs 362; פ״י Verbs 365; פ״נ Verbs 367; ע״ו Verbs 368;
    ע״ע Verbs 370; ל״ה Verbs 370; Quadriradical Verbs 373.

ג. Verbs Formed from Guttural Roots 373
    I-Guttural Verbs 373
    Strong Verbs 373; Verbs ע״ו 376; Verbs ע״ע 376; Verbs ל״ה 377
    II-Guttural Verbs 379
    Strong Verbs 379; פ״י Verbs 380; פ״נ Verbs 381; ל״ה Verbs 381
    I- and II-Guttural Verbs 382
    III-Guttural Verbs 382
    Strong Verbs 382; Verbs פ״י 385; Verbs פ״נ 386; Verbs ע״ו 387
    I- and III-Guttural Verbs 387
    II- and III-Guttural Verbs 388
    Quadriradical Verbs 388

ד. Pronominal Suffixes on Verbs 389
    A. All Verbs Except III-Guttural and ל״ה 389
    Perfect 389; Imperfect 391; Imperative 394
    B. III-Guttural Verbs 395
    Perfect 395; Imperfect 396; Imperative 398
    C. Verbs ל״ה 398
    Perfect 398; Imperfect 400; Imperative 401

ה. Verbal Nouns 402
    A. Verbs Formed from Non-Guttural Roots 402
    Active Participle 402; Passive Participle 405; Infinitive 405
    B. Verbs Formed from Guttural Roots 408
    Active Participle 408; Passive Participle 412; Infinitive 413

The Noun

א.	Nouns Formed from Non-Guttural Roots	418
	A. Nouns from Single Radical Roots	418
	B. Nouns from Biradical Roots	418
	C. Nouns from Triradical Roots	419
	Without Affixes 419; With Prefixes 430; With Suffixes 432; With Prefixes and Suffixes 438	
	D. Nouns from Roots with Four or Five Radicals	440
ב.	Nouns Formed from Guttural Roots	440
	A. Nouns from Biradical Roots	440
	B. Nouns from Triradical Roots	441
	I-Guttural	441
	Without Affixes 441; With Prefixes 448; With Suffixes 448; With Prefixes and Suffixes 451	
	II-Guttural	452
	Without Affixes 452; With Prefixes 454; With Suffixes 455; With Prefixes and Suffixes 456	
	I- and II-Guttural	457
	III-Guttural	457
	Without Affixes 457; With Prefixes 459; With Suffixes 460; With Prefixes and Suffixes 462	
	I- and III-Guttural	462
	II- and III-Guttural	463
	Nouns from Roots with Four or Five Radicals	463

INVENTORY OF FORMS

THE VERB

א. Roots of the Verbs

This list is intended to assist the reader in doing the following: (a) obtain an overview of the stems derived from each root, with an eye to a comparison of the Samaritan tradition with the Jewish tradition; (b) locate the place of each verb with two weak radicals in the lists of conjugated forms which follow, since the class under which the conjugated forms are listed appears next to each such verb in the following list (see, e.g., אב״י and יצ״א); (c) examine the corpus of Samaritan roots required by the grammatical analysis but without exact parallels in the Pentateuchal linguistic traditions of the Jews, since such Samaritan roots appear alongside their closest counterparts in Jewish Hebrew separated by a virgule.

קל	ארג	הפעיל		קל	אבי(ל״ה)
קל	ארך	פיעל		קל	אבל
הפעיל		נפעל		התפעל ב	
קל	ארר(ע״ע)	פיעל ב	אלם	פיעל	אבק
פיעל ב		קל	אמן	קל	אגר
קל	ארש	הפעיל		הפעיל	אדם
פיעל		נפעל		קל	אדר
קל	אשם	קל	אמץ	נפעל	
הפעיל		הפעיל		קל	אהב
קל	אשר	פיעל	אמר	פיעל ב	
קל	אתי	קל		קל	אהל
קל	אתר	נפעל		פיעל	אוי(ל״ה)
קל	באש	קל	אנח	התפעל	
הפעיל		קל	אני(ל״ה)	קל	אול/אהל
קל	בגד	התפעל	אמן(ע״ע)	הפעיל	אול
הפעיל	בדל	התפעל	אנף	פיעל	
נפעל		קל	אסף	הפעיל	אוץ(ע״ו)
נפעל	בהל	פיעל ב		הפעיל	אור
קל	בוא(ע״ו)	נפעל		נפעל ב	אות(ע״ו)
הפעיל		התפעל ב		קל	אזל
קל	בז	קל	אסר	נפעל	
הפעיל		נפעל		הפעיל	אזן
קל	בן	קל	אפד	קל	אחז
נפעל		קל	אפי(ל״ה)	פיעל ב	
קל	בז	נפעל		נפעל	
הפעיל	בזי	התפעל	אפק	פיעל ב	אחר
נפעל	בחן	קל	אצי(ל״ה)/אוץ	פיעל	איב
קל	בחר	קל	ארב	קל	אכל

קל	דוי(ל"ה)	קל	גבל	קל		קל		קל	בטא
קל	דח	הפעיל		פיעל ב	גבע	קל ב			בטח
הפעיל	דוף/הדף	פיעל ב		פיעל		קל		פיעל	ביר/באר
קל	דכך	קל	גבר	פיעל		קל		קל	בכי
קל	דלא	נפעל ב	גד	קל		קל ב			
קל	דלק	קל		נפעל ב		פיעל		פיעל	בכר
פיעל	דמי	הפעיל		פיעל		פיעל		נפעל ב	
קל	דמם	התפעל ב		הפעיל		נפעל ב		קל	בלי
קל	דפק	קל	גדל	קל		קל		פיעל	בלל
קל	דקק	הפעיל		פיעל		פיעל			
הפעיל		קל	גרע	פיעל		קל		קל	בלע
קל ב	דקר	קל	גדף	נפעל		קל		נפעל	במי
קל	דרך	פיעל	גז/גח	קל ב		נפעל		נפעל ב	
קל	דרש	קל		קל		קל			
נפעל		הפעיל	גוע	נפעל		נפעל ב		פיעל	במן
קל ב	דשא	קל	גוע/נגע	נפעל ב		פיעל		קל	בעט
קל	רשן	הפעיל		פיעל		קל		קל	בעי
פיעל		קל	גור	פיעל		קל		קל	בעל
הפעיל	הדף	הפעיל		הפעיל		קל		קל	בער
קל	הדר	נפעל ב	גור/גרר	נפעל ב		קל		הפעיל	
קל	הרי(ל"ה)	קל	גז/גח	קל		הפעיל		נפעל	
קל	הום	קל	גז	קל		נפעל			
הפעיל		קל	גול	פיעל		הפעיל			
הפעיל	הון	פיעל	גלח	פיעל		נפעל			
קל	היי(ל"ה)	התפעל		פיעל		קל		קל	בצק
נפעל		קל	גלי	התפעל		נפעל		קל	בצר
קל	הלד	פיעל		פיעל		קל		פיעל ב	
פיעל		נפעל		פיעל		פיעל ב			
התפעל		התפעל		קל		נפעל		קל	בקע
קל	הלד/ילד	פיעל	גל/גלל	נפעל		פיעל		קל ב	בקר
פיעל	הלל	פיעל	גלל	פיעל		קל ב		פיעל	בקש
פיעל	הלל/חלל	התפעל		פיעל		פיעל		קל	ברא
הפעיל	הסס	הפעיל	גמא	הפעיל		קל		נפעל	
קל	הפך	קל	גמל	קל		נפעל		קל	ברד
נפעל		הפעיל		נפעל		קל		קל	ברח
התפעל ב		נפעל		קל		קל		הפעיל	
קל	הרג	קל	גנב	קל		הפעיל		קל	ברך
קל	הרי	נפעל		נפעל		קל		הפעיל	
קל	הרס	נפעל ב		הפעיל		הפעיל		פיעל	
קל	זבד	פיעל ב	געל	פיעל		פיעל		נפעל	
קל	זבח	קל	גער	נפעל ב		נפעל		קל	בשל
קל	זבל	פיעל	גרם	התפעל		התפעל		הפעיל	
הפעיל	זהר	קל	גרע	קל		הפעיל		נפעל	
קל	זוב	נפעל		הפעיל		נפעל		פיעל	
קל	זוד	קל	גרש	פיעל		נפעל ב			
הפעיל		פיעל		פיעל		פיעל		התפעל	בשש/בוש
קל	זוך	קל	דבק	הפעיל		התפעל		קל	בתר
קל	זור/זרה	הפעיל		הפעיל		הפעיל		פיעל ב	גאי
קל	זחח	נפעל		פיעל		קל		נפעל	גאל
קל	זחל	פיעל	דבר	קל		קל		קל	
קל	זכר	נפעל	דגי	פיעל ב		פיעל ב			גבה
קל ב		הפעיל	דוב	נפעל		נפעל			
הפעיל		קל	דוד/נדד	קל		קל			

קל	חרד	קל	חיי(ל"ה)	נפעל		זלל
הפעיל		הפעיל		קל		זמם
קל	חרי	קל	חכם	פיעל ב		זמם/זמן
הפעיל	חרם	התפעל		פיעל ב		זמר
נפעל ב		קל	חלי	קל		זנב
נפעל	חרף	הפעיל	חלל	פיעל		זני
קל	חרץ	פיעל		קל		זנק
הפעיל	חרש	נפעל		הפעיל		זעם
קל	חרת	קל	חלם	פיעל		זעף
קל	חשך	הפעיל	חלף	קל		זקן
קל	חשב	קל	חלץ	קל		זרח
פיעל		הפעיל		קל		זרי
נפעל		נפעל		פיעל		זרע
התפעל		קל	חלק	קל		
הפעיל	חשך	הפעיל		הפעיל		
נפעל	חשל	פיעל		נפעל		
קל	חשק	קל	חלש	קל		זרק
פיעל		קל	חמד	קל		חבא
קל	חתי	נפעל		נפעל		
קל	חתם	קל	חמל	התפעל ב		
הפעיל		קל	חמם	קל		חבב
התפעל	חתן	קל	חמץ	קל		חבט
נפעל	חתת	קל	חמר	קל		חבל
קל	טבח	קל	חמש	פיעל		
קל	טבל	הפעיל		פיעל		חבק
קל	טבע	קל		קל		חבר
קל	טהר	הפעיל		נפעל		
פיעל ב		קל	חני	הפעיל		חבש
התפעל		הפעיל		פיעל		
קל	טוב	פיעל	חנך	קל		חגג
קל	טוח	קל	חנן	קל		חגר
פיעל	טוי(ל"ה)	הפעיל		נפעל		
קל	טור/נטר	התפעל		קל		חדי
הפעיל	טחח	הפעיל	חנף	קל		חדל
קל	טחן	קל	חסי	קל		חרש
הפעיל	טלא	הפעיל	חסל	הפעיל		חוט/חטא
קל	טמא	קל	חסם	קל		חול
פיעל		פיעל		קל		חום
נפעל ב		קל	חספס	קל		חוס
התפעל		הפעיל	חסר	קל		חרש
קל	טמן	קל	חפד	קל		חזי
הפעיל		קל	חפז	קל		
קל	טען	קל	חפף	קל		חזק
קל	טרף	קל	חפץ	הפעיל		
נפעל		קל	חפר	פיעל		
נפעל	יאל	פיעל	חפש	נפעל		
פיעל	יבם	קל	חפש	התפעל		
קל	יבש	קל	חצב	קל		חטא
קל	יגע	קל	חצי	הפעיל		
קל	יגר	פיעל		פיעל		
התפעל ב		פיעל	חקק	התפעל		חטא/טחח
הפעיל	ידי(ל"ה)	קל	חקר	פיעל		
התפעל		קל	חרב	קל		חטב

שורש	בניין	שורש	בניין	שורש	בניין	שורש	בניין
ידע	קל	ירק	קל				פיעל
	הפעיל	ירש	קל	כסף	נפעל		נפעל ב
	נפעל		קל	כעס	הפעיל		התפעל
	התפעל	ישב	קל	כפל	קל		נפעל
יהב	קל		הפעיל	כפץ/קפץ	קל		הפעיל
יחם	קל		נפעל	כפר	קל		פיעל ב
יטב	קל	ישב/שוב	הפעיל		פיעל ב		נפעל
	הפעיל	ישן	קל	כרי	קל		קל
יכח	נפעל		נפעל	כרע	קל		קל
יכל	קל	ישע	הפעיל	כרת	קל		הפעיל
ילד	קל		פיעל		הפעיל		נפעל
	הפעיל		נפעל		נפעל		פיעל
	התפעל ב	ישר	קל		קל		נפעל ב
ילד	קל	יתן	קל	כשי	קל		קל
	הפעיל	יתר	הפעיל	כשל	הפעיל		פיעל
יני(ל"ה)	הפעיל		נפעל	כשף	פיעל		נפעל ב
ינק	קל	כאב	קל	כתב	קל		קל
	הפעיל	כבד	קל	כתת	קל		קל
יסד	נפעל ב		הפעיל	כתת	קל ב		פיעל ב
יסף	קל		פיעל ב	לאי	נפעל		קל
	הפעיל		נפעל	לבן	קל	כבי	נפעל
יסר	פיעל		הפעיל	לבש	קל	כבס	הפעיל
	נפעל		פיעל		הפעיל		פיעל
יעד	הפעיל	כבש	נפעל ב	להט	פיעל ב		נפעל
	נפעל		קל	להי(ל"ה)	קל		הפעיל
יפע	הפעיל		נפעל ב	לוי(ל"ה)	קל		קל
יפת	קל	כהי(ל"ה)	קל		הפעיל		נפעל ב
ירא(פ"י)	קל	כהן	נפעל ב	לוח	קל		קל
יצב	הפעיל		פיעל	לוש	הפעיל	כון	הפעיל
יצג	התפעל ב		נפעל	לחך	פיעל ב		פיעל
יצק	קל		התפעל	לחם	פיעל ב		נפעל
יצר	הפעיל	כזב	פיעל		נפעל		התפעל
יקד	קל	כחד	הפעיל	לחץ	פיעל ב		פיעל
יקע	קל		נפעל	לכד	קל		הפעיל
יקץ	קל	כחש	פיעל ב	למד	קל		נפעל
יקש	נפעל		נפעל		פיעל		קל
ירא(פ"י)	קל	כלא	קל	לן/לון	קל		קל
	נפעל	כלי	קל	לעט	הפעיל		פיעל
	התפעל		פיעל	לקח	קל		נפעל ב
ירא/ירי	קל	כלכל	פיעל	לקט	פיעל		נפעל
ירד		כלם	נפעל	מאן	פיעל ב		נפעל
	הפעיל	כמר	נפעל	מאס	נפעל		קל
ירי(ל"ה)	הפעיל	כנס	קל	מדד	קל		פיעל ב
ירם	קל	כנע	נפעל	מהמה	התפעל		
		כסי	הפעיל				

פיעל ב			פיעל		פיעל ב		מהר
נפעל ב			קל	משי	קל		מוט
התפעל			קל	משך	קל		מול
פיעל ב	נחם		קל	משל	הפעיל		מוס/מסס
נפעל ב			פיעל	משש	הפעיל		מור
התפעל			נפעל	מתק	קל		מוש
פיעל ב	נחש		פיעל ב	נאף	הפעיל		מות/המם
קל	נטי(ל"ה)		פיעל ב	נאץ	קל		מות
הפעיל			הפעיל	נבט	הפעיל		
פיעל			התפעל	נבי(ל"ה)/נבא	קל		מחי
קל	נטע		קל	נבך/בוך	התפעל		
קל	נטש		קל	נבל	פיעל ב		מחץ
פיעל			פיעל		הפעיל		מטר
קל	נכח		הפעיל	נגד	קל		מכך/מוך
קל	נכי(ל"ה)		פיעל	נגח	פיעל		מכר
הפעיל			קל	נגע	נפעל ב		
פיעל			הפעיל		התפעל		
קל	נכל		פיעל		קל		מלא
התפעל			קל		פיעל		
פיעל	נכסף/כסף		נפעל	נגף	פיעל ב		
הפעיל	נכר		קל	נגש	נפעל		
התפעל			הפעיל		קל		מלח
קל	נמג/מוג		קל	נגש	הפעיל		
קל	נמל/מול		הפעיל		נפעל ב		מלט
קל	נמס/מסס		קל	נדב	קל		מלך
קל	נסב/סבב		קל	נדח	פיעל		מלל
הפעיל	נסג/סוג		קל	נדף	קל		מלק
נפעל	נסח		קל	נדר	נפעל		מני
פיעל	נסי(ל"ה)		קל	נהג	קל		מנע
קל	נסך		פיעל ב		נפעל		
הפעיל			פיעל ב	נהל	קל		מסר
קל	נסע		התפעל		נפעל		
הפעיל			הפעיל	נוא(ע"ו)	הפעיל		מעט
קל	נער		קל	נוד(ע"ו)	נפעל		
הפעיל	נפח		קל	נוח(ע"ו)	קל		מעך
קל	נפל		הפעיל		קל		מעל
הפעיל			הפעיל		פיעל ב		
התפעל			פיעל ב	נוי(ל"ה)	קל		מצא
קל	נפץ		קל	נוס(ע"ו)	הפעיל		
פיעל ב	נפש		הפעיל		נפעל		
קל	נצב		קל	נוע(ע"ו)	נפעל		מצי
פיעל ב			הפעיל		קל		מקק
פיעל			הפעיל	נוף(ע"ו)	הפעיל		מרא/מאר
קל	נצי(ל"ה)		קל	נזי(ל"ה)	קל		מרד
פיעל			קל	נזל	קל		מרח
נפעל ב			הפעיל	נזר	נפעל		מרט
הפעיל	נצל		נפעל		קל		מרי
פיעל			פיעל ב	נחב/חבא	הפעיל		
נפעל ב			קל	נחי(ל"ה)	פיעל		
התפעל			הפעיל		קל		מרק
קל	נצר		קל	נחל	פיעל		מרר
קל	נקב		הפעיל		קל		משח

עלי	קל	סכן	הפעיל	נקד	קל
	הפעיל	סכר	נפעל ב	נקי(ל״ה)	קל
	נפעל	סכת	הפעיל		פיעל
עלל	פיעל	סלח	קל		נפעל ב
	התפעל		נפעל	נקם	קל
עלם	הפעיל	סלף	פיעל	נקף	הפעיל
	נפעל	סמך	קל	נקר	נפעל ב
	נפעל ב	סעד	קל	נקש	נפעל ב
	התפעל	ספד	קל	נשא	קל
עלף	התפעל	ספח	פיעל		הפעיל
עמד	קל	ספי	הפעיל		התפעל
	הפעיל		פיעל	נשג	הפעיל
עמס	קל		נפעל	נשא(פ״נ)	הפעיל
עמר	התפעל	ספן	קל	נשב	פיעל
ענה	קל	ספק	קל	נשי(ל״ה)	קל
	הפעיל	ספר	קל		פיעל
	פיעל		פיעל ב	נשך	קל
	נפעל		נפעל		הפעיל
	נפעל ב		פיעל		פיעל
	התפעל	סקל	קל	משל	קל
ענן	קל		נפעל	משק	קל
	הפעיל	סרח	קל		פיעל
	פיעל		נפעל	נתח	פיעל
ענק	הפעיל	סרר	קל		קל
ענש	פיעל	סתם	קל	נתך	קל
עפל	נפעל ב	סתר	הפעיל	נתן	קל
עפף/עוף	קל		נפעל		נפעל
עפף	הפעיל	עבד	קל	נתץ	קל
עצב	פיעל		פיעל		פיעל
	קל		נפעל	נתק	קל
עצם	התפעל	עבט	קל	נתר	פיעל
עצר	קל		הפעיל	נתש	קל
	קל		נפעל	סבא	קל
עקב	נפעל	עבי	קל	סבב	קל
עקד	פיעל	עבר	קל	סבל	פיעל
	הפעיל		פיעל	סגר	קל
עקר	קל		התפעל		הפעיל
ערב	קל		קל		נפעל
ערך	קל	עדף	הפעיל	סוב/סבב	קל
	הפעיל	עוד	הפעיל	סוך	הפעיל
	הפעיל	עח	הפעיל		קל
ערל	קל	עול	קל		הפעיל
ערם	נפעל	עוף/עיף	קל	סול/סלל	התפעל
ערף	קל	עוץ	הפעיל	סוף	הפעיל
ערץ	קל	עור	הפעיל	סור	קל
עשי	קל		פיעל		הפעיל
	נפעל	עזב	קל	סות	הפעיל
עשק	התפעל	עזר	קל	סתר	קל
עשר	הפעיל	עטי	קל		פיעל ב
	פיעל	עטף	הפעיל		נפעל
עשק	קל		הפעיל	סכך	קל
עשר	הפעיל	עכר	פיעל	סכל	הפעיל

שורש	בניין	שורש	בניין	שורש	בניין
עתק		פרע	קל	קבר	קל
עתר	קל		פיעל		פיעל ב
	קל	פרץ	קל		נפעל
	הפעיל		פיעל	קדד	קל
פאר	פיעל ב	פרק	קל	קדח	קל
פגל	קל		פיעל	קדם	קל
	התפעל ב		התפעל	קדש	קל
פגע	קל		קל		הפעיל
	פיעל ב	פרש	קל		פיעל
פגש	קל	פרשׂ	פיעל		נפעל ב
	קל ב	פשׂי	קל		התפעל
פדי	קל ב		קל ב		הפעיל
	הפעיל	פשט	קל	קהל	
	נפעל		הפעיל		נפעל
פוג	קל	פתח	קל	קהת	נפעל
פול/נפל	קל		הפעיל	קוא(ע״ו)	קל
פוץ	קל		פיעל	קוב/קבב	קל
	הפעיל		נפעל ב	קוד	קל
פור	קל	פתי	קל	קרי	פיעל
פז	קל		הפעיל		נפעל
פחד	קל		נפעל	קול/קלל	קל
פחז	פיעל ב	פתל	קל	קום/נקם	קל
פחא	קל	פתר	קל	קום	קל
פלא	נפעל	פתת	קל		הפעיל
פלג	נפעל ב	צבא	נפעל	קוץ	קל
פלי	הפעיל		קל	קטן	הפעיל
פלל	פיעל	צבי	קל	קטף	קל
	התפעל	צבר	קל	קטר	פיעל
פני	קל	צדי	הפעיל		הפעיל
	קל ב	צדק	התפעל	קלל	פיעל ב
	פיעל	צוד	קל		קל
פסח	קל		קל ב		הפעיל
פסל	קל	צוי(ל״ה)	פיעל		פיעל
פעל	פיעל ב	צוף	הפעיל		נפעל
פעם	נפעל	צוף/צפי	הפעיל	קמץ	קל
פצי	קל		קל	קנא	קל
פצל	קל ב	צוק	הפעיל		הפעיל
פצע	קל		קל		פיעל
פצר	קל ב	צור	פיעל	קני	קל
פקד	קל	צחק	הפעיל	קסם	קל
	הפעיל	צלח	קל	קפא	קל
	נפעל	צלל	קל	קצי	הפעיל
	התפעל ב	צמא	קל	קצע	קל
פקח	פיעל ב	צמד	נפעל		פיעל
	נפעל	צמח	קל	קצף	קל
פרד	הפעיל		הפעיל		הפעיל
	נפעל ב		נפעל	קצץ	קל
פרח	קל	צנף	פיעל ב		פיעל
פרי	קל	צעק	פיעל	קצר	קל
	הפעיל	צפי	פיעל		נפעל
פרם	קל	צפן	קל	קרא	קל
פרס	הפעיל	צרע	פיעל		הפעיל
		צרר	קל		נפעל
			הפעיל	קרא/קרי	קל
			קל		
		קבב	פיעל ב		
		קבל	פיעל		
		קבץ	נפעל ב		
			פיעל ב		

קרב	קל		רור	קל		שכך	קל
	הפעיל		רחב	הפעיל		שכל	הפעיל
	פיעל		רחם	פיעל ב			
	נפעל ב		רחף	פיעל ב		שכר	קל
קרח	קל		רחץ	קל		שמח	קל
קרי/קרא	נפעל		רחק	קל		שנא	קל
קרי	קל			הפעיל			
	הפעיל		רחש	פיעל ב			פיעל
	נפעל		רכב	קל		שער	קל
	פיעל			הפעיל		שפן	קל
קרן	קל		רכך	קל		שרט	קל
קרע	פיעל		רכס	פיעל		שרי	קל
	נפעל ב		רכש	קל		שרף	קל
קשי	קל		רמי	קל			נפעל
	הפעיל		רמם	הפעיל		שאב	פיעל ב
	פיעל		רמש	קל		שאל	קל
	נפעל ב			הפעיל			הפעיל
קשר	קל						פיעל ב
	פיעל ב		רנן	קל		שאר	הפעיל
קשש	הפעיל			הפעיל			נפעל
ראי/ירא	קל		רעב	קל		שבי	קל
ראי	קל ב		רעי	נפעל			נפעל
	הפעיל		רעע	קל		שבע	קל
	נפעל			הפעיל			
רבב	קל		רעץ	פיעל ב		שבץ	נפעל
רבי	קל		רפא	קל		שבר	פיעל
	הפעיל			נפעל			
	פיעל		רפי	נפעל			הפעיל
רבך	פיעל		רפף	הפעיל			פיעל
רבע	קל		רצח	קל			נפעל
	הפעיל		רצי	קל		שבת	קל
רבץ	קל			הפעיל			הפעיל
רגז	קל			נפעל		שגג	קל
	נפעל ב		רצע	קל		שגי	קל
	התפעל		רצץ	קל		שגי/שגע	פיעל
רגל	קל			התפעל		שדף	קל
	פיעל		רקח	פיעל		שוב	קל
רגם	קל		רקע	פיעל			הפעיל
רגן	פיעל		רקק	קל		שוט	קל
רגע	נפעל ב		רשע	הפעיל		שוף	קל
רדי	קל		שבע	קל		שור	קל
רדף	קל		שגב	קל			הפעיל
רוב	קל		שוא(ע"ו)	קל		שות	קל
רוח	הפעיל		שור	קל			הפעיל
	הפעיל		שוח	קל		שזר	פיעל
רוי(ל"ה)	קל		שום	קל		שחוי	התפעל
רום	קל			הפעיל		שחט	קל
	הפעיל		שור/שרר	התפעל			נפעל
	פיעל		שוש	קל		שחל/משל	פיעל ב
רוע	הפעיל		שחט	קל		שחק	קל
רוץ	קל		שטי	קל		שחת	קל
	הפעיל		שטם	קל			הפעיל
רוק	הפעיל		שטן	קל			נפעל

נפעל		הפעיל		התפעל		
פיעל	שקץ	קל	שמם	קל		שטף
פיעל	שקר	הפעיל		נפעל		
קל	שרץ	נפעל ב		קל		שכב
פיעל	שרת	קל	שמן	קל		שכח
קל	שתי	קל	שמע	נפעל		
הפעיל		הפעיל		קל		שכך
נפעל		פיעל		הפעיל		
קל	שתת	נפעל		קל		שכל
פיעל ב	תאי	פיעל	שמץ	הפעיל		
קל	תוך	קל	שמר	פיעל		
קל	תום/תמם	נפעל		קל		שכם
קל	תור	קל	שנן	הפעיל		
קל	תלי	פיעל		קל		שכן
הפעיל	תלל	קל	שסע	הפעיל		
נפעל ב	תמה	פיעל		פיעל		
קל	תמך	קל	שעי	הפעיל		שכר
פיעל		קל ב		נפעל		
קל	תמם	נפעל	שען	פיעל ב		שלב
קל	תעב	קל	שפט	קל		שלח
פיעל ב		קל	שפך	פיעל		
קל	תעי	נפעל		הפעיל		שלך
הפעיל		פיעל	שקד	קל		שלם
פיעל	תעתע	קל	שקי	הפעיל		
קל	תפר	הפעיל		פיעל		
קל	תפש	קל	שקל	קל		שלף
נפעל		נפעל	שקע	פיעל		שלש
קל	תקע	קל	שקף	הפעיל		שמר
		הפעיל		נפעל ב		

ב. Verbs Formed from Non-Guttural Roots
(בלא כינויי הפעול)

						קל עבר
			זקן כרת כתב פגש פקד קבר קטן	zåqánti	א	
משל פקד פרם פרץ פרש קצף קרב			שכב שכל			
רדף רכב שכב שכן שמן שפט שפך			גנב	gånibtá	ב	
שקל			דלק כתב פרץ רכב שמן	dålåqtá		
דרך קצר קרב שבת שכב	tidråk	ה	קצף	qēṣəf	ד	
גנב שמר	nignåb	ו	שכב שכן שלם	såkəb		
כרת שרף שמר	tikråton	ז	גדל גזל דרך דרש זכר זקן זרק כרת	gådál		
בצר גנב דרש מרד ספר פקד	tibṣəru		לבש סמך פצל פקד פתר קבר קרב			
פרם קצר קרב שרף שבר שמר שפך			קרן רכש שכר שרף שבת שטף שכב			
שרץ	yišrəṣu	ט	שמר שפך			
למד	yilmådon					
זרק למד משל סמך פרש קבר רגם	yizråqu		קרב	qårbát	ה	
רדף שרט שרף שבר שבת שכב שפט			משך שׂגב	måšåka		
גנב	wtignáb	ב	שבת	šåbåtá		
גדל גנב דבק זרק טבל כבד כבר לכד	wyigdál	ד	גמל זכר לכד	gåmálnu	ו	
מלך סמך ספק פסל פקד פרץ פרש			גבר	gēbēru	ט	
פתר צבר קבר קדש קצף קרב רדף			גבל גזל גזר מלך מרד סגר פקד קבר	gåbålu		
שטם שבת שכב שכם שכן שמר שפט			קדם קרב רדף רכש שרף שכל שמר			
שקל שקף תמך			שפך שרץ			
גנב כרת לבש קשר רבץ שכב	wtignáb	ה	כבד	kåbåda*	י	
קרב	wtiqråbon	ז	בצק	båṣåqå*		
שרץ	wyišrəṣu	ט	זכר כתב פקד שכב שכן שפט	wzåkárti	א	
גדל טבל כרת כתב לכד משך סמך	wyigdálu		דרש זכר זרק כפל כפר כרת כתב	wdåráštá	ב	
ספר צבר קבר קרב רגם רדף שכם			משל סמך ספר פרץ פרש קרב שרף			
שכן שמר שפט שפך שקף תפר			שמר שפך			
קרב רכב	wtiqråbinna	י	גבר	wgēbər	ד	
לבן	nilbåna	ו	דבק	wdåbəq		
כרת	nikråtá		גדל דשן זרק טבל כתב לבש מלך	wgådál		
כתב פסל קרב שׂרף תפשׂ	wiktåba	א	סמך ספר פרש פשט קמץ רדף שׂרף			
קבר	wiqbårá		שכב שמר שפך שרץ תפש			
לכד שׂרף שכב	wnilkåda	ו	שכל	wšåkála	ה	
כרת שבר	wnikråtá		ספר קרב שבת	wsåfårå		
			זכר טבל למד ספר סקל קצר קשר	wzåkártimma	ז	
			רדף שכב שמר שפט			
קל ציווי			שרץ	wšērəṣu	ט	
כתב שכם	iktåb	ב	רבץ רגם	wrēbåṣu		
קבר קרב שכן	qēbår		דרש זרק כשל למד סמך פקד פרש	wdåråšu		
ספר קבר	wsēfår		רגז רדף שרף שמר שפט שפך			
פסל	afsəl					
פקד רדף	fåqåd					**קל עתיד**
שכב	šēkåbi	ג	גדל דרש פרש קדש רדף שכל שמר	igdál	א	
זכר כתב כשל משך סמך קבר רגם שמר	zēkåru	ז	בצר גזל גנב דרש זמר זרק כפץ	tibṣår	ב	
שרץ	wšērəšu		כרת כתב לבש למד מלך משל ספר			
שבר	wšēbåru		פקד קצף קצר קרב רדף שׂרף שבת			
שכב	šēkåba	ב	שכב שמר שפט שפך			
			שמר	åtišmår		
קל סביל עבר			גבל גדל גנב טרף לבש למד מלך	yigbål	ד	
פקד	fēqəd	ד				
טרף	ṭårəf					
זרק	zåråq					
מרק שטף	wmåråq					

קל ב עתיד

א	ēzåkår	זכר
ב	tēzåkår	זכר
ד	yēbåqår	בקר
ז	tēzåkåru	זכר
ד	wyēdåqår	דקר זכר פצל פצר
ט	wyēfåṣåru	פצר
א	wēzåkårå	זכר

הפעיל עבר

א	abdilti	בדל כבד סכן קדש
	ēzåkårti	זכר
ב	askiltå	סכל קצף
ד	abdəl	בדל סגר פקד פרד קרב שלך שמד
	åmṭər	מטר פרס קטר
ה	albīša	לבש
	åfrīså	פרס
ז	aqṣeftimma	קצף
ט	ibšīlu	בשל
	aqrību	קרב
	åfrīsu	פרס
א	wåkritti	כרת סתר פקד שבת שמד
ב	wåbdiltå	בדל גבל לבש פשט קטר קרב
ד	wåsgər	סגר קטר קרב שלך
ה	wåbdīlu	קרב
	wåbdeltimma	בדל קרב שבת שכם
ט	wåfṣīṭu	פשט צדק קטר שלך

הפעיל עתיד

א	astər	סתר שבת שכר שמד
	åṣdəq	צדק
ב	tabdəl	בדל זכר כרת סגר פקד קדש קרב שלם
	tåqṭər	קטר שבת שמט
ג	taqrəb	קרב
ד	yabdəl	בדל כרת פקד קדש קרב שמד
	yådbəq	דבק קטר
ה	taqdəš	קדש רמש
ז	taqrībon	קרב שלך
	tagmīlu	גמל כרת פרד קרב שכל שבר שלך שמד
	tåšbītu	שבת
ט	yaqdīšu	קדש קרב
א	wabdəl	בדל פקד
ב	wtagdəl	גדל
ד	wyabdəl	בדל ברך גמל כבד לבש סגר סתר פקד קרב רכב שבר שכן שלך
	wyåṭmən	טמן מטר פשט קטר
ה	wtalbəš	לבש שלך
ו	wnaqrəb	קרב
ט	wyaqrību	קרב שכל שלך
	wyåfšīṭu	פשט
א	wagdīla	גדל שלך

הפעיל ציווי

ב	agbəl	גבל סכת פקד קרב שקף
	wåqrəb	קרב שלך
ז	aqrību	קרב שלך

פיעל עבר

א	barrikti	ברך דבר למד שכל
ב	barriktå	ברך גרש דבר
	šåbbårtå	שבר
ד	baqqəš	בקש ברך דבר כבד פרש שכל
	makkår	מכר
	båttår	בתר שבר
ה	dabbēra	דבר
ו	dabbirnu	דבר
ז	dabbertimma	דבר מכר קדש שכל שלם
ט	dabbēru	דבר מכר קדש
	låqqēṭu	לקט
	tåmmåku	תמך
א	wbarrikti	ברך גרש דבר קדש
	wšåbbårti	שבר
ב	wbaqqištå	בקש ברך בשל דבר קדש קטף שבץ שלם
ד	wbarrək	ברך דבר כבד מכר קדש שלם שרת
ה	wgarrēša	גרש
ז	wbaqqeštimma	בקש ברך דבר כבד למד קדש
	wšåbbårtimma	שבר
ט	wbaššēlu	בשל דבר רשן כבס שרת
	wlåqqēṭu	לקט

פיעל עתיד

א	ēbarrək	ברך דבר קדש שלם
ב	tēbaqqəš	בקש ברך בשל דבר מכר
	tēlåqqəṭ	לקט קבץ שבץ
	tēšåbbår	שבר שקר
ד	yēbarrək	ברך גרם גרש דבר כבס מכר שלם
ה	tēšakkəl	שכל
ו	nēdabbər	דבר
ז	tēdabbēron	דבר
	tēbaqqēšu	בקש ברך בשל
	tēšåqqēṣu	שקץ
	tēšåbbåron	שבר
	tēšåbbåru	שבר שקר
ט	yēlammēdon	למד
	yēlammēdu	למד מכר שרת
	yēlåqqēṭu	לקט
א	wēbarrək	ברך
ב	wtēdabbər	דבר
ד	wyēbaqqəš	בקש ברך גרש דבר זנב כזב מכר סלף קדש קרב שרת
	wyēbattår	בתר
	wyēlåqqəṭ	לקט קבץ
	wyēšåbbår	שבר
ה	wtēdabbər	דבר

	wtēraggēnu רגן	ז
	wyēbarrēku ברך גרש דבר כבס מכר רגל רגן רכס	ט
	wyēlåqqēṭu לקט	
	ēdabbēra דבר	א
	wēdabbēra דבר	
	wēšåbbårå שבר	

פיעל ציווי

	barrək ברך גרש דבר קדש	ב
	wbarrək ברך	
	baššēlu בשל דבר פרק	ז
	låqqēṭu לקט	
	makkēra מכר	ב

פיעל סביל עבר

| | baššēla בשל | ה |

פיעל ב עבר

| | kåbəd כבד ספר | ד |
| | wkåfər כפר | |

פיעל ב עתיד

	ēkåfər כפר	א
	tēkåfər כפר ספר	ב
	yēkåfər כפר	ד
	yēzåmēnu זמן	ט
	wyēkåfər כפר ספר	ד
	wnēsåfər ספר	ו
	wyēsåfēru ספר	ט
	ēkåfēra כפר	א

פיעל ב ציווי

	kēbåd כבד כפר	ב
	wkēfår כפר	
	sēfåru ספר	ז

פיעל ב סביל עבר

| | kåfår כפר | ד |

פיעל ב סביל עתיד

| | yēkåfər כפר | ד |
| | tēqåṭər קטר | ה |

נפעל עבר

	niggånåbti גנב פתל	א
	naksiftå* כסף	ב
	niffåqåd פקד שבר	ד
	nitfåša תפש	ה
	nikkåmåru כמר	ט
	wniddåråšti דרש	א
	wniššåmårtå שמר	ב
	wnikkåfər כפר	ד
	wnikkåråt כרת שבר	
	wnistårå סתר	ה

	wnikkåråtå כרת	
	wnizzåkårtimma זכר שמר	ז
	wnikkåråtu כרת	ט

נפעל עתיד

	ikkåbəd כבד סתר	א
	tiddåbəq דבק	ב
	tiqqåbår קבר	
	yiggånəb גנב דבק טרף כרת ספר צנף שרף שפך	ד
	yibbåšår בצר מרט סקל פקד שבר שטף	
	tikkåbəd כבד כלם כרת שרף	ה
	tissågår סגר סקל	
	niddårəš דרש	ו
	nissåtår סתר	
	tiddåbēqu דבק	ז
	yiddåbēqu דבק שרף	ט
	wyiggåməl גמל צמד	ד
	wyiqqåbår קבר שכר	
	wtiddåbəq דבק שרף	ה
	wtissågår סגר קבר קצר	
	wyimmåtēqu מתק	ט
	wyimmåsåru מסר שכר	
	wikkåbēda כבד	א

נפעל ציווי

	iššåmår שמר	ב
	ibbådēlu בדל	ז
	iššåmåru שמר	

נפעל ב עבר

	nimmakkår מכר	ד
	niffållåga פלג	ה
	nibbårrådu פרד	ט
	wniqqåddåšti קדש שמר	א
	wnimmakkår מכר	ד
	wniggånnåb גנב קרב	
	wnikkåbbåša כבש	ה
	wnibbårråku ברך קדש	ט

נפעל ב עתיד

	immållåṭ מלט	א
	yibbakkår בכר מכר	ד
	yibbårråk ברך כבס פרד קדש	
	tibbaššål בשל מכר	ה
	tikkåbbås כבס	
	tiššåmmådon שמד	ז
	yimmakkåru מכר	ט
	yibbårrådu פרד	
	wyissakkåru סכר רגז	
	wyiggåbbåru גבר פרד קדש	

נפעל ב ציווי

| | immållåṭ מלט פרד | ב |

365

	יכל tūkål		
ג	ילד tēlådi ילד		
	ילד åtēlåki		קבץ iqqåbbåṣu	ז
ד	ישב yiššåb		**התפעל עבר**	
	יטב ינק ירש ישר yīṭåb		ברך wētbårråk	ד
	ילד yēlåk ירד		מכר קדש wētmakkertimma	ז
	יכל yūkål		ברך wētbårråku	ט
	יטב å'īṭåb		**התפעל עתיד**	
ה	ישב tiššåb		צדק niṣṭåddåq	ו
	ילד tēlåd ילד		רגז titraggåzu	ז
ו	יכל nikkål		קדש yitqåddåšu	ט
	ילד nēlåk ירד		פרק wyitfårråqu	
	יכל nūkål		**התפעל ציווי**	
ז	ישב tiššåbu		פרק itfarråqu	ז
	ירש tīråšon		קדש itqåddåšu	
	ירש tīråšu		**התפעל ב עבר**	
	ילד tēlåkon		פקד itfåqådu	ט
	ילד tēlåku			
	ישב tåšåbu		**פעלי פ״י**	
ט	ירש yīråšu		**קל עבר**	
	ילד yēlåku			
	יכל yūkålon		ילד יגר יכל ילד yågårti	א
	ילד åyēlåku		יגר yågårtå	ב
א	יקץ ישב wiqqåṣ		יפת yēfət	ד
ב	יכל wtūkål		יסף yåsəf	
ד	ישב wyiššåb		יכל יצק ירד ישב yåkål	
	יטב ירש ישן wyīṭåb		ישב yēbēša	ה
	ילד wyålåk		ישב yēbēšåt*	
ה	ילד ילד ירד ישב wtålåd		יסף yåsēfa	
ו	ישב wniššåb		יכל ילד yåkåla	
	ירם wnīråm*		ירד ירש ישב yårådnu	ו
ז	ישב wtåšåbu		ישב yåšåbtimma	ז
ט	יטב ירש wyīṭåbu		ילד yēlēdu	ט
	ילד wyålåku		יכל ירד ירש ישב yåkålu	
			ירד wyårådti	א
קל עתיד			יכל יצק ירש ישב wyåkåltå	ב
י	ילד ילד wtålådinna		ילד wyålådti	ג
א	ילד ירד ēlåka		יסף wyåsəf	ד
ו	ילד ירד nēlåka		יצק יצר ירד ישב wyåṣåq	
א	ילד ירד wēlåka		ילד wyålåda	ה
ו	ילד wnēlåka		ירד ירש ישב wyårådnu	ו
קל ציווי			ירש ישב wyåråštimma	ז
ב	ילד lik		ילד wyēlēdu	ט
	ילד wlik		ירד ישב wyårådu	
	ילד lek			
	ילד wlek		**קל עתיד**	
	ישב šab			
	ישב wšab		ילד ילד ירד ēlåd	א
	ירד ירש råd		יכל ūkål	
ג	ילד līki		ילד å'ēlåk	
	ישב šēbi		ישב tiššåb	ב
ז	ילד līku		ילד ירד tēlåk	

ילך wlīku
ירד שב rēdu
ירש wråšu
ילך līka ב
ילך wlīka
ישב šēbå
ירד råda

קל סביל עבר
יתן yētən ד
ילד yåləd
ילד yålåda ה
ילד yēlīdu ט

קל סביל עתיד
יצג yiṣṣåg ד

הפעיל עבר
ישב ūšabti א
יצב aṣṣibtå ב
ילד ūladtå
ילד ūləd ד
ישב ūšabnu* ו
יטב īṭību ט
ירש u'ūrəš ד
יטב wīṭåbnu ו
ירד ירש u'ūredtimma ז
ירד u'ūrīdu ט

הפעיל עתיד
יטב īṭəb א
ילד יסף ירש ūləd
יטב tīṭəb ב
ילד יסף יתר tūləd
ילד ירש יתר yūləd ד
יסף יקד tūsəf ה
יסף tūsīfon ז
ילד יסף ירש יתר tulīdu
יסף ירד yūsīfu ט
יטב wīṭəb א
ילך u'ūlək
יצג wyaṣṣəg ד
יצב wyåṣṣəb
ילד ילך ישב wyūləd
ינק wtīnəq ה
יקד ירד wtūqəd
ילד יסף ירד ירש יתר wyūlīdu ט
יצג aṣṣīga א

הפעיל ציווי
ירד ישב ūrəd ב
ירד ūrīdu ז

הפעיל סביל עבר
יטב å'īṭåb ד
ירד uwwårəd
ילד uwwålēdu ט
ירד wēwwårəd ד

פיעל עבר
ילד yalləd ד
יסף יסר wyassafti א
יסף wyassiftå ב
ירק ישב wyarrēqa ה
יסר wyåssåru ט

פיעל עתיד
יסר yiyyåssår ד

פיעל ציווי
יבם wyabbəm ב

נפעל עבר
יתר nūtår ד
יסף wnuwwåsåf
יסף wnūsīfa ה
ישן wnūšåntimma ז

נפעל עתיד
יקש ירש tuwwåqəš ב
ילד yuwwåləd ד
יצק יתר yuwwåšåq
יסר tuwwåsåru ז
ילד yuwwålēdu ט
ילד wyuwwåləd ד
יתר wyuwwåtår

התפעל ב עבר
יצב wittīṣåbu ט

התפעל ב עתיד
יגר tittīgår ב
יצב yittīṣåb ד
יגר tittīgåru ז
יצב wyittīṣåb ד
יצב wtittīṣåb ה
ילד יצב wyittīlådu ט

התפעל ב ציווי
יצב ittīṣåb ב
יגר יצב wittīgår
יצב ittīṣåbu ז
יצב wittīṣåbu

367

			פעלי פ"נ		
				קל עבר	
			נתן nåtåtti	א	
			נדר נתן nådårtå	ב	
			נשך nēšək	ד	
			נגש נדב נפל נתך נתן någåš		
			נתן nētīna*	ה	
			נדר nēdårå		
			נדב נפל נפץ nådåba		
			נמג nēmēgu	ט	
			נגש נכל נסב נפל נצב נתן någåšu		
	נתן wtånu		נתן wnåtåtti	א	
ב	נגש נתן gåša		נתן wnåtåttå	ב	
	נשק wšåqå		נגש נמס נסב נפל משל נתן wnågåš	ד	
	נקב nēqåba		נגש נפל נתן wnågåša	ה	
	קל סביל עבר		נתן wnåtannu	ו	
ד	נמל נתן nēməl		נמל נפל נתן wnåmåltimma	ז	
ה	נתן nētīna		נגף נגש נפל נצב נתן wnågåfu	ט	
ט	נמל נקב נתן nēmīlu			קל עתיד	
ה	נתן wnētīna		נתן ittən	א	
ז	נגף נתן wnūgeftimma		נתן tittən	ב	
	קל סביל עתיד		נבל נדר נסך tibbål		
ד	נקם yiqqåm		נתן yittən	ד	
ט	נתץ yittåṣu		נגף נגש נדר נזל נפל נקם משך נשק yiggåf		
	הפעיל עבר		נתן tittən	ה	
א	נגד aggitti		נדר נפל tiddår		
ב	נגד aggidtå		נתן nittən	ו	
	נצל åṣṣiltå		נפל alnibbål		
ד	נגד נכר aggəd		נתן tittēnu	ז	
	נצל åṣṣəl		נתץ tittåṣon		
ה	נשׂג aššīga		נגש נדר נסך tiggåšu		
ט	נשׂג aššīgu		נתן yittēnu	ט	
א	נגד נצל wåggitti		נגש נסך נפל yiggåšu		
ב	נגד wåggidtå		נצר yånṣēru*		
ד	נבט נגד מר נשׂג wåbbəṭ		נתן wittən	א	
ה	נשׂג wåššīga		נתן wtittən	ב	
ז	נגד wåggedtimma		נתן wyittən	ד	
ט	נבט נגד נצל wåbbīṭu		נגף נגש נדר נטש נפל נקב משך wyiggåf		
	הפעיל עתיד		נתן wtittən	ה	
א	נגד נשׂג aggəd		נגש נפל wtiggåš		
	נבט åbbəṭ		נתן wyittēnu	ט	
ב	נגש נכר נסג משך taggəš		נגש נפל wyiggåšu		
	נבט tåbbəṭ		נגש wtiggåšinna	י	
ד	נגד נגש נזל מר נכר נפל נשׂג yaggəd		נתן wittēna	א	
	נבט נצב yåbbəṭ			קל ציווי	
ה	נשׂג taššəg		משל šal	ב	
ז	נכר נקף takkīru		נתן wtån		
ט	נגד yaggīdu		נקם nēqåm		
ב	נגד wtaggəd		נתן tåni	ג	
ד	נגד נגש נכר נפל נשׂג wyaggəd		נגש נתן gåšu	ז	
	נצל wyåṣṣəl				
ה	נגד wtaggəd				
	נבט wtåbbəṭ				
ו	נגד wnaggəd				
ט	נגד נגש נשׂג wyaggīdu				
א	נגד waggīda				
	הפעיל ציווי				
	נבט ēbåṭ*				
ב	נכר נסך akkər				

	מות שוב	matnu	ו		נגד	aggīdi	ג
	סור שוב תור	sartimma	ז		נגד	aggīdu	ז
	קום	qåmtimma			נגד נגש	aggīda	ב
	מות	mētu	ט				
	סור	sāru		**הפעיל סביל עתיד**			
	גור זוד טוב מוש נוס קול קום רוב שום שוט שות תוך תום תור	gåru			נגד	wyiggåd	ד
	קול	åqålu		**פיעל עבר**			
	מות	wmitti	א		לשב	naššibtå	ב
	שום שוב שות	wšamti			נצב	wnaṣṣibtå	
	שום שוב	wšamtå	ב		נצל	wnåṣṣeltimma	ז
	מול קום	wmåltå			נתץ	wnåttåṣtimma	
	שוד	wsådåtå			נתץ	wnåttåṣu	ט
	מות נוס סור שוב	wmat	ד	**פיעל עתיד**			
	מול קום רום שום	wmål			נכר	yēnakkēru	ט
	מות	wmēta	ה		לשק	wyēnaššəq	ד
	שוב	wšāba			נבל לשך	wyēnabbēlu	ט
	מוט	wmåṭå			נצל	wyēnåṣṣēlu	
	מות	wmatnu	ו	**פיעל ב עתיד**			
	מול נוס סור שום שוב	wmaltimma	ז		נפש	wyēnåfɔš	ד
	מות	wmētu	ט	**נפעל עתיד**			
	סור	wsāru			נתן	yinnētən	ד
	נוס קום שום שוב	wnåsu			נגף	tinnågēfu	ז
קל עתיד					נזר	wyinnåzēru	ט
	גור מות סור שוב	ēgor	א	**נפעל ב עתיד**			
	שום שות	åšəm			נקש	tinnåqqåš	ב
	טור קום	tiṭṭor	ב		נצל	yinnåṣṣål	ד
	גור מות נוס סור צור קום שוב	tēgor			נקר	tinnåqqår	ה
	שום שות	tåšəm			נצל	wtinnåṣṣål	
	גור דון זוב מוש מות נוס סור צוד קום שוב	yēgor	ד	**התפעל עבר**			
	דון שום שור שות	yådən			נפל	itnåbbålti	א
	שוש שור	yåšåš		**התפעל עתיד**			
	מול	yåmol			נכר	wyitnakkår	ד
	זוב מוט מות שוב	tēzob	ה		נכל	wyitnakkålu	ט
	מות סור שוב	nēmot	ו		נצל	wyitnåṣṣålu	
	לון	nallən			נפל	witnåbbåla	א
	פוץ	nåfoṣ		**פעלי ע"ו**			
	מות שוב	tēmūton	ז	**קל עבר**			
	גור מות סור שוב תור	tēgūru			שום	šamti	א
	רוב	tårībon			גור קוץ	gårti	
	שום	tåšīmu			גור	gårtå	ב
	מות	yēmūton	ט		מות נוס סור שוב	mat	ד
	מות נוס סור קום	yēmūtu			גור לון קום רוץ רוד שום שוש שות	går	
	שום	yåšīmu			מות	mēta	ה
	שום	wåšəm	א		שוב	šåba	
	מות רום שוב	wyēmot	ד				
	לון	wyallən					
	שום	wyåšəm					
	גור זור מול מוש מות נוס סוב סוך	wyåågår					
	פוג פוץ צוץ רוץ קוד קום קוץ רוץ שוב						

369

		הפעיל עתיד		שׁוֹם	wtåšəm	ה
א	mēqī	קום שׁוּב		דוד מות קום רום רוץ שׁוּב	wtådåd	
	těåm	מות קום רוק		סוב שׁוּב	wnēsob	ו
ב	tīmət	מות קום נוף שׁוּב		שׁוֹם	wnåšəm	
	takkən	כן לך		שׁוּב	wtåšåbu	ז
ד	yīməs	מוס מור מות סור פור קום שׁוּב		נוס פור שׁוּב תור	wyēnūsu	ט
	yazzəd	זור לך		לך	wyallīnu	
	yåṣṣəf	צוּף		בן רוב שׁוֹם	wyåbīnu	
	yåsəf	סוּף רום		מוּל מות נוס סור פוּל קוד קום קוץ שׁוֹם	wyåmålu	
ז	tīqīmu	קום שׁוּב		שׁוּב	ēšūba	א
	tårīmu	רום		שׁוֹם	åšīma	
ט	yīnīsu	נוס קום		מות נוס	åmūta	
	yazzīdu	זור		שׁוּב	wēšūba	
	yårībon	רוב		שׁוֹם	wåšīma	
	yåṣīqu	צוק רום		קום	wnēqūma	ו
ד	wyīmət	מות נוס נוף סור פור קום שׁוּב				
	wyazzəd	זור		קל ציווי		
	wyåbəz	בן רום				
ה	wtīsər	סור		שׁוֹם	šim	ב
	wtåsəf*	סוּף		שׁוֹם	wšim	
ו	wnīšəb	שׁוּב		גוּר קום שׁוּב	gor	
ז	wtazzīdu	זור		מות צוּד קום שׁוּב	wmot	
ט	wyīkīnu	כן שׁוּב		לוּשׁ קום שׁוּב	lūši	ג
				בן לך שׁוֹם שׁוּר	bīnu	ז
		הפעיל ציווי		לך שׁוֹם	wlīnu	
ב	īsər	סור שׁוּב		סור קום שׁוּב	sūru	
	wīkən	כן קום		קום שׁוּב	wqūmu	
	ērəm	רום		שׁוֹם	šīma	ב
ז	īsīru	סור		קום שׁוּב	qūma	
	ērəmu	רום				
	åšīru	שׁוּר		הפעיל עבר		
		הפעיל סביל עבר		כן קום	īkinti	א
ד	ʔuwwånəf	נוף		רום	årimti	
	ʔuwwåqåm	קום רום שׁוּב		נוף	īniftå	ב
	wēwwåmət	מות		נוס נוף סור פוּר צוּף קום שׁוּב	īnəs	ד
				מות	īmettimma	ז
		הפעיל סביל עתיד		מוס	īmīsu	ט
ד	yūmåt	מות		קוץ רום	åqīṣu	
	yuwwåsåk	סך רום שׁוּת		סור קום שׁוּב	wīsirti	א
ט	yūmåtu	מות		מות	wåmitti	
ד	wyuwwåšåm	שׁוֹם		רוק	wårēqåti	
				מות נוף קום	wīmittå	ב
		נפעל ב עתיד		רום	wårimtå	
ד	yiggåwwår	גוּר		שׁוּב	wīšībūtå	
				שׁוּב	wī:šībūtå	
		התפעל עתיד		מות נוף סור פוּר קום שׁוּב	wīmət	ד
ב	tištūrår	שׁוּר		פוּץ	wī:fəṣ	
ה	wtitkūnən	כן		רום	wårəm	
				סור	wīsīra	ה
				רום	wåremtimma	ז
				מות	wīmittən	ח
				כן פוּר קום שׁוּב	wīkīnu	ט

פעלי ע"ע

קל עבר
א	שמן	šanti
ד	דקק תמם	dåq
	שגג	šågåg
ה	קצץ	qåṣṣå
ו	תמם	tamnu
	בזז	båzåznu
ט	בזז צלל	båzåzu
א	שכך	wšakti
	צרר	wṣårti
ב	סכך צרר קצץ	wsåktå
ד	מכך תמם	wmåk
ז	מדד	wmådåtimma
ט	דכך	wdakku
	מדד צרר שמם	wmådådu

קל עתיד
א	קבב	aqqåb
ב	בזז גזז	tibbåz
ד	מכך רכך רקק	yimmåk
ה	סבב שמם	tissåb
ז	לנן	tillånu
ט	מקק תמם	yimmåqu
	דמם	yīddåmu
י	סבב	tissåbinna
א	קדד קלל	wiqqåd
ד	גזז דמם דקק לנן סכך רבב שתת תמם	wyiggåz
ה	קלל רבב תמם	wtiqqål
ט	בזז כתת לנן רנן שכך תמם	wyibbåzu
	מדד פזז	wyēmaddu
א	כתת	wikkåta

קל ציווי
	פתת	fåtåt
ז	צרר	ṣåråru
ב	קבב	qēba

הפעיל עבר
ד	חלל	åttål
ז	לנן	allentimma
א	שכך שמם	wåššikti
ד	צרר	wåṣṣår

הפעיל עתיד
ד	גדד	yaggəd
	רמם רפף	wyarrəm

הפעיל ציווי
ב	רפף	arrəf
	קלל	waqqəl
ז	רנן	arnīnu

פיעל עבר
א	פלל	fållålti
ב	משש	maššištå
ד	קלל	qalləl
	בשש	baššåš
	מלל	mållel
	בלל	bållål
ט	גלל	wgallēlu
	קצץ	wqåṣṣåṣu

פיעל עתיד
ב	קלל	tēqalləl
ד	משש קלל	yēmaššəš
	משש קלל	wyēmaššəš
ט	מרר קשש	wyēmarrēru

פיעל ב עבר
ד	זמם	zåməm

נפעל עבר
ד	קלל	wniqqål

נפעל ב עבר
ט	שמם	wniššammu

התפעל עתיד
ט	בשש	yitbaššåšu
ד	פלל	wyitfållål
ט	רצץ	wyitråṣṣåṣu
א	פלל	witfållåla

התפעל ציווי
ב	פלל	itfållål

התפעל ב עתיד
ז	גדד	titgådēdu

פעלי ל"ה

קל עבר
א	קני	qånīti
	שתי	šåtīti
ב	קני	qånītå
	בני כשי נטי פרי שרי	bånītå
ג	שטי	šåṭīti
ד	בכי בני פשי צדי קני	båka
	נטי רמי שתי תלי	nåṭå
ה	בלי זני נטי פצי פשי קשי	bålåtå
ז	בכי מרי שתי	båkītimma
ט	בלי בני נכי פני פרי שבי	bålu
א	פני שתי	wfånīti
ב	שבי	wšēbītå
	בני רבי תלי	wbånītå

		ד	wzåna זני פני	
בכי wtēbēku	ז	ה	wnåṭå נטי נקי פרי שתי תלי	
בכי wyēbēku	ט		wnåqåṭå נקי פצי צבי	
פני wyåfånu		ו	wfårīnu פרי	
פני wēfåna	א	ז	wråbītimma רבי שתי	
פני wnēfåna	ו	ט	wzånu זני רדי שתי	

הפעיל עבר

נכי akkīti	א		

קל עתיד

נטי ēṭi	א	
לשי tišša	ב	
tibni בני מרי פרי רבי שתי		
נטי tēṭi		
פני tēfån		
taqni קני רדי		
tirbi רבי שטי	ג	
yišša לשי	ד	
yibni בני פני פרי פתי רבי שקי שתי		
yakli כל כרי קני		
tizni זני פני שתי	ה	
nibni בני שתי	ו	
tifnu פני	ז	
tašgu שגי		
yirbon רבי	ט	
yašgu שגי		
wišti שתי	א	
wyåṭ נטי	ד	
wyibni בני		
wyiqna קני		
wyardi רדי שבי		
wyåfån פני		
wtåṭ נטי	ה	
wtišti שתי		
wništi שתי	ו	
wyibnu בני פרי רבי רדי שתי	ט	
wyakru כרי שבי		

akkīti נכי	א
akkītå נכי	ב
akkå נכי	ד
afzå בזי קרי קשי רבי	
ašqåṭå שקי	ה
ikku נכי	ט
wåkkīti נכי	א
wåflīti פלי פרי רבי	
u'ūrīti ירי	
wazzītå מזי	ב
wåkkītå נכי	
wålwītå לוי שקי	
wåzzå מזי	ד
wåfla פלי	
wåšqå שקי	
wårṣåṭå רצי	ה
wåšqinnu* שקי	ו
wåkkītimma נכי	ז
wåqrītimma קרי	
wåkku נכי	ט
wåznu זני שקי	

קל ציווי

bēni בני פרי קני	ב
wrēbi רבי	
bēnu בני פני פרי	ז
wfēru פרי רבי רדי	
nēṭå נטי	ב
wnēṭå נטי	
šåṭå שתי	

הפעיל עתיד

išqi שקי	א
ūdi ירי	
tirbi רבי	ב
takki נכי	
talwi לוי ספי	
tårṣi רצי	
takki נכי	ג
yirbi רבי	ד
yazzi מזי נכי	
yafti פתי	
tårṣi רצי	ה
našqi שקי	ו
tirbu רבי	ז
taksu כסי קשי	
tūnu יני	
yašqu שקי	ט
yårṣu רצי	
yūru ירי	
wakki נכי	א
wyazzi מזי נכי	ד
wyašqi שקי	
wyakkē'u נכי	
wtašqi שקי	ה

קל ב עתיד

ēfēdi פרי	א
tēfēdi פרי	ב
tēfēši פשי	ג
yēfēši פשי	ד
yēbēku בכי	ט
wyēbēki בכי	ד
wtēbēki בכי	ה

			ו	נכי	wnakki	
	wyēkalla	כלי	ז	מרי	wtamru	
	wyēṣåbbi	צפי	ט	נכי	wyakku	
ה	wtēkassi	כסי	י	שקי	wtašqīyyinna	
	wtēkalla	כלי				
ו	wnēballi	בלי		**הפעיל ציווי**		
ט	wyēbakku	בכי כסי נסי				
			ב	מזי	azzi	
	פיעל ציווי			נכי	wakki	
			ג	נטי	åṭi	
ב	zarri	זרי	ז	רבי שקי	arbu	
ז	kallu	כלי				
				הפעיל סביל עבר		
	פיעל ב עבר					
			ד	נכי	ukkå	
א	ṣåbīti	צוי				
ד	ṣåba	צוי		**הפעיל סביל עתיד**		
א	wṣåbīti	צוי				
ב	wṣåbītå	צוי	ד	רצי	yårṣi	
ד	wṣåba	צוי	ט	רצי	yårṣu	
	פיעל ב עתיד			**פיעל עבר**		
א	ēṣåbi	צוי	א	דמי כלי פני קוי	dammīti	
ב	tēṣåbi	צוי	ד	כלי	kalla	
ד	yēṣåbi	צוי		כסי	kasså	
א	wēṣåbi	צוי		גלי נסי צפי	gållå	
ד	wyēṣåbi	צוי		נסי	annåsså	
	wyēṣåba	צוי	ה	נסי	nissåtå	
ט	wyēṣåbu	צוי		כסי	kassåtå	
				גלי	gållåtå	
	פיעל ב ציווי		ז	כלי נסי	kallītimma	
			ט	כלי	kallu	
ב	ṣåbi	צוי		טוי	ṭuwwu	
	wṣåbi	צוי	ב	כסי פני	wkassītå	
				צפי	wṣåbbītå	
	פיעל ב סביל עבר		ד	כלי	wkalla	
				כסי	wkasså	
א	ṣåbīti*	צוי		גלי צפי	wgållå	
			ה	בכי כסי	wbakkåtå	
	נפעל עבר		ו	כסי	wkassīnu	
			ט	כסי פני	wkassu	
ד	niššåba	שבי				
	niggålå	גלי		**פיעל עתיד**		
ה	nibnåtå	בני				
	niffådåtå	פדי	א	זרי כלי קשי	ēzarri	
ד	wnårṣi	רצי		כלי	ēkalla	
				רבי	ēråbbi	
	נפעל עתיד		ב	גלי כסי	tēgalli	
				כלי	tēkalla	
ב	tissåfi	ספי		צפי	tēṣåbbi	
ג	tibbåni	בני	ד	גלי נקי	yēgalli	
ר	yiqqåri	קרי	ז	נסי	tēnassu	
	yimmåni	מני מצי פדי שתי	ט	בכי	yēbakku	
ה	tiggåli	גלי כבי		נצי	yēnåṣṣu	
ז	tissåfu	ספי	א	כלי	wēkalli	
ט	yiqqåbu	קוי		רבי	wēråbbi	
	wyiddågu	דגי	ד	בכי גלי כסי	wyēbakki	
	נפעל ב עבר					
ט	wnillawwu	לוי				

373

	נפעל ב עתיד				התפעל עתיד	
א	בני ibbanni			ט	ידי wētbaddu	
ב	כסי לוי נקי tikkassi					
ד	לוי קשי yillawwi		ד	גלי wyitgalli	
א	בני wibbanni		ה	כסי wtikkassi	
ה	קשי wtiqqašši		ט	נבי wyitnabbu	
	כלי wtikkalla					
ט	כלי לוי wyikkallu			הפעלים הרבעיים	
	נצי wyinnåṣṣu			פיעל עבר	
י	כלי wtikkallinna		ב	נכסף naksiftå*	
			א	כלכל wkalkilti	
	נפעל ב ציווי				
ג	נקי innaqqi			פיעל עתיד	
			א	כלכל ēkalkəl	
	התפעל עבר		ד	כלכל wyēkalkəl	
ד	ידי wētbåddå				

ג. Verbs Formed from Guttural Roots
(בלא כינויי הפעול)

פא גרונית
השלמים

	קל עבר					
א	הלך ålikti			אכל אמר wåkålti	
	אכל אמר הרג חפץ åkålti			ערך wåriktå	
	חלם חפר עבד עמד ˁålåmti			הלך הרג wåliktå	
ב	הלך הרג åliktå			אכל אמר אפד הדר חבר חגר חדל חפר חקר חשק עבד wåkåltå	
	אבד אכל אמר חפץ åbådtå				
	אמר å:mårtå		ד	אשם ערך wåśəm	
	חלם חסר חצב חשך עבד עמד עצם ˁålåmtå			אכל אמר ארב אשם חדל חזק חשב עבר עזב עזר wåkål	
ד	אשם הלך åśəm		ה	הלך wēlåka	
	אכל אמר ארש הלך הפך חבר חדל חזק חלק חמץ חפץ åkål			אכל wåkåla	
	חלם חשך עבד עזב עמד עצר ערב עשק ˁålåm			אמר אסר אשם חלץ wåmårå	
ה	אבד åbåda			אכל wåkålåt	
	אמר אסר åmårå		ו	הלך wåliknu	
	אזל åzålåt			אמר wåmårinnu*	
	עמד ˁåmåda		ז	ערל wåreltimma	
	חשק ˁåśåqå			הלך wålektimma	
ו	הלך åliknu			אבד אכל אמר עבד wåbådtimma	
	אבד åbådnu		ט	אשם wåśēmu	
	חלם ˁålåmnu			אכל אמר הרג חסר עבד עמד ערך ערף wåkålu	
ז	הלך ålektimma				
	אכל åkåltimma			קל עתיד	
ח	עזב ˁåzåbtən		א	חלק עבר ēlləq	
ט	אכל אמר ארך הל הרג חרב åkålu			אכל אמר ēˀūkəl	
א	חבר חכם חפר עבד עזב עקר ˀåbåru*		ב	הרס חלק חמד חסם חצב עבד עבר ערץ עשק tērrås	
	הלך הרג wålikti			אגר אדר הדר הרג חבל חדל חמל tågår	
				הדר חבט חסר עבד עזב עמד taddår	
				אכל אמר taˀūkəl	
			ד	אמץ חלק חמד חמץ חרץ עבר yēmmåṣ	
				חדל חפץ yådål	

374

	wnābbåda עבר			yåbbåd אבד חסר עזב עמד ערף		
				yå'ūkəl אכל אמר		
	קל ציווי		ה	tēbbår עבר		
ב	ēmår אמר חדל חזק עמד			tåbbåd אבד עזב עמד		
	wēmåṣ אמץ הלך			tå'ūkəl אכל אמר		
	åzåq חזק		ו	nēbbår עבר		
	ēmåri אמר			nåråg הרג		
ג	ērågu הרג חזק עבד עמד			nåbbåd עבר		
ז	wēmåṣu אמץ הרג עבד			nå'ūkəl אכל אמר		
	wåkålu אכל		ז	tērråṣon ערץ		
ב	wēkåla אכל			tēṣṣåbu עצב ערץ		
				tåbbådon עבר		
	קל סביל עבר			tårågu הרג חפז		
ד	ēmər אמר הפך			tåbbådon אבד		
	'åbəd עבר			tåbbådu עבר		
ה	ēfīka הפך			tå'ūkēlon אכל אמר		
	åråša ארש חפש			tå'ūkēlu אכל אמר		
ד	wēmər אמר		ט	yērråsu הרס		
				yådålon חדל		
	הפעיל עבר			yåssåron חסר		
א	åšširti עשר			yåbbådu אבד עזב עמד ערף		
	å:kålti אכל			yå'ūkēlon אכל		
ד	å:sər חסר חתם עבד ערף			yå'ūkēlu אכל אמר		
	åzən אזן		א	wåššåk חשך		
	årrəš חרש			wē'ūkəl אכל אמר		
	å:mən אמן		ב	wtå'ūkəl אכל אמר		
ז	å:mentimma אמן		ד	wyēllåm חלם חלק חלש חרד עבד		
א	wåzziqti חזק			wyåbbåd עבר		
	wåttårti עתר			wyåsår אסר אפד הפך הרג חבר חגר חפר		
	wå:rimti חרם			wyåzzåb עזב עמד עתק עתר		
ב	wåbbiṭṭå עבט עבר עמד			wyå'ūkəl אכל אמר		
	wåriktå ארך		ה	wtåmål חמל		
	wåbbištå* חבש חזק			wtåmmåd עמד		
	wå:zintå אזן			wtå'ūkəl אכל אמר		
ד	wåmməd עמד ערך		ו	wnēllåm חלם		
	wåmən אמן			wnå'ūkəl אכל אמר		
	wåbbəd אבד חזק חרש		ז	wtågåru חגר		
ה	wåzzīqa חזק			wtåmmådon עמד		
ז	wårektimma ארך			wtå'ūmēru אמר		
ט	wåbbīru עבר		ט	wyēllåmu חלם חרד		
	wåliṣu חלץ			wyåbådu אבד הרג חפד חפר עבד עמס עפל		
	wåmēnu אמן			wyåssåru חסר עבד עמד עצם		
				wyå:dålu חדל		
	הפעיל עתיד			wyå'ūkēlu אכל אמר		
א	åbbər 'עבר עתר		י	wtåmmådinna עמד		
	åzzəq חזק			wtå'ūkēlinna אכל אמר		
ב	tånnəq ענק		א	ēbbåra עבר		
	tåmən אמן אמץ חרם			ēbbårå עבר		
	tårrək ארך חרש			ē'ūkēla אכל		
ד	yånnəf חנף עלם עמד ערך			wēråga הרג		
	yårəm חרם			wē'ūkēla אכל אמר		
	yårrək ארך חרש		ה	wtåmårå חמר		
ז	tabbīdu אבד		ו	wnēbbårå עבר		

375

	tånnīfu חנף עבד עבר ענן		
	tårrīkon ארך חרש		
ט	yåbbīdu עבד עלם		
	yåšīmu אשם		
	yåmēnu אמן		
	yårrīkon ארך		
	yå:mēnu אמן		
ב	wtålləf חלף		ה	tåkkəl אכל
ד	wyålləf חלף עבר עמד עקד ערך			tåbbår עבר
	wyåməš חמש חרם		ז	tåbbēdon אבד
	wyåzzəq חזק			tåbbåru עבר
ה	wtåšək חשך		ט	yåkkēlu אכל
ט	wyåbbīdu עבד עבר			yåbbåru עבר
	wyåmēnu אמן		ד	wyåbbəq אבק חבק חבש חפש
	wyånnīṭu חנט			wyåbbår עבר
	wyå:mēnu אמן		ה	wtåbbår עבר
ו	wnårīma חרם			wtållək הלך
			ט	wyårrēku ערך
	הפעיל ציווי			wyåzzēqu חזק
ב	årəm חרם			wyåbbåru עבר
	åzzəq חזק			
ז	åttīru עתר			פיעל ציווי
	wållīfu חלף		ב	'abbår עבר
	åzīnu אזן		ג	wazzīqi* חזק
	å:līṣu חלץ		ז	'abbåru עבר
ח	åzīna אזן			wåbbåru עבר
ב	å:zīna אזן			
				פיעל סביל עבר
	פיעל עבר		ט	'abbēdu עבר
א	'arrikti ערך			
	'åbbårti עבר			פיעל ב עבר
ד	abbəd אבד		ד	åsəf אסף
	ålləq חלק		ב	wåsiftå אסף
	'åbbår עבר		ד	wåsəf אסף
ו	'åbbårnu עבר			
ז	'aššebtimma חשב עבר			פיעל ב עתיד
	'åbbårtimma עבר		ב	tåsəf אסף
א	wabbidti אבד		ו	nåsəf אסף
	wayyabti איב		ד	wyåsəf אסף
	wåbbårti עבר		ט	wyåsēfu אסף
ב	wabbidtå אבד			
ד	wamməṣ אמץ			פיעל ב ציווי
	wåššåq חשק עבר		ב	åsēfa אסף
ז	wabbedtimma אבד			
	wåbbårtimma עבר			נפעל עבר
ט	wåbbådtimma עבר		ד	niyyåsåf אסף הפך
	wannēšu ענש		ה	niyyåṣårå עצר
			ו	niyyåšåbnu חשב
	פיעל עתיד		ט	niyyåråmu ערם
ב	tåššår עשר		ב	wniyyåsåftå אסף
	tårrəš ארש		ד	wniyyåfåk הפך חשב
ד	yåbbəl חבל		ז	wniyyåsåftimma אסף
	yåbbår עבר		ט	wniyyåsåfu אסף הפך
				נפעל עתיד
			ב	tiyyåsåf אסף עבט
			ד	iyyåkəl אכל אמר
				tiyyåsəf אסף אסר חבר חגר חשב עבד
			ה	tiyyåkəl אכל
				tiyyåsåf אסף חשב

קל עתיד

ה	חוס tå'os	
ד	אול wyå'ol*	

הפעיל עבר

א	עוד å'idti
ב	עוד å'idtå
ד	עוד å'ɔd
ט	אור wå'īru

הפעיל עתיד

ד	עור yā'ər
ר	אור yå'ər
ט	אור yå'īru
ד	אול אור הום wyå'əl
ז	הן wtåyyīnu
ט	אוץ wyå'īṣu
א	עוד wå'īda

הפעיל ציווי

| ב | עח 'ā'əz |
| ד | עוד å'ɔd |

פיעל עבר

| א | אול uwwalti |
| ד | אול uwwål |

פיעל עתיד

| ד | עור yāwwər |

נפעל ב עתיד

| ו | אות nēwwåt |
| ט | אות yēwwåtu |

פעלי ע"ע

קל עבר

| ד | חנן ånån |
| ז | חגג wā'egtimma |

קל עתיד

א	ארר ē'år
ב	חגג tāg
ד	ארר חתת tē'år
ד	חמם yåm
ה	עפף tāf
ז	חגג tāggu
ט	חגג wyāggu

קל ציווי

| ב | ארר ēra |
| | ארר årā |

ו	חלץ niyyålåṣ
ז	חזק חלץ tiyyåzåqu
ט	אסף חשב iyyåsåfu
ד	אכל אמר wiyyåkəl
	אסף הפך חזק wiyyåsåf
ה	אזל חזק עצר wtiyyåzål
ט	אסף הפך wiyyåsåfu

נפעל ציווי

| ב | אסף wiyyåsåf |
| ז | אסף אסר iyyåsåfu |

נפעל ב עבר

| ד | עלם wniyyållåm |

נפעל ב עתיד

| א | עמש iyyannəš |
| ד | חרם iyyårråm |

התפעל עבר

א	הלך ētållåkti
ד	אנף ētånnåf
ט	הלך עשק ētållåku
א	הלך wētållåkti
ב	עלם wētållåmtå
ד	הלך עמר wētållåk
ז	חזק wētåzzåqtimma

התפעל עתיד

ב	חתן עמר tētåttån
ד	חשב yētåššåb
ו	חכם nētåkkåm
ד	אנף אפק הלך חזק עבר עצב wyētånnåf
ה	עלף wtētållåf
ט	עצב wyētåṣṣåbu

התפעל ציווי

| ב | הלך ētållåk |
| ז | חתן wētåttånu |

התפעל ב עבר

| ה | אסף iyyåsēfa |

התפעל ב עתיד

| ד | אבל wyētåbål |
| ט | אבל wyētåbålu |

פעלי ע"ו

קל עבר

ד	חוש waš
ה	חום wåmå
ט	חול wålu

377

קל סביל עתיד

ד wyår ארר

הפעיל עבר

א å'ilti חלל
ב å'iltå חלל
ד å'əl חלל
א wå'inti חנן

הפעיל עתיד

א å'ən חנן
ב tå'əl חלל
ד yå'əl חלל חנן
ה tå'əl חלל
ד wyå'ɔs הסס
ד wyå'əl חלל
י wtå'ēlinna חלל

הפעיל ציווי

ב å'əl חלל

פיעל עבר

ב 'allåltå חלל
ד 'aləl חלל
ב walliltå חלל

פיעל עתיד

ב tālləl חלל
 tūləl עלל
ד yālləl חלל עפף
ז tālīlu חלל
ט yālīlu חלל
 wyāllēlu הלל

התפעל עבר

א ētållålti עלל

התפעל עתיד

א wētånnåna חנן

פעלי ל"ה

קל עבר

א 'aššīti עשי
 å'īti הי הרי
ב 'aššītå עשי
 åbītå עלי אבי
 å'ītå הי
ג 'aššīti עשי
ד ayya הי
 'āna עני עשי
 åna אני
 åbå אבי אפי חלי חרי

 'ålå עלי
ה ayyåtå הי
 åråtå הרי
 'ålåtå עלי עשי
ו 'aššīnu עשי
 'ålīnu עלי
 å'īnu הי
ז 'aššītimma עשי
 'ālītimma עלי
 åbītimma אבי הי
ח 'aššītən עשי
ט isyu חסי
 ayyu הי
 'āyu חי עלי עני עשי
 ånu חני
 wåyyu הי
א wå'īti הי
ב waššītå עשי
 wā'ītå חי עלי עני
 wåfītå אפי הי חצי
ד wī חי
 wēyya הי
 wāsa עשי
 wåyå חי חרי עלי
ה wēyyåtå הי
 wayyåtå חי
 wålåtå עלי עני עשי
ו waššīnu עשי
 wālīnu עלי
 wå'īnu הי
ז waššītimma עשי
 wālītimma עלי
 wå'ītimma הי
ט wāyu חי עלי עני עשי
 wåfu אפי חני
 wåyyu הי

קל עתיד

א ēyyi הי עלי עשי
ב tiyya חי
 tēyyi הי עשי
 tānna עני
 tā:la עלי
 tåzi חזי
 tåbbå אבי
ג tēššən עשי
ד yī חי
 yår חרי
 yiyya חי
 yēyyi הי עלי עשי
 yēṭṭå עטי
 yālli עלי
 yānna עני

		היי ayyu				היי yå'i
		חיי wāyu				אבי yåbå
	הפעיל עבר					חזי yåzzi
א		חיי 'ā'īti	ה			חיי tiyya
ב		עלי āllītå				היי עשי tēyyi
ד		עלי ållå				אבי tåbbå
ז		חיי 'ā'ītimma	ו			היי עלי עשי nēyyi
ב		עלי wāllītå	ז			חיי tiyyon
ד		עלי wållå				אפי tēfu
ז		עלי wāllītimma				עשי tēššon
	הפעיל עתיד					עשי tēššu
א		עלי 'ālli				עלי tāllu
ב		חיי עלי tāyyi				אבי חני tåbu
ז		חיי עלי tāyyon				היי tåyyu
		עלי tāllu	ט			עשי yēššon
ט		חיי yāyyu				עשי yēššu
א		חיי עלי wāyyi				עלי עני yāllu
ד		עלי wyālli				חצי yåṣṣon
ו		חיי wnāyyi				עלי חני yåyyu
ח		חיי wtāyyinna	י			היי tåyyinna
ט		עלי wyāllu				עשי tēššīyyinna
י		חיי wtāyyinna	א			היי עלי עשי wēyyi
	הפעיל ציווי		ד			חיי wyī
ב		עלי 'ālli				חרי עלי עני עשי wyād
		עלי wālli				חני חרי wyån
ז		חיי 'āyu				חצי wyā'oṣ
	פיעל עבר					אתי חתי wyåttå*
ד		עני 'anna				היי wyå'i
		חצי 'åṣṣå	ה			חיי wtī
ז		עני wannītimma				עלי עני עשי wtāl
ט		עני wannu				הרי wtår
		חצי wåṣṣu				חיי wtiyya
	פיעל עתיד					היי wtēyyi
ב		עני tānni				היי wtå'i
ה		אוי tåwwå	ו			חיי wniyya
ז		עני tānnu				היי עלי עשי wnēyyi
ט		עני yānnu	ז			עלי עני wtāllu
	נפעל עבר		ט			עשי wyēššu
ב		היי nå'ītå				עלי עני עשי wyāllu
ד		עלי niyyålå				אפי wyåfu
ה		היי nēyyåtå				היי חני wyåyyu
ט		עשי niyyåšåtå				חזי wyå:zu
		עשי niyyåšu	י			היי wtåyyinna
ד		עלי wniyyålå				הרי wtå:rinna
	נפעל עתיד			**קל ציווי**		
ד		עשי iyyāši	ב			חיי wiyya
		עני iyyāne				הוי עלי עשי ēbi
						הוי עלי עשי wēbi
			ג			הוי עלי עשי ēbi
						עשי wēši
			ז			אפי חני עלי עשי ēfu
						עלי עשי wēlu

379

ד	wyē'bār בחר בעט			ה	tiyyāši עשי	
	wyē'rås̱ רחץ שחט			ט	tiyyåfi אפי	
	wyå'gå̱r גער				iyyāšon עשי	
ה	wtē'bār בער מעל			י	iyyālu עלי עשי	
ט	wyērås̱ṣu רחץ שחט				tiyyāšīyyinna עשי	
					tiyyåfīyyinna אפי	

קל ציווי

נפעל ציווי

ב	bār בחר
ז	ṭånu טען
	wsådu סער רחץ
	wšåṭṭu שחט
ב	zåmå זעם

| ז | iyyālu עלי |

נפעל ב עתיד

| ה | tiyyanna עני |

הפעיל עבר

התפעל עבר

ד	å'rīb רחב שאר שחת
	å'bēš באש
ה	årīqa רחק
ז	åbēštimma באש
ט	åqīlu קהל רחק
א	wårēbti רחב
ב	wåqēltå קהל
	wåẕårtå זהר
ה	wåmī:ṭa מעט
ז	wåẕårtimma זהר

| ט | ētåwwu אוי |
| ז | wētåwwītimma אוי |

התפעל ציווי

| ג | wētånni עני |

הפעיל עתיד

עין גרונית

א	å'šīt שחת
ב	tå'mīṭ מעט שחת
	tå'rēq רחק
	åtå'šīt שחת
ד	yå'bīr בער מעט רחב שאר
ז	tåbīru בער מעט רחק
	tåšīttu שחת
ט	yåšīru שאר
ד	wyå'qīl קהל
	wyå'bēš באש
ה	wtå'bēš באש
ט	wyåqīlu קהל

השלמים

קל עבר

א	bārti בער
ד	bār בחר
	rås̱ רחץ שחת
ה	bāra בער
ט	bā:ru בחר
	šåtu שחת
ב	wbārtå בער בחר
ד	wṭårtå טהר פחד רחץ שחט שחק
	wbēš באש
	wbār בער
	wṭår טהר כהן רחץ שחט שחת
ה	wmāla מעל
ז	wšåttimma שחת
ט	wṭånu טחן רחץ
	wkånnu כהן שחט

הפעיל ציווי

קל עתיד

ב	å'qīl קהל
	wå'qīl קהל
ז	åqīlu קהל

פיעל ב עבר

א	ē'bār בחר זעם
ב	tē'bār בער
	tē'fåd פחד שחט
ד	yē'bār בחר
	yē'ṭår טהר רחץ רחק שחט
ה	tē'māl מעל
	tē'ṭår טהר
ז	tēšåṭṭu שחט
ט	yērås̱ṣu רחץ שחט
א	wē'šåṭ שחט

א	mā'is̱ti מחץ
	s̱å'iqti צחק
ב	fā'iztå פחד פעל
ג	gå'iltå גאל מאן מהר שאל
	s̱å'iqti צחק
ד	fā'ɔl פעל
	mā'ɔn מאן צעק שאל
ה	gā'ēla געל

380

טהר צעק tå'ēra	
ז מאס מעל mā'estimma	
מאן må'entimma	
ח מהר må'irtən	
ט מאס מעל mā'ēsu	
א רחם wrā'imti	
גאל wgå'ilti	
ב שאל wšå'iltå	
ד כחש מחץ wkå'əš	
גאל טהר שאל wgå'əl	
ה גאל wgå'ēla	
טהר wtå'ēra	
ז טהר מהר wtå'ertimma	

פיעל ב עתיד

א שאב רחם ērå'əm
ב תעב tētā'əb
tēfå'ər פאר צעק שאל
ד שחל רחף מחץ לחם לחך yēlā'ək
גאל צחק שאל yēgå'əl
ה רעץ להט נעל tēgå'əl
ז מאס לחץ לחם כחש tēkā'ēsu
א שאל wēšå'əl
ד לחם wyēlā'əm
מהר צעק שאל wyēmå'ər
ה שאב לחץ כחש wtēkā'əš
מהר צחק wtēmå'ər
ו שאל צעק wnēṣå'əq
ט מהר צעק שאל wyēmå'ēru

פיעל ב ציווי

מהר må'ər
ב מחץ må'eṣ
שאל šå'əl
ג מהר må'ēri
ז מהר må'ēru

נפעל עבר

ד שאר niš'står
ה שחת niššåtå
ט בהל nibbå:lu
ד שען wniš'šān
גאל wnig'ål
לחם wnallā'əm
ז שאר wniššårtimma

נפעל עתיד

ד בער yib'bār
מעט שחט yim'måṭ
מאן גאל yiggå'əl
ה שאר tiš'står
ו כחד nik'kåd
ז שחת tiššåton

בחן סחר tibbånu
ט קהת yiqqåtu
י שאר tiššårinna
ב כחד wtik'kåd
מאן wtimmå'ən
ד כהן קהל שאר wyik'kån
מאן wyimmå'ən
ה פעם רעב wtib'bām
קהל שחת wtiq'qål
ט בחן סחר קהל שאר wyibbånu
כחש wyikkā'ēšu

נפעל ציווי

ב לחם allā'əm
ז שען wiššā'īnu

התפעל עבר

ז שחת wēššåttimma
ט טהר wiṭṭå'ēru

התפעל עתיד

ז טהר tiṭṭå'ēru

התפעל ציווי

ז טהר wiṭṭå'ēru

התפעל ב ציווי

ב פאר it'får

פעלי פ״י

קל עתיד

י יחם wyåminna

קל ציווי

ז יהב ēbu
יהב wåbu
ב יהב åbå

הפעיל סביל עבר

ט יעד uwwā'ēdu
ד יעד wēwwā'əd

נפעל עבר

ו יאל nuwwalnu
א יעד wnuwwā'idti
ט יעד wnuwwā'ēdu

נפעל עתיד

א יעד uwwā'əd

381

	גאי ראי gå:		פעלי פ"נ	
ה	ראי rå:tå		קל עבר	
ו	ראי rå'īnu		נהג någ	ד
ז	ראי rå'ītimma		קל עתיד	
ט	ראי rå'u		נער wyå'når	ד
י	כהי kātta*		הפעיל עתיד	
א	מחי wmā'īti		נחל yå'nīl	ד
	ראי wrå'īti		נחל yå:nīlu	ט
ב	ראי wrå'ītå		פיעל ב עבר	
ד	מחי wmā:		נחם נחש nā'imti	א
	ראי wrå:		נהל נהב nå'iltå	ב
ז	ראי wrå'ītimma		נאץ nā'ēṣu	ט
ח	ראי wrå'ītən		נחל wnå'iltå	ב
ט	ראי wrå'u		פיעל ב עתיד	
	קל עתיד		נאף tēnā'ɔf	ב
א	מחי רעי ē'mī		נאף נהג נחש yēnā'ɔf	ד
ב	מחי tē'mī		נחש tēnā'ēšu	ז
ד	בעי yē'bī		נהג wtēnā'ɔg	ב
ט	רעי yē'rū		נאץ נהג נחם wyēnā'ɔṣ	ד
א	מחי wē'mī		נפעל ב עתיד	
ד	שעי wyåsa		נחל tin'nål	ב
ה	להי wtalla		נחם yin'nām	ד
	חעי wtåtå		נחל yin'nål	
י	כהי רעי wtåkīyyinna		נחל nin'nål	ו
	קל ציווי		נחל yinnålu	ט
ב	ראי rē'i		נחם wyin'nām	ד
	ראי wrē'i		נפעל ב ציווי	
	נחי nå'i		נחם win'nām	ב
ז	רעי rū		התפעל עבר	
	ראי rē'u		נחל itnålu	ט
	ראי wrē'u		נחל wētnåltimma	ז
	קל סביל עתיד		התפעל עתיד	
ד	ראי yårå'i*		נחם yit'nām	ד
	קל ב עתיד		נחל titnålu	ז
א	ראי ērē'i		נחל yitnålu	ט
ב	ראי tērē'i		נחם wyit'nām	ד
ד	ראי yērē'i		נהל itnåla	א
ה	ראי tērē'i			
ז	ראי tērē'u		פעלי ל"ה	
ט	ראי yērē'on		קל עבר	
	שעי yåšå'u		ראי rå'īti	א
	ראי yērē'u		נחי ראי nå'ītå	ב
א	ראי wērē'i		שעי šå	ד
ד	ראי wyēre			
ה	ראי wtēre			
ו	ראי wnērē'i			
ז	ראי wtērē'u			
ט	ראי wyērē'u			
	לאי wyallā'u			
	שעי wyåšå'u			

		ט	אחז wyā'ēzu
	פיעל ב ציווי		
		ב	אחז wā'ɔz
		ז	אחז wā'ēzu
	נפעל עבר		
		ט	אחז wnā'ēzu

למד גרונית

השלמים

		קל עבר
א	שמע šāmātti	
	שכח סלח sålātti	
	קרא מצא ברא bårātti	
ב	שמע šāmāttå	
	משח מצא måšåttå	
ד	שמע מנע māna	
	פסח משח גוע gåba	
	ברא bårå ברא ברח דלא כרע מצא פרח צמח
	תקע קרא	
	åšāma שמע	
ה	מלא må'lā	
	zå'rå זרע מצא פרח קדח קרא
	שמע šāmānnu	
	גוע gåbānnu	
	מצא måṣånnu	
ז	שמע šāmāttimma	
	שנא sånāttimma	
ט	qāfā'u שמע קפא
	ṭåbā'u טבע מלא צבא
	måṣā'u מצא קרא
א	שמע wšāmātti	
	פסח wfåsātti	
	קרא wqårātti	
ב	זבח wzēbāttå	
	שמע שבע wšābāttå	
	שכח wšåkāttå	
	wmåšåttå משח סלח משה פתח קרא שמח
ג	קרא wqårātti	
ד	טמא wṭēma	
	רצח רצע wrēṣå	
	שמע שבע wšāba	
	פסח wfåsa	
	wzårā זרע מצא פרח קרא שמח
ה	טמא wṭē'mā	
	שמע פתח wfā'tā	
	שבע wšā'bāt	
	wbå'lā בלע מלא	
	מצא wmå'ṣå	

הפעיל עבר			
ד	ראי ar'rå		
	תאי å'tå		
הפעיל סביל עבר			
ב	ראי arråttå		
ד	ראי åri		
	ראי wå'rī		
פיעל ב עתיד			
ז	תאי tåtå'u		
נפעל עבר			
ד	ראי nirrå'i		
ט	ראי nirrå'u		
ד	ראי wnirrå'i		
ה	ראי wnirråttå		
ט	לאי wnallā'u		
נפעל עתיד			
א	ראי irrå'i		
ד	ראי yirrå'i		
ה	ראי tirrå'i		
ט	ראי yirrå'u		
א	ראי wirrå'i		
ד	ראי wyirrå'i		
ה	ראי wtirrå'i		
התפעל ב עתיד			
ד	מחי yim'mī		
	מחי wyim'mī		
ט	מחי wyim'mū		

פא ועין גרוניות

		קל עתיד
ד	אהל wyå'ol*	
פיעל ב עבר		
א	אהב å'ibti	
ב	אהב å'ibtå	
ד	אחז 'ā'ɔz	
	å'ɔb אהב אחר	
ב	אהב wå'ibtå	
ז	אהב wå'ebtimma	
פיעל ב עתיד		
ב	אחר tå'ɔr	
ד	אחר yå'ɔr	
ז	אחר tå'ēru	
א	אחר wå'ɔr	
ד	אהב wyå'ɔb	
ה	אחז wtā'ɔz	

383

			ו	שמע wšāmānnu		
	קל ציווי		ז	זבח זרע wzēbāttimma		
ב	מלא קרא mēli			קרא שמח תקע wqåråttimma		
	ברח סלח רפא שמע bēra		ט	זבח טמא שמע wzēbā'u		
	שמע wšēma			שבע wšābā'u		
	שמח šåmå			מלא wmålā'u		
	שכח wšåka			קרא תקע wqårå'u		
	טבח wṭåbå					
ז	זבח שמע zēbā'u				קל עתיד	
	מלא mēlå'u					
	שמע wšēmā'u		א	קרא רפא שמע iqra		
	מלא wmēlā'u			מצא imṣå		
	פגע wfågā'u		ב	זבח זרע מלא מלח פגע פתח קרא tizba		
ח	קרא qē'rīn			שמע		
	שמע šē'mān			מצא רצח timṣå		
	שמע wšē'mā			שנא tåšna		
				שמע åtišma		
	קל סביל עתיד		ד	ברא yibri		
ד	מצא wyimṣå			גוע גרע מלא משח סלח פלא פרח yigba		
				פרע פתח קרא רפא שמע		
	קל ב עתיד			טמא מצא רצח yiṭmå		
ד	בטא yēbēṭå			צמח yåṣ'ma		
ה	דשא tēdēši			פלא åyifla		
			ה	פרח tifra		
	הפעיל עבר			טמא מצא tiṭmå		
ד	שבע ašbi		ו	זבח זרע קרא שמע nizba		
	צלח åṣli			מצא nimṣå		
	צלח åṣ'lī			שמע tiš'mūn		
ט	מצא åmṣiyyu			גרע זבח זרע פרע קרא שבע שמע tigrā'u		
ד	שבע wåšbi			מצא timṣå'u		
	צלח wåṣ'lī			תקע tatqā'u		
ט	רשע wåršiyyu		ט	קרח yiq'rū		
				שמע yiš'mūn		
	הפעיל עתיד			זבח קרא שמע yizbā'u		
ב	רבע tirbi			קצע yiqṣå'u		
	צלח tåṣ'lī			תקע yatqā'u		
ה	זרע צלח צמח tåz'rī			מצא timṣåna		
ד	שבע wyašbi		א	מלא קרא wimla		
	פתח wyafta		ד	בלע ברא ברח גוע זבח זרע מלא פתח wyibla		
	צמח wyåṣ'mī			קרא רפא שבע שמע		
ט	מצא wyåmṣiyyu			מצא wyimṣå		
				זרח wyazra		
	הפעיל ציווי			צמא wyåṣma		
ב	קרא iqra		ה	בלע ברח מלא פתח קרא שמע wtibla		
				טמא wtiṭmå		
	פיעל עבר		ו	פתח wnifta		
א	שלח šallātti		ט	זבח מלא פתח קרא שמע wyizbā'u		
ב	שלח šallattå			מצא wyimṣå'u		
ד	שלח šalla			שנא wyåšnā'u		
	טמא ṭåmma		י	קרא wtiqrāna		
	קנא qånnå			בלע דלא מלא קרא wtiblā'inna		
ה	שלח šal'lā		ו	זבח niz'bā		
ו	שלח šallānu		א	שמע waš'mā		
ז	שלח šallāttimma		ו	זבח wniz'bā		

			ט	qarrā'u קרע		
			א	ṭåmmā'u טמא		
	nirråfa רפא			wšallåtti שלח	א	
	nimmåṣå מצא קרא		ד	wgalla גלח פרע שלח שסע		
	anniššāma שמע			wṭåmma טמא		
	niššābā'u שבע	ט		wqånnå קנא		
	nibbåqå'u בקע ברא מצא		ה	wgal'lā גלח שלח		
	wniššāba שבע שמע	ד	ט	wqarrā'u קרע שלח		
	wnissåla סלח רפא שכח					
	wniggårå גרע מצא קרא			**פיעל עתיד**		
	wniggå'rå גרע זרע	ה				
	wnifṭånu פלא	ו	א	ēšalla שלח		
	wnimmåṣå'u מצא	ט		ēmålli מלא		
	wnēfåqå'u פקח		ב	tēmašša משח נתח פתח שלח		
				tēṭåmmi טמא		
	נפעל עתיד		ד	yēgalla גלח רקח שלח		
			ז	tēgad'dūn גרע		
	iššāba שבע	א		tēšallā'u שלח		
	timmāna מנע שבע	ב		tēṭåmmiyyu טמא		
	tiššåka שכח		ט	yēgallā'u גלח		
	yiqqāri קרא	ד		yēṭåmmiyyu טמא		
	yikkāna כנע שבע		א	wēšalla שלח		
	yiššåka שכח		ד	wyēgalla גלח משח קרע שלח		
	yiggårå גרע זרע מצא			wyēmålli מלא		
	tiššāba שבע	ה	ה	wtēqanni קנא		
	tiššåka שכח			wtēšalla שלח		
	tizzårå זרע מצא סרח		ט	wyēqannā'u קנא קרע רקע שלח שמע		
	niggårå גרע	ו	ו	nēšal'lā שלח		
	tiššābā'u שבע	ז	א	wēšal'lā שלח		
	tiššåkā'u שכח					
	yiššāmā'u שמע	ט		**פיעל ציווי**		
	yimmåṣå'on מצא					
	yiqqårå'u קרא		ב	šalla שלח		
	wtiššåka שכח	ב		målli מלא		
	wyiqqāri קרא	ד	ז	šallā'u שלח		
	wyiššāba שבע					
	wtimmåli מלא	ה		**פיעל סביל עבר**		
	wtibbåqå בקע שקע					
	wyiššābā'u שבע	ט	ט	šallā'u שלח		
	wyiṣṣåbā'u צבא					
	wyibbåqå'u בקע			**פיעל ב עבר**		
	נפעל ציווי		ב	målåttå מלא		
			ד	måla מלא		
	iššāba שבע	ב	ב	wmålåttå מלא		
			ד	wmåla מלא		
	נפעל ב עבר					
				פיעל ב עתיד		
	niṭṭåmmåtti טמא	א				
	niṭṭåm'mā טמא	ה	ט	yēmålā'u מלא		
	niffattā'u פתח	ט	ד	wyēfåga פגע		
	niṭṭåmmā'u טמא			wyēbåqå בקע פקח		
	wniṭṭåm'mā טמא	ה	ט	wyēmålā'u מלא פגע		
	wniṭṭåmmåttimma טמא	ז	י	wtēfåqåna פקח		
	נפעל ב עתיד			**נפעל עבר**		
	tirraggi רגע	ב	א	niššābātti שבע		
	yiqqarra קרע	ד	ב	niššābåttå שבע		
	tiṭṭåmmā'u טמא	ז	ד	niššāba שבע שמע		

ט תמה wyittammā'u

התפעל עבר
ה טמא iṭṭåm'mā
ד גלח wētgalla

פעלי פ"י

קל עבר
א ידע yādåtti
  יצא yåṣåtti
ב ידע yādåttå
  ירא yårītå*
  יצא yåṣåttå
ד ידע yāda
ה יצא ירא yå'ṣå
  יצא ירא yåṣå
ו ידע yādånnu
  יצא yåṣånnu
ז ידע yādåttimma
  יצא ירא yåṣåttimma
  ידע åyādåttimma
ח ידע yādåttən
ט ידע yādå'u
  יצא ירא yåṣå'u
ב ידע wyādåttå
  יצא ירא wyåṣåttå
ד ידע wyāda
ה יצא wyå'ṣå
ז ידע wyādåttimma
ט ידע wyādå'u

קל עתיד
א ידע idda
  יצא iṣṣå
ב ידע tidda
  יצא tiṣṣå
  ירא tīra
ג ירא tīrā'i
ד ידע yidda
  יצא yiṣṣå
ה יצא tiṣṣå
ו ידע nidda
ז ידע tid'dūn
  ידע tiddā'u
  יצא tiṣṣå'u
  ירא tīrā'on
  ירא tīrā'u
ט ידע yiddā'u
  יצא yiṣṣå'u
א ירא wå'īra
ד ידע wyidda

  יצא wyiṣṣå
  ירא wyīra
ה יצא wtiṣṣå
  יקע wtåqå
ו ידע wnidda
ט ידע wyiddā'u
  יצא wyiṣṣå'u
  ירא wyīrā'u
י ירא wtūrā'inna
  יצא wtåṣå'inna
א ידע id'dā
  ידע wid'dā

קל ציווי
ב ידע dā
  יצא ṣå
  יצא wṣå
ז ידע wdā'u
  יצא ṣå'u

הפעיל עבר
א יצא ūṣåtti
ב יכח ūkåttå
  יצא ūṣåttå
ד יצא ūṣi
  יכח יצא ū'kī
ז יצא ūṣåttimma
ט יצא ūṣiyyu
א יצא u'ūṣåtti
ב ידע u'ūdåttå
  יצא u'ūṣåttå
ד יכח יפע יצא u'ūki
  יכח u'ūkī
ז יצא u'ūṣåttimma
ט יצא u'ūṣiyyu

הפעיל עתיד
א יצא ūṣi
  יצא ū'ṣī
ב יצא tūṣi
  יכח tū'kī
ד יצא yūṣi
ה יצא tūṣi
ו יצא nūṣi
ז יצא tūṣiyyu
ד יצא wyūṣi
  ידע לשע wyū'dī
ה יצא wtūṣi
ט יכח יצא wyūkiyyu

הפעיל ציווי
ב יצא ūṣi
ז יצא ūṣiyyu

386

			הפעיל סביל עבר		
ה	לקח נגע נשא tiqqa		ד	ידע uwwāda	
ו	לקח niqqa				
ז	לקח נגע נשא tiqqā'u		הפעיל סביל עתיד		
ט	לקח נגע נסע נשא yiqqā'u		ד	ידע yūda	
א	לקח נשא wiqqa				
ד	לקח נסע נשא wyiqqa		נפעל עבר		
	נטע wyiṭṭå		א	ידע nūdātti	
ה	לקח נשא wtiqqa		ד	ידע nūda	
ו	לקח wniqqa			ידע wnuwwāda	
ט	לקח נסע נשא wyiqqā'u		ז	ישע wnuwwāšāttimma	
	נסע nis'sā				
	נסע wnis'sā		התפעל עתיד		
			א	ידע ittūda	
קל ציווי			ז	ירא tittūrā'u	
ב	לקח נשא qā				
	לקח נשא wqā		פעלי פ"נ		
ג	נשא šā'i				
ז	לקח נסע נשא qā'u		קל עבר		
	לקח נסע wqā'u		א	לקח lēqātti	
	לקח lēqā'u			נשא nåsātti	
ב	לקח lēqa		ב	לקח lēqāttå	
				נשא nåsāttå	
קל סביל עבר				נטע nåṭåttå	
ב	לקח lēqītå		ד	לקח lēqa	
ד	לקח lēqi			נגע נסע נשא שנא någa	
ה	לקח lēqiy'yā			נטע nåṭå	
			ה	נשא nå'šā	
קל סביל עתיד			ו	לקח lēqānnu	
ד	לקח yiqqa*		ט	לקח lēqā'u	
ה	לקח wtuqqå			נסע נשא nåsa'u	
			א	לקח wlēqātti	
הפעיל עבר				נשא wnåsātti	
ז	נגע wiggāttimma		ב	לקח wlēqāttå	
ט	נשא wåššiyyu			נדח wnådåttå	
			ג	לקח wlēqātti	
הפעיל עתיד			ד	לקח wlēqa	
ד	נסע נפח wyassa			נסע נשא wnåsa	
ט	נדח wyaddiyyu			נדח wnådå	
			ה	לקח wlē'qā	
פיעל עבר			ו	לקח wlēqānnu	
ד	נתח natta		ז	לקח wlēqāttimma	
ט	נתח wnattā'u			נשא wnåsāttimma	
				נטע wnåṭåttimma	
פיעל עתיד			ט	לקח wlēqā'u	
ד	נגח yēnagga			נסע נשא wnåsā'u	
	נגע wyēnagga				
			קל עתיד		
נפעל עבר			א	לקח נשא iqqa	
ז	נסח wnissåttimma		ב	לקח נשא tiqqa	
				נטע tiṭṭå	
התפעל עתיד			ד	לקח נגע נשא yiqqa	
ד	נשא yitnašša				
ז	נשא titnaššā'u				
ג	נשא wtitnašša				

פעלי ע״ו

קל עבר

א	bātti	בוא
ג	bātti	בוא
ד	bā	בוא
ה	bā:	בוא קוא
ו	bānnu	בוא
ז	bāttimma	בוא
ט	bā'u	בוא
ב	wbåttå	בוא
ד	wbā	בוא
ז	wbāttimma	בוא
ט	wbā'u	בוא שוא
	wṭå'u	טוח

קל עתיד

א	å'bū	בוא
ב	tå'bū	בוא
ד	yå'bū	בוא נוח
ה	tēqi	קוא
ו	tå'bū	בוא
ו	nå'bū	בוא
ז	tābā'u	בוא
ט	yābā'u	בוא
י	tābā'inna	בוא
א	wå'bū	בוא
ד	wyanna	נוח
	wyāba	בוא
	wyå'ga*	גוע
ה	wtēqi	קוא
	wtanna	נוח
	wtāba	בוא
ו	wnå'bū	בוא
ז	wtābā'u	בוא
ט	wyannā'u	נוע
י	wyābā'u	בוא
	wtābā'inna	בוא

קל ציווי

ב	bā	בוא
ג	wbā'i	בוא
ז	bā'u	בוא
	wbā'u	בוא

הפעיל עבר

א	ībåtti	בוא
ב	ībåttå	בוא
ד	ībi	בוא
	anni	נוא
ז	ībåttimma	בוא
ט	ībiyyu	בוא
א	wīnētti	נוח
	wībåtti	בוא
ב	wībåttå	בוא
ד	wībi	בוא
	wånni	נוח
	wån'nī	נוח
ה	wībiyya	בוא
ז	wībåttimma	בוא
	warrāttimma	רוע
ט	wībiyyu	בוא

הפעיל עתיד

א	ībi	בוא
	åri	רוח
ב	tībi	בוא
ג	tībi	בוא
ד	yībi	בוא
	yanni	נוא נוח
	yan'nī	נוח
ז	tībiyyon	בוא
	tībiyyu	בוא
	tanniyyon	נוא
ט	yībiyyon	בוא
	yībiyyu	בוא
	yåriyyon	רוח
י	tībiyyinna	בוא
א	wībi	בוא
ד	wyībi	בוא
	wyåri	רוח
	wyå'rī	רוח
ה	wtågi*	גוע
ט	wyībiyyu	בוא
	wyanniyyu	נוא נוח

הפעיל ציווי

ב	ībi	בוא
	wånni	נוח
ז	anniyyu	נוח
	wībiyyu	בוא
ב	anniy'yē lli	נוח

הפעיל סביל עבר

ד	uwwāba	בוא
ט	uwwābā'u	בוא
ד	wēwwāba	בוא

פא ולמד גרוניות

קל עבר

א	ēṭåtti	חטא
	'åṭīti	חטא
ד	'åṭå	חטא
ו	'åṭīnu	חטא
ז	'åṭītimma	חטא

ט	חטא ʻåṭåʼu			
א	חטא wåṭīti		קל עתיד	
ב	חטא wåṭītå		ד	רעע zḥḥ yazza
ה	חטא wēʼṭå		ה	רעע tirra
ז	חטא wåṭītimma			רעע tarra
			ד	רעע wyarra
	קל עתיד			
ד	חטא yēṭṭi			הפעיל עבר
ה	חטא tēṭṭi		א	רעע arrātti
ז	חטא tēṭṭiyyu		ב	רעע arrāttå
	חטא tēṭṭåʼu		ד	רעע åra
א	חבא wåʼibba		ז	רעע arrāttimma
ט	אנח wyåːnåʼu			
				הפעיל עתיד
	הפעיל עתיד		ו	רעע narri
ז	חטא tåṭṭiyyu		ז	רעע tarriyyu
ט	חטא yåṭṭiyyu		ט	רעע wyarriyyu
	פיעל עבר			הפעלים הרבעיים
ד	חטא wåṭṭå			
				התפעל עבר
	פיעל עתיד		ו	מהמה itmåmånu
ד	חטא wyåṭṭi			
				התפעל עתיד
	נפעל עבר		ד	מהמה wyitmåmå
ב	חבא nåʼibtå*			
				התפעל עבר
	התפעל עתיד		ב	שחוי wēštåbbītå
ד	חטא yētåṭṭå		ז	שחוי wēštåbbītimma
ז	חטא tētåṭṭåʼu		ט	שחוי wēštåbbu
ט	חטא wyētåṭṭåʼu			
				התפעל עתיד
	התפעל ב עתיד		ב	שחוי tištåbbi
ד	חבא wyētåbå		א	שחוי wištåbbi
			ד	שחוי wyištåbbi
	עין ולמד גרוניות		ו	שחוי wništåbbi
			ט	שחוי wyištåbbu
	קל עבר		י	שחוי wtištåbbīyyinna
ד	רעע rā*			
ה	רעע wrāː			

ד. Pronominal Suffixes on Verbs

The order in which the forms cited below appear is determined by their suffixes (see the list of abbreviations above, p. XXX, section [1]). The reader should bear in mind that in a combination such as "ב+א", the element on the left represents the pronominal suffix, and it is, therefore, the primary determinant of the order of forms. Each such pair of abbreviations appears only once alongside the first finite form listed, and is not repeated with each stem.

א. Verbs Except III-Guttural and ל"ה

עבר

קל

ד+ב   שׂוּם såmåk

אמר å:måråk
ילד עבד yålådåk
עבד wåbådåk
נתן wnåtånåk

הפעיל

פוץ īfīṣåk
ילך ūlīkåk
יתר u'ūtīråk
פוץ שוב wīfīṣåk
שמד wåšmīdåk

פיעל

ברך barrēkåk
ברך קבץ wbarrēkåk

פיעל ב

אהב å'ēbåk
אהב wå'ēbåk
רחם wrā'ēmåk
שאל wså'ēlåk

קל

ט+ב   גמל רדף gåmålok
עבד wåbådok
רדף wrådåfok

הפעיל

אבד abbīdok
שמד ašmīdok
נשג wåššīgok

קל

א+ג   הרג årigtək

קל

א+ד   שׂוּם šamtiyyu

עבר

קל

ב+א   זכר עזב zåkårtåni
עבד wåbådtåni
קבר wqåbårtåni

הפעיל

זכר wåzkirtåni

פיעל

ברך נטש barriktåni

קל

ד+א   חנן ånåni
דון שׂוּם dånåni
אכל åkēlåni
זבר עצר zåbådåni
שמר wšåmåråni

קל

ט+א   אשר åšårūni
הרג עזב wårågūni
סקל wsåqålūni

פיעל ב

כעס kā'ēsūni
נאץ wnā'ēṣūni

קל

א+ב   נתן עבר שכר nåtåttək
שׂוּם wšamtək
נתן שמר wnåtåttək

הפעיל

עמד 'å:mådtək
שוב wīšibtək

פיעל

ברך wbarriktək

yålidtiyyu ילד			wṭå'ēru טהר	
nåtåttiyyu נתן סמך				
wnåtåttiyyu נתן			åkålittu אכל	קל ד+ה
	הפעיל			
wåṣṣigtiyyu יצג				קל
wåkådēttiyyu כחד			wregåmē'u רגם	ט+ד
	פיעל		wåkålē'u אכל	
wbarriktiyyu ברך				הפעיל
wgarreštiyyu גרש			akkīrē'u נכר	
		קל	ūrīdē'u ירד	
wåråftu ערף		ב+ד		
wqåbittu קוב				קל
wsåqåltu סקל			nåtåttiyya נתן	א+ה
wnåtåttu נתן				
wåkålittu אכל				קל
	הפעיל		wbålåtå בלע	ב+ה
wīšibtu שוב			wyåråštå ירש	
	פיעל			פיעל
wqaddištu קדש			wnaṭṭištå נטש	
	פיעל ב			
wåsiftu אסף				קל
		קל	årårå ארר	ד+ה
zā:mu זעם		ד+ד	wbāla בלע	
qåbu קוב			wåkēla אכל	
årågu הרג			wnåtåna נתן תפש	
nåtånu נתן				הפעיל
wšåmu שום			å'īda עוד	
wšåṭṭu שחט			wåmmīda עמד	
wåbådu עבד			wåggīša נגש	
wzåråqu זרק נתן			wåqrība קרב	
	הפעיל			פיעל
īdīfu דוף			'aššēba חשב מכר	
akkīru נכר			wyabbēma יבם	
ašmīdu שמד				
åṣṣīlu נצל				קל
wåmmīdu עמד ערך			'åfåruw'wā חפר	ט+ה
wåggīšu נגש נפל נשג			wnåluw'wā נחל	
wåbdīlu בדל סגר קרב			wåkåluw'wā אכל	
	פיעל		wsåqåluw'wā סקל	
barrēku ברך דבר חלל חנך				פיעל ב
barrēkē'u ברך			wnå'iltånu נחל	ב+ו
wmakkēru מכר קדש				הפעיל
	פיעל ב		åṣṣīlånu נצל	ד+ו
å'ēbu אהב				פיעל
			makkērånu מכר	

		עתיד		
קל	נתן nåtåttimma		קל	
א+ט	עזב wåzåbtimma		א+ב	קבר tiqbårinni
	דפק wdåfåqtimma		הפעיל	
פיעל ב			שבר tašbīråni	
	גאל מאס gā'eltimma		קל	
קל			א+ד	זבל yizbålinni
ב+ט	שום wšamtimma			מוש yēmūšinni
	עבד wåbådtimma			הרג yårågåni
	ירש כתב סקל קשר wyåråštimma			עבד wyābbådåni
הפעיל				שום wyåsīmåni
	ירש u'ūreštimma		הפעיל	
	נשג wåššegtimma			נצל wyåṣṣīlåni
	לבש wålbeštimma		פיעל	
פיעל				עקב wyāqqēbåni
	אבד wabbedtimma			ברך wyēbarrēkåni
	גרש קדש שנן wgarreštimma		פיעל ב	
קל				אהב yå'ēbåni
ד+ט	שות šåtimma			נאץ yēnā'eṣinni
	הום wåmimma		קל	
	לבש נתן wlåbåšimma		ה+א	דבק tidbåqinni
הפעיל			פיעל	
	פוץ פור īfīšimma			ברך tēbarrēkinni
	סגר שמד asgīrimma		קל	
	נחל ånīlimma		ט+א	הרג yårågūni
	קטר wåqṭīrimma		קל	
פיעל			א+ב	עבד ēbbådåk
	מכר makkērimma			שום åšīmåk
קל				עזב 'åzåbåk
ה+ט	גנב gånbåtimma			מוש wēmūšåk
קל			הפעיל	
ט+ט	שער šårumma			עוץ å'īṣåk
	סתם såtåmumma			עוץ wā'īṣåk
	עבד wåbådumma		פיעל	
	שפט wšåfåṭumma			ברך ēbarrēkåk
הפעיל				ברך wēbarrēkåk
	קרב aqrībumma		פיעל ב	
	שאל wåsīlumma			כבד ēkåbēdåk
פיעל			קל	
	גרש garrēšumma		ד+ב	נתן yittēnåk

391

	עשׂר 'āššīrinnu			ירשׁ yīråšåk
	ירשׁ u'ūrīšinnu			שׁוף yēšūfåk
	שׁלך wašlīkē'u			עבד yēbbådåk
		פיעל		שׂום yåšīmåk
	גרשׁ ēgarrēšinnu			עזב yåzåbåk
	גרשׁ wēgarrēšinnu			שׁמר wyišmåråk
	ברך wēbarrēkē'u			רעב wyårå:båk
	רום wērūmēminnē'u			עזר wyåzzåråk
		קל		קל ב
	נתן tittēninnu	ב+ד		פגשׁ yēfågåšåk
	קבב tiqqåbinnu			הפעיל
	דרשׁ קבר שׂרף שׁפך tidråšinnu			קום yīqīmåk
	תעב tētå:binnu			סות yassītåk
	שׁוף tēšūfinnu			רפף yarrēfåk
	שׂום tåšīminnu			שׁחת yåšīttåk
	הרג עזב tårråginnu			חנן yå'ēnåk
	אכל tå'ūkēlinnu			נחל yånnīlåk
				נגד wyaggīdåk
		הפעיל		אכל wyåkīlåk
	שׁוב tīšībinnu			חנן wyå'ēnåk
	עבט tåbbīṭinnu			פיעל
	רוב wtårībē'u			ברך yēbarrēkåk
		פיעל		קבץ yēqåbbēṣåk
	חלל tållīlinnu			ברך wyēbarrēkåk
	בקשׁ ברך tēbaqqēšinnu			כון wyēkūnēnåk
	שׁקץ tēšåqqēṣinnu			פיעל ב
	חלל wtållēlē'u			נהג yēnå'ēgåk
		קל		שׁאל yēšå'ēlåk
	נתן yittēninnu	ד+ד		פיעל
	נדב yiddåbinnu			ברך tēbarrēkåk
	דרשׁ שׁמר yidråšinnu			ה+ב
	שׂום yåšīminnē'u			פיעל ב
	אכל yå'ūkēlinnu			שׁאל tēšå'ēlåk
	נתן wyittēnē'u			קל
	משׁק שׁתת wyiššåqē'u			רדף yirdåfok
	זרק טמן שׂרף wyizråqē'u			עבד yåbbådok
	שׁחט wyēšåṭṭē'u			ט+ב
	מושׁ wyēmūšē'u			פיעל
	שׂום wyåšīmē'u			שׁרת wyēšarrētok
	הרג טחן wyåråġē'u			קל
	צור wyåṣårinnē'u			דרשׁ idråšinnu
		קל ב		ערב ērråbinnu
	פגשׁ wyēfågåšē'u			שׂום åšīminnu
		הפעיל		שׁור åšūrinnu
מור מות נוף פור קום yīmīrinnu				הפעיל
	ינק yīnīqē'u			שׁוב īšībinnu
	גדר yaggīdinnu			
	סגר קרב yasgīrinnu			

	רכב yarkībē'u		
	דוף yåddīfinnu*		
	חלף חסל ערך yållīfinnu		
	קטר yåqṭīrinnu		
	קום yåqīminnu		
	אכל אמץ yåkīlē'u	הפעיל	
	נצל wyåṣṣīlu	כעס yåkīsē'u	
	מות נוף wyīmītē'u	רוב רוץ wyåŕībē'u	
	פקד שלך wyafqīdē'u		
	עמד wyåmmīdē'u	פיעל	
		חלל yållīlē'u	
	פיעל	שרת yēšarrētē'u	
	חלל yållīlinnu	מרר wyēmarrērē'u	
	חנך yånnīkinnu*		
	סבב yēsūbēbinnē'u	קל	
	חבק wyåbbēqē'u	נתן ittēninna	א+ה
	בנן ברך קדש wyēbannēnē'u	ירש īråšinna	
		קבר wiqbårå	
	פיעל ב		
	גאל yēgå'ēlinnu	הפעיל	
	נהג wyēnå'ēgē'u	שוב īšībinna	
	שאל wyēšå'ēlē'u	חוט 'å'īṭinnå	
	קל	קל	
	תפש wtitfåšē'u	ה+ד	נתן tittēninna	ב+ה
		אכל tå'ūkēlinna	
	הפעיל		
	ירש tūrišmu	הפעיל	
	ינק wtīnīqē'u	שוב tūšībinna	
	צפן wtåṣfīnē'u	שמט tåšmīṭinna	
		נחל tånīlinna	
	קל		
	הרג wnåråğē'u	ו+ד	פיעל	
		מכר tēmakkērinna	
	הפעיל		
	שלך wnašlīkē'u	קל	
		נתן yittēninna	ד+ה
	פיעל	ירש yīråšinna	
	מכר nēmakkērinnu	אכל yå'ūkēlinna	
		נתן wyittēna	
	פיעל ב	שתת wyiššåtå	
	לחם wnēlå'imnu*		
		הפעיל	
	קל	סור קום yīsīrinna	
	חגג tåggē'u	ז+ד	עוד yå'īdinna	
	אכל tå'ūkēlē'u	קטר yåqṭīrinna	
		נחל yånīlinna	
	פיעל	נכר wyakkēra	
	לקט tēlåqqēṭē'u	רום wyårēma	
	קל	פיעל	
	רגם yirgåmē'u	ט+ד	שלם yēsallēminna	
	אכל yå'ūkēlē'u	חשב wyåššēba	
	שטם wyištåmē'u	למד wyēlammēda	
		פיעל ב	
		מהר yēmå'ērinna	
		אהב wyå'ēba	

393

קל

ט+ה	ירש yīråšuw'wā		
	אכל yå'ūkēluw'wā		
	לכד wyilkåduw'wā		

הפעיל

ב+ו	עבר tābbīrånu

קל

ד+ו	שטם yištåmånu

הפעיל

אכל yåkīlånu

פיעל ב

נחם yēnå'ēmånu

קל

ה+ו	אכל tå'ūkēlånu

קל

ט+ו	סקל yisqålånu

קל

ט+ז	עזר wyåzzårūkimma

קל

א+ט	שום wåšīmimma

הפעיל

חלק כעס ålīqimma
שלך שמד wašlīkimma
פוץ wå:fīṣimma

פיעל

ברך ēbarrēkimma
ברך wēbarrēkimma
שבר wēšåbbårimma

קל

ב+ט	פקד tifqådimma
	צור tēṣūrimma
	הרס tērråsimma
	עבד tåbbådimma

הפעיל

שוב tīšībimma
חרם tårīmimma
חנן tå'ēnimma

פיעל

למד tēlammēdimma

קל

ד+ט	אחז yāzzåmu
	לבש yilbåšimma
	שום yåšīmimma
	אכל yå'ūkēlå:mu
	נתן wyittēnimma
	נתש wyittåšimma
	כתב פקד רדף wyiktåbimma
	שחט wyēšåṭṭimma

הפעיל

שמד yašmīdimma
יצג נכר נשג wyaṣṣīgimma
לבש רכב שלך שמד wyalbīšimma
עבר wyābbīrimma
נצל wyåṣṣīlimma
נחל wyånīlimma

פיעל

גרש yēgarrēšimma
אבד wyåbbēdimma
ברך wyēbarrēkimma

קל

ה+ט	אכל tå'ūkēlimma
	שום wtåšīmimma

קל

ו+ט	עבד wnābbådimma

קל

ט+ז	רגם tirgåmumma
	אכל tå'ūkēlumma

קל

ט+ט	ירש yīråšumma
	נתן wyittēnumma
	כתת wyikkåtumma
	סתם wyiståmumma
	ירש wyīråšumma

הפעיל

שאל wyåšī:lumma

פיעל

גרש wyēgarrēšumma

ציווי

קל

ב+א	הרג ērågåni

חזק wazzīqē'u*		הפעיל	
		נצל åṣṣīlåni	
	הפעיל	לוט ålīṭåni	
ינק wīnīqē'u	ג+ד	שוב wīšībåni	
	קל		פיעל
אכל ēkålē'u	ז+ד	ברך barrēkåni	
	פיעל		קל
למד wlammēda	ב+ה	קבב wqåbinnu	ב+ד
	קל		הפעיל
אכל wēkåluw'wā	ז+ה	שלך ašlīkē'u	
כבש wkēbåšuw'wā		עלי wållē'u	
	פיעל ב		פיעל
סחר så'ēruw'wā		כן kūnēnu	
		אמץ wammīṣē'u	

ב. III-Guttural Verbs

שמע ידע yādāttək		עבר	
לקח wlēqāttək			קל
	הפעיל	נשא wnåšāttåni	ב+א
יצא ūṣåttək			הפעיל
	פיעל	ידע ūdāttåni	
שלח šallāttək		יצא u'ūṣåttåni	
	קל		פיעל
מנע må'nāk	ד+ב	שלח šallattåni	
נשא nå'šāk			קל
קרא qå'råk		לקח lēqānni	ד+א
	הפעיל		הפעיל
שבע שמע ašbiyyåk		בוא ībbiyyåni	
יצא ūṣiyyåk		נשא aššiyyåni	
בוא wībiyyåk		שבע ašbiyyåni	
	קל		פיעל
נגע någānok	ו+ב	שלח šallāni	
	קל		קל
מצא wmåṣå'ok	ט+ב	מצא måṣå'ūni	ט+א
	קל		פיעל
שמע wšāmāttiyyu	א+ד	קנא qånnå'ūni	
	הפעיל		קל
בוא ībåttiyyu		לקח lēqāttək	א+ב
ידע u'ūdāttiyyu			
בוא wībåttiyyu			

	שלח wšal'lā			פיעל ב	
		קל	מלא målāttiyyu		
ידע yā'dā	ט+ה			קל	
		קל	ידע yādāttu	ב+ד	
לקח lēqåṭṭånu	ב+ו		מצא wmåṣåttu		
		הפעיל		הפעיל	
בוא ībåṭṭånu			נוח wīnēttu		
יצא ūṣåṭṭånu				קל	
		פיעל	נשא nåšā'u	ד+ר	
שלח šallaṭṭånu			ידע yādā'ē'u		
		הפעיל	רצח wrēṣå'u		
יצא ūṣiyyånu	ד+ו		טבח wṭåbē'u		
		פיעל		הפעיל	
שלח šallānu			בוא ībiyyu		
		קל	נוח wånniyyu		
מצא måṣåṭṭånu	ה+ו			פיעל	
		קל	פרע farrā'u		
שמע šāmåṭṭimma	א+ט		שלח šallā'ē'u		
		הפעיל	חטא wåṭṭå'u		
ידע u'ūdåṭṭimma	ב+ט		טמא wṭåmmā'u		
נוח wīnēttimma				קל	
		קל	מצא wmåṣå'ē'u	ט+ד	
ברא bårå'imma	ד+ט			קל	
		הפעיל	מצא måṣåṭṭiyya	א+ה	
יצא ūṣīyyimma				קל	
נוח wånnīyyimma			מצא måṣåṭṭå	ב+ה	
		קל	מצא wmåṣåṭṭå		
מצא måṣåṭṭimma	ה+ט			הפעיל	
		הפעיל	בוא wībåṭṭå		
בוא ībiyyånumma	ו+ט			פיעל	
		קל	שלח wšallāttā		
ידע yādā'umma	ט+ט			קל	
		הפעיל	לקח lē'qā	ד+ה	
בוא wībiyyumma			שנא šå'nā		
			מצא må'ṣå		
	עתיד		לקח wlē'qā		
		קל	שנא wšå'nā		
שמע yišmānni	ד+א		מצא wmå'ṣå		
				הפעיל	
			בוא wībiyya		
				פיעל	
			שלח šal'lā		

הפעיל	שבע wyašbiyyånì	יצא	wyūṣiyyē'u
פיעל	שלח wyēšallānni	פיעל	
		גלה שלח	yēgallā'innu
פיעל		טמא	yēṭåmmā'innu
ז+א	שלח wtēšallūni	חטא	wyåṭṭiyyē'u
קל		שלח	wyēšallā'ē'u
א+ב	לקח iq'qāk	נפעל	
	ידע wid'dāk	שכח	wyiššåkå'ē'u
הפעיל		קל	
	שבע wašbiyyåk	ה+ד	מלא timlā:mu
פיעל		הפעיל	
	שלח ēsal'lāk	בוא	wtībiyyē'u
	שלח wēsal'lāk	קל	
קל		ז+ד	זבח tizbā'ē'u
ד+ב	לקח yiq'qāk	הפעיל	
	קרא åyiq'rāk	ט+ד	קנא yaqniyyē'u
הפעיל			נוח wyanniyyē'u
	בוא yībiyyåk	הפעיל	
	נדח yaddiyyåk	ב+ה	tībiyyinna
	יצא wyūṣiyyåk	קל	
פיעל		ד+ה	לקח yiqqā'inna
ו+ב	שלח wnēšallāk		מצא wyim'ṣå
הפעיל			לקח wyiq'qā
א+ד	בוא ībiyyinnu		שנא wyåš'nā
קל		הפעיל	
ב+ד	לקח tiqqā'innu		בוא yībiyyinna
	זבח tizbā'innu		בוא wyībiyya
פיעל			יצא wyūṣiy'yā
	שלח tēšallā'innu	פיעל	
קל		שלח	wyēsal'lā
ד+ד	קרא yiqrānnu	קל	
	נשא yiššā'ē'u	ה+ה	לקח wtiq'qā
	לקח wyiqqā'ē'u		פתח wtif'tā
	מצא wyimṣå'ē'u	קל	
	תקע wyatqā'ē'u	ט+ה	גבה wyigbā'uw'wā*
הפעיל		הפעיל	
	בוא yībiyyinnu		בוא wyībiyyuw'wā
	רשע yaršīyyinnu	הפעיל	
	בוא wyībiyyē'u	ד+ו	בוא wyībiyyånu
	נוח wyanniyyē'u		שמע wyašmiyyånu
			יצא wyūṣiyyånu

397

	פיעל			פיעל
ט+ע	רקע wyēraqqāʾumma		שלח	wyēšallānu
	פיעל ב			פיעל ב
	מלא wyēmålāʾumma		פגע	yēfågånnu
	הפעיל			קל
ד+י	ישע wyūšīyyinna		בלע	tiblānu
			קרא	tiqrånnu
	ציווי			הפעיל
	קל		קנא	aqniyyimma
ב+א	שמע šāmānni		שמע	wašmiyyimma
	הפעיל			קל
	ידע ūdiyyåni		ירא	tūrāʾimma
			נטע	wtiṭṭå:mu
	פיעל			הפעיל
	שלח šallāni		בוא	tibyå:mu
	הפעיל			קל
ג+א	גמא agmiyyåni		כנע	yiknāʾimma
	קל		לקח	wyiqqāʾimma
ז+א	שמע šēmāʾūni		מצא	wyimṣåʾimma
	פיעל		נוע	wyannāʾimma
	שלח šallūni			הפעיל
	קל		בוא	yībiyyimma
ב+ר	נשא šåʾēʾu		יצא	yūṣiyyimma
	בקע wbåqåʾēʾu			פיעל
	הפעיל		שלח	yēšallāʾimma
ז+ה	יצא ūṣiyyuwʷā		משח שלח	wyēmaššāʾimma
	קל			קל
ב+ט	לקח qåʾimma		בלע	tiblā:mu
	כלא kēlāʾimma		בלע	wtiblāʾimma
				קל
			ירא	tūrāʾumma
				פיעל
			שלח	tēšallāʾumma

ג. Verbs ל״ה

	הפעיל			עבר
	נכי akkītåni			קל
	פיעל ב		רמי	råmītåni
	צוי ṣåbītåni	ב+א		

		קל			קל
ד+ד	עשׂי ק 'āšē'u		א+ד	נחי nå:ni	
	נחי nå'ē'u				הפעיל
	עשׂי wāšē'u			פרי ifrå̊ni	
	קרי wqārē'u			נחי ånå̊ni	
		הפעיל		נכי wå̊kkå̊ni	
	נכי akkē'u				פיעל
	נכי wå̊kkē'u			נשׁי niššå̊ni	
		פיעל			פיעל ב
	כסי kassē'u			צוי ṣå̊bå̊ni	
	נסי nå̊sså̊'ē'u				הפעיל
	כסי wkassē'u			נכי wå̊kkūni	
		פיעל ב	ט+א		הפעיל
	צוי ṣå̊bē'u		א+ב	ראי arrå̊ttək	
		פיעל		ירי u'ūrītək	
ב+ה	עני 'annīta			רבי wå̊rbītək	
		קל			פיעל
ד+ה	שחת wšå̊tå̊			כלי wkallītək	
		הפעיל			פיעל ב
	פרי wå̊få̊då̊			צוי ṣå̊bītək	
		פיעל			קל
	עני 'an'nā		ד+ב	עשׂי 'å̊šå̊k	
		קל		ראי wrå̊k	
ט+ה	כרי kå̊ruw'wā				הפעיל
		הפעיל		ראי ar'rå̊k	
ב+ו	חיי 'ā'ītå̊nu			רבי wå̊rå̊bbå̊k	
	עלי 'āllītå̊nu				פיעל ב
		הפעיל		צוי ṣå̊bå̊k	
ד+ו	ראי arrå̊nu			צוי wṣå̊bå̊k	
	עלי 'å̊llå̊nu				הפעיל
		פיעל ב	ט+ב	עלי 'å̊llok	
	צוי ṣå̊bå̊nu				קל
		קל	א+ד	משׁי må̊šīttiyyu	
א+ט	עשׂי 'åššītimma			ראי rå̊'ītiyyu	
		פיעל ב			פיעל ב
	צוי ṣå̊bītimma			צוי ṣå̊bītiyyu	
		קל			פיעל
ב+ט	עשׂי waššītimma		ב+ד	נסי nassītē'u	

הפעיל				
נכי wåkkītimma				
קל		קל		
ד+ט		ה+ב	tånnåk עני	
נחי nå'imma				
ראי rå'imma		הפעיל		
פיעל		ט+ב	yūdok ידי ירי	
כסי kasså:mu		קל		
פיעל ב		א+ד	ēmīyyinnu מחי	
צוי ṣåbimma		קל ב		
			ērē'innu ראי	
עתיד			wērē'innu ראי	
הפעיל		הפעיל		
ב+א	tållåni עלי		akkinnu נכי	
	wtårṣīni רצי	פיעל		
קל ב			ēnassinnu נסי	
ד+א	yērē'inni ראי	פיעל ב		
הפעיל			ēṣåbinnu צוי	
נחי yånåni			wēṣåbinnu צוי	
ראי yarriyyåni			wēnåbē'u נוי	
קל ב		קל		
ה+א	wtērē'inni ראי	ב+ד	tilwannu לוי	
קל			tēššinnu עשי	
א+ב	wēššåk עשי		tiqnā'ē'u קני	
הפעיל		קל ב		
ראי ar'råk			tērē'innu ראי	
עלי 'ållåk			tēfēdinnu פדי	
פיעל		הפעיל		
כלי ēkållåk			tūninnu יני	
פיעל ב		פיעל		
צוי ēṣåbåk			tēṣåbbinnu צפי	
קל		קל		
ד+ב	yilwåk לוי	ד+ד	yā:ninnu עני	
קל ב			wyāššē'u עשי	
	wyåfådåk פדי		wyiqnā'ē'u קני	
הפעיל		הפעיל		
נכי yikkåk			yakkinnu נכי	
פרי רבי wyifråk			wyållē'u עלי	
עני wyā:nåk			wyarriyyē'u ראי	
		פיעל		
			yēkassinnu כסי	
			wyēkassē'u כסי	
			wyēṣåbbē'u צפי	

401

פיעל ב	צוי wyēṣåbånu		פיעל ב	צוי yēṣåbē'u
				צוי wyēṣåbē'u
פיעל			הפעיל	
ט+ו	עני wyānnēnu		ה+ד	שקי wtašqiyyē'u
פיעל			הפעיל	
ט+א	כלי wēkallimma		ו+ד	נכי nakkinnu
פיעל ב				שקי našqinnu
ט+ב	צוי tēṣåbimma			נכי wnakkinnu
הפעיל			פיעל	
ט+ד	נכי wyakkimma		ה+ב	כלי tēkallinna
פיעל			קל	
	כסי yēkassiyyå:mu		ה+ד	עשי wyāša
	צפי wyēṣåbbimma			
פיעל ב			קל ב	
צוי wyēṣåbimma			ראי yērē'inna
הפעיל				ראי wyē'rā
ט+ו	נכי wnakkimma		פיעל	
הפעיל			עני wyānna
ט+ט	נכי wyakkumma		הפעיל	
	ראי wyå:rumma		ה+ה	עני wtā:na
			קל	
ציווי			ה+ו	עשי wnēššinna
קל			קל ב	
ב+א	מחי mīni		ה+ט	ראי yērē'uw'wā
הפעיל			קל	
	ראי arriyyåni		ו+ד	רדי yardinnu
הפעיל			הפעיל	
ג+א	שקי ašqiyyåni			נחי yå:nēnu

ה. Verbal Nouns

For each type of verbal noun — the participle and the infinitive — the forms are organized according to the same general headings ("guttural roots" and "non-guttural roots") and classes as those applied to the finite verbs. Nonetheless, an effort has been made to avoid generating an overabundance of rubrics for the classes, since the transition from class to class is evident from even a cursory look at the roots recorded in Hebrew letters. It should be borne in mind that the verbal nouns derived from quadriradical roots are listed after the triradical roots in the same section.

א. Verbs Formed from Non-Guttural Roots

א. הבינוני הפועל

	שפט šūfåṭīkimma	ר+ז			קל
	שפט šūfåṭīyyimma	ר+ט	כתב רכב רמש שכב שכן שפך kētəb		
			רבץ rēbåṣ		
	הפעיל		גנב טרף שכב שכן gånəb		
	בדל קרב mabdəl		דרש כרת משל קסם שמר תפש dåråš		
	מטר פרס קטר måmṭər		פקד פתר רדף fūqəd		
	זכר måzåkər		שפט šūfåṭ		
	קדש קרב שבר ammaqdəš		פתר fåtårå*		
	שכל maškēla	נ	רמש arrēməš		
	פרס måfrīsåt	ס+נ	משל קרב ammåšål		
	זכר måzåkīråt		זרק רמש שכב שכן azzūrəq		
	שכן maškinta	ה	שפט aššūfåṭ		
	קדש קרב maqdīšəm	ר	שרץ aššūrəṣ		
	קצף måqṣīfəm		שמר åšūmər		
	קרב maqrībi	ס+ר	שפט åšūfåṭ		
	פרס wmimmåfrīsi		גנב wgånəb		
			דרש wdåråš		
	פיעל		פתר רדף wfūtər		
	גרש דבר מכר garrəš		שרף שכב waššūrəf		
	בקש למד måbaqqəš		שפט walšūfåṭ		
	גדף דבר כשף שרת amgaddəf		רבץ rēbīṣåt	נ
	דבר ammådabbər		גבר gēbēra		
	שלם wamšalləm		רמש arråmšət		
	כשף amkaššēfa	נ	רמש שרץ arrūmīšåt		
	רבך amrabbēkət		רכב rikbu	ד
	ברך ambarrēkək	ג	שפך šafku		
	ברך wambarrēkək		רכב wrikbu		
	קדש שרת amqaddēšu	ד	קרב qårbəm	ר
	שרת wamšarrētu		רבץ שבר rēbīṣəm		
	קדש amqaddeškimma	ז	שפט šūfåṭəm		
	קדש amqaddēšimma	ט	דבק addēbīqəm		
	דבר dabbērəm	ר	משל קסם ammåšåləm		
	בקש måbaqqēšəm		שפט aššūfåṭəm		
	רגל amraggēləm		שפט waššūfåṭəm		
	בקש דבר ammåbaqqēšəm		תפש tēfēši	ס+ר
	כשף walmåkaššēfəm		שמר šåmēri		
	רגל kamraggēləm		פרש שפט fåråši		
	דבר dabbērot	נ+ר	שמר walšåmēri		

403

		amšåbbēṣot* שבץ	
		åmšåbbēṣot* שבץ	
		måbaqqēši בקש	ר+ס
		פיעל ב	
		amqåbårəm קבר	ר
		נפעל	
		nikbåd כבד	
		annikbåd כבד שקף	
		anniṣṣåmēdəm צמד	ר
		wnikbådəm כבד	
		wannistårəm סתר	
		annistårot סתר	ר+נ
		קל	
		yēšəb ישב	
		yūšəb ישב	
		abyūšəb ישב	
		ayyēšəb ישב	
		ayyånəq ינק	
		ayyūrəd ירד	
		wyånåq ינק	
		wayyēšəb ישב	
		alyūšəb ישב	
		yēšībåt ישב	נ
		yēbēša יבש	
		yåriššåt ירש	
		yålēdåt ילד	
		ayyålēdåt ילד	
		åyånåqå ינק	
		yūsīfəm יסף	ר
		yūrēšəm ירש ישב	
		ayyūšēbəm ישב	
		wyårēdəm ירד	
		yūšēbi ישב	ר+ס
		yūšēbiyya ישב	ר+ה
		הפעיל	
		måṣṣəb יצב	
		mīnqåt ינק	נ
		ammūlīkåk ילד	ב
		mīniqta ינק	ה
		mūrīšimma ירש	ט
		mīnqot ינק	ר
		פיעל	
		åmyallēdət ילד	נ
		amyåssåråk יסר	ב
		åmyallēdot ילד	ר+נ
		lamyallēdot ילד	
		låmyallēdot ילד	

נפעל

nūšån ישן
annūtår יתר
annuwwåləd ילד
wannūtår יתר
nūšåbåt ישב נ
annūtårət יתר
wannūtårət יתר
annūtårəm יתר ר
annuwwålēdəm ילד

קל

nēfəl נפל נצב נתן
någəf נגף נדף נתן
nåṣår נצר נתן
nūtən נתן
annēfəl נפל
annūdər נדר משך נתן
wnåqåb נקב
nēṣība נצב נ
nåfålåt נפל
nēfīləm נצב ר
annēgīšəm נגש נצב
wannēgīšəm נגש
nēgīši נגש ר+ס
nēgīšo נגש ר+ד

הפעיל

maggəd נגד נסג
måṣṣəl נצל
måṣågåt נשג נ

קל

går גור דן זוב זוך רום
aggår גור זוב
aṣṣod צוד
wnad נוד
wråm רום
wazzåb זוב
zåka זוך נ
zåbå זוב רום
qå'ēma קום
baqqå'ēma קום
aqqå'ēma קום
zåbåt זוב ס+נ
qåmək קום ג
arråməm רום ר
aqqå'ēməm קום
qåmo קום ר+ד

הפעיל

mīqəm קום שוב
mårəm רום

	waddåbå דוי				kåmīšəb שוב	
	alzūna זני				wamgīråt גור	נ+ס
	qånåk קני	ב			mårīqəm רוק	ר
	wåfådåk פרי				wmådībot דוב	נ+ר
	qånē'u קני	ד				
	båkəm בכי זני נצי	ר		**נפעל**		
	azzånəm זני				nåbon בון כון	
	aqqārot קרי	נ+ר			wnåbon בון	
					nåkūnəm כון	ר
הפעיל					wnåbūnəm בון	
	makki נכי					
	wmazzi מי נכי			**התפעל**		
	måṭi נטי				mistūlål סול	
	ammakki נכי					
	marbi רבי שקי שתי			**קל**		
	ammarbi רבי שקי				måk מכך	
	mukkå נכי	נ			zūlål זלל סרר	
	mafriyyåk פרי	ב			aṣṣårår צרר	
	makkē'u נכי שקי	ד			assūbåb סבב	
	makkəm נכי מרי רבי	ר			aššūgīgåt שגג	נ
	ammašqəm שקי				ṣåråråk צרר	ג
					ṣåråṛəm צרר	ר
פיעל					sūkēkəm סכך	
	mēkassi כסי				gåzåzi גזז	נ+ס
	båmēkassi כסי					
	amnassi נסי שגי			**הפעיל**		
	åmkassi כסי				miqqēllå קלל	
	ammēkassi כסי				mallēnəm לנן	ר
	wmēkassi כסי					
	wammēkassi כסי			**פיעל**		
	mēkassē'u כסי	ד			måmaššəš משש	
	wmēkassē'u כסי				amqaššəš ששש	
	åmarrəm מרי	ר			ammēqalləl קלל	
	amkalliyyot כלי	נ+ר			wamqalləl קלל	
	åmnaqqiyyot נקי				wamqallēlək קלל	ג
	wkallot כלי					
	amnaqqiyyūto נקי	נ+ר		**קל**		
	wamnaqqiyyūto נקי				qāni קני	
					båki בכי פרי רבי	
פיעל ב					båna בני לשי פני	
	amṣåbi צוי				aqqāni קני	
	amṣåbiyya צוי	נ			wmūra מרי	
	amṣåbåk צוי	ב			kannēši לשי	
					alqāni קני	
נפעל					qåša קשי	נ
	wnåmṣi מצי				ṣåba צבי	
	narfəm רפי	ר			dåbå דוי	
	wanniglå'ot גלי	נ+ר			zūna זני	
					arrē'bå* רוי	
התפעל					wråbå רבי	
	mitnabbəm נבי	ר			wzūna זני	

405

ב. הבינוני הפעול

		קל			קל
	ילד ayyåləd		*gēdəl גדל סגר		
			gēnob גנב		
		קל	bårok ברך גזל כנס כפל כתב ספן פגל קבר		
	nēgəf נגף		šbar שרף		
	nēqod נקד		wbårok ברך גזל כרת		
	annūšək משך		afšīlå בשל	נ
	wnēqod נקד		šērīfa שרף		
	wnåtoq נתק		qāšūra קשר		
	nēbīkəm נבך נגף נמל נתן	ר	gårūša גרש שלף		
	nēqūdəm נקד		akkåtūba כתב		
	nētūnot נתן	ר+נ	wgårūša גרש		
	annēqūdot נקד		gēnūbåt גנב	ס+נ
		הפעיל	wgēnūbåt גנב		
	mūsåbot סוב		šēmīrəm שמר	ר
	ammūšåb שוב		fārūməm פרם		
		קל	kåtūbəm כתב		
	kētət כתת		bakkåtūbəm כתב		
	bålol בלל		affēqīdəm פקד		
	wkåtot כתת רצץ		akkåtūbəm כתב שרף		
	bålūla בלל	נ	wbårūdəm ברד		
	ṣårårot צרר	ר+נ	waqqāšūrəm קשר		
	bålūlot בלל		båṣīrot בצר	ר+נ
			wbåṣīrot בצר שדף		
		קל	wabbåṣīrot בצר		
	tålo תלי		fēqīdi פקד	ר+ס
	nåṭuwwi נטי רצי		gårūšī גרש		
	aššēbi שבי		ṭåmūni טמן		
	wgålo גלי		wšåfūni שפן		
	nåṭuwwiyya נטי	נ		פיעל
	annåṭuwwiyya נטי		ambaššål בשל שזר שלש		
	tåluwwəm תלי	ר	ambårråk ברך		
	kåšibyot שבי	ר+נ	amšallåšåt שלש	נ
		הפעיל	amšaqqådəm שקד	ר
	ammukkå נכי			פיעל ב
	ammukkå נכי	נ	ammåqåšårot קשר	ר+נ
		פיעל	amšålåbot שלב	
	amṣåbbəm צפי	ר	amgåballot* גבל קבל	

ג. המקור

					קל
	wlišmårå שמר		rēgåm רגם		
	lidråš דרש כרת כתב לבן לבש מסר סבל		zēkor זכר שמר		
	ספד ספר פתר קבר קצר קרב רגל		gånəb גנב טרף		
	רגם שטן שבר שכב שכן שמר שפט		dåråš דרש זכר מלך משל סקל פקד קבר		
	fēqūdi פקד	א	gånob שכר שכב שמר		
	afsabri שבר		båfēqad פקד		
	liškåni שכן		åmålok מלך		
	baškåbåk שכב	ב	wšēmor שמר		
	båmūšåk משך		wlišmår שמר		
	lišṭånåk שטן שמר		wlēmšål* משל		

			ד	qåbåru קבר	
walkåfər כפר				båbigdu בגד	
alkåfər כפר				wmiššamru שמר	
kåbēdåk כבד	ב		ה	baškåba שכב	
afkåfēråk כפר				lētfåša* תפש	
			ז	kåqåråbkimma קרב	
נפעל			ט	abrådåfimma רדף	
naksəf* כסף					
iggåməl גמל כרת			**הפעיל**		
wlēddåbēqa דבק					
bēkkåbēdi כבד	א			istår סתר	
				baškən שכן	
נפעל ב				akbəs כבס סכן קרב שלך שמט	
ibbårråd פרד				wlåbdəl בדל שמד	
immakkår מכר				låbdəl בדל כרת קטר קרב שכל שמד	
iššammåd שמד			א	låqdīšåni קדש	
lēmmållåṭ מלט			ב	ašmīdåk שמד	
			ד	båfrīdu פרד	
קל				aqrību קרב שמד	
rēdət ירד ישב				akbēsu כבס	
yåråd ירד ירק				åṣfīnē'u צפן	
yūkål יכל				låqrību קרב שמד	
yēbēšåt* יבש			ו	låšmīdånu שמד	
ablēdət ילד ירד ירש ישב			ז	båqrebkimma קרב	
åyūkål יכל			ט	båqrībimma קרב	
wabrēdət ירד				ašmīdimma שמד	
lallēdət ילד ילד					
alṣåqåt יצק			**פיעל**		
millēdət ילד ירד ישב					
liktåk ילד	ב			birrok ברך בתר	
abliktåk ילד ישב				garrəš גרש דבר שלם	
abrēdētu ירד	ד			råbbot רבי	
kåšåbtu ישב				wbiššol בשל	
lēdēta ילד ירד	ה			wmakkər מכר	
ablēdēta ילד				wšåbbår שבר	
alrišta ירש				walbarrək ברך	
afšibtånu ישב	ו			kådabbər דבר	
afšēbetkimma ישב	ז			lillamməd למד	
				lillåqqəṭ לקט	
הפעיל				albakkår בכר	
īṭåb יטב				albarrək ברך דבר פרש קדש שכן שרת	
aṣṣīga יצג			א	afdēbåri דבר	
ūlēdət ילד			ב	dabbēråk דבר	
līṭəb יטב יסף			ד	båbirrūku ברך	
lūrəd ירד ירש				afdabbēru דבר קדש שלם שרת	
līṭībåk יטב	ב			alšammēṣu שמץ	
bīṭību יטב	ד		ה	kådabbēra דבר	
ūlīdu ילד ירש				almakkēra מכר	
lūrīšimma ירש	ט		ז	afdabberkimma דבר	
			ט	afdabbērimma דבר קדש שרת	
פיעל					
alyåssårå יסר			**פיעל ב**		
yabbēmi יבם	א			sēfər ספר	
alyåssåråk יסר	ב			kåbəd כבד	
abyallidkən ילד	ח			mikkåfər כפר	

					נפעל	
	båmol מול			bēwwåləd ילד		
	åmol מול				נפעל ב	
	alšəm שום			ayyåssåda יסד	ה	
	lallən לחן				קל	
	alšåš שוש			tat נתן		
	alboz בח גור נוס צוד קום שוב תור			nåbål נבל נתן		
	låmol מול			nåton נתן		
	mittor תור			aftət נתן		
	šatti שות	א		afgiššåt נגש		
	šūbåk שוב	ב		waltət נתן		
	wafqūmåk קום			walnåfål נפל		
	šūbu שוב	ד		lingåf נגף		
	båmålu מול			altət נתן		
	wafqūma קום	ה		alnēdår נדר		
	tåmimma תום	ט		mittət נתן		
	afqūmīyyimma קום			miggiššåt נגש		
		הפעיל		tatti נתן	א	
	īmər מור מות פור קום שוב			altitti נתן		
	bīdəf* דוף			mittatti נתן		
	å'īšəb שוב			aftittåk נתן	ב	
	wlīšəb שוב			waltittåk נתן		
	līdəf* דוף מות נוף סוף סור פור קום שוב			tattu נתן	ד	
	årēmi רום	א		gåštu נגש		
	kårēmi רום			aftittu נתן		
	åmītu מות	ד		bingåfu נגף		
	līmītu מות			abnēqåbu נקב		
	līmītånu מות	ו		altitta נתן	ה	
	īnefkimma נוף	ז		afgeštimma נגש	ט	
	båremkimma רום				הפעיל	
	līferkimma פור			åṣṣəl נצל		
	līmītimma מות	ט		wåṣṣəl נצל		
		פיעל		låggəd נגד נגש מר נצל		
	bayyår ביר			miyyåbbəṭ נבט		
		התפעל		låṣṣīlåk נצל	ב	
	ištūrår שור			azzīru מר	ד	
		קל		låṣṣīlu נצל		
	qåb קבב תמם				פיעל	
	gådod גדד			alnaššəq נשק		
	alqåb קבב			alnattår נתר		
	algoz גז				התפעל	
	alṣårår צרר			wlētnabbål נפל		
		הפעיל			קל	
	addåq דקק			šim שום		
	åttål תלל			sar סור		
	båsåmå שמם	ה		zåb זוב רום		
	åsåmå שמם			sob סוב שוב		
		פיעל				
	alqalləl קלל קשש					

	נכי akkūtu	ד		סבב alsūbåb	
	נכי שקי låkkūtu			קלל alqallēlåk	ב
	נטי נכי קשי låṭṭūta	ה			התפעל
	זני lēznūta*				
	ירי lū:rūtimma	ט		גלל lētgållål	קל
		פיעל			
	נכי nakki			פשי fåša	
	כלי נסי ספי kallot			פדי fådå	
	כלי kåkallot			נקי wnåqå	
	בכי גלי כסי ספי albakkot			בני זני מני פני שתי libnot	
	נטי alnåṭṭot			צבי alṣåbåt	
	נסי nassūtåk	ב		בלי båliti	א
	נסי walnassūtåk			נטי abnēṭåtti	
	כלי kallūtu	ד		דוי dåbåtå	ה
	כלי kåkallūtu				הפעיל
	כסי alkassūtu				
	בכי walbakkūta	ה		רבי arbi	
	כלי נסי kallūtimma	ט		נכי akkå	
	כלי walkallūttimma			נכי רבי akkot	
	כלי alkallūtimma			קצי åqṣot	
				רבי warbi	
		פיעל ב		פדי wåfådå	
	צוי alṣåbåt			רבי wlårbot	
	צוי ṣåbåtu	ד		ירי wlūrot	
		פיעל		נטי נכי שקי låṭṭot	
				ירי lūrot	
	נכסף naksəf*			נכי miyyakkot	
				נכי båkkūti	א

ב. Verbs Formed from Guttural Roots

א. הבינוני הפועל

	חרב wårēba			פא גרונית	
	אכל åkēlu				
	אכל wåkēlu	ד			קל
	עבר עבר עמד ʿābēdəm	ר		אבל ēbəl	
	עדף עמד ʿā:dēfəm			עבד עמד ʿåbəd	
	אמר הלך åmērəm			עבר עדף עמד ʿā:bəd	
	אכל הלך å:kēləm			אכל ארג הלך הרג åkəl	
	אשם åšåməm			אמן אסף הלך å:mən	
	אתר å:tūrəm*			אמר åmår	
	הלך ålēkåt	ר+נ		אמר å:mår	
	חבר åbērot			חלם עבר עמד ʿålåm	
		הפעיל		עבר ʿå:bår	
	עבר måbbər			עדף bādəf	
	חזק חרד måzzəq			ארג wårəg	
	חרש wmårrəš			עדף ʿā:dēfåt	
	אכל ammåkīlåk	ב		אכל åkēla	
	אמן måmēnəm	ר		אכל åkēlåt	נ
	אמן må:mēnəm			אכל הלך חבר å:kēlåt	

409

			פיעל		
	חלל mållēlåt	נ	abbəd אבד חבל		
	חלל mållēlåk	ב	måbbəd אבד		
	ענן ammånnēnəm	ר	'åbbår עבר		
	חלל mållēliyyå	ר+ה	wåkkəl אכל		
			ammållēkå הלך	נ	
	פיעל ב		måbbēdəm עבר	ר	
	ארר ammåråɾəm*	ר			
			פיעל ב		
	התפעל		måsəf אסף		
	אנן kåmtannēnəm	ר	målamməm אלם	ר	
	קל		**נפעל**		
	עשׂי 'åši		nēmmåd חמד		
	עשׂי 'å:ši		nå:mən אמן		
	חני åna		niyyåsåf אסף		
	חלי ålå		nå:dåri ארר		
	עלי ålå		annåmən אמן		
	עני å'åni		wnēmmåd חמד		
	עשׂי wåši		wnåkkəl אכל		
	אפי wå:få		wnå:låm עלם		
	עשׂי låši		nårrēfåt חרף	נ	
	הרי årå		anniyyåkēlåt אכל		
	חני ånəm	ר	wnå:låmå עלם		
	עלי עשׂי åləm		annåšləm חשל	ר	
	עלי עשׂי 'å:ləm		nå:zēləm אזל		
	עלי 'ålləm		wnåmēnəm אמן		
	אפי חני å:fəm		wnåmēnot אמן	נ+ר	
	אצי åṣuwwəm				
	חני wå:nəm		**התפעל**		
	עלי ålot	ר+נ	mētållåk הלך		
	עלי עשׂי 'å:lot				
	הרי åri*	ר+א	**התפעל ב**		
			ammētåfēkət הפך		
	הפעיל				
	עלי målli		**קל**		
	עלי ammålli		īf עוף		
	עלי mållåt	ס+נ			
	עלי ammållåk	ב	**הפעיל**		
	עלי mållot	ר+נ	må'əd עוד		
	עלי mimmålli	ר+ס			
			קל		
	נפעל		ånon חנן		
	עשׂי niyyåši		ūbåb חבב		
			u'ūfåf חפף		
	התפעל		wånon חנן		
	אוי ammētåwwəm	ר	årērək ארר	ג	
			wårērək ארר		
	פיעל				
	מחספס måsfəs		**פיעל**		
			månnən ענן		
עין גרונית			mūqåq חקק		
			båmūqåq חקק		
	קל		wmūqåq חקק		
	בער bår				
	זעף zīfəm	ר			
	סחר sērrəm				

410

קל
רעי תעי rā'i
ראי rå'i
כהי kå'å
רעי arrā'i
נ   כהי kå'å
רעי rā'iyya
ג   רעי rā'ɔk
ר   רעי rā'ɔm
רעי rå'ɔm
רעי arrå'ɔm
ראי arrå'ɔm
ראי wrå'ɔm
נ+ר   כהי ראי kå'ot
ראי arrå'ot
ר+א   רעי rā'i

הפעיל
ראי må'rī

נפעל
ראי annirrå'i

פיעל
תעתע kammētåttå

התפעל
ר   שחוי mištåbbəm

פא ועין גרוניות

פיעל ב
אהב wå'ɔb
אחז 'ā'ēzāt
אהב å'ēbåt
ר   אהב å'ēbəm
ר+א   אהב lå'ēbi
ר+ד   אהב lå'ēbo

נפעל
אחז nā'əz

למד גרונית

קל
שבע שמח šēbi
זבח zēba
בטח רצח bēṭå
זבח שמע zāba
מלא måli
מלא שנא måla
ברח פרח קנא bårå

כאב kå'ebəm
שחק šå'ūqəm
ס+ר   זחל zå'ēli

הפעיל
רחב שחת må'rīb
מעט שחת ammå'mīṭ
בער åmå'bīr
מעט wammå'mīṭ
שחת almå'sīt
ט   שחת måšīttimma
ר   שחת måšīttəm

פיעל ב
שאב šā'ɔb
גאל מאן שאל gå'əl
גאל miggå'əl
גאל צחק aggå'əl
טהר åmṭå'ər
מהר wmåmå'ər
צחק kåmṣå'ɔq
נ   רחף רחש amrā'ēfāt
ד   גאל gå'ēlu
ר   לחץ lā'ēṣəm
צעק ṣå'ēqəm
נ+ר   שאב ašša'ēbot

נפעל
שאר anniš'šår
לחם annillā'əm
שאר wanniš'šår
ר   שאר anniššårəm
שאר wanniššårəm
נ+ר   שאר anniššårot

התפעל
טהר ammiṭ'ṭår
טהר lammiṭ'ṭår

נפעל
יעד annuwwā'ēdəm

הפעיל
נחל mån'nīl

פיעל ב
נאף נחש annā'ɔf
נ   נאף wannā'ēfāt
ר+א   נאץ amnā'ēṣi

התפעל
נחם mit'nām

	מצא ånimṣå				רצח arrēṣå	
	מצא annimmåṣå				שבע שמע aśśåba	
	פלא nifʻlåt	נ			צמח aṣṣåmå	
	פלא niflåʾot	ר+נ			צמא aṣṣåʻmå	
	מצא annimmåṣåʾot				שבע wšēbi	
	פלא niflåʾūti	ר+א			מלא wmåli	
		קל			שׂע wšåsa	
	ידע yåda				סבא wsūba	
	ירא yåri				זבח kåzēba	
	יצא yåṣå				ברח båʻrēt	נ
	ירא yūra				שמע šåʻmåt	
	יצא yūṣå				פרח fåʻråt	
	ירא ayyåri				מלא måliyya	
	יצא ayyūṣå				שׂע wšåʻså	
	יגע wyåḡi				שׂע wšåʻsåt	
	יצא wayyūṣå				מצא måṣåʾi	א
	ידע yåʻdåt	נ			רפא rēʻfåk	ב
	יצא yåʻṣåt				שנא såʻnåk	
	יצא ayyūʻṣåt				מצא måṣåʾu	ד
	יצא yūṣåʾəm	ר			זבח שמע zåʻbīm	ר
	יצא ayyūṣåʾəm				מלא måʻlīm	
	ידע wyåʻdīm				שמע aššåʻmīm	
	יצא yåṣåʾot	ר+נ			טבח aṭṭåʻbīm	
	ידע yådåʾi	ר+ס			רפא arrēfåʾəm	
	יצא ירא yåṣåʾi				צבא aṣṣåbåʾəm	
		הפעיל			מצא ammūṣåʾəm	
	ישע mūʻšī				מלא malyot	ר+נ
	יצא ammūʻṣī				מלא målåʾot	
	יצא ammūṣiyyåk	ב			צמח ṣåmåʾot	
	יצא mūṣīyyimma				צבא aṣṣåbåʾot	
	יצא mūṣåʾi	ר+ס			מלא wammalyot	
		נפעל			זבח zåbi	ר+ס
	ירא nūra					הפעיל
	ישע annuwwåša				ברח mabri	
	ירא wnūra				זרע mazʻrī	
	ירא wannūra				צלח måṣli	
	יכח wnūʻkåt*	נ			מלח mamʻlēt	נ
	ירא annūråʾot	ר+נ			מרא måmʻrēt	
		קל				פיעל
	לקח lēqa				שלח šalla	
	נסע נשא nåsa				שלח amšalla	
	נגע נשׂא annūga				קנא åmqanni	
	נגע נשׂא wannūga				שלח wåmšalla	
	נסע wnåsa				ספח amsabʻbēt*	נ
	נגע wnūga				ספח åm̊sabʻbēt*	
	נגע annūʻgåt	נ			שנא wlamšannåʾi	א
	נכח wnūʻkåt*	ב			שנא amšannåʾək	ג
	נדח nēʻdåk	ב			שנא wamšannåʾo	ד
	נדח nēdåʾəm	ר				נפעל
					גרע niggårå	

בוא abbā'əm			נשא נסע nåsā'əm
בוא wabbā'əm			נשא annūšā'əm
בוא bā'ot	נ+ר		נשא nåšā'ot	ר
בוא abbā'ot			נשא nåšā'i	ס+ר
בוא bā'i	ס+ר		לקח lūqā'i
	הפעיל			התפעל
גוע mågi*			לקח mitlaq'qēt	נ
בוא mībi				קל
בוא mībiyyåk	ב		בוא נוע bā
			בוא abba
פא ולמד גרוניות			בוא wabba
			בוא bā:	נ
	פיעל		בוא ab'bā
חטא ammåṭṭi			בוא bā'əm	ר

ב. הבינוני הפעול

עול uwwållåt	נ+ר		פא גרונית
	קל			קל
ארר åror			אכל ēkəl
ארר wåror			עקד ēqod
ארר årūrå	נ		'āroṣ חרץ חרת חתם עצר עשק
	קל		חתם 'ā:tom
עשי 'āšuwwi			אסר חלץ åsor
עשי 'āšuw'wā	נ		עשק å'āšoq
			אסר åsūri
עין גרונית			עזב wāzob
	קל		ערף 'ā:rūfa	נ
טחן ṭå'on			חגר ēgīrəm	ר
מעך wmā'ok			עקד ēqūdəm
שחט šå'ūṭå	נ		עטף 'āṭūfəm
שחט aššå'ūṭå			אסר חלץ åsūrəm
בעל bīlåt	ס+נ		אסר å:sūrəm
	הפעיל		חצב åṣūbəm
ראי mir'rå			עקד å'ēqūdəm
			חמש wēmīšəm
פא ועין גרוניות			אסר חלץ åsūri	ס+ר
	קל			הפעיל
אהב å'ūba	נ		אדם mådamməm	ר
			אדם ammådamməm
למד גרונית				פיעל
	קל		ארש mårråša	נ
סרח פרע פתח sāru			ארש ammårråša
			חשק måššåqəm	ר
				קל
			חוש īšəm	ר

413

	ר+ס	קרא qaryā'i		זרע	zå'rī
		פיעל		פצע	fåṣa*
		ammēṣårrå צרע		טבח מרח	ṭå'bū
		amṣår'råt צרע		משח	ammåṣi
	ר+נ	amgabbā'ot* גבע פתח		מצא	wmåṣi
		åmgabbā'ot* גבע		טלא	wṭå'lū
		ammēqiṣṣå'ot גבע	נ	שנא שלח	šånuw'wā
		wamgabbā'ot* גבע		שנא	aššånuw'wā
		almēqiṣṣå'ot קצע		שנא	waššånuw'wā
		הפעיל	ר	שנא	laššånuw'wā
				משח	må'sīm
	נ	mū'ṣåt יצא		מלא	måluwwəm
				משח	ammå'sīm
		הפעיל		טלא	wṭåluwwəm
				טלא	waṭṭåluwwəm
	ר	mūbā'əm בוא	ר+נ	טלא	waṭṭåluwwot

ג. המקור

	ד	aklu אכל		פא גרונית	
		åmådu' עמד הפך חדש עמד הרג עבד		קל	
	ו	miyyåbådnu עבר		הרג	ērāg
		båkålånu אכל הרג		עבר עבד	'ābod
	ז	aklåkimma אכל		הרס	årrås
		båkålkimma אכל		הלך	ålək
		wlåkålkimma אכל		עבד אכל אמר אשם הרג עצר	åbåd
	ט	båkålimma אכל		חבל עזב	åbål
		låbbådimma עבד		הלך	ålok
		הפעיל		אכל	båkål
		åbbəṭ' עבט עלם ענק		אמר	bē'ūmər*
		årəm חרם		אכל	wåkål
		å:mən* אמן		אכל חשב	wlåkål
		årrəš חרש		עבד	wlåbbåd
		bīdəf* הדף		אמר	līmor
		bå:rək ארך		עבד עבר	lēbbåd
		wbā:ṭəf עטף		עבד עמד	låbbåd
		wbå:rək ארך		עבט	låboṭ
		līdəf* הדף		הלך	lålək
		låbəd עבד		אכל אסר הרג חבר עזב	låkål
		låbbəd אבד		עבר	lå:bår
	ב	abbīdåk אבד		חטב חנט עבד עמד	låṭṭåb
	ד	abbīdu אבד		עבר	lēbbåda
		ålīṣu* חלץ		הלך עבר	miyyēlåk
		låbbīdu אבד		עזב	miyyåzåb
	ו	'abbīrånu' עבר	א	הפך	åfēki
		פיעל		הרג	ålårågåni
			ב	אכל	aklåk
		abbəd אבד		אסף	båsfåk
		annəš' עלש		עבר	bå:båråk
		aššår' עשר		הרג	lårågåk
		åbbår' עבר		עבר	lå:båråk

עלי lā:lot
עשי lāššot
היי lāyyot
עלי bāllūtåk   ב
היי wlåyyūtåk
עשי ʻaššūtu   ד
עלי ʻālūtu
עשי lāššūtu
עשי bā:šūta   ה
עשי lāššūta
חני ånūtīnu   ו
עשי lāššotkimma   ז
היי ayyūtimma   ט
היי båyyūtimma
עשי lāššūtimma

הפעיל

עלי ʻāllot
עלי wbāllot
חיי wliyyot
חיי liyyot
עלי lā:lot
עלי bāllūti   א
עלי bāllūtåk   ב
עלי wbāllūtu   ד
עלי wlālūtu
חיי wliyyūtīnu   ו
חני lånotkimma   ז

פיעל

עני ʻanna
עני ʻannūtåk   ב
עני ʻannūtimma   ט

עין גרונית

קל

שחת såt
שאל šåʼål
תעב wtåb
בער מעל alʼbår
כהן סהר רחץ שחט alʼkån

הפעיל

רחק שאר åʼrīq
קהל שחת båʼqīl
קהל wbåʼqīl
שחת låʼšīt
באש lībīšåni   א
שחת åšīttåk   ב
שאר åšīrinnu   ד
כעס låkīsu
שחת låšītta   ה

עבר båbbår
עשר låššår
עבר ʻåbbåri   א
אבק båbbēqu   ד
עבר båbbårkimma   ז

פיעל ב

אסף båsefkimma   ז

נפעל

אסף iyyåsåf

התפעל

אפק lētåbbåq
עלם lētållåm

התפעל ב

אסף bētåsēfu*

קל

הום lå:mimma   ט

הפעיל

עוד åʼåd
אור låʼər

קל

עמן bånåni   א

הפעיל

חלל miyyåʼēlåk   ב
חלל åʼēlimma   ט

פיעל

חלל walləl

נפעל

חלל låʼlū   ד

התפעל

חנן bētånnånu   ד

קל

היי ayyot
עשי aššot
היי ayyu
עלי עני ålot
עלי ålå
עשי miyyaššot
היי mīʼayyot
היי båyyot
חני wbånot
עשי wlåššot
עני lånot

415

	פיעל ב
	gå'əl גאל מאן מהר צעק
	kēlā'ək לחך
	alšā'əb שאב
	alṭå'ər טהר מהר צחק
ד	alṭå'ēru טהר
ט	båmā'ēlimma מעל
	alṭå'ērimma טהר

נפעל

| | iš'såt שחת |
| | lēllā'əm לחם |

התפעל ב

| | wlētfå'ērət פאר |

קל

| | yåm יחם |
| ה | alyåminna יחם |

נפעל

| ט | bēwwā'ēdåtimma יעד |

קל

| | al'nål נחל |

הפעיל

| | bån'nīl נחל |
| ד | ånīlu נחל |

פיעל ב

| | nā'əš נחש |
| ד | alnā'ēmu נחם |

התפעל

| | lēt'nåm נחם |

קל

	mā: מחי
	rå: ראי
	rå'ot ראי
	rå'u ראי
	alrā'ot ראי
	alrå'ot ראי
	mirrå'ot ראי
א	rå'īti ראי
	kårå'ūti ראי
ב	rå'ūtåk ראי
ד	abrāttu ראי
	kårå'ūtu ראי
ה	kårå'ūta ראי
	alrå'ūta ראי
ט	abrå'ūtimma ראי

	הפעיל
ד	arråttu ראי

נפעל

	arrå'ot ראי
	lērrå'ot ראי
ז	lērrå'otkimma ראי

התפעל

| | lētmåmå מהמה |

התפעל

| | lēštåbbot שחוי |

למד גרונית

קל

	fāta פתח שמע
	šåka שכח
	må'lāt מלא
	dålå דלא פרח
	afsāma שמע
	afgåba גוע
	wbåmå'lāt מלא
	wrēfa רפא
	wšāma שמע
	wlišma שמע
	kåsāma שמע
	kåbåla בלע
	libra ברח גוע זבח סלח פלא קרא שמע
	lir'bā רבע
	limṣå מצא
	albēṭå בטא
	alṣaba צבא
ב	šā'bāk שבע
	båbē'rāk ברח
ד	šāmā'u שמע
	måšā'u משח
	båbērā'u ברח פגע
	afsāmā'u שמע
	wkåšāmā'u שמע
	kåsāmā'u שמע
ו	qåránnu קרא
ז	båmåṣåkkimma מצא
ט	kåšāmākkimma שמע
	kåšāmā'imma שמע

פיעל

	šalla שלח
	ṭåmma טמא
	afšalla שלח
	wafšalla שלח

	הפעיל		שלח alšalla	
ידע יכח ū'dī			שלח afsallā'i	א
לשע wlū'šī			שלח šal'lāk	ב
יצא lūṣi			שלח afšal'lāk	
יצא būṣå'i	א		קנא afqånnå'u	ד
ידע ūdiyyåk	ב		שלח kåšallā'u	
יצא būṣiyyåk			שלח alšallā'u	
יצא būṣå'u	ד		טמא alṭåmmā'u	
יצא lūṣiyyånu	ו		שלח šal'lā	ה
יצא kå'ūṣīyyimma	ט		שלח alšallānu	ו
יצא lūṣīyyimma			טמא afṭåmmākkimma	ז
			שלח šallā'imma	ט
	התפעל		טמא afṭåmmā'imma	
ידע bēttūda			שלח alšallā'imma	
				פיעל ב
	קל		מלא walmåla	
נשא šāt			מלא almåla	
נשא al'šāt			מלא almå'lāt	
נשא nåša			מלא må'lāt	ס
נשא af'šāt			מלא båmålā'ūtimma	ט
נסע abnåsa				
לקח al'qēt				נפעל
נגע wnūga			שבע iššāba	
נסע wabnåsa			מצא immåṣå	
נדח alnēdå			רפא lērråfa	
נגע alnūga			ברא ibbårå'imma	ט
נשא minnåša			ברא bēbbårå'imma	
לקח qåttək	ג			
נשא šåttu	ד			התפעל
לקח afqåttu			גלח itgallā'u	ד
נגע abnēgā'u				
לקח alqēttu				קל
לקח alqētta	ה		ידע dāt	
נסע abnåsā'imma	ט		ידע ad'dāt	
			ידע waf'dāt	
	הפעיל		ידע yāda	
נדח låddiyyåk	ב		יצא ירא yåṣå	
			יצא ṣiyyåt	
	קל		יצא afṣiyyåt	
בוא bā			ידע åyūda	
בוא bå'bū			יצא kåṣiyyåt	
בוא åba			יצא alṣiyyåt	
בוא wbåba			יצא afṣiyyåti	א
בוא wlå'bū			יצא kåṣiyyåti	
בוא נוח kå'bū			יצא ṣiyyåtåk	ב
שוח al'šū			יצא afṣiyyåtåk	
בוא lå'bū			ידע dåttu	ד
בוא båbā'i	א		יצא ṣiyyåtu	
בוא båka	ב		יצא afṣiyyåtu	
בוא bå'bāk			יצא wafṣiyyåtu	
בוא bā'u	ד		ידע aldātta	ה
בוא båbā'u			יצא afṣiyyåtkimma	ז
בוא bånnu	ו		יצא afṣiyyåtimma	ט

417

ז	בוא bākkimma		ז	בוא ībiyyåkimma
	בוא båbākkimma		ט	נח līnēttimma
ט	בוא bā'imma			
	בוא båbā'imma			פא ולמד גרוניות
י	בוא båbā'inna			
				קל
	הפעיל			חטא lēṭṭå
	בוא ībi			
	נח bån'nī			**פיעל**
	נוא anni			חטא *'åṭṭå
	בוא lībi			חטא låṭṭå
	רוח lå'rī			
	בוא mībi			**הפעיל**
ב	בוא wlībiyyåk			טחח *'åṭṭå
	בוא lībiyyåk			lå'rī
ד	נוע lånniyyu			

THE NOUN

א. Nouns Formed from Non-Guttural Roots

א. משורש בן עיצור אחד

ב	bā	ה		ב	b°	
ל	lā			כ	k°	
ב	bånu	ו		ל	l°	
ל	lånu			ב	bī	א
ב	båkimma	ז		ל	lī	
כ	kåkimma			ב	båk	ב
ל	låkimma			ל	låk	
ב	bimma	ט		ב	bek	ג
ל	låmu			ל	lik	
ב	bēmma			ל	lek	
ל	lēmma			ל	līki	
ב	bēnna	י		ב	bū	ד
כ	kå'inna			ל	lū	
ל	lēnna			ל	låmu	

ב. משורש בן שני עיצורים

מוֹ	kåmok	ב		שֶׁה	šī	
מוֹ	kåmē'u	ד		שֶׁה	šiyyu	ד
מוֹ	kåmuwwa	ה		פֶּה	fā	
מוֹ	kåmūnu	ו		פֶּה	fī	ס
שֵׁם	šem			פֶּה	fiyyi	א
שֵׁשׁ	šeš			פֶּה	fiyyåk	ב
דָּת	dat			פֶּה	fiyyu	ד
יָד	yad			פֶּה	fiyyē'u	
יֵשׁ	yaš			פֶּה	fiyya	ה
שָׁם	šam			פֶּה	miffīkimma	ז
יָד	yed			פֶּה	fīyyimma	ט
יֵשׁ	yåšåt			פֶּה	alfīyyinna	י
שֵׁם	baššəm			מוֹ	mū	
יָד	yēdi	א		מוֹ	kåmūni	א

419

	yēdīnu	ר+ו		שֵׁם	šēmi	
	yēdīkimma	ר+ז	ב	יָד	yēdåk	
	yēdīyyimma	ר+ט		יָשׁ	yåšåk	
	šēmūtimma			שֵׁם	šēmåk	
וָו	båb °			יָד	yēdǝk	ג
וָו	båbǝm	ר	ד	יָד	yēdu	
וָו	båbi	ר+ס		יָשׁ	yašnu	
וָו	båbīyyimma	ר+ט		שֵׁם	šēmu	
קֶבֶה	qāb-a		ה	יָד	yēda	
מְתִים	mēt-ǝm °			שֵׁם	šēma	
מְתִים	mēti	ר+ס	ו	יָד	wyēdånu	
מַיִם	m-em		ז	יָד	abyedkimma	
מַיִם	mem	ר		יָשׁ	yåškimma	
מַיִם	mī	ר+ס	ט	יָד	yēdimma	
מַיִם	mīmǝk	ר+ג		שֵׁם	šēmimma	
מַיִם	mīmo	ר+ד	ר	יָד	yēdǝm	
מַיִם	mīmīyyimma	ר+ט		יָד	yådot	
				שֵׁם	šēmot	
			ר+ס	יָד	yēdi	
			ר+ד	יָד	yēdo	
			ר+ה	יָד	yēdiyya	

ג. משורש בן שלושה עיצורים

1. הפשוטים

עִיס	afkīsåk			דַּי	dī	
זַיִת	zītǝk	ג	ר	דַּי	dem	
בֵּין	bīnu	ד		בֵּין	bin	
בַּיִת	bītu			בַּיִת	bit	
זֵר	alzirru			גַּד	gid	
מִין	almīnu			זַיִת	zit	
רִיב	abrību			זֵר	zir	
מִין	almīnē'u			עִיס	kis °	
בַּיִת	bīta	ה		עַר	kir °	
מִין	almīna			מִין	min °	
צַד	afṣiddå			נִין	nin °	
בֵּין	bīnånu	ו		צַד	ṣid	
בֵּין	wbinkimma	ז		רִיב	rib	
רִיב	wribkimma			רִיק	riq	
בֵּין	bīnimma	ט		רִיק	riq	
בַּיִת	battǝm	ר		תַּשׁ	tiš	
זַיִת	zītǝm			בַּיִת	bet	
עַר	kirrǝm			בַּיִת	bīta	
רִיב	rībot			בֵּין	bīni	א
תַּשׁ	wtīšǝm			בַּיִת	bīti	
בַּיִת	batti	ר+ס		נִין	walnīni	
צַד	ṣiddi			בֵּין	bīnåk	ב
בַּיִת	battǝk	ר+ג		בַּיִת	bītåk	
צַד	ṣiddo	ר+ד				
צַד	miṣṣiddiyya	ר+ה				
בֵּין	bīnåtånu	ר+ו				
בַּיִת	battīnu					

מַד	mad °			בַּיִת	battīkimma	ר+ז
מַן	man			צַד	afṣiddīkimma	
מַס	mas °			בֵּין	bīnåtimma	ר+ט
מַר	mar °			בַּיִת	battīyyimma	
מֵת	mat			מִין	almīnīyyimma	
נַד	nad			גִּיד	**ged**	
פַּס	fas °			גֵּר	ger	
רַק	raq °			דִּין	den	
שַׂר	šak °			דַּיִשׁ	deš	
שַׁד	šad °			מֵת	met	
שַׁן	šan			גֵּר	ner °	
שַׁשׁ	šaš			סִיר	ser	
כֹּל	bakkål			צַיִד	ṣed	
עַן	ken			צִיץ	ṣeṣ	
לֵב	leb			צַן	ṣen °	
מַן	almån			קַיִץ	qeṣ	
מַר	wmirra	נ		קִיר	qer	
עַן	bēni	א		קֵן	qen	
עַן	kinni			קֵץ	qeṣ	
לֵב	libbi			שַׁד	šed °	
מִן	mimminni			גֵּר	gir	
מֵת	mitti*			מֵת	mēta	נ
עַן	bēnåk	ב		צַיִד	miṣṣīdi	א
גַּג	algiggåk			גֵּר	wgīråk	ב
עַן	kinnåk			קֵן	qinnåk	
לֵב	libbåk			גֵּר	gīru	ד
מִן	mimmåk			דַּיִשׁ	afdīšu	
מֵת	mittåk*			צַיִד	ṣīdu	
עַן	bēnək	ג		קֵן	qinnu	
צַד	kiddək			גֵּר	gīrəm	ר
עַן	bēnu	ד		מֵת	mītəm	
גַּג	giggu			גֵּר	nīrot	
כֹּל	kallu			סִיר	assīrot	
עַן	kinnu			צַן	walṣinnəm	
לֵב	libbu			קִיר	afqīrot	
מִן	mimminnu			קֵן	qinnəm	
שַׁן	šinnu			שַׁד	alšīdəm	
מֵת	mittu*			סִיר	sīrūto	ר+ד
עַן	bēna	ה		קִיר	qīrūto	
צַד	kidda			גֵּר	nīrūtiyya	ר+ה
כֹּל	kallå			בֵּן	**ban**	
מִן	mimminna			גַּג	gag °	
עַן	binna*			גַּף	gaf °	
עַן	bēnånu	ו		דָּג	dag °	
כֹּל	kallånu			צַד	kad °	
מִן	mimmånu			כֹּל	kal	
כֹּל	kallåkimma	ז		עַן	kan	
מִן	mikkimma			עַן	kan °	
כֹּל	kallimma	ט		לֵב	lab	
לֵב	libbimma					
מִן	miyyimma					
כֹּל	kallinna	י				

421

פַּת	fåt			לֵב	libbinna	
צָב	ṣåb			מִן	miyyinna	
צֵל	ṣål			בֵּן	bånəm	ר
צַר	ṣår			כֵּן	kånəm	
צוּר	ṣår			מַס	massəm	
קָשׁ	qåš			מַר	marrəm	
רַב	råb			פַּס	fassəm	
רֹב	råb			שֵׁר	alšikkəm	
רַד	råk			שֵׁר	šiddəm	
רֹךְ	råk			שֵׁן	šinnəm	
שַׂק	šåq			רַק	wraqqot	ר+נ
שַׂר	šår			בֵּן	båni	ר+ס
שֵׁר	šår °			דָּג	dēgi	
תֵּל	tål			מַד	mådi	
תָּם	tåm			בֵּן	båni	ר+א
חֹם	tåm			בֵּן	bånək	ר+ג
תֹּף	tåf			בֵּן	båno	ר+ד
תֹּר	tår			עֵף	afgabbo	
יָם	yåmå			בֵּן	båniyya	ר+ה
דַּק	daqqa	נ		בֵּן	båbånīnu	ר+ו
זָר	zarra			בֵּן	bånīkimma	ר+ז
רַב	råbbå			בֵּן	bånīyyimma	ר+ט
רַד	arråka			שֵׁן	šinnīyyimma	
בַּד	albaddi	א		בַּד	**båd**	
עַף	kabbi			בַּז	båz	
נַס	nåsi			בַּר	bår	
צַר	alṣårri			גַּד	gåd	
בַּד	albåddåk	ב		גַּז	gåz	
צַר	ṣårrək	ג		גַּל	gål	
רֹב	råbbək			גַּן	gån	
בַּד	albaddu	ד		דּוֹר	dår	
דָּם	dammu			דַּל	dål	
עַף	kabbu			דָּם	dåm	
שַׂק	šiqqu			דַּק	dåq	
בַּד	albadda	ה		זַג	zåg	
דָּם	damma			זָר	zår	
עַף	kabba			טַל	ṭål	
תֹּף	ṭåbbånu	ו		טַף	ṭåf	
בַּד	albåddåkimma	ז		יָם	yåm	
דָּם	dåmkimma			כַּף	kåf	
תֹּף	ṭåfkimma			כַּר	kår	
רֹב	mirråbkimma			לַג	låg	
בַּד	albaddimma	ט		מָן	mån	
דָּם	dammimma			נַס	nås	
תֹּף	ṭåbbimma			נֵץ	nåṣ	
בַּד	albaddinna	י		סַל	sål	
בַּד	baddəm	ר		סַף	såf	
דָּם	damməm			סַף	såf	
זָר	bazzarrəm			פַּר	får	
יָם	yåmməm					
עַף	kabbot					

שׁוֹק	šoq	סַל	assalləm
שׁוֹר	šor	פַּר	abbarrəm
שׁוּר	šor	פַּת	fattəm
תָּוֶךְ	tok	רַב	råbbəm
טוֹב	ṭuba	דַּךְ	rakkəm
טוֹב	ṭubåt	שַׂר	såṛəm
טוֹב	ṭubi	שַׂר	afsåṛəm
מוּל	mimmuli	חֹף	aftabbəm
מָוֶת	muti	תֹּר	tarrəm
קוֹל	quli	דַּל	dallot	ר+נ
קוֹל	qulåk	דַּק	daqqot
שׁוּר	šuråk	רַב	råbbot
דּוֹד	dudu	עֵד	baddi	ר+ס
זוּב	zubu	דָּם	dammi
יוֹם	abyumu	כַּף	kabbi
מָוֶת	mutu	סַל	salli
קוֹל	qulu	שַׂר	šåri
שׁוּר	šuru	עֵד	baddo	ר+ד
תָּוֶךְ	tuku	כַּף	kabbo
זוּב	zuba	צַר	ṣårro
קוֹל	qula	דָּם	dammiyya	ר+ה
תָּוֶךְ	aftuka	כַּף	kabbiyya
מָוֶת	mutånu	צַר	ṣårrinu	ר+ו
צוּר	kåṣurånu	דָּם	dammiyyimma	ר+ט
קוֹל	qulånu	כַּף	kabbiyyimma
תָּוֶךְ	aftukånu	שֹׁק	šiqqiyyimma
קוֹל	afqolkimma	בּוֹר	bor
תָּוֶךְ	aftukåkimma	גּוּר	gor
מָוֶת	båmutimma	דּוֹד	dod
סוֹד	afsudimma	דּוֹר	dor
צוּר	ṣurimma	זוּב	zob
קוֹל	qulimma	טוֹב	ṭob
תָּוֶךְ	waftukimma	טוּב	ṭob
בּוֹר	burot	טוּר	ṭor
דּוֹר	aldurot	יוֹם	yom
טוֹב	ṭubəm	כּוּר	kor
טוּר	ṭurəm	לוּז	loz
יוֹם	yumåt	לוֹט	loṭ
סוּס	susəm	מוֹט	moṭ
צוּר	ṣurəm	מוּל	mol
קוֹל	qulot	מוּם	mom
קוֹץ	quṣəm	מָוֶת	mot
יוֹם	yumå'əm	מַס	mos
טוֹב	ṭubot	נוּר	nor
טוּר	ṭuri	ר+נ	סוֹד	sod °
דּוֹר	afduruto	ר+ס	סוּס	sos
סוּס	alsuso	ר+ד	צוּר	ṣor
דּוֹר	durutikimma	ר+ז	קוֹל	qol
דּוֹר	aldurutimma	ר+ט	קוֹץ	qoṣ
דּוֹר	dudiyyinna	ר+י	קוֹר	qor
וָלָד	wlad °		
וָלָד	wlåda	ה		

423

צְבִי	ṣåbi			כְּלִי	kīli	
צָלִי	ṣåli			לֵוִי	lībi	
שָׂדֶה	šådi			פְּרִי	fīri	
שָׂדַי	šådi			כְּלִי	kīli	א
שָׁנִי	šåni			כְּלִי	kīlək	ג
רָזָה	råza	נ		כְּלִי	kīləm	ר
שֵׁנִי	šēni	ס		לֵוִי	allībəm	
מְרִי	maryåk	ב		כְּלִי	kīlo	ר+ד
שָׂדֶה	šådåk			פְּרִי	fīro	
שָׂדֶה	šåde'u	ד		כְּלִי	kīliyya	ר+ה
מֹנֶה	månəm	ר		פְּרִי	fīriyya	
שָׂדֶה	aššådot			כְּלִי	kīlīkimma	ר+ז
גְּדִי	gadyi	ר+ס		כְּלִי	kīlīyyimma	ר+ט
דְּלִי	middalyo	ר+ד		בְּכִי	bēki	
מָנָה	måne			נְקִי	nēqi	
נָוֶה	nåbe			נָשִׁי	nēši	
שְׁבוּ	šåbu			פדי	fēdi °	
שֶׁמֶשׁ	šīməš			קְרִי	qēri	
דָּגָן	dīgån			שְׁבִי	šēbi	
דָּגָן	dīgånåk	ב		שֵׁנִי	šēni	
קִיטוֹר	qīṭor			שְׁנִי	šēnət	נ
בֶּטֶן	bēṭən			פדי	wfidyu	ד
בֶּתֶר	bēṭər °			שְׁבִי	šibyu	
גְּבִיר	gēbər			שְׁבִי	šibya	ה
דֶּגֶל	dēgəl			שְׁנִי	šēnəm	ר
דֶּלֶת	dēlət			יָפָה	yēfa	
דֶּרֶךְ	dērək			יָפָה	yēfət	ס+נ
זֵכֶר	zēkər			יָפָה	yēfot	ר+נ
זֶפֶת	zēfət			נְקוִי	nēqo °	
טֶרֶם	ṭērəm			נקוי	wnēquttå	ב
יֵצֶר	yēṣər			נקוי	nēquwwəm	ר
יֶקֶב	yēqəb			קָלִי	qåli	
יָרֵךְ	yērək			קָנֶה	qåni	
יָרָק	yērəq			קָשִׁי	qåši	
יָרָק	yērəq			קְשִׁי	qåši	
יָחַד	yētəd °			קָשָׁה	qåša	נ
פָּלִיל	kēləl			קָנֶה	qånəm	ר
כֶּשֶׁב	kēšəb			קָשֶׁה	qåšot	ר+נ
כֶּתֶף	kētəf			קָנֶה	qåni	ר+ס
לֶקֶט	lēqət			קָנֶה	qåniyya	ר+ה
מֶגֶד	mēgəd			קָנֶה	wqånūtimma	ר+ט
מֶכֶס	mēkəs			גְּדִי	gådi	
מֶלֶךְ	mēlək			דְּלִי	dåli °	
נֶגֶב	nēgəb			מֹנֶה	måni °	
נֶגֶד	nēgəd			מְרִי	måri °	
				סְנֶה	såni	
				פָּרָה	fåri	

דֶּרֶךְ	dirku			גֶּגֶף	nēgəf	
יֵצֶר	yiṣru			נָדִיב	nēdəb	
יָרַד	yirku			מָזִיר	nēzər	
גֶּגֶד	kånigdu			גֶּסֶךְ	nēsək	
גֶּסֶךְ	nisku			נָפִיל	nēfəl °	
קָרֵב	qirbu			גֹּפֶךְ	nēfək	
רֶגֶל	riglu			נָצִיב	nēṣəb	
רָכֵב	rikbu			מֶשֶׁךְ	nēšək	
שָׁכֵן	šēkīnu			גֶּתֶק	nētəq	
בֶּטֶן	båṭna	ה		סַפִּיר	sēfər	
יָרַד	yirka			פָּלִיט	fēləṭ	
קָרֵב	afqirba			פָּקִיד	fēqəd	
רֶגֶל	rigla			צֶדֶק	ṣēdəq	
קָרֵב	afqirbånu	ו		צָמִיד	ṣēməd	
דֶּרֶךְ	aldirkåkimma	ז		קֶדֶם	qēdəm	
קָרֵב	afqirbåkimma			קֹדֶשׁ	qēdəś	
רֶגֶל	rēgelkimma			קֶצֶף	qēṣəf	
זָכַר	zakrimma	ט		קֶרֶב	qērəb	
מֶכֶס	wmaksimma			רָבִיב	rēbəb °	
גֶּסֶךְ	niskimma			רֶגֶל	rēgəl	
רֶגֶל	riglimma			רֶכֶב	rēkəb	
קָרֵב	qirbinna	י		רָכִיל	rēkəl	
דֶּלֶת	dålåtəm	ר		רֶמֶשׂ	rēməš	
דֶּרֶךְ	dērēkəm			רָקִיק	rēqəq	
יָרַד	yērēkəm			שָׁכֵן	šēkən	
יָחַד	yētēdot			שָׁלִישׁ	šēləš °	
כֶּשֶׂב	kiśbəm			שָׁפֵךְ	šēfək	
כָּתֵף	katfot			שֶׁרֶץ	šērəṣ	
גֶּסֶךְ	wniskəm			תֶּבֶל	tēbəl	
נָפִיל	annēfīləm			תֶּבֶן	tēbən	
פָּלִיט	fēlīṭəm			תֶּנֶךְ	tēnək	
פָּקִיד	fēqīdəm			גֶּגֶב	nigba	
צָמִיד	ṣēmīdəm			קֶדֶם	qidma	
רָבִיב	wkarrēbībəm			קֹדֶשׁ	qēdīša	נ
רֶגֶל	rēgåləm			דֶּרֶךְ	dirki	א
רֶגֶל	argåləm			זָכַר	zakri	
שָׁלִישׁ	wšēlīšəm			יָרַד	yirki	
יָרַד	walyērēkūti	ר+ס		גֶּגֶד	alnigdi	
נָדִיב	nēdībi			קָרֵב	afqirbi	
רֶגֶל	wrēgåli			רֶגֶל	alrigli	
רָקִיק	wrēqīqi			בֶּטֶן	båṭnåk	ב
רֶגֶל	abrēgåli	ר+א		דֶּרֶךְ	dirkåk	
דֶּרֶךְ	dērēkək	ר+ג		יָקֵב	wmiyyiqbåk	
רֶגֶל	rēgålək			גֶּגֶד	nigdåk	
רֶגֶל	dēgålo	ר+ד		מָזִיר	nēzīråk	
דֶּרֶךְ	dērēko			קָרֵב	afqirbåk	
יָחַד	yētēdūto			רֶגֶל	riglåk	
כָּתֵף	katfūto			בֶּטֶן	båṭnək	ג
גֶּסֶךְ	wnisko			יָרַד	yirkək	
רֶגֶל	rēgålo			בֶּתֶר	bitru	ד
שָׁלִישׁ	šēlīšo					
יָרַד	yērēkiyya	ר+ה				
יָחַד	yētēdūtiyya					

425

דָּבָר	kådēbårək		
גֶּדֶר	nēdårək		
לֵבָב	lēbåbu	ד	
דֶּרֶך	nidru		
נֶזֶר	nizru		
שְׁכֶם	šikmu		
שְׁכֶם	šikma	ה	
שָׁלָל	šēlåla		
לֵבָב	lēbåbnu	ו	
גְּלָל	afgēlålkimma	ז	
לֵבָב	lēbåbkimma		
לֵבָב	lēbåbimma	ט	
שְׁכֶם	šikmimma		
בֶּגֶד	bēgådəm	ר	
גָּדֵל	gēdalləm		
דָּבָר	dēbårəm		
מֶם	annēzåməm		
קֶרֶס	baqqēråsəm		
קֶרֶשׁ	qēråšəm		
בֶּגֶד	bēgådi	ר+ס	
דָּבָר	dēbåri		
מֶם	nēzåmi		
קֶרֶס	qēråsi		
קֶרֶשׁ	qēråši		
בֶּגֶד	bēgådo	ר+ד	
דָּבָר	dēbåro		
קֶרֶס	qēråso		
קֶרֶשׁ	qēråšo		
גֶּדֶר	nēdåriyya	ר+ה	
בֶּגֶד	bēgådīkimma	ר+ז	
דָּבָר	dēbårīkimma		
גֶּדֶר	nēdårīkimma		
בֶּגֶד	bēgådīyyimma	ר+ט	
דָּבָר	dēbårīyyimma		
גֶּדֶר	nēdårīyyimma		
גְּלָל	abnēkålīyyimma		
שְׁתִי	**šē'tåy**		
גְּבוּל	**gēbol**		
זָכוּר	zēkor °		
יְבוּל	yēbol °		
יְסוֹד	yēsod		
יָתוֹם	yētom		
כְּרוּב	kērob		
לְבוּשׁ	lēboš °		
גְּבוּל	gēbūlåk	ב	
זָכוּר	zēkūråk		
גְּבוּל	gēbūlu	ד	
לְבוּשׁ	lēbūšu		
זָכוּר	zēkūra	ה	
יְבוּל	yēbūla		
גְּבוּל	gēbolkimma	ז	
מָזִיר	nēzīriyya		
נֶסֶך	wniskiyya		
רֶגֶל	rēgåliyya		
דֶּרֶך	dirkīkimma	ר+ז	
נֶסֶך	walniskīkimma		
רֶגֶל	rēgålīkimma		
רֶגֶל	aldēgēlīyyimma	ר+ט	
יָחַד	wyētēdūtimma		
נֶסֶך	wniskīyyimma		
רֶגֶל	rēgålīyyimma		
בֹּקֶר	**bēqar**		
בֶּגֶד	**bēgåd**		
גָּדֵל	gēdål °		
גֶּדֶר	gēdår		
גְּלָל	gēlål		
דָּבָר	dēbår		
זֶרֶת	zēråt		
פוּס	kēwås		
כִּכָּר	kēkår		
לֵבָב	lēbåb		
מָטָר	mēṭår		
גֶּדֶר	nēdår		
מֶם	nēzåm		
נֶזֶר	nēzår		
נֵכֶל	nēkål °		
גֶּכֶר	nēkår		
נָקָם	nēqåm		
לֶשֶׁר	nēšår		
סֵתֶר	sētår		
פֶּטֶר	fēṭår		
פֶּרֶט	fēråṭ		
פֶּרֶך	fēråk		
פֶּרֶס	fērås		
קֶטֶף	qēṭåf		
קֶרֶס	qērås °		
קֶרֶשׁ	qēråš		
רֶשֶׁף	rēšåf		
שְׁכֶם	šēkåm		
שֵׂכָר	šēkår		
שֶׁלֶג	šēlåg		
שֶׁלֶך	šēlåk		
שָׁלָל	šēlål		
שָׁלֹשׁ	šēlåš		
דָּבָר	dēbåri	א	
לֵבָב	lēbåbi		
גְּלָל	afgēlålåk	ב	
לֵבָב	lēbåbåk		
גְּלָל	afgēlålək	ג	

צַדִּיק	ṣådəq			גְּבוּל	gēbūlot	ר
קֹדֶשׁ	qådəš			יָתוֹם	yētūməm	
קָצִיר	qåṣər			כְּרוּב	kērūbəm	
שָׂכִיר	šåkər			גְּבוּל	algēbūlūtiyya	ר+ה
שָׂרִיד	šårəd			קֶרֶן	qārən °	
שַׁבָּת	šåbət °			קֶשֶׁת	qåšət	
שָׁלֵם	šåləm °			קֶשֶׁת	qašti	א
שָׁלֵם	šåləm °			קֶשֶׁת	wqaštåk	ב
שֶׁמֶן	šåmən			קֶשֶׁת	qaštu	ד
שָׁפָל	šåfəl			קֶרֶן	qārēnot	ר
שֹׁרֶשׁ	šårəš			קֶרֶן	qārēno	ר+ד
תָּמִיד	tåməd			קֶרֶן	qārēnūto	
תָּמִים	tåməm			קָדֹשׁ	qådoš	
תָּמָר	tåmər °			קָרוֹב	qårob	
תַּנִּין	tånən			קָרוֹב	qårūbəm	ר
גֹּרֶן	gårån ʿåṭåd*			בְּדִיל	bådəl	
תָּמִיד	tåmīda			בָּכִיר	båkər	
בָּכִיר	abbåkīra	נ		בָּצִיר	båṣər	
כָּבֵד	kåbēda			בְּדֹשׁ	gådəš	
לָבָן	låbēna			גֶּפֶן	gåfən	
צַדִּיק	ṣådīqa			גֹּרֶן	gårən	
שָׁלֵם	šalmå			גֶּרֶשׁ	gårəš	
תָּמִים	tåmīma			זָקֵן	zåqən	
יֶלֶד	yålīdi	א		טֶרֶף	ṭårəf	
כֶּסֶף	kasfi			טֶרֶף	ṭårəf	
מַקֵּל	båmåqīli			יֶלֶד	yåləd	
נֶפֶשׁ	nafši			יָלִיד	yåləd	
קֹדֶשׁ	qådēši			יָשָׁר	yåšər °	
גֹּרֶן	miggirnåk	ב		כָּבֵד	kåbəd	
כֶּסֶף	kasfåk			כֶּלֶב	kåləb	
כֶּרֶם	kårmåk			כָּנָף	kånəf	
מֶלֶךְ	malkåk			כֶּסֶף	kåsəf	
נֶפֶשׁ	nafšåk			כֶּרֶם	kårəm	
פָּתִיל	wfåtīlåk			לָבָן	låbən	
קֹדֶשׁ	qådēšåk			מֶכֶר	måkər °	
קָצִיר	qåṣīråk			מֶלֶךְ	målək	
קֹדֶשׁ	qådēšək	ג		מַקֵּל	måqəl	
שָׂכִיר	walšåkīrək			מַתָּן	måtən	
כֶּסֶף	kasfu	ד		נָטָף	nåṭəf	
כֶּרֶם	karmu			נֶפֶשׁ	nåfəš	
מֶלֶךְ	malku			סָבִיב	såbəb	
נֶפֶשׁ	nafšu			סֹלֶת	sålət	
פֶּרֶשׁ	faršu			סֵמֶל	såməl	
קֹדֶשׁ	alqådēšēʾu			סַפִּיר	såfər	
שַׁבָּת	šabtu			סָרִיס	sårəs	
גֶּרֶשׁ	miggirša	ה		פֶּרֶשׁ	fårəš °	
נֶפֶשׁ	nafša			פָּתִיל	fåtəl	
סֹלֶת	missilta					
פֶּרֶשׁ	farša					
קָצִיר	qåṣīra					
שֶׁמֶן	šåmēna					

427

כָּנָף	afkånåfīyyimma	ר+ט		כֶּסֶף	kasfånu		ו
כֶּסֶף	kasfīyyimma			נֶפֶשׁ	nafsånu		
מֶלֶךְ	målēkīyyimma			כֶּסֶף	kasfåkimma		ז
נֶפֶשׁ	abnafsūtimma			נֶפֶשׁ	nåfeškimma		
קֹדֶשׁ	qådēšīyyimma			קָצִיר	qåṣerkimma		
יֶלֶד	yålīdīyyinna	ר+י		גֶּפֶן	gåfnimma	ט
בָּדָד	bådåd			מֶכֶר	makrimma		
בָּצָל	båṣål °			נֶפֶשׁ	nafsimma		
בָּצָק	båṣåq			פֶּרֶשׁ	faršimma		
בָּקָר	båqår			שָׁלָם	šalmimma		
בָּרָד	båråd			זָקֵן	zåqīnəm		ר
בֶּרֶךְ	båråk °			יֶלֶד	ayyålīdəm		
בָּרָק	båråq			ישיר	yåšīrəm		
בֶּשֶׂם	båšåm			כָּנָף	kånåfəm		
בֹּשֶׂם	båšåm			כָּנָף	kånåfot		
בָּשָׂר	båšår			כֶּרֶם	kårēməm		
גֶּבֶן	gåbån			מֶלֶךְ	målēkəm		
גֶּבֶר	gåbår			מֹתֶן	mimmåtēnəm		
גָּדֹל	gådål			נֶפֶשׁ	nafsot		
גָּזָל	gåzål			פָּתִיל	fåtīləm		
גֶּזֶר	gåzår °			צַדִּיק	ṣådīqəm		
גָּמָל	gåmål			קֹדֶשׁ	qådēšəm		
גֹּפֶר	gåfår			שָׁלָם	šalməm		
גָּרָב	gåråb			תָּמִים	tåmīməm		
גֶּשֶׁם	gåšåm			תֹּמֶר	tåmērəm		
דָּבָר	dåbår			תַּנִּין	tånīnəm		
דְּבַשׁ	dåbåš			לָבָן	låbēnot		ר+נ
דֶּשֶׁן	dåšån			מַקֵּל	bammåqīlot		
זָבַד	zåbåd			שָׁלָם	šalmot		
זָכַר	zåkår			תָּמִים	tåmīmot		
זָמַר	zåmår			זָקֵן	zåqīni		ר+ס
זָנָב	zånåb			יֶלֶד	miyyålīdi		
זָקֵן	zåqån			יָלִיד	yålīdi		
יָבָם	yåbåm °			כָּנָף	kånåfi		
לָשׁוֹן	yåšån			מֶלֶךְ	målēki		
יָשָׁר	yåšår			מֹתֶן	måtēni		
ישׁר	yåšår			סָרִיס	såīsi		
יָתַד	yåtåd			קֹדֶשׁ	qådēši		
יֶתֶר	yåtår			שֶׁמֶן	miššåmåni		
כָּבֵד	kåbåd °			זָקֵן	zåqīnək		ר+ג
כֶּבֶשׂ	kåbåš			כֶּרֶם	alkårēmək		
כֶּסֶל	kåsål °			יֶלֶד	yēlīdo		ר+ד
כֹּפֶר	kåfår			כָּנָף	kånåfo		
מָשָׁל	måšål			מֹתֶן	båmtåno		
מֶשֶׂק	måšåq			סָרִיס	såīso		
נָבָל	nåbål			קֹדֶשׁ	qådēšo		
סָבַךְ	såbåk			יֶלֶד	wyålīdiyya		ר+ה
סֵבֶל	såbål °			זָקֵן	wafzåqīnīnu		ר+ו
				נֶפֶשׁ	nafsūtīnu		
				זָקֵן	zåqīnīkimma		ר+ז
				מַקֵּל	wmåqīlīkimma		
				מֹתֶן	måtēnīkimma		
				נֶפֶשׁ	nafsūtīkimma		

זָקֵן	zåqånkimma			פֶּגֶר	fågår °	
בָּקָר	båqrimma	ט		פֶּדֶר	fådår	
בָּשָׂר	båšårimma			פֶּרֶץ	fåråṣ	
זָקֵן	zåqånimma			פֶּתֶן	fåtån °	
יֶתֶר	wyatrimma			צֶלֶם	ṣålåm	
שֶׁבֶר	šabrimma			צֶמֶר	ṣåmår	
בַּעַל	abbåṣåləm	ר		צְרֹר	ṣårår °	
בֶּרֶךְ	abbåråkəm			קֶבֶר	qåbår	
בָּרָק	wbåråqəm			קָטָן	qåṭån	
גֶּבֶר	ågåbårəm			קֶמַח	qåmåṣ °	
עֵזֶר	aggåzårəm			קֶסֶם	qåsåm °	
גָּמָל	gåmåləm			קֹצֶר	qåsår	
זָכָר	azzåkårəm			קֶרֶן	qårån °	
כָּבֵד	kåbådəm			שָׂכָר	šåkår	
כֶּבֶשׂ	kåbåšəm			שֵׁבֶט	šåbåṭ	
כֶּסֶל	akkåsåləm			שֶׁבֶר	šåbår	
סֵבֶל	såbålot			שֶׁגֶר	šågår	
פֶּגֶר	affågårəm			שָׁפָל	šåfål °	
פֶּתֶן	fåtånəm			שָׁתָם	šåtåm	
צְרֹר	ṣårårot			קָטָן	qåṭanna	נ
קֶבֶר	qåbårəm			שָׁפָל	wšåfåla	
קֶמַח	alqåmåṣəm			בָּשָׂר	wbåšåri	א
קֶסֶם	qåsåməm			יָבָם	yåbåmi	
גָּמָל	miggåmåli	ר+ס		קֶבֶר	afqabri	
פֶּגֶר	fågåri			שָׂכָר	šakri	
צֶלֶם	ṣålåmi			בָּקָר	båqråk	ב
קֶרֶן	wqåråni			בָּשָׂר	båšåråk	
שֵׁבֶט	šåbåṭi			גֹּרֶל	gådlåk	
שֵׁבֶט	šåbåṭək	ר+ג		שָׂכָר	šakråk	
גָּמָל	gåmålo	ר+ד		גָּמָל	gåmålək	ג
שֵׁבֶט	alšåbåṭo			שָׂכָר	šakrək	
קֶבֶר	qåbårīnu	ר+ו		צֵק	biṣqu	ד
גֶּשֶׁם	gåšåmīkimma	ר+ז		בָּשָׂר	båšåru	
סֵבֶל	alšåbålūtīkimma			גֹּרֶל	gådlu	
פֶּגֶר	fågårīkimma			דֶּשֶׁן	aldišnu	
שֵׁבֶט	šåbåṭīkimma			זָנָב	afzånåbu	
גָּמָל	wgåmålīyyimma	ר+ט		זָקֵן	zåqannu	
סֵבֶל	afsåbålūtimma			מָשָׁל	måšålu	
קֶסֶם	wqåsåmīyyimma			פֶּדֶר	fidru	
שֵׁבֶט	šåbåṭīyyimma			צֶלֶם	afṣålåmu	
בְּכוֹר	**båkor**			קֶבֶר	qabru	
גָּדוֹל	gådol			קֶמַח	qåmṣu	
דָּרוֹם	dårom			שָׂכָר	šakru	
כָּבוֹד	kåbod			שֶׁבֶר	šabru	
נָבוֹב	nåbob			בָּשָׂר	båšårå	ה
צְרֹר	ṣåror			יָבָם	yåbåmå	
קָלוֹט	qåloṭ			בָּקָר	wbåbåqrånu	ו
רְכוּשׁ	råkoš			בָּשָׂר	wbåšårnu	
שָׂרוּג	śårog			צֶלֶם	afṣåråmånu	
שָׁלוֹם	šålom			בָּקָר	båqråkimma	ז
תְּמוֹל	tåmol			בָּשָׂר	båbåšårkimma	

גָּדוֹל	gådalla		נ
בְּכוֹר	båkūri		א
כָּבוֹד	kåbūdi		
בְּכוֹר	båkūråk		ב
כָּבוֹד	kåbūdåk		
בְּכוֹר	båkūru		ד
כָּבוֹד	kåbūdu		
רָכוּשׁ	råkūšu		
רָכוּשׁ	råkūšimma		ט
בְּכוֹר	mibbåkūrot		ר
גָּדוֹל	gådalləm		
גָּדוֹל	gådallot		ר+נ
בְּכוֹר	båkūri		ר+ס
יוֹבֵל	yūbəl		
גּוֹזָל	gūzål		
גּוֹרָל	gūrål		
כּוֹכָב	kūkåb		
כּוּמָז	kūmåz		
כְּפָר	kūfår		
כֹּפֶר	kūfår		
שׁוֹטֵר	šūṭår°		
שׁוֹפָר	šūfår		
גּוֹרָל	gūrålot		ר
כּוֹכָב	kūkåbəm		
שׁוֹטֵר	wšūṭårəm		
כּוֹכָב	kåkūkåbi		ר+ס
שׁוֹטֵר	šūṭåri		
שׁוֹטֵר	wšūṭårək		ר+ג
גּוֹזָל	gūzålo		ר+ד
שׁוֹטֵר	šūṭåro		
שׁוֹטֵר	wšūṭårīkimma		ז+ז
מְרִי	mirri		
שַׂדַי	šiddi		
צָרִי	ṣårri		
גּוֹי	guwwi		
גּוֹי	guwwəm		ר
גּוֹי	guwwi		ר+ס
גּוֹי	afguwwīyyimma		ר+ט
צִנִּים	ṣinnəm°		
קָדִים	qiddəm		
צִנִּים	ṣinnīmot		ר
כִּנּוֹר	kinnår		
רַגְזָ	riggåz		
שִׂיד	šiyyåd		
בִּכּוּר	bikkor		
בֶּרֶךְ	birrok°		

גִּבּוֹר	gibbor		
גִּלּוּל	gillol°		
דְּרוֹר	dirror		
כִּיּוֹר	kiyyor		
לָשׁוֹן	liššon		
פְּרוּר	firror		
צִבּוֹן	ṣibbon°		
צִפּוֹר	ṣibbor		
רִמּוֹן	rimmon		
שָׂרוּג	širrog°		
שִׁקּוּץ	šiqqoṣ°		
תַּנּוּר	tinnor		
צִפּוֹן	ṣibbūna		
בֶּרֶךְ	birrūki		א
בְּכוֹר	bikkūrək		ג
תַּנּוּר	waftinnūrək		
לָשׁוֹן	liššūnu		ד
גִּבּוֹר	aggibbūrəm		ר
צִפּוֹר	ṣibbūrəm		
רִמּוֹן	arrimmūnəm		
שָׂרוּג	širrūgəm		
רִמּוֹן	rimmūni		ר+ס
בֶּרֶךְ	birrūko		ר+ד
גִּלּוּל	gillūlīkimma		ר+ז
גִּלּוּל	gillūlīyyimma		ר+ט
לָשׁוֹן	lilliššūnūtimma		
שִׁקּוּץ	šiqqūṣīyyimma		
יָבֵשׁ	yabbəš°		
יַיִן	yayyən		
יָמִין	yammən		
לַפִּיד	labbəd		
סֶלַע	salləm		
קָדֵשׁ	qaddəš°		
קָרֵב	qarrəb		
שָׂרַד	šarrəd		
שָׁלֵם	salləm		
שָׁמֵן	šammən		
יָמִין	wayyammīna		
שָׁמֵן	åšammīna		נ
קָרֵב	afqarrībi		א
יָמִין	yammīnåk		ב
יַיִן	miyyayyēnu		ד
יָמִין	yammīnu		
קָרֵב	qarrību		
יַיִן	yayyēnimma		ט
יָמִין	miyyammīnimma		
יָבֵשׁ	wyabbīšəm		ר
לַפִּיד	allabbīdəm		
קָדֵשׁ	qaddīšəm		

שֶׁקֶל	ašqəl			כִּכָּר	kakkår		
שֶׁקֶץ	ašqəṣ			לְשַׁד	laššåd		
תֹּכֶן	atkən			פְּלַל	fallål °		
שֶׁקֶל	ašqēləm	ר		רֹכֶב	rakkåb		
פְּסִיל	afsīli	ר+ס		שַׁקָּר	šaqqår		
פְּסִיל	wafsīlīyyimma	ר+ט		פְּלַל	fallåləm	ר	
שָׁפָן	a-šfan			רָבִיד	råbbəd		
לֶשֶׁם	a-lšåm			שַׁלִּיט	ṣållәṭ		
גֶּשֶׁר	anšår			גַּנָּב	gannåb		
סֵפֶר	asfår			לַטָּשׁ	låṭṭåš		
שָׂפָם	asfåm			פָּרָשׁ	fårråš °		
שֶׁקֶר	ašqår			קַסָּם	qåssåm		
סֵפֶר	miyyasfåri	א		רַקָּם	råqqåm		
סֵפֶר	miyyasfåråk	ב		שַׁבָּת	šåbbåt		
אֲשׁוּר	å-šor °			שַׁבָּת	šåbbåtkimma	ז	
אֲשׁוּר	åšūrəm*	ר		לָשׁ	wlåṭṭåšəm*	ר	
				פָּרָשׁ	fårråšəm		
	עיצורים עם תנועות			שַׁבָּת	šabbētot		
				שַׁבָּת	šabbētūti	ר+א	
יָקוּם	yē-qom			פָּרָשׁ	fårråšo	ר+ד	
יַנְשׁוֹף	ya-nšof			שַׁבָּת	šabbētūtiyya	ר+ה	
מָגֵן	am-gən			שַׁבָּת	afsabbētūtīkimma	ר+ז	
מֹרֶךְ	mi-rråk			כּוֹס	kuwwås		
מֵיטָב	mī-ṭåb			צִנָּאר	ṣuwwår		
מֵיתָר	mītår °			צִנָּאר	ṣuwwåråk	ב	
מֵיתָר	mītåro	ר+ד		צִנָּאר	ṣuwwåru	ד	
מֵיתָר	mītåriyya	ר+ה		יְרַקְרַק	yēråqråq		
מֵיתָר	mītårīyyimma	ר+ט		יְרַקְרַק	yēråqråqot	ר+נ	
מִישׁוֹר	mī-šor			פְּתַלְתֹּל	fåtåltål		
מָסָךְ	mē-sək			כָּסוּי	kassuwwi		
מִקְנֶה	ma-qni			צָפוּי	ṣåbbuwwi		
מִרְמָה	marmi						
מִשְׁנֶה	mašni				2. המוספים בראשם		
מַשְׁקֶה	mašqi						
מִשְׁתֶּה	mašti				תנועות (> א, ה)		
מִקְנֶה	maqni	א		אֵיתָן	ī-tån		
מִקְנֶה	maqnək	ג		הֵיטֵב	īṭåb		
מִקְנֶה	maqnē'u	ד		אֵיתָן	ītånu		
מִקְנֶה	maqnīnu	ו		רָפֶה	a-rfi		
מִקְנֶה	maqnīkimma	ז		שְׁפִי	ašfi		
מִקְנֶה	maqnīyyimma	ט		הַרְבֵּה	a-rbå		
מִגְרָשׁ	ma-grəš			פְּסִיל	afsəl °		
מַזְלֵג	mazləg °			פֶּסֶל	afsəl		

431

מִשְׁכָּן	wmaškånūtək	ר+ג		מִזְרָק	mazrəq		
מִשְׁפָּט	mašfåṭo	ר+ד		מכרת	makrət °		
מִכְשׁוֹל	ma-kšol			מַמְזֵר	mamzər		
מַלְקוֹשׁ	malqoš			מִמְכָּר	mamkər		
מִשְׁקוֹל	mašqol			מִשְׁקָל	mašqəl °		
מַשְׂקוֹף	mašqof			מִמְכָּר	mamkēru		ד
מַבּוּל	ma-bbol			מִשְׁקָל	mašqēlu		
מַטְמוֹן	må-ṭmon			מִשְׁקָל	mašqēla		ה
מַטֶּה	må-ṭṭi			מִשְׁקָל	mašqēlimma		ט
מַטֶּה	måṭṭåk	ב		מַזְלֵג	ammazlēgot		ר
מַטֶּה	måṭṭē'u	ד		מִזְרָק	ammazrēqot		
מַטֶּה	måṭṭot	ר		מִגְרָשׁ	magrēši		ר+ס
מַטֶּה	måṭṭūtimma	ר+ט		מִזְרָק	mazrēqi		
מַתָּן	må-ttån °			מַזְלֵג	wmazlēgūto		ר+ד
מַתָּן	måttånimma	ט		מִזְרָק	wmazrēqūto		
מדי	må-di			מכרת	makrētīyyimma		ר+ט
מֵלִיץ	må-ləṣ			מִגְרָשׁ	magrēšīyyinna		ר+י
מָזוֹן	må-zon			מִגְדָּל	ma-gdål		
מָכוֹן	måkon			מִדְבָּר	madbår		
מָלוֹן	målon			מִדְרָךְ	madråk		
מָצוֹק	måṣoq			מִכְבָּר	makbår		
מָצוֹר	måṣor			מִכְתָּב	maktåb		
מָקוֹם	måqom			מִסְפֵּד	masfåd		
מָקוֹר	måqor			מִסְפָּר	masfår		
מָקוֹם	måqūmi	א		מִקְבָּר	maqbår		
מָקוֹם	måqūmåk	ב		מִקְדָּשׁ	maqdåš		
מָקוֹם	måqūmu	ד		מִקְלָט	maqlåṭ		
מָקוֹם	almåqūma	ה		מֶרְכָּב	markåb		
מָקוֹם	måqūmimma	ט		מִשְׁכָּב	maškåb		
מָקוֹם	ammåqūmot	ר		מִשְׁכָּן	maškån		
מָקוֹם	båmåqūmīnu	ר+ו		מִשְׁמָר	mašmår		
מָקוֹם	almåqūmūtimma	ר+ט		מִשְׁפָּט	mašfåṭ		
מִבְצָר	må-båṣər			מִקְדָּשׁ	maqdåši		א
מִבְצָר	måbåṣīrəm	ר		מִשְׁכָּן	maškåni		
מָדוּהַ	må-duwwi			מִשְׁפָּט	mašfåṭi		
מוֹקֵשׁ	mū-qəš			מִשְׁכָּב	maškåbək		ג
מוּסָד	mū-såd °			מִשְׁפָּט	mašfåṭək		
מוּסָר	mūsår			מִקְדָּשׁ	maqdåšu		ד
מוֹפֵת	mūfåt			מִקְלָט	maqlåṭu		
מוֹשָׁב	mūšåb			מִשְׁכָּב	båmaškåbu		
מוֹפֵת	mūfåti	א		מִשְׁפָּט	kåmašfåṭu		
מוֹשָׁב	mūšåbåk	ב		מִשְׁכָּב	båmaškåba		ה
				מִסְפָּר	masfårkimma		ז
				מִקְדָּשׁ	maqdåškimma		
				מִשְׁמָר	mašmårkimma		
				מִסְפָּר	båmasfårimma		ט
				מִשְׁפָּט	kåmašfåṭimma		
				מִשְׁפָּט	mašfåṭən		י
				מִשְׁפָּט	wmašfåṭəm		ר
				מִשְׁכָּב	maškåbi		ר+ס

שֵׁנָה	šēna °			מוּשָׁב	mūšåbu	ד
שָׁנָה	šēna			מוּשָׁב	mūšåbimma	ט
דָּגָה	afdēgət	ס		מוֹפֵת	wmūfåtəm	ר
שֵׁנָה	šēnåt			מוּסָד	mūsådi	ס+ר
שֵׁנָה	šanti	א		מוֹשָׁב	mūšåbūtīkimma	ז+ר
שֵׁנָה	miššintu	ד		מוֹשָׁב	båmūšåbūtimma	ט+ר
שֵׁנָה	šēnåtu			מֵזִיד	na-zzəd	
שֵׁנָה	šēnåtå	ה		תְּבַלּוּל	ti-bballål	
גֵּבָה	gēbot	ר		תֵּימָן	tī-mån	
שֵׁנָה	šēnəm			תִּירָשׁ	tīråš	
שֵׁנָה	šēnåt			תִּירָשׁ	tīråšåk	ב
שֵׁנָה	šēnåtå'əm			תַּשְׁבֵּץ	tē-šåbbəṣ	
שֵׁנָה	šēni	ס+ר		תּוֹשָׁב	tū-šåb	
שֵׁנָה	šēno	ד+ר		תּוֹשָׁב	waltūšåbək	ג
בָּמָה	båm-a °			תּוֹשָׁב	wtūšåbəm	ר
מִדָּה	måda					
קָמָה	qåma °			3. המוספים בסופם		
קָמָה	qåmåt	ס				
בָּמָה	båmåtimma	ט			תנועות	
בָּמָה	båmot	ר				
מִדָּה	mådot			נָכְרִי	nikr-i	
בָּמָה	båmåti	ס+ר		נָכְרִי	nikriyya	נ
בָּמָה	båmåtūkimma	ז+ר		נָכְרִי	kannikriyyot	נ+ר
דּוּדָה	dūd-a °			שַׂלְוִי	šalw-i	
זוּנָה	zūna °			שִׁשִּׁי	šišš-i	
טוֹבָה	ṭūba			שְׁלִישִׁי	šēlīš-i	
סוּפָה	sūfa			שְׁלִישִׁי	aššēlīšət	נ
קוֹמָה	qūma			יָשְׁפֵה	yašf-e	
קוּרָה	qūra			בִּינָה	bīn-a °	
שֻׁבָּה	šūba			בֵּיצָה	bīṣa °	
קוּרָה	qūråti	א		טִירָה	tīra °	
דּוּדָה	dūdåtåk	ב		לַיְלָה	līla	
שֻׁבָּה	šūbåtåk			שִׁיבָה	šība	
דּוּדָה	dūdåtu	ד		שִׁירָה	šīra	
קוֹמָה	qūmåtu			תֵּבָה	tība	
קוֹמָה	qūmåtå	ה		שִׁיבָה	šībåt	ס
זוּנָה	zūnåtīkimma	ז+ר		תֵּבָה	tībåt	
טוֹבָה	wṭūbūtimma	ט+ר		שִׁיבָה	šībåti	א
כְּשִׂבָּה	kiśb-a			בִּינָה	wbīnåtkimma	ז
לִבְנָה	libna			בֵּיצָה	bīṣəm	ר
לִבְנָה	libna			טִירָה	ṭīrūtimma	ט+ר
נְקָמָה	niqma °			גַּבָּה	gēb-a °	
סִתְרָה	sitra			דָּגָה	dēga	
פִּשְׂתָּה	fišta					
קִדְמָה	qidma °					
לִבְנָה	libnåt	ס				
נְקָמָה	niqmåt					
קִדְמָה	qidmåt					
לִבְנָה	libnəm	ר				

שְׁלֹשָׁה	šēlåšåtkimma		ז	פִּשְׁתָּה	fištəm		
שְׁלֹשָׁה	šēlåšåtimma		ט	לִבְנֶה	millibnīkimma		ר+ז
בְּתוּלָה	bētūl-a			קָרְבָה	qårb-a °		
גְּבוּרָה	gēbūra °			קָרְבָה	afqårbåtimma		ט
לְבוּנָה	lēbūna			מָרָה	mirr-a		
סְגֻלָּה	sēgūla			מָרָה	mirra °		
לְבוּנָה	lēbūnta		ה	שִׁשָּׁה	šišša		
בְּתוּלָה	bētūlot		ר	מָרָה	mirråt		ס
גְּבוּרָה	wkågēbūrūtək		ר+ג	שִׁשָּׁה	šiššåt		
גְּדֵרָה	gådīr-a °			מרה	martu		ד
יַלְדָּה	yålīda			גַּנָּה	gann-a °		
סְבִיבָה	såbība			זָרָה	zarra		
צְדָקָה	ṣådīqa			כַּלָּה	kalla °		
סְבִיבָה	såbībåt		ס	כָּלָה	kalla		
צְדָקָה	ṣådīqåt		א	סֻכָּה	sakka °		
צְדָקָה	ṣådīqåti		ב	פִּנָּה	fanna °		
צְדָקָה	afṣådīqåtåk			פָּרָה	farra		
גְּדֵרָה	gådīrot		ר	כַּלָּה	kaltåk		ב
סְבִיבָה	såbībūti		ר+א	כַּלָּה	kaltu		ד
סְבִיבָה	såbībūtīyya		ר+ה	גַּנָּה	kågannot		ר
סְבִיבָה	såbībūtīnu		ר+ו	סֻכָּה	sakkot		
סְבִיבָה	såbībūtīkimma		ר+ז	פָּרָה	farrot		
סְבִיבָה	såbībūtīyyimma		ר+ט	כַּלָּה	kallūtu		ר+ד
				פִּנָּה	fannūto		
בְּרָכָה	båråk-a						
גְּנֵבָה	gånåba °			מַסָּה	måss-a °		
יְבָמָה	yåbåma °			צָרָה	sårra		
יוֹנָה	yåbåna			מַסָּה	måssåt		ס
כִּבְשָׂה	kåbåša			צָרָה	sårti		א
נְבֵלָה	nåbåla			צָרָה	wsårrot		ר
נְדָבָה	nådåba						
נְקֵבָה	nåqåba			דַּכָּה	dukk-a		
פְּצֵלָה	fåṣala °			גְּנֵבָה	gēnīb-a °		
קְלָלָה	qålåla			דְּבִירָה	dēbīra °		
שִׂמְלָה	šåmåla			טְרֵפָה	ṭērīfa		
שְׁגָגָה	šågåga			נְבֵלָה	nēbīla		
שְׂדֵמָה	šådåma °			שְׂרֵפָה	šērīfa		
קְלָלָה	qålålå			שְׁרֵקָה	šērīqa		
בְּרָכָה	båråkåt		ס	שְׁפֵלָה	šēfīla		
נְדָבָה	nådåbåt			נְבֵלָה	abnēbīlåt		ס
קְלָלָה	qålålåt			שְׂרֵפָה	šērīfåt		
שִׂמְלָה	šåmålåt			נְבֵלָה	nēbiltåk		ב
בְּרָכָה	båråkti		א	נְבֵלָה	nēbiltu		ד
בְּרָכָה	båråktåk		ב	נְבֵלָה	nēbilta		ה
קְלָלָה	qålåltåk			נְבֵלָה	nēbeltimma		ט
שִׂמְלָה	šåmåltåk			דְּבִירָה	middēbīrūtək		ר+ג
בְּרָכָה	kåbåraktu		ד				
גְּנֵבָה	afgånåbtu			שְׁלֹשָׁה	šēlåš-a °		
יְבָמָה	yåbåmtu			שְׁלֹשָׁה	šēlåšåt		ס
שִׂמְלָה	šåmåltu						

זִמְרָה	mizzimrāt	ס		שָׁגְגָה	šågågtu	
זִמְרָה	wzimrāti	א		שָׁגְגָה	šågågtimma	ט
גְוִיָה	gibyūtūnu	ר+ו		בְּרָכָה	abbåråkot	ר
פְּלֵיָה	kaly-å °			כְּבָשָׂה	kåbåšot	
קִרְיָה	qaryå			פְּצָלָה	fåṣålot	
קִרְיָה	miqqaryåt	ס		קְלָלָה	aqqålålot	
פְּלֵיָה	kalyot	ר		שִׂמְלָה	šåmålot	
פַּרְסָה	fårs-å			שְׁדֵמָה	wmiššådåmot	
פַּרְסָה	fårsot	ר		נְדָבָה	wnådåbūtək	ר+ג
שׂרטה	šurṭ-å			שִׂמְלָה	šåmålūto	ר+ד
גֵּרָה	girr-å			נְדָבָה	nådåbūtīkimma	ר+ז
נִדָּה	niddå			שִׂמְלָה	šåmålūtīkimma	
צִדָּה	ṣiddå			נְדָבָה	nådåbūtimma	ר+ט
קִדָּה	qiddå			שִׂמְלָה	šåmålūtimma	
קִצָּה	qiṣṣå			מְלִילָה	millīl-a °	
קֵצָה	qiṣṣå			מְלִילָה	millīlåt	ר
נִדָּה	niddåt	ס		גְּבִירָה	gēbirr-a °	
קֵצָה	qiṣṣå			כְּבֵרָה	kēbirra °	
קֵצָה	qiṣṣåʾēʾu	ד		פְּקֵדָה	fēqidda °	
נִדָּה	niddåtå	ה		קְבֵרָה	qēbirra °	
דִּבָּה	dåbb-å			כְּבֵרָה	kēbirråt	ס
מִדָּה	måddå			פְּקֵדָה	fēqiddåt	
מַצָּה	måṣṣå			קְבֵרָה	qēbirråt	
נִצָּה	nåṣṣå			גְּבִירָה	gēbirråti	א
קַבָּה	qåbbå			גְּבִירָה	gēbirråtək	ג
קַצָּה	qåṣṣå °			קְבֵרָה	qēbirråtu	ד
דִּבָּה	dåbbåt	ס		גְּבִירָה	gēbirråtå	ה
קַבָּה	qåbbåtå	ה		קְבֵרָה	qēbirråtå	
דִּבָּה	dåbbåtimma	ט		פְּקֵדָה	wfēqiddåtimma	ט
מַצָּה	måṣṣot	ר		קְבֵרָה	afqēbirråtimma	
קַצָּה	qåṣṣot			יַבָּשָׁה	yåbbåš-a	
קַצָּה	qåṣṣūto	ר+ד		יְרֻשָׁה	yårišš-a	
טוה	ṭuww-å			יְרֻשָׁה	yårišš-åtu	ד
רִמָּה	rummå			שְׁנִינָה	šånāʾīn-a	
פְּלֵיטָה	fēlīṭ-å			גֵּרָה	gīr-å	
בְּכִירָה	båkīr-å			נִצָּה	nåṣ-å °	
בְּכִירָה	kåbåkīråtu	ד		סָרָה	sårå	
נְשָׁמָה	nåšēm-å			צָרָה	sårå °	
נְשָׁמָה	nåšēmåt	ס		צָרָה	afṣåråt	ס
גְּזֵרָה	gåzar-å			נִצָּה	abnåṣtu	ר
רְבָבָה	råbåbå			גְוִיָה	giby-å	
שְׁמָמָה	šåmåmå			זִמְרָה	zimrå	
רְבָבָה	råbåbot	ר		זִמְרָה	zimrå °	
				צִדְיָה	ṣidyå	
				שִׁבְיָה	šibyå	

435

			בְּכוֹרָה	båkūr-å		
			בְּכוֹרָה	båkūråti	א	
יָמִים	yåməm		בְּכוֹרָה.	båkūråtåk	ב	
פָּנִים	fånəm		בְּכוֹרָה	båkūråtu	ד	
שָׁמַיִם	såməm					
שְׁקָקִים	aššåqəm		דְּבוֹרָה	dūbēr-å °		
יָמִים	yåmīma		דְּבוֹרָה	addūbērəm	ר	
פָּנִים	fånīma					
יָמִי	yåmi	ר+ס	קְטֹרָה	qiṭṭår-å		
פָּנִי	fåni					
שָׁמַי	wšåmi		בִּכּוּרָה	bikkūr-å °		
יָמַי	yåmi	ר+א	בִּכּוּרָה	bikkūrot	ר	
פָּנַי	fåni					
יָמֶיךָ	yåmək	ר+ג	פְּטֹרָה	fēṭidd-å		
פָּנֶיךָ	fånək		שְׁמִטָּה	šēmiṭṭå		
שָׁמֶיךָ	såmək					
יָמָיו	yåmo	ר+ד	קְשִׂיטָה	qaššīṭ-å		
פָּנָיו	fåno					
יָמֶיהָ	yåmiyya	ר+ה	זִקְנָה	zåqånn-å		
פָּנֶיהָ	fåniyya		זִקְנָה	zåqåntu	ד	
יָמֵינוּ	alfånīnu	ר+ו				
יָמֵיכֶם	yåmīkimma	ר+ז	עיצורים עם תנועות			
פָּנֵיכֶם	fånīkimma					
שָׁמֵיכֶם	såmīkimma		רַגְלַי	riggål-āʾi		
פָּנֵיהֶם	fånīyyimma	ר+ט				
שׁוּלַיִם	šūl-əm °		שְׁלִישִׁי	šēlīʿš-åy °		
שׁוּלַי	šūli	ר+ס	שָׁלֵשׁ	šēlīʿsåy °		
שׁוּלָיו	šūlo	ר+ד	שְׁלִישִׁי	wšēlīšåʾəm	ר	
			שָׁלֵשׁ	šēlīšåʾəm		
בְּשָׂמִים	bašm-əm					
תְּרָפִים	tarfəm		דּוּדָאִים	dū'd-īm		
בְּשָׂמִים	bašməm	ר	דּוּדָאִים	dū'dīm	ר	
תְּרָפִים	attarfəm		דּוּדָאִים	dū'dī	ר+ס	
בְּטָנִים	båṭn-əm		פִּדְיוֹם	fid'w-īm		
בְּטָנִים	båṭnəm	ר	פִּדְיוֹם	affid'wīm	ר	
			פִּדְיוֹם	fidwi	ר+ס	
כִּירַיִם	kirr-əm		פִּדְיוֹם	fidwīyyimma	ר+ט	
פָּנִים	kinnəm					
שְׁתַּיִם	šiṭṭəm		רֵיקָם	rīq-əm		
שִׁשִּׁים	šiššəm		רֵיקָם	rīqəm	ר	
שְׁתַּיִם	šittəm					
כִּירַיִם	wkirrəm	ר	שָׁנַיִם	šēn-əm		
פָּנִים	kinnəm		שָׁנַיִם	šēnəm	ר	
שְׁתַּיִם	šiṭṭəm		שָׁנַיִם	šēni	ר+ס	
שִׁשִּׁים	šiššəm		שָׁנַיִם	šēnīnu	ר+ו	
שְׁתַּיִם	šittəm		שָׁנַיִם	šēnīkimma	ר+ז	
שְׁתַּיִם	šitti	ר+ס	שָׁנַיִם	šēnīyyimma	ר+ט	
מָרִים	marr-əm		יָמִים	yåm-əm		
סַמִּים	samməm		פָּנִים	fånəm		
תָּמִים	tamməm		פָּנִים	fånəm		
מָרִים	ammarrəm*	ר	שָׁמַיִם	såməm		
סַמִּים	samməm		שְׁקָקִים	såqəm		

שַׁגָּם	šåg-åm		תַּמִּים	attamməm	
יוֹמָם	yūm-åm		תַּמִּים	tammək	ר+ג
שִׁלְשׁוֹם	šalš-om		פְּקֻדִים	fēqād-əm	
גָּרְזֶן	garz-ən		פְּקֻדִים	affēqādəm	ר
צִפֹּרֶן	ṣēfēr-ən °		פְּקֻדִים	fēqādi	ר+ס
	ṣēferniyya	ר+ה	פְּקֻדִים	fēqādo	ר+ד
			פְּקֻדִים	fēqādīkimma	ר+ז
פִּתְרוֹן	fitr-ån °		פְּקֻדִים	fēqādīyyimma	ר+ט
קִנְיָן	qinyån		מְרֹרִים	mērår-əm	
פִּתְרוֹן	fitrånu	ד	פְּלִילִים	felåləm	
קִנְיָן	qinyånu		שְׁלִישִׁים	šēlåšəm	
קִנְיָן	wqinyånimma	ט	מְרֹרִים	mērårəm	ר
פִּתְרוֹן	fitrånəm	ר	פְּלִילִים	båfēlåləm	
			שְׁלִישִׁים	šēlåšəm	
כִּבְשָׂן	kåbåš-ån		בְּתוּלִים	bētūl-əm	
קָרְבָּן	qåråbån		כְּפוּרִים	kēfūrəm	
קָרְבָּן	qåråbåni	א	בְּתוּלִים	bētūləm	ר
קָרְבָּן	qåråbånåk	ב	כְּפוּרִים	akkēfūrəm	
קָרְבָּן	qåråbånək	ג	בְּתוּלִים	bētūli	ר+ס
קָרְבָּן	qåråbånu	ד	בְּתוּלִים	båbētūliyya	ר+ה
קָרְבָּן	qåråbåna	ה	זְקֵנִים	zåqīn-əm	
קָרְבָּן	qåråbånimma	ט	זְקֵנִים	zåqīnəm	ר
קָרְבָּן	qåråbånīkimma	ר+ז	מְרֹרִים	mårūr-əm	
קָרְבָּן	qåråbånīyyimma	ר+ט	מְרֹרִים	mårūrəm	ר
דִּישׁוֹן	dīš-on		תּוֹפִינִים	tūfēn-əm °	
זָדוֹן	zīdon		תּוֹפִינִים	tūfēni	ר+ס
קִיצוֹן	qīṣon °		בִּכּוּרִים	bikkūr-əm	
תִּיכוֹן	tīkon		כְּפוּרִים	kibbūrəm	
קִיצוֹן	aqqīṣūna	נ	בִּכּוּרִים	bikkūrəm	ר
יָגוֹן	yåg-on		כְּפוּרִים	kibbūrəm	
רָצוֹן	råṣon		בִּכּוּרִים	bikkūri	ר+ס
רָצוֹן	alråṣūnu	ד	שְׁלָמִים	šēlamm-əm	
רָצוֹן	alråṣonkimma	ז	שְׁלָמִים	šēlamməm	ר
רָצוֹן	wabråṣūnimma	ט	שְׁלָמִים	šēlammi	ר+ס
			שְׁלָמִים	šēlammək	ר+ג
פִּדְיוֹן	fidy-on		שְׁלָמִים	šēlammo	ר+ד
פִּקָּדוֹן	fiqdon		שְׁלָמִים	šēlammīkimma	ר+ז
פִּתְרוֹן	fitron		שְׁלָמִים	šēlammīyyimma	ר+ט
זִכָּרוֹן	zakr-on		שִׁבֳּלִים	šabbēl-əm	
יֵרָקוֹן	yēråq-on		שִׁבֳּלִים	šabbēləm	ר
יְשִׁימוֹן	yåšīm-on		זְקֵנִים	zåqånn-əm °	
שִׁדָּפוֹן	šådåf-on		זְקֵנִים	alzåqånno	ר+ד
שִׁדָּפוֹן	šåfåfon		שׁוּמִים	šuwwåm-əm	
			שׁוּמִים	aššuwwåməm	ר

צָרֶבֶת	ṣårrēb-ət			שַׁבָּתוֹן	šåbbåt-on	
בַּת	b-at			כִּלָּיוֹן	kalliyy-on	
בַּת	bitti	א		שִׁגָּעוֹן	šaggiyyon	
בַּת	bittåk	ב		צִיצִת	ṣīṣ-ət	
בַּת	bittu	ד		צִיצִת	ṣīṣiyyot	ר
בַּת	wbintu			בְּכִית	bēk-ət ○	
בַּת	bitta	ה		בְּרִית	bērət	
בַּת	bittånu	ו		רֶשֶׁת	rēšət	
בַּת	båbatkimma	ז		שְׁבִית	šēbət ○	
בַּת	bånot	ר		שָׁלִית	šēlət ○	
בַּת	bånūti	ר+א		שֵׁנִית	šēnət	
בַּת	bånūtåk	ר+ב		בְּרִית	bērīti	א
בַּת	wbånūtək	ר+ג		בְּרִית	wbērītåk	ב
בַּת	bånūto	ר+ד		בְּכִית	bēkītu	ד
בַּת	bånåtiyya	ר+ה		בְּרִית	bērītu	
בַּת	bånūtīnu	ר+ו		שָׁלִית	wafšēlitta	ה
בַּת	bånūtīkimma	ר+ז		שְׁבִית	wšēbetkimma	ז
בַּת	bånūtimma	ר+ט		קֶשִׁית	kåš-ət	
פָּרָת	får-åt			תָּלִית	tålət ○	
כְּתֹבֶת	kitb-åt			תָּלִית	tålītåk	ב
דַּלֶּקֶת	dålåq-åt			גָּפְרִית	gifr-ət	
יְכֹלֶת	yåkålåt			שִׁלְשִׁית	šilšət	
יַבֶּשֶׁת	yåbbåš-åt			גָּזִית	gizz-ət	
דְמוּת	dēm-ot			כְּרִיתֻת	kērīt-ət	
דְמוּת	afdēmūtu	ד		צְמִיתֻת	ṣēmītət	
דְמוּת	wkådēmūtånu	ו		פָּרֹכֶת	fårēk-ət	
מָלוֹת	mål-ot			יוֹתֶרֶת	yūtår-ət	
פָּדוּת	fådot			קוֹמְמִית	qūmåmət	
מְכַסּוֹת	maks-ot			כִּסָּמֶת	kissåm-ət	
כְּסוּת	kass-ot			כַּפֹּרֶת	kibbårət	
קָשְׁוֹת	qaššot			כֻּתֹּנֶת	kittånət	
כְּסוּת	kassūtåk	ב		קְטֹרֶת	qiṭṭårət	
כְּסוּת	kassūtu	ד		כֻּתֹּנֶת	kittåntu	ד
כְּסוּת	kassūta	ה		כֻּתֹּנֶת	kittånot	ר
קָשְׁוֹת	qaššot	ר		כֻּתֹּנֶת	afkittånūtimma	ר+ט
קָשְׁוֹת	wqaššūto	ר+ד		יַרְכִית	yērakk-ət ○	
מְרֹרוֹת	mērår-ot			ירכית	wyērakkētu	ד
מְרֹרוֹת	mērårot	ר		בָּרֶקֶת	barrēq-ət	
טֹטָפֹת	ṭåṭåf-ot			יַבֶּלֶת	yabbēlət	
מַלְכוֹת	målåkot ○			יַלֶּפֶת	yallēfət	
מַלְכוֹת	målåkūtu	ד		תְּכֵלֶת	takkēlət	
טֹטָפֹת	alṭåṭåfot	ר				

מַמְלָכָה	mamlåkåt	ס	כְּבֵדוֹת	kåbūd-ot	
מֶרְכָּבָה	markåbåt		מַגְדָן	magdån-ot	
מַמְלָכָה	mamlåkti	א	מִגְדָן	wmagdånot	ר
מַמְלָכָה	mamlåktu	ד	שְׁרִירוּת	šarrīr-ot	
מֶרְכָּבָה	markåbtu		גְּבָלוֹת	gåball-ot	
מַמְלָכָה	mamlåkåt	ר	בִּלְתִּי	bil-ti	
מַגֵּפָה	ma-ggīf-a		זוּלָתִי	zūl-åti	
מַסֵּכָה	massīka				
מַגֵּפָה	maggīfūti	ר+א			
מַסֵּכָה	massīkūtimma	ר+ט	4. המוספים בסופם ובראשם		
מַצֵּבָה	må-ṣṣīb-a		(לפי סדר הסופיות)		
מַצֵּבָה	måṣṣībåt	ס			
מַצֵּבָה	måṣṣībūtīyyimma	ר+ט			תנועות
מַתָּנָה	må-ttån-a		פְּרָזִי	a-frizz-i	
מַתָּנָה	kåmåttånåt	ס	אַכְזְרִי	a-kzarr-i	
מַתָּנָה	måttånot	ר	שָׂפָה	a-šf-a	
מַתָּנָה	måttånūtīkimma	ר+ז	שָׂפָה	ašfåt	ס
מְסִלָּה	må-sīl-a		שָׂפָה	ašfåtu	ד
מְרִיבָה	mårība		שָׂפָה	ašfåtəm	ר
מְרִיבָה	båmårībåt	ס	שָׂפָה	ašfåtək	ר+ג
מְצֻלָּה	må-ṣal-a °		שָׂפָה	ašfåtiyya	ר+ה
מֻקְשֶׁה	måqåša				
מַשְׂגֵּה	måšåga		נְקָרָה	a-nqīr-a °	
מְצֻלָּה	bammåṣålot	ר	נְקָרָה	banqīrot	ר
מְנוּסָה	må-nūs-a °		מְדוּכָה	a-mdūk-a	
מְנוּסָה	månūsåt	ס	מִצְוָה	mē-ṣåb-a	
מוֹקְדָה	mū-qīd-a		מִצְוָה	mēṣåbot	ר
מוֹרָשָׁה	mū-råš-a		מִצְוָה	mēṣåbūti	ר+א
תִּלָּנָה	ti-llån-a °		מִצְוָה	mēṣåbūtək	ר+ג
תִּלָּנָה	tillånot	ר	מִצְוָה	mēṣåbūto	ר+ד
תִּלָּנָה	tillånūtīkimma	ר+ז	מְנוֹרָה	mē-nūr-a	
תִּלָּנָה	tillånūtimma	ר+ט	מְנוֹרָה	mēnūråt	ס
תְּמִירָה	tē-mīr-a °		מִסְפָּה	ma-sf-a	
תמירה	wtēmīråtu	ד	מִקְנֶה	maqna °	
תְּבוּנָה	tē-būn-a		מִקְנֶה	maqnåt	ס
תְּמוּנָה	tēmūna		מִקְנֶה	maqnåtu	ד
תְּנוּפָה	tēnūfa		מַסָּה	ma-ss-a	
תְּקוּמָה	tēqūma		מַסָּה	båmassot	ר
תְּקוּפָה	tēqūfa		מַמְלָכָה	ma-mlåk-a °	
תְּרוּמָה	tērūma		מֶרְכָּבָה	markåba °	
תְּשׁוּמָה	tēšūma °		מִשְׁכָּבָה	maškåba	
תְּשׁוּקָה	tēšūqa °				
תְּמוּנָה	tēmūnåt	ס			

שְׁפָטִים	a-šfåṭ-əm		
שְׁפָטִים	ašfåṭəm	ר	
מְגָרִים	mē-garr-əm ○		
מְגָרִים	mēgarri	ר+ס	
מְגָרִים	mēgarri	ר+א	
מְגָרִים	mēgarrək	ר+ג	
מְגָרִים	mēgarrīyyimma	ר+ט	
מְכַנְסִים	ma-knēs-əm ○		
מְכַנְסִים	maknēsi	ר+ס	
מִשְׁפָתִים	ma-šfåṭ-əm		
מִשְׁפָתִים	ammašfåṭəm	ר	
נַפְתָלִים	ni-ftål-əm ○		
נַפְתָלִים	niftåli	ר+ס	
אֶתְנַן	i-tn-an		
נְקָיוֹן	a-nqiyy-on		
אַשְׁמֹרֶת	i-šmår-ət		
תְכֻנָת	a-tkēn-ət ○		
תְכֻנָת	wbatkantu	ד	
מַשְׂכִּית	ma-šk-ət		
מַשְׂכִּית	maškiyyūtimma	ר+ט	
מִסְגֶרֶת	ma-sgēr-ət		
מִסְכֶּנֶת	maskēnət		
מַתְכֹנֶת	matkēnət		
מִסְגֶרֶת	almasgirtu	ד	
מַתְכֹנֶת	båmatkanta	ה	
מִשְׁמֶרֶת	ma-šmår-ət		
מִשְׁמֶרֶת	mašmårti	א	
מִשְׁמֶרֶת	mašmårtåk	ב	
מִשְׁמֶרֶת	mašmårtu	ד	
מִשְׁמֶרֶת	wmašmårtimma	ט	
מִצְנֶפֶת	må-ṣnēf-ət		
מוֹלֶדֶת	mū-lēd-ət		
מוֹלֶדֶת	mūlēdēti	א	
מוֹלֶדֶת	mūlēdētåk	ב	
מוֹלֶדֶת	wmūladtåk	ד	
מוֹלֶדֶת	mūlēdētu	ד	
מוֹלֶדֶת	walmūlēdētånu	ו	
תַבְנִית	ti-bn-ət		
תַרְבִּית	tirbət		
תַבְנִית	aftibnītimma	ט	

תְנוּפָה	tēnūfåt		
תְקוּפָה	tēqūfåt		
תְרוּמָה	tērūmåt		
תְשׁוּמָה	aftēšūmåt		
תְרוּמָה	tērūmåti	א	
תְשׁוּקָה	tēšūqattək	ג	
תְשׁוּקָה	tēšūqåttu	ד	
תְרוּמָה	tērūmåtimma	ט	
תְרוּמָה	tērūmåtīkimma	ר+ז	
תַרְדֵמָה	ta-rdīmm-a		
תוֹדָה	tū-d-a		
תוֹרָה	tūra		
תוֹרָה	tūdåt	ס	
תוֹרָה	tūråt		
תוֹרָה	wattūrot	ר	
תוֹרָה	wtūrūti	ר+א	
תוֹרָה	wtūrūtək	ר+ג	
תוֹרָה	tūrūto	ר+ד	
מַסְוֶה	må-sūwʷ-ā		
אַזְכָרָה	ē-zåkår-å		
אַזְכָרָה	ēzåkårtā	ה	
מִטָה	mē-ṭ-å		
מִטָה	mēṭåttək	ג	
מִקְוֶה	ma-kw-å		
מִקְוֶה	maqwå		
מִקְוֶה	makwåt	ס	
מְזוּזָה	må-zūz-å		
מְשׂוּרָה	måšūrå		
מְזוּזָה	måzūzot	ר	
מַכָּה	mu-kk-å		
מַכָּה	makkot	ר	
מַכָּה	makkūtåk	ר+ב	

עיצורים עם תנועות

נָשִׁים	i-nš-əm		
נָשִׁים	inšəm	ר	
נָשִׁים	inši	ר+ס	
נָשִׁים	inši	ר+א	
נָשִׁים	inšo	ר+ד	
נָשִׁים	inšīnu	ר+ו	
נָשִׁים	inšīkimma	ר+ז	
נָשִׁים	inšīyyimma	ר+ט	
שָׁקֵד	a-šqīd-əm		
שָׁקֵד	ašqīdəm	ר	

	maškåråtåk	מַשְׂכֹּרֶת	ב	tå-nšēm-ət	תִּנְשֶׁמֶת	
	tū-ld-åt	תּוֹלֶדֶת		a-fqår-åt	בְּקֹרֶת	
	tūldåt	תּוֹלֶדֶת	ר	aškåbåt	שְׁכֹבֶת	
	tūldūtimma	תּוֹלֶדֶת	ר+ט	aškåbtåk	שְׁכֹבֶת	ב
	a-šq-ot	הַשְׁקוֹת		aškåbtu	שְׁכֹבֶת	ד
	a-šfīk-ot	שְׁפָכוֹת		ma-mkēr-åt	מִמְכֶּרֶת	
	mī-nq-ot	מֵינִקֹת		ma-mšål-åt	מֶמְשָׁלָה	
	ti-rb-ot	תַּרְבּוֹת		maškåråt °	מַשְׂכֹּרֶת	
				maškåråti	מַשְׂכֹּרֶת	א

ד. משרשים בני ארבעה וחמישה עיצורים

	šåmån-a	שִׁמְנָה		kirkåb	כַּרְכֹּב	
	šåmånåt	שִׁמְנָה	ס	filgåš	פִּילֶגֶשׁ	
	lå'l-ā °	לֶלָאָה		kirkåbu	כַּרְכֹּב	ד
	lålā'ot	לֶלָאָה	ר	wfilgåšu	פִּילֶגֶשׁ	
	šåmån-əm	שְׁמָנִים		affilgåšəm	פִּילֶגֶשׁ	ר
	šåmånəm	שְׁמָנִים	ר	barzəl	בַּרְזֶל	
	sinnuwwår-əm	סַנְוֵרִים		karməl	כַּרְמֶל	
	afsinnuwwårəm	סַנְוֵרִים	ר	taršəš	תַּרְשִׁישׁ	
	širšår-ət °	שַׁרְשֶׁרֶת		kaftår	כַּפְתֹּר	
	širšårot	שַׁרְשֶׁרֶת	ר	kaftarriyya	כַּפְתֹּר	ר+ה
	qašqēš-ət	קַשְׂקֶשֶׂת		kaftarrīyyimma	כַּפְתֹּר	ר+ט
	ṣånṣēn-ət	צִנְצֶנֶת		såfsåf	אַסְפַּסֻף	
	gilgål-åt	גֻּלְגֹּלֶת		dårdår	דַּרְדַּר	
	algilgålūtimma	גֻּלְגֹּלֶת	ר+ט	ṣålṣål	צְלָצַל	
	dūgīfåt	דְּגִיפַת		qådqåd	קָדְקֹד	
	mardåror	מָרְדְּרוֹר		qålqål	קַלְקַל	
				qådqådåk	קָדְקֹד	ב
				sånåfər	סַנְפִּיר	
				qinnåmon	קִנָּמוֹן	
				šēmīn-i	שְׁמִינִי	
				aššēmīnət	שְׁמִינִי	נ

ב. Nouns Formed from Guttural Roots

א. משורש בן שני עיצורים

el	אֶל		il	אֵל	
eṣ	עֵץ		it	אֵת	
å'īṣ	עֵץ		iṣ	עֵץ	
īli	אֵל	א			

441

אָמָה	åm-å		
אָמָה	åmåti	א	
אָמָה	åmåtåk	ב	
אָמָה	åmåtu	ד	
אָמָה	åmåtå	ה	
אָמָה	wåmå'ūtək	ר+ג	
אָמָה	wåmå'ūto	ר+ד	
אָמָה	wåmå'ūtīkimma	ר+ז	
כֹּחַ	kå		
חֵץ	iṣ °		
עֵד	id		
עֵד	ed		
עֵד	wīda	נ	
חֵץ	iṣṣi	א	
חֵץ	iṣṣəm	ר	
עֵד	īdəm		
חֵץ	wiṣṣo	ר+ד	

אֶת	ūti		
אֶת	ūtåk		ב
עֵץ	īṣåk		
אֶת	ūtək		ג
עֵץ	īṣək		
אֶת	ūtu		ד
אֶת	ūta		ה
עֵץ	īṣa		
אֶת	ūtånu		ו
אֶת	itkimma		ז
אֶת	ūtimma		ט
אֶת	ūtīyyinna		י
אֶל	bå'īləm		ר
עֵץ	īṣəm		
עֵץ	īṣi	ר+ס	
עֵץ	īṣo	ר+ד	
אֵשׁ	aš		
אֵשׁ	bēš		
אֵשׁ	ēšu		ד
אִשָּׁה	ēš-i		
אִשָּׁה	lēši		א

ב. משורש בן שלושה עיצורים

פ"א גרונית

1. הפשוטים

אַיִל	īl		
אַיִן	īn		
אִישׁ	īš		
הֵן	īn		
חַיִל	īl		
חַיִל	īl		
חֵיק	īq °		
עַיִט	īṭ		
עַיִן	īn		
עִיר	īr		
עִיר	īr °		
אַיִן	īninni	א	
אִישׁ	īši		
עַיִן	īni		
אַיִן	īnåk	ב	
חֵיק	īqåk		
עַיִן	īnåk		
אִישׁ	īšək	ג	
עַיִן	īnək		
אַיִן	īninnu	ד	
חַיִל	īlu		

חֵיק	īqu		
עַיִן	īnu		
עִיר	īru		
עִיר	īru		
אַיִן	īninna	ה	
אִישׁ	īša		
חֵיק	īqa		
עַיִן	īna		
עִיר	īra		
עַיִן	īnånu	ו	
אַיִן	inkimma	ז	
אַיִן	īnimma	ט	
חַיִל	īlimma		
עִיר	īrimma		
אַיִל	īləm	ר	
עַיִן	īnəm		
עִיר	'ā:rəm		
עִיר	wīrəm		
עַיִן	īnot		
עִיר	'arrəm		
אַיִל	īli	ר+ס	
עַיִן	īni		
עִיר	'arri		
עִיר	'arrək	ר+ג	
חַיִל	wīlo	ר+ד	
עַיִן	īno		

אֵת	itta			עִיר	ʿarro		
חָם	åmiyya			עַיִן	īniyya	ר+ה	
עַם	imma			עִיר	larriyya		
אָב	åbīnu	ו		עַיִן	wīnīnu	ר+ו	
אֵת	ittånu			עַיִן	īnīkimma	ר+ז	
הֵן	innånu			עִיר	ʿarrīkimma		
עַם	immånu			עַיִן	īnīyyimma	ר+ט	
אָב	åbīkimma	ז		עִיר	ʿarrīyyimma		
אַף	miyyåfkimma			**אָב**	**ab**		
אֵת	atkimma			אָד	ad		
הֵן	winnåkimma			אַט	aṭ °		
עַם	immåkimma			אִי	ay °		
אָב	åbīkən	ח		אֵל	al		
אָב	åbīyyimma	ט		אֵם	am		
אַף	abbimma			אַף	af		
אֵת	ētimma			אֵת	at		
הֵן	winnimma			הֵן	an		
עַם	immimma			חָם	am °		
עֵת	bēttimma			עֵז	az		
אָב	åbīyyinna	י		עַם	am		
אָב	åbot			עֵת	at		
אַף	abbəm	ר		אַט	lēṭṭå		
אֵז	åʾizzəm			עֵת	bēt		
אִי	ayyi	ר+ס		אָב	åbi	ס	
אָב	åbūti	ר+א		אָב	åbi	א	
אֵל	īli			אֵם	immi		
אָב	åbūtək	ר+ג		אַף	abbi		
אֵל	īlək			אֵת	itti		
אָב	åbūto	ר+ד		הֵן	innåni		
אֵל	īlo			עַם	immi		
אַף	babbo			אֵם	immåk	ב	
אֵל	īliyya	ר+ה		אַף	abbåk		
אָב	åbūtīnu	ר+ו		אֵת	ittåk		
אֵל	īlīnu			הֵן	innåk		
אָב	åbūtīkimma	ר+ז		עַם	immåk		
אֵל	īlīkimma			אָב	åbək	ג	
אָב	åbūtimma	ר+ט		אַף	abbək		
אֵל	īlīyyimma			אֵת	ittək		
אַף	abbīyyimma			הֵן	innək		
אֵל	īlīyyinna	ר+י		חָם	åmək		
הַר	**år**			עֵז	wizzək		
חֹל	ål			עַם	immək		
חֹם	åm			אָב	åbiyyu	ד	
חֵן	ån			אֵם	immu		
חֹק	åq			אַף	abbu		
הַר	å:rå			אֵת	ittu		
הַר	åri*	א		עַם	immu		
חֹק	åqqåk	ב		עֵת	bēttu		
חֵן	innu	ד		אָב	åbiyya	ה	
חֹק	åqqåkimma	ז		אֵם	imma		
חֹק	åqqimma	ט		אַף	abba		
הַר	årəm	ר					

עָז	ūnūtimma	ר+ט		חֹק	aqqəm	
עוֹר	ūrūtimma			הַר	åri	ר+ס
חַג	ʻag			חֹק	aqqi	
חַי	ʻay			הַר	båråri	
עַד	ʻad			חֹק	aqqo	ר+ד
עֹד	ʻad			הַר	wmiyyēråriyya	ר+ה
עַז	ʻaz			**אוֹב**	ob	
עֹז	ʻaz			אוֹר	or	
עַל	ʻal			אוּר	or °	
עַם	ʻam			חוּט	oṭ	
חַי	ʻayyå	נ		אוּר	uʼūrək	ג
עַז	ʻazza			אוֹב	åʼūbot	ר
חַג	ʻaggi	א		אוּר	åʼūrəm	
עַד	ʻādi			**אוֹן**	ūn °	
עֹז	ʻazzi			אוֹת	ūt	
עַם	ʻammi			הוֹד	ūd °	
חַג	baggåk	ב		חוֹל	ūl	
עֹז	bazzåk			חוּם	ūm	
עַם	ʻammåk			חוֹף	ūf	
עַם	ʻåmmåk			חוּץ	ūṣ	
עַם	ʻamməkk	ג		עוֹד	ūd	
עַם	ʻammu	ד		עֹל	ūl	
עַם	ʻamma	ה		עָוֹן	ūn	
עֹז	ʻazzåkimma	ז		עוֹף	ūf	
עַם	ʻammimma	ט		עוֹר	ūr	
חַי	ʻayyəm	ר		עֹל	ūl	
עַם	ʻamməm			חוּץ	miyyoṣ	
חַי	ʻayyot	ר+נ		חוּץ	åʼūṣå	
עַל	ʻāli	ר+ס		אוֹן	ūni	א
עַם	ʻammi			אוֹד	būdinni	
עַל	ʻāli	ר+א		עָוֹן	ūni	
עַל	ʻālək	ר+ג		הוֹד	miyyūdåk	ב
עַל	ʻālo	ר+ד		עוֹד	ūdåk	
עַם	miyyammo			אוֹן	ūnu	ד
עַל	ʻāliyya	ר+ה		עוֹד	ūdinnu	
עַם	ʻammiyya			עָוֹן	ūnu	
עַל	ʻālīnu	ר+ו		עוֹר	ūru	
עַל	ʻālīkimma	ר+ז		עֹל	ūlu	
עַל	ʻālīyyimma	ר+ט		עָוֹן	ūna	ה
עַל	ʻālīyyinna	ר+י		עוֹר	ūra	
עֵצָה	īṣå			עֹל	olkimma	ז
חֲצִי	ēṣi			עוֹד	åʼūdimma	ט
חַצִי	iṣyu	ד		עָוֹן	ūnimma	
אפה	åfi			אוֹת	ūtot	
חָזֶה	åzi			עָוֹן	ūnot	
חֹלִי	åli			עוֹר	ūrot	
חֲרִי	åri			אוֹת	ūtūti	ר+א
חֹרִי	åri			אוֹת	ūtūto	ר+ד
חָזֶה	å:zot	ר		עָוֹן	lūnīnu	ר+ו
				עָוֹן	ūnūtīkimma	ר+ז

אֹזֶן	bēzni	ר+ס		חֲלִי	wåləm	
אֱצִיל	ēṣīli			אַקּוֹ	åqu	
חֵלֶב	ēlåbi			חֲמָר	īmår	
עָקֵב	ʿåqåbi			חֹמֶר	īmår	
אֹזֶן	bēzēni			אָבִיב	ēbəb	
חלם	ēlåmo	ר+ד		אֵבֶל	ēbəl	
חלם	ēlåmūtīnu	ר+ו		אדם	ēdəm °	
אֹזֶן	bēznīkimma	ר+ז		אֹזֶן	ēzən	
אֹזֶן	bēznīyyimma	ר+ט		אֹזֶן	ēzən	
אֹזֶן	bēzēnīyyimma			אֱלִיל	ēlə l°	
הֶבֶל	bēbålīyyimma			אָפִיל	ēfəl °	
חֵלֶב	ēlåbīyyinna	ר+י		אֱצִיל	ēṣəl °	
הֲלֹם	ēlåm			אֵצֶל	ēṣəl	
חָלָל	ēlål			הֶבֶל	ēbəl °	
עֵבֶר	ēbår			חֵלֶב	ēləb	
עֵנָב	ēnåb			חלם	ēləm °	
עֲנָק	ēnåq			חֵלֶף	ēləf	
חָלָל	ēlåləm	ר		חֶסֶד	ēsəd	
עֵנָב	ēnåbəm			עֵגֶל	ēgəl	
עֲנָק	ēnåqəm			עֵמֶק	ēməq	
עֵנָב	ēnåbi	ר+ס		עֵמֶק	ēməq	
חָלָל	ēlålīyyimma	ר+ט		עָקֵב	ēqəb	
עֵבֶר	ibrīyyimma			עָקֵב	ēqəb	
עֵנָב	ēnåbīyyimma			עֶרֶב	ērəb	
אָדָם	ēdom			עֶרֶב	ērəb	
אֱנוֹשׁ	ēnoš			עֵשֶׂב	ēšəb	
חֲלוֹם	ēlom			אדם	idma	נ
חמוד	ēmod			אֹזֶן	bēzni	א
חֲמוֹר	ēmor			אֵצֶל	išli	
עֲבוּר	ēbor			חלם	bēlmi	
חֲמוֹר	ēmūråk	ב		אֹזֶן	iznåk	ב
עֲבוּר	bēbūråk			חֶסֶד	isdåk	
עֲבוּר	bēbūrək	ג		חֶסֶד	isdək	ג
חֲמוֹר	ēmūru	ד		אֹזֶן	iznu	ד
עֲבוּר	bēbūra	ה		חֵלֶב	ilbu	
עֲבוּר	bēbūrimma	ט		חלם	ilmu	
אֱנוֹשׁ	ēnūšəm	ר		חֶסֶד	isdu	
חֲמוֹר	ēmūrəm			אֵצֶל	išla	ה
חֲמוֹר	ēmūrīnu	ר+ו		חֵלֶב	ilba	
חֲמוֹר	ēmūrīyyimma	ר+ט		אֹזֶן	iznimma	ט
עֲבִי	ʿåbi			חֵלֶב	ilbimma	
עֲדִי	ʿådi			אֹזֶן	wēzēnəm	ר
עָלֶה	ʿåli			אֱלִיל	ēlīləm	
עָנִי	ʿåni °			חֵלֶב	åʾēlåbəm	
עֳנִי	ʿåni °			חלם	åʾēlåmot	
עֲנִי	ʿanyi	א		חֶסֶד	åʾēsådəm	
עֲדִי	idyåk	ב		עֶרֶב	åʾirbəm	
עֲנִי	lanyåk			אָפִיל	ēfīlot	ר+נ
עֲנִי	ʿanyək	ג				

445

Hebrew	Transliteration	Code
עֵדִי	idyu	ד
עֵדִי	idyimma	ט
עֲנִי	ʿanyimma	
חָשׁוּק	āšoq °	
חָשׁוּק	wāšūqīyyimma	ר+ט
עָנוּ	ʿānu	
אַבִּיר	åbər	
אֶבֶן	åbən	
אַדִּיר	ådər	
אֶדֶן	ådən	
אֵיד	åyəd °	
אֶלֶף	åləf	
אמן	åmən °	
אָמֵן	åmən	
אֹמֶר	åmər	
אָמָשׁ	åməš	
אָסִיף	åsəf	
אָסָם	åsəm °	
אֹפֶן	åfən	
אֶפֶס	åfəs	
אֶפֶס	åfəs	
אֶרֶז	årəz	
אֶרֶךְ	årək	
אֶרֶךְ	årək	
אֶרֶץ	årəṣ	
אֲשֶׁר	åšək	
אֹשֶׁר	åšər	
חֹדֶשׁ	ådəš	
חָזָק	åzəq	
חָמָס	åməs	
חֹמֶץ	åməṣ	
חֹמֶץ	åməṣ	
חֹמֶר	åmər	
חֵמֶת	åmət	
חָצִיר	åṣər	
חָצֵר	åṣər	
חֶרֶב	årəb	
חֵרֶם	årəm	
חֹשֶׁךְ	åšək	
חֹשֶׁן	åšən	
אֶרֶץ	åršå	
חָזָק	åzēqa	נ
אֹמֶר	åmēri	ס
אֶרֶץ	årši	א
אֲשֶׁר	båšīri	
חָמָס	åmēsi	
חֶרֶב	arbi	
אָסָם	båsīmåk	ב
אֶרֶץ	årṣåk	
חֶרֶב	årbåk	
אֹרֶךְ	arku	ד
אֶרֶץ	årṣu	
חֶרֶב	arbu	
אֹרֶךְ	arkå	ה
אֶרֶץ	årṣå	
אֶרֶץ	åreṣkimma	ז
אֵיד	åydimma	ט
אמן	åmēnimma	
אֶרֶץ	årṣimma	
אֶבֶן	åbånəm	ר
אַדִּיר	ådīrəm	
אֶדֶן	ådēnəm	
אֶלֶף	ålåfəm	
אָרֶז	kårēzəm	
אֶרֶץ	årṣot	
חֹדֶשׁ	ådēšəm	
חֹמֶר	åmērəm	
חָצֵר	å:ṣīrəm	
אֶבֶן	åbåni	ר+ס
אֶדֶן	ådēni	
אֶלֶף	ålåfi	
אֶפֶס	åfēsi	
חֹדֶשׁ	lådēši	
אֶלֶף	ålåfək	ר+ג
אֶבֶן	åbåno	ר+ד
אֶדֶן	ådēno	
אֶבֶן	åbåniyya	ר+ה
אֶדֶן	ådēniyya	
חֹדֶשׁ	ådēšīkimma	ר+ז
אֶדֶן	ådēnīyyimma	ר+ט
אֶרֶץ	bårṣūtimma	
חָצֵר	båṣīrūtimma	
אָבָק	åbåq	
אֲגַם	ågåm °	
אָדָם	ådåm	
אֹדֶם	ådåm	
אֹכֶל	åkål	
אָסָר	åsår	
אָפָר	åfår	
אֶשֶׁל	åšål	
אָשָׁם	åšåm	
אֲשֶׁר	åšår °	
הָדָר	ådår	
חֶבֶר	åbår	
חָזָק	åzåq	
חָלָץ	ålåṣ	
חָלָק	ålåq	
חֵלֶק	ålåq	

עֲגִיל	ʿāgəl			חֹמֶר	å̊mår		
עָמַת	ʿāmət			חֹסֶר	å̊sår		
עֹרֶב	ʿārəb			חֶרֶט	å̊raṭ		
עֹרֶב	ʿārəb			חָשָׁב	å̊šåb		
עָרֵל	ʿārəl			חָתָת	å̊tåt		
עָרֹם	ʿārəm °			עֹמֶר	å̊mår		
עֶרֶשׂ	ʿārəš			אֹכֶל	aklå̊k		ב
עָשָׁן	ʿāšən			אֲשֶׁר	å̊šårå̊k		
חָכָם	ʿākēmå̊t		נ+ס	חֵלֶק	å̊lå̊qå̊k		
עֶבֶד	ʿabdi		א	חֵלֶק	miyyå̊lå̊šək		ג
חתים	ʿātīmå̊k		ב	אָשָׁם	å̊šåmu		ד
חֹתָן	ʿātēnå̊k			חָתָת	wå̊tå̊tkimma		ז
עֶבֶד	ʿabdå̊k			אֹכֶל	aklimma		ט
עֶבֶד	å̊bdå̊k			אָשָׁם	å̊šåmimma		
חֹתָן	ʿātēnu		ד	חֵלֶק	å̊lqimma		
עֶבֶד	ʿabdu			אָנֹם	å̊:gå̊məm		ר
עֶרֶשׂ	ʿaršu			חָשָׁב	wå̊šå̊bi		ר+ס
עָשָׁן	ʿašnu			אָסֶר	å̊så̊riyya		ר+ה
חֹתָן	ʿātintu		נ	אָנֹם	å̊gå̊mīyyimma		ר+ט
עֶבֶד	ʿabdå̊kimma		ז	אָדֹן	å̊don		
חָכָם	ʿākēməm		ר	אַלּוּף	å̊lof		
עֶבֶד	ʿābēdəm			אָרֹן	å̊ron		
עָרֵל	ʿārēləm			חֹמֶט	å̊moṭ		
עָרֹם	ʿārēməm			אָדֹן	å̊danni		א
עֶבֶד	ʿåbå̊dəm			אָדֹן	å̊dannək		ג
חָכָם	ʿākēmi		ר+ס	אָדֹן	å̊:dūnəm		ר
עֶבֶד	å̊bå̊di			אָדֹן	å̊danni		ר+ס
עֶבֶד	å̊bå̊di		ר+א	אַלּוּף	å̊lūfi		
עֶבֶד	å̊bå̊då̊k		ר+ג	אָדֹן	å̊danno		ר+ד
חֹתָן	ʿātēno		ר+ד	אָדֹן	å̊danniyya		ר+ה
עֶבֶד	å̊bå̊do			אָדֹן	lå̊dannīyyimma		ר+ט
חָכָם	ʿākēmiyya		ר+ה	אַלּוּף	å̊lūfīyyimma		
עֶבֶד	å̊bå̊dīkimma		ר+ז				
חָכָם	ʿākom			אוֹצָר	ūṣår °		
חָרֹם	ʿārom			חוֹתָם	ūtå̊m		
עָבֹט	ʿāboṭ			חֹפֶן	ūfå̊n °		
עָרֹם	ʿārom			עדן	ūdå̊n °		
עָרֹם	ʿārom			עוֹלָם	ūlå̊m		
עָשׂוֹר	ʿāšor			עֹמֶר	ūmår		
עַתּוּד	ʿātod °			אוֹצָר	ūṣåru		ד
עָבוֹט	ʿābūṭu		ד	עדן	miyyūdå̊ni		ר+ס
עַתּוּד	ʿātūdəm		ר	אוֹצָר	būṣårūti		ר+א
חֶבֶל	å̊bəl			חֹפֶן	ūfå̊no		ר+ד
אָטָד	å̊ṭå̊d			חֹפֶן	ūfå̊nīkimma		ר+ז
חֹבֶר	å̊bår			חָכָם	ʿåkəm		
חָגָב	å̊gåb			חֶרֶשׂ	ʿårəš		
חָדָשׁ	å̊dåš			חתים	ʿåtəm		
חָלָב	å̊låb			חֹתָן	ʿåtən		
חֹמֶר	å̊mår			חֹתָן	ʿåtən		
				עֶבֶד	ʿåbəd		

עָמַד	immåd °			עָנָב	ʿågåb	
אוֹיֵב	uyyåb			עֶדֶר	ʿådår	
אוֹיֵב	iyyåbi	א		עֵזֶר	ʿåzår	
עָמַד	immådi			עָמָל	ʿåmål	
אוֹיֵב	iyyåbåk	ב		עָנָן	ʿånån	
אוֹיֵב	iyyåbək	ג		עָנָף	ʿånåf °	
אוֹיֵב	iyyåbo	ר+ד		עָפָר	ʿåfår	
אוֹיֵב	wiyyåbīnu	ר+ו		עֶצֶם	ʿåṣåm	
אוֹיֵב	iyyåbīkimma	ר+ז		עָקָר	ʿåqår	
אוֹיֵב	iyyåbīyyimma	ר+ט		עָקָר	ʿåqår	
אֵזוֹב	izzob			עָקֵשׁ	ʿåqåš	
אֵפוֹד	ibbod			עָרֵב	ʿåråb	
אָתוֹן	itton			עָרֵךְ	ʿåråk	
הִלּוּל	illol °			עוֹרֶף	ʿåråf	
אָתוֹן	ittunåk	ב		עָשָׁר	ʿåšår	
אָתוֹן	ittunu	ד		חֶדֶר	ʿå:dårå	
אָתוֹן	ittunot	ר		חָדָשׁ	ʿådåsa	
הִלּוּל	illuləm			עָקָר	ʿåqrå	
עָנִי	ʿanni			עֵזֶר	bazri	א
עָנִי	ʿanni			עָמָל	ʿåmåli	
עָנִי	ʿannīnu	ר+ו		עֶצֶם	ʿåṣåmi	
חָסִיד	assəd °			עֵזֶר	ʿåzråk	ב
חָסִיד	assīdåk	ב		עָנָן	wånånåk	
אַגָּן	aggån °			עָפָר	ʿåfåråk	
אַיָּל	ayyål			עֶרֶךְ	ʿårkåk	
אַגָּן	baggånot	ר		עוֹרֶף	ʿårfåk	
חֹטֶב	åṭṭåb			עָפָר	ʿåfåru	ד
חָמֵשׁ	ʿamməš			עֶרֶךְ	ʿarku	
עִוֵּר	ʿawwər			עוֹרֶף	ʿarfu	
עָמִית	ʿammət °			עָמָל	ʿåmålånu	ו
עָשִׁיר	ʿaššər			עוֹרֶף	wåråfkimma	ז
עָמִית	ʿammītåk	ב		חָנָב	kågåbəm	ר
עָמִית	ʿammītu	ד		חֶדֶר	wmiyyådårəm	
חֹשֵׁב	ʿaššåb			חָדָשׁ	ʿådåsəm	
עָנָג	ʿannåg			עֶדֶר	ʿådårəm	
עָנָג	wånnågå	נ		עֶצֶם	ʿåṣåmåt	
עָבוֹת	ʿabbot			חֶדֶר	wbådåri	ר+ס
עָבוֹת	ʿabbot			עֶדֶר	ʿådåri	
עַמּוּד	ʿammod			עָנָף	wånåfi	
עָבוֹת	ʿåbētot	ר		עֶצֶם	ʿåṣåmūti	ר+א
עַמּוּד	ʿāmmūdəm			עֶצֶם	wåṣåmūtīyyimma	ר+ט
עַמּוּד	ʿammūdi	ר+ס		חֻמָשׁ	ʿåmoš	
עַמּוּד	ʿammūdo	ר+ד		עֶצֶם	ʿåṣom	
עַמּוּד	ʿammūdiyya	ר+ה		עֶצֶם	ʿåṣom	
עַמּוּד	ʿammūdīyyimma	ר+ט		עֶצֶם	wåṣūməm	ר
				חָנִיךְ	ʿanyåk °	
				חָנִיךְ	ʿanyåko	ר+ד
				אוֹיֵב	iyyåb °	
				אִלֵּם	illåm	

מַחֲנֶה	må:-ni			חֶלֶד	ʿållad	
מַחֲנֶה	månək	ג		חֹנֶט	ʿånnåṭ °	
מַחֲנֶה	må:nēʾu	ד		חָרָשׁ	ʿårråš	
מַחֲנֶה	må:not	ר		חנט	ʿånnåṭəm	ר
מַחֲנֶה	må:nīyyimma	ר+ט		עֲשָׂאִי	ʿåšāʾi	
מָאוֹר	må-ʾor			אֲדַמְדָּם	ådåmdåm	
מָאוֹר	måʾūrot	ר		אדמדם	ådåmdåmət	נ
מַאֲכָל	må:-kål			אדמדם	ådåmdåmot	ר+נ
מַחֲזֶה	må-zzi					
מַחְסֹר	må-ssår °			2. המוספים בראשם		
מַעֲבָר	måbbår					
מַחְסֵר	måssåru	ד		תנועות (> א, ה)		
מַחֲבַת	må-ʾēbåt			חָרִישׁ	i-rrəš	
מָעוֹן	mū-n			חֹרֶף	irrəf	
תַּעַר	tā-r			חֶרֶשׁ	irrəš	
תַּעֲנֻג	tā-nnåg			חֶרֶס	i-rrås	
תַּחְמָס	tå-mos			חֲזִיר	a-zzer	
				חָזָק	azzəq	
				חֹזֶק	azzəq	
3. המוספים בסופם				עֹשֶׁר	ʿa-ššer	
		תנועות				
				עיצורים עם תנועות		
חֹרִי	år-i			יַחְמוּר	yå-mor	
חָפְשָׁה	ifš-i			מַעַן	mā-n	
חָפְשִׁי	ifši			מַעַן	almānkimma	ז
אַרְבֶּה	arb-i			מַעֲשֶׂה	mā-šši	
עִתִּי	ʿāt-i			מַעֲשֶׂה	måššək	ג
חֲמִישִׁי	ēmīš-i			מַעֲשֶׂה	kåmåššēʾu	ד
עֲרִירִי	ērīri			מַעֲשֶׂה	måššom	ר
עֲשִׁירִי	ēšīri			מַעֲשֶׂה	måššo	ר+ד
חֲמִישִׁי	åʾēmīšət	נ		מַעֲשֶׂה	mimmåššīnu	ר+ו
עֲרִירִי	ērīrəm	ר		מַעֲשֶׂה	måššīkimma	ר+ז
אֲדֹנִי	ådån-i			מַעֲשֶׂה	kåmåššīyyimma	ר+ט
עָזְנִיָּה	azn-iyya			מַחְשֹׂף	mā-ššəf	
אֵיבָה	iyyåb-e			מַעֲלָל	mållǎl °	
אִמָּה	īm-a			מַעֲלָל	mållēlək	ג
אֵיפָה	īfa			מַעְיָן	mā-yyån	
				מַעֲשֵׂר	måššår	
				מַעֲשֵׂר	mimmåššåru	ד
				מַעְיָן	måyyånot	ר
				מַעֲשֵׂר	måššårūtīkimma	ר+ז

אֵלָה	īla			אָמְרָה	ēmīråtåk	ב	
חִידָה	īda	○		אֶבְרָה	ēbīråtu	ד	
אֵיפָה	īfåt	ס		עֲבֹדָה	ēbīdåtu		
אֵימָה	īmåti	א		עֲבֹדָה	ēbīdåtkimma	ז	
חִידָה	bīdot	ר		עֲבֹדָה	ēbīdåtimma	ט	
				הֲפִיכָה	ēfīkot	ר	
אָלָה	ål-a			חֲלִיפָה	ēlīfot		
אָלָה	miyyålåti	א					
אָלָה	wbålåtu	ד		הֲפֵכָה	åfīk-a		
אָלָה	ålot	ר		חֲסִידָה	åsīda		
				עַלְמָה	ålīma		
חוֹמָה	ūm-a						
חוֹמָה	ūmåtåk	ב		אֲפֻדָּה	åfēd-a	○	
				חֲגֹרָה	ågēra	○	
עֶגְלָה	igl-a			חָרְבָּה	årēba		
עֶדְנָה	idna			חֲשֵׁכָה	åšēka		
עֶגְלָה	iglåt	ס		אֲפֻדָּתוֹ	åfēdåtu	ד	
				חֲגֹרֹת	ågērot	ר	
עָלָה	ʿāl-a						
עָלָה	ʿålåt	ס		אָכְלָה	åkål-a		
עָלָה	ʿålåtåk	ב		חֶמְלָה	åmåla	○	
עָלָה	ʿålåtu	ד		חֶמְלָה	båmålåt	ס	
עָלָה	ʿålåtimma	ט					
עָלָה	ʿålot	ר		אֱמוּנָה	åmūn-a		
עָלָה	ʿålūtək	ר+ג		חֲלוּשָׁה	ålūša		
עָלָה	ʿålūto	ר+ד					
עָלָה	ʿålūtīkimma	ר+ז		עֲלִילָה	ālīl-a		
				עֲלִילָה	ālīlåt	ס	
חֶלְקָה	ålq-a	○					
חֶלְקָה	ålqåt	ס		עֲגָלָה	ʿāgēl-a		
				עֲגָלָה	ʿāgēlot	ר	
אִשָּׁה	išš-a						
עָנָה	igga	○		אֲגֻדָּה	ēgidd-a	○	
אִשָּׁה	iššåt	ס		אַלְמָה	ēlimma	○	
אִשָּׁה	išti	א		חֲמִשָּׁה	ēmišša		
אִשָּׁה	ištåk	ב		חֲנֻכָּה	ēnikka		
אִשָּׁה	ištu	ר		אֲגֻדָּת	ēgiddåt	ס	
עָנָה	iggot			חֲמֻשָּׁה	ʿamšåt		
				חֲנֻכָּה	ēnikkåt		
אָמָה	amm-a	○		אַלְמָה	ēlimmåti	א	
אָמָה	ammət	ס		אַלְמָה	ålamməm	ר	
אָמָה	låmmåtimma	ט		אַלְמָה	ēlimmåtīkimma	ר+ז	
אֶבְרָה	ēbīr-a			אַרְבֶּה	ēråbb-a	○	
אָמְרָה	ēmīra			אַרְבֶּה	wēråbbot	ר	
אֹפֶל	ēfila						
הֲפִיכָה	ēfīka	○		חֲרָדָה	åridd-a		
חֲלִיפָה	ēlīfa	○					
חֶרְפָּה	ērīfa			עֲרִיסָה	ʿāriss-a		
עֲבֹדָה	ēbīda			עֲרִיסָה	ʿārissūtīkimma	ר+ז	
עֲבֹדָה	ēbīda						
עֲבֹדָה	ēbīdåt	ס		אַיָּלָה	ayyåʾl-ā		
אָמְרָה	ēmīrti	א		חָכְמָה	ikm-å		
עֲבֹדָה	ēbīdåti			עֶרְוָה	irbå		

אֲשָׂרָה	åšårå			חָכְמָה	ikmåt	ס
חֲלָלָה	ålålå			עֶרְוָה	irbåt	
אֲדָמָה	ådåmåt	ס		עֶרְוָה	irbåtåk	ב
אַשְׁמָה	låšåmåt			עֶרְוָה	irbåtu	ד
אֲדָמָה	ådåmåtåk	ב		עֶרְוָה	irbåtå	ה
אַשְׁמָה	åšåmtu	ד		חָכְמָה	ikmåtkimma	ז
אֲדָמָה	ådåmåtimma	ט		עֶרְוָה	irbåtən	י
אֲדָמָה	ådåmūtīnu	ר+ו		אֱלִיָה	alyå	
אֲדָמָה	ådåmūtīkimma	ר+ז		אֲנִיָה	anyå ○	
עֶבְרָה	ʿåbår-å			אֲרִיָה	aryå	
עֲלָטָה	ʿålåṭå			אֲנִיָה	anyot	ר
עֲרָבָה	ʿåråbå			עֳנָה	ʿån-å ○	
עָרְמָה	ʿåråmå			עֹנָה	wånåtå	ה
עֲשָׂרָה	ʿåšårå			חָרְבָה	årb-å	
עֲשָׂרָה	ʿåšåråt	ס		חִטָּה	iṭṭ-å	
עֶבְרָה	wåbåråtimma	ט		חִטָּה	iṭṭəm	ר
עֲשָׂרָה	ʿåšårot	ר		אַיָּה	ayy-å	
עֲרָבָה	wåråbi	ר+ס		אָמָּה	åmm-å	
אֲבֵדָה	ēbidd-å			חֻקָּה	åqqå	
אֲבֵדָה	ēbiddåt	ס		אָמָה	wåmå	
חֲבוּרָה	ʿabbūr-å			אָמָה	båmmåt	ס
חֲבוּרָה	labbūråti	א		חֻקָּה	aqqåt	
עָרְלָה	ʿārill-å			חֻקָּה	åqqåt	
עָרְלָה	ʿārillåt	ס		חֻקָּה	baqqūti	א
עָרְלָה	ʿārillåtu	ד		אָמָה	ammot	ר
עָרְלָה	ʿārillåtkimma	ז		חֻקָּה	baqqot	
עָרְלָה	ʿārillåtimma	ט		אָמָה	åmmåtåʿom	
				חֻקָּה	aqqūti	ר+א
	עיצורים עם תנועות			חֻקָּה	aqqūto	ר+ד
עֶשְׂרִים	išr-əm			חֻקָּה	wbaqqūtīyyimma	ר+ט
עֶשְׂרִים	išrəm	ר		אַוָּה	uww-å ○	
עֲדָשִׁים	ʿadš-əm ○			אַוָּה	uwwåt	ס
עֲדָשִׁים	ʿad šem	ר		חַיָּה	ʿayy-å	
חַיִּים	ʿayy-əm			חַיָּה	ʿayyåt	ס
חַיִּים	ʿayyəm	ר		חַיָּה	ʿayyåtimma	ט
חַיִּים	ʿayyi	ר+ס		חַלָּה	ʿåll-å	
חַיִּים	ʿayyi	ר+א		חַלָּה	ʿållåt	ס
חַיִּים	ʿayyək	ר+ג		חַלָּה	ʿallot	ר
חַיִּים	ʿayyo	ר+ד		אֲשֵׁרָה	åšīr-å ○	
חַיִּים	bayyayya	ר+ה		אֲשֵׁרָה	wåšīrīyyimma	ר+ט
חַיִּים	ʿayyīkimma	ר+ז		אֲדָמָה	adåm-å	
חַיִּים	ʿayyīyyimma	ר+ט		אֲנָפָה	ånåfå	
אֲנָשִׁים	ēnåš-əm			אֲנָקָה	ånåqå	
אֲנָשִׁים	ēnåšəm	ר		אַשְׁמָה	åšåmå	
אֲנָשִׁים	ēnåši	ר+ס				

אֲנָשִׁים	ēnå̊šo		ר+ד
עֲפָלִים	ʿåfå̊l-əm		
עֲפָלִים	wbåfå̊ləm		ר
חֲמָשִׁים	ēmišš-əm		
חֲמָשִׁים	ēmiššom		ר
אִישׁוֹן	īš-å̊n		
חָמָן	åmm-å̊n		
חָמָן	åmmå̊nīkimma		ר+ז
אַלּוֹן	å̊l-on		
אָסוֹן	å̊son		
הָמוֹן	å̊mon		
חַלּוֹן	å̊lon		
אֶבְיוֹן	iby-on		
עִשָּׁרוֹן	išron		
אֶבְיוֹן	ibyūnå̊k		ב
עִשָּׁרוֹן	išrunəm		ר
אֶבְיוֹן	ibyūni		ר+ס
חָרוֹן	ʿår-on		
חָרוֹן	ʿårūnå̊k		ב
עַרְמוֹן	ʿarm-on		
עִצָּבוֹן	ʿå̊så̊b-on		
עֵרָבוֹן	ʿårå̊bon		
עִצָּבוֹן	ʿå̊så̊būnək		ג
עֶלְיוֹן	illiyy-on		
הֵרָיוֹן	arriyy-on		
הֵרָיוֹן	warriyyūnək		ג
אַדְמוֹנִי	ådå̊m-ūni		
חֲצִית	ēṣ-ət		
אֱמֶת	åm-ət		
אֱמֶת	wåmētu		ד
עוֹפֶרֶת	ūfå̊r-ət		
עִוֶּרֶת	ʿawwēr-ət		
חֲמִישִׁית	ēmīš-å̊t		
עֲשִׂירִת	ēšīrå̊t		
חֲמִישִׁת	ēmīšåtu		ד

אַדֶּרֶת	ådå̊r-å̊t		
עֲצֶרֶת	ʿå̊ṣå̊r-å̊t		
עֵדוּת	īd-ot		
אֵדוּת	ēd-ot		
חרפות	ērīf-ot		
חרפות	ērīfūti		א
חמידות	åmīd-ot		
עֲתִידוֹת	ʿåtīd-ot		

4. המוספים בראשם ובסופם
(לפי סדר הסופיות)

. תנועות

מְחִיָּה	mi-yy-a		
מַעֲלָה	mā:-la		
מַעֲלָה	mā:la		
מְעָרָה	mā:ra		
מַעֲלָה	båmå̊lot		ר
מַעֲרָכָה	mā-rrēk-a		
מַחֲלָה	må̊:-l-a		
מַחֲלָה	må̊:la		
מַחֲלָה	wbåmå̊:lot		ר
מַחֲשָׁבָה	må̊-ššå̊b-a		
מַחְשָׁבָה	må̊ššå̊bot		ר
תְּחִלָּה	tē-ll-a		
מֶחֱצָה	mē-ṣṣ-å̊		
מְהוּמָה	må̊:-m-å̊		
מַחְתָּה	må̊-tt-å̊		
מַעֲקֶה	måqqå̊		
מַחְתָּה	måttot		ר
מְעוֹנָה	mū-n-å̊		
תַּאֲוָה	tē-ww-å̊		
תְּהִלָּה	tēllå̊		
תַּאֲוָה	tēwwå̊t		ס
תְּהִלָּה	tēllå̊tå̊k		ב
תְּהִלָּה	tēllå̊t		ר

בְּעִיר	bīr °			תהללה	tē-llå̄l-å °	
זְאֵב	zīb			תהללה	wbattēllålot	ר
צָעִיף	ṣīf			תַּאֲוָה	tå̄-ww-å̄	
צָעִיר	ṣīr					
שָׂעִיר	šīr				עיצורים עם תנועות	
צָעִיר	waṣṣīra	נ				
צָעִיר	ṣīri	א		מֹאזְנַיִם	mū-zå̄n-əm °	
בְּעִיר	bīru	ד		מֹאזְנַיִם	mūzå̄ni	ר+ס
צָעִיף	ṣīfa	ה		חִפָּזוֹן	i-bbå̄z-on	
בְּעִיר	wbīrå̄nu	ו		עִוָּרוֹן	iwwå̄ron	
בְּעִיר	bīrkimma	ז		חֲרֹשֶׁת	a-rrē̊š-ət	
בְּעִיר	bīrimma	ט		מְחִית	mā-ʾ-ət	
שָׂעִיר	aššīrəm	ר		מַחְמֶצֶת	mā-mmē̊ṣ-ət	
שָׂעִיר	šīri	ר+ס		מַעֲרֶכֶת	mārrēkət	
בַּעַד	bēd			מַעֲרֶכֶת	mārrēkot	ר
טַעַם	ṭēm			מַחְתִּית	må̄-tt-ət °	
לֶחֶם	lēm			מַחְתִּית	må̄tītu	ד
נַחַל	nēl			מַחְתִּית	wmå̄ttiyyūto	ר+ד
רָחֵל	rēl °			מַחְתִּית	må̄ttiyyūtiyya	ר+ה
רֶחֶם	rēm			מַחֲצִית	må̄-ʾē̊ṣ-ət	
רַעַד	rēd			מַחֲצִית	må̄ʾēṣītu	ד
תַּחַת	tēt			מַחֲצִית	må̄ʾēṣītå̄	ה
בַּעַד	bēddi	א		מַחֲצִית	mimmå̄ʾēṣītimma	ט
לֶחֶם	lēmmi	ב		מְגֵרַת	må̄:-gēr-ət	
בַּעַד	bēddå̄k			מַאֲכֶלֶת	må̄-kkēl-ət	
לֶחֶם	lēmmå̄k	ג		מַהְפֶּכֶת	mī-fk-å̄t	
רָחֵל	rēllək			מַחְבֶּרֶת	må̄:-bēr-å̄t	
תַּחַת	tēttək			מַחְבֶּרֶת	må̄:bårtu	ד
בַּעַד	bēddu	ד		מַחְתֶּרֶת	må̄-ttå̄r-å̄t	
טַעַם	ṭēmu					
לֶחֶם	lēmu				עין גרונית	
רֶחֶם	rēmma	ה			1.א. הפשוטים	
לֶחֶם	lēmmå̄nu	ו				
לֶחֶם	lēmmå̄kimma	ז		רֵעַ	rē °	
בַּעַד	bēddimma	ט		רֵעַ	rēk	ב
נַחַל	wbannēlləm	ר		רֵעַ	rēʾu	ד
רָחֵל	rēlləm			בְּאֵר	bir	
נַחַל	nēlli	ר+ס		בְּאֵר	ber	
תַּחַת	tētto	ר+ד		בְּאֵר	bīrot	ר
תַּחַת	tēttiyya	ר+ה				
תַּחַת	tēttīyyimma	ר+ט				
בַּעַל	bāl					
יַחַד	yād					
יַעַר	yār					
מָחָר	mār					
מְעַט	māṭ					
מַעַל	māl					
נָחָשׁ	nāš					
נַעַל	nāl					

453

רֹחַב	råb		
רָחֹק	råq		
שְׂאֹר	šår		
שְׂאֹר	šår		
שָׁחַם	šåm		
שַׁחַד	šåd		
שַׁחַר	šår		
שָׁחֹר	šår		
תֹּאַר	tår		
תַּחַת	tåt		
רֹאשׁ	råmi		
רָחָב	wråbbå	נ	
טַאן	tånnåk	ב	
פַּחַד	fådåk		
רֹחַב	råbbu	ד	
שְׂאֹר	alšåru		
טֹהַר	țårå	ה	
רֹחַב	råbbå		
רֹחַב	råbbå		
שְׂאֹר	šårå		
לַחַץ	låṣṣånu	ו	
פַּחַד	fådkimma	ז	
לְאֹם	låmməm	ר	
נָהָר	annårot		
רַהַט	barråṭṭəm		
תַּחַת	tåtto	ר+ד	
תַּחַת	tåttiyya	ר+ה	
לַהַט	ablåṭīyyimma	ר+ט	
נָהָר	nårūtimma		
תַּחַת	tåttūyyimma		
בָּחוּר	būr		
תְּהוֹם	tūm		
תְּהוֹם	tū:mot	ר	
בֹּהוּ	bēʾu		
תֹּהוּ	tēʾu		
יָעֶה	yāʾi		
לְחִי	lāʾi °		
תָּאִי	tāʾi		
לְחִי	wallāʾəm	ר	
יָעֶה	wyāʾo	ר+ד	
מְאֹד	mēʾod		
צֹאן	ṣēʾon		
רֹאשׁ	rēʾoš		
רָחוּם	rēʾom		
צֹאן	ṣēʾūni	א	
רֹאשׁ	rēʾūši		
מְאֹד	mēʾūdåk	ב	
צֹאן	ṣēʾūnåk		

נַעַר	når		
פַּעַם	fåm		
קָהָל	qål		
רָעָב	råb		
שַׂעַר	šår		
שַׁחַף	šåf		
שַׂעַר	šår		
תַּחַשׁ	tåš		
מְעַט	åʾmåṭ		
נַעַל	nā:lək	ג	
שַׂעַר	šårək		
נַעַל	nā:lu	ד	
שַׂעַר	šåru		
בַּעַל	bāla	ה	
שַׂעַר	wšāra		
קָהָל	qālkimma	ז	
קָהָל	wafqā:limma	ט	
נָחָשׁ	annåššəm	ר	
נַעַר	annā:rəm		
פַּעַם	fåmməm		
שַׂעַר	šårəm		
תַּחַשׁ	tåššəm		
בַּעַל	bålli	ר+ס	
נַעַר	nā:ri		
בַּעַל	bålo	ר+ד	
נַעַר	nā:ro		
פַּעַם	fåmmūto		
נַעַר	abnā:rīnu	ר+ו	
נַעַל	nā:līkimma	ר+ז	
שַׂעַר	afšārīkimma		
יְאֹר	yår		
יְאֹר	yårīyyimma	ר+ט	
בֹּהַק	båq		
זָהָב	zåb		
טַאן	țån °		
טֹהַר	țår °		
לְאֹם	låm		
לַהַט	låṭ		
לַחַץ	låṣ		
נְאֻם	nåm		
נָהָר	når		
סַהַר	går		
פַּחַד	fåd		
צֹהַר	ṣår		
צַעַר	ṣår		
רֹאשׁ	råm		
רַהַט	råṭ °		
רֹחַב	råb		
רָחָב	råb °		

בָּחִיר	bayyår °		רֹאשׁ	rē'ūšåk	
בָּחִיר	mibbayyåro	ר+ד	צֹאן	ṣē'ūnu	ד
			רֹאשׁ	rē'ūšu	
2. המוספים בראשם			רֹאשׁ	rē'ūša	ה
			צֹאן	afṣē'ūnånu	ו
יִצְהָר	yå-'ṣår		צֹאן	ṣē'onkimma	ז
יִצְהָר	wyåṣåråk	ב	רֹאשׁ	rē'oškimma	ט
מִרְעֶה	mē-'ri		צֹאן	ṣē'ūnimma	
מִבְחָר	mē-'bār		רֹאשׁ	rē'ūšimma	
מַטְעָם	mē-'ṭåm °		רֹאשׁ	råšəm	ר
מַטְעָם	mēṭåmməm	ר	רֹאשׁ	råši	ר+ס
			רֹאשׁ	råšīkimma	ר+ז
מַרְאָה	må-'rī		רֹאשׁ	råšīyyimma	ר+ט
מֶרַע	må'rī °				
מַרְאֶה	mårē'u	ד	יָחִיד	yå'əd °	
מֶרַע	mårē'u		פַּעַס	kå'əs	
מַרְאָה	måriyya	ה	מָחִיר	må'ər	
מַרְאָה	wmårēnna	י	מְעִיל	må'əl	
מַרְאָה	båmårå'ot	ר	נַחַשׁ	nå'əš	
			פֹּעַל	få'əl	
מִנְעָל	må-'nål °		שָׂעִיר	šå'ər	
מִנְעָל	månålləḳ	ג	שָׁחִין	šå'ən	
			יָחִיד	yå'īdåk	ב
מִבְחָן	må-'bån °		פֹּעַל	få'ēlu	ד
מַלְאָךְ	må'låk		נַחַשׁ	annå'ēšəm	ר
מִשְׁחָת	må'såt °		שָׂעִיר	šå'īrot	ר+נ
מַלְאָךְ	målåkki	א			
מַלְאָךְ	målåkkək	ג	טָהוֹר	ṭå'ər	
מַלְאָךְ	målåkku	ד	כֹּהֵן	kå'ən	
מִבְחָן	åmåbånəm		מֹהַר	må'ər	
מַלְאָךְ	målåkkəm	ר	פְּאֵר	få'ər	
מִשְׁחָת	måsåttəm		צָהֹב	ṣå'əb	
מַלְאָךְ	målåkki	ר+ס	טָהוֹר	ṭå'ēra	נ
			כֹּהֵן	kå'ēnəm	ר
מִשְׁעוֹל	må-šā'əl		טָהוֹר	ṭå'ērot	ר+נ
			פְּאֵר	få'ēri	ר+ס
מַכְאוֹב	må-kå'ob °				
מַכְאוֹב	må'kå'ū'bū	ד	בֹּהֶן	bå'on	
			גָּחוֹן	gå'on	
מוֹעֵד	mu-wwəd		טָהוֹר	ṭå'or	
מוֹעֵד	muwwēdi	א	פַּעַס	kå'os	
מוֹעֵד	muwwēdi	ר+ס	רָחוֹק	rå'oq	
מוֹעֵד	båmuwwēdīkimma	ר+ז	רָחוֹק	rå'ūq	נ
			גָּחוֹן	gå'ūnåk	ב
מוֹעֵד	mu-wwad		רָחוֹק	arrå'ūqəm	ר
מוֹעֵד	almuwwāda	ה	רָחוֹק	arrå'ūqot	ר+נ
מוֹעֵד	båmuwwādimma	ט			
מוֹעֵד	walmuwwādəm	ר	תְּאֹם	tiyyåm	
מוֹעֵד	båmuwwādo	ר+ד	תְּאֹם	tiyyåməm	ר
			שְׁאוֹל	šiyyol	

		נֵעְמָה	nēmm-a				3. המוספים בסופם
		תֶּחְרָה	tērra				
		נְחֻשָׁה	nāšš-a				תנועות
		טָהֳרָה	ṭårr-a°		תֵּחְתִי	tētt-i°	
ד	טָהֳרָה	ṭårråtu			תֵּחְתִי	tēttəm	ר
		פְּעֻלָּה	faʾēl-a°		יָעֲנֶה	yān-e	
ס	פְּעֻלָּה	faʾēlåt			לַעֲנֶה	lā:n-e	
		גְּאֻלָּה	gaʾēl-a		עֵדָה	īd-a	
		לֶהָבָה	laʾēba		ס	עֵדָה	īdåt	
		צְחוֹקָה	ṣaʾēqa		ב	עֵדָה	īdåtåk	
		צְעָקָה	ṣaʾēqa		ד	עֵדָה	īdåtu	
ס	גְּאֻלָּה	gaʾēlåt		ר	עֵדָה	åīdot	
		לֶהָבָה	ablaʾēbåt		ר+ד	עֵדָה	wīdūto	
		צְעָקָה	ṣaʾēqåt			בְּעֵרָה	bīr-a	
ד	גְּאֻלָּה	gaʾiltu			צְעִירָה	ṣīra°	
		צְעָקָה	ṣaʾiqtu			שְׂעִירָה	šīra°	
ה	צְעָקָה	ṣaʾiqtå		ס	שְׂעִירָה	šīråt	
ט	צְעָקָה	ṣaʾeqtimma		ד	צְעִירָה	kåsīråtu	
		תּוֹעֵבָה	tuwwēb-a			נַעֲרָה	nā:r-a	
ט	תּוֹעֵבָה	tuwwēbūtimma			קְעָרָה	qā:ra	
ר	תּוֹעֵבָה	tuwwēbot			שָׂעֳרָה	šā:ra	
		דָּאָה	d-ā:		ס	קְעָרָה	qā:råt	
		עֵצָה	īṣ-å°		ר	קְעָרָה	qā:rot	
ר+ט	עֵצָה	īṣūtīyyimma			שְׂעֹרָה	šārəm	
		חֵמָה	åm-å		ר+ד	קְעָרָה	qā:rūto	
ס	חֵמָה	åmət		ר+ה	נַעֲרָה	wnā:rūtiyya	
א	חֵמָה	åmåti			בֶּהָלָה	båːl-a	
ד	חֵמָה	wbåmåtu			נַחֲלָה	nå:la	
		תְּאֵנָה	tīn-å			קְהִלָּה	qå:la°	
		זִמָּה	zåm-å		ס	נַחֲלָה	nå:låt	
		רֶחֱמָה	råmå			קְהִלָּה	qå:låt	
		שְׁאֵרָה	šårå		ב	נַחֲלָה	nå:låtåk	
		צָאָה	ṣiyy-å°		ד	נַחֲלָה	nå:låtu	
ב	צָאָה	ṣiyyåtåk		ו	נַחֲלָה	nå:låtnu	
		כְּהֻנָּה	kånn-å		ט	נַחֲלָה	nå:låtimma	
		רַחְצָה	råṣṣå		י	נַחֲלָה	nå:låtən	
ס	כְּהֻנָּה	kånnåt		ר+ז	נַחֲלָה	abnå:lūtīkimma	
ז	כְּהֻנָּה	kånnåtkimma			בְּהֵמָה	bīmm-a	
ט	כְּהֻנָּה	kånnåtimma		ס	בְּהֵמָה	bīmåt	
		מֵאָה	m-å:		ב	בְּהֵמָה	bīmtåk	
		פֵּאָה	få:		ד	בְּהֵמָה	bīmtu	
ס	מֵאָה	måt		ה	בְּהֵמָה	bī:måta	
					ז	בְּהֵמָה	bīmåtkimma	
					ט	בְּהֵמָה	bīmåtimma	
					ר	בְּהֵמָה	bīmot	
					ר+ו	בְּהֵמָה	bīmūtīnu	

תַּחְתִּית	tētt-ət	פֵּאָה	fåt
נְחֹשֶׁת	nāšš-ət	פֵּאָה	må'ot	ר
בַּהֶרֶת	bå'ēr-ət	פֵּאָה	affå'ot	
מָחָרַת	må'ērət	פֵּאָה	fåti	ר+ס
בַּהֶרֶת	bå'ērot	ר		
קָאָת	q-āt		עיצורים עם תנועות	
פְּחֶתֶת	fåt-åt	מֵעִים	m-īm °	
שְׁחֶלֶת	šå'ēl-åt	סְאִים	sīm	
רְעוּת	rā'-ot °	רֵחַיִם	rīm	
רְעוּת	rā'ūta	ה סְאִים	sīm	ר
גֵּאוּת	gå'-ot °	רֵחַיִם	rīm	
רחבות	råbot	מֵעִים	bå'mīk	ר+ג
שארות	šårot	נְעָרִים	nā:r-əm °	
גֵּאוּת	gå'ūtåk	ב נְעָרִים	minnā:ro	ר+ד
גֵּאוּת	wafgå'ūtu	ד נְעָרִים	abnā:riyya	ר+ה
		נְעָרִים	minnā:rīnu	ר+ו
4. המוספים בסופם ובראשם		צָהֳרַיִם	ṣērr-əm	
		רַחֲמִים	rēmməm	
מְלָאכָה	må-låk-a	צָהֳרַיִם	afṣērrəm	ר
מְלָאכָה	målåkåt	ס רַחֲמִים	rēmməm	
מְלָאכָה	målåktåk	ב רַחֲמִים	rēmmo	ר+ד
מְלָאכָה	målåktu	ד גֶּחָלִים	gå'ēl-əm °	
מִלְחָמָה	må-lāmm-a	גֶּחָלִים	gå'ēli	ר+ס
מִלְחָמָה	målā'imtu	ד מָאתַיִם	mått-əm	
מִלְחָמָה	målā:mot	ר מָאתַיִם	måttəm	ר
תַּבְעֵרָה	tē-bā:r-a	כהן אן	kå'ēn-ån	
אֶצְעָדָה	ē-ṣidd-å	דְּאָבוֹן	dīb-on	
תְּלָאָה	te-liy'y-å	רְעָבוֹן	rā:b-on	
מִשְׁעֶנֶת	må-šā:n-ət °	גָּאוֹן	gå'-on	
מִשְׁעֶנֶת	måšā'intu	ד גָּאוֹן	gå'ūnåk	ב
מִשְׁעֶנֶת	wbåmåšā:nūtimma	ר+ט פַּעֲמוֹן	fāmm-on	
מֵרֵאשֹׁת	må-råš-ət °	פַּעֲמוֹן	affāmmūnəm	ר
מֵרֵאשֹׁת	måråšītu	ד פַּעֲמוֹן	fāmmūni	ר+ס
מֵרַחֲשֹׁת	am-rā'ēš-åt	רִאשׁוֹן	rå'īš-on	
מִשְׁאֶרֶת	må-šå:r-åt	רִאשׁוֹן	rå'īšūna	נ
מִשְׁאֶרֶת	wmåšå:råtåk	ב רִאשׁוֹן	rå'īšūnəm	ר
מִשְׁאֶרֶת	wbåmåšårūtåk	ר+ג רִאשׁוֹן	arrå'īšūnot	ר+נ
מִשְׁאֶרֶת	måšårūtimma	ר+ט רֵאשִׁית	råš-ət	
		רֵאשִׁית	råšītimma	ט

457

אַחַר	å᾿ūrīyyimma			תּוֹעָפוֹת	tu-wwēf-ot	
אַחַר	å᾿ūrīyyinna	ר+י		תועפות	kåtuwwēfot	ר

פא ועין גרוניות

אָחֲזָה	åzz-a		
אחזה	åzzåt	ס	
אחזה	åzzåtu	ד	
אחזה	åzzåtkimma	ז	
אחזה	åzzåtimma	ט	

אָח	ʿā	
אח	ʿā᾿i	ס
אח	ʿā᾿i	א
אח	ʿāyåʾk	ב
אח	miyyåʾåk	
אח	ʿā᾿o	ד
אח	ʿåyånu	ו
אח	ʿåyåkimma	ז
אח	ʿā᾿əm	ר
אח	ʿā᾿i	ר+ס
אח	ʿā᾿i	ר+א
אח	ʿā᾿ək	ר+ג
אח	ʿā᾿o	ר+ד
אח	ʿåyyå	ר+ה
אח	ʿā᾿īnu	ר+ו
אח	ʿā᾿īkimma	ר+ז
אח	ʿāyyimma	ר+ט

אַהֲבָה	å᾿ēb-a	
אהבה	miyyå᾿ēbåt	ס
אהבה	bå᾿ēbåttu	ד

אַחֲרוֹן	å᾿ēr-on	
אחרון	bå᾿ērinna	נ
אחרון	å᾿ērinnəm	ר

אַחֲרִית	å᾿ēr-ət	
אחרית	å᾿ērīti	א
אחרית	bå᾿ērītåk	ב
אחרית	wå᾿ērītu	ד
אחרית	å᾿ērītimma	ט

אָחֳרָנִית	å᾿ēr-innət	

אֶחָד	ʿād	
אחז	ʿāz	
אחד	ʿādəm	ר

אַחַת	ʿ-āt	

אָחוּ	ā᾿u °	

אָחוֹת	ʿā᾿-ot	
אחות	ʿā᾿ūti	א
אחות	ʿā᾿ūtåk	ב
אחות	ʿā᾿ūtu	ד
אחות	ʿā᾿ūta	ה
אחות	ʿā᾿ūtånu	ו
אחות	ʿā᾿ūtimma	ט

אַחַר	å᾿ər	
אַחַר	å᾿ər	
אחר	å᾿ērət	נ
אחר	å᾿ērəm	ר
אחר	å᾿ērot	ר+נ

אֹהֶל	å᾿ol	
אָחוֹר	å᾿or	
אַחַר	å᾿or °	
אהל	å᾿ūlək	ג
אהל	å᾿ūlu	ד
אהל	å᾿ūləm	ר
אהל	å᾿ūli	ר+ס
אחור	å᾿ūri	
אחר	å᾿ūri	
אחר	å᾿ūri	ר+א
אחר	å᾿ūrək	ר+ג
אחר	å᾿ūro	ר+ד
אחר	å᾿ūriyya	ר+ה
אחר	å᾿ūrīnu	ר+ו
אהל	bå᾿ūlīkimma	ר+ז
אחר	å᾿ūrīkimma	
אהל	å᾿ūlīyyimma	ר+ט

למד גרונית

1. הפשוטים

פִּיחַ	fī	
רֵיחַ	rī	
שִׂיחַ	šī	
רֵיחַ	riyyånu	ו

כֹּחַ	kū	
רוּחַ	rū	
שׂוֹחַ	šū °	
שָׁוְא	šū	
כח	kuwwi	א
רוח	ruwwi	
כח	afkuwwåk	ב
רוח	abruwwåk	
כח	wafkuwwu	ד

לָקַח	lēqā'i			רוּחַ	ruwwu	
פֶּשַׁע	fēšā'i			כֹּחַ	kuwwa	ה
דֶּמַע	wdē'māk	ב		כֹּחַ	kuwwåkimma	ז
זֶרַע	zē'rāk			רוּחַ	arruwwå'ot	ר
זֶבַח	zē'bīk	ג		שׁוּחַ	aššuwwəm	
זֶרַע	zē'rīk			סֶלַע	sīla	
זֶבַח	zē'bū	ד		צֶלַע	ṣīla	
זֶרַע	zērā'u			צֶלַע	ṣīlā'u	ד
גֶּגַע	nēgā'u			צֶלַע	ṣīlā'ot	ר
נֹכַח	nēkā'u			צֶלַע	ṣīlā'ūto	ר+ד
רֶשַׁע	rēšā'u			גָּבִיעַ	gēbi	
זֶרַע	zē'rā	ה		טָמֵא	ṭēmi	
זֶבַח	zēbākkimma	ז		נָבִיא	nēbi	
זֶרַע	zērākkimma			פֶּסַח	fēsi	
פֶּשַׁע	alfēšākkimma			פֶּקַח	fēqi	
זֶרַע	afzērā'imma	ט		טָמֵא	ṭēmiy'yā	נ
זֶבַח	zē'bīm	ר		גָּבִיעַ	gē'bī	א
טָמֵא	ṭēmā'əm			נָבִיא	nibyåk	ב
יָרֵחַ	yē'rīm			נָבִיא	nibyåkimma	ז
לוּחַ	lē'būt			גָּבִיעַ	gē'bīm	ר
גֶּגַע	nēgā'əm			נָבִיא	nibyəm	
גֻּתַח	annē'tīm			גָּבִיעַ	gēbiyya	ר+ה
פֶּקַח	fēqā'əm			סָפִיחַ	sē'fī °	
קֶלַע	qē'līm			סָפִיחַ	sē'fī	ס
רֶשַׁע	arrēšā'əm			סָפִיחַ	sēfiyya	ר+ה
זֶבַח	zē'bī	ר+ס		דֶּמַע	dēma °	
קֶלַע	qē'lī			דֶּשֶׁא	dēša	
גֻּתַח	nēto	ר+ד		זֶבַח	zēba	
גֻּתַח	alnētiyya	ר+ה		זֶרַע	zēra	
זֶבַח	wzēbīkkimma	ר+ז		טָמֵא	ṭēma °	
זֶבַח	zēbīyyimma	ר+ט		יָרֵחַ	yēra	
פֶּשַׁע	fēšāyyimma			לוּחַ	lēba °	
בֶּטַח	bēṭå			לָקַח	lēqa °	
בֶּצַע	bēṣå			מֶלַח	mēla	
מֶצַח	mēṣå			גֶּגַע	nēga	
פֶּתַח	fētå			נֹכַח	nēka	
שֶׁבַע	šēbå			גֻּתַח	nēta °	
מֶצַח	mēṣå'u	ד		פֶּקַח	fēqa °	
מְלוֹא	mē'lū			פֶּשַׁע	fēša	
קָמַח	qāma			פֶּתַח	fēta	
קָרַח	qāra			קֶלַע	qēla °	
שָׂבַע	šāba			רֶגַע	rēga	
שָׁבַע	šāba			רוּחַ	rēba	
שָׁמַע	šāma			רֶשַׁע	rēša °	
שֶׁמַע	šā'māk	ב		רָשָׁע	rēša	
בטיח	båṭi °			זֶבַח	zē'bī	א
בָּרִיא	båri °					
בָּרִיחַ	båri					

מָלֵא	må'lū °			גָּמָא	gåmi		
יָצוּעַ	yåṣuwwi	א		בָטִיחַ	abbå'īm	ר	
זָרוּעַ	zåruwwåk	ב		בָּרִיחַ	bar'yīm		
זָרוּעַ	zåruwwu	ד		בָּרִיא	baryot	ר+נ	
מָלֵא	wmåluw'wā	ה		בָּרִיא	bar'yī	ר+ס	
זָרוּעַ	zåruwwi	ר+ס		בָּרִיחַ	baryo	ר+ד	
כֶּרַע	kūra °			גָּבֹהַּ	gåba °		
תּוֹלָע	tūla °			גָּבֵהַּ	gåba		
כֶּרַע	kūrā'əm	ר		טָמֵא	ṭama		
תּוֹלָע	tū'līm			טָנֵא	ṭana		
כֶּרַע	kūrā'o	ר+ד		טֹפַח	ṭafa		
תֵּשַׁע	tišša			יָגֵעַ	yåga		
נִיחֹחַ	niy'yå			כָּסֵא	kåsa		
נִיחֹחַ	niyyå'i	א		צָבָא	ṣåba		
נִיחֹחַ	niyyå'īkimma	ר+ז		שָׂבֵעַ	såba		
פָּתוּחַ	fittu °			שָׂשַׂ	šåsa		
שָׁבוּעַ	šibbu			גָּבֹהַּ	gå'bā	נ	
שָׁבוּעַ	šibbuwwå'əm	ר		יָגֵעַ	yå'gāk	ב	
פָּתוּחַ	fittuwwi	ר+ס		כָּסֵא	kåsā'u	ד	
רֹקַח	raqqa			צָבָא	ṣåbā'u		
שָׁנָא	šanna °			צָבָא	ṣåbā'imma	ט	
שָׁנָא	šannā'ək	ג		גָּבֹהַּ	aggåbā'əm	ר	
שָׁנָא	šånā'īnu	ו		צָבָא	ṣåbā'ot		
שָׁנָא	šannā'īkimma	ז		גָּבֹהַּ	aggåbā'ot	ר+נ	
שָׁנָא	šannā'i	ר+ס		צָבָא	ṣåbā'ūti	ר+א	
שָׁנָא	alšannā'i	ר+א		צָבָא	ṣåbā'ūtīkimma	ר+ז	
שָׁנָא	alšannā'o	ר+ד		צָבָא	ṣåbā'ūtimma	ר+ט	
רָקוּעַ	raqqu °			בָּקַע	båqå		
רָקוּעַ	raqquwwi	ר+ס		טֶבַח	ṭåbå		
				טֹרַח	ṭårå °		
	2. המוסיפים בראשם			יָרֵחַ	yårå		
				סֶרַח	sårå		
	(תנועות (א > ה			פֶּצַע	fåṣå		
אֶפְרֹחַ	i-fra °			פֶּרַח	fårå		
אֶצְבַּע	iṣba			פֶּרַע	fårå		
אֶצְבַּע	biṣ'bāk	ב		צָמֵא	ṣåmå		
אֶצְבַּע	iṣ'bū	ד		צֶמַח	såmå		
אֶפְרֹחַ	ifrå'əm	ר		רֶמַח	råmå		
נָשִׂיא	a-nši			פֶּצַע	alfåṣā'i	א	
רָקִיעַ	arqi			טֹרַח	ṭåråkkimma	ז	
נָשִׂיא	anšiyyā'əm	ר		פֶּרַח	fåriyya	ר+ה	
נָשִׂיא	anšiyyā'i	ר+ס		צֶלַע	ṣålu		
נָשִׂיא	anšiyyāyyimma	ר+ט		צָרַע	ṣåru		
אֶזְרָח	a-zra			רֶבַע	råbu		
אַרְבַּע	arba			שָׂרוּעַ	såru		
				זָרוּעַ	zå'rū		
				יָצוּעַ	yå'ṣū		

תְּשִׁיעִי	tišˈš-ī			פֶּסַח	afsa	
תְּשִׁיעִי	attišˈšīt	נ		שֶׁפַע	a-šfå̄	
יְרִיעָה	yå̄riyy-a					
יְרִיעָה	yå̄riyyot	ר			עיצורים עם תנועות	
בִּקְעָה	bēˈq-ā			מְשַׁלֵּח	mē-šalla	
טָמְאָה	ṭēˈmā			מִזְבֵּחַ	ma-zba	
טְמֵאָה	ṭēˈmā °			מִזְרָח	mazra	
נְקִיאָה	nēˈqā °			מַלְקָח	malqa	
רְשָׁעָה	rēˈšā °			מִקְרָא	maqra	
טָמְאָה	afṭēˈmå̄t	ס		מִזְבֵּחַ	ammazˈba	
נְקִיאָה	nēˈqāt			מִזְרָח	mazˈrā	
רְשָׁעָה	abrēˈšāt			מִזְבֵּחַ	mazˈbī	א
טָמְאָה	ṭēmāttu	ד		מִזְבֵּחַ	mazˈbāk	ב
רְשָׁעָה	rēšāttu			מִזְבֵּחַ	mazbā'ot	ר
טָמְאָה	ṭēmå̄ttå̄	ה		מִקְרָא	maqrā'i	ר+ס
טָמְאָה	ṭēmå̄ttimma	ט		מִזְבֵּחַ	mazbā'ūtīyyimma	ר+ט
נְקִיאָה	nēqāttimma					
בִּקְעָה	wbēqā'ot	ר		מַרְצֵעַ	ma-rṣå̄	
גִּבְעָה	gå̄ˈb-ā			מַסָּע	må̄-sa	
מִנְחָה	må̄ˈnā			מַשָּׂא	må̄ša	
מִשְׁחָה	må̄ˈšā			מַשָּׂא	må̄ša	
מְשִׁחָה	må̄ˈšā			מַשָּׂא	må̄šā'u	ד
שְׂנֻאָה	šå̄ˈnā			מַשָּׂא	må̄šākkimma	ז
שִׁבְעָה	šå̄ˈbā °			מַשָּׂא	må̄šā'imma	ט
שִׁבְעָה	šå̄ˈbā			מַסָּע	må̄sā'i	ר+ס
גִּבְעָה	gå̄ˈbāt	ס		מַשָּׂא	må̄sā'i	
מִנְחָה	må̄ˈnāt			מַסָּע	almå̄sā'o	ר+ד
מִשְׁחָה	må̄ˈsāt			מַסָּע	må̄sāyyimma	ר+ט
שְׂנֻאָה	afså̄ˈnāt			מֹרָא	må̄-ˈrå̄ °	
שִׁבְעָה	så̄ˈbāt			מֹרָא	wmå̄rå̄kkimma	ז
מִנְחָה	må̄nātti	א		מֹרָא	wbå̄må̄rå̄'əm	ר
מִנְחָה	må̄nāttu	ד		מָבוֹא	må̄-ˈbū	
שְׂנֻאָה	wmiššå̄nāttu			מָנוֹחַ	må̄ˈnū	
מִנְחָה	wmå̄nātta	ה				
מִנְחָה	må̄nāttimma	ט		מִבְטָא	må̄-bēṭå̄	
מִשְׁחָה	må̄šåttimma					
גִּבְעָה	aggå̄bā'ot	ר		מוֹצָא	mū-ṣå̄	
שִׁבְעָה	så̄bā'ot			מוֹצָא	mūṣå̄yyimma	ר+ט
מִנְחָה	må̄nā'ūtək	ר+ג				
מִנְחָה	walmå̄nā'ūtīkimma	ר+ז			3. המוספים בסופם	
שִׁבְעָה	afså̄bā'ūtīkimma					
תִּשְׁעָה	tišˈš-ā				תנועות	
תִּשְׁעָה	altišˈšāt	ס		רְבִיעִי	rēˈb-ī	
זְוָעָה	zuwˈw-ā			שְׁבִיעִי	šēˈbī	
שַׁוְעָה	šuwˈwā °			שְׁבִיעִי	waššēˈbīt	נ
שַׁוְעָה	šuwwāttimma	ט				

461

מְלֵאִים	mallā�ef-əm			יְשׁוּעָה	yēšuw'w-ā	
מְלֵאִים	mallā'əm	ר		שְׁבוּעָה	šēbuw'wā	ס
מְלֵאִים	mallā'īkimma	ז+ר		יְשׁוּעָה	yēsuwwåt	
קִשּׁוּאִים	qāšuww-əm			שְׁבוּעָה	šēbuwwåt	
קִשּׁוּאִים	aqqāšuwwəm	ר		שְׁבוּעָה	miššēbutti	א
שְׁלוּחִים	šåluww-əm °			יְשׁוּעָה	alyēšuwwåtåk	ב
שְׁלוּחִים	šåluwwiyya	ה+ר		יְשׁוּעָה	yēsuwwåttu	ד
שִׁבְעָתַיִם	šibbuww-åtå̊'əm			מְלֵאָה	måliy'y-ā	
שִׁבְעָתַיִם	šibbuwwåtå'əm	ר		מְלֵאָה	målītåk	ב
סָלְעָם	sā'l-ām			זְרוּעָה	zåruw'w-ā °	
פִּתְאָם	fē't-åm			זְרוּעָה	zåruwwåtu	ד
שְׁנִינָה	šånā'-īṇa			לְטָאָה	låṭ-å	
שִׁלְחָן	šå'l-ān			בְּרִיָּה	biry-å	
צִמָּאוֹן	så̊mā'-on			לביה	libyå	
תִּמָּהוֹן	tammiyy-on			נְבִיאָה	nēbiyy-å	
יִדְּעוֹנִי	yidd-ū:ni			פְּלִיאָה	fåliyy-å	
יִדְּעוֹנִי	wyiddū:nəm	ר		קִנְאָה	qē'n-å	
צְפִיחִית	ṣē'f-īt			רְוָחָה	rē'bå	
רְבִיעִית	rē'bīt			שְׁבוּעָה	šē'bå	
קָרַחַת	qā'd-ēt			קִנְאָה	qēnåtti	א
שַׁפַּחַת	šā'fēt			קִנְאָה	wqēnåttu	ד
סַפַּחַת	sab'b-ēt			קִנְאָה	qē'nåt	ר
טַבַּעַת	ṭåb'b-ēt			בִּקְעָה	bå̊'q-å	
צָרַעַת	ṣår'rēt			יִרְאָה	yå'rå	
טַבַּעַת	ṭåbbēttu	ד		צָרָה	så̊'rå	
טַבַּעַת	ṭåbbē'ot	ר		שִׂמְחָה	så̊'må	
טַבַּעַת	ṭåbbē'ūtīyyimma	ט+ר		יִרְאָה	yå'råt	ס
זֵעָה	z-āt			יִרְאָה	wyåråttåk	ב
שְׂאֵת	šāt			יִרְאָה	yåråttu	ד
נְכֹאת	nē'k-āt			שִׂמְחָה	så̊mā'ūtīkimma	ז+ר
קָרַחַת	qā'r-āt °			קָרְחָה	qū'r-å	
קָרַחַת	afqārāttu	ד		קָרְחָה	qur'-å	
גַּבַּחַת	gå̊'b-āt °					
גַּבַּחַת	afgåbāttu	ד			עיצורים עם תנועות	
תּוֹלַעַת	tū'l-āt			רֶבַע	rēbiy'y-åy °	
פַּרְעַת	far'r-āt			רֶבַע	rēbiyyå'əm	ר
פַּרְעַת	far'råt	ר		שִׁבְעִים	šå̊'b-īm	
				שִׁבְעִים	šå̊'bīm	ר
				תִּשְׁעִים	tiš'š-īm	
				כִּלְאַיִם	kēlā'-əm	
				כִּלְאַיִם	kēlå'əm	ר

מְלָקְחִים	må-lqå̊-əm°		קְרָאת	qē'r-åt	
מְלָקְחִים	målqåyyå	ר+ה	קְרָאת	alqēråtti	א
תּוֹצָאת	tū-ṣå̊-ət°		קְרָאת	alqēråttåk	ב
תּוֹצָאת	tūṣå̊'ītu	ד	קְרָאת	alqēråttu	ד
פָּרַחת	a-fʼr-āt		קְרָאת	alqēråttå	ה
מְרְקָחת	am-raqʼq-āt		קְרָאת	alqēråttånu	ו
מְרְבָּעת	mi-rrē'b-āt		קְרָאת	alqēråtkimma	ז
מַשָּׂאת	mā-'š-āt		קְרָאת	alqēråttimma	ט
מַשָּׂאת	må'šāt	ר			

4. המוספים בסופם ובראשם

תנועות

מַשָּׂאת	må-'š-āt°		
אַמְתַּחת	a-mʼt-å̊t		
אַמְתַּחת	bamtåtti	א	
אַמְתַּחת	amtåttu	ד	
אַמְתַּחת	amʼtåt	ר	
אַמְתַּחת	amtåttūnu	ר+ו	
אַמְתַּחת	amtåttūkimma	ר+ז	

אַרְבָּעה	a-rʼb-ā	
שִׂפְחה	ašʼfā	
אַרְבָּעה	arʼbāt	ס
שִׂפְחה	ašʼfāt	
שִׂפְחה	ašfātti	א
שִׂפְחה	ašfåttək	ג
שִׂפְחה	ašfāttu	ד
שִׂפְחה	ašfātta	ה
שִׂפְחה	å̊šfå̊'ot	ר
שִׂפְחה	ašfātto	ר+ד

פא ולמד גרוניות

חָח	'ā	
אֱלֹהַ	ēla	
חֵטְא	ēṭå̊	
חֵטְא	ēṭå̊'i	א
חֵטְא	ēṭå̊'u	ד
חֵטְא	ēṭå̊'imma	ט
אֹרַח	å̊rå̊	
חַטָּא	'åṭṭå̊	
חַטָּא	'åṭṭå̊'əm	ר
תַּחֲלָא	tē-llå̊°	
תַּחֲלָא	tēllå̊'iyya	ר+ה
חַטָּאה	ē'ṭ-å̊	
חֶטְאָה	ē'ṭå̊	
חַטָּאה	ē'ṭå̊	
חֶמְאָה	å̊'m-å̊	
אָרְחה	å̊'rå̊	
חֶמְאָה	å̊måt	ס
אָרְחה	å̊'råt	ס
אֱלֹהִים	ēluww-əm	
אֱלֹהִים	ēluwwəm	ר
אֱלֹהִים	ēluwwi	ר+ס

מִשְׁפָּחה	ma-šʼf-ā	
מִשְׁפָּחה	mašʼfēt	ס
מִשְׁפָּחה	mašfātti	א
מִשְׁפָּחה	mašfāttu	ד
מִשְׁפָּחה	wmimmašfāttimma	ט
מִשְׁפָּחה	mašʼfūt	ר
מִשְׁפָּחה	almašfūtto	ר+ד
מִשְׁפָּחה	almašfūttīkimma	ר+ו
מִשְׁפָּחה	mašfūttimma	ר+ט
מְנוּחה	må̊-nuwʼw-ā	
תְּנוּאה	ti-nnuwʼw-ā	
תְּרוּעה	tirruwʼwā	
תְּרוּעה	wtirruwwåt	ס
תְּנוּאה	tinnuwwåti	א
תְּבוּאה	tē-buwʼw-å̊°	
תְּבוּאה	tēbuwwåt	ס
תְּבוּאה	tēbuwwåtåk	ב
תְּבוּאה	tēbuwwåtu	ד
תְּבוּאה	tēbuwwåtå	ה
תְּבוּאה	tēbuwwåt	ר
תְּבוּאה	tēbuwwåtīnu	ר+ו

עיצורים עם תנועות

אַרְבָּעים	a-rʼb-īm	
אַרְבָּעים	arʼbīm	ר

463

		עין ולמד גרוניות		ēluwwi	אֱלֹהִים	ר+א
פַּח	fī °			ēluwwåk	אֱלֹהִים	ר+ב
פַּח	fīm	ר		ēluwwiyyu	אֱלֹהִים	ר+ד
פַּח	fiyyi	ר+ס		ēluwwīnu	אֱלֹהִים	ר+ו
לֵחַ	lā °			ēluwwīkimma	אֱלֹהִים	ר+ז
לַח	lā			ēluwwīmu	אֱלֹהִים	ר+ט
רֵעַ	rā			ēluwwīyyinna	אֱלֹהִים	ר+י
רֹעַ	rā			ˁåṭ-åt	חַטָּאת	
רַע	rā:	נ		ˁåṭåtåk	חַטָּאת	ב
לֵחַ	lā·e	ד		ˁåṭåtu	חַטָּאת	ד
לַח	lā·əm	ר		ˁåṭåtimma	חַטָּאת	ט
רַע	rā·əm			ēˈṭ-åt	חַטָּאת	
רַע	rā·ot	ר+נ		ēṭåtti	חַטָּאת	א
רָעָה	r-ā:			ēṭåttu	חַטָּאת	ד
רָעָה	rāt	ס		ēṭåttimma	חַטָּאת	ט
רָעָה	abrātti	א		ēˈṭåt	חַטָּאת	
רָעָה	rāttu	ד		wlēṭṭåˀūtīnu	חַטָּאת	ר+ו
רָעָה	rāˀot	ר		ēṭåˀūtīkimma	חַטָּאת	ר+ז

ג. משרשים בני ארבעה וחמישה עיצורים

חֲצֹצְרָה	åṣīṣår-a °		אֶשְׁכּוֹל	iškol		
חֲצֹצְרָה	åṣīṣårot	ר	אֶשְׁכּוֹל	wiškūli		ר+ס
חַכְלִילוּ	iklīl-u		אֶשְׁכּוֹל	iškūlūtiyya		ר+ה
חֶלְבְּנָיה	albin-ya		חַרְצֻן	arṣən °		
אַרְנֶבֶת	arnēb-ət		חַרְצֻן	miyyårṣinnəm		ר
אַלְמָנוּת	ilmēn-ot °		אַבְרֵךְ	abråk		
אַלְמָנוּת	ilmēnūta	ה	חַרְגֹּל	argål		
עַשְׁתֹּרֶת	ištårr-ot °		חַרְטֹם	årṭåm °		
עַשְׁתֹּרֶת	weštårrot	ר	חַרְטֹם	årṭåmməm		ר
רַעֲנָן	rā:nən		חַרְטֹם	årṭåmmi		ר+ס
יַהֲלֹם	yēllåm		חֶרְמֵשׁ	ˁarməš		
מְטַחֲוֵי	am-ṭuwwi		עֲרָפֶל	ˁarfəl		
אֲבַעְבֻּעוֹת	å-babbāˀ-ot		עַקְרָב	ˁåqråb		
אֲבַעְבֻּעוֹת	åbabbāˀot	ר	חַלָּמִישׁ	ēlåməš		
אַחְלָמָה	å:lēm-a		אַבְנֵט	åbånəṭ		
גְּבַעַל	gēˈbāl		אַבְנֵט	åbånīṭəm		ר
שְׂמֹאל	šēmål		עֲטַלֵּף	åṭåləf		
שְׂמֹאל	aššēmåla		עַכָּבוֹר	åkåbor		
			אַלְמָנָה	ilmēn-a		
			אַלְמָנָה	ilmēnot		ר

קֶעְקַע	qå:qå		שְׂמֹאל	šēmålu	ד
אַרְגָּמָן	argåmån		שְׂמֹאל	wmiššēmålimma	ט
שַׁעַטְנֵז	šåṭnəz		בִּלְעַד	bå'lād °	
שְׁקַערוּר	šåqårår °		בִּלְעַד	bålāddi	א
שְׁקַערוּר	šåqårårot	ר	בִּלְעַד	wbålāddək	ג
עֲזָאזֵל	ēzåzəl		שְׂמָאלִי	šēmål-i	
צְפַרְדֵּעַ	ṣēfår'dā °		חַרְחֹר	åruwwår	
צְפַרְדֵּעַ	ṣēfårdā'əm	ר	קַרְקַע	qarqa	
			בְּדֹלַח	bådla	
			בְּלִיַּעַל	bå'līl	

The Plural Ending *åt* ('-*ắt*, '-*āt*)

These nouns are given according to their actual forms, with the root of each noted as well so as to enable the reader to find the references to them in *LOT* IV. See above 1.5.2.5 and also 4.3.14.

bamtåttīnu			tēbuwwåt	בוא
amtåttīkimma			tēbuwwåtīnu	
bamtåttīkimma			bīnåtånu	בן
mētåttək	נטי		bīnåtimma	
må'šāt	נשא		ålēkåt	הלך
mimmå'šāt			tēllåt	הלל
uwwållåt	עול		ē'ṭåt	חטא
'åṣåmåt	עצם		zūnåtīkimma	זני
far'rāt	פרע		yūmåt	יום
qē'nåt	קנא		yūmå'əm	
aqqē'nåt			tūldåt	ילד
tērūmåtīkimma	רום		mamlåkåt	מלך
wtērūmåtīkimma			millīlåt	מלל
šēnåt	שני		am'tåt	מתח
			amtåttīnu	

ADDENDA AND CORRIGENDA

[p. 311 §5.5.3 ll. 1–3];

šilšət שלשית (SP Nu 15:6,7; 28:14 is a segholate noun with the addition of the fem. ending ת-. Its cognates in form and meaning are Aramaic תלתא (2 Kgs 11:5), תלת < תלתות with the addition of the ending ות-, e.g., ST Nu ibid.; תרין תלתותין (y. ʿEruvin 20); Syriac תולתא ; Arabic ثُلْث. TH שֶׁלֶשׁ and שְׁלֹשָׁה are personal names (2 Kgs 11:5). In the light of the above mentioned examples it appears that in the older stage of Hebrew the segholate pattern was used to express fractions, but later it was replaced by the ordinal numbers in the fem. form. Thus, silšət must be understood as the only remnant of that stage and not as a product of defective spelling

Prof. Simon Hopkins informs me that a similar situation prevails in the Neo-Aramaic dialects. They do not continue the use of *qutlā* for fractions, but replace it by ordinal numbers, syntactical means, or even by loans from surrounding languages.

[p. 356 left column]: לנן/לון:

Precise application of the method of morphological analysis long accepted in the study of Hebrew requires us to assume that in the Hebrew represented by the Tiberian vocalization, forms such as וַיָּלֶן (Ex 17:3) and הֲלִינֹתֶם (Nu 14:29) are derived from לו"ן, whether meaning "lodge, pass the night" or "murmur, complain," while the form תִּלֻּנּוֹת (Nu 14:27)/ תְּלֻנֹּת (Ex 16:12) is derived from לנ"ן. Nonetheless, medieval Jewish grammarians of Hebrew (see, for example, Ibn Janāḥ and David Qimḥi) assigned both types to a single root, לו"ן, both in their grammars and in their lexicons, and in this they have been followed ever since by the authors of all biblical grammars and dictionaries. Only Nöldeke, *Beiträge*, 42, n. 2, offered the hypothesis that the original root of the forms meaning "murmur, complain" is לנ"ן, based on the constant *defective* spelling in SP. Our knowledge of the Samaritan pronunciation, unavailable to Nöldeke at the time, confirms his hypothesis. Cf., e.g., [p. 370 right column], קל עתיד, l.10, לנן (represented by *wyiggå̄z*), and [p. 438 left column], the plural noun form *tillå̄not* (תלנות), in contrast with, e.g, [p. 462 right column], *tirruw'wā* = TH תְּרוּעָה.

[p. 372 right column], הפעיל עתיד, l. 6, חלל wyå'el ד, (TH וַיָּחֶל).

The form might indicate a derivation from חל"ל or חו"ל, but the Samaritan tradition, too, interprets the verb in Gn 8:10 as "wait." On the interchange of verb classes, see 2.15.1.

Add there ([p. 372 right column, הפעיל עתיד]): חנן yå'ən (Dt 28:50). The given pronunciation implies *Hif'il*, as is also clearly indicated by the form å'inti (TH חַנֹּתִי) and by the spelling החנתי in various SP manuscripts.

[p. 380 left column], הפעיל סביל עבר, l. 2, יעד wēwwå'əd:

This form could be derived from the root עו"ד with no change of meaning; see 2.15.1, and cf. Arabic وعد ("warn").

[p. 382 left column], קל עבר, l. 27:

קרא, representing wqåråttå (וקראת — Gn 17:19, Dt 20:10), is listed here properly along with משח wmåšåttå, but wqårāttå (וקראתה — SP Dt 31:29, TH וְקָרָאת), should also be represented several lines lower under ה. The latter form is, of course, an outcome of the blending of the ל"א and ל"ה classes, similar to the TH form הֶחְבָּאַתָה (Jos 6:17).

[p. 386 right column], ll. 11–12 התפעל עתיד, and [p. 416 left column], l. 13 התפעל:

The verbs listed under these rubrics are most probably *Hittaf'al* forms; cf. 2.4.7, 2.4.14.

[p. 387 right column] קל עתיד:

l. 11 נוח wyanna ד and l. 15 נוח wtanna ה are *Hif'il* forms.

[p. 411 left column] הפעיל:

The form in the fifth line, יצא mūṣå'i ס+ר, is probably not a participle but a substantive. See 12.12.12.

[p. 448 right column] l. 1:

חֹלֶד For 'allad read ållåd.

ABBREVIATIONS AND BIBLIOGRAPHICAL REFERENCES

Journals, Books, Series

AbrN	*Abr-Nahrain*
AHw	W. von Soden, *Akkadisches Handwörterbuch*. Wiesbaden, 1965–1981
ArOr	*Archiv Orientální*
BASOR	*Bulletin of the American Schools of Oriental Research*
BDB	F. Brown, S. R. Driver, and C. A. Briggs, *Hebrew and English Lexicon of the Old Testament*. Oxford, 1907
Bibl	*Biblica*
BiOr	*Bibliotheca Orientalis*
BJPES	*Bulletin of the Jewish Palestine Exploration Society*
BL	H. Bauer and P. Leander, *Historische Grammatik der hebräischen Sprache des Alten Testamentes*. Halle, 1922
BSLP	*Bulletin de la Société de Linguistique de Paris*
BZAW	*Beihefte zur Zeitschrift für die Alttestamentliche Wissenschaft*
CAD	*Chicago Assyrian Dictionary*
CPA	Christian Palestinian Aramaic (also known as Palestinian Syriac)
DJD	*Discoveries in the Judaean Desert*
EI	*Eretz Israel*
EJ	*Encyclopaedia Judaica*. New York, 1971
GKC	*Gesenius' Hebrew Grammar*, ed. E. Kautzsch, trans. A. E. Cowley. Oxford, 1910
GvG	C. Brockelmann, *Grundriss der vergleichenden Grammatik der semitischen Sprachen*, 2 vols. Berlin, 1908–1913
HAR	*Hebrew Annual Review*
IOS	*Israel Oriental Studies*
JAOS	*Journal of the American Oriental Society*
JM	P. Joüon and T. Muraoka, *A Grammar of Biblical Hebrew*, 2 vols. Rome, 1991
JQR	*Jewish Quarterly Review*
JRAS	*Journal of the Royal Asiatic Society*
JSS	*Journal of Semitic Studies*
KAI	H. Donner and W. Röllig, *Kanaanäische and Aramäische Inschriften*[3], 3 vols. Wiesbaden, 1971

KB³	L. Koehler, W. Baumgartner et al., *Hebräisches und aramäisches Lexikon zum Alten Testament³*, 6 vols. Leiden, 1967–1996
LOT	Z. Ben-Ḥayyim, *The Literary and Oral Tradition of Hebrew and Aramaic Amongst the Samaritans*, 5 vols. Jerusalem, 1957–1977 [Hebrew]
MélPhLJ	*Mélanges de philosophie et de litterature juives*
MMT	*Miqṣat Ma'aśe Ha-Torah* DJD 10, ed. E. Qimron and J. Strugnell. Oxford, 1994
ScrHier	*Scripta Hierosolymitana*
Sef	*Sefarad*
SVT	*Supplements to Vetus Testamentum*
Tībåt Mårqe	תיבת מרקה *[Tībåt Mårqe]: A Collection of Samaritan Midrashim*, edited, translated and annotated by Z. Ben-Ḥayyim. Jerusalem, 1988 [Hebrew]
ZA	*Zeitschrift für Assyriologie*
ZAW	*Zeitschrift für die Alttestamentliche Wissenschaft*
ZDMG	*Zeitschrift der Deutschen Morgenländischen Gesellschaft*

Baer-Strack, *Dikduke Ha-Teamim* = S. Baer and H. L. Strack, *Dikduke Ha-Teamim des Aharon ben Moscheh ben Ascher*. Leipzig, 1879

Barth, *Nominalbildung* = J. Barth, *Die Nominalbildung in den semitischen Sprachen*. Leipzig, 1889

Bendavid, "Unusual Vocalisation" = A. Bendavid, "On the Unusual Vocalisation of a Poem," *Tarbiẓ* 29 (1960), 250–260 [Hebrew]

Ben-Ḥayyim, "Samaritan Poems" = Z. Ben-Ḥayyim, "Samaritan Poems for Joyous Occasions," *Tarbiẓ* 10 (1939), 190–200, 333–374 [Hebrew]

——, "Medial Šəwa" = Z. Ben-Ḥayyim, "The Medial Šəwa and Gemination in Hebrew," *Lěšonénu* 11 (1940), 83–93 [Hebrew]

——, "Samaritan Hebrew" = Z. Ben-Ḥayyim, "Samaritan Hebrew," *Lěšonénu* 12 (1943–1944), 45–60, 113–126 [Hebrew]

——, "Ha'azinu," = Z. Ben-Ḥayyim, "The Song *Ha'azinu* in Samaritan Hebrew," *Lěšonénu* 15 (1947), 75–86 [Hebrew]

——, *Studies* = Z. Ben-Ḥayyim, *Studies in the Traditions of the Hebrew Language*. Madrid and Barcelona, 1954

——, "Samaritan Vowel System" = Z. Ben-Ḥayyim, "The Samaritan Vowel System and Its Graphic Representation," *ArOr* 22 (1954), 515–530

——, "Rules of Šəwa" = Z. Ben-Ḥayyim, "On the Rules of Šəwa of R. Judah Ḥayyūj," *Lěšonénu* 20 (1956), 135–138 [Hebrew]

——, "Tradition" = Z. Ben-Ḥayyim, "La tradition samaritaine et sa parenté (avec les autres traditions de la langue hébraïque)," *MélPhLJ* 3–4 (1958–1962), 89–128

——, "Theory of Vowels" = Z. Ben-Ḥayyim, "R. Sa'adia Ga'on's Theory of Vowels," *Lěšonénu* 18 (1952–1953), 89–96 [Hebrew]

——, "Penultimate Stress" = Z. Ben-Ḥayyim, "On the Originality of Penultimate Stress," 150–160 in *Henoch Yalon Jubilee Volume*, ed. S. Lieberman et al. Jerusalem, 1963 [Hebrew]

——, "Observations" = Z. Ben-Ḥayyim, "Observations on the Hebrew and Aramaic Lexicon from the Samaritan Tradition," SVT 16 (1967) [Hebräische Wortforschung: Festschrift zum 80. Geburtstag von Walter Baumgartner], 12–24

——, "Contribution" = Z. Ben-Ḥayyim, "The Contribution of the Samaritan Inheritance to Research into the History of Hebrew," *Proceedings of the Israel Academy of Sciences and Humanities* 3:6 (1968), 162–174

——, "Palestinian Aramaic and Samaritan Poetry" = Z. Ben-Ḥayyim, "Studies in Palestinian Aramaic and Samaritan Poetry," 39–68 in *Hayyim (Jefim) Schirmann Jubilee Volume*, ed. S. Abramson and A. Mirsky. Jerusalem, 1970 [Hebrew]

——, "Hebrew Grammar" = Z. Ben-Ḥayyim, "Hebrew Grammar," *EJ* 8 (1971), cols. 78–124

——, "Sfire" = Z. Ben-Ḥayyim, "Comments on the Inscriptions of Sfire," *Lěšonénu* 35 (1971), 243–253 [Hebrew]

——, "Some Problems" = Z. Ben-Ḥayyim, "Some Problems of a Grammar of Samaritan Hebrew," *Bibl* 52 (1971), 229–252

——, "Reflections" = Z. Ben-Ḥayyim, "Reflections on the Vowel System in Hebrew," *Sef* 46 (1986) [Volumen en Homenaje à Prof. Pérez Castro], 71–84

——, "Verdrängung" = Z. Ben-Ḥayyim, "Verdrängung der ersten Person durch die dritte im Aramäischen der Targumim?" חכמות בנתה ביתה *Studia Semitica necnon Iranica Rudolpho Macuch septuagenario dedicata ab amicis et discipulis*, ed. M. Macuch et al. Wiesbaden, 1989

——, *Struggle* = Z. Ben-Ḥayyim, *The Struggle for a Language*. Jerusalem, 1992 [Hebrew]

——, "More about the Seghol" = Z. Ben-Ḥayyim, "More about the Seghol and Related Matters," *Hebrew Linguistics* 33–35 (1992) [Studies on the Hebrew Language Through its History Dedicated to Gad B. Sarfatti], 153–159 [Hebrew]

Ben Yehuda, *Thesaurus* = E. Ben Yehuda, *Thesaurus totius hebraitis et veteris et recentioris*. 16 vols. Jerusalem, 1908–1959

Bergsträsser, *Grammatik* = G. Bergsträsser, *Hebräische Grammatik*. 2 vols. Leipzig, 1918–1929

Blau, "Passive Participle" = J. Blau, "The Passive Participle with Active Meaning," *Lěšonénu* 18 (1953), 67–81 [Hebrew]

——, "Notes on Changes" = J. Blau, "Notes on Changes in Accent in Early Hebrew," *Hayyim (Jefim) Schirmann Jubilee Volume*, ed. S. Abramson and A. Mirsky. Jerusalem, 1970 [Hebrew], 27–38

Brockelmann, *LS* = C. Brockelmann, *Lexicon Syriacum*.² Halle, 1928

——, "Neuere Theorien" = C. Brockelmann, "Neuere Theorien zur Geschichte des

Akzents und des Vokalismus im Hebräischen und Aramäischen," *ZDMG* 94 (1940), 332–371

Brønno, *Studien* = E. Brønno, *Studien über hebräische Morphologie und Vokalismus auf Grundlage der zweiten Kolumne der Hexapla des Origenes.* Leipzig, 1943

Dalman, *Grammatik* = G. Dalman, *Grammatik des jüdisch-palästinischen Aramäisch²*, Leipzig, 1905

Diening, *Hebräische* = F. Diening, *Das Hebräische bei den Samaritanern: Ein Beitrag zur vormasoretischen Grammatik des Hebräischen.* Stuttgart, 1938

Dietrich, *Bibelfragmente* = M. Dietrich, *Neue Palästinische punktierte Bibelfragmente.* Leiden, 1968

Dotan, *Diqduqe Haṭṭěʿamim* = A. Dotan, *Diqduqe Haṭṭěʿamim of Ahǎron ben Moše ben Ašér.* Jerusalem, 1967 [Hebrew]

Epstein, *Grammar* = J. N. Epstein, *A Grammar of Babylonian Aramaic.* Jerusalem, 1960 [Hebrew]

——, *Introduction* = J. N. Epstein, *Introduction to the Text of the Mishna².* Jerusalem and Tel Aviv, 1964 [Hebrew]

Florentin, *Shomronit* = M. Florentin, *"Shomronit": A Grammatical Description and Lexical Characterization.* Ph.D. thesis. Tel Aviv University, 1990 [Hebrew]

Gesenius, *De Pentateuchi samaritanae origine* = W. Gesenius, *De Pentateuchi samaritanae origine, indole et auctoritate commentatio philogico-critica.* Halle, 1815

Haneman, *Morphology* = G. Haneman, *A Morphology of Mishnaic Hebrew According to the Tradition of the Parma Manuscript [De Rossi 138].* Tel Aviv, 1980 [Hebrew]

Kahle, *Geniza* = P. E. Kahle, *The Cairo Geniza².* Oxford, 1959

Kister, "Lexical Problems" = M. Kister, "Lexical Problems: Early and Late," *Tarbiz* 61 (1991), 45–59 [Hebrew]

Kohn, *Pentateucho samaritano* = S. Kohn, *De Pentateucho samaritano eiusque cum versionibus antiquis nexus.* Dissertatio inauguralis, Leipzig, 1865

Kutscher, *Isaiah Scroll* = E. Y. Kutscher, *The Language and Linguistic Background of the Isaiah Scroll (1QIsaᵃ).* Leiden, 1974 (=Jerusalem, 1959 [Hebrew])

Macuch, *Grammatik* = R. Macuch, *Grammatik des samaritanischen Hebräisch.* Berlin, 1969.

Morag, *Yemenite* = S. Morag, *The Hebrew Language Tradition of the Yemenite Jews.* Jerusalem, 1963 [Hebrew]

Moreshet, *Lexicon* = M. Moreshet, *A Lexicon of the New Verbs in Tannaitic Hebrew.* Ramat-Gan, 1989 [Hebrew]

Moscati, *Introduction* = S. Moscati et al., *An Introduction to the Comparative Grammar of the Semitic Languages: Phonology and Morphology.* Wiesbaden, 1969.

Nöldeke, "Aussprache" = "Über die Aussprache des Hebräischen bei den Samaritanern," *Nachrichten von der Königl. Gesell. d. Wissenschaften* 23 (1868), 485–504

——, *Grammatik* = T. Nöldeke, *Mandäische Grammatik*. Halle, 1875
——, *Beiträge* = T. Nöldeke, *Beiträge zur semitischen Sprachwissenschaft*. Strassburg, 1910
——, *Neue Beiträge* = T. Nöldeke, *Neue Beiträge zur semitischen Sprachwissenschaft*. Strassburg, 1910
——, "Texte" = T. Nöldeke, "Texte im aramäischen Dialekt von Maʿlūla," *ZA* 31 (1917–1918), 203–230
Orlinsky, "*Qal* Infinitive Construct" = H. M. Orlinsky, "The *Qal* Infinitive Construct and the Verbal Noun in Biblical Hebrew," *JAOS* 67 (1947), 107–126
Petermann, *Versuch* = J. H. Petermann, *Versuch einer hebräischen Formenlehre nach der Aussprache der heutigen Samaritaner*. Leipzig, 1868
Revell, "Studies" = E. J. Revell, "Studies in the Palestinian Vocalization of Hebrew," in *Essays on the Ancient Semitic World*, ed. J. W. Wevers and D. B. Redford. Toronto, 1971, 51–100
Sarauw, *Akzent* = C. Sarauw, *Über Akzent und Silbenbildung in den älteren semitischen Sprachen*. København, 1939
Schulthess, *Lexicon* = F. Schulthess, *Lexicon syropalaestinum*. Berlin, 1903
——, *Grammatik* = F. Schulthess, *Grammatik des christlich-palästinischen Aramäisch*. Tübingen, 1924
von Gall, *Pentateuch* = A. von Gall, *Der Hebräische Pentateuch der Samaritaner*. Gießen, 1918
Waltke, *Prolegomena* = B. K. Waltke, *Prolegomena to the Samaritan Pentateuch*. Ph.D. thesis, Harvard University, 1965
Yalon, *Vocalization* = H. Yalon, *Introduction to the Vocalization of the Mishna*. Jerusalem, 1964 [Hebrew]
——, *Studies* = H. Yalon, *Studies in the Hebrew Language*. Jerusalem, 1971 [Hebrew]
Yeivin, *Babylonian Vocalization* = I. Yeivin, *The Hebrew Language Tradition as Reflected in the Babylonian Vocalization*, 2 vols. Jerusalem, 1985 [Hebrew]

Editions Cited

Hilkhot Reʿu = *Sefer Halakhot Pesuqot ʾo Hilkhot Reʿu*, ed. A. Schlossberg. Versailles, 1886
Kitāb al-Lumaʿ = *Kitāb al-Lumaʿ*, ed. J. Derenbourg. Paris, 1886
Kitāb al-Mustalḥaq = *Kitāb al-Mustalḥaq*, ed. J. and H. Derenbourg. Paris, 1880
Kitāb al-Muwāzana = Isḥāq Ibn Barūn, *Kitāb al-Muwāzana*, ed. Kokowzoff, 1890
Kitāb al-ʾUṣūl = *Kitāb al-Uṣūl*, ed. A. Neubuer. Oxford, 1875
Maḥberet = Menaḥem ben Saruq: *Maḥberet. Edicion critica e introduccion*, ed A. Sáenz-Badillos, Granada, 1986
Mekhilta de-R. Yishmaʿel = *Mekhilta deRabbi Ismael*, ed. Horowitz–Rabin. Breslau,

1930

Mikhlol = David Qimḥi, *Mikhlol*, ed. I. Rittenberg. Lyke, 1862
MS Kaufmann = G. Beer, *Faksimile Ausgabe des Mischnacodex Kaufmann A50*. The Hague, 1929
MS Lowe = *The Mishna of the Palestinian Talmud*, ed. W. H. Lowe. Cambrige, 1883
Pesiqta de Rav Kahana = *Pesikta de Rav Kahana*, ed. B. Mandelbaum, 2 vols. New York, 1962
Ṣaḥut = Abraham Ibn 'Ezra, *Sefer Ṣaḥut*, ed. Lippmann. Fürth, 1827
Sefer Ha-Riqma = Jonah Ibn Janāḥ, *Sefer Ha-Riqma*. 2 vols., trans. R. Judah Ibn Tibbon, ed. M. Wilensky; 2nd ed. with notes by D. Tene. Jerusalem, 1964
Sefer Zikkaron = *Sefer Zikkaron*. ed. W. Bacher. Berlin, 1888
Sifra = *Sifra or Torat Kohanim According to Codex Assemani LXVI*, ed. L. Finkelstein. New York, 1953
Sifre Deuteronomy = *Siphre ad Deuteronomium*, ed. L. Finkelstein. Berlin, 1939
Sifre Numbers = *Sifre d'Be Rab, I: Siphre ad Numeros adjecto Siphre zutta cum varis lectionibus et adnotationibus*, ed. H. S. Horovitz. Leipzig, 1917
Words of Aḥiqar = A. E. Cowely, *Aramaic Papyri of the Fith Century B.C.* Oxford, 1904

Biblical Books

		Nah	Nahum
Gn	Genesis	Zeph	Zephaniah
Ex	Exod	Hag	Haggai
Lv	Leviticus	Zech	Zechariah
Nu	Numbers	Mal	Malachi
Dt	Deuteronomy	Ps	Psalms
Jos	Joshua	Prov	Proverbs
Jud	Judges	Ru	Ruth
1 Sa	1 Samuel	Cant	Canticles (Song of Songs)
2 Sa	2 Samuel		
1 Kgs	1 Kings	Eccl	Ecclesiastes (Qohelet)
2 Kgs	2 Kings	Est	Esther
Isa	Isaiah	Dan	Daniel
Jer	Jeremiah	Neh	Nehemiah
Ezek	Ezekiel	1 Chr	1 Chronicles
		2 Chr	2 Chronicles

Rabbinic Hebrew

m.	Mishna
t.	Tosefta
b.	Babylonian Talmud
y.	Palestinian Talmud (Jerusalem Talmud)

Other Abbreviations

BH	Babylonian Hebrew
CPA	Christian Palestinian Aramaic (also known as Palestinian Syriac)
DSS	Dead Sea Scrolls
f.	folio
fem.	feminine
IPA	International Phonetic Alphabet
l.	line
LSH	Late Samaritan Hebrew
masc.	masculine
MH	Mishnaic Hebrew
MS	manuscript
MT	Masoretic Text
pl.	plural
PS	Proto-Semitic
SA	Samaritan Aramaic
SAV	Samaritan Arabic Version
SH	Samaritan Hebrew
sing.	singular
SP	Samaritan Pentateuch
ST	Samaritan Targum
TH	Tiberian Hebrew
v	vowel
1QapGen	Genesis Apocryphon from Qumran Cave 1
1QIsa^a	Great Isaiah Scroll from Qumran Cave 1
1QS	Rule of the Community from Qumran Cave 1
1st	1st person
2nd	2nd person
3rd	3rd person
ø	zero vowel

INDEX OF PASSAGES

References are to page numbers

A. Samaritan Sources

Pentateuch (including both the Samaritan and Jewish versions)

Genesis		3:13	44n.45	6:13	76
1:2	37	3:16	30, 92, 229, 274, 286	6:14	117n.37
1:5	68			6:15	174
1:16	8	3:19	179	6:16	285, 310
1:18	208, 211	3:21	9, 37	7:3	166
1:20	157n.85	3:23	179	7:11	82
1:21	37, 107	3:24	37	7:18	128
1:24	8	4:6	174n.110	8:3	206
1:26	47n.51	4:7	92, 330	8:5	103n.13
1:28	191	4:9	44n.45	8:7	215, 270
1:30	8	4:15	312	8:10	466
2:3	47n.51	4:16	68	8:17	143, 160
2:9	38	4:17	77	8:22	250
2:11	37	4:18	140	9:5	295
2:12	164	4:23	187	9:6	192
2:18	47n.51	4:24	181, 312	9:22	250
2:21	37	4:26	177, 179	9:24	143
2:23	179, 181	5:4	30	9:27	253n.10
3:5	135	5:19	309	10:5	245
3:6	37	5:29	196	10:21	177
3:7	135	6:1	177	10:23	14n.21
3:9	319	6:3	322, 343n.9	10:25	179, 323
3:11	37	6:6	77	10:30	174
3:12	226	6:7	10n.15, 130, 131	11:3	77

I thank Mr. Ohad Cohen for preparing the index and verifying the Biblical quotations in the text.

11:4 38, 77	18:6 298	23:6 162, 163, 184, 209
11:6 158	18:12 57, 217	23:8 184, 247, 266
11:9 178	18:17 197	23:10 190n.148
11:31 230	18:18 217	23:11 184
12:2 38	18:21 317	23:13 184
12:3 57, 87, 223	18:25 317	24:3 190n.148
12:4 139	18:27 150	24:5 138
12:10 108	19:4 158	24:7 88, 91
12:15 44, 83, 181	19:9 209	24:8 93, 138, 293
12:16 66, 139, 181	19:11 164	24:9 229
13:7 190	19:13 327	24:12 187
13:8 174	19:14 190	24:14 146, 165
13:9 143	19:15 229n.7	24:15 180
13:12 150	19:16 68, 123, 131	24:18 84, 165
13:14 64n.90	19:19 167, 228, 324n.2	24:20 255
13:18 150	19:20 89, 174, 321	24:21 197
14:5 283	19:30 325	24:23 257
14:10 261	19:31 267	24:27 92
14:13 192	19:32 54	24:36 209
14:23 34, 250	19:33 237	24:43 43, 228
15:1 262	20:3 90	24:45 228
15:4 228, 262	20:6 209	24:46 164
15:5 146	20:9 20	24:51 174
15:10 212	20:10 354	24:55 312
15:11 139	20:13 88	24:65 237
15:18 169	20:16 189, 193n.156	24:67 232
16:2 166	20:17 139	25:13 229
16:4 91	21:6 58, 109	25:16 269, 295
16:6 123	21:7 139, 317	25:25 36
16:10 217	21:16 88	25:31 183
16:11 9n.14, 20n.28	21:17 229	25:34 299n.76
16:13 317	21:18 9, 124	26:2 9
16:29 9n.14	21:19 135	26:10 108
17:10 215	21:23 34, 113	26:26 198
17:12 317	21:28 235	26:28 174, 217
17:13 215, 317	21:29 225n.2, 235	26:35 258
17:17 317	21:38 234	27:3 295
17:19 466	22:9 321	27:8 197
17:26 145	22:13 125	27:12 50, 155
17:27 145	22:18 87	27:15 76
18:2 256	22:21 14n.21	27:19 185, 186

27:23 229
27:27 230, 295
27:31 169, 174
27:33 196, 319
27:36 317, 320
27:45 337n.5
28:12 190
28:14 301
28:22 124
29:8 161
29:9 94, 197
29:19 186
29:21 175n.113
29:24 229
29:27 312
30:3 142
30:11 160n.92, 316
30:14 298
30:15 317
30:20 88
30:38 173
30:41 235
31:19 155, 215
31:21 77
31:22 163
31:23 325n.3
31:26 43
31:27 116
31:30 108, 116
31:36 152
31:37 132
31:39 281n.49
31:40 147, 250
31:42 134, 283, 327
31:45 152
31:49 174
32:7 155
32:9 293
32:12 327
32:13 182n.133, 214
32:16 279
32:23 229
32:26 142
32:27 169
33:1 172
33:8 238
33:13 22, 88, 202
33:14 315
34:15 153
34:21 142
34:22 153
34:23 153
34:24 14n.21
34:29 160
34:30 210
35:1 209
35:3 39, 269
35:5 92
35:8 269
35:16 214
35:22 210
36:11 279n.47
36:24 217
37:2 37
37:3 37
37:7 38, 82
37:17 10n.15, 233, 283
37:18 329
37:19 237
37:20 88, 137, 231
37:24 326
37:27 174
37:29 313n.2
37:33 88, 137, 179, 209
37:34 209
38:11 230
38:14 283
38:18 84, 256
38:21 237, 283
38:23 132
38:24 44, 181, 283, 293, 306n.4
38:25 84
39:1 140, 162, 230
39:15 186, 205, 331
39:18 186, 205, 331
39:21 76
40:6 194
40:10 198n.163
40:14 275n.45
40:15 177, 178, 208
40:17 93
40:20 142, 179
41:9 111
41:19 93
41:21 234, 235
41:23 263
41:28 181, 237
41:33 174
41:45 266, 282n.49
41:51 161, 164
41:54 157
41:55 130
42:1 144
42:8 90
42:11 226
42:16 37
42:18 167, 327
42:19 37
42:21 269
42:22 328
42:24 37
42:25 91
42:34 38
42:35 201, 289
42:36 235
42:38 230
43:3 215
43:7 209
43:10 37, 131
43:11 319
43:12 37, 179
43:14 222

43:28 155	48:14 217	3:2 176n.116, 179, 271
43:29 157	48:22 293	3:7 70
43:33 136, 267	49:1 223	3:9 9n.14
43:34 174n.110	49:4 158	3:15 86
44:3 148, 182	49:5 87n.118, 276	3:21 9n.14
44:4 327	49:6 74, 223, 293	3:22 14
44:8 220	49:7 123, 233	4:1 124
44:10 202	49:9 108, 151	4:24 215
44:12 181	49:10 131	4:25 15
44:16 88	49:11 281	5:7 57
44:20 283n.52	49:12 283	5:8 146
44:23 38	49:14 108	5:9 223
44:33 174	49:15 39, 268, 323	5:10 190
44:34 295	49:17 192, 286	5:13 65, 202, 220
45:1 140	49:18 150, 159	5:16 330
45:2 223	49:19 156, 209	5:21 174
45:5 279	49:20 260, 293, 321, 323	5:22 134
45:11 37	49:21 70	6:24 83
45:12 238	49:22 104, 198, 268	7:5 92, 146, 217
45:18 185	49:23 90, 151, 152n.79	7:15 222, 330
45:19 177	49:25 301	7:22 223
45:21 38	49:26 316	7:27 18
45:26 124	49:33 217	7:28 84, 92, 107
46:3 214	50:3 135, 263	8:1 70, 187
46:7 89, 230n.7, 230	50:4 264, 269	8:12 186
46:22 293	50:10 39	8:13 285
46:27 179, 323	50:11 190	8:14 285
46:30 216n.195, 217	50:23 179	8:16 51n.59
47:1 93	50:25 133	8:17 43
47:13 109, 156		8:22 90, 232
47:14 189	Exodus	9:3 167
47:19 300	1:7 160, 327	9:8 44
47:21 123, 268	1:10 81, 131	9:16 160, 181, 211
47:23 317	1:14 64n.89, 182	9:18 214
47:24 310, 311	2:3 161, 340	9:28 90
47:26 310, 311	2:4 144	9:29 327
47:27 138	2:7 279	9:31 144
48:1 178	2:9 143, 230	9:32 144
48:2 181	2:10 231	9:33 144, 223
48:6 88	2:13 214	10:15 37, 140
48:10 104	2:20 187, 232, 319	10:19 109

11:6 167	16:21 158	23:5 108
12:4 289	16:29 190	23:6 146
12:8 326	16:31 284	23:14 252
12:9 212	16:32 137	23:16 213
12:14 157	17:3 465	23:22 150, 155n.83
12:34 201	17:9 81	23:23 129
12:37 284	17:14 184, 217	23:24 208
12:42 189	17:16 259	23:27 216n.194
13:3 274	18:9 172	23:33 142
13:15 262	18:22 327	24:1 179
13:16 228	18:25 166	25:3 8
13:18 311	19:1 325n.3	25:4 74
13:19 211	19:3 171	25:5 91, 201
13:21 215	19:5 54	25:9 202
14:4 123	19:9 209	25:10 92
14:5 44, 181	19:11 142	25:11 74
14:12 209	19:13 143, 181	25:18 77
14:16 186	19:15 91, 316, 325	25:40 325n.3
14:24 157	19:17 89	26:2 14
15:1 151, 152, 186	19:20 342	26:13 92
15:2 153, 166	19:22 87	26:14 197
15:4 311	20:5 284	26:18 279n.47
15:5 170, 236	20:20 275n.45	26:23 201
15:6 281	20:21 111	26:30 181
15:8 193, 222	20:22 164n.97, 284	27:20 197
15:9 135, 149, 233	20:23 162	28:2 211
15:10 145, 236	21:13 77	28:3 135
15:11 270	21:19 209, 210	28:5 327
15:12 282	21:22 14, 254	28:7 125
15:13 237	21:29 179, 229	28:11 59
15:14 39, 117	21:33 162	28:14 59, 90, 92, 201, 279
15:15 145	22:4 162	
15:16 122, 237	22:5 125, 193	28:22 260, 289
15:17 58, 91, 150, 233, 236, 325n.3	22:6 312	28:24 264n.33
	22:8 8, 312	28:28 156
15:24 156	22:9 77	28:32 135
15:26 207	22:11 8, 9	29:8 76
15:31 118	22:12 332	29:9 123, 201
16:12 465	22:20 8	29:13 197, 198n.163
16:15 239	22:24 8	29:33 179
16:20 156	23:2 146	29:35 135

30:7	214	
30:9	74	
30:32	178, 275	
30:34	197, 284	
30:38	49, 81	
31:17	145	
32:1	150	
32:2	297	
32:6	209	
32:7	159	
32:10	74	
32:11	174	
32:12	92, 109, 216, 231n.11	
32:17	215, 327	
32:18	270	
32:24	239	
32:33	239	
32:34	209	
33:1	159	
33:2	113	
33:4	48	
33:16	135	
33:22	155	
34:10	328, 332	
34:23	325, 327	
34:27	184, 189	
34:29	209n.184, 214	
34:30	214	
35:17	294	
35:25	91n.129	
35:26	88, 161, 233n.14	
36:5	245, 248n.5	
36:7	245	
36:8	210, 258, 340	
36:29	201	
38:11	201	
38:26	309	
38:28	309	
39:1	323	
39:2	323	
39:3	323	
39:17	264n.32	
39:40	295	
40:3	155	

Leviticus

1:4	74, 331	
1:6	111	
1:13	110	
1:15	116, 331	
2:2	89, 257	
2:16	257	
3:4	197	
3:9	197	
4:2	234	
4:13	193	
4:16	327	
4:31	163	
5:4	209, 210	
5:15	160	
5:21	9	
5:23	9	
5:24	9, 235	
5:26	9	
6:2	9, 142	
6:3	248, 283	
6:5	9	
6:13	212	
6:15	182	
6:18	9	
6:19	45	
6:21	177, 179, 182	
7:9	9	
7:15	157n.84	
7:38	217	
8:35	182	
9:24	156	
10:13	182	
10:17	328	
10:19	90	
10:20	90	
11:7	153, 201	
11:16	280	
11:19	33	
11:21	54, 260	
11:23	252	
11:26	201	
11:30	238, 318	
11:35	91, 181	
11:38	179, 180	
11:46	189	
11:47	193	
12:2	217, 232, 328	
12:4	191n.151	
12:5	296, 312	
12:7	127	
12:8	127, 132	
13:3	182	
13:4	182	
13:6	59, 127	
13:7	217	
13:10	182	
13:14	218	
13:17	182	
13:24	279	
13:25	182	
13:49	181	
13:55	212	
13:56	212	
13:57	198	
13:58	117	
14:8	173, 319	
14:10	232	
14:11	123	
14:13	171	
14:14	171	
14:21	195	
14:26	142	
14:37	92	
14:42	319	
14:43	216	
14:45	145	

14:47   192
14:48   216
14:49   211
15:3   22, 215
15:19   196
15:23   199, 326
16:4   90, 125, 223
16:19   84
16:21   140, 248, 301
16:27   328
17:3   87
17:10   186
17:13   14
18:9   250
18:10   225n.2
18:28   152
19:7   181
19:9   203
19:12   158
19:13   179
19:14   74
19:15   327
19:18   146, 152
19:19   133
19:20   33, 145, 179, 217, 270
19:22   181
19:23   181
19:25   137, 213
19:27   181, 323
19:28   270
19:29   135, 217, 328
19:35   14
20:14   238
20:23   156
20:26   111
21:1   49, 224
21:4   216
21:5   270
21:10   135, 143
21:14   49n.52

21:20   199, 280
22:6   74
22:8   123
22:25   93, 181
22:41   282
23:13   299
23:29   179, 223
23:39   211
23:41   155
23:43   214
24:20   146
25:4   172
25:6   14
25:14   204
25:21   325n.4
25:22   325
25:27   113, 223
25:30   284
25:33   68
25:36   280
25:37   280
25:44   130n.49, 162
25:45   178
26:9   284
26:13   113, 315
26:18   307
26:22   156, 223, 299
26:25   179
26:26   208
26:31   156
26:33   149
26:36   277
26:39   238
26:43   126n.44, 224
27:2   228n.6
27:8   123
27:22   328
27:23   231
27:26   223
30:11   171
33:13   136

35:30   166

Numbers
1:17   179
2:2   252
2:10   310
2:34   43
3:13   216n.195
3:49   285, 298
3:51   70, 298
4:9   257n.17
4:20   207
4:36   309
5:7   140
5:12   36, 128
5:13   116, 125, 194
5:15   142, 174n.107, 278
5:18   76, 196
5:20   237
5:22   210, 217
5:28   144, 223, 328
5:31   144
6:5   122, 199
6:19   33, 136, 329
6:25   157
7:11   82
7:89   218n.198
8:19   214
9:14   68
9:15   216
10:2   203, 209
10:8   109, 149, 156
10:9   90
10:31   232
11:1   126
11:4   265
11:5   88, 256
11:8   316
11:15   86, 209, 226
11:16   140, 185
11:21   284

11:31	36, 63, 152	19:15	44	23:10	91, 174, 291
11:32	206n.180	19:17	39	23:11	212
12:1	330	19:20	177	23:13	186, 231, 236
12:12	174	20:3	205	23:18	283
12:15	126	20:5	232	23:19	151
13:2	172n.105	20:13	224	23:23	259
13:18	274	20:14	133	23:24	294n.66
13:21	172n.105	20:24	303	23:27	155, 231
13:24	90	21:1	162, 194	23:35	133
13:27	134	21:4	196n.160, 216	24:1	152
13:30	142, 210	21:5	232, 236	24:5	148
13:39	142	21:8	200	24:6	159
14:3	126, 211	21:9	145	24:13	211
14:13	84	21:16	185	24:15	283
14:14	163, 190	21:17	40, 43, 186	24:19	123, 162, 163
14:15	149	21:22	146	24:24	245
14:16	270	21:27	118, 153	25:1	157
14:21	224	21:30	141, 220	25:2	105
14:27	465	21:32	208	25:3	88
14:28	297	22:4	317	25:8	232
14:29	149, 465	22:6	157n.85, 181, 186, 217	25:13	319
14:33	232, 235, 289			25:14	182, 197
14:34	91	22:7	259	25:15	269, 295
14:35	156	22:9	238	25:17	186
14:37	195	22:11	113, 186	25:18	144
14:45	271	22:13	209, 210	25:34	295
15:6	465	22:14	87, 209, 210	26:5	93
15:7	465	22:15	87, 143, 202	26:9	214
15:15	317	22:16	209, 210	26:20	283n.51
15:35	203	22:22	120, 192, 208	26:31	14n.21
16:13	216	22:23	146	26:54	180
16:14	329	22:26	146, 206n.180, 208, 209, 216	26:65	140
16:30	133			27:1	105
17:2	332	22:32	158, 208	27:20	295
17:3	9, 332	22:37	74	28:5	22
17:22	157n.84, 173	22:38	209, 210	28:6	22
17:25	258	22:41	77	28:14	467
18:2	7	23:1	186	28:24	22
18:16	94	23:3	88, 121, 239, 264	30:3	204, 212
19:10	213	23:7	184, 186	30:6	149, 215
19:13	177	23:8	128, 155, 156, 239	30:11	20

31:7	223	1:45	173	7:8	162, 208
31:19	57, 83, 295	1:46	173	7:15	257
31:26	199, 202	2:3	215	7:22	231n.11
31:47	68	2:4	186, 190n.149	7:24	123
32:13	224	2:5	144	7:26	130, 213
32:17	202	2:9	144	8:3	130, 164
32:24	259	2:10	93	8:5	143
32:30	125	2:12	303	8:11	207
33:34	288	2:15	215, 216	8:14	325
33:54	146n.64	2:16	148	8:17	259
34:13	146n.64	2:24	183, 186	9:4	213
34:17	70	2:29	191	9:7	77n.107
35:5	68, 155	2:31	157	9:14	186
35:8	317	2:34	89, 211, 315, 321	9:17	111
35:27	191	2:37	128n.46, 329, 332	9:20	157
35:33	182, 192	3:20	152, 173	9:21	155, 156, 190, 194, 317
36:3	140	3:23	157	9:26	51n.59, 84
36:4	140	3:24	270	9:28	209
36:8	91	3:25	175n.113	10:1	184
		3:28	122, 185	10:3	162
Deuteronomy		4:10	209	10:6	131
1:4	191	4:11	50	10:7	131
1:5	9, 211, 213	4:17	153	10:8	111
1:7	14, 192	4:19	113	10:17	84
1:11	143	4:25	131, 140	11:8	125
1:12	319	4:26	117	11:15	120, 132
1:13	186	4:32	77n.107	11:22	83, 211
1:16	166	4:33	317	12:3	134, 145
1:17	166	4:34	317	12:6	272
1:19	172	4:35	92, 181	12:7	91
1:20	191	4:39	149	12:10	149
1:21	183, 186	5:9	297	12:11	81, 84
1:28	149, 154	5:12	103, 206, 209, 212	12:17	272
1:30	130	5:22	232	13:6	127
1:32	194	5:24	226	13:7	152
1:33	218	6:11	135	13:9	138
1:38	185	6:17	207	14:1	157
1:39	155, 215	6:19	213	14:15	280
1:41	130, 151	6:24	167, 231, 232	14:21	120
1:42	130	7:2	157	14:22	124
1:44	156, 271	7:5	145		

14:23 137, 231	21:14 134,	27:1 209
14:28 231	21:15 139, 180	27:4 88
15:6 89, 125	21:20 193n.156, 214	27:9 167
15:7 90, 295	22:2 113, 125	27:16 196
15:9 307	22:9 224	27:18 197
15:10 156, 209	22:12 166	27:19 146, 249
15:11 92, 262	22:21 328	27:25 190
15:18 166	22:23 68, 295	28:7 93
15:19 156	22:28 179	28:11 295
16:1 206	22:29 63, 90, 159	28:12 166
16:5 295	23:2 44, 201, 274, 289, 290	28:22 123
16:15 199		28:27 164
16:19 146	23:5 192	28:28 197, 286
17:2 211	23:13 250n.7	28:29 199
17:4 177	23:14 250n.7, 251	28:34 197
17:5 164, 233	24:1 284	28:35 164
17:12 207	24:2 120, 318	28:37 283
17:17 164	24:3 284	28:40 165
17:20 215	24:5 19, 122, 184, 329	28:43 164
18:3 166, 297	24:9 209	28:59 257
18:6 14	24:10 209	28:63 134
18:10 259	24:13 94n.136	28:40 20n.28
18:18 166	24:17 146, 246	28:50 466
18:21 329	25:2 332	28:52 156
19:1 233	25:3 44, 156, 332	28:54 143, 156
19:18 263	25:5 132, 326	28:56 156, 161, 206, 212, 279
19:19 158	25:6 166	
20:3 48	25:7 43	28:63 144, 152
20:5 123, 172	25:8 43	28:65 15, 135, 286
20:8 154, 155	25:9 163	28:67 214
20:14 68, 156, 331	25:11 224	29:17 198
20:16 331	25:12 155	29:18 194
20:19 208, 211	25:18 159, 194, 223	29:22 279
21:2 173, 189	26:6 90	29:24 214
21:3 19, 56, 179	26:7 262	29:28 159
21:7 104	26:8 277n.46	30:1 149
21:8 118	26:12 124	30:9 152, 215
21:9 130	26:14 259	30:13 122
21:10 160	26:17 137	30:20 211
21:12 288	26:18 137	31:4 111
21:13 139	26:27 297	31:8 122

31:14 89, 187
31:17 269
31:18 211, 214
31:20 36
31:21 105
31:24 215
31:29 132, 211, 466
32:2   223, 270, 325
32:3   186
32:5   48
32:6   55n.70, 153, 224
32:7   84, 209, 269, 303
32:8   103, 146, 204
32:10 15, 123, 147, 173, 280
32:11 151
32:12 70
32:14 268n.38
32:16 325
32:17 325
32:18 162, 164
32:20 19, 175, 270
32:22 142, 224
32:24 268
32:26 175
32:28 192
32:31 14, 220n. 202, 254
32:32 261
32:33 268, 274
32:35 66
32:36 120, 332
32:37 160
32:41 148
32:42 264
32:43 74, 145, 186
32:51 128
33:3   148, 270
33:5   126
33:6   174
33:7   19, 184
33:9   270
33:10 272
33:11 151, 239
33:16 175, 281n.49, 316
33:17 257n.18, 281, 297
33:18 19, 184
33:20 289
33:21 164
33:22 162
33:24 174
33:25 81
33:26 194, 270
33:27 111, 326
33:29 193n.156, 319
34:4   160
34:7   104
34:12 277n.46

The Samaritan Targum

Genesis
2:23   15n.23
2:25   15n.23
3:9   319
8:7   270
9:14   64n.89
12:16 139, 181
13:7   190
13:9   143
17:10 215
17:13 215
18:12 217
19:9   209
19:22 228n.6
20:9   20
20:16 193n.156
21:7   139
21:24 88
22:17 207n.183

23:8   247
23:16 87n.118
23:33 319
24:21 197
25:34 299n.76
26:28 207n.183
31:42 320n.15
32:13 182n.133
33:8   238
33:19 146
37:24 326
38:14 283
38:17 285
38:21 283
41:45 266, 282n.49
41:51 164n.98
42:21 269
42:22 329
43:3   207n.183, 215n.194

43:14 222n.207
44:3   182
44:20 283n.52
45:19 177n.118
46:30 217
48:11 245n.13
49:11 281n.49
49:12 283
49:19 209
49:22 198
50:11 190

Exodus
1:14   182
2:20   319
4:25   15
5:23   259
7:15   331
9:3   167

Index

9:18   214
12:4   14
12:34 201
15:4   311
15:9   233
18:27 166
20:22 164n.97
21:22 254n.13
23:17 327
23:27 216n.194
28:22 289
28:24 88
32:25 215n.192
34:27 184n.136
34:29 209n.184
36:5   248n.5
36:8   210

Leviticus
6:3   248
6:15   182
6:21   179, 182
8:35   182
10:13 182
11:26 201
11:30 238
11:38 180n.128
12:7   127
12:8   127
13:49 181

14:26 142
19:25 213n.189
19:29 217, 328
20:14 238
25:44 130n.49
26:36 277
26:39 238
26:43 224
27:2   228n.6

Numbers
3:49   285
5:13   116, 194
5:15   142
5:22   210
5:28   328
6:5   199
12:15 126
13:21 172n.105
13:22 116
13:30 142n.59
14:3   211
14:14 190
21:1   194
21:30 141n.58
22:9   238
22:13 210
22:26 206n.180, 209
26:54 180n.129
30:3   212

32:35 133n.50
32:52 123
33:52 123
35:30 166n.103
35:33 182

Deuteronomy
1:5   213
4:10   210
5:12   212
9:21   194
19:18 263n.28
20:16 331
21:3   19
22:28 180
25:5   326
26:17 137
26:18 137
28:37 283
28:56 206n.180
32:2   165
32:10 280
32:31 254n.13
32:33 274
33:5   126
33:11 239
33:24 174n.108
33:27 326
34:12 277n.46

The Samaritan Arabic Version

Genesis
3:16   207n.183
8:7   270
9:27   253n.10
17:10 215
17:13 215
18:12 217
19:22 208n.6

20:9   20
20:16 193n.156
21:7   139
22:17 207n.183
24:21 197
24:55 312
25:34 299n.76
26:28 207n.183

30:3   262n.25
31:42 327
32:13 182n.133
33:8   238
37:24 326
38:14 283
38:21 283
41:28 180n.130

41:45 261
41:51 164n.98
42:22 329
43:3 207n.183
43:17 222n.207
44:20 283n.52
45:2 223
45:19 177n.118
46:7 230
46:30 217
48:11 254n.13
49:11 282n.49
49:12 283

Exodus
1:14 182
2:20 319
4:25 15
7:15 331
9:3 167
9:18 214
12:34 201
15:9 233
18:27 166
20:22 164n.97
21:22 254n.13
23:8 247
23:27 216n.194
23:28 269
28:22 289
29:33 180
32:25 215n.192
34:27 184n.136
34:29 209

36:5 248n.5

Leviticus
6:21 179, 182
8:35 182
10:13 182
11:26 201
11:30 238
11:38 180n.128
12:7 127
12:8 127
14:26 142
19:25 213n.189
19:29 217, 328
25:21 325n.4
26:36 277
26:39 238
26:43 224

Numbers
3:49 285
5:13 116, 194
5:15 142
5:22 210
6:5 199
12:15 126
13:21 172n.105
13:22 116
13:30 142n.59
14:3 211
19:13 179
19:20 179
21:1 194
21:17 187

21:30 141n.58
22:9 238
22:13 210
22:26 206n.180, 209
23:8 239
24:15 283
30:3 212
32:35 133n.50
35:30 166n.103
35:33 182

Deuteronomy
2:37 128n.46
9:21 194
18:21 329
19:18 263n.28
21:3 19
22:28 180
26:17 137
26:18 137
28:37 283
28:56 206n.180
32:2 165
32:10 157n.88, 280
32:18 164n.98
32:31 254n.13
32:33 274
33:5 126
33:7 19, 184
33:11 239
33:24 174n.108
33:26 194
33:27 326
34:12 277n.46

B. Non-Samaritan Sources

Joshua
2:6 186
6:17 466

10:13 169
11:14 18
19:13 301

19:45 97n.4
21:10 310
21:11 253

24:15   203

Judges
2:3   268n.41
5:7   103
6:32   147
8:10   308
12:6   37n.22
13:6   107
20:25   308
20:43   58

1 Samuel
1:6   161
1:9   204
1:20   79
3:8   51n.59
4:15   104
6:12   142
8:15   124
13:21   287
14:22   109
14:33   20
14:36   186
15:23   211
17:41   209
18:29   143
18:30   141
19:17   236
25:18   202
31:3   141n.57

2 Samuel
1:26   132
6:1   143
12:20   51n.59
19:33   220
21:20   248n.5
22:38   175n.113
23:6   235

1 Kings
2:40   186, 301
6:19   316
7:37   235
11:9   163
11:20   198
17:14   316
20:6   81

2 Kings
2:10   176n.116
2:12   127
2:14   319
3:11   313n.2
7:14   192
10:7   88n.109
10:10   319
11:5   465
12:9   214
13:17   141, 204
16:6   289
16:7   196
23:4   158
25:23   258

Isaiah
1:4   17
1:20   176
3:15   321
3:16   158, 202
3:17   235
5:4   159
8:4   204
9:2   315
13:19   203n.174
14:11   197
14:31   295
25:6   159
26:19   75
27:3   58
28:12   204

29:1   75
30:18   315
31:5   18
32:11   183
33:4   347
34:14   15
41:2   163
42:24   204
44:18   216
45:23   307
47:13   235
54:4   235
56:3   163
56:6   203
58:9   205
59:10   175
62:9   114
63:14   216
63:19   154

Jeremiah
1:5   141
1:6   204
2:15   104
2:20   103
2:27   139
2:35   327
6:7   246
7:10   18
8:13   213
9:2   110
10:17   288
11:15   228, 235
13:10   18n.27
22:15   58, 109
22:24   236
23:13   118
25:34   235
29:14   164
31:31   18
37:7   314

37:21 204
41:6 209
42:2 204
42:10 220
44:17 299n.75
50:34 211

Ezekiel
1:14 202
5:12 235
6:8 235
6:9 157n.87
13:20 233n.12, 235
14:5 17
16:4 91n.127
16:19 104
16:22 103
16:31 235
16:53 235
19:2 294n.66
20:36 327
21:29 211
23:16 175
23:20 175
23:48 117, 233n.12
25:4 140
27:6 91
32:28 116, 117
34:17 226
35:9 220
40:12 320
40:16 235
40:43 58, 287
45:13 244n.4

Hosea
10:10 117n.37
13:3 114

Micah
4:6 67

Nahum
2:14 235

Zephaniah
1:2 213
1:14 18

Haggai
1:6 204

Zechariah
5:11 178, 336n.4
7:5 236
7:7 237
10:5 196
10:6 220

Malachi
3:6 197n.161, 222

Psalms
8:2 214
11:7 233, 235
14:1 58n.79
17:10 235
18:31 58
18:33 314
18:34 57
18:36 317
18:38 175n.113
18:39 57
18:46 56
18:48 57
21:11 235
27:14 105n.18
29:2 56
31:25 58, 105n.18
32:1 220
32:7 56
32:9 57
41:5 183

48:14 152
49:9 141
50:15 183
50:21 204
55:20 123
62:4 114
66:6 175
75:1 51n.59
78:30 313n.2
86:2 183
89:30 317
89:52 58
94:10 117n.37
95:10 157n.87
101:5 114
106:28 117
115:7 155
118:11 155
140:3 153n.81
144:12 254

Proverbs
1:22 138
9:7 117n.37
10:12 117n.37
17:4 219
23:15 187
24:31 287
27:1 140
28:23 284n.53
30:6 141

Job
9:15 114
9:18 58
15:7 310
20:18 259
20:23 233, 235
20:26 138
23:2 258

33:25 181	8:11 161	2:6 169
33:31 51n.59	8:12 20	2:13 169, 175
39:18 59	11:3 62, 163n.95	3:10 202
39:24 15	12:11 287	11:5 283n.51
		12:45 203

Canticles
1:7   64n.89
4:9   104
5:2   91n.127

Esther
1:6   58
1:17 160
7:4   254

1 Chronicles
7:36 311
9:5   283n.51
10:3 141n.57
20:6 248n.5

Ruth
2:9   219
4:7   150

Daniel
1:10 150
1:16 287
2:15 202
5:15 196
6:18 181
7:5   178

2 Chronicles
1:4   126n.44
24:10 204
30:3 248n.5
35:13 88n.109

Lamentations
1:16 68n.89
3:48 142

Ecclesiastes
3:18 126n.44
4:2   18
5:10 217

Nehemiah
1:7   204
1:10 176

Ben Sira

14:13 206n.180
40:9   265

Dead Sea Scrolls

1QIsa[a]
   103, 206n.180, 220
45:23 262

1QPs[a]
       177

Copper Scroll
9:14   322
10:5   322

1Q5, 1Q5a, 1Q5b
       230n.8

Mishna

Berakhot
1:2   205n.178
3:2   238

Kil'ayim
3:1   287n.57

Terumot
10:1   268n.37

Ma'aser Sheni
5:1   201

Shabbat
1:11   219
10:5   188n.140
13:6   188n.140

Sukka
1:3   136, 253

Beṣa
1:4   256n.16

Rosh Ha-Shanah
3:7   319

Yevamot
12:3   132

Nedarim
10:7   205

Qiddushin
4:14   155n.83

Makkot
3:5   165 n.99, 270n.42
3:10   332

'Avoda Zara
1:4   188n.140

Avot
1:1   64n.89
5:9   290

Kelim
29:4   285

Miqwa'oth
9:2   254

Yadayim
4:5   24

Tosefta

Berakhot
1:14   218n.198

Ma'aser Sheni
1:18   210n.186

Bikkurim
2:2   188n.140
2:5   188n.140

Hagiga
2:5   315

Bava Qamma
6:8   188n.140

Bava Batra
8:18   155n.83

Kelim
4:5   279

Palestinian Talmud (Jerusalem Talmud)

Berakhot
1:1 (2c)   194

Peah
1:1 (15b)   166n.102

Kil'ayim
1:1 (26a)   194

Ma'asrot
3:1 (54a)   237n.17

Shabbat
3:6   205

Yevamot
1:6   326

Nedarim
(38c)   315

Sanhedrin
2:4   321n.16

Nidda
1:5 (49a)   279

Babylonian Talmud

Shabbat
128a   285

Sanhedrin
106a   294n.66

Shavu'ot
34b   315

'Avoda Zara
58b   336

Hullin
4a   1

Nidda
31a   328

Targum Onqelos

Genesis
23:6   164
27:33 319

31:22 163
40:10 261
43:11 319

Leviticus
4:31   163
27:2   228n.6

Palestinian Targum

Genesis
49:21 293

Numbers
21:20 174n.109

Targum to Isaiah
10:16 142n.61
58:9   205

Septuagint

Genesis
30:11 160n.92
50:2   264
Deuteronomy
32:42 264
33:10 272

2 Samuel
15:32 67
2 Kings
2:14   319
7:14   192
10:10 319

Jeremiah
5:8   268n.37
Ezekiel
25:4   140

Hexapla

Psalms
18:39 322

36:2   253
36:10 253

49:5   253n.12

Inscriptions

Sefire
KAI 224:17   91n.128, 259

Eshmun'azar of Sidon
KAI 14:6   256